Somme: Into the Breach

Hugh Sebag-Montefiore was a barrister before becoming a journalist and then a historian. His bestselling book *Enigma: The Battle for the Code* describes how the Allied cryptographers cracked the German Enigma code. Another of the great events of the Second World War was the subject of his next bestseller, *Dunkirk: Fight to the Last Man*.

He lives in North London with his wife and three children. More details can be found on his website: http://www.hughsebagmontefiore.com.

Somme

Into the Breach

HUGH SEBAG-MONTEFIORE

VIKING
an imprint of
PENGUIN BOOKS

*For Aviva Burnstock, my wife, for Saul, Esther and Abraham,
my children, and for Stephen Sebag-Montefiore, my late father,
who so wanted this story to be told*

VIKING

UK | USA | Canada | Ireland | Australia
India | New Zealand | South Africa

Viking is part of the Penguin Random House group of companies
whose addresses can be found at global.penguinrandomhouse.com.

First published 2016
001

Set in 11.5/14.25 pt Bembo Book MT Std
Typeset by Jouve (UK), Milton Keynes
Printed in Great Britain by Clays Ltd, St Ives plc

A CIP catalogue record for this book is available from the British Library

Hardback ISBN: 978–0–670–91838–6
Trade paperback ISBN: 978–0–670–91839–3

www.greenpenguin.co.uk

Penguin Random House is committed to a
sustainable future for our business, our readers
and our planet. This book is made from Forest
Stewardship Council® certified paper.

Contents

List of Illustrations

Section 1

Section 2

List of Maps

Maps

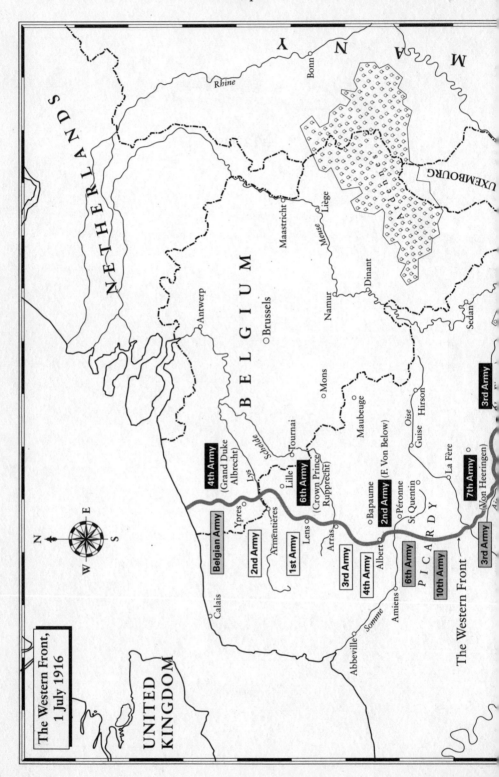

The Western Front, 1 July 1916

Map 1   xv

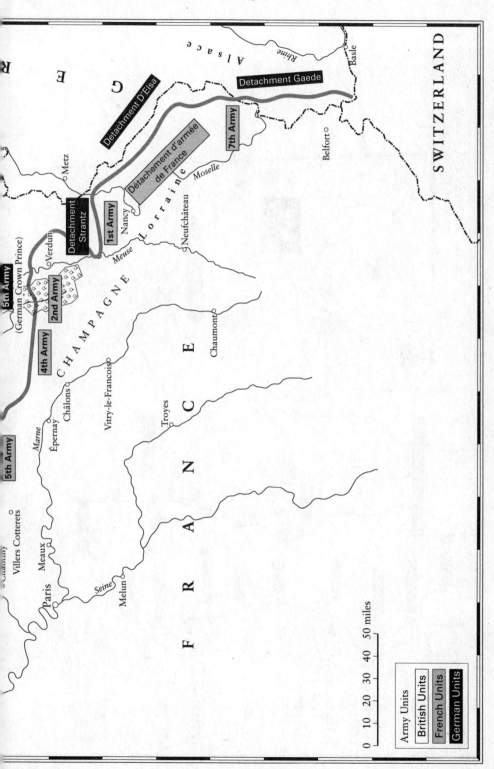

Army Units

British Units

French Units

German Units

0 10 20 30 40 50 miles

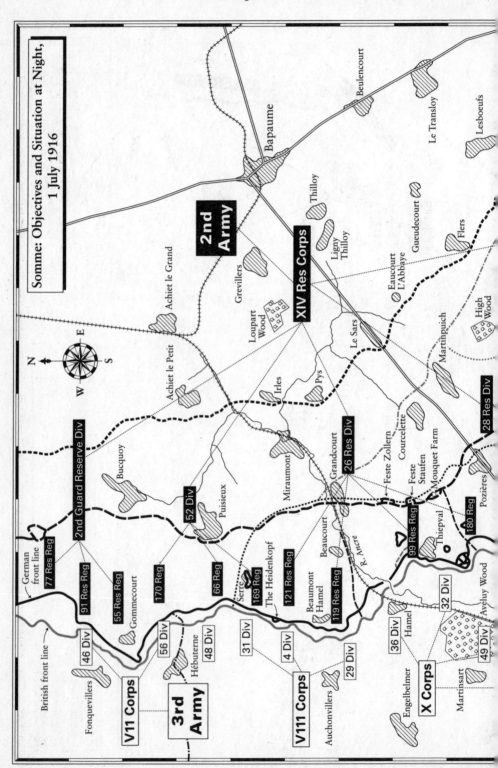

Somme: Objectives and Situation at Night, 1 July 1916

2nd Army

XIV Res Corps

3rd Army

V11 Corps

V111 Corps

X Corps

German front line

British front line

77 Res Reg

2nd Guard Reserve Div

52 Div

26 Res Div

28 Res Div

91 Res Reg

55 Res Reg

170 Reg

66 Reg

169 Reg

121 Res Reg

119 Res Reg

99 Res Reg

180 Reg

46 Div

56 Div

48 Div

31 Div

4 Div

29 Div

36 Div

32 Div

49 Div

Bapaume

Beulencourt

Le Transloy

Lesboeufs

Thilloy

Ligny Thilloy

Gueudecourt

Flers

Eaucourt L'Abbaye

High Wood

Grevillers

Achiet le Grand

Achiet le Petit

Loupart Wood

Le Sars

Martinpuich

Irles

Pys

Feste Zollern

Courcelette

Feste Staufen

Mouquet Farm

Bucquoy

Puisieux

Miraumont

Grandcourt

Thiepval

Pozières

Serre

The Heidenkopf

Beaucourt

R. Ancre

Beaumont Hamel

Hamel

Aveluy Wood

Fonquevillers

Gommecourt

Hébuterne

Auchonvillers

Engelbelmer

Martinsart

N E S W

Map 2   xvii

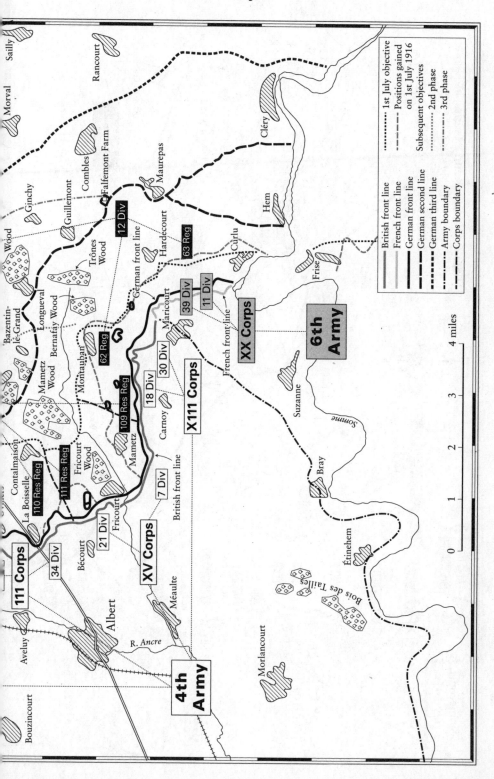

Legend:

- British front line
- French front line
- German front line
- German second line
- German third line
- Army boundary
- Corps boundary

- 1st July objective
- Positions gained on 1st July 1916
- Subsequent objectives
- 2nd phase
- 3rd phase

4 miles
0   1   2   3

Morval, Sailly, Rancourt, Combles, Falfemont Farm, Maurepas, Cléry, Hem, Frise, Ginchy, Guillemont, Trônes Wood, Hardecourt, 63 Reg, Curlu, 12 Div, German front line, 62 Reg, Maricourt, 39 Div, 11 Div, Wood, Bazentin-le-Grand, Longueval, Bernafay Wood, Mametz Wood, Montauban, 109 Res Reg, 30 Div, 18 Div, Carnoy, French front line, XX Corps, Suzanne, Somme, 6th Army, Mametz, 111 Res Reg, Fricourt Wood, X111 Corps, 7 Div, British front line, Bray, Contalmaison, La Boisselle, 110 Res Reg, Fricourt, 21 Div, XV Corps, Étinehem, 111 Corps, 34 Div, Bécourt, Méaulte, Albert, R. Ancre, Morlancourt, Bois des Tailles, 4th Army, Aveluy, Bouzincourt

Map 3

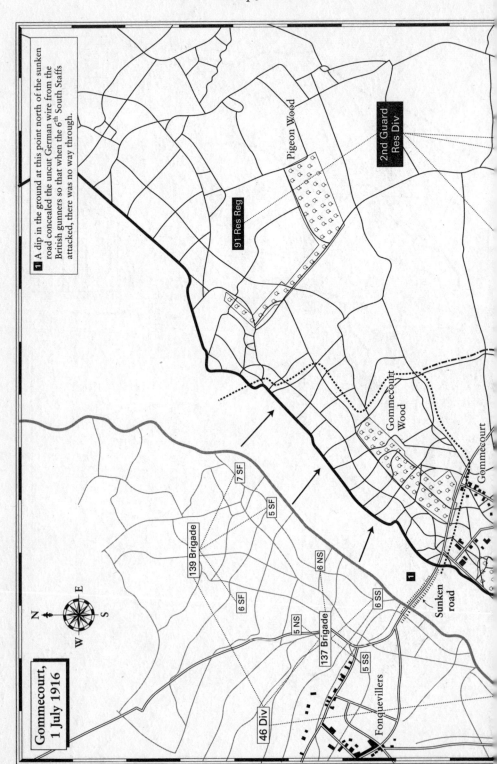

Gommecourt, 1 July 1916

N
W — E
S

46 Div

139 Brigade

7 SF

6 SF

5 SF

5 NS

137 Brigade

6 NS

6 SS

5 SS

Fonquevillers

1 Sunken road

Gommecourt

Gommecourt Wood

91 Res Reg

Pigeon Wood

2nd Guard Res Div

1 A dip in the ground at this point north of the sunken road concealed the uncut German wire from the British gunners so that when the 6th South Staffs attacked, there was no way through.

Map 3

xix

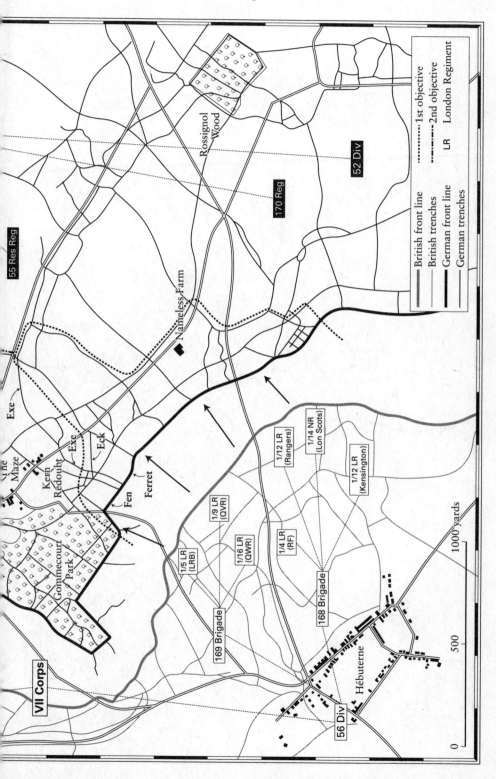

Map 3

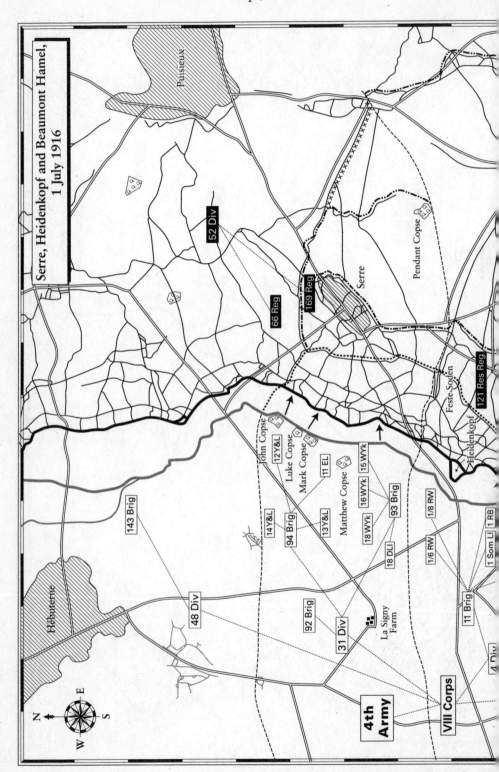

Serre, Heidenkopf and Beaumont Hamel, 1 July 1916

Map 4   xxi

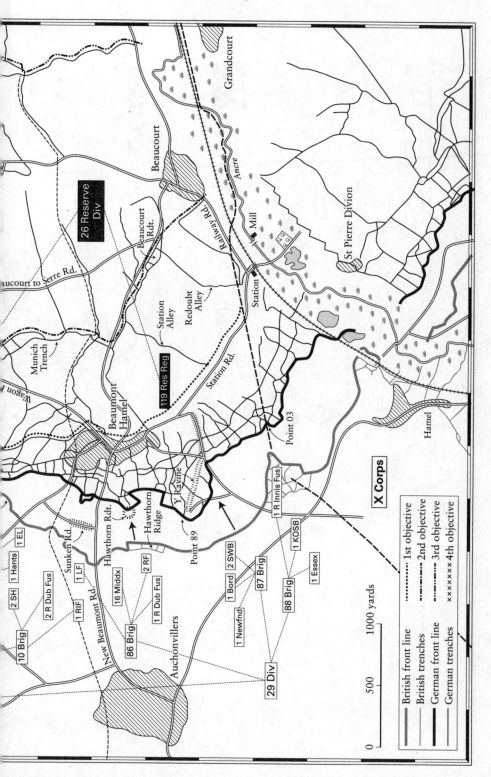

Grandcourt

Beaucourt

26 Reserve Div

Beaucourt Rdt.

aucourt to Serre Rd.

Station Alley

Redoubt Alley

119 Res Reg

Station Rd.

Munich Trench

Wagon

Beaumont Hamel

Ancre

Mill

Station

St Pierre Divion

Point 03

Hamel

X Corps

Y Ravine

Point 89

Hawthorn Rdt.

Hawthorn Ridge

1 R Innis Fus

1 KOSB

1 Essex

2 SWB

87 Brig

1 Bord

88 Brig

1 Newfnd

29 Div

1 EL

1 Hants

2 SH

2 R Dub Fus

Sunken Rd.

1 RIF

1 LF

16 Middx

2 RF

1 R Dub Fus

10 Brig

86 Brig

New Beaumont Rd.

Auchonvillers

Railway Rd.

Beaucourt Rdt.

	British front line
	British trenches
	German front line
	German trenches

········ 1st objective
─ ─ ─ 2nd objective
─ · ─ 3rd objective
xxxxxxx 4th objective

0   500   1000 yards

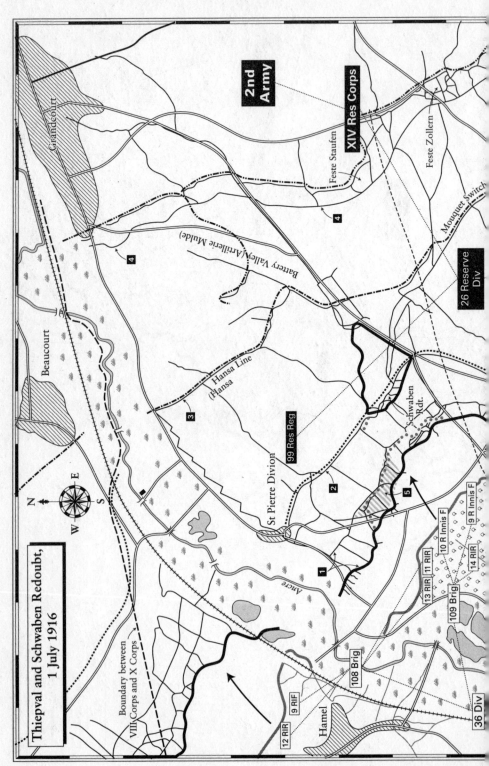

Thiepval and Schwaben Redoubt,
1 July 1916

Map 5   xxiii

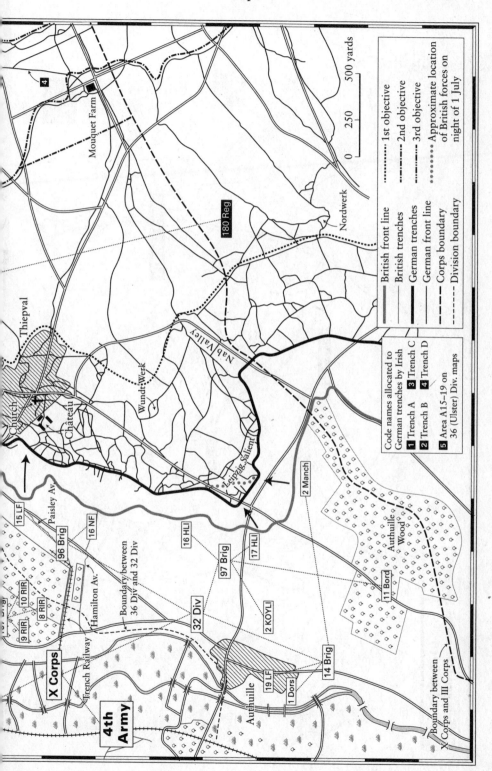

Code names allocated to
German trenches by Irish

1 Trench A   **3** Trench C
2 Trench B   **4** Trench D
5 Area A15–19 on
36 (Ulster) Div. maps

········· British front line
——— British trenches
▬▬▬ German trenches
— — German front line
—·—·— Corps boundary
– – – Division boundary

········· 1st objective
– – – 2nd objective
–··–··– 3rd objective
•••••• Approximate location
of British forces on
night of 1 July

0   250   500 yards

Map 6

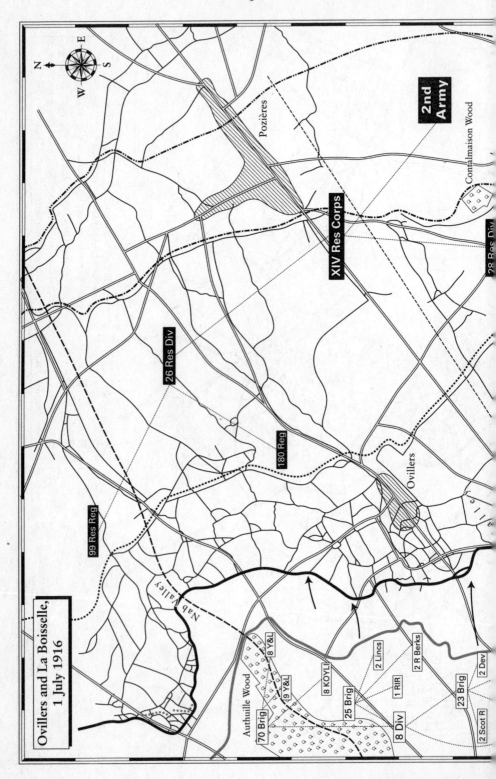

Ovillers and La Boisselle,
1 July 1916

Map 6   XXV

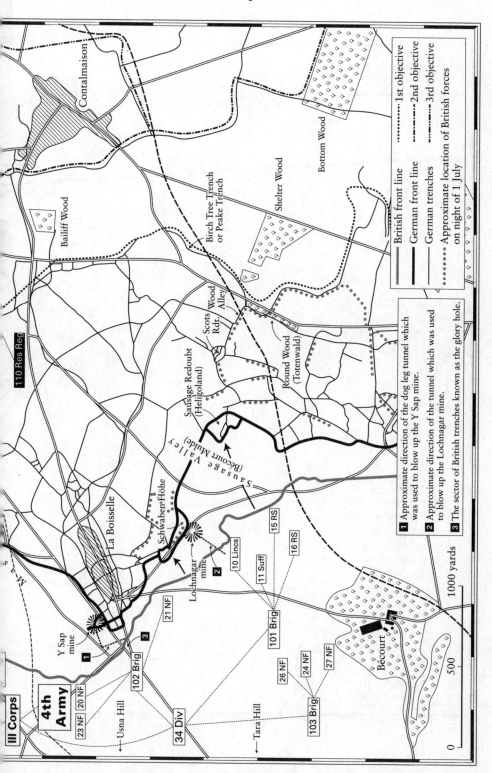

III Corps

4th Army

1 Approximate direction of the dog leg tunnel which was used to blow up the Y Sap mine.

2 Approximate direction of the tunnel which was used to blow up the Lochnagar mine.

3 The sector of British trenches known as the glory hole.

British front line
German front line
German trenches
Approximate location of British forces on night of 1 July

········ 1st objective
-·-·-·- 2nd objective
------- 3rd objective

Contalmaison

Bailiff Wood

La Boisselle

Schwaben Höhe

110 Res Reg

Birch Tree Trench or Peake Trench

Scots Wood Rdt. Alley

Sausage Redoubt (Heligoland)

Shelter Wood

Bottom Wood

Round Wood (Totenwald)

Sausage Valley (Bécourt Mulde)

Lochnagar mine

Y Sap mine

Usna Hill

Tara Hill

34 Div

23 NF
20 NF
21 NF
102 Brig
26 NF
24 NF
27 NF
103 Brig
10 Lincs
11 Suff
101 Brig
15 RS
16 RS

Bécourt

0   500   1000 yards

Map 7

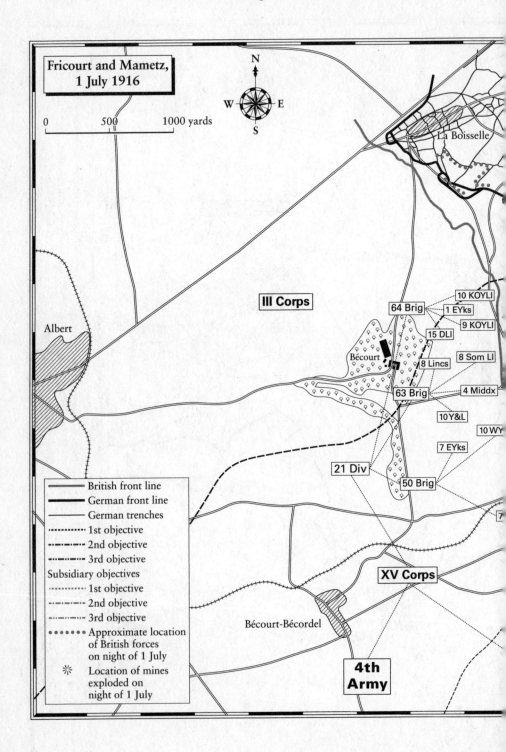

**Fricourt and Mametz,
1 July 1916**

0   500   1000 yards

N
W · E
S

III Corps

La Boisselle

Albert

Bécourt

64 Brig

10 KOYLI
1 EYks
9 KOYLI
15 DLI
8 Som LI
8 Lincs
63 Brig   4 Middx
10 Y&L
10 WY
7 EYks
21 Div   50 Brig

British front line
German front line
German trenches
1st objective
2nd objective
3rd objective
Subsidiary objectives
1st objective
2nd objective
3rd objective
Approximate location
of British forces
on night of 1 July
Location of mines
exploded on
night of 1 July

XV Corps

Bécourt-Bécordel

**4th
Army**

Map 7 xxvii

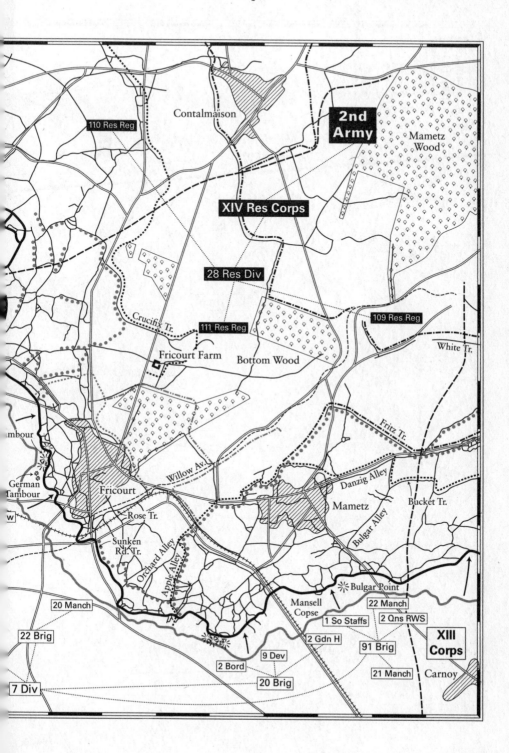

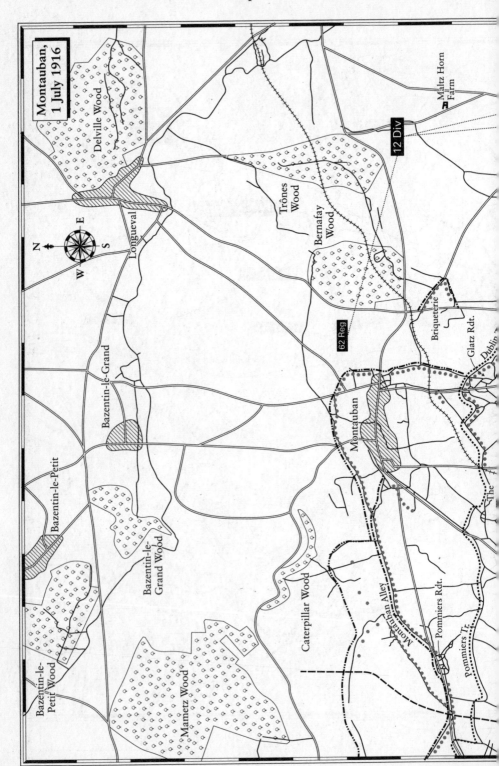

Map 8 xxix

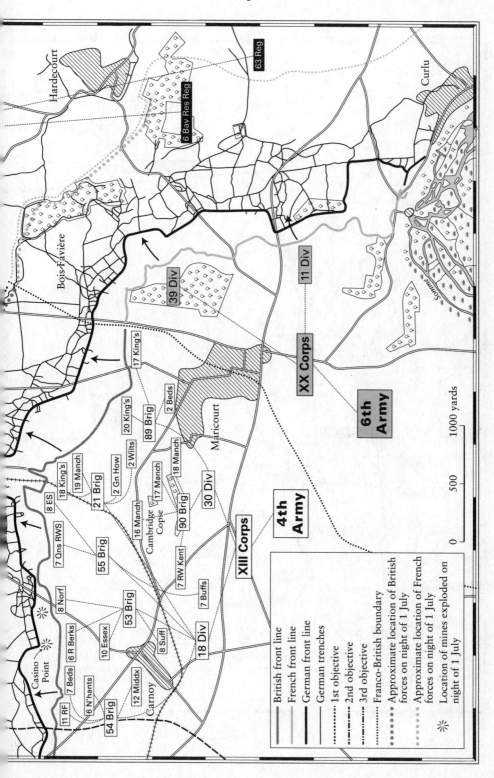

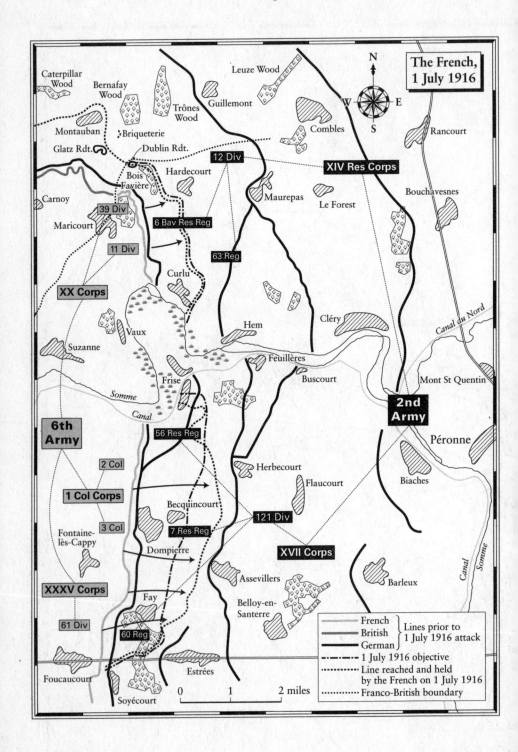

The French,
1 July 1916

N
W   E
S

Caterpillar
Wood

Bernafay
Wood

Leuze Wood

Trônes
Wood

Guillemont

Combles

Rancourt

Montauban

Briqueterie

Glatz Rdt.

Dublin Rdt.

Bois
Favière

Hardecourt

12 Div

Maurepas

Le Forest

XIV Res Corps

Bouchavesnes

Carnoy

39 Div

6 Bav Res Reg

Maricourt

11 Div

XX Corps

63 Reg

Curlu

Vaux

Hem

Cléry

Canal du Nord

Suzanne

Feuillères

Buscourt

Mont St Quentin

Frise

Somme

2nd
Army

Canal

56 Res Reg

Péronne

6th
Army

2 Col

Herbecourt

Flaucourt

Biaches

1 Col Corps

3 Col

Becquincourt

7 Res Reg

121 Div

Fontaine-
lès-Cappy

Dompierre

XVII Corps

XXXV Corps

Assevillers

Barleux

Fay

Belloy-en-
Santerre

Canal   *Somme*

61 Div

60 Reg

Foucaucourt

Estrées

French
British
German

Lines prior to
1 July 1916 attack

Soyécourt

0   1   2 miles

1 July 1916 objective
Line reached and held
by the French on 1 July 1916
Franco-British boundary

Map 10   xxxi

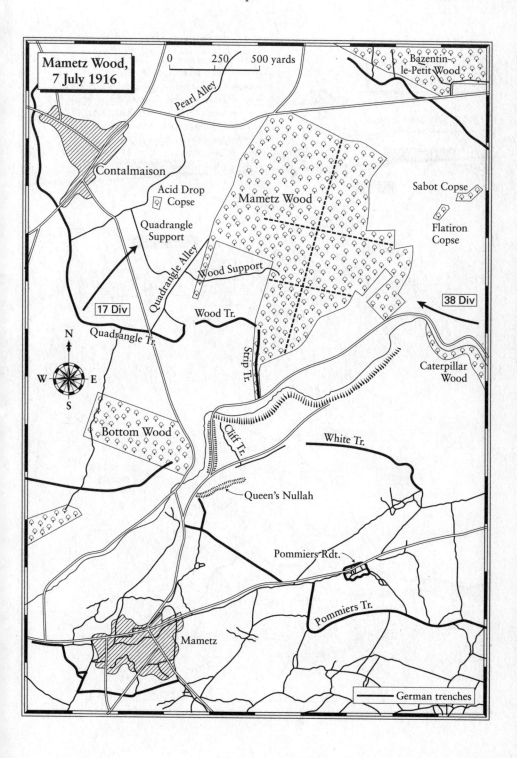

Mametz Wood,
7 July 1916

0   250   500 yards

Pearl Alley

Bazentin-
le-Petit Wood

Contalmaison

Acid Drop
Copse

Mametz Wood

Sabot Copse

Flatiron
Copse

Quadrangle
Support

Quadrangle Alley

Wood Support

17 Div

Quadrangle Tr.

Wood Tr.

38 Div

N
W   E
S

Strip Tr.

Caterpillar
Wood

Bottom Wood

Cliff Tr.

White Tr.

Queen's Nullah

Pommiers Rdt.

Mametz

Pommiers Tr.

German trenches

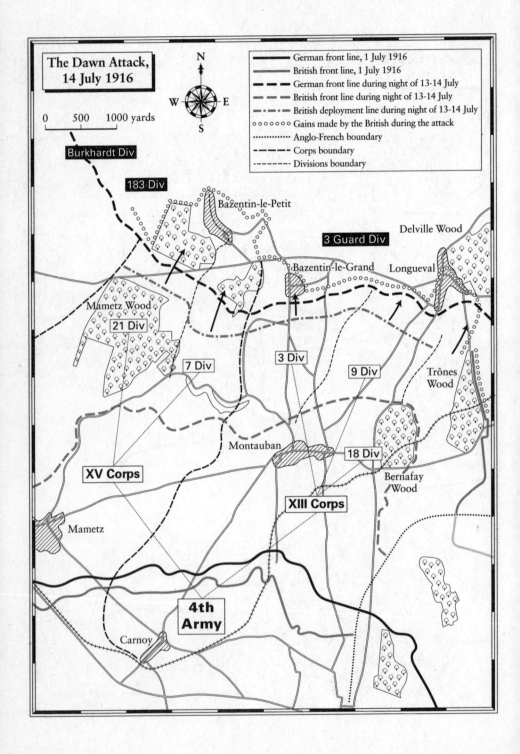

The Dawn Attack, 14 July 1916

0   500   1000 yards

German front line, 1 July 1916
British front line, 1 July 1916
German front line during night of 13-14 July
British front line during night of 13-14 July
British deployment line during night of 13-14 July
Gains made by the British during the attack
Anglo-French boundary
Corps boundary
Divisions boundary

Burkhardt Div

183 Div

Bazentin-le-Petit

Delville Wood

3 Guard Div

Bazentin-le-Grand

Longueval

Mametz Wood

21 Div

7 Div

3 Div

9 Div

Trônes Wood

Montauban

18 Div

XV Corps

Bernafay Wood

XIII Corps

Mametz

4th Army

Carnoy

Map 12

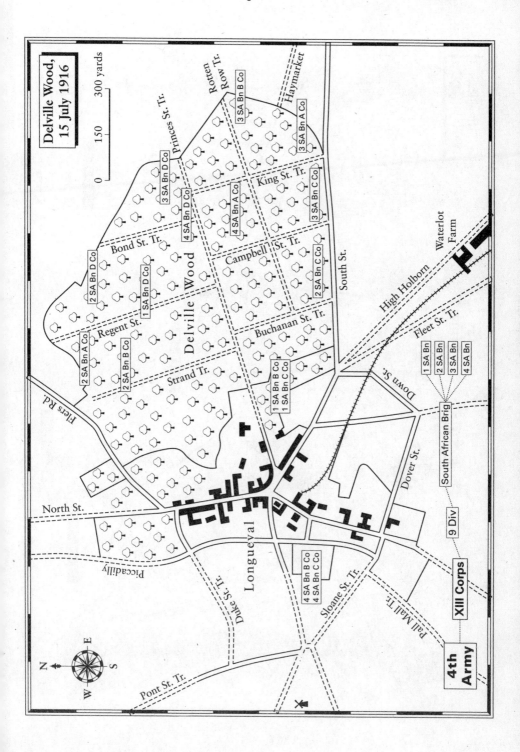

Delville Wood, 15 July 1916

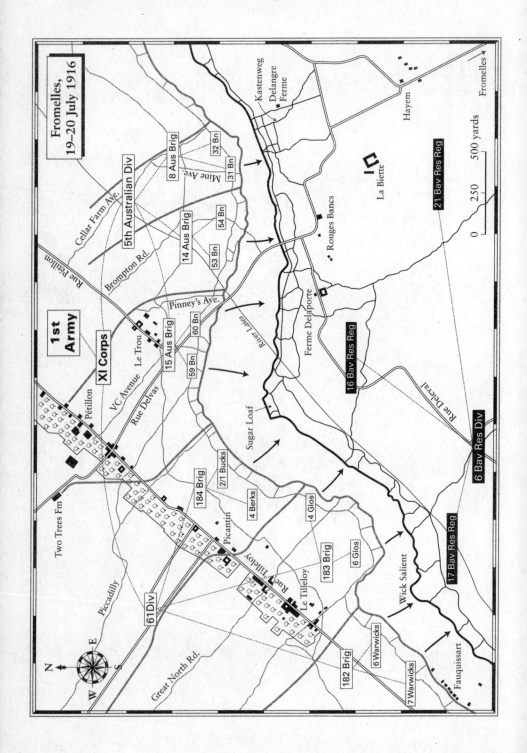

Fromelles, 19–20 July 1916

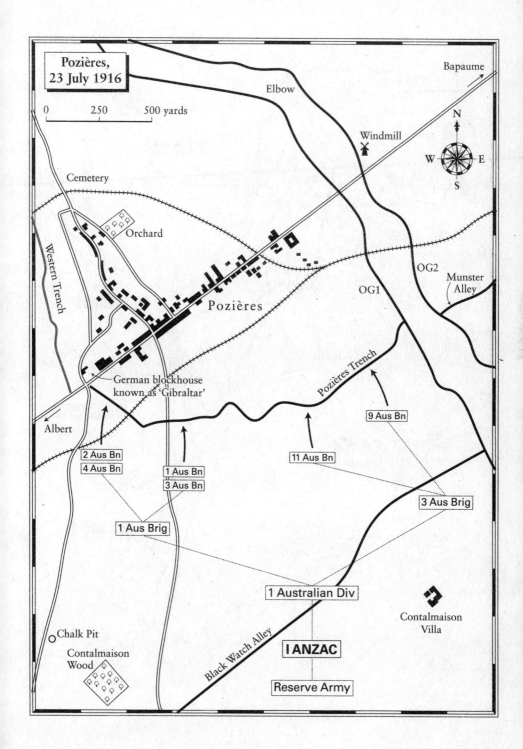

Map 14

XXXV

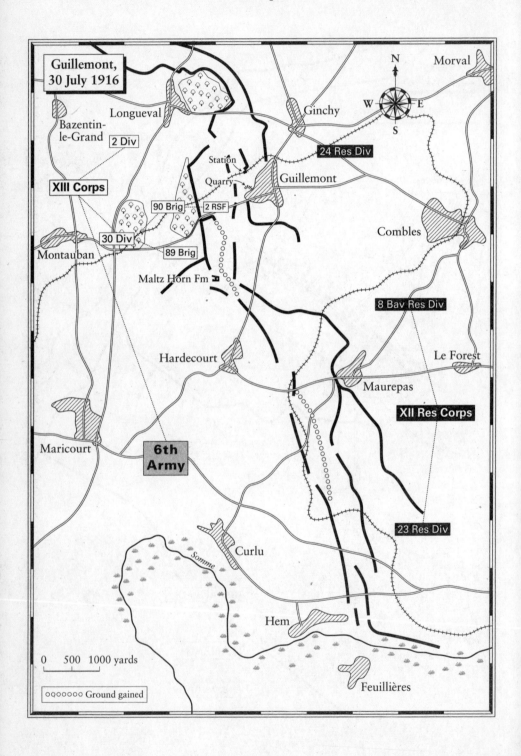

Guillemont,
30 July 1916

Morval

N
W ─ E
S

Longueval

Bazentin-
le-Grand   2 Div   Ginchy

XIII Corps   24 Res Div

                              Station
                              Quarry   Guillemont

90 Brig   2 RSF   Combles

30 Div
89 Brig

Montauban

Maltz Horn Fm

                                                8 Bav Res Div

Hardecourt

                                         Le Forest

                                   Maurepas
                                                XII Res Corps

Maricourt

6th
Army   23 Res Div

                                   Curlu

                    Somme

                              Hem

0   500 1000 yards

○○○○○○○ Ground gained

                                   Feuillières

Map 16 xxxvii

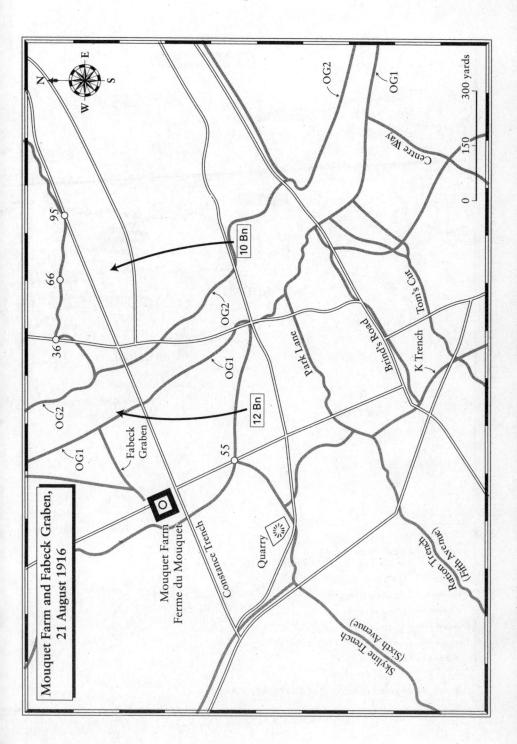

Mouquet Farm and Fabeck Graben,
21 August 1916

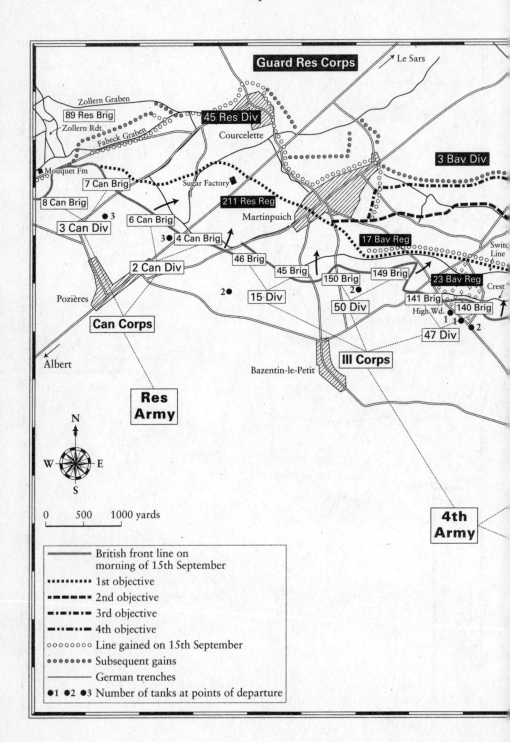

Guard Res Corps

Le Sars

Zollern Graben

89 Res Brig

45 Res Div

Zollern Rdt.

Fabeck Graben

Courcelette

3 Bav Div

Mouquet Fm

7 Can Brig

Sugar Factory

8 Can Brig

211 Res Reg

● 3

6 Can Brig

Martinpuich

3 Can Div

3 ● 4 Can Brig

17 Bav Reg

Switc
Line

2 Can Div

46 Brig

45 Brig

150 Brig

149 Brig

23 Bav Reg

Crest

Pozières

2 ●

15 Div

2 ●

141 Brig

140 Brig

Can Corps

50 Div

High. Wd.

1 ●

2

47 Div

Albert

Bazentin-le-Petit

III Corps

Res
Army

N

W ⊕ E

S

4th
Army

0   500   1000 yards

——— British front line on
       morning of 15th September

········· 1st objective

------ 2nd objective

-·-·-·- 3rd objective

-··-··- 4th objective

ooooooo Line gained on 15th September

●●●●●●● Subsequent gains

——— German trenches

●1 ●2 ●3 Number of tanks at points of departure

Map 17   xxxix

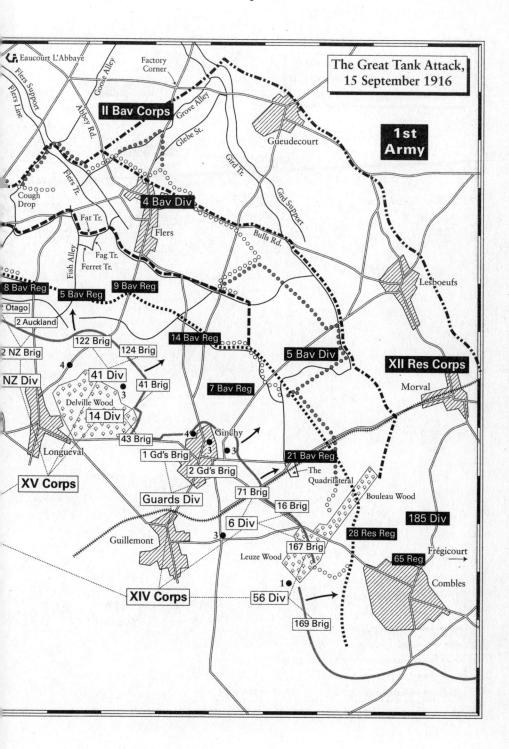

The Great Tank Attack,
15 September 1916

1st Army

Eaucourt L'Abbaye

Factory Corner

II Bav Corps

Gueudecourt

Flers Support

Flers Line

Goose Alley

Abbey Rd.

Grove Alley

Glebe St.

Gird Tr.

Gird Support

Flers Tr.

4 Bav Div

Cough Drop

Fat Tr.

Flers

Bulls Rd.

Lesboeufs

Fag Tr.

Fish Alley

Ferret Tr.

8 Bav Reg

5 Bav Reg

9 Bav Reg

Otago

2 Auckland

122 Brig

124 Brig

14 Bav Reg

5 Bav Div

XII Res Corps

2 NZ Brig

41 Div

41 Brig

4

7 Bav Reg

Morval

NZ Div

Delville Wood

3

14 Div

43 Brig

4

Ginchy

Longueval

1 Gd's Brig

3

3

21 Bav Reg

XV Corps

2 Gd's Brig

The Quadrilateral

Bouleau Wood

Guards Div

71 Brig

16 Brig

185 Div

6 Div

28 Res Reg

Guillemont

3

167 Brig

65 Reg

Frégicourt

Leuze Wood

XIV Corps

1

56 Div

Combles

169 Brig

Map 18

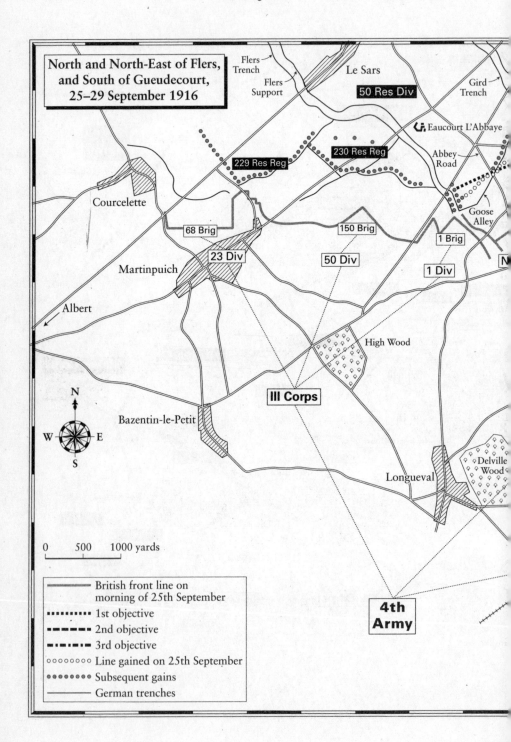

North and North-East of Flers,
and South of Gueudecourt,
25–29 September 1916

Flers Trench

Flers Support

Le Sars

50 Res Div

Gird Trench

Eaucourt L'Abbaye

230 Res Reg

Abbey Road

229 Res Reg

Goose Alley

Courcelette

68 Brig

150 Brig

1 Brig

N

23 Div

50 Div

1 Div

Martinpuich

Albert

High Wood

N

W   E

S

III Corps

Bazentin-le-Petit

Delville Wood

Longueval

0   500   1000 yards

British front line on
morning of 25th September

1st objective

2nd objective

3rd objective

Line gained on 25th September

Subsequent gains

German trenches

4th
Army

Map 18   xli

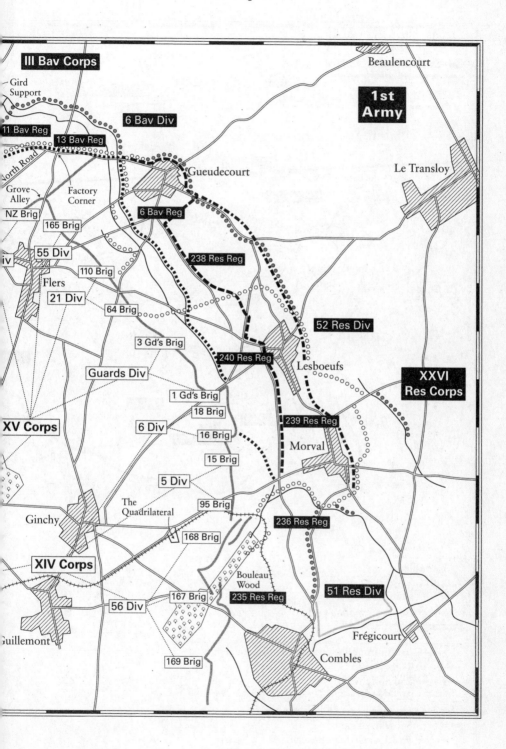

III Bav Corps

Gird
Support

11 Bav Reg

13 Bav Reg

6 Bav Div

North Road

Grove
Alley

Factory
Corner

NZ Brig

165 Brig

Gueudecourt

6 Bav Reg

Le Transloy

1st
Army

Beaulencourt

55 Div

iv

110 Brig

Flers

21 Div

64 Brig

3 Gd's Brig

Guards Div

1 Gd's Brig

18 Brig

XV Corps

6 Div

16 Brig

15 Brig

5 Div

95 Brig

Ginchy

The
Quadrilateral

168 Brig

XIV Corps

56 Div

167 Brig

Guillemont

169 Brig

238 Res Reg

240 Res Reg

Lesboeufs

52 Res Div

239 Res Reg

Morval

236 Res Reg

Bouleau
Wood

235 Res Reg

XXVI
Res Corps

51 Res Div

Frégicourt

Combles

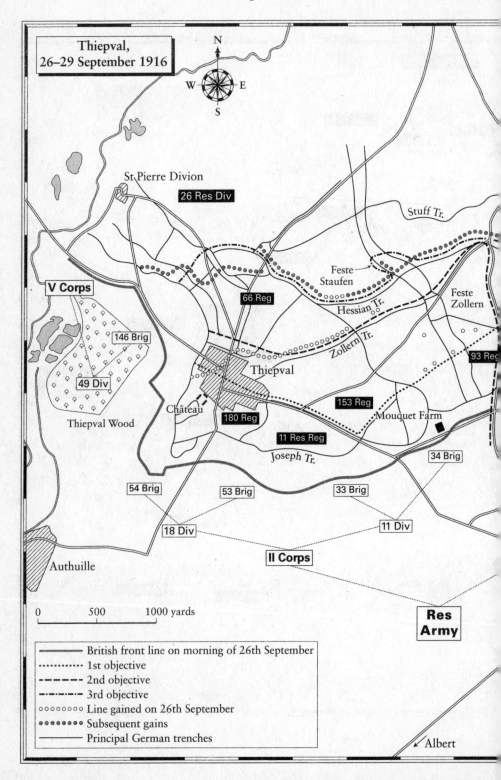

**Thiepval,
26–29 September 1916**

N
W   E
S

St Pierre Divion

26 Res Div

Stuff Tr.

V Corps

Feste
Staufen

Feste
Zollern

146 Brig

66 Reg

Hessian Tr.

49 Div

Zollern Tr.

93 Reg

Thiepval

Thiepval Wood

Château

153 Reg

180 Reg

Mouquet Farm

11 Res Reg

Joseph Tr.

34 Brig

54 Brig

53 Brig

33 Brig

18 Div

11 Div

Authuille

II Corps

Res
Army

0   500   1000 yards

———— British front line on morning of 26th September
.... 1st objective
– – – – 2nd objective
–·–·–·– 3rd objective
ooooooo Line gained on 26th September
•••••••• Subsequent gains
———— Principal German trenches

Albert

Map 19   xliii

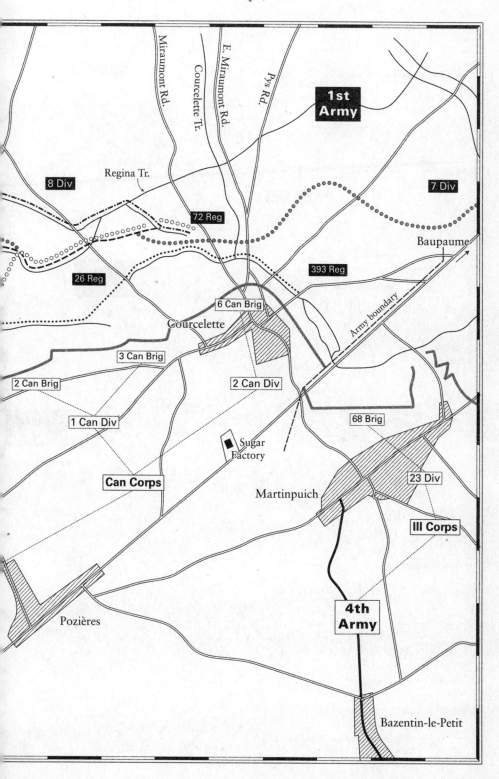

Miraumont Rd.

Courcelette Tr.

E. Miraumont Rd.

Pys Rd.

1st Army

Regina Tr.

8 Div

7 Div

72 Reg

Baupaume

393 Reg

26 Reg

Army boundary

6 Can Brig

Courcelette

3 Can Brig

2 Can Brig

2 Can Div

68 Brig

1 Can Div

Sugar Factory

23 Div

Can Corps

Martinpuich

III Corps

Pozières

4th Army

Bazentin-le-Petit

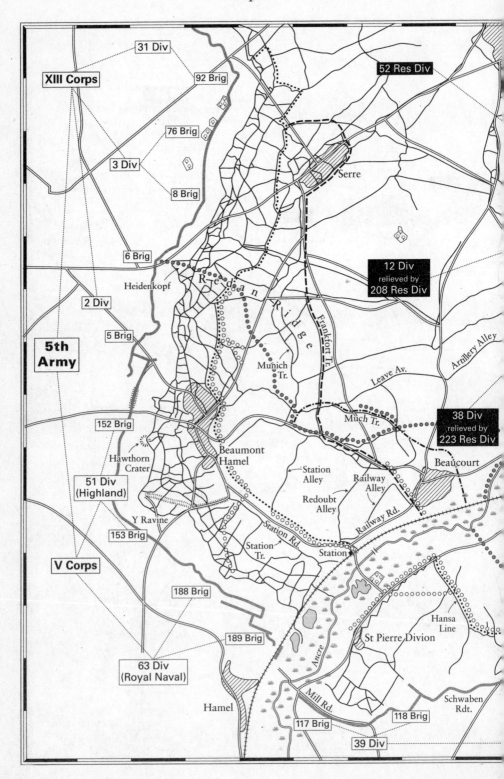

XIII Corps

31 Div
92 Brig
76 Brig
3 Div
8 Brig
6 Brig

52 Res Div

Serre

12 Div
relieved by
208 Res Div

Heidenkopf

R e d a n

Munich
Tr.

Frankfort Tr.

R i d g e

Leave Av.

Artillery Alley

2 Div

5 Brig

5th
Army

152 Brig

Much Tr.

38 Div
relieved by
223 Res Div

Hawthorn
Crater

Beaumont
Hamel

Station
Alley

Railway
Alley

Beaucourt

51 Div
(Highland)

Redoubt
Alley

Railway Rd.

Y Ravine

153 Brig

Station Rd.

Station
Tr.

Station

V Corps

188 Brig

Hansa
Line

189 Brig

St Pierre Divion

63 Div
(Royal Naval)

Hamel

Ancre

Mill Rd.

Schwaben
Rdt.

117 Brig

118 Brig

39 Div

Map 20

xlv

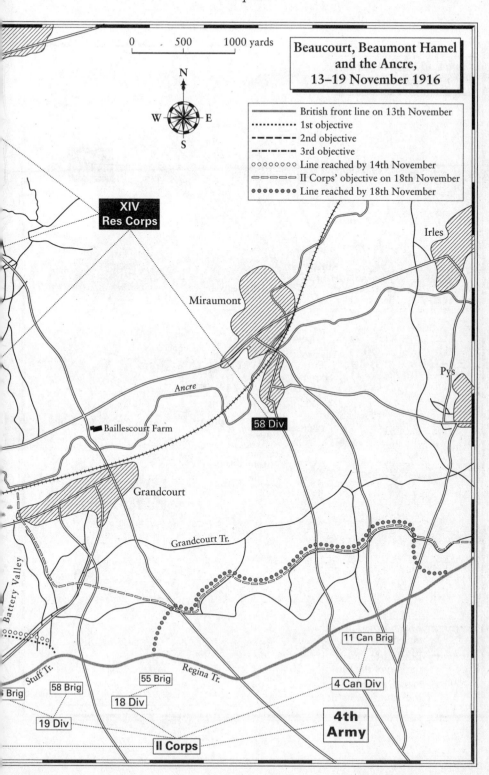

0   500   1000 yards

N
W — E
S

**Beaucourt, Beaumont Hamel
and the Ancre,
13–19 November 1916**

——————— British front line on 13th November
·················· 1st objective
– – – – – 2nd objective
–·–·–·– 3rd objective
ooooooooo Line reached by 14th November
======= II Corps' objective on 18th November
●●●●●●● Line reached by 18th November

**XIV
Res Corps**

Irles

Miraumont

Pys

Ancre

■ Baillescourt Farm

58 Div

Grandcourt

Grandcourt Tr.

Battery Valley

11 Can Brig

Stuff Tr.

58 Brig   *Regina Tr.*

Brig   58 Brig   55 Brig   4 Can Div

18 Div

19 Div

II Corps   **4th
Army**

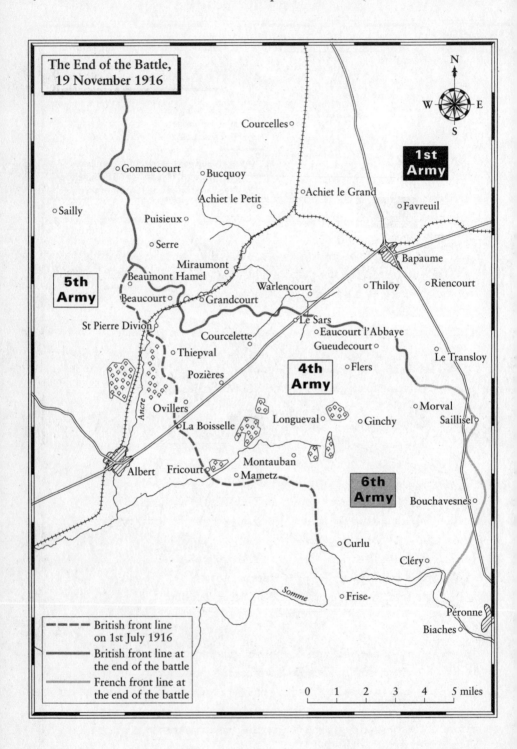

**The End of the Battle,
19 November 1916**

N
W   E
S

Courcelles

1st
Army

Gommecourt

Bucquoy

Achiet le Grand

Sailly

Achiet le Petit

Favreuil

Puisieux

Serre

Miraumont

Beaumont Hamel

5th
Army

Thiloy

Riencourt

Beaucourt

Grandcourt

Bapaume

St Pierre Divion

Warlencourt

Le Sars

Eaucourt l'Abbaye

Courcelette

Gueudecourt

Le Transloy

Thiepval

Pozières

4th
Army

Flers

Ovillers

Morval

Saillisel

La Boisselle

Longueval

Ginchy

Albert

Fricourt

Montauban

Mametz

6th
Army

Bouchavesnes

Curlu

Cléry

Ancre

Somme

Frise

Péronne

Biaches

- - - British front line
on 1st July 1916

—— British front line at
the end of the battle

—— French front line at
the end of the battle

0   1   2   3   4   5 miles

Note to the Reader

ANZ – see NZ ANZ
ATL – see NZ ATL
AWM – Australian War Memorial, Canberra
Churchill College – Churchill Archives Centre, Churchill College,
    Cambridge
Fourth or 4th Army Papers or Records – The Fourth Army Records of
    Lord Rawlinson, in IWM Documents 20537
Generallandesarchiv Karlsruhe – Landesarchiv Baden-Württemberg:
    Generallandesarchiv Karlsruhe
Hauptstaatsarchiv Stuttgart – Landesarchiv Baden-Württemberg:
    Hauptstaatsarchiv Stuttgart
IWM – Imperial War Museum, London
Liddle Archive or Collection – Liddle Collection, Leeds University
    Library
NAM – see NZ NAM
NSW – State Library of New South Wales, Sydney, Australia
NZ ANZ – Archives New Zealand, Wellington, New Zealand
NZ ATL – Alexander Turnbull Library, Wellington, New Zealand
NZ NAM – National Army Museum, Waiouru, New Zealand
Personal file for Australian soldier – personal file in National Archives of
    Australia, Canberra
Red Cross file for Australian soldiers – Australian Red Cross Society:
    Wounded and Missing Enquiry Bureau files via AWM website
SLV – State Library of Victoria, Melbourne, Australia

★ ★ ★

Because many of the accounts and other documents quoted in this book
were not written for publication, words and punctuation necessary to
make them easy to read or comprehensible have often been omitted by
their authors. Alternatively the grammar is faulty. I have taken the liberty of correcting punctuation where this has occurred, but when I have

added a word to help the sense, I have placed it in square brackets, and when I have omitted a word or phrase, or moved a word or phrase within the quotation, I have marked this action by inserting three dots. I have used round brackets inside a quotation if I am explaining the meaning of what is quoted.

1: Great Expectations

Beaumont Hamel, 1 July 1916

(See map 4)

At 7.19 a.m. on 1 July 1916, the tension in the British trenches opposite the German stronghold of Beaumont Hamel reached fever pitch. Expectations of victory had never been higher. The 'Big Push' was about to begin.

For seven days, as part of the softening-up process before the great advance, British and French artillery had been pounding the German front line to the north and south of where it was bisected by the River Somme. However, the point where the German line scaled the heights that dominate Beaumont Hamel, a sleepy French village 11 miles north of the river, was receiving some of the closest attention. It was one of several German strongpoints where British miners, supported by the infantry, were hoping to administer the *coup de grâce*.

Unbeknown to the Germans, the miners had hacked their way through the chalk, until they had hollowed out a 350-yard-long tunnel that ran from behind their own line, east of the village of Auchonvillers, to beneath the part of the heights known as Hawthorn Redoubt, on the German side of No Man's Land (see map 4).[1] Then, having packed the mine with 40,000 pounds of explosives, and having connected wiring, detonators and guncotton primers, they had scuttled back to the area behind the British front parapet. There, they joined the other 230,000 British soldiers, who along with their French counterparts to the south, represented the largest strike force assembled since the German invasion of France in 1914.[2] Now the British infantry were only waiting for the commanders of the tunnelling companies controlling this mine, and the mines secreted under a series of other strongpoints in the German front line, to push down their plungers, before they charged over the top.

Geoffrey Malins, a British cameraman, who at this crucial juncture had come to the British front line to film Hawthorn Redoubt, the strongpoint on the Beaumont Hamel heights that was to be exploded (see map 4), described for posterity what some soldiers were expecting to be the defining moment of the war, in the following terms:

Time 7.19 a.m. My hand grasped the handle of the camera . . . Another thirty
seconds passed. I started turning the handle . . . My object in exposing half a minute before . . . [zero hour] was to get the mine from the moment it broke ground.
I fixed my eyes on the Redoubt. Any second now. Surely it was time. It seemed to
me as if I had been turning for hours . . . Why doesn't it go up? I looked at my
exposure dial. I had used over a thousand feet. The horrible thought flashed
through my mind that my film might run out before the mine blew. The thought
brought beads of perspiration to my forehead . . . Then it happened.

The ground where I stood gave a massive convulsion. It rocked and swayed. I
gripped hold of my tripod to steady myself. Then, for all the world like a gigantic
sponge, the earth rose in the air . . . hundreds of feet. Higher and higher it rose . . .
[Then], with a horrible grinding roar, the earth fell back upon itself, leaving in its
place a mountain of smoke . . .[3]

The explosion certainly stunned the German defenders, who were already
struggling to cope with the regular bombardment. According to one of the
survivors in the 119th Reserve Infantry Regiment, the 26th Reserve Division unit that manned the Redoubt:

[It made] such a loud bang . . . that it was clear it was not made by the firing of any
gun. It was accompanied by an enormous smoke cloud which reared up into the
air in front of [our] . . . 9th Company, while stones rained down onto the
position . . . The explosion killed the men in three of the Company's sections . . .
and entombed those in the dugouts nearby . . . [Afterwards], the surrounding
field was as white as if it had just snowed, and, cut out of the side of the hill, [we
could see] the yawning mouth of an [enormous] crater, 50–60 metres across and
20 metres deep.

The explosion was the signal for the attack. Wave after wave of enemy troops
emerged from the British trenches and walked towards us, their bayonets glinting
in the sun . . .[4]

The cameraman on the British side of No Man's Land, Geoffrey Malins,
also reported the infantrymen's advance:

[After] the earth was down, I swung my camera round on to our own parapets.
[Men] . . . were [climbing] over [them] . . . and streaming along the skyline . . .
Then another signal rang out, and from the trenches immediately in front of me,
[more of] our wonderful troops went over the top. What a picture it was! They

went over as one man . . . [and crossed] . . . the ground in swarms . . . still smoking cigarettes. One man actually stopped in the middle of No Man's Land to light up again.

The Germans had by now realized that the great attack had come. Shrapnel poured into our trenches. They had even got their crumps . . . into . . . our boys before they were half way across No Man's Land. But still they kept on.

At that moment my spool ran out. I gave it to my man in a dugout to take care of, impressing on him he must not leave it under any circumstances. If anything unforeseen happened [to me], he was to take it back to Headquarters.[5]

But Malins was not the only British witness to the great events unfolding. An account written by a signaller, stationed in a forward position a few hundred yards to the south, takes up where Malins' statement was cut off:

I [had] watched . . . the lads mount the firestep, and . . . spring up the ladders onto the parapet . . . with mixed feeling[s] . . . Many slid . . . back [as soon as] they . . . reached the top, killed or wounded . . . The survivors [had] worked their way through our barbed wire in the face of the fierce shell and machine-gun fire, leaving [behind] many of their pals . . . They went up the long incline in perfect order, dropping to the ground every now and then, as if on an exercise on Salisbury Plain, regardless . . . of the intense shelling and small arms fire around and ahead of them. The line thinned as men fell, but [it] never faltered, [and] at last they vanished from sight, into the inferno on the ridge beyond . . . All that we could see was the bursting of heavy shells, and [over the sound of the artillery, we heard] . . . the rattle of machine guns and small arms fire.[6]

One of the German machine-gunners, whose weapon was 'rattling' on the next height, a mile and a half to the north, in the trench sector protecting the hilltop village of Serre, was Unteroffizier Otto Lais. He described how the distinctive 'calm, solid, regular tacking' of the machine guns could be heard 'above all [the] . . . rumbling, growling . . . and wild banging of the [artillery and infantry guns]: "tack-tack tack-tack". One gun "tacked" with a slower rhythm, while another gun "tacked" faster . . . It was an ominous melody as far as the enemy was concerned. Whereas it reassured and calmed our infantry.'[7]

No account has yet come to light by any member of the British unit, the 2nd Battalion, the Royal Fusiliers, whose men rushed forward to occupy the lips of the gigantic crater, gouged out of the chalk, on Hawthorn Ridge.

Perhaps none of them survived, or perhaps what they observed was too awful for them to want to replay it in their mind's eye in all its gory details.[8] However, the following description of the aftermath of the explosion, by the aforementioned witness in the German 119th Reserve Regiment, suggests that there must have been at least one exquisite moment for the attackers, when they would have believed that all the digging underground – at great personal risk – had been worthwhile:

Near the crater, the British soldiers encountered no resistance . . . [This was because] the [9th] Company's 3rd platoon had been trapped in a big dugout where three of the four exits had been buried. The sentry was trying to break out of the fourth exit, which had been reduced to a very small hole, [when the first British soldiers reached the German position] . . . Before he could get out, he was killed with a thrust from a [British] bayonet, and his falling corpse knocked down the men who were standing on the [dugout] stairs behind him. A German officer retaliated by shooting the sentry's assailant in the face with a flare, a response which prompted the attackers to lob hand grenades and smoke bombs into the dugout. But the trapped Germans refused to surrender, banking on their regiment to send up reinforcements to rescue them.[9]

Subsequent events proved they were right not to give in immediately. Even as the Germans cowered in their subterranean refuge, hoping against hope that their attackers would run out of hand grenades before blasting them to kingdom come, British fortunes all of a sudden nosedived: the waves of British attackers in the northern sectors of their line, who had advanced at 7.30 a.m., zero hour for all troops not in the vanguard attacking the area around the mine on Hawthorn Ridge, were swept aside by a wall of bullets fired by the German machine-gunners, isolating those who had advanced ten minutes earlier, just after the mine exploded.

Evidence of this comes from Otto Lais, the machine-gunner protecting Serre. The following extract from his account describes how, after repulsing the first British attack, the relatively few guns operated by him and his fellow machine-gunners dashed British attempts to take Serre once and for all:

After the confusion and panic caused by our unexpected resistance, and the heavy casualties, the English redeployed. Then, for the next two hours, wave after wave of their troops attempted to beat down our door. They fearlessly ran towards our positions, only to be shot down before they could get past our wire. [Only] the most intrepid made it to within 20 . . . metres of our guns.

Those following took shelter behind their fallen comrades, some of whom were still groaning and moaning. Many of these men whimpered as they hung, fatally wounded, on the remnants of our wire. The survivors took refuge behind the small slope by our wire, where, like mad men, they fired at us without taking the time to aim their guns carefully . . . We fired at the stakes holding up the wire . . . and our bullets ricocheted onto the slope occupied by the English. It was not long before the enemy fire coming from behind the slope petered out . . .

[However] new waves emerged [from the English trenches] . . . only to sink back behind their parapets. [Then their] officers ran forward, in a [vain] attempt to inspire their men to follow their example . . . Numerous helmets became visible, but they disappeared again immediately after bullets from rifles and machine guns sprayed the position, where they had been taking cover. After that, no more English officers left their trenches, the sight of the battlefield demoralizing any would-be attackers.

Lais' account of 1 July concludes with what he witnessed that evening:

Our losses were very heavy, but the enemy's were unimaginable. Whole companies and battalions of English troops lay on the ground, having been mown down in lines, swept away. No Man's Land in between the English and German positions was full of miserable scenes. There was no more fighting. It was as if the surfeit of misery had frozen any action . . .

An English medical team appeared . . . with an unfolded Red Cross flag . . . Where to begin? Whimpering men were calling out from nearly every square metre of ground. Our own medical orderlies helped out, wherever they were needed. The victims, who moments before had been [regarded as a threat because they were] the enemy, were now just injured fellow human beings, who could be handed over to their own countrymen [without fear of reprisals].[10]

No Man's Land opposite Hawthorn Redoubt and the area around the crater, which was swiftly reclaimed from the British, could only be described as 'horrific' by the writer of the 119th Reserve Regiment's regimental history. He went on to report that 'Poison gas [released by the British troops during the days before the attack] had whitened [No Man's Land] . . . and made the grass look as if it was corroded. Corpses, dressed in khaki brown uniforms, and wounded soldiers, lay in hundreds between the enemies' lines.' Piles of the dead from both sides lay beside the chalk that was heaped up around the rim of the crater. The only redeeming feature from the German point of view was the re-emergence from the earth of one of their buried officers with a few of his men. 'They dug themselves out just as the last of their supply of air was about to be used up.'[11]

Given the extremity of the torment experienced on the battlefield, it is astonishing how long it took for accurate news of the disaster to reach those in command. The contrast between the nightmarish chaos in and between the front lines, and what initially filtered back to the British commanders miles to their rear, could not have been more striking. There had been what amounted to mass slaughter of a substantial proportion of the British VIII Corps' troops, who had tried and failed to capture the German front lines at the northern end of the Somme front. That did not just apply to the men with VIII Corps' 29th Division, who had been attacking the German trenches to the north and south of the mine on Hawthorn Ridge, near Beaumont Hamel. It also aptly described the plight of VIII Corps' 31st Division, whose annihilation opposite Serre, the next village to the north, has been described by machine-gunner Otto Lais.

Yet for a considerable time the headquarters of the 4th Army, the unit under General Sir Henry Rawlinson that was supposed to be masterminding the attack from its chateau in Querrieu, some 14 miles south-west of the Hawthorn Redoubt, was oblivious to the pain and suffering on the front line. At 8 a.m. its first situation report relating to VIII Corps complacently concluded: 'The whole of the Corps reported over the German front line.'[12]

It was 11.30 a.m. before the 4th Army war diarists sounded a note of caution, stating in relation to the 29th Division: 'Enemy have retaken front line and cut off troops that got through.'[13] Over three hours passed before the 4th Army recorded, at 3 p.m., that the bulk of the 29th and 31st Division troops were 'back in our own front line'.[14] However, as late as 10 p.m. on the night of 1–2 July, orders were still being given to the 31st Division telling them to 'attack . . . and try to join up with two battalions still believed to be in Serre', even though no such units were there.[15]

Similar excessively optimistic reports glossed over the horrendous casualties sustained without material gain opposite many of the other strongholds in the German front line attacked by British troops on 1 July.[16] The only true breakthrough made by British forces occurred at the southern end of the Somme line, near the villages of Montauban and Mametz.

(The French also broke through to the south of the 4th Army.)[17] But even in and around these two villages the victory was inconclusive, because Rawlinson failed to authorize renewed attacks quickly enough beyond the prearranged objectives of the first day. This permitted the Germans to regroup before the breach in their line could be widened and exploited.

Due to the frustratingly slow communication back from VIII Corps' front line, it is not surprising, given what appears in the 4th Army war diary, to discover that the first words in General Rawlinson's personal diary for 1 July, recording his view of the events up to 9.20 a.m., reads: 'The battle has begun well . . . We captured all the front line trenches easily.'[18] The second entry, made at 12.15 p.m., was equally optimistic, asserting that 'The VIII Corps has taken Serre.' Only at 3.15 p.m. did Rawlinson come closer to the truth: 'The VIII Corps have been pushed out of Serre and Beaumont Hamel.'

An equally ill-informed view of operations may have prompted Rawlinson's superior, the British Commander-in-Chief General Sir Douglas Haig, to comment the next day that the British casualties 'cannot be considered severe in view of the numbers engaged and the length of line attacked'. But this was on the basis that he believed there were 'only' 40,000 men killed, wounded or missing.[19] Later analysis showed that casualties on 1 July 1916 were in excess of 57,000 (including at least 19,000 men killed), a huge total for just one day of operations, and one that certainly could not be sustained on a daily basis during what was likely to be a lengthy campaign.[20]

How had it come to this? How could the British Army with its overwhelming numerical superiority (nineteen British infantry divisions fighting against five German divisions), and with the tactical advantage of being able to choose the time and the place to launch its attack so that it could maximize its troops' efficiency by preparing for the battle, have contrived to lose more men in a single day than it had ever lost before?[21] And why had it failed to follow up the one decisive breakthrough made on 1 July, the exploitation of which might perhaps have justified such high casualties?

2: Paradise Lost

England and Northern France, November 1915–May 1916

(See map 1)

At the beginning of 1916, that is six months before the commencement of the 'Big Push', the British Expeditionary Force (the BEF) in France and Belgium consisted of thirty-eight infantry and five cavalry divisions (in excess of 987,000 men). They held around 67 of the 87 miles of trenches that stretched between Boesinghe, near Ypres, Belgium, in the north and the Somme near Curlu, France, in the south.[1] The trenches to the south were held by the French Army, and they ran all the way to France's border with Switzerland. The Belgian and French Armies held the trenches to the north.[2]

This long line of trenches was the legacy of the German attempt in August 1914 to invade and take over Belgium and France. Thanks to British, French and Belgian resistance – which encompassed celebrated actions such as the BEF's retreat from the area around Mons in Belgium in August 1914, as well as the Anglo-French counter-attack on the Marne in France the following month – the German advance was halted. Whereupon both sides dug in on the terrain they then occupied, thereby putting an end to what is sometimes referred to as the war of movement. The result was a stalemate, with British, French and Belgian trenches snaking from north to south through Belgium and France opposite an equally long German line.

Subsequent attempts by the Germans, and the French and British Armies, to cut through the entrenched lines opposing them, had proved fruitless, raising the question: would it ever be possible? The French and British generals believed they could break the deadlock, if they were only given enough guns and ammunition, provided they did not repeat the errors made in the previous operations. With that in mind, in the course of a conference at Chantilly, France, in December 1915, they reached an agreement as to what they should do next. The two countries would mount a major offensive during 1916 at more or less the same time as the Russian planned offensive on the Eastern Front.

Such plans required more boots on the ground. Over the next months, the British recruitment drive led to a dramatic increase in the size of the

BEF. By 1 July 1916, the date when the planned offensive commenced, the number of men under British command on the Continent had risen to in excess of 1,488,000. They were divided up into fifty-eight divisions. The commander of each of these divisions controlled three brigades, which in turn contained four battalions, battalions being the units of around 700 to 1,000 men who actually did the fighting in the front line. These divisions were in turn controlled by the commanders of eighteen corps, and these corps answered to the commanders of four armies (see map 1).[3] All of these troops acted under the direction of the British General Headquarters (GHQ) commanded by General Sir Douglas Haig.

Given that many of the regular full-time British troops had become casualties during the initial German offensive, the core of the British Army in 1916 consisted of inexperienced volunteers. Their units are sometimes referred to collectively as the New Armies. They largely consisted of the men raised following the fabulously successful recruitment campaign featuring the charismatic Secretary of State for War, Field Marshal Earl (Horatio Herbert) Kitchener, as well as some of the so-called 'Derby men'. These were the last volunteers recruited pursuant to a scheme instigated by Lord Derby, Director General of Recruiting, shortly before conscription was introduced for single men in Britain in January 1916. Conscription was only extended to cover married men four months later.[4]

Many of the pre-conscription volunteers served in Pals battalions, the generic name given to those battalions whose recruits had a link either with a particular profession or an area. This enabled volunteers to enlist alongside friends and acquaintances. The downside was that these Pals battalions, like the other recruits raised by Kitchener, were full of novices who knew nothing of army life, let alone what it took to survive and fight in trenches. There was also the risk that if casualties in any particular unit were high, whole families or even whole communities could be more or less wiped out.

The top British generals cited the rudimentary training offered to these new recruits as the reason why they adopted pedestrian tactics on the battlefield. But that excuse was far from being the only explanation for what went wrong. Long before the beginning of the planned offensive, there was abundant evidence suggesting that the British Army was not the efficient force it was portrayed to be, and if more politicians had served in the ranks as well as on the generals' staffs, the government would have been in the know as well.

It is easy to see why Members of Parliament might not want to muck in with the lower ranks, or even with the junior officers. The facilities laid on for them in France were often basic to say the least. A portrait of the kind of privations and primitive conditions that the newly arrived soldiers had to put up with can be gleaned from the diaries and letters of four soldiers who served in the same battalion: the 22nd Battalion, the Manchester Regiment, one Pals battalion that was to be entrusted with a particularly important role in the attack being planned.

Like many of the Pals battalions, the 22nd Manchesters, also known as the 7th Manchester Pals, contained a substantial number of middle-class professionals, some of whom were already making their mark in civilian life when war was declared. They included a barrister who was to become a Member of Parliament and the government's Solicitor General after the war, a future editor of the *New Statesman* and two university lecturers.

Most of these professionals and intellectuals were officers. However, Harry Tawney, a left-wing university lecturer of economic history, whose work would one day lead to him being referred to as one of the brains behind the post-war Labour Party, refused to take the commission offered to him, preferring to serve initially as a private and subsequently as a sergeant. It is largely thanks to Tawney that we know about some of the hardships men in the ranks had to endure, as well as the inefficiencies within the Army which were particularly galling for those who were often dismissively referred to as the 'poor bloody infantry'.

If one can believe the reassuring letters that Tawney sent to his wife Jeannette before going to France, he handled the trench-digging training exercises surprisingly easily for a man approaching middle age who was not used to physical exercise. He was thirty-four years old at the time of writing. In one such letter he wrote: 'It was quite hard work digging them. One uses a pick and a spade. But I found I could do it as well as the others and am only a little stiff today.'[5]

He found grenade-throwing practice more exacting. It involved 'getting into trenches and throwing small bags filled with earth as imitation bombs,' Tawney informed Jeannette. 'It is more difficult than it sounds, for the trenches are very narrow and deep, and if one knocks the side, one would probably be blown up.'[6] However, both activities were preferable to 'squad drill of which we are all heartily sick',[7] Tawney concluded.

His battalion left Lark Hill, the army base on Salisbury Plain, on 10 November 1915, and after a brief delay in Folkestone the men were shipped to Boulogne, the entry port for many of the BEF units sent to

France. The departure was particularly hard to bear for those with young families. The resulting homesickness prompted Charlie May, a twenty-seven-year-old captain in the 22nd Manchesters, to scribble a series of heartfelt entries addressed to his wife Maude in the diaries he wrote up each day he was away from his family. It is an extraordinary record, given that unlike so many World War I diaries it does not just list the day's events. It provides a full account of May's hopes and anxieties, and contains countless professions of love both for Maude and for Pauline, their newly born daughter.

'When shall we meet again?' he wrote wistfully on the eve of the battalion's departure for France, continuing: 'When will the time come when we can once more set up our home and recommence our life of utter happiness? Ah Maudie, how little I realized where happiness lay until this old war came along and it was denied me.'[8]

The letter that Tawney wrote to his sister Mildred on 22 November 1915 describes the conditions that the members of his battalion had to endure on their arrival in France:

When we first landed, we had two rather bad days. First an awful night under canvas in rain which lasted for about 24 hours and made the whole place a swamp. Then after about 4 hours in cattle trucks, a march of some 15 miles in which we contrived to lose our way. Since then . . . we are billeted with . . . the peasants. I and another sergeant sleep in a little hut, one half of which is occupied by a pig, [albeit] a very clean and quiet one . . . We sleep on straw with a blanket each.[9]

Captain May, who was less enamoured with the simplicity of peasant life, and who appears to have regarded his absence from his idealized home as something akin to paradise lost, analysed their resting place less enthusiastically. According to his diary, Brucamps, the village where they had ended up (sixteen miles north-west of Amiens), stank because of the mounds of dung piled up beside each house.[10] Its inhabitants were filthy. Not that you could blame them. There was no running water, and May's men had to design and dig their own sewage system. Bracing route marches were necessary to ward off the icy cold. Within days of their arrival, the ground was carpeted with snow. To add insult to injury, the peasants overcharged the battalion for the firewood that the soldiers had to burn to keep warm, only lowering the price after some hard bargaining. This prompted May, referring to a stereotype that was then commonplace amongst the officer class, to complain: 'I think the French peasantry [must] have Hebrew blood in their veins in degrees of varying intensity.'[11]

Complaints about the cost of firewood must have been the last subject on the minds of recruits on their way to the Somme from sunnier climes. The reinforcements that were to swell the ranks of the BEF prior to the battle were not all from Britain. There were also soldiers from British dominions such as South Africa and Canada, and by the beginning of 1916 the Australian and New Zealand contingents in Egypt, who were eventually to serve under British command in France, contained well in excess of 100,000 men.[12]

The following account of the scene at Sydney's Wooloomooloo Wharf on 30 September 1915 as Private R. W. Harpley, an Australian Imperial Force recruit, left Australia, highlights the wave of patriotism which swept through the dominions after the news reached them that their mother country needed their help if they were to overcome their common enemies, the Germans and the Turks:

Just before entering the Wharf, all civilians were stopped . . . So the . . . farewell took place in the main street . . . We then boarded the transport ship *Argyleshire* . . . When all were aboard, the people were allowed onto the Wharf. They streamed in until the Wharf was just one mass of people . . . Almost everyone had a roll of streamers. These they threw up to the soldiers on the boat until there [were] . . . streamers of every colour imaginable from one end of the ship to the other . . . It presented the most beautiful sight I have ever witnessed.

It had such a glorious effect as the boat was swinging out that I believe it brought tears from every soldier's eyes, mine being no exception. It was about 10.30 a.m. when we moved off from the Wharf. We then put out to middle harbour and anchored until 5 p.m. when we finally set out on our long voyage to Egypt.[13]

The following extract, from a letter written by Leslie Kenney almost three months earlier, records how tears of a different kind were shed as he and his fellow signallers, part of the New Zealand Expeditionary Force's 6th Reinforcement troops, left Wellington in New Zealand. His letter starts with the words 'Dear Mother', and continues:

I will never forget our departure from Wellington Wharf. During our parade through the principal streets of Wellington, I was proud to be among the boys. I only realized in a dim sort of way what had caused so many people to assemble along our route. It was easy to call a cheerful 'Goodbye' to the many people whom I recognized, to the girls, Len, Ern and the kiddies. Even when I called out to you just before going onto the Wharf, I was so sure of seeing you on board, and saying 'goodbye' properly, that I hadn't given the final parting a thought.

So when I got on board, I scrambled . . . onto one of the lifeboats where I was sure of being seen . . . I semaphored Len as to your whereabouts . . . He [semaphored] back that you were too upset to see me . . . The news came as a blow. It was . . . not until then that I realized your share of the sacrifice. I kept on deck somehow until the ship cleared the wharf.

The last few minutes of leaving were like a huge and awful nightmare. The swaying, yelling people crowded on that wharf, and that beastly band assembled on that crane platform playing patriotic airs, the ship's frantic whistling as she cast off and backed slowly out, simply smothered with khaki clad men on her side nearest the Wharf, and with a list as if she would capsize any minute, is a memory which will last a lifetime.[14]

At least the 22nd Manchesters and the Australasians had time to acclimatize before going into action. That was a luxury denied to men like Private Arthur Wrench, who on 15 November 1915 was shipped from Southampton to Le Havre, the other commonly used route for the BEF's reinforcements. He was to make up the numbers in the 4th Battalion, the Seaforth Highlanders, part of the 51st Highland Division.

Before he had time to enquire why more men were needed, Wrench was whisked off to the Béthune sector, and within two days of arriving in France, found himself marching towards the front. He had to learn the ropes quickly.

The more experienced soldiers roared with laughter when, on the way, Wrench remarked that he could hear the rumbling of thunder in the distance. That was his first introduction to the sound of gunfire. No one was laughing when during Wrench's first night in the trenches, the company sergeant-major asked for volunteers to bury the dead in No Man's Land. Wrench's account states that he only stepped forward because he thought the sergeant-major was being facetious. But it was no joke. 'There were plenty of them there . . . ,' he wrote:

[Before burying them] we . . . [had to take] off their identity disks and . . . [give] them to the Company Sergeant Major . . . We heaped the earth over perhaps 50 bodies before we were spotted [by the Germans], and sent back to our trench by [their] machine-guns. It was the most gruesome sight imaginable to come into this so suddenly, and see these men lying mutilated and half decomposed, and black with the effects of poison gas.

It was all the more shocking for men such as Wrench, because it was the first time they had been outside their comfort zone. He himself had never travelled abroad before. It is not surprising, then, that for such men life away from the trenches was equally perplexing. Wrench was also appalled by his fellow soldiers' drinking habits, especially those who drank until they passed out on the floor.

It was only after he and his comrades were drenched during a compulsory church service that Wrench relented a little. He could understand why, in these circumstances, they might wish to drink away their sorrows afterwards, acknowledging that 'this other "spiritual" happiness' was necessary 'to counteract the ill effects of the drenching and cold [encountered] on the church parade'.

His growing tolerance for the soldiers' habits did not, however, stretch to his comrades' preoccupation with women. On 14 December 1915, nearly a month after arriving in France, Wrench wrote:

I am disgusted . . . with all the discussions and stories the fellows generally indulge in, and if they are not talking objectionably about the virtues of any particular girls in the village, they may be telling their experiences with other disreputable females in certain houses. Tonight some of us were squatted round a table in an estaminet drinking coffee and blathering to Mademoiselle Floré Lété, who is an incorrigible flirt. She showed us a few dozen photographs of different British soldiers, which she hurriedly hid in her blouse as her mother appeared.[15]

Perhaps it was fortunate he was not with the 1st Battalion, the Lancashire Fusiliers, when they were given permission to sample the nightlife in Armentières two months later. According to the Lancashire Fusiliers' Corporal George Ashurst, the estaminet he visited was full of soldiers, all drinking what they referred to as ' "vinn" blanc'. However, the real attraction was the five women up in the bedrooms. 'The steps leading up to the bedrooms were full. [There was] a man on every step waiting . . . [his] turn,' Ashurst reported. All was going well until the battalion's padre walked in. He was horrified by what he observed and asked 'Have none of you any mothers? Have none of you any sisters?' The padre then flounced out, promising to report what he had seen to the colonel, which he duly did. It was the last time they were allowed out for the whole evening. A curfew was subsequently imposed two hours after dark.[16]

The privates in the 22nd Manchesters, and presumably those in other units, might have enjoyed similar horizontal refreshment had they been left to their own devices. A note that Captain Charlie May wrote in his diary on 15 November 1915 stated that Canaples (11 miles north-west of Amiens), the village where his men spent much of their leisure time that month, had a 'café wherein two young ladies dispense drinks, or just as readily, photographs of themselves in the nude'. To this he added the observation:

It was not possible for me to sample either of the chief wares of the café, but I understand it has been [full] ... of my ... company, and the only reason why any of its stock is [still] in the possession of its proprietors, is the acute penury of my high-minded privates, who have not been paid for over a fortnight. I had intended paying them this morning, but a wise Providence decreed that I should forget the Acquittance roll. Thus a prolonged [period of] depravity has been avoided.[17]

Wrench's chastity and Ashurst's tale of unbridled lust and the poverty-stricken Manchesters' frustration probably represented only half the story. One wonders whether the sexual exploits of Eddie Bigwood, a private in the 7th Battalion, the Worcestershire Regiment, were more typical. Like many who enlisted under the Derby recruitment scheme, he had enlisted as a soldier on his eighteenth birthday, and had had little, if any, experience of a sexual nature involving women before he was shipped to France. That was what made a trip to White Star, a brothel in Rouen, so appealing. However, when the clanging of a bell as he and his mates entered the brothel prompted four or five beautiful girls to come running down the corridor to greet them, clad only in wispy transparent lace, the 'virgin' soldiers turned tail and ran for their lives.[18]

The prospect of being chased by nubile young women was not confined to houses of ill repute. The Anglo-Irish officer Frank Crozier, at the time in question a major in the 9th Battalion, the Royal Irish Rifles, has described how the young daughter of the house, where he was billeted on arriving in France, took to visiting him when he was in bed. She wore nothing but her nightdress. On the first night she used the pretext that she was bringing him a hot-water bottle. The next night she was slightly more direct, asking him whether he was happily married, and whether he had any children. Crozier could not help but observe how 'her long hair nestles round her neck and over her shoulders'. Fearing that he would not be able to resist her a third time, and knowing 'it is a dirty bird who fouls its own nest', he quit the billet before he was tempted to do something he might regret. It was only later that he learned it was routine for many billets to offer sex as an optional extra.[19]

Some British soldiers found that the French girls on the game were less of a threat outside the confines of a brothel. Lieutenant Lawrence Gameson, a doctor with the 45th Field Ambulance unit, recalled how while doing a bit of sightseeing, which involved walking around the cathedral in Amiens, 'a little caressing lady took my arm, and asked: "Where are you going darling?" I told her and passed on', without feeling harassed or intimidated. 'These girls for the most part do not solicit in the cruder London manner,' he commented. 'Rather they suggest in a way entirely without offence that they are at your service.'

Having said that, Gameson's journal also contains an account of how one French prostitute tipped a bottle of scent over a fellow officer. This did not go down well with their colonel. At dinner that night, he sniffed disapprovingly and said 'Fisher, really!'[20]

While drinking French beer and wine and sleeping with French women spiced up long evenings spent out of the trenches, there was plenty of time during the day to concentrate on the main reason for coming to France: how to break through the German line and how to hold a position once it was taken. Digging trenches, shooting and practising moving through a wood were all on the training agenda, as was advancing on replicas of No Man's Land and the enemy front line. Great pride was taken in making one's own unit the best in the division.[21]

However, sometimes even the keenest soldier tired of the comradeship and communal living. Captain Charlie May's diary makes it only too clear how he chafed against the enforced lack of privacy. On New Year's Eve 1915–16 he would have given almost anything to have been left to his own devices. Solitude would have permitted him to daydream about what it would be like at home. As he confessed to Maude, who he hoped would one day read what he had written, May was happiest when slipping away on Lizzie, his horse, and riding through the countryside around Canaples so that he could, as he put it:

imagine that you were with me and that we had the open countryside to stroll through as so often we have done in the dear days before all the world were soldiers . . . I thought of you as we strolled there, Lizzie with her reins slack wandering where she would . . . and I longed that you could have been with me for I know how you would have loved it and how happy we two would have been. The green rides of Epping came back to me in a flash. You in that black spotted muslin dress you used to wear looking cool and lovely, so that I just asked nothing more than to walk along and gaze at you dumbly, like any simple country lout gazes at his maid.[22]

Such romantic yearnings were evidently absent from the letters he actually sent to Maude. On 13 January 1916, May wrote in his diary:

I have a letter from you tonight in which you ask if I love you . . . My dear girlie. How can you ask me such a question? To me, it seems so impossible you could ever think otherwise. And yet. I expect my letters are rather matter of fact, and contain little reiteration of my affections. I must try and write more softly . . . I can understand . . . you hunger for letters more full of unadulterated love, more truly personal missives, less everyday and plain. Here . . . one is liable to forget that personal outlook. We are all so absolutely in the same boat that one gets to look upon enforced separation from one's dear ones as an affliction common to all, and therefore to be borne as such.

I long . . . to see you, to clasp you in my arms and hug you. And I long with all my heart to see my Baby, my sweet, pure and precious Pauline. Her little pert face looks up at me from out her photo so lifelike that I can see her as though she was in this very room . . .

There. I have given myself the pip, as I knew I should. Too long dwelling on things such as these are not good for one here. It is better not to think too much if one would bear a smiling face about one's work.[23]

Perhaps 'thinking too much' was the reason why Major Frank Merriman, the barrister in the battalion, always looked so miserable. He constantly had a 'doleful' expression, and rarely if ever smiled.[24] Never could a man have been so inappropriately named. That put him on a collision course with Captain Alfred Bland, his subordinate in the battalion's A Company, who according to May, 'grins from morn to eve, swears he is enjoying himself top-hole, and I believe, really is'.[25]

Merriman and Bland's personality clash was highlighted by their different reaction to the battalion being ordered to move from its original position on the Somme to one further to the east opposite Mametz. In spite of the fact that the relocation meant they would have to forget all they had learned about their original sector, Bland thought the move would be 'great fun' and a 'great experience', whereas Merriman pessimistically stated: 'If this transfer is accomplished without a very grave disaster, I shall be surprised.'[26]

Matters came to a head between them on 18 January 1916. May's diary entry for that day stated: 'Poor Bland is in rather serious trouble. Major Merriman has charged him before the CO with using insubordinate language, a most serious [allegation] . . . if it is true.'[27] Bland countered by secretly giving to the 91st Brigade's staff captain his version of what had happened.[28] A hint of what he told the staff captain is contained in a remarkable letter that Bland sent to his wife Violet on the same day. It included the following damning analysis of Merriman's character:

He is of the genus fox, weasel, stoat, ferret and rat . . . He is cunning, smooth faced, double tongued, uncertain in temper, ferocious, predatory and given to burrowing underground. He is a born intriguer, rejoicing in pulling secret wires, striving to undermine other people's reputations, gloating over their mistakes, making the worst of their errors, always imagining evil, always eagerly searching after vicious motives, stooping to wilful invention to cover up any mistakes of his own, and piling up damnation for others if thereby he can save his own face . . .

He is a parasite. He makes friends of those who will improve his future prospects . . . He ignores or pushes aside all others . . . He gets the ear of the powers that be, and by subtle suggestion and careful deference, worms his way into their confidence and having won his way maintains his position by deliberately artless flattery, constant court and persistent attentions . . . In fact my dear, he is the rankest poison I have ever met . . .

He is working day and night to out our present Second in Command and to take his place . . . So he plays eternal court to the CO, busies himself with the Second in Command's job . . . and takes every chance of improving the occasion, catching up any casual word of criticism and hastening to clinch it with a wise head nodding and murmured agreement. Oh he is a detestably false creature . . .[29]

What Violet made of Bland's character assassination has not been recorded. Certainly, to a dispassionate third party it appears hyperbolic, even comic. However, the fact that Bland and Merriman were supposed to be preparing to go over the top together, which might require one of them to risk his life to save the other, made the enterprise very dangerous. Because Merriman was loathed by all the other officers, and mocked by the 'other ranks' to the extent that in Bland's opinion 'they will never follow him', the situation became even more untenable.

There were, it seemed, only two ways out. Either Merriman would be 'accidentally' shot by one of his own men, a real prospect according to another of Bland's letters to Violet,[30] or Merriman would disgrace himself in the trenches. In yet another letter to his wife, Bland observed that during their last visit to the front line, Merriman had had 'the jumps', suggesting that his nerve was about to fail him.[31]

Eventually, a third option presented itself. During a subsequent stint in the front line, Merriman was so unpleasant and difficult that his company's NCOs were in open revolt. Two of them refused to go back into the front line with him again and applied for a transfer to another unit. That gave Bland the opening he had been waiting for. He sent a report on Merriman to the colonel.

Merriman was reprimanded and shortly afterwards he applied to join the 4th Army's headquarters as its judge advocate, leaving the way clear for Bland to take over his command.[32] It was the right result for the Army, but it had taken a long time to sort out, raising questions about whether similar problems were prevalent within other units, and even further up the hierarchy.

Harry Tawney's experiences certainly suggested that something was badly wrong. His letters are full of grievances concerning Army inefficiency. Even a simple act such as handing out plates and clothing resulted in inordinately long delays: 'People in the Army seem to have absolutely no idea of time and no capacity for organizing anything at all,' he complained to his wife Jeannette. 'With a little foresight the whole business could have been done in about half an hour', instead of the two long hours it had taken.[33]

Much more serious, given that the men were about to participate in an offensive, was the failure to provide adequate equipment. By all accounts the first spell of the 22nd Manchesters in the trenches was traumatic, not because of any assault by the Germans, but because it was wet and muddy and because appropriate clothing had not been supplied. 'It would not be so bad if the Army had any idea of how to dress soldiers,' Tawney told Jeannette. 'But in this, as in other matters, they appear to know nothing about their own silly business. What one ought to wear is fisherman's oilskins with waders up to our chest. The great coats they give us suck up all the water and mud there is, and become, after a few hours, of an intolerable weight.'[34]

In another letter concerning the same spell in the trenches, which Tawney wrote to his friend and brother-in-law William Beveridge (already a respected economist, who later achieved immortal fame as the author of the Beveridge Report, the basis of the modern welfare state), he grumbled:

Their incompetence in these minor practical matters is . . . astonishing . . . As to packs, an even more important matter, for it is the marching which 'kills' most men, instead of a rucksack hanging down the middle of one's back, what we are given is a thing like a lady's hatbox, an evil thing at all times, but an instrument of torture on one's back.

Oh, these soldiers! Perhaps they are good at astronomy or poetry . . . But as to war! If only they would clear out and leave it to be settled by a committee of civilians! . . . Their cardinal rule is never to admit a mistake or to accept any suggestion from anyone who cannot give it as an order. What is called discipline is mainly, after a few elementary matters have been learned, a code of rules for preventing any sort of new idea struggling into the august presence of the authorities.

The pedagogic vices − . . . [little] ability, cocksureness, ignorance of the ordinary affairs of men, predominate in some high military quarters to a degree which would cause explosive laughter in civil life.

And one might . . . smile. One might even . . . laugh, while these great little men stamp and fume, and gnaw their moustaches, and abuse their subordinates for their [own] mistake, and behave like the schoolmaster of fiction [were it not so serious]. I see one of these [men] fairly often. He has the power to send some 1000 men to be killed. And I come away between laughter and tears.[35]

One can easily imagine Jeannette Tawney dining out on one incident covered in the letter her husband sent her shortly before Christmas 1915:

Today the Quartermaster sent for me and began scolding me for not taking over various properties which do not exist in the usual army style, meeting every attempt to explain with: 'Don't answer me back', and finally threatening to take me before the CO. (Tawney was supposed to find suitable billets for the battalion when out of the line.)

He is a vulgar little animal, who has probably never been accustomed to exercise any authority, and behaves to one as the baser sort of *nouveau riche* behave to their domestic servants. You can imagine the kind of beast and its ways. What is more to the point, he does not appear to know his job, and is therefore doubly severe on his subordinates. He was very angry with me because he lost his temper, and I had the impudence not to be frightened.[36]

However, in spite of all the threats, Tawney was not reduced to the ranks, and his wife probably marvelled at how he was able to transform an ugly argument into an amusing anecdote. But behind the laughter he was making a serious point. The British New Armies were full of incompetent officials. It might not matter if they abused their subordinates unfairly concerning the minor administrative matters such as those mentioned by Tawney. But it could be a matter of life and death if such individuals were ever let loose with a gun in the trenches.

This was something that Lieutenant Edgar Lord, of the 15th Battalion, the Lancashire Fusiliers, was soon to find out. He learned from bitter personal experience just how dangerous it could be to share the same field, let alone the same trench, with some of his brother officers. During the first half of 1916, Lord was one of several hundred officers and NCOs who had the misfortune to be invited to Beauval (around 15 miles north of Amiens) to watch an exhibition of a new weapon: the Stokes light mortar, which could be used to lob 50-pound bombs shaped like toffee apples (they consisted of a spherical bomb attached to a long pipe) over the German parapets into their trenches:

We sat down in a field near . . . [where] the Trench Mortar Battery . . . personnel . . . were preparing for the show . . . when suddenly we heard [the] . . . cry: 'Run for it!' . . . I . . . had only gone a few yards when I felt rather than heard a tremendous explosion . . . An enormous roar rent the air, earth and pieces of metal flying everywhere . . . Everyone there was hit with either or both. Two more explosions followed . . .

When we gathered our scattered wits . . . my right thigh felt as if it had been beaten with a heavy stick . . . [and] the [right] leg of my trousers felt warm and sticky . . . A few yards away a man lay groaning across a few strands of barbed wire . . . I bandaged him [up. Then] . . . I had to ask Doncaster to attend to [my] two small wounds . . . As the pain became more severe, I found it more comfortable to lie on my stomach. It was at least an hour before the ambulances arrived to take us away. Only one man was killed outright, but several died later from the seventy or eighty casualties.

Only later did Lord discover the cause of the explosions. An officer had accidentally 'released a striker which fired a ten-second fuse. Instead of throwing the shell into an empty emplacement or traverse, he dropped it where it was, among all the bombs – and ran for it.' He escaped without a scratch![37]

The only 'crime' that matched not knowing how to handle a weapon with which you were entrusted was rashly putting the lives of the men under your command at risk. Before the 'Big Push' started, there were many commanding officers who fell into this latter category. That meant Lieutenant-Colonel H. G. Powell, commander of the newly formed 8th Battalion, the East Surrey Regiment, was one of several senior officers who did not measure up. In September 1915 he shocked 2nd Lieutenant P. G. Heath, who at eighteen years of age was one of his youngest subalterns, into disobedience when he instructed him via his company commander to supervise the digging of a trench joining up two salients in the front line at 8 o'clock that night. Given that at 8 p.m. it was still broad daylight, Heath was understandably appalled. 'I could feel myself trembling,' he later wrote in his memoirs, 'for the order practically amounted to a death sentence for me and my platoon.' Fortunately, the colonel quickly revoked the order when he heard what Heath had to say about it, but it was just one of a string of incidents which made it clear that this battalion, like many others, had to fear its own officers almost as much as the Germans.[38]

It should be emphasized that most of Harry Tawney's wrath was not aimed at the battalion officers below the rank of colonel. '[The] poor devils . . . are kicked about like we are,' he wrote to William Beveridge:

But I never met anyone who had been in the game for a year or so, who did not damn the staff. Of course one never has much direct evidence of their incompetence. That is the worst of the military system. One never can bring one's superiors, the men who make the really big blunders to book. And as there is not, and cannot be, any military public opinion in England . . . they escape scot free, or with nothing worse than a peerage! . . .

There are so many strands pointing in the same direction, from the imbecil[ic] waste of time over training, to . . . tragic affairs such as Neuve Chapelle [the first of several British attempts to break through the German line during 1915], I fancy there must be something in the general feeling that the Higher Command is not up to the game.[39]

When Beveridge received this letter in England, he might have wondered whether Tawney was exaggerating. But in fact Tawney had made a good point. Behind the superficial veneer of competence presented to the outside world by the British Army's top brass, which led the politicians and most British citizens to hope that they had everything under control, there really was something very worrying going on.

3: A Gentleman's Agreement

Northern France, February–May 1916

(See map 1)

The British Army's inefficiency, when it came to organizing the most basic actions, might have been excused if only its generals had sensibly carried out their most important task of all: the planning of the great attack.

Unfortunately, unbeknown to the public in general, and in particular to those poor soldiers who would have to go over the top, the fault line, which ran through the Army's middle ranks, stretched right to the top. Although to outside observers there seemed to be unity within the high command concerning how the attack should be conducted, there were hidden fissures deep down beneath the surface resulting from the divergent strategies of Britain's top generals.

On the one hand, there were the flamboyant views of General Sir Douglas Haig, the fifty-five-year-old Commander-in-Chief of the BEF, the eternal optimist. He was adamant that any attack plan should be ambitious, and should be calibrated so that there was at least the chance of a decisive break-through. If the plan worked, he wanted the *coup de grâce* to be administered by his beloved cavalry, the branch of the Army where he had earned his spurs.

On the other hand, there were the more pessimistic opinions voiced by General Sir Henry Rawlinson, the fifty-two-year-old commander of the British 4th Army, the unit selected by Haig to carry out the Somme attack. If asked, he might have agreed that Haig was the British Army's equivalent of Don Quixote, because like Cervantes' fictional anti-hero, Haig did not face up to the real nature of what he had to attack.[1] Lessons learned from making previous assaults on the Western Front had convinced Rawlinson that Haig's plan to break through the German multilayered trench systems in one great rush, while desirable in theory, was unachievable in practice.

The 4th Army's commander believed the most that could be accomplished on the first day of the Somme attack was the penetration of the front network of German barbed wire and trenches (often referred to misleadingly as their front or 1st Position, 'system' or 'line', even though it contained several trenches running more or less parallel with each other). The reason for Rawlinson's relatively unambitious approach was his realization that to be sure of taking a trench system, his artillery had first to cut the protective wire and pulverize the trenches. It was hard to accomplish this if the trench system targeted was too far away from the artillery, as was the case with the Germans' 2nd Position on the Somme, particularly if it could not be seen from the British line. That explains why Rawlinson advocated pausing after capturing the first position while the artillery was dragged forward. Only then could the next stage of the attack commence, which would involve the softening up of part of the German second line, before the second assault went in.

Rawlinson famously referred to his strategy as 'bite and hold'. It required the attacker to bite off one line of the German trench system at a time, and when selecting the objective, not to be too greedy.[2]

The different expectations of Haig and Rawlinson certainly made the planning of the attack more complicated. But those expectations did not inevitably mean that the approach of one of the generals had to be totally ignored. Compromises reached after such creative tension can often capture the good points of both sides of the argument.

However, for creative tension to produce constructive results, it is essential that the opinions of both sides are given equal weight. That was not the case in this instance. During the year leading up to April 1916 when the Somme plan was formulated, Haig had established a hold over Rawlinson way in excess of what should have been the case given their relative status. It meant the 4th Army's commander was constrained when it came to challenging Haig's tactics.

The seeds of Haig's unhealthy ascendancy, and of the resulting disaster that eventually ensued on the first day of the Battle of the Somme on 1 July 1916, were sown at the time of the BEF's very first major attack in France. During the advance towards Neuve Chapelle on 10 March 1915, Rawlinson had made a mistake. He instructed the general of one of the divisions within his IV Corps to use a unit to back up the assault on the German front system, when it should have been kept back so that it could carry on the advance after the 1st German Position was breached. Rawlinson had compounded his error by blaming the subordinate major-general.

Matters came to a head when the major-general complained that he was unfairly being made a scapegoat, and Rawlinson, humiliated, was forced to apologize. Field Marshal Sir John French, the then commander of the BEF, was all for sacking Rawlinson, but Haig, who as commander of the 1st Army was Rawlinson's immediate superior, successfully argued he should be given another chance. Haig's verdict, noted in his diary, was that 'Rawlinson is unsatisfactory in this respect, loyalty to his subordinates. But he has many other valuable qualities for a commander on active service.'[3]

However, there were consequences. Although Haig's intercession meant that Rawlinson was reprieved, it effectively neutered him. Unless there was a dramatic change in circumstances, never again could he challenge Haig without transgressing the unwritten rule between gentlemen. This states that if a man saves your life or reputation, then you must treat him like a brother and never betray him.

Rawlinson would have been particularly susceptible to the obligations imposed on him by such a rule. He was the archetypal English gentleman of the old school, whose actions, and sense of right and wrong, were strongly influenced by his family and their history. It was his family he had to thank for the baronetcy he had inherited, and their values would have been reinforced by the lessons about morality and chivalry he would have picked up while a pupil at Eton. Britain's most prestigious public school was famous for the way it transformed the sons of rich and aristocratic families into pillars of the community. Although Haig, who had been a pupil at Clifton College, a less well-known public school, did not belong to the Old Etonian 'club', his money, contacts, and subsequent education and position meant that he was to be treated as if cut from the same cloth.

The rule that required Rawlinson to pay back Haig in kind would have been all the more applicable in this case, because of the way Haig's support acted as a shield against Sir John French on an ongoing basis. It was clear that French had a grudge against Rawlinson. Haig had told Rawlinson that Sir John had referred to a previous incident where Rawlinson had displeased him; in October 1914, Rawlinson had, wisely as it turned out, not complied with French's order to 'move on' Menin, Belgium, during the battles that are known as 1st Ypres, and this had angered French. Now French wanted Rawlinson to be told that this was to be his last warning.[4] The mental torture inflicted on Rawlinson by this comment was exacerbated by the fact that for weeks afterwards, whenever their paths crossed, French had either totally ignored him or was studiously cold towards him. This naturally led Rawlinson to fear that French would seize on some other pretext to have him sent home.

It prompted Rawlinson to write in his diary: 'I know Sir John will never forgive me for what I did at Menin, because he knows he was wrong and I was right. He is a vindictive little person and harbours resentment for years, so I don't fancy I shall get any help from him.'[5]

Throughout this very difficult period, Rawlinson was comforted by the knowledge he had Haig's support. That had been made abundantly clear to him. As Rawlinson recorded in his diary, after mentioning Sir John's verdict, Haig had 'then said he was quite prepared to fight my battles for me, and I might have every confidence in him. It was very good of him and I am certain I have a good friend and staunch ally . . . [thanks to] his strong character and personality.'[6]

Rawlinson's daily jottings in his diary refer back to Haig's steadfastness concerning this incident time and again. Whenever French's behaviour made him feel insecure, he would add a note repeating in substance the mantra he had recorded after his talk with Haig: 'I feel quite sure I shall get justice in DH's hands.'[7]

With the benefit of hindsight, Haig's promise that he would fight Rawlinson's battles for him has a sinister ring about it, given what transpired. As will be demonstrated below, Haig was able to use his hold over Rawlinson to dominate him, and to require him to fight the Somme battle in the way he desired. However, at the time when Haig made the promise, it is likely that the thought that this might be the end result never entered Rawlinson's mind.

The fact that Rawlinson could not challenge him might not have mattered so much had Haig not become so sure that his strategy in 1916 was the correct one. This confidence was partly a product of his religious belief. On the eve of the Battle of the Somme, he would write to his wife Doris: 'I think it is . . . Divine help which gives me tranquillity of mind, and enables me to carry on without feeling the strain of responsibility to be too excessive. I try to do no more than do my best and trust to God.'[8] As events would reveal, such tranquillity of mind when faced with opposing views could be very dangerous.

There may have been another reason why Haig was so confident that his tactics were correct: three months before he looked at Rawlinson's plan for the Somme attack, Haig's sister Henrietta informed him that their dead brother George had contacted her via a medium: he wanted Haig to know that God was letting Napoleon advise him.[9] Whether or not Haig positively believed the medium was telling the truth, it would not be surprising if the possibility gave his confidence a boost.

But Haig's willingness to trust his own judgement was also influenced by his upbringing and education.[10] As the rich scion of one of Scotland's best-known whisky dynasties, the Haig Distillery being the family business, he was used to having what he wanted and doing things his own way.

This sense of entitlement did not spring from a belief that he was especially intelligent. Although, unusually for a regular soldier, he had been a student at Oxford University (1880–3), where he read French, Political Economy and Classical History, there is some suspicion that he owed his place more to his name and connections than to his brain. He took a so-called pass degree, rather than an honours degree, which would have required his work to be graded, and Brasenose, the Oxford college he attended, was known to be interested in providing an education for those who were more of a sporty than an academic disposition.

While up at Oxford, Haig certainly showed more interest in what was happening on the polo field (he played polo for the university), and in drinking clubs such as the Bullingdon, than in lecture halls. There was little chance of his shining in the debating chamber or the theatre, where other high-flyers cut their teeth. Haig was shy and often tongue-tied, to such an extent that some have called him inarticulate.

However, neither his inability to express himself fluently nor his limited academic prowess stood in the way of his being accepted within the top strata of British society. Thanks to his sister Henrietta, who had married a friend of Edward, the Prince of Wales – subsequently Edward VII – Haig was a regular guest at parties attended by the royal family, a privilege that also led to his being on speaking terms with Edward's son, who in 1910 was to be crowned George V.

It was only after he had come down from Oxford, while serving in the cavalry, that Haig experienced his first major setback. His initial attempt to secure a place at the prestigious Staff College at Camberley was scuppered because he failed his Maths exam. While there was a good excuse for what happened – the exam was unexpectedly made more difficult that year – it raises questions as to whether he had the desire, or capacity, to rigorously analyse a difficult problem. Fortunately for Haig, his admirers in the Army did not see it like that, and he was eventually given one of the Staff College places that were in the gift of the Adjutant-General.[11]

While there, Haig was such an able student that he was already being talked about as a commander-in-chief in the making. And afterwards he was helped on his way, as was the norm for talented young officers, by various high-flyers in the Army who were to become his patrons. One such patron was the Quartermaster-General Sir Evelyn Wood, who had realized Haig was going to rise far after reading some of the thoughtful papers he wrote about the cavalry. Another was John French, a cavalry officer, who would himself rise to

the top of the Army, becoming Commander-in-Chief of the British Expeditionary before Haig took over from him in December 1915. French gave Haig
a leg up just when he needed it after Haig had in his turn saved French's Army
career, and prevented him from being declared bankrupt, by lending him
£2,500. In 1899, when French went to fight in the Boer War as head of the
cavalry, Major Haig accompanied him as his Chief Staff Officer.

But it was lessons learned from a series of events on the Western Front,
during the months before he became the Commander-in-Chief, that were
to make the biggest impact on Haig's self-belief and confidence. What he
learned from the 1st Battle of Ypres, at the end of October 1914, had nothing to do with the part he as corps commander had played in the rearguard
action that held up the Germans. Rather the battle taught him that the
Germans had thrown away their great opportunity to break through the
British line because they did not have sufficient reserves at hand to penetrate the gap they had created.[12]

In his capacity as commander of the 1st Army, Haig had also seen how
the failure to handle reserves correctly had halted the advance of Rawlinson's IV Corps after its breakthrough at Neuve Chapelle. Although his
own forces were not on the receiving end during the 2nd Battle of Ypres in
April 1915, Haig learned similar lessons from the German failure there to
exploit their breakthrough achieved thanks to the use of gas.[13] Last but not
least, the fact that he had been asked to replace Sir John French as the BEF's
Commander-in-Chief due to Sir John's failure to make reserves available to
exploit the breach in the German line at Loos on 25 September 1915, only
served to emphasize the same point. All these events left Haig with the
unshakeable conviction that whatever the resistance from his own side, he
should never fail to exploit an opening through lack of ambition at the
planning stage.

Haig would have preferred to make his first advance as the BEF's
Commander-in-Chief in the Ypres sector rather than on the Somme. A
breakthrough in Flanders would have given him more scope to disrupt
German operations behind the front-line systems. However, bearing in
mind Lord Kitchener's instructions on his being appointed, which contained the order that he must 'support and co-operate with the French',
Haig felt obliged to accede to the request by General Joseph Joffre, the
sixty-four-year-old Commander-in-Chief of French forces, that they
should make their big push together on the Somme.[14]

When this offensive was first discussed, the French were offering to take the lead, attacking with forty divisions on a 25-mile front, leaving British forces to cover the remaining 14 miles targeted with twenty-five of their divisions.[15] However, the German attack at Verdun on 21 February 1916 changed all that. French efforts to defend Verdun (see map 1) meant that available French units ebbed away, leaving Haig wondering at one point whether the Somme offensive would end up being an all-British attack with no French participation.[16]

Fear that Britain would be bled dry led some members of the British Cabinet's War Committee to withhold their consent for such a massive undertaking. It was only the passing of time without a suitable alternative strategy being agreed, together with pressure from the French, that finally persuaded the War Committee on 7 April 1916 to give Haig the go-ahead for his Somme campaign.[17]

It would have made sense for the War Committee to have appointed a representative who would have been privy to all Haig's correspondence concerning the planning of the great attack. If they had taken that precaution, it is possible that both Haig and his immediate boss, General Sir William Robertson, the Chief of the Imperial General Staff, would have resigned in protest on the grounds that the Commander-in-Chief was not being trusted.

Haig and Robertson were certainly not above challenging the politicians' supremacy. In May 1916 there was a stand-off between the two soldiers and the War Committee over whether the politicians had the right to tell Haig to make do with fewer horses on the Continent. There was a shortage of shipping, and the shortfall would have been reduced if no more horses were sent out to the Western Front. The discovery that the War Committee were thinking of looking at such a subject prompted Haig to write a letter to Robertson saying that the question of how many horses he needed was his responsibility. The Army Council supported its Commander-in-Chief.

Not surprisingly, this upset the majority on the War Committee. David Lloyd George, one of its members, accused Haig of being 'insolent', and stated that the effect of this letter was to tell the War Committee 'to mind their own business' and not to interfere with Haig's. That was 'most improper . . . They had a perfect right to investigate any matter connected with the war that they pleased.' A constitutional crisis was only avoided after Robertson diplomatically requested that Haig should not be reprimanded since he had only expressed his views in a private letter that was never intended to be shown to the War Committee. The War Committee members agreed, and eventually no action was taken. More significantly, Haig, helped by Robertson, had effectively barred the politicians from monitoring the way he exercised his command, a development that was to have unfortunate consequences.[18]

It meant there was what Rawlinson referred to as a kind of military dictatorship run by Haig and General Robertson.[19] Once the politicians handed over the reins of power to them, permitting Haig and Robertson to fight the battle, there was no effective means of controlling them. The situation was made all the more dangerous because Robertson, the man who sweet-talked the War Committee into approving the Somme offensive against their better judgement, did not check that Haig was keeping to the letter of what was effectively the small print of the politicians' agreement. Robertson had only persuaded the War Committee to back the offensive at the beginning of April 1916 by promising its members that their Commander-in-Chief would be prudent. 'If he was convinced that the French intended to leave all the fighting to him, then he would shut down at once,' he told them. 'General Haig was properly alive to the situation and would not do any foolish thing.'[20]

Then, at the end of May 1916, when faced with the French generals' demand that the British 'should make some big movement' and Joffre's comment that the French 'force at Verdun was now reduced to 22 divisions', Robertson told the War Committee what appears to have been another white lie. Although Haig had just written to him stating that he was hoping to use his cavalry to exploit any success enjoyed by the infantry, Robertson calmed the nerves of the War Committee members by telling them that Haig had 'no idea of any attempt to break through the German lines'. According to Robertson, Haig would restrict himself to 'dégager' (relieving) the French.[21] The French generals were afraid they would not be able to carry on fighting if the Germans were not diverted away from Verdun by the Somme attack.[22]

By the time the War Committee approved the principle of the offensive on 7 April, Haig had already seen Rawlinson's first draft of the Somme attack plan, which had been forwarded to him four days earlier.[23] It was a curious mixture of restraint and recklessness. It was restrained in that in the southern half of the front, the assault was to be restricted to an attack on the German front-line system, the one exception being that the village of Contalmaison, which was east of the front system, would be targeted as well. The focus on the front line meant that although the front would run from

the Maricourt salient in the south to Serre in the north, there would be no
attempt to take the German second trench system, south of the road running from Albert to Bapaume, which bisected the centre of the area to be
attacked (see map 2, and note 24 which describes what is meant by the Maricourt salient).[24] The second system south of the road was more than
4,000 yards from the British front line, making it harder for the artillery to
take out than the second system north of the road which (as shown in map
2) was for the most part nearer, in some places much nearer.

Even north of the road, the attack was in the first instance to be confined to the front system. The troops would only be authorized to attack
the second system after the first system had been captured, and the renewed
advance prepared, a process that Rawlinson estimated might take three
days.

The targeting of the village of Contalmaison, which, as mentioned
above, was to be the most ambitious target south of the road, and the village of Pozières, which straddled the road, was particularly crucial since
they would become important bases for the subsequent attack on the second
trench system south of the road. The latter advance would only be attempted
after the objectives specified in the plan had been taken.

The reckless nature of the plan sprang from the fact that some of the key
lessons gleaned from the failed operations on the Western Front during
1915 had been ignored. One such lesson had been enunciated by
Brigadier-General Charles Budworth, who at the time had been Rawlinson's artillery adviser within IV Corps. In a report sent to Rawlinson after
the Battle of Loos in September–October 1915, the last of the four offen-
sives masterminded by Rawlinson and Haig in that year, Budworth had
stated that Rawlinson could not be sure of obliterating a trench so that it
could be taken without heavy losses unless he used one heavy howitzer for
each 100 yards of front.[25] (In simple terms, a howitzer is a 'gun' whose shells
do not fly directly from the gun barrel to their target, but which instead
loop up into the air before falling steeply onto it.) When Budworth specified that these howitzers must be 'heavy', he was referring to those whose
calibre (internal diameter) was in excess of 6 inches.

Rawlinson's plan, while implicitly paying homage to Budworth's recommendation, disregarded it. The 4th Army commander had extended the
definition of heavies to include 6-inch howitzers. That sleight of hand
would have enabled Rawlinson to claim, without any justification, that the
number of howitzers possessed by the 4th Army to cover the front selected

by him complied with Budworth's specification. Using the Rawlinson definition of 'heavy', he was able to claim he had at least 200 'heavy' howitzers (those with a calibre of 6 inches or more). If each 'heavy' howitzer could cover 100 yards of front, this meant that Rawlinson ostensibly had sufficient firepower to take out 20,000 yards of front-line trenches.[26]

It was this calculation, and the knowledge that he could use in excess of 160,000 men (more than eight men per yard attacked) from the seventeen infantry divisions he had been told were at his disposal, which gave Rawlinson the statistics he needed to underpin the front he had chosen for his attack. It was to be the east of Mametz to Serre line, which from south to north measured around 20,000 yards.[27]

Rawlinson's adaptation of the Budworth ruling might have been acceptable if there had been any controversy about whether the 6-inch howitzers could stand in for the heavier artillery. But there was no uncertainty about this. Budworth's report stated unequivocally: 'I am not of the opinion that any artillery, except howitzers of the heaviest nature, are likely to cause material damage to German trenches . . . The fire of 6" howitzers . . . is no doubt demoralizing and to a limited extent destructive to the enemy's personnel . . . but its destructive effect on deep trenches is distinctly limited.'[28]

Even after stretching Budworth's ruling in this way, Rawlinson realized he had still fallen short of what he knew Haig would expect. 'I . . . doubt his acquiescing in the scheme without my convincing him verbally,' he scrawled in his diary on 3 April 1916, the day when he sent in the plan. Next day he added: 'I daresay I shall have a tussle with him over the limited objective, for I hear he is inclined to favour the unlimited with the chance of breaking the German line.'[29]

Perhaps he would have made more effort to produce what he knew would be expected had he not been fortified four days earlier by a meeting with the Secretary of State for War, Field Marshal Kitchener. This was a man whom Rawlinson did not just respect for what he had done concerning the recruitment of the New Armies, but who during the earlier part of Rawlinson's career had been a much admired mentor. Kitchener had told Rawlinson that given the French were not in a position to undertake what he called a big offensive, 'it would be unwise of us to make an attack "au fond", incurring 50 or 60,000 casualties which could not be replaced'.[30]

Rawlinson's argument in favour of his less ambitious plan was certainly persuasive. In his proposal he argued:

It does not appear to me that the gain of 2 or 3 more kilometres of ground is of much consequence, or that the existing situation is so urgent as to demand that we should incur very heavy losses in order to draw a large number of German reserves against this portion of our front. Our object rather seems to be to kill as many Germans as possible with the least loss to ourselves, and the best way to do this appears to me to be to seize points of tactical importance, which will provide us with good observation and which we may feel quite certain the Germans will counter attack . . . under disadvantages which will conduce to heavy losses [on their side].

But Rawlinson lessened his chances of convincing his Commander-in-Chief to accept his – and Kitchener's – approach by failing to specify all of the risks that would have to be taken if a more ambitious plan were to be adopted. He did not, for example, go on to give a complete analysis as to why a deeper attack was tantamount to having a 'gamble'. His report refers to there being 'serious risks' should he attempt to attack both the first and second systems north of the road 'in one rush'. But what he was principally referring to was the risk of incurring 'very heavy losses' in front of the second system if the barbed wire protecting it had not been destroyed before the system was attacked. No mention was made of the even more fundamental danger referred to in the following questions: would the targeting of the second system as well as the first system before the advance commenced dilute the strength of the artillery barrage on each yard of trench within the first system, to the extent that Rawlinson's troops would be stopped in their tracks or mowed down by the German guns before they even reached the first system?

It was Rawlinson's failure to deal with this crucial issue that permitted Haig to believe that he had answers for all the problems that might emerge as a result of making a deeper thrust. In Haig's reply, which was included in the letters written by his right-hand man, Lieutenant-General Lancelot Kiggell, the Chief of the General Staff, he brushed aside Rawlinson's warning, albeit using the quaintly formalized language of the day, requiring 'that further consideration may be given to the possibility of pushing our first advance further than is contemplated in your plan'.[31]

Of all the changes that Haig was requesting this was the most controversial. He wanted the German second system to the north of the Albert to Bapaume road to be taken on the first day, rather than several days later, as suggested in Rawlinson's original proposal. Although Haig – and

Kiggell – were too decorous to state that explicitly in their letters, Rawlinson immediately understood what they were after. On 14 April 1916, the day he received their orders, he scribbled in his diary: 'It is clear that DH would like us to do the whole thing in the rush.'[32]

Width was also a problem. Haig wanted the attack to be made on a wider front than Rawlinson had proposed. He asked Rawlinson to see whether he could include an attack on Gommecourt, the village to the north of Serre, which was the northern limit in Rawlinson's first draft, and he ordered Rawlinson to link up with the adjacent attack by the French to the south. With that in mind, he wanted the southern portion of the attack to be extended to include the capture of Montauban and the nearby Briqueterie.

As if that was not ambitious enough, Haig asked Rawlinson to start thinking about where he would advance after the first day's attack. He wanted Rawlinson to adopt the overall strategy for the campaign, which required British forces to turn towards the east after the German positions between Montauban and Fricourt had been taken (the initial attack in the south would involve an advance from south to north).

As for the risks specified by Rawlinson, Haig claimed they could be provided for by bringing up supporting troops and artillery, which could for example withstand any counter-attack that might be launched by the enemy. 'It is . . . wiser to act boldly in order to secure at the outset points of tactical value which it may be possible to reach, rather than to determine beforehand to stop short of what may prove to be possible in order to avoid risks,' Haig directed.[33]

Notwithstanding Rawlinson's failure to point out the most important pitfall inherent in the extra depth of the thrust that Haig was requesting, no one can say that prior to the attack the 4th Army commander did not himself appreciate the dangers which were part and parcel of Haig's demand. Three and a half weeks after reading the Commander-in-Chief's response to his plan, whilst informing Haig that he would need five extra heavy howitzer batteries to cover the additional 2,500 yards of extra front within the Montauban sector (the number of 'guns' presumably having been arrived at with reference to the Budworth formula of one howitzer per 100 yards), Rawlinson informed Haig that the extension also involved his covering an additional 13,500 yards of support and communication trenches.[34] This reply, sent to GHQ on 10 May 1916, showed that Rawlinson fully understood the principle that if the attack was to go deeper into the German lines, there would be more trenches for the artillery to target.[35]

The fact that he fully appreciated the risks Haig was asking him to take is perhaps even clearer if one refers to the following extract from the entry concerning the Montauban extension that Rawlinson wrote in his diary on 18 April 1916, the day before he sent off his comments on the changes requested by Haig:

I am not at all sure that we can undertake this further objective with the guns we shall have. If we have to do too much, we shall water down the bombardment to such an extent that we may not get in. So I am rather inclined to oppose Montauban in the first objective. I know it will make the negotiations with the French more difficult, but I am responsible for the attack by this Army and must deprecate taking on too much.[36]

But for some unexplained reason, Rawlinson did not explicitly apply the principles underlying his diary note, and the aforementioned 10 May letter to GHQ, to the extra depth Haig was requiring him to tackle during the first day of the attack on the northern half of the Somme front.

This failure was repeated in the memorandum that Rawlinson sent Haig on 19 April 1916. In it he stated that while he could cater for the extra yards of front in the Montauban sector, by using one of the divisions he had originally earmarked for the reserves, it would be impossible without the provision of extra guns. But there was no reference to how the extra depth of the attack requested by Haig to the north of the Albert–Bapaume road made it essential that he should be given extra artillery for that as well. The following extract shows how Rawlinson merely reiterated the incomplete analysis of risk already mentioned in the original plan:

It still seems to me that an attempt to attain more distant objectives, that is to say the enemy's second line system . . . involves considerable risks. I however fully realize that it may be necessary to incur these risks in view of the importance of the object to be attained. This will no doubt be decided by the Commander-in-Chief and definite instructions sent to me in due course.[37]

The only points on which Rawlinson would not give way related to the suggested attack on Gommecourt (he stated he did not have the resources to include it in his plan), and the form of the artillery softening-up process.

In his original plan Rawlinson had favoured a bombardment of between forty-eight and seventy-two hours over the alternative, a hurricane onslaught lasting just five to six hours. Haig had queried whether the former option might forewarn the Germans of what was to come, only for Rawlinson in his considered reply to counter that the hurricane version would not give the gunners time to cut the wire in front of the German trenches, which would take several days. Furthermore, it would be impossible to do that at the same time as bombarding the German trenches. The bombardment would throw up dust and smoke, concealing the wire from the artillery observers, who needed to see clearly in order to be able to direct the gunners' shells onto it.[38]

Haig would eventually give in to Rawlinson on both these points.[39] Gommecourt would be attacked by Lieutenant-General Edmund Allenby's 3rd Army, and Rawlinson could carry out his methodical bombardment. But because Rawlinson never challenged Haig's implied demand that he should attack the second system north of the road during the first day of the attack, it stayed in the plan.

Rawlinson's failure to make his case properly and stand his ground on this important issue raises questions concerning his competence and integrity. Did he realize that Haig's plan was so impractical that it unnecessarily put the lives of his men at risk, yet refuse to challenge it robustly because of his personal circumstances? Did the gentleman's code of honour require him to let Haig win the argument over the depth of the attack as a reward for saving Rawlinson's career in the wake of the Neuve Chapelle affair? And did this trump his duty to protect his men by insisting the plan should be workable? Or was Rawlinson so overwhelmed by the huge task he had been set that he really did not appreciate the scale of the shortage of artillery? The aforementioned analysis of his concerns relating to the Montauban extension suggests that the former explanation is more likely than the latter.

Whichever is correct was beside the point as far as the situation of the British infantrymen was concerned. Following what had been planned by their two most senior generals, they were to be ordered to attack a German defence system, consisting of deep trenches and dugouts, which far from being obliterated, as they would be assured was the case, in many areas would not even be touched. It was a disaster waiting to happen.

4: The Build-Up

The Somme, April–June 1916

(See map 7)

Whatever their views of their leaders, most British soldiers at least started off believing that their generals could be trusted to support them with an adequate artillery barrage. Or they gave them the benefit of the doubt. When the 22nd Manchesters' Captain Charlie May, whose battalion was holding the front line opposite Mametz, was told on 13 April 1916 that his unit would have to cover a wider front during the coming attack than had previously been anticipated, he wrote in his diary: 'The Staff appear very confident of our superiority in guns . . . All we can hope is that their confidence may be justified.'[1]

However, this trust, which meant so much to soldiers in the front line, was quickly dissipated if a commander blotted his copybook. There was plenty of scope for that to happen during the lead-up to the big attack, especially in those units ordered to mount preliminary operations. The battalions holding the front line were frequently ordered to send their men out on probing trench raids. These raids were partly carried out to capture German soldiers, or to report on the state of the German barbed wire and their dugouts for intelligence purposes. But they were also viewed as a test, a kind of dress rehearsal for the big day, to check out the relative strengths of the opposing forces.

In the course of one such raid during the night of 2–3 June, the 22nd Manchesters attacked the enemy's trenches at Bulgar Point, the site of a German listening post near Mametz (see map 7), following what May described as a 'terrific bombardment'.[2] In spite of this and of intensive training before the operation on a replica of the German trenches, the raid went spectacularly wrong. Out of the sixty-four men who went out into No Man's Land, there were thirty-one casualties including all four officers, two of whom were killed.[3]

Given that all these officers came from Captain Alfred Bland's A Company, one can imagine the sense of foreboding that must have dominated his wife's thoughts after reading his letter giving her the bad news. Although Bland did not say it in so many words, he was in effect telling her that by the law of averages his own days might also be numbered. 'It's extraordinary. All the original A Company officers are gone,' he wrote:

and I alone am left. Yes, at one blow, we have lost 4 officers [in a raid] . . . As a show it was a success. They did considerable damage, obtained two prisoners and dealt destruction to a great many more. The only hitch was the enemy wire, which had not been cut [in the right place] by the artillery . . .

[Lieutenant Eric] Street, was last to leave the Boche trench, ran [the] greatest risks and got [caught] fast in the wire. Burchill went across to help him and received a fatal stomach wound, and [Lieutenant Edmund] Cansino did likewise, and so far as we know was killed in attempting to save Street.[4]

Given the anguish which such a letter must have provoked, it was fortunate perhaps that Bland spared his wife the gory details. Some of them can be reconstructed from Captain May's record of what he observed through the trench telescope when he peered over the parapet the next day:

Poor Street, Cansino and one other unidentified [man] can be plainly seen tangled in a heap among the German wire right under their parapet. A Boche sentry is mounted over them, and keeps popping his head up every now and then to have a look at them. I saw him first through the telescope, and the sudden apparition of his great face caused me to think him a fiend from hell gloating over his victims . . . Street was a married man with three children, and Cansino was also married (with a baby on the way). It's a sad business.[5]

But what added insult to injury was the ill-informed explanation proffered by a major presumably acting under the instructions of Lieutenant-General Henry Horne, XV Corp's fifty-five-year-old commander, who as the only artillery officer to command a corps on the Somme should have known better. Instead of admitting the true cause, which as May and Bland could have told him was the failure by the artillery to cut through the German barbed wire in the right place, the following extract from Horne's condolences sought to blame faulty intelligence: 'The fact that the air photo [taken by the Royal Flying Corps] did not reveal the existence of the trench described as Reserve Supply in the report is most unfortunate. Had it not been for this, the raid would have been conducted with but little loss.'[6]

The casualties in the course of the Bulgar Point raid were just one of a series of traumatic events that members of the 22nd Manchesters witnessed before the main attack. At first, much of what went wrong was swept under the carpet so that their families would not be alarmed. Entries in their diaries and correspondence are full of statements confirming they were in a relatively safe section of the front.

Lieutenant William Gomersall, another officer from the battalion whose letters survive, even went so far as to describe his actions in the trenches as if they were a game played during a kind of action holiday. In one letter that he sent to his younger brother and sisters in December 1915, he thanked them for their welcome birthday gift of chocolate, adding:

I only wish I could send you a souvenir or something from here . . . Next time I go up into the trenches, I shall have to try and remember to send a birthday present from each of you through a rifle to those beastly old Germans, and say that one from Mabel, that one from Enid and that from Eddie. What do you say? . . .

I am getting just like I was when I was your age . . . [I am] mudlarking for all I'm worth. [I am] up to [my] . . . eyes in it in the trenches. The majority of us couldn't be seen except [for] our faces and shoulders for cakes of mud . . . I splash and mess about in [the] mud, and am getting to enjoy it as much as you . . . [I] feel just like a bunny . . . rabbit when I burrow in[to] my dugout to go to sleep, or run away from the Germans when they start to be nasty and throw things at us. They are not sportsmen are they?

In another letter that Gomersall sent to young Eddie on Christmas Day 1915, he wrote:

No Eddie old man I am not killed. You needn't worry. I'm having a fine time out here, almost as comfortable as being in England. I will write you many more letters yet, if you only write to me, and then when I come home we shall have a right jolly fine time. What do you say?

I saw [Santa Claus] . . . a few days ago . . . and told him to call at 69 Queen's Road, Urmston . . . and leave something there for all of you . . . As he is out here, he may be a little late in coming, but tell me if he did come in your next letter will you old sport.

I hope you are having a real good time. I am. I have bought . . . a turkey and will have a fine feed tonight and . . . I've got dates, muscatels [raisins], chocolates, butterscotch [and] cakes, and then from May in London, I've got a Christmas pudding, more chocolate, dates and cigars. So you can see I have . . . got more than my share and I wish you were all here to share . . . them [with me].[7]

But as time passed, with both sides patrolling No Man's Land each night and letting off their guns, it was inevitable that eventually someone would get hurt. Captain Charlie May had a taste of what was to come, after one of the officers found a dead German sniper during the night of 21 February 1916. 'They got his rifle, shoulder straps etc.,' he wrote in his diary. Four days later he recorded the sequel: 'Cotton came in to breakfast with us. He brought the little bible which Burchill had taken from the body of the dead German on the night of his patrol exploit . . . It was a kind of children's testament filled with gaudy prints . . . On the fly leaf was the name Hermann Stampa . . . and over this in a child's handwriting the word "Dada". War is very sad . . . I suppose he had a wife and kiddie somewhere, filled with pride for the daddy who was a soldier, and now stricken with grief for the daddy who is missing.'[8]

Five and a half weeks later there was another incident, only this time the injuries were closer to home. On 6 April, the day before the War Committee finally signed off on the Somme offensive, the Germans shelled the 22nd Manchesters' positions opposite Mametz, killing three NCOs and wounding three men. 'I saw the killed go down the line,' May recorded in his diary. 'It was a pitiful sight . . . English soldiers battered to pieces . . . Gresty, a lad who was a sergeant of mine before he went to D [Company] . . . was about the worst. His poor body was full of gaping holes. It was very, very sad.'[9]

Because most of May's correspondence is missing, we may never know what, if anything, he mentioned to his wife Maude about these tragic events. If he kept them from her, one can say for certain that Gomersall was less reticent. Concerning the 6 April incident, he spelt out the following details to his family:

Towards the end of the strafe, I had been talking to . . . [the] three [NCOs] cracking jokes and generally making light of the whole thing in front of the men . . . and during the few moments I was away, one ripping fellow, a lance corporal, passed me and went to them and, picking up a chunk of a shell quite hot which had just dropped beside him, said: 'Nearly got a Blighty that time Sergeant', and then burst into laughter at his escape. At the same moment my other sergeant, a public school boy, joined the three, accompanied by a private. And then a high explosive shell . . . burst right bang among them. I returned a few minutes later to find my platoon sergeant, Sergeant Gresty, killed outright, two corporals . . . also killed, Corporal Gandy and the private wounded, and my other sergeant . . . an absolute nervous . . . [wreck, his condition brought on by] . . . the terrific shock. They were soon removed, but . . . I shall never forget the sight of them as long as I live.[10]

Given the frankness of his disclosures, it is not surprising to hear that Gomersall's parents, who had been lulled into complacency by his previous correspondence, were horrified to hear what he was being subjected to. They were so unhappy with what he had told them that Gomersall felt obliged to apologize for upsetting them. 'I am sorry to hear my Thursday letter filled you with sadness,' he wrote. ' . . . I hate to feel I have made you think of such things, and perhaps I ought not to have mentioned it . . . Please try and . . . forget all about it. Such things happen daily . . . That happened to be right in my own platoon. When all is said and done, we were really very fortunate, and I should think that scarcely 1 per cent of enemy shells ever do any damage.'[11]

Captain Alfred Bland also became increasingly indiscreet. It had not started that way. He had even gone so far as to withhold a rather frightening letter he had written to his wife in February 1916. If Violet had received it, she would have heard how on one occasion German shells rained down on the area he was inspecting behind the front line, the last missile missing him by just a few yards. Bland, who always saw the good side of every aspect of life, regarded the fact that he had not been hurt in spite of the shell landing so close to him as a good sign. Only a direct hit would kill him, the blast from near misses being smothered by the soft earth. That made it much more unlikely he would be injured or killed. 'The chances of walking into one are terribly remote,' he wrote. 'It's [no] . . . more dangerous than the 5th of November, unless you have . . . bad luck, as in crossing Piccadilly Circus [an accident] might happen to the civilest of civilians.'

Nevertheless the letter remained with him in France until, hardened by the tragedies he witnessed, Bland eventually could not understand why he had ever thought his wife should not see it. On 18 June he sent it to her, along with the letter he was writing to her that day.[12]

Five days earlier Bland had written to Violet to explain how he only kept sane by making a conscious effort to shut down his emotions. It was not just the sight of:

those two lads as they were last seen the day after [the Bulgar Point raid] lying dead on the German wire . . . The other day a trench mortar of ours was defectively charged. Result: the 60 pound projectile just toppled over the gun muzzle, exploded, and ignited a good 100 in [a] store nearby. The explosion shook the earth for a mile a[round] . . . obliterated 20 yards of trench, [and left behind] . . . a huge crater. One of my men . . . was buried and killed. I supervised . . . digging [him] . . . out.

One becomes absolutely callous. You chat with a sentry, move on and a moment after he is dead. You send out a wiring party under a trusted sergeant. In half an hour that sergeant has a chance bullet through his head.

But . . . the cause is good. The end will come. We make the most of all good things that come our way. We love each other. We sing and laugh and chat, and eat and drink. We avoid unpleasant thoughts, because unpleasant things are too close and frequent, [and] we are all homesick.[13]

Shortly after Bland wrote about his stiff upper lip, the orders covering the big attack were at long last handed down to the battalion's company commanders. 'It is to be quite soon, within a fortnight I believe,' May wrote in his diary.[14] He had already guessed that the time for the offensive was approaching. Since 7 June, leave had been shortened and granted less frequently, and numerous troops were moving forward, filling the district around the Bois de Tailles, where the 22nd Manchesters were resting.[15]

As for the ammunition for the artillery, it was, as May put it: 'pouring up, that for the heavies by motor transport, that for the lighter fry, by wagon and limber. Two convoys of the latter, each of them fully 500 yards in length, passed the Bois at sundown,' he wrote on 16 June. 'It was a great sight.' It inspired him to comment: 'It is marvellous this marshalling of power, this concentrated effort of our great nation . . . to the end of destroying our foe. The greatest battle in the world is on the eve of breaking. Please God it may end successfully for us.'[16]

Even as May watched, new arrangements were being made by the British and French commanders for the deployment of all this firepower. Three days earlier, because of the vulnerability of the French at Verdun, and a linked political crisis in Paris, the date for the Somme attack had been hurriedly scheduled for 25 June. The attack date was only put back to 29 June late on 16 June, after situation reports came in stating that circumstances on the ground at Verdun – and in the French Chamber – had been stabilized.[17]

This correlation between the state of the fighting at Verdun and the 'Big Push' underlined how the two great battles had become inextricably linked.

The Somme offensive may have started off being just another attempt to take the fight to the Germans. But by mid-June it was as much a diversionary attack as an attempt to break through. If the offensive achieved nothing else, it was hoped it would at least force the Germans to transfer their reserves away from Verdun, thereby rescuing the French, and enabling them to keep fighting.

Whether or not the latest date change had anything to do with the 22nd Manchesters' move the next day back into the relative comfort of the billets at Bonnay, some six miles south-west of Albert, the move softened May's heart and prompted him on 17 June to write another entry that was particularly aimed at Maude: 'I must not allow myself to dwell on the personal . . . But I do not want to die. Not that I mind for myself. If it be that I am to go, then I am ready. But the thought that I may never see you or our darling baby again turns my bowels to water. I cannot think of it with even the semblance of equanimity.'[18]

Captain Bland also had cold feet. The next day he informed Violet: 'Even after six months of active service, I cannot properly reconcile my heart to extinction.'[19] That did not stop him enjoying the short time he had before the trial that lay ahead. The fact that he knew survival was not guaranteed made the short period of respite in Bonnay all the sweeter. While they had the chance, he and the other officers with horses went out riding. He described the route thus in his letter of 18 June: 'The way runs through fields of richest wheat, sprinkled with cornflower and poppy, scabious and charlock, vetch and clover, our dear geraniaciae, herb Robert . . . and all the sky blue pinks. Below us lies the river occasionally visible through the deep woodland green, exquisite.'[20]

But Bland appears to have been even more ecstatic after discovering that he really had triumphed over Major Merriman. In a letter to Violet that he started on 22 June, just hours before the beginning of the softening-up bombardment for the big attack, Bland mentioned that: 'Merriman turns up now and then . . . He is still technically Officer Commanding [A] Company, but I am king de facto. The C.O. said the other day, in reference to future movements: "You'll take the Company, Bland, whether Merriman comes back before or not. I'm not going to have him upsetting [it] . . . again." I laugh inwardly, you know not how much, when I turn back to past events . . . and think of tables turned.'[21]

By 23 June the build-up had reached fever pitch. The Bray to Corbie road became, in May's words, 'one incessant stream of heavy laden motor lorries'. It was a stirring sight. 'It should certainly not be for want of ammunition if this time we do not make a huge success of the venture,' he wrote in his diary, little realizing that Rawlinson had been ordered to cut back the planned bombardment due to a shortage of ammunition. Three days earlier the 4th Army, at Haig's request, had cancelled some of the concentrated artillery bombardments Rawlinson had counted on to destroy the German trenches. The majority of the bombardment by heavy howitzers on the second day of the softening-up bombardment were also cancelled.[22]

This further curtailment of the artillery, which had been inadequate enough without the reduction, was worrying. As Haig stressed in one of his final messages to the 4th Army's corps, Rawlinson had been given, if not an open goal to aim at, a never-to-be-repeated window of opportunity: British intelligence was claiming that the enemy holding the trenches opposite the 4th Army consisted of a surprisingly small force, just thirty-two battalions belonging to some five divisions. This meant that when Rawlinson's troops first attacked, he and the eighteen divisions initially made available to him would, in Haig's words, have 'considerable numerical superiority'.[23]

If Haig had known the reason for this uncharacteristic German oversight, his exhortation might have been even more emphatic. The oversight only existed because of an anomaly, an aberration that was likely to be swept away at any minute: General Erich von Falkenhayn, the fifty-four-year-old German Chief of the General Staff in charge of the German Army, had temporarily taken leave of his senses by backing his intuition, and favouring it over the kind of hard-headed analysis of the facts that is second nature to most Prussians. Falkenhayn was Prussian-born, and before the war had risen to be his country's War Minister. It was this extraordinary phenomenon, a Prussian leader who ignored the facts, that gave Haig's armies a chance in a lifetime, in spite of all the errors he and Rawlinson had made.

Falkenhayn's intuition told him to ignore all the evidence which suggested that the British and French were planning to make their counter-stroke on the Somme, following on from the German attack at Verdun. Such disregard for the facts horrified his critics, who feared that if Falkenhayn's 'mania' went unchecked, he could end up losing Germany the entire war.

One of his harshest critics was Prince Rupprecht, the outspoken forty-seven-year-old Crown Prince of Bavaria and commander of Falken-hayn's 6th Army. This unit was located just to the north of the German 2nd Army under General Fritz von Below, which held the trenches opposite Rawlinson's troops, and the French to the south. Rupprecht cited a string of factors at the beginning and in mid-June that all pointed to the Somme being the next Anglo-French target in the near future. Amongst the most persuasive evidence was a statement by Arthur Henderson, the Labour Party minister within Britain's coalition government, who, at the begin-ning of June 1916, spoke to a meeting of munition workers. When asked why the Whitsun holiday should be taken after the end of July rather than in June, he had apparently replied: 'How curious we all are. It should suffice to say we have only asked for a postponement until the end of July. This fact alone should speak volumes.' 'This does speak volumes,' Rupprecht commented in his diary. 'It contains the clear proof that in a few weeks there is going to be a great English offensive.'

It appeared to corroborate agent reports stating that the attack would be made after Whitsun. But it was far from being the only evidence. First and foremost there was the sharp increase in the number of trains arriving behind the enemy lines, suggesting that troops, weapons and ammunition were being transported into the area. Then there were the reports that fresh trenches were being dug, and the French civilians south of the Somme were being moved out of the area. English troops withdrawn from opposite the 6th Army had been seen moving towards the Somme. The observation that a crack French regiment had been seen digging in south of the Somme also looked ominous. Last but not least, shortly before the commencement of the preliminary bombardment, Rupprecht learned that the French had cancelled all leave prior to 30 June.

Some of what Rupprecht was hearing was probably fed back to him from the first and second positions on the Somme itself. The German sol-diers there could not fail to notice how the build-up was progressing. In his post-action report Sergeant Karl Eisler of the Reserve Field Artillery Regi-ment 29, who occupied an observation post in a tower near the chateau at Contalmaison, reported: 'From 20 May onwards we saw the frenzied activ-ity behind the British front lines. From our observation post . . . we watched endless columns of lorries passing each day between Bray-sur-Somme and Albert. These convoys often contained 100 vehicles. We [also] frequently saw vast artillery columns which were so long, it took them more than three hours to pass a given point.'[24]

Even evidence as compelling as that did not convince the sceptics. Some of them insisted that the death of Lord Kitchener, Britain's Secretary of State for War – who had drowned on 5 June 1916 west of the Orkney Islands after the armoured cruiser bearing him to Russia for a conference hit a mine and sank – put an end to British offensive plans, in part because only he knew what the plans were. This was 'full of inner contradictions and was based on stupid rumours,' commented Rupprecht. It was not possible for such a vast enterprise to rely on just one man.

However, Rupprecht only fully appreciated how irrational Falkenhayn's views were when the German Chief of the General Staff and the Kaiser, Wilhelm II, visited the 6th Army's headquarters at Douai ten days later. In the course of the meeting, Falkenhayn told Rupprecht he believed that no French general would ever contemplate an offensive which would involve trampling over French and Belgian soil, and he argued that Alsace-Lorraine in Germany was a much more likely target for any offensive by the French Army. Falkenhayn said this even though, as Rupprecht recorded in his diary, Rupprecht told him the French thought that Alsace-Lorraine was just as French as the Somme.

Rupprecht heard Falkenhayn's final verdict on the next Anglo-French offensive when he talked to General Max von Boehn, whose IXth Reserve Corps was part of Rupprecht's 6th Army. According to Boehn, the Kaiser, who had just been briefed by Falkenhayn, had beckoned him as he was about to board his train at Douai's railway station, and had said to him: 'I gather you [the 6th Army] are about to be attacked . . .' Given such irrational views, it was no wonder that Falkenhayn, who could only be described by Rupprecht as very 'stubborn', had refused to reinforce the German troops on the Somme, in spite of the frequent requests coming from the local commander there, the 2nd Army's General von Below.[25]

Unaware what was going on in the German camp, Rawlinson's greatest concern on 23 June 1916 was the weather. At 2.30 p.m. there was such a violent wind that a British plane was driven before it over enemy lines, and the loud claps of thunder convinced some soldiers that the preliminary barrage had started already.[26]

That night A. J. Peters of the 7th Battalion, the South Lancashire Regiment, was sitting in B and D Company's mess in the former billiard room of the Café d'Univers in Molliens-au-Bois (seven miles north-east of Amiens) when an orderly marched in carrying two fat packets. They turned out to be the preliminary instructions for the two companies. 'Of course there was at once great speculation as to what day "Z" would be,' Peters later recalled:

We knew there was to be a 6 day bombardment which helped us in our calculations . . . The general [consensus] was that it would be Wednesday or Thursday in the following week.

That night we had a game of bridge and afterwards I sat up pretty late talking . . . When we [finally] turned out to go to our billets, the sky over Albert was bright with flashes. We could hear nothing although it was a still night, but we then had no doubt that the show had started.[27]

It seems likely that Peters either misremembered the day of the week when he saw the flashing in the sky or that he saw some guns firing before the softening-up bombardment commenced, because the main pre-attack bombardment started up during the morning of 24 June.

The South Lancashires were some 15 miles from the front lines when it started. Roland Ingle, a thirty-year-old 2nd lieutenant in the 10th Battalion, the Lincolnshire Regiment, another Pals unit also known as the Grimsby Chums, was closer to the action; however, being to the west of Albert, he was still to the rear of the area likely to be targeted by German guns. As a schoolmaster, and one who had come down from Cambridge with a first in Classics, he was used to reading and writing essays. And at around 5.30 p.m. on 24 June, with the shelling still hotting up, he settled down in the open air and recorded his impressions thus:

The bombardment for the Big Push has just begun. I am sitting . . . on an old plough in a half-tilled field watching the smoke of the shells rising over the German lines. There is a very wide view from here . . . and you can see . . . our own bit of front [south of La Boisselle] beyond the wood I have often mentioned [Becourt Wood], and a mile or more to left and right. In the hollow straight [ahead] . . . lies the town [Albert] with its broken church. It is a pleasant, rather cloudy day after a night of heavy rain, and the light breeze blowing from the west lessens for us the sound of the guns . . . There are poppies and blue flowers in the corn just by, [in] a part of the field which is cultivated, and on the rise towards the town [there] is a large patch of yellow stuff that might be mustard and probably isn't. On the whole the evening is a pleasant one for a stroll with the larks singing.[28]

Not surprisingly, conditions were completely different on the other side of No Man's Land, where the shells were landing.

'The enemy guns suddenly started flashing brightly,' artillery observer Sergeant Karl Eisler reported, recording the position as he saw it from the tower linked to the chateau at Contalmaison:

There were countless streaks of lightning above us accompanied by yelling, moaning, hissing and splintering sounds.

The English gunners were focusing on our rear, and on our . . . observation positions which they knew about already, as well as the communication trenches leading up to them and the village itself, locations which had been spared previously.

The rushing, splintering and cracking followed by the loud bangs made by the exploding shells of all types and calibres all around us were louder than anything I had heard in the previous two years of war. That made it very frightening . . .

The Contalmaison château was targeted by shells of all sorts of shapes and sizes. When it was hit, the whole building shook, and a cloud of brick dust rose up into the air making it hard to see what was happening. [Then] more shells came screaming overhead. They landed initially on the outskirts of Pozières, and subsequently on the village itself so that it disappeared behind clouds of smoke.

Shortly afterwards heavy shells obliterated the last houses in our village [Contalmaison]. And all around us we could see large clouds of smoke caused by the exploding shells . . . and one could hear the cracking and crashing sounds of the bombardment.[29]

The systematic destruction of the villages held by the Germans, and their lines of communication, would not have surprised any of the British soldiers who had seen their artillery's shells appearing to wipe out their targets one by one. It was a welcome sight after such a long time waiting. Captain Charlie May's diary records how the bombardment was celebrated by some of the 22nd Manchester officers, still located far away from the action, at Morlencourt (some three miles south of Albert): 'Tonight (24 June) we had a little reunion of all the "old boys",' he wrote. 'We sat round a table and sang all the old mess songs of Morecambe, Grantham and Salisbury [the places where they had been trained before coming out to France]. It was top-hole, and we all loved each other.'[30]

The next day May climbed onto the ridge above Morlencourt and

watched with relish as German front-line strongholds in the villages of La
Boisselle, Fricourt and the 22nd Manchesters' own target, Mametz, disappeared into the clouds of smoke thrown up by the exploding shells. The
following description in his diary enables one to appreciate just how easy it
was for British commanders to be seduced into believing that when the
time came to advance there would be no opposition left to fight:

The hillsides over there are under a haze of smoke already. [It is made by] shells,
which bursting, throw up . . . white puffs, black puffs, brown puffs and grey. Puffs
which start as small downy balls and spread sideways and upwards till they dwarf
the woods. Darts of flame and smoke – black smoke these last, which shoot . . .
high into the air like giant poplar trees.

The shooting was magnificent. Time and again, the explosions occurred right
in the Hun trenches. By Mametz Wood, an ammunition dump must have been
struck. The [resulting] . . . smoke column was enormous. Mametz itself one cannot see. It is shrouded in a multi-coloured pall of smoke all of its own.[31]

Perhaps the excessively optimistic British commanders should have been
ordered to watch the bombardment from where the 22nd Manchesters'
Sergeant Harry Tawney was standing on 25 May. His underwhelmed
response to that evening's shelling appears in the following extract from
the letter he sent to his wife Jeannette the next day:

Far away, [some] . . . miles off, one could see the faint, pale lines of trenches, and
above them the puffs [made] . . . by our shells, like surf on a coast. It was odd to
think that this was war, what the papers call a 'severe bombardment', and that . . .
[the] Germans were wondering if they would ever see their families again.

On so large a landscape, the wrath of men seemed extraordinarily ineffective,
and life infinitely more powerful than death, so that one forgot one had come to
see the bombardment, and looked instead at the sunset and poplars and light on
the distant downs.[32]

Given that the reason why Tawney had climbed up to the ridge above
Morlencourt was to admire the British bombardment, it was ironic that the
one feature in this huge landscape that really grabbed his attention was
Albert's church, which had been shelled by the Germans. Its unnatural,
awkward, clumsy silhouette, the result of its tower having been damaged
and its transept smashed, reminded him of 'a windmill with only one sail

left' or 'a face distorted by disease', the analogies unconsciously reflecting his fear about what German guns might do to the limbs and faces of British soldiers during the attack.[33]

The shelling continued late into the night, and whatever its shortcomings when viewed in daylight from a long way off, it impressed Roland Ingle that night when he once again climbed the hill west of Albert and saw how 'sharp flashes like sheet lightning showed our guns firing', while 'all along the horizon, there were red flashes of the shells falling on their target'.[34]

On 26 June, with just two clear days remaining before the original date scheduled for the attack (29 June), British soldiers all along the front were writing their last letters home, warning their families that they might be out of touch for a while. Charlie May's was no exception. It began with the words 'My darling Maudie', and carried on: 'Just one last little note for some days, since after tonight, I will have no chance of writing for the best part of a week.' He then referred to the bombardment:

The biggest show of the war is now on. The greatest bombardment the world has ever seen is banging and booming away in the valley, and on the hill over yonder. No-one has whispered it before, but you'll know all about it and what we have achieved by the time you have received this. At present, we are lying behind the line, waiting to go up for the assault. In the assault, the Battalion has the position of honour, [on] the right of the Division (7 Division), and B [Company] has been chosen as the right of the Battalion, in the leading line . . .

I little thought in those far off days in Morecombe that I should ever rise to have such a trust given to me. The Company is the envy of the Battalion, and the Battalion is [the envy] of the whole Division. To be the right of the finest division of the British Army is no small honour dearest, and I know you will be as proud of it as we are.

For myself Maudie, I pray [to] God in all humility that I may do my job well, achieve my objectives, hold them and generally carry out our orders correctly and successfully.

He signed off the letter with the words: 'All the love and devotion of my heart and soul to you my dear Wife and to our darling Baby. Know that I will think of you all the time. Au revoir my love. Your loving hubby, Charlie.'[35]

May's letter reached Maude on 30 May, the day after the original 'Z' day, which as mentioned in Chapter 5, was postponed until 1 July because of the bad weather. She wrote back that very night:

My darling Charlie . . .

For some time past I have been dreading such news as you have given me in your letter . . . but I have always tried to put it out of my mind and to think that you might be spared taking part. That your company . . . would hold such an important position in the assault, I never dreamed of, and . . . when I think of all the danger you are encountering at the present time, my heart beats with fear. My dearest, I am trusting in God and praying, Baby with me, that you will be spared to come through these terrible days of fighting safe and well, and return to us . . .

Well, the time we have all been waiting for has come. The papers are full of raids, artillery work etc . . . but so far no news of a big infantry assault . . .

Would it be possible to give my best wishes to your men? If at all poss., try to do so. And tell any who come to, or near, London to let me know their whereabouts.

My whole soul goes out to you my heart's dearest tonight in love and trust and longing. God will be good to us. He will keep little Pauline's Daddy safe . . . My own, my love. Your wife Maude.[36]

While all this correspondence was criss-crossing across France and England, and the English Channel, the British battalions that were to carry out the assault began to move up towards the front line. This prompted Charlie May on 27 June to write:

The Battle of Mametz I suppose may really be taken as having now commenced. True, it has been working up, so far as artillery activity is concerned, for the last three days. But as no infantry have yet come in, I take it that I give no offence to anyone if I call the period ending today 'preliminary proceedings'.

From today, however, the battle should begin to show definite shape. Infantry are now moving up, small parties as yet it is true, but still the infantry. Runners and wire cutters, signallers and dump guards have already gone. The assaulting troops follow tomorrow . . .[37]

5: Fatal Flaw

The Somme, June–early morning 1 July 1916

(See map 2)

From time immemorial, monarchs and great leaders have sought out the most efficacious means to make their troops fight bravely in battle. However, by the time of the Somme, the British Army had become too big to be inspired by one man. Each corps commander, each major-general and each lieutenant-colonel had to fire up his men in his own way.

Some of the speeches that were made before what so many referred to as the 'Big Push' have been lost with the men who heard them. However, there are a few that have been immortalized in documents or the accounts of soldiers who were affected by them.

Hubert Rees, the 94th Brigade's thirty-four-year-old commander, circulated to the Pals battalions acting under his command an open letter shortly before sending them in to assault the heights in and around the village of Serre, the 4th Army's northernmost target. It included the words:

You are about to attack the enemy with far greater numbers than he can oppose to you, supported by a huge number of guns . . . You are about to fight in one of the greatest battles in the world, and the most just cause . . . Remember that the British Empire will anxiously watch your every move . . . Keep your heads, do your duty, and you will utterly defeat the enemy.[1]

Henry de Beauvoir de Lisle, the fifty-one-year-old major-general in charge of the 29th Division, whose troops were responsible for the Beaumont Hamel sector, evidently remembered past exploits of the 1st Battalion, the Lancashire Fusiliers, when two days before the attack he spoke to them near Mailly Wood.[2] This was the unit that had won six Victoria Crosses in one day during the Gallipoli campaign.[3] He started his address to them thus: 'I cannot allow the Battalion, of which I am so proud, to enter this great battle without coming to wish you good luck.' He went on:

We are now taking part in the greatest battle in which British troops have ever fought. At this great time, all the previous engagements during this and former wars sink into insignificance. The forces that are engaged in this 4th Army are five times as large as the whole of the original Expeditionary Force. We came out in August 1915 with 4 divisions, and here we have 21 . . .[4]

All that military thought and science can do to make this a great success has been done. For the first time we have got into place as many guns as we can, and with unlimited ammunition.[5] In this Corps alone we have 600 guns.[6] . . . We are firing away 40,000 tons of artillery ammunition. In other words one and a half million rounds. In this Corps alone, if all the ammunition were placed in lorries, they would occupy 46 miles of road . . .

As you go into . . . battle, I want you to remember what you are fighting for. You are not only fighting to add to the glories won by past generations of the Lancashire Fusiliers. You are not only fighting to maintain the honour of the 29th Division which won its laurels on the Gallipoli Peninsula. You are fighting for your country . . . You are fighting for humanity. We are fighting against oppression, fighting for truth, honour and justice . . .

Our higher commanders know – I know – that all their arrangements cannot win victory. Victory must be won by the infantry.

Officers and men . . . To you has been [given] . . . the most difficult task. That of breaking the hardest part of the enemy's shell. And I expect you to break that shell in the German first system of trenches.

Officers and men. I wish you the best of luck, and leave you with the highest confidence that what any man [can] . . . do, you will do for your country.[7]

But perhaps even more impressive was the series of speeches by Lieutenant-General Sir Aylmer Hunter-Weston, VIII Corps' fifty-one-year-old commander, described in the following extract from the 30 June 1916 letter to his wife Grace:

Today, I went round eight battalions of the New Army (31st Division) that are to form part of my assaulting line. They have never yet been in battle and I therefore went and gave them an inspiriting address with most excellent results. I felt I had got them.

A heavy task to speak to 8 separate battalions and 2 machine gun batteries, over 8000 men, in the open air. It took all the morning, motoring and walking round and making those speeches. Fortunately my voice stood the heavy strain, and I was given the power to strike the right note and to enthuse the men. It is a valuable gift to be able to speak fairly well.[8]

A soldier who heard the speech delivered to the 16th Battalion, the West Yorkshire Regiment (the 1st Bradford Pals), remembers that Hunter-Weston 'stood on a box and . . . went on about having the true attack spirit'. Also 'the old words like fighting for Britain's honour came out'. And he underlined that the Germans knew nothing about honour: it was they who had started the war. That was why 'God was on our side.' Fortunately, the attack's success was a foregone conclusion, Hunter-Weston had forecast: 'Not even a rat would be left alive in the German trenches after our bombardment.'[9]

The only discordant note was the reference to shirkers. 'He said anyone who funked the attack and didn't go forward would be shot on the spot.' The military police would be watching.[10]

There were many other similar speeches. Most reiterated the message: We have destroyed the Germans with our guns. Now all you have to do is to walk over to their trenches. There will be no opposition.

If the British commanders had any qualms about what they were saying to their men, they certainly put on a good act. General Hunter-Weston, while talking to Lieutenant-Colonel Freeth of the 2nd Lancashire Fusiliers on 30 June about the large number of Germans seen in the front line opposite the 4th Division, interjected: 'Splendid Freeth. The enemy's trenches are full of Germans? They'll be blown to pieces by the morning.'[11] Another officer, who overheard the conversation, passed on this welcome news to the men in his company. 'It put us all in good heart,' he said later. 'In fact, we thought this must be the start of the end of the War!'[12]

However, not everyone was convinced. General Beauvoir de Lisle may have spoken optimistically to his men, but he claims he was less sanguine when talking to his superiors. After reading the official historian's version of his division's actions at Beaumont Hamel, de Lisle sent him the following comments:

Before the attack, Rawlinson came to visit me . . . I told him I was gravely dissatisfied with the artillery plan which in my opinion was inadequate, and too prolonged to be effective. I also highly disapproved of the [Hawthorn Redoubt] mine being exploded 10 minutes before the attack, as this would give the Germans warning. He said he would consider this last point, but I would find the artillery preparation more than sufficient.

A few days later Haig came with Rawlinson and I repeated my objections. Haig appeared to agree with me and seemed anxious about the success of the attack north of the Ancre.[13]

If survivors' accounts are to be believed, there were also a substantial proportion of assault troops who did not believe what their commanders were telling them. Take Percy Jones, a private soldier in the 1st/16th Battalion, the London Regiment (Queen's Westminster), for example. Scribbled into his diary under 26 June is a description of how his battalion had been rehearsed again and again on how they were going to snatch Gommecourt, at the extreme north of the line, from the Germans. To make the rehearsal more realistic, a piece of land near Halloy (11 miles north-west of Amiens) had been commandeered, and marked with the relative positions of the British front line and the German trenches. Then Jones and his brothers in arms were required to take them 'several times a day'.

His account continues: 'General Snow (the VII Corps commander) and his staff . . . [tell] us that we shall have practically no casualties, because all the Germans will have been killed by our artillery barrage . . . We know, however, that the Germans have dugouts 40 feet deep, and I do not see how the stiffest bombardment is going to kill them all off . . . If the Germans obstinately refuse to die and make way for us, our scheme will become impractical.'

When Jones mentioned this to his sergeant-major, he at least had the decency to come clean: 'Sergeant Major Froome . . . agreed with me, and called our practices "Damned foolery and [a] waste of good corn" [the practices involved trampling over fields full of wheat]. Nearly all the boys have no faith in the carefully drawn up plans of attack and consolidation.'

That being the case, it seems almost incredible that no one objected. 'They are all determined to go on until something stops them,' Jones concluded.[14]

Given his pessimistic analysis of their prospects, it is not surprising that Jones took care to write a last letter to his family, only to be delivered if he failed to come back. In the letter he described how on 29 June, the night before they moved up for the attack, the men in his battalion had met up in a café behind the front line: 'We . . . sang all the old songs, perhaps for the last time. We are . . . true friends, because the trials of trench life have made us know one another. We hope to meet again in a day or two, but it is quite plain that in the meantime, some of us will have gone west.'

He terminated his correspondence with the words: 'I am afraid I have been rather slack in answering letters. So when you meet any of my friends, please apologize for me and say that I know I have always had better friends than I deserved. Goodbye, and good luck to all.'[15]

Jones and his colleagues were far from being the only British soldiers who did not take their commanders' assurances at face value. Even more worrying was the demoralizing effect that the generals' ill-informed forecasts were having on some of the more discerning mid-ranking officers. They could hardly be expected to back the attack plan by putting their men's lives on the line, if they did not agree that what was proposed was feasible.

While writing to his wife Hilda, Lieutenant-Colonel Kyme Cordeaux, the newly appointed commanding officer of Roland Ingle's battalion (10th Lincolns), contrasted the vulnerability of the Somme's unprotected bird life with that of the Germans in the 'fortresses' they had hewn out of the chalk on the other side of No Man's Land. Cordeaux, who had inherited his interest in birds from his father, an eminent ornithologist, wondered 'what the little fledgling swallows in the nest above my bed think of it all. They will be deaf for the natural time of their lives. We shall soon know . . . what the effect is on the Boche. I am inclined to believe that his dugouts are too deep down for him to have suffered much.'[16]

If only Haig and his generals had been as perspicacious. But perhaps that is a criticism which can only be made with the benefit of hindsight. Even now it is hard to find detailed German accounts that describe exactly what was going on in the German trenches during the bombardment. One of the most revealing was written by F. L. Cassel, a twenty-seven-year-old Jewish lieutenant, who was serving in the 99th Reserve Regiment, part of the 26th Reserve Division, at the end of June 1916. He was based in the Thiepval South sector of the line when the bombardment started.

Unlike some accounts, which puffed up the bravery of German soldiers in an effort to appeal to the supporters of Adolf Hitler, during whose dictatorship many were written, Cassel's was written during the 1920s, before the rise of National Socialism made the glorification of German physical – and martial – exploits an obsession or a cult. It was then translated into English, after he had somehow survived the Holocaust and emigrated to England. That, together with the way Cassel was treated while he was in the Army, meant he had little incentive to write a romanticized version of what had really taken place on the German side of No Man's Land.

His account starts by revealing that during World War I, a form of insti-
tutionalized anti-semitism was already built into the culture fostered
within the German Army. The staff at the school where he was training to
be an officer during 1915 were not allowed to recommend that a Jewish
soldier could be promoted above the rank of NCO. As a result Cassel was
promoted later than his peers, only becoming a lieutenant after being
awarded the Iron Cross for bravery in the wake of a defensive action following the explosion of a mine under his trench.

Before being accepted into the regimental fold, Cassel also had to endure
weeks of being ostracized at meal times because he refused to comply
with the old-fashioned custom, still prevailing in some regiments, which
required him to address his superiors in the third person. However, by the
time the bombardment commenced on 24 June 1916, these teething problems had been long forgotten, and he had become the commander of one of
his regiment's positions in the front system, consisting of several lines of
trenches interspersed with deep dugouts. These dugouts, which were some
three metres beneath the surface, and were entered by climbing down
eighteen to twenty stairs, were believed to offer complete protection from
the blast of the enemy's shells, although the jury was out over whether soldiers inside could survive a direct hit. Dugout entrances were certainly
vulnerable, which was why with typical German efficiency many of the
dugouts had at least two exits.

When the bombardment started on 24 June, Cassel, along with the others
in his trench, had no idea that this was the preliminary softening-up process before a big attack. The shells sailed overhead into the regiment's back
areas, leaving the front line unscathed. 'We thought it was not our business,' he commented. 'We perhaps even enjoyed the thought that people
behind there, who [until then had] had it so good, should get a bit of the
medicine we usually had to accept.'

It was only after the shelling continued all day and all night, and then
carried on for several more days and nights, that the penny dropped.
During the first three days and nights, no food could be brought up to the
front-line position, and the Germans had to make do with the 'iron rations'
they always carried around with them. At that point, 'we began to look at
the situation as critical,' Cassel reported. 'It appeared they wanted first to
starve us and then to shoot us out of our positions.' It was only during the
third night that the German lines of communication were re-established,
enabling food to be supplied during hours of darkness.

However, no sooner had this need been satisfied than their lives were made uncomfortable for another reason. The shelling began to focus on destroying their trenches. Given that the German regiment were spending most of the time inside their dugouts, this did not represent a direct existential threat. But according to Cassel, 'it was not very pleasant!' The almost continuous banging made by the 'drum fire' was not only monotonous but made it hard to sleep, in spite of his men feeling very tired. Officers such as Cassel were also kept awake by the suspicion that the sentries who had been ordered to stand near the top of the dugout steps, so that they could warn their superiors if the enemy was approaching, would not do their job properly. Cassel was only being realistic when he observed, 'Not all men are heroes.'

One evening, during the bombardment, there was a gas alarm, which was accompanied by the cry: 'Everyone into the trenches with gas masks!' 'In front of us all along the line, a greenish yellow cloud rolled slowly towards us,' Cassel recalled. ' "She" was hesitating. "She" did not want to go uphill.' Luckily for him, and his men, the artillery fire on the trench was not too intense at that moment, and within an hour or so the gas had been dispersed by the wind, enabling them to resume their hibernation in their dugouts.

But were the dugouts secure? In the following extract from his account, Cassel describes how he found out:

One afternoon [during the bombardment], I was lying on my wire bedstead. I heard the . . . boom of a heavy gun, the awesome whiz and swish of a rising heavy missile. Then the earth was quaking, and while the dirt was falling through the boards, [overhead] I saw the beams above me bend and slowly descend by about 10 cm. My heart seemed to stop. Now comes the end. But the catastrophe did not come. After the momentary paralysis was gone, I left my bed and went into the trench. Rather die in the open air, .than be crushed between the boards. In the evening, I went and inspected the rampart above my dugout, and found a crater with a diameter of several meters made by . . . [an 8-inch shell], a dud. Had it exploded, whoever was in the dugout would [not] have seen daylight . . . before the day of resurrection![17]

Cassel's testimony suggests that the larger British shells probably could destroy at least some of the German dugouts, but only if there was a direct hit. The dugout exits were also vulnerable. However, the problem for the

British, as General Rawlinson had pointed out following the Battle of Loos (September–October 1915), was that 'it is impossible to locate even from air photographs where these exits are . . . Their destruction is therefore a matter of chance.'[18]

Rawlinson's clear-sighted analysis as early as 1915 made it all the more surprising that, almost a year later, many of the senior officers in his army were still training their men, and basing their tactics, on the assumption that all front-line opposition would be neutralized before the attack on the Somme.

Even Rawlinson was not aware of another problem, which threatened to be just as damaging to the attack's prospects. German records made available after the war have revealed the stunning results produced by their intelligence officers during the big attack's preliminary bombardment. Thanks in part to the streamlined procedures in place for interrogating captured British prisoners and disseminating what they disclosed, the intelligence officers were able to extract crucial information from those soldiers apprehended in No Man's Land, and to circulate it quickly enough for it to play a significant role in the blunting of the much-anticipated big attack.

The first of these intelligence coups revolved around the capture of Victor Wheat, a twenty-two-year-old miner. During the night of 23–24 June 1916, he had been out in No Man's Land opposite the German stronghold of Gommecourt, the northernmost village that was due to be targeted during the attack. He and the other men from his unit, the 1st/5th Battalion, the North Staffordshire Regiment, were complying with an order from the 46th Division to dig an advanced assembly trench, the idea being that they would be nearer to the enemy when the time came to advance. However, while they were digging, they were targeted by German gunners, and Wheat was one of the covering party's twenty-four casualties.[19] Left by his comrades to make his own way home, Wheat had apparently become confused due to the loss of too much blood, and had ended up inadvertently heading towards the German line. At least that was what he told the Germans, who found him near their front line later that night.

If Wheat had been allowed to recover before being subjected to an interrogation, who knows what might have transpired. However, the following extract from the German report in their records reveals that he was barely given time to catch his breath before being questioned: 'The prisoner was in a very vulnerable state, because he was in pain and had lost a lot of blood. When he talked about the attack, he was experiencing a renewed wave of light-headedness. This can only give us more confidence in what he was telling us.'

Such a statement in an intelligence report raises the question: did the interrogators intentionally withhold treatment until he had told them what they needed to know? Whether or not such tactics were applied during the first hours after he was captured, Wheat eventually sang like a canary. The interrogator concluded his report with the words: 'The prisoner is fed up with the way he has been treated by the English, and has made this statement voluntarily.'

The following information, disclosed during Wheat's first interrogation, probably before the start of the pre-attack bombardment, was already damaging enough as far as British plans were concerned: 'The English attack will definitely start during the next 2 to 3 days. It will be preceded by a 4 to 5 day bombardment.' But it was during the subsequent interrogation that Wheat gave the evidence which effectively sealed the fate of thousands of British soldiers who would be advancing on Gommecourt at zero hour.

The report dated Sunday 25 June 1916 starts with the words: 'The prisoner had rested and was freshly bandaged.' It continues:

On being questioned about the English 'Big Push', he confirmed that it would be over the next few days, probably on Wednesday (28 June). He only knows specifics concerning his own brigade (46th Division's 137th Brigade): Gommecourt is to be isolated by attacks, one from the north and another from the south . . . The objective is the wood behind the trenches. When asked how he knew about this, he stated that they had practised the attack in woods and trenches behind the front line.

The practice had evidently not catered for gas being used. Wheat could only say it would be used 'in those locations where it is necessary'.[20]

Wheat could talk freely about all of this because he was confident that he would not be rescued in the course of the coming attack. The British were commanded by the same general (Haig) who had failed at Loos, leading Wheat and his comrades to assume they would do no better this time.

The Germans on the Somme became even more convinced they knew when they were to be attacked after capturing one British soldier, and two more men whom they linked with the Newfoundland Regiment, during the night of 27–28 June.[21] German records tell us that this time, their most fruitful informant was Josef Lipman, a twenty-three-year-old carpenter.

He is described in the German interrogation report as a Jew, whose Russian parents had brought him to England when he was two years old. Lipman had enlisted in the Army in 1914, and at the time he was captured, he was serving in the 2nd Battalion, the Royal Fusiliers regiment.[22] This unit, which was part of the 29th Division's 86th Brigade, was located, as indicated in Chapter 1, opposite the Hawthorn Redoubt.

It says a lot for the secrecy maintained by the 252nd Tunnelling Company that Lipman did not appear to know anything about the Hawthorn Redoubt tunnel. The German report of his interrogation, dated Wednesday 28 June 1916, contains nothing about mining. By way of contrast, it is so specific about the date of the coming attack that it would have made sickening reading for any British readers who happened to see it contemporaneously.

Unlike Victor Wheat, who seems to have been captured unwillingly, Lipman's desertion was not just voluntary; it was premeditated. The German interrogation report states that Lipman did not want to play any part in the coming offensive. That explains why he had volunteered to join the seventeen-man raiding party, which had been ordered to seize a soldier from the German front line for intelligence purposes. He was hoping the raid would give him the chance to desert.

It was a risky strategy. German defenders fired at the raiders, before they had even reached the enemy's barbed wire, and according to Lipman most of them were killed. But it gave Lipman the chance he had been waiting for. While the survivors were taking cover, Lipman peeled off, and eventually, after shouting out in German that he wanted to defect, rather than to attack, he was permitted to enter the German line.

Like Wheat, he was processed very quickly, which was essential if the Germans were to benefit from what Lipman had to tell them. The information he divulged could not have been more precise. According to the report by the German interrogator: 'On Friday last week (23 June), the prisoner learned from the order issued by his battalion commander that the big attack by British forces would commence this Thursday (29 June), early in the morning, between 5 and 6 a.m. The attack would be preceded by an artillery bombardment lasting 5 days and 4 nights.'

And if there was still any doubt about whether gas would be used, the report continued:

Since last Saturday (24 June) his battalion has released gas on several occasions, most recently yesterday morning. There were now no more full gas cylinders left.

Shortly before the attack, lots of smoke generators will be burned which, as the British know, will lead us to open fire, and they will only launch the attack when the firing eases off.[23]

The only key aspect of Lipman's report that was wrong related to the specification of the attack front: he overestimated the area to be attacked in the north, and underestimated it to the south. He told the Germans the attack would be between Albert and Arras, whereas Wheat, more accurately, said that as well as covering Gommecourt, the British would also seek to capture the area 30–50 miles to its south. (Even Wheat's description was slightly misleading. The Anglo-French front was approximately 21 miles as the crow flies.)[24]

Lipman also mistakenly overstated the number of casualties. His battalion's war diary states that there were no fatalities, only one man wounded, and one missing (Lipman).[25] This error would only have been important if the Germans had found out. If they had, it might have led them to suspect that the whole operation was a ruse, designed to mislead them. As it was, they accepted Lipman's version of the facts without question.

Details of these interrogations were quickly circulated to the units along the front. Consequently, far from being in the dark about when the attack was expected, when dawn broke on 29 June, the German defenders were stood to.[26]

Perhaps it was lucky then, from the British viewpoint, that after breakfast on 28 June it began to rain, as Rawlinson put it in his diary, 'in torrents'. After consulting with the sixty-four-year-old General Ferdinand Foch, the commander of France's Northern Group of Armies, who was effectively Rawlinson's opposite number, he decided it was far too wet for a major offensive and postponed the attack until 7.30 a.m. on 1 July.[27]

Later that same day, Captain Charlie May, who along with the other assault troops in the 22nd Manchesters was still some way back from the front line, in the Bois de Tailles, wrote in his diary: 'We were to move up tonight to take up our positions . . . But we have not moved. At the last moment, came an order: Stand by. And so here we are still, the artillery pounding on as ever.'[28]

Of all the 22nd Manchester soldiers whose accounts survive, Sergeant Harry Tawney, who had been so critical of the Army's organization, was the most philosophical about the delay. Writing to his wife Jeannette on 29 June, he told her he was still in his 'bivouac in the wood (not so bad as it looks, a little green cage of bent branches and a tarpaulin on the top, and myself and two sergeants inside)'. After imploring her not to worry, he continued: 'For myself, I feel that you and I, and all men, are what our forefathers called in the hands of the Lord, and I am not troubled . . . The only thing which occasionally worries me is anxiety that I should fail in my small duties.'[29]

Two days later, at 5.45 a.m., just hours before zero hour, Charlie May recorded details of the movement he and the entire attack force had been waiting for:

We marched up last night, the most exciting march imaginable. Guns all around us crashed and roared, till sometimes it was impossible to hear oneself speak . . . Fritz of course strafed back in reply causing us . . . a few casualties . . .

It is a glorious morning and is now broad daylight. We go over in two hours' time. It seems a long time to wait, and I think, whatever happens, we shall all feel relieved once the line is launched . . . Our gunnery has wrecked . . . his front trenches all right, but we do not yet seem to have stopped his machine-guns. [They] . . . are pooping off all along our parapet as I write. I trust they will not claim too many of our lads before the day is over.[30]

But even as the weather cleared, another dark cloud blotted out the metaphorical sunshine. During the lead up to 1 July, various reports had reached Rawlinson's intelligence officers indicating that the Germans were intercepting British telephone and 'buzzer' messages.[31] German prisoners captured by British patrols had revealed that this had enabled them to anticipate bombardments by British artillery, and to repulse British raids. It was known that the German Army was using Arendt listening apparatus, codenamed 'Moritz', and that one such device was located in the village of La Boisselle.[32]

If the British Army had been an efficient organization, this would have led to the enforcement of an absolute ban on secret messages being sent prior to the attack anywhere near the front line, except in accordance with strict rules. But as we have seen, the administration of the British Army in 1916 was far from being efficient. Even if senior commanders were clear-sighted enough to realize that an order should be given, as was the case concerning the banning of secret messages, there was no fail-safe enforcement procedure in place to ensure that the rules were not broken. This state of affairs conspired to produce a deadly combination: on 22 June,

III Corps' general staff thought it had taken all necessary security measures on this subject when it warned all of its major-generals, including the commander of the 34th Division, that 'Telephone circuits are easily tapped and are consequently very dangerous for the transmission of secret information.'[33] Yet when, during the early hours of 1 July, the following compromising 4th Army message was circulated by III Corps' 34th Division, no one thought anything of it:

In wishing all ranks good luck, the Army Commander desires to impress on all infantry units the supreme importance of helping one another and holding on tight to every yard of ground gained. The accurate and sustained fire of the artillery during the bombardment should greatly assist the task of the infantry.[34]

The message was picked up by the German operators manning the Arendt apparatus in La Boisselle, and within minutes warnings were being sent to German units all along the front that an attack was imminent.[35] Ironically, the message, apparently intended by Britain's latter-day Henry (Rawlinson) to have the same morale-boosting properties as Henry V's much more stirring 'Once more unto the breach, dear friends' speech (delivered to the troops prior to the Battle of Agincourt in Shakespeare's eponymous play), was to have quite the opposite effect. Intercepted as it was by the Germans, the message at a stroke deprived the British soldiers who had to go over the top at 7.30 a.m. on 1 July of one of their most important tactical advantages: the element of surprise. When they advanced to attack the enemy's trenches, the German soldiers would be there waiting for them.

6: The First Blows

The Somme, 1 July 1916

(See maps 1, 2, 4 and 6)

For many Germans, the first indication that they were about to be attacked was the sight of what they took to be clouds of poison gas floating across No Man's Land towards them. The horror that this evoked at dawn on 1 July 1916, overlaying as it did the terror already experienced following the British and French bombardment, was recorded by an artillery observer based in Contalmaison. This was Sergeant Karl Eisler, of the 28th Reserve Division's 29th Field Artillery Regiment, whose description of the intensity of the preliminary bombardment has already been cited in Chapter 4:

A wall of milky white drifted slowly towards us . . . until the hollows stretching from Pozières to Fricourt were filled with a veil of 'gas fog' . . . It smelt very strongly of bitter almonds. We believed it must be prussic acid, [a worrying thought since] we knew that our gas masks provided no protection against it.

As the first rays of the morning sun lit up the sky, the terrifying flood of gas increased in size, climbing higher and higher, until we too were submerged by it. One could barely see further than 10 metres.

[It was accompanied by] powerful enemy artillery fire along the whole front . . . The roaring of the guns grew louder and louder, until the diabolical bellowing sound . . . combined with the blasts made by the exploding shells . . . threatened to rip the whole world off its hinges and turn everything upside down.

The roaring became so loud that it was impossible to hear oneself speak, and at the same time we could not see anything because of the fog . . .

We waited tensely, wondering what would happen next . . . realizing that this day might be our last.[1]

Eisler was not alone in voicing that sentiment. As zero hour approached, similar scenes were experienced, and similar questions asked, by German soldiers at many of the strongpoints dotted along the front. However, those who donned their gas masks, fearing they would be poisoned or suffocated, were playing into their attackers' hands. Whereas there had been gas attacks before the main attack, on the morning of 1 July it was in most cases either a natural morning mist or smoke that was blinding them. Evil-smelling and revolting certainly, if it was the latter, but designed to conceal the attackers and to terrorize, rather than to kill the defenders.[2]

It was this smoke that, shortly before 7.30 a.m., billowed out of the British lines and enveloped the villages at Gommecourt and Mametz, and at some of the other spots where British commanders believed their troops crossing No Man's Land would be most vulnerable. In some places the smokescreen was thicker than in others. We know, for example, that there were breaks in the protective veil, during the critical first phase of the attack, just to the south of the fortified salient protruding from the German line between Beaumont Hamel and Serre. The Germans referred to this spot as the Heidenkopf (the name of the officer who built up the position), and the British the Quadrilateral (see map 4). According to Lieutenant Beck of the German 121st Reserve Regiment, who was observing the enemy's movements from a reinforced one-man observation tower, located a short distance behind the front line:

At first . . . I could not see anything because of the fog and gases . . . [However] during moments when the fog temporarily cleared, I could see that masses of English troops had assembled in their trenches. Groups of them dressed in their battle equipment were lounging around on the edges of their trenches, chatting, joking and smoking. [Then] the shelling became stronger, until . . . it swept over us with the intensity of a hurricane. All of a sudden . . . there was a violent tremor under our feet – caused by the explosion [of the mine on Hawthorn Ridge] . . . while the shelling lifted from our front trenches so that it could target our rear. Seconds later, the slope opposite us resembled an ant heap gone mad, as wave after wave of British troops advanced towards our positions which were still shrouded in the fog and smoke. I told my battalion that the attack was beginning, but no sooner had I done so than the underground cable connecting me to the rear was cut.

[As I watched] parts of the first English wave, acting under the umbrella of the artillery fire and the fog, reached our front trench, where they overran the dugout . . . just to the left of the Heidenkopf, and attacked the 3rd Company from the flank and rear.[3]

At least Lieutenant Beck had had enough time to warn his superiors. German observers at Gommecourt, the village at the northern end of the British attack line, did not have the luxury of seeing what was coming their way. In that portion of the front, the clouds of smoke produced by the lighting of smoke candles, and by the throwing, and firing, of smoke bombs into No Man's Land, could not have been much denser.[4] That was what had been demanded by the commanders of both the British divisions involved in the sector.[5] It was seen as being particularly important for troops within the five London battalions from the 56th (1st London) Division, which were to spearhead the advance to the south of the village. They had been ordered to advance up to 750 yards, approximately half of it across No Man's Land, where there would be no protective obstacle between the men and the German guns.[6]

The last moments leading up to the advance by one of them, the 1st/9th Battalion, the London Regiment (Queen Victoria's Rifles), was subsequently chronicled by Captain R. H. Lindsey-Renton as follows:

At 6.25 [a.m.] the final intensive bombardment started . . . It was . . . a most wonderful sight. Our shells appeared to be falling everywhere and the German trenches were enveloped in clouds of smoke with earth, bricks and trees shooting up into the air whenever a big shell burst.

All the troops [in the reserve position] in the old front line were standing on the firestep gleefully surveying the scene. At 7.20 [a.m.], the smoke barrage began, and five minutes later had extended all along the line. At 7.30 [a.m.], the attack commenced, the front line men advancing over the top . . . calmly and slowly . . . just as though they were on parade . . . [They were watched by] the reserve men, who stood up on the parapet cheering . . . as the troops gradually disappeared in[to] the smoke.[7]

The sight of thousands of British troops marching towards them might have been expected to strike terror into the hearts of the Germans defending their positions on the other side of No Man's Land. Instead, account after account confirms that the approaching enemy, and the lifting of the English barrage off the front trenches, galvanized them. As the 169th Regiment's machine-gunner, Otto Lais, located in the southern portion of the Serre sector (just to the south of Gommecourt), put it:

We were finally liberated from the nightmare posed by the . . . [7] . . . days of drumfire . . . No longer were we stuck like a mouse caught in a trap, incarcerated inside [our] caved in dugouts. No longer did we have to quake, as each explosion hit the ground, making a noise which sounded like a hammer striking a helmeted skull. No longer did we have to calm men down by hugging them tight, or tying them down because they had almost been driven mad by the banging and splintering . . . the suffocating atmosphere, and the vibrating dugout walls which made them want to rush screaming and shaking out of their holes [where they had been imprisoned even though] the open air meant braving [flying] iron and [for those who were hit] death.

[Instead] there was a choking in every throat, an urge, which finally emerged [from the men's mouths] as the liberating battle cry: 'They are coming!'[8]

It was a cry that was repeated again and again, all along the attack line to the south, as more and more British troops, over a vast area, were seen to be advancing. Four miles to the south, on the other side of the River Ancre, in the German 99th Reserve Regiment's trenches, south of Thiepval, that same haunting cry 'They are coming!' dissipated Lieutenant F. L. Cassel's lethargy in an instant. Moments before, he had been lying listlessly in the same dugout where he had effectively been imprisoned for the past week, listening to the dull booms of the guns and the subsequent shattering explosions. The shrill battle cry woke him from his reverie. Grabbing his helmet, belt and rifle, he raced up the steps to the trench outside. He later described what he witnessed as he rushed to the surface: 'On the steps [there was] something white and bloody. In the trench [there was] a headless body.' It was the remains of the sentry who had 'paid for his vigilance with his life'. One of the last shells fired at the front trenches by the British artillery before it had swept to the rear 'had torn [off] his head . . . [It was] his brain [that was] lying on the [dugout] steps.'

'We rushed to the ramparts,' Cassel reported, expecting to have to repulse hordes of savage infantrymen hurtling towards him. Instead he saw a spectacle that amazed him. There were plenty of 'khaki-yellows', as he called them, all right. But rather than running stormtroopers, they were burdened down with equipment and were advancing 'slowly' as if they believed they could 'march across our bodies into the open country'.

'But no boys, we are still alive!' Cassel wrote, recalling the indignation that the British soldiers' apparent insouciance provoked:

The 'moles' come out of their holes. Machine-gun fire tear[s] holes in their rows. [When] they discover our presence, [they have to] throw themselves on[to] the ground in front of our trenches [or what] once . . . were . . . trenches, [but which] now [are] a mass of craters, [where they are] welcomed by [our] hand grenades and gun fire, and have . . . to sell their [own] lives . . . [if they want to advance any further].[9]

But there were some Germans who would never have the satisfaction of hearing anyone shout 'They are coming!' One of the last sounds some of the German garrison guarding the village of La Boisselle may have heard this side of eternity, over and above the booming of the British and German guns, was the throbbing, buzzing noise made by the engine inside an approaching enemy plane. The eighteen-year-old British pilot, Lieutenant Cecil Lewis, was flying his Morane Parasol reconnaissance plane over the village, when, at 7.28 a.m. precisely, one of the most iconic events of 1 July took place: somewhere, 8,000 feet below where he was flying, a tunnelling company commander pushed down the plunger, which was to detonate the largest pair of mines ever exploded under the German trenches.[10] Shortly afterwards, another huge mine went up. Lewis later described how they affected him:

We were looking at the [La] Boisselle Salient. And then suddenly . . . there was an ear-splitting roar . . . [and] the whole earth heaved up, and up from the ground came what . . . looked . . . like two enormous cypress trees . . . silhouettes, great dark cone-shaped lifts of earth, [climbing] 3, 4, 5000 feet. And then, a moment later, we struck the repercussion wave . . . and it flung us . . . [to] one side away from the blast. A moment later . . . the second mine [exploded. Once] again [we heard] the roar . . . [and saw] the strange gaunt silhouette invading the sky. Then the dust cleared, and we saw the two white eyes of the craters. The barrage had lifted to the second line trenches, the infantry went over the top, the attack had begun.[11]

7: False Dawn

Serre, 1 July 1916

(See maps 1, 2 and 4)

The final hours leading up to the attack on the extreme left of the sector targeted by Rawlinson's 4th Army triggered a moment of introspection from the officer in charge of this northern wing. On 30 June 1916, after VIII Corps' commander Lieutenant-General Sir Aylmer Hunter-Weston had spoken to the last of the Pals battalions within his 31st Division, which were to attack Serre the next day, he wrote a letter to his wife, Grace, to tell her his innermost thoughts on what was about to take place:

Tomorrow is the great day . . . By this time tomorrow another great page in history will be turned. Everything promises well for the success of the great venture . . . Never have I entered a battle with so many chances in our favour.

The result is in the hands of God, but I can say that all that can be done to ensure success has been done by Haig and Rawly, and by my staff.

Difficulties, disappointments, contretemps and heavy losses there are sure to be. But I rejoice in difficulties and pray God I may be given strength and judgment to put right matters that require to be put right as the difficulties arise.[1]

He went on to tell Grace what he would be doing, as the 50,000 infantrymen within his corps went into battle.[2] They had the following objectives: his southernmost unit, the 29th Division, which Hunter-Weston had himself once commanded, during the April 1915 landings at Gallipoli, was to attack the area around Beaumont Hamel, the village near the big mine (see Chapter 1, p. 1). His 4th Division troops were waiting to the north of the 29th Division's battalions. They were to attack the Heidenkopf strongpoint in the salient at the same time as the northernmost assault in his corps was mounted by the 31st Division.

Its troops were to advance towards the heights crowned by the village of Serre, with a view to capturing it, and establishing a defensive flank facing NNE, protecting the northern limits of the 4th Army's advance. Two battalions from his corps' fourth unit, the 48th Division, to the north of the 31st Division, were not to advance at 'zero hour', but were to make it look as if they were about to, by discharging smoke from their trenches (see map 4 for pre-attack positions).[3]

Hunter-Weston's letter to Grace continued:

At 7.30 [a.m.], the infantry will assault . . . I shall myself be getting up . . . at the time after a . . . restful night. I shall breakfast quietly at that château [in Marieux], far from the sound of guns, and shall have nothing to do with war till the reports of where we have succeeded and where we have failed come in, and the situation is put before me by my staff on the map.[4] [It is] very different from the idea of an old fashioned general with battles on a small scale where the commander was looking at the little battlefield himself.[5]

Given what we know about what happened on 1 July, it is perplexing to hear an experienced commander such as Hunter-Weston being so complacent and optimistic. Could he really have been so naive about the difficulties his men would encounter? The answer, not even hinted at in the British official history of the war, is to be found in those of his private papers stored in vaults of the British Library in London. They reveal a very different picture to the narrative that is normally told about this controversial general.

Hunter-Weston, often referred to by his nickname Hunter-Bunter, may have utilized speech patterns that made him seem like a throwback to a past era – his sentences were full of flamboyant exclamations such as 'How Jolly!', 'Capital!', and, when talking about a shell, 'What a nice little chap!', all delivered in cut-glass King's English. He may have been ridiculed for being the archetypal ignorant and bloodthirsty upper-class buffoon, one of many who were given the reins of power within the British Army during the war years. But his papers show that he sometimes exhibited very sound judgement: he had the uncanny knack of being able to analyse the plan for a big pre-prepared attack, and say whether it would succeed.

The fact that he had turned up in his Rolls Royce, his magnificent bushy moustache bristling, with his glamorous young wife in tow, on his first day as the 29th Division's commander shortly before the troops were to be transported to Gallipoli in 1915, may have made it hard for his men to take him seriously.[6] But behind the scenes it was Hunter-Weston who tried to save the lives of all the men in the division by writing a candid report before the operation started, urging his superiors to call it off.[7] His recommendation could not have been more correct. Gallipoli turned out to be a disaster for both Britain and Australia, who lost thousands of men there, many of them while following Hunter-Weston's orders, without any realistic prospect of defeating the Turks.

Hunter-Weston was, initially at least, equally pessimistic about VIII Corps' chances on the Somme. The following extracts from the report he sent to Rawlinson's 4th Army headquarters on 25 March 1916 represents a damning indictment of the strategy Haig eventually persuaded Rawlinson to accept: 'Even after the best artillery operation on a position which consists of so many lines of wire and trenches, and which has in it 3 strong villages, we must expect to lose many men before taking the line of German trenches that crown the Serre-Beaucourt ridge . . . We shall be lucky if we have a brigade in hand when we reach . . . the ridge.'

That was why he stated emphatically that the advance to the German 2nd position (the Serre–Grandcourt ridge), 2,000 yards behind the first objective (the Serre–Beaucourt ridge) over an open rolling valley, would be 'foolish generalship' unless his corps was allocated a fifth division to add to the four he already had, so that a fresh division could make the final assault. Another essential requirement was the pulling forward of sufficient artillery to the first objective, so that it could cover the subsequent advance to the Serre–Grandcourt ridge.

As if that was not clear enough, Hunter-Weston concluded:

I am strongly opposed to a wild rush by the advanced line of troops for an objective 4000 yards away from their trenches of departure. Even if they get over the intervening line of trenches, the remnant of the line that started cannot but arrive as a widely spread and disordered rabble, with no power to overcome even a feeble resistance in the enemy back trenches, and with but little chance of being able to maintain themselves therein.[8]

These were strongly held views backed up by hard logic. Nevertheless, just over two weeks later, there had been a dramatic shift in the way the attack was being analysed at VIII Corps' headquarters. On 12 April 1916, Hunter-Weston's chief of staff, Brigadier-General 'Jerry' Hore-Ruthven, wrote the following critique that seems to paint a picture of the likely outcome of the attack in a much more positive light:

It is assumed that the intensive preliminary bombardment, and the élan of the assaulting infantry, will carry them through to the first objective within half an hour of the commencement of the assault . . .

It is assumed that the artillery bombardment will pin the troops holding the front line to their positions, and at the same time batter down Beaumont Hamel and Serre to such an extent as to nullify all resistance in these two villages.[9]

If this really does represent a dramatic shift in attitude, rather than the stating of assumptions so that another point could be examined – the report goes on to analyse the likely movement of German reserves and its impact on the attack – it raises the question: what made Hunter-Weston and his staff change their minds?

It is likely that Haig's conversation with Hunter-Weston, when he visited VIII Corps' headquarters at Marieux on 8 April, may have started the ball rolling. After hearing Hunter-Weston's reservations about the plan, Haig sought out Rawlinson and effectively ordered him to nobble Hunter-Weston. Haig insisted that Hunter-Weston must take both objectives in 'one single effort', failing which the German 2nd position would be manned by German reinforcements before the attack on it had even started.[10]

There is no record of what Rawlinson said to convince Hunter-Weston that, at the very least, the first objective could be attained (the critique by Hunter-Weston's chief of staff still maintained it would be hard to take the German 2nd position without bringing up the artillery), but it more than likely had something to do with what Rawlinson would have categorized as the generous number of howitzers and guns allocated to VIII Corps, and his forecast concerning the effect they would have on the German trenches.

In spite of his own original reservations about Haig's alterations to his plan, by 19 July even Rawlinson had been persuaded that, after the thousands of shells fired at the enemy lines, German defenders would not be able to put up much of a fight. On that day he scribbled out a note that quantified the weight of the shells which would have rained down on the German positions before the end of the preliminary bombardment (40,000 tons), leading him to conclude: 'There should not be much left of his defences at the end of it.'[11]

A few days later, Hunter-Weston proudly informed Grace just how many guns had been entrusted to his corps: 'I have in all under my command . . . 600 pieces of ordnance less 4 i.e. 596 . . . a very formidable array of ordnance for one army corps. Would that I had had 1/6th of these at Gallipoli. [If I had had them] we should have been through to

Constantinople, and the war would by now have been very much nearer its end than it is at present.'[12]

Although the guns mentioned by Hunter-Weston included mortars as well as heavy howitzers and guns, and the lighter field artillery used for cutting the German wire, it was a massive number compared with what he had been expecting. It was this that appears to have transformed him from arch-opponent to fervent supporter of the attack, blinding him to the plan's defects.

There are also grounds for concluding that some kind of trade-off was going on between Hunter-Weston and Haig and Rawlinson. As the day of reckoning approached, VIII Corps' performance on the wire-cutting and counter-battery front became more and more worrying. That appeared to be the reason why the corps' attempts to conduct raids had been so unsuccessful. On 28 June, Haig, commenting on this inability to reach the German trenches, wrote in his diary, following a visit to Hunter-Weston's headquarters: 'Although raids had been ordered to be made and had been organized, not one had yet entered enemy's lines!'

In the same diary entry Haig mentioned his hopes that delaying the attack for two days would give VIII Corps the chance to improve its performance. However, there was no reason for optimism in the sectors under two of the corps' generals: Haig stated that he thought two of VIII Corps' major-generals, Major-General de Lisle of the 29th Division and Major-General O'Gowan of the 31st Division, were 'poor'.

Nevertheless, Haig's diary entry next day revealed that in spite of his complaints, which Rawlinson had discussed with Hunter-Weston, VIII Corps' commander was 'quite satisfied and confident'. Haig's diary contains no evidence of any confrontation between the two men. This leads one to wonder whether they had reached some kind of accommodation: Hunter-Weston would not criticize the plan if Haig and Rawlinson did not haul him over the coals for his inadequate pre-attack preparations.

Some of Hunter-Weston's subordinates were less accommodating. There were certainly some who believed his attack plan needed tweaking. In his after-action report, Brigadier-General Hubert Rees, who had been asked to stand in as commander of the 31st Division's northern unit (94th Brigade) for the Serre operation, recalled mentioning one omission in particular:

A few days before the attack, I pointed out to General Hunter-Weston that the assembly trenches stopped dead on the left of 94 Brigade, and that not a spade had been put into ground between me and the subsidiary attack at Gommecourt. Worse still, no effort at wire cutting was made on that stretch either. A child could see where the flank of our attack lay to within ten yards.[13]

Rees also recollected having 'a severe argument' with his corps commander over the principle that his plan did not allow for hold-ups, even though, unbeknown to the 94th Brigade commander, this was more or less the very same point that Hunter-Weston had mentioned to Haig in May when he had opposed the plan.[14]

In spite of this, Rees' objection was given short shrift: 'I was looked upon as something of a heretic for saying that everything had been arranged . . . except for the unexpected, which usually occurs in war. One of my criticisms . . . was that the time allowed for the capture of each objective was too short.' He had to capture the first four trenches protecting Serre within twenty minutes. Twenty minutes later he had to move again, with a view to taking the next 800 yards, including Serre itself, within just over half an hour. Finally, his troops had twenty minutes to capture an orchard on a knoll 300 yards further. Eventually, 'I induced him to give me an extra ten minutes for the capture of . . . [the] orchard.'

Having said that, Rees did concede that he never dreamt the plan, defects or no defects, would end up being such a disaster. 'A great spirit of optimism prevailed in all quarters,' he admitted ruefully.[15]

Both Rees and Hunter-Weston might have been a lot less sanguine about the 31st Division's prospects if they had known who had been prowling around in front of the British front line during the night before the attack. According to a report in the war diary of the German unit responsible for the Serre sector (the 52nd Division's 169th Regiment):

At 4 a.m. (German time – one hour ahead of the times used by the English) – during the night 30 June to 1 July, an officer whose surname is . . . Ackermann along with an under officer and three other ranks crossed over from the southern front line trench (in section S4, see map 4) into the English front line. No-one was in the English trench. However there was something going on in their second trench. The German patrol was not spotted. When opposite the northern front line trench Ackermann cut the tape which ran from the second English trench . . . into the area in front of S3 (see map 4), and they brought part of the tape back with them.[16]

The significance of the tape would have been evident to the Germans. It went without saying that the most likely reason why the tape would have been pegged down in such a location was that it was needed to show the infantry where they were to line up prior to an imminent attack. It was the sighting of this tape together with the circulation of the intercepted good-luck message from General Rawlinson (mentioned in Chapter 5) that set the 169th Regiment's alarm bells ringing.

The war diarist described what happened next:

At about 5 a.m. (German time) thick 'fog' which became thicker and thicker came over from the direction of the enemy's trenches and enveloped our positions masking the area in front of us.

That settled it. We stood to. The men who didn't have to stand guard sat on the stairs leading down to the dugouts with their guns on their knees and with sacks of hand grenades beside them.

If the English thought they could demoralize us by their 'carpet' shelling, they could not have been more wrong. Never was the desire to fight . . . stronger than at this time when we were blockaded. Without exception everyone was just itching to get at the enemy . . .

After a while the 'fog' dispersed and the sun could be seen shining through. At about 7.30 a.m. (German time), intense drum fire commenced, and it spread over the whole position. That told us all that the time when we could seek our revenge was fast approaching. Our last-minute preparations included the building up of reserve stocks of ammunition and hand grenades. And then we were ready for action.[17]

The single demoralizing factor they could not get round was that, as one German officer recorded, 'The British horizon was full of tethered balloons, and the air was buzzing with enemy aircraft.' As a result, the British could see the Germans' every move.[18] It was a state of affairs that was to hamper the German defences whenever visibility was good.

Meanwhile, on the other side of No Man's Land, the British troops who were to invest Serre were making their final preparations. Its commanders could rest assured that the Pals battalions in the 31st Division's southernmost unit, the 93rd Brigade, would certainly not fail because of a lack of fitness. They were one of the most sporty groups in the BEF, including in their ranks four footballers who had played First Division football (three of them being English or Scottish internationals, and the fourth a soccer gold medallist at the 1912 Olympic Games), and four cricketers, who either before or after the war played for England.[19]

Perhaps hoping to replicate the kind of last-minute pep talks they would have been given by their football club managers and cricket team captains, Major-General Wanless O'Gowan, 31st Division's fifty-one-year-old commander, shouted out his last instructions to some of them as, at around 6.30 p.m. on 30 June, they marched off from Bus-lès-Artois (about 17 miles north-east of Amiens) on the way to the front line. It was always the same old message: 'Good luck men. There is not a German left in the trenches. Our guns have blown them all to hell!'[20]

The leading assault troops within the northernmost brigade (Brigadier-General Rees' 94th Brigade) included the 11th East Lancashire Regiment (the Accrington Pals). Pumped up with confidence by all the optimistic speeches, and like most British troops, willing to see the funny side of life even at the worst of times, they had joked and laughed as they tramped up to the front line on the night of 30 June–1 July. Little did they realize what the Germans had in store for them.

The fact that they were soaking wet, through having to march along communication trenches that according to the war diary were 'knee deep in mud which had become glutinous', did not stop them calling out quips as they passed the artillery, such as: 'What do you want bringing back: a German helmet? Or [perhaps] an officer's wrist watch?'[21]

Once safely installed in the front-line assembly trenches early in the morning of 1 July, they had to wait for several long hours before the countdown started for the attack. Shortly after 7 a.m. the men in one of the assembly trenches who were passing the time singing were interrupted by the warning call: 'Twenty minutes to go boys!'[22] Ten minutes later there was another reminder: 'Ten minutes to go!'[23]

It was only after this call that the German machine-gunners opened up. They were now sucked in by the start of the British gunners' final 'hurricane' bombardment, and the appearance of the first waves of British troops who at 7.20 a.m. climbed over the top and advanced.[24]

Even so, Brigadier-General Rees, who was in charge on the left, still clung to the hope that his men would somehow prevail. As the final softening-up barrage opened up, ten minutes before zero hour, he climbed up out of his dugout some 600 yards back from the front line to watch the spectacle he had helped to create. 'It was magnificent,' he wrote later in his

Personal Record of the day's events. 'The trenches in front of Serre changed shape and dissolved minute by minute under the terrific hail of steel. I began to believe in the possibility of a great success.'[25]

In some ways the advance of the subsequent waves of British troops, which began during the next minutes, was even more heroic than the slow, measured marching forward of the vanguard. They had to leave the safety of their trenches after the enemy had been alerted as to what was coming their way. Those Accrington Pals who were to make up the subsequent waves were still smoking and joking when '5 minutes!' and then '3 minutes!' was called out. One of the Accrington Pals was Harry Roberts, a thirty-eight-year-old colliery engineer from Burnley. As he later reported, by that stage 'Germans were sweeping the . . . trench top with their machine-guns, and shells were bursting all around.' Nevertheless when the Pals heard the final call 'Over you go lads!', over they went, in most cases without hesitation. 'We were in the last of four waves,' he recalled. 'And to see those waves! It was just as you would see four long lines of soldiers in peace times. On we went in a steady walk. The bullets from the German machine guns just looked like one glistening fan as they flew through the air . . .' At least that was what they looked like as he lay on the ground having been shot through the shoulder. The sight led him to comment afterwards: 'I marvel at us getting so near the enemy as we did.'[26]

The leading left-hand battalion of 94th Brigade was the 12th Battalion, the York and Lancaster Regiment (the Sheffield City Pals). Private Reginald Glenn, a signalman who accompanied the battalion's second wave, has described how it took some time for the penny to drop:

We were told to walk. We'd to carry the rifle at the high port . . . The first line went [first. I saw] they were walking slowly . . . Then they all lay down. [At first] I thought they'd had different orders [to us. I only realized why they acted as they did later]. They lay down because they were shot . . . [They were] either killed or wounded. They [had been] . . . mown down [by the German] machine guns . . . like corn. [At the time] we didn't know they were dead and dying [although] we could hear the clatter of [the guns. That explains why] our line [also] . . . went forward. [And] the same thing . . . more or less . . . happened with our party.[27]

Glenn's life was saved because he lay down, thinking he was complying with orders given to the others in his wave. He did not advance any further. The survivors were eventually told to go back to where they had started, and Glenn accompanied them. Not many of the Sheffield City Pals made it to the German wire, and those who did found it to be mostly uncut.[28] Only a few entered the first German trench. It seems likely that the same is true of the Accrington Pals on their right, in spite of the wire in front of them having been adequately cut.[29]

Even fewer of the troops in the 93rd Brigade, to the right of the Accrington Pals, made any such headway.[30] The Germans, who had been expectantly waiting on their dugout steps, and their artillery saw to that, as is made clear by the following accounts by some of the Leeds Pals (15th West Yorkshires), whose 10th and 13th Platoons formed the spearhead of the Brigade's attack:

At about 7.15 . . . [our 19-year-old 2nd Lieutenant, Tom] Willey passed down the order 'Get ready 13' as casually as though on an ordinary parade. We then filed out, up the scaling ladder, through the gap in our own wire, and to our place as the first wave, in advance of our wire. Mr Willey said 'Ten paces interval, boys', and it was done just as though on manoeuvres.[31]

Another participant, Private Arthur Hollings, described how the Germans started firing as soon as they climbed out of the trench:

For over an hour just preceding our platoon going over the 'lid', it seemed to us as if nothing could live in their first line trench. Individual shells could not be heard. It was just one continuous scream overhead, and roaring and ripping of bursting shells across the way . . . [However], no sooner had the first lot got over the parapet, than the Germans opened up a terrific bombardment, big shells and shrapnel, and their parapet was packed with Germans exposing themselves over the top to their waist[s. They] . . . opened rapid fire . . . It seemed impossible for a square inch of space to be left free from flying metal.[32]

Nevertheless, after filing out of the trench and spreading out, they obeyed the order to lie down for about ten minutes. Then, as Hollings reported: 'At the end of that time, young Willey jumped up, and waving his revolver, shouted: "Come on 13. Give them hell!"', and led them towards the German trenches. They did not get far. According to the battalion's war diary, one hundred yards beyond the British front-line trench was the limit of their progress for all but the most intrepid and fortunate.[33]

The war diarist of the German 169th Regiment chronicled how his unit's foot soldiers, like Lieutenant F. L. Cassel south of Thiepval (see Chapter 6, p. 69), were spurred into frenetic activity by the same war cry Cassel had found so stirring: 'They are coming!' 'The men rushed out of the dugouts and climbed onto the trench fire steps,' the diarist recorded:

Now at long last we could take the initiative. We could take some positive action and exact our revenge. We shot at the enemy as if on a shooting range, very calmly and accurately . . . Almost every shot found its target . . .

The first and second waves of the approaching solders were swept away by our gunfire. We were helped by our artillery, whose shells dropped right into their midst, blowing them to pieces . . . Some were even hit before they started. They didn't even make it to their own front line thanks to our guns, which were trained on the spots where they come into view.[34]

The German war diarist's account has been corroborated by the reports filed by several British soldiers. For example, Sergeant-Major George Cussins from the 16th Battalion, the West Yorkshire Regiment (1st Bradford Pals), 93rd Brigade's left-hand support unit, confirmed that 'five minutes before [zero hour, at] 7.25 [a.m.], the enemy machine gun, rifle fire and shrapnel was directed against the parapet of our assembly trench – the southern half of Bradford Trench causing us to suffer considerably. A lot of men never got off the ladder, but fell back, and many fell back from the parapet while getting over.'[35]

When the German war diarist refers to 'our guns', he appears to be talking principally about the 169th Regiment's machine-gunners. That is why the testimony of Otto Lais, one of the best-known accounts by a World War I machine-gunner, is so important. Although it could be dismissed as unreliable propaganda, written as it was in the Nazi era during World War II, with the express aim of showing the younger generation of Germans how it was possible for brave and determined soldiers to overcome a superior force, it nevertheless provides the details that are missing from many of the less detailed war diaries.

If nothing else, it enables us to appreciate how just a few machine-gunners could dominate a battlefield filled with hostile advancing soldiers. In one telling passage, Lais reports that the gun team which he was profiling, located beside the Mailly-Maillet to Serre road (to the south of the 31st Division's front), fired no fewer than 20,000 machine-gun bullets during 1 July. That explains why troops within the 93rd Brigade, the 31st

Division's southernmost unit, struggled to make it past their own wire, let alone into the German trenches.

According to Otto Lais, until 1 July 1916 the machine-gunners, in the 169th Regiment at least, had been accused of not mucking in. For example, they were exempted from the unpopular task of carrying heavy shells up to the front. But that all changed in the course of the great attack, and the following extracts from his account gives us an inkling why that was so.

The account starts by describing the reaction of one of the German machine-gun teams as the first wave of British soldiers began advancing towards them. 'We quickly shot off 250 rounds, 1000 rounds, 3000 rounds,' Lais tells us. The gunners fired until the barrel of their gun was 'red hot', and their commander, Under Officer Koch, shouted out 'Bring the reserve barrel!'

Koch was to play a vital role in maximizing the gun's firepower. Not only did he procure the speedy replacement of the machine-gun parts during the battle, but he also drove on junior members of the team, until it seems they would do anything, and sacrifice everything, if only they could escape the lashing of his tongue.

After around 5,000 rounds were fired, the overheated barrel needed changing again. And this was not all that was hot. The water that was supposed to be cooling the gun mechanism was boiling. It was almost impossible to carry on pressing on the gun's trigger. 'The machine-gunner's hands were burned, half cooked,' Lais tells us. But still their commander showed no mercy: 'Keep firing, or die!' he yelled. That was easier said than done. All the more so because:

the water in the gun 'jacket' which was supposed to cool the gun became so hot it began to evaporate. And in the heat of the battle the hose which carried away the steam became disconnected from the water 'kettle' in which the steam was supposed to be transformed back into liquid. A hissing fountain of steam shot up into the air above us, making us an easy target for the enemy. We were only saved because the sun which was behind us was shining in their faces.

It was not long before the water had almost entirely evaporated. 'Where is the water?' bawled the irate commander, and on seeing there was none, he screamed 'Get the Seltzer!' By this he meant the mineral water, part of the men's 'iron ration', stored in the dugouts. His subordinates apologetically replied: 'There's none left, Sir. All the iron rations have been consumed.'

As Lais observed, this was a potential disaster. Until this point the machine-gunners had almost single-handedly held back the approaching hordes. It was true that 'the English were lying in their hundreds in the craters in front of our trenches, but new waves of enemy soldiers were still flooding out of the trenches on the other side of No Man's Land. We had to carry on shooting, or else.'

The crisis spurred one of the machine-gunners into action. He 'took the water kettle, jumped into a crater and urinated into it. A second man topped up the kettle with his urine.' They brought the kettle back to the gun in the nick of time. Lais continued:

Some English soldiers were closing in on them and were close enough to attack them with hand grenades. Hand grenades flew in all directions. But while this was going on, the barrel was changed, the water in the jacket replenished.

Load the gun . . . Don't get stressed and mess that up. Say out loud what needs to be done . . . Push forward the bolt. Get the belt . . . safety catch to the right . . . Tak tak tak tak. The gun was firing again. Once more it fired into the dip in front of us.

But the crisis had not passed. It was evident that these machine-gunners were not the only ones experiencing this problem. As Lais could see, 'Jets of steam were shooting up into the air from almost all the regiment's machine guns. Their hoses had likewise either been ripped or shot away.'

Added to that there was a new problem:

The machine gunners' hands were so burned that the skin on their fingers hung down in ribbons. What were once their left thumbs became shapeless swollen lumps of meat thanks to their having to repeatedly press down on the safety catch. Cramp became a problem caused by the need to hang on to the machine guns' vibrating hand grips.

As the number of bullets fired reached the 18,000 mark, the man who was feeding the ammunition belt into the machine gun was shot through the head. It was his fall that led to the twisting of the belt, and the jamming of the gun. However, even this setback was not allowed to interrupt the flow. 'His corpse was dragged to one side,' Lais explained. Another man took his place, removed the loading mechanism, reloaded the gun, and then started firing it again.[36]

Whatever one makes of Lais' claim that it was the German machine-gunners who decided the battle for Serre, Brigadier-General Rees, whose principal focus was the left side of the British attack, where his own brigade was advancing, was deeply impressed by the German artillery. It was 'the most frightful artillery display that I had [ever] seen,' he noted in his personal record of the disaster, 'a perfect wall of explosive along the [entire] front of my brigade and the 93rd'.[37]

That may explain why he became increasingly sceptical about the claims emanating from Major-General O'Gowan, the 31st Division's commander, that some of his men had a foothold in or near Serre itself. These claims were not wholly without foundation. At 8.25 a.m., the occupants of one of the division's observation posts had reported seeing in Serre what they took to be a 'small party' of British soldiers. They were identified as being British because the sun was seen glinting off what looked like the shiny triangles some of the men wore on their clothing so that they could be easily identified from the air.

This sighting appeared to corroborate a 'coded' signal sent by the crew in an aircraft that dropped a flare over Serre at 8.19 a.m., presumably because they believed British troops had reached the village.[38] Shortly after 10 a.m. there were reports from three officers that Serre was being shelled by the enemy.[39]

What was common to all these reports was that none suggested that the troops in Serre were doing any fighting. Nevertheless, notwithstanding the fact that Brigadier-General Rees, the commander nearest the village, was positive that there really was no substantial British presence there, Major-General O'Gowan persisted in believing there was. In keeping with the unjustified optimism that had already played such a damaging role prior to the attack, it was O'Gowan's appraisal of the situation, rather than Rees', which found its way to Hunter-Weston at VIII Corps' headquarters, and then via him to Rawlinson and Haig.[40]

Even so, the optimism that was swirling around inside the 31st Division's headquarters could not alter the facts on the ground. When shortly after midday O'Gowan ordered 94th Brigade to endeavour to make contact with the troops who were understood to be in Serre, Rees categorically refused to comply, citing as justification the 'lack of definite reports from our front about this'. As far as Rees was concerned, it was just one of a series of the 'wildest reports . . . rife' at the division's headquarters at this time.

Amongst the others was a rumour that Rees' headquarters had been captured by the enemy. Rees was also exasperated by yet another order from O'Gowan later that day telling him to send some troops to bomb the Germans out of the 93rd Brigade's front-line trenches. 'I expostulated,' Rees reported on hearing of this order, and argued that the front trenches did not exist any more. But it was only shortly before the operation was about to begin that he managed to challenge O'Gowan in person. To the 'considerable amazement' of Rees, O'Gowan agreed with him, whereupon Rees remarked that in that case he should be excused so that he could countermand the attack 'which you have just ordered me to make'.[41]

As Rees acknowledged, it was all part and parcel of the 'unbalancing effect of the disaster', which had seen the casualties of the 31st Division's two assaulting brigades rise to approaching 3,500 men (including approximately 1,700 men who had either been killed or were missing).[42]

Even that figure, extracted from the reports filed with the brigades' war diaries, was subject to change as men who were thought to have died turned up from No Man's Land, and men who were believed to have survived, died.

Whether dead or alive, the soldiers' families back home could not wait to find out what had happened to their beloved sons, brothers, husbands and boyfriends, especially if they had featured on the casualty list. The worst fears of the families of two well-known sportsmen were to be cruelly realized: the cricketer Major (his first name) Booth, the up-and-coming England all-rounder, was missing and never reappeared; and the footballer Evelyn Lintott, who had played for the English national team, had also died.

Their last moments were described in the *Yorkshire Evening Post* in the following terms:

Lieutenant Lintott's death was particularly gallant. He led his men with great dash, and when hit the first time, he declined to take the count. Instead he drew his revolver and called for greater effort. Again he was hit, but struggled on, but a third shot finally bowled him over.

Lieutenant Booth too though in sore agony from a shell fragment which penetrated the shoulder and must have touched the heart tried his utmost to go forward but pitched forward helplessly after going a few yards. He and Lintott were two gallant sportsmen who knew how to die – but then so did all the boys.[43]

One family left on tenterhooks was that of Lieutenant Morris Bickersteth, a twenty-five-year-old in the same unit as Booth and Lintott: the 15th West Yorkshire Regiment (the Leeds Pals), the leading assault battalion in the

93rd Brigade. Shortly after the attack had failed, the battalion's chaplain sent the family a telegraph stating: 'I have tried to find some good news of your son, but I can only find the worst. He is missing. I am making all enquiries but I have not much hope. You must prepare Leeds for splendid and heroic news but oh so terribly sad.'

The next day the chaplain wrote again to say: 'I thought I had better send you another line as you will be in suspense, but it is only to say that still no news is forthcoming of Morris. More men have come in, and say they saw him fall. His servant looked at him after he had fallen and felt sure he was killed.'

It was only on 3 July that the chaplain was able to come up with definite news: 'Now there is no doubt whatsoever. Morris is killed. I saw his brother [Julian] this afternoon and gave him full particulars.'

Captain Julian Bickersteth's subsequent letter told the family the full story, gleaned from a conversation he had had with Private Bateson, an eighteen-year-old from the same company. Morris had been in one of the support waves. When their time came, Morris had sent his men on their way with a 'Come on lads. Here's to a short life and a gay one', only to come to a halt a few yards after leaving the front line, where the remnants of the previous wave lay wounded or dead.

While they were lying there, Bateson had asked Morris for permission to go back as he had been wounded, whereupon Morris wrote him a chit and told him to go back as best he could. It was just then that a 'bullet struck him in the back of the head. A second later another bullet passed right through his head, coming out through his forehead. He just rolled over without a word or sound, and Bateson was able to see that he was quite dead. [He had been] killed instantly.'[44]

No one could say that the Bickersteth family were lucky. Any family who loses a twenty-five-year-old son is blighted. But one can say that they were fortunate in one sense. What is even worse than losing a beloved child or husband is to be left in suspense for a long time. Given the number of casualties during the attack on Serre, there must have been many families who fell into this latter category. One officer whose family were put through it in this way was the thirty-one-year-old Robert Tolson, who like Morris Bickersteth was a lieutenant in the Leeds Pals.[45]

The first telegraph telling the Tolson family that something was wrong was wired the day after the battle for Serre, on 2 July. The same chaplain who had written to the Bickersteths informed Robert Tolson's wife Zoe that he had apparently been wounded. The chaplain ended the letter: 'You will probably see him soon.'[46]

However, eight days later the chaplain wrote to Zoe Tolson again to tell her that Robert was in fact missing. 'Six men told me that they knew he had been wounded but was brought in. But all was confusion [after the battle] and I am afraid it is too true that he was not brought in. I have searched the hospitals and find no trace of him and we can only say he is missing.'[47]

On 13 July, Zoe's hopes must have been raised again by a letter from the 93rd Brigade. It stated that her husband had been wounded and sent to a hospital, adding: 'I think he is all right or we would have heard.'[48] However, another letter from the battalion chaplain sent five days later would have brought her crashing down to earth. It commiserated with her on his death.[49]

On 22 July another officer from the battalion gave the Tolson family some idea of what Robert had been through. Like Morris Bickersteth, Robert Tolson was in the last wave, and had made it past the front line. 'He could not have gone further than our wire but in that short distance anything could have happened. Our front line was being shelled. Shrapnel and every kind of missile at the command of the enemy [was] . . . bursting on every side. The wounded who could not get out of the trench to the dressing station were liable to be buried as the trench was blown in. I am sorry to say that many were buried in this way.'[50]

At the end of the month the Tolson family were still waiting for news. On 27 July a cousin with the BEF, Newcombe Wright, went over to talk to those in the battalion who had survived. He then wrote to Robert's father, Whiteley Tolson, telling him what he had found out. Apparently the battalion had been more or less 'wiped out' by machine-gun fire:

Robert's company (A Company) caught it worst and . . . only two or three of his platoon ever came back and those wounded. Only two officers escaped and none of these saw Robert . . . One man of his company, but not of his platoon who got back unhurt told me that as he was lying out in front of our wire, a wounded man who was trying to get back to our trenches told him that Mr Tolson was shot through the neck. None of our men reached the German wire and immediately after the attack the German artillery barraged No Man's Land and on our front line trench knocking it in and burying many of the wounded who had managed to get back. The man did not think there was much chance of anyone who was out coming through alive.

There is just one gleam of hope but personally I am afraid I should not think much of it. I am told that although the Germans when the barrage stopped would not let our stretcher bearers beyond our own wire their parties picked up a very few wounded of ours. They were watched by our men who did not fire on them as they were bandaging and looking after our wounded. It is just within the bounds of possibility that Robert was picked up by them.

However, Newcombe Wright did have a lead. One of Robert's men, a man called Spence, had been wounded and was currently in a specified hospital in Bristol. 'If I were you, I would at once go to Bristol to enquire . . . But I should not waste any time as the man is not seriously wounded and may be discharged to duty at any time.'[51]

By this time, Robert's father had more or less given up hope. On 28 July he wrote to his older son Gerald: 'Personally my hopes that Robert is a prisoner are faint . . . No private soldier suggests with any force there is any possibility of Robert being a prisoner. If mentioned at all, it is said in a comforting sort of way as a last resource.'[52]

In a subsequent letter Whiteley Tolson revealed the pain he was suffering. 'It was a murderous situation to charge into No Man's Land with the Germans so well prepared with machine guns . . . Robert was sacrificed and many a hundred besides. It makes me have a sinking sick feeling to imagine his end, perhaps bleeding to death for Newcome heard he was wounded in the neck.'[53] But Robert's father still could not let the matter rest. As he wrote to Gerald, 'Zoe . . . still clings to the hope that Robert is a prisoner.'[54]

It was only on about 5 September that the family had a breakthrough. They received a letter from the Red Cross stating that a Private Jepson who was in a hospital in Epsom had fallen into a trench right onto the dead body of Lieutenant Tolson.[55] A letter was swiftly sent to Private Jepson asking for a meeting. And on 8 September, Jepson wrote back agreeing to meet outside the hospital gates the following Sunday.

On 11 September, Gerald wrote to tell his uncle Legh what Jepson had seen. During the attack he had been wounded on his face and had ended up falling into a trench, which he thought was the German first trench. He had landed on Robert's dead body. 'Robert was stretched out face downwards arms extended. His body was cold and stiff and his eyes were closed.'[56]

Whiteley wrote back to his son Gerald, who had also filled him in: 'Words fail me to express my horror of his dreadful end. There is no glory in it for me. [It was] downright wicked murder!'[57]

The problem with Jepson's account was that he had been half blinded by the blood coming from the wound on his face. However, approximately six weeks later an even clearer report came in from a lance corporal. According to this man, he had seen Robert lying in the British front-line trench. 'I took him to be dead,' he said. 'I cannot understand how he has been reported missing unless the trench was blown in and he got buried.'[58]

However, it was only in March the following year that definitive proof was discovered of Robert Tolson's death. After the Germans moved out of Serre, his body was recovered and he was given a proper burial.[59]

Given the number of young men who died during the attack on Serre, it is likely that there were lots of other families who, like Whiteley Tolson, felt that their loved ones had been recklessly sacrificed. Nevertheless one wonders whether even their torment could have compared with that suffered by the families of two young men whose lives were ended intentionally by a group of killers authorized by their own side: a British firing squad.

During the month of June 1916 Privates Herbert Crimmins and Arthur Wild, aged thirty-two and twenty-four respectively, were acting as ration carriers in the 18th Battalion, the West Yorkshire Regiment (2nd Bradford Pals), on the Somme. At around midday on the eve of the battle, all the ration carriers in the battalion were warned not to leave the camp at Bus-lès-Artois. Unwisely, Crimmins and Wild disobeyed that order and at around 2 p.m. crept out to one of the local estaminets. They had not returned by 4 p.m. when the officer responsible for them received the order to march to the front line two hours later. After staying in the estaminet until it closed for the remainder of the afternoon, the two privates went to sleep in a nearby cornfield, only waking at dusk. Too frightened to go back to their battalion immediately, they moved around the Somme rear area for three days before finally handing themselves in on 4 July.

That meant Crimmins and Wild missed the attack on Serre, and they were both charged with desertion, their court martial taking place on 21 August 1916. It is not clear whether they were represented at the hearing. Nor is the extent to which two crucial pieces of evidence were challenged.

An NCO testified that before they went to the estaminet, he had told Crimmins and Wild to be ready to go to the front-line trench area at 5.45 p.m. If that was true, it could be argued that they had deliberately intended to avoid the impending action. This was a significant point given that Haig subsequently stated that notwithstanding the rule permitting the absolute penalty for any man who was absent without leave, men would only be executed if they deserted deliberately.

But had they? One can imagine an experienced lawyer, had he been available, casting doubt on the veracity of the NCO's statement. It does seem a bit unlikely that a corporal would have known about the plan to move to the trenches before his superior officer heard about it.

The second crucial statement was made by Arthur Wild, the younger of the two men. He claimed that he had not given himself in after sleeping off the effects of the drink firstly because he was fearful of the consequences and secondly because he feared he could not 'stand the noise of the guns'. Once again this evidence could have been incriminating. If it meant that Private Wild – and Crimmins – knew before they absconded that they were about to go up where the guns were firing, it could be said they had deserted deliberately. On the other hand, if Wild merely meant to say that neither he nor his friend had been told about the imminent move to the front line, but they merely wanted to be temporarily free of the constant fear of being sent there, that might well have fallen outside Haig's definition of what was inexcusable.

If the recommendations of the court martial had been presented to the two men's brigadier and the intervening commanders up to Haig without further comment, it is probable, notwithstanding the ambiguous nature of the above-mentioned evidence, that they would have escaped any serious punishment. Although the court condemned them to death, it unanimously recommended clemency because Crimmins had such a good character and Wild could be excused for being nervous of the guns, having recently recovered from shell shock.

However, when their commanding officer sent the court-martial papers to their brigadier, he added derogatory comments about both men based on evidence that had not been submitted to the court. He also used these comments to justify his judgement that both men had deserted deliberately. It is possible, given what has been said about the ambiguity of the evidence, that his judgement was correct, although a more humane person might have found a way to let the men off because of the mitigating circumstances. However, what cannot be justified is the way the commanding officer reached his verdict, depriving the men of the chance to argue their case, making it a blatant breach of the rules of natural justice.

It was probably this allegation of deliberate desertion that sealed the two culprits' fate, and it is perhaps no surprise that on seeing it, the 93rd

Brigade's commander John Ingles, and eventually Haig, recommended that the death sentence should be carried out. The two men were shot by firing squads on 5 September 1916.

After their execution, they were buried nearby. However, General Wanless O'Gowan is said to have kicked away flowers placed by their graves muttering 'These men are best forgotten.' Arthur Wild's family are said to have responded by paying for the following inscription to be engraved on his gravestone: 'Not forgotten by those who loved him best.'[60]

8: Hunter-Bunter's Folly

Beaumont Hamel, 1 July 1916

(See maps 1, 2 and 4)

Of all the images that highlight how the flower of British youth was sacrificed on 1 July 1916, none are more iconic than those purporting to show the young men of the 1st Battalion, the Lancashire Fusiliers Regiment, in 'a sunken road' in the middle of No Man's Land, gearing up for their assault on the village of Beaumont Hamel.

Whether or not the filming was carried out just before the great attack was launched, as the caption in the official Battle of the Somme film suggests, the fact that British soldiers were able to approach so near to the German front line without being rumbled was a triumph. It was an ingenious idea, which made the most of the British miners' extraordinary digging prowess, ensuring the main pathway to this strategically important spot was not over the top. To reach it undetected, men could pass through one of the many tunnels that the tunnelling companies working in most of the Somme sectors had cut through the chalk, all part of the effort to take the German defenders unawares.

The cinematographer who filmed the waiting Fusiliers was the same Geoffrey Malins who would so memorably record his impressions of the great mine exploding under Hawthorn Ridge (see Chapter 1, p. 1). Both the tunnel leading to the sunken road and the tunnel to Hawthorn Ridge were within the same sector. It was controlled by the British 29th Division, the 1st Lancashire Fusiliers being one of the units leading the assault in that division's 86th Brigade (see map 4).

Malins claims he visited the tunnel linked to the sunken road at dawn on 1 July. Afterwards, he described it in the following terms:

The tunnel was no more than two feet and six inches wide and five feet high. Men inside were passing ammunition from one to the other in an 'endless' chain . . . They were wet with perspiration, steaming in fact: working like Trojans . . . It was only by squeezing past the munition bearers that we were able to proceed at all . . . In some places it was impossible for more than one [person] to crush through at a time.

The journey through the tunnel was only the beginning. After emerging into daylight at the other end, Malins had to 'wriggle' along a shallow communication trench, dragging his camera behind him. 'The ground sloped downwards,' he recalled, until 'the end of the sap came in sight . . . [There], running at right angles on both sides, was [the sunken road] . . . overgrown with grass and pitted with shell holes. The bank immediately in front was lined with the stumps of trees and a rough hedge, and there lined up . . . were the Lancashire Fusiliers.'

According to Malins, he quickly shot his iconic film before hurrying to retrace his steps. This time the tunnel was full of soldiers, and it was hard to see where he and his guide were going: 'We groped our way along as best we could,' Malins remembered. 'It was only possible to get my tripod and camera along by passing it from one to another. Then, as the men stooped low, I stepped over them, eventually reaching the other end and daylight.'[1]

It was already around 6.30 a.m., less than an hour before his next cue: he had to be back behind the British front line if he was to film what was to be his *pièce de résistance*: the explosion of the mine under the Hawthorn Redoubt, which even before it took place, promised to be one of the defining moments of the battle, if not the whole war.

The digging out of the tunnel from behind the British line to beneath the Hawthorn Redoubt was an even more prodigious feat than more minor works such as the tunnel to the sunken road. Miners had also built a series of relatively shallow tunnels at intervals along the whole front, which were designed to be used as covered communication trenches across No Man's Land just before or after zero hour. Because the Hawthorn Redoubt tunnel was only started at the beginning of April 1916, shortly before Rawlinson's attack plan was finalized, it had been touch-and-go whether it would be completed in time.

There was no difficulty in digging out the first part of the tunnel. After his men had been digging for less than a month, Captain Rex Trower, commander of the 252nd Tunnelling Company, boasted: 'This Company has every record for the Army beaten by the driving in the Hawthorn Mine. In this, we made in [one] 24 hour . . . period, 200 feet in one week of 7 days, 322 feet in fourteen days, and 565 feet in 26 days. This is one tunnel with one face only, and the length to destroy the enemy trench will be 1,055 feet.'[2]

Three and a half weeks later, however, meeting the deadline was less assured. Rex Trower reported: 'Extraordinary difficulty is being encountered with mine H3. The length is now 900 feet . . . Work is being carried on silently by wetting the face and working the chalk out with bayonets. This face is now entirely flint and progress is very slow.'[3]

Captain Trower was worried that if any noise was made, which would occur if the miners worked too fast, the Germans would hear them and would dig a counter-mine. He was right to be concerned. Documents captured after the 1 July 1916 attack told British intelligence that German miners had been instructed to stop work three times for up to half an hour during each eight-hour shift so that they could listen out for British mining.

With typical German efficiency, these listening periods were to be synchronized with the listening periods in all neighbouring mines. This was achieved by using a simple code within each mine. The miners were to knock a given number of times on the timbers inside their mine to indicate a listening period was beginning or ending. These knocks were to be repeated until the miners in the neighbouring tunnel responded by knocking the prescribed number of times in their turn. This told the miners from the first mine that their coded message had been received.[4]

Notwithstanding the resulting delay, Trower's men eventually reached their target in good time. By 22 June 1916 the 80-foot-deep mine was packed with 40,600 pounds of ammonal, ready to be exploded.[5]

The question then arose as to when the mine should be blown up. The first plan was to explode it several hours before the attack, or even the evening before.[6] This was vetoed by GHQ on the advice of the Inspector of Mines, who feared that the resulting crater would be occupied by the Germans. They had shown themselves to be much quicker at taking over craters made by exploding mines than the British.[7]

Subsequent events proved that it would have been much better to have blown up the mine just before zero hour, in accordance with what the 29th Division's commander, Beauvoir de Lisle, the major-general in charge of the sector, claims he suggested.[8] However, prior to the battle, there was concern in some quarters that blowing up such an enormous mine just before an attack might end up killing as many British soldiers as Germans.[9] Eventually, the fateful decision was taken by VIII Corps' commander, Lieutenant-General Sir Aylmer Hunter-Weston, to order the mine to be exploded at 7.20 a.m., ten minutes before zero hour, an act that the Inspector of Mines subsequently referred to as 'Hunter-Bunter's folly'.[10] For it warned the Germans, who were cooped up in their dugouts, that the British were about to attack.

'Hunter-Bunter' made another significant error. If the British artillery had carried on firing at the German front line – apart from in the vicinity of the mine crater, where the infantry were advancing, just after the mine exploded – until zero hour, it is just possible they would have pinned down the garrison in their dugouts until the British leading units were upon them.

However, apparently to preserve the unity of the advances by all units in the corps after they passed the German front line, the decision was taken to lift the heavy artillery for the entire corps off the German front trenches at 7.20 a.m., and half of the 29th Division's lighter 18-pounder guns off the front trenches in the division's sector at 7.27 a.m. Thus, the front-line trenches in the 29th Division's sector were to have very limited artillery firing at them at the crucial moment: just before the bulk of the British forces in that area advanced.[11] The consequences of these decisions rippled over the entire 29th Division front, except for the area around the crater attacked by the 2nd Royal Fusiliers (the right-hand unit of the 86th Brigade, the 29th Division's left brigade).

The lack of progress made by the 1st Lancashire Fusiliers, 86th Brigade's northernmost unit, whose advanced position in the sunken road had given rise to so much hope, typified the difficulties experienced by all the division's leading battalions. At zero hour their troops in the sunken road climbed over the top. They were followed by the battalion's support waves, who advanced from the British front line, around 180 yards to the west of the road. The battalion's war diarist did not mince his words about how they fared:

The leading waves of B and D Companies [who had been in the sunken road] had a few moments of grace . . . Then the enemy machine gun opened up and a storm of bullets met the attack. The third and fourth lines of B and D Company [advancing from the British front line west of the sunken road] were practically wiped out within a few yards of [the] sunken road . . . Only some wounded managed to crawl back.[12]

George Ashurst was one of the Fusiliers whose journey from a support trench behind the British front line to the sunken road was hampered by the hail of machine-gun fire. 'We bent low in the [communication] trench and moved forward,' he wrote after the action:

Fritz's . . . shrapnel shells seemed to [be] burst[ing] on top of us. Shouts of pain and calls for help could be heard on all sides . . . We stepped over mortally wounded men who tried to grab our legs as we passed, [and] . . . we squeezed to one side of the trench while wounded men struggled by us anxious to get gaping wounds dressed . . . Men uttered terrible curses even as they lay dying from terrible wounds . . . Others sat at the bottom of the trench shaking and shouting, not wounded but unable to bear the noise, the smell and the horrible sights.

And that was all before he had even reached the front line. Ashurst later recalled how he, and the other men in his company, then had to advance over the top to the sunken road. 'I was zigzagging . . . expecting at any minute to get hit, holding my head down . . . so a bullet would hit my tin hat . . . Run! That was the only thing in my mind . . . [until] . . . I . . . miraculously, breathlessly reached the sunken road . . . almost diving into its shelter.'

It was only then that he registered the disaster that had unfolded in the last few minutes. 'The whole road was strewn with dead and dying men,' Ashurst wrote later:

Some were talking deliriously, others calling for help and asking for water . . . Then I heard the Colonel calling out for all fit men to line the bank of the road. He was waving his revolver menacingly . . . He called for a signaller. One stepped up . . . 'Get to the top of that road and signal for reinforcements' he thundered. Without a moment's hesitation, the signaller obeyed. But as he raised his flags to send the first letter . . . [he] dropped back into the road, riddled with bullets.

A similar fate awaited most of the men in the support battalion, who were supposed to back up the Lancashire Fusiliers, and the surviving Fusiliers who at 8.15 a.m. were ordered to make the battalion's second thrust from the sunken road.[13] Only one officer and ten other ranks from this second 'thrust' reached the German wire. Ashurst's life was spared because, on discovering after a short time that he was the last man still advancing, he was able to take refuge in a shell hole. From there he could look back over the battlefield. It was not a pleasant sight. Scattered over the area between where he was and the British trenches there were 'hundreds of dead . . . and wounded'. Worse still, many were in great pain. When the sound of the guns died down, he could hear the wounded men's 'heart-rending cries'.

That would have been that for the rest of the day, until nightfall, had Ashurst not seen a mass of men fleeing back to the British front line on the battalion's right (probably a group from the 2nd Royal Fusiliers, 86th Brigade's right-hand assault unit who retired during the morning).[14] Fearing that if he stayed out in front, he might be caught in any artillery barrage fired to support a renewed British attack, Ashurst took a chance and raced back too, ending up having to fling himself down into the sunken road once again.[15]

It was lucky that Lieutenant-Colonel Meredith Magniac, Ashurst's thirty-six-year-old commanding officer, was a robust fellow. The fact that his father was a general must have helped. Fighting was in Magniac's blood. Before the war, he himself had been a keen cricketer, without rising to the heights achieved by some of the sportsmen in the Pals battalions who were attacking Serre (see Chapter 7, p. 77); he had only played in one first-class fixture.[16] Nevertheless, given that what Magniac had just witnessed was slaughter on the scale of that seen in the wake of the charge of the Light Brigade during the Crimean War, he must have been amazed when he first saw the following order from Brigadier-General Weir De Lancey Williams, his out-of-touch commander. It reached him at 11.45 a.m. at White City, the bank behind the British front line, into which had been built the series of dugouts used as unit headquarters, as well as a casualty clearing station:

There will be another bombardment of the front line from 12 noon until 12.30 p.m. At 12.30 p.m., you must attack again with every man you can raise.

I suggest you go for the north end of Beaumont Hamel, as I hear the 4th Division have progressed at that side . . .

Whatever costs you must hold the sunken road. Many of the enemy have retired and troops on the right and left are progressing. Hammer away at him and he'll go!

Evidently horrified by what he had read, Lieutenant-Colonel Magniac quickly replied:

My previous reply has not reached you.

I have in sunken road now 75 men and 1 officer. In my other trenches about 50 men.

I have tried two advances covered by Stokes and Lewis guns. Both have failed. We are mown down by Machine Gun fire, and only get a few yards beyond sunken road.

If you wish, I will of course attack . . . I consider it is bound to fail. Machine guns are behind debris in village and rake the front.

On seeing this, Brigadier-General Williams sent a rapid response via his brigade major: 'Reference your note. G.O.C does not under the circumstances wish you to attack.' Unfortunately for the Fusiliers, the reply was not rapid enough. It did not reach Magniac until just after 1 p.m., that is after the time of the attack. Therefore he had little option but to order one of the few officers in his battalion who was still standing to advance from the British front line at 12.30 p.m. with the twenty-five men still available. The idea was that if the officer and his men reached the sunken road, Magniac would throw in the seventy-five men waiting there, and then they would all advance together in one last do-or-die attempt to capture the German front line.

The battalion's war diarist justified Magniac's decision thus: 'Although there was no chance of achieving anything on our own front, there were about 700 men in our trenches opposite the Hawthorn Redoubt, and to help them it seemed necessary to attract as much machine gun fire as possible on ourselves.'

Predictably, as soon as the advance began from the British front line, the machine guns started up again. The officer only had four men with him when he reached the sunken road. As for the troops on their right, the war diarist commented acidly that they 'never moved, and so our sacrifice was in vain'. Magniac, who by this time was back in the sunken road, called off the attack when he saw how few men he had at his disposal.[17]

In the course of this doomed attack, the Lancashire Fusiliers sustained over 500 casualties. But in some ways the failure of the advance on their right, by the 2nd Royal Fusiliers, their sister company within the 86th Brigade, was even more upsetting. Thanks to the explosion of the Hawthorn Redoubt mine, the vanguard of the Royal Fusiliers had reached the German front line and neutralized the soldiers inside the first dugout they came to (see Chapter 1, p. 4). They were backed up by the survivors of their support battalion, the 16th Middlesex Regiment, which had suffered heavy losses following them across No Man's Land.

If only the British artillery had been ordered to lay down a barrier of fire immediately behind the German front network of trenches in this sector, the terrorized garrison, isolated and with no prospect of being reinforced, might have been persuaded to give in. The Royal Fusiliers could then have consolidated their position, and who knows what would have been the result. A secure British foothold in the German front line near the Hawthorn Redoubt crater would certainly have opened up the possibility of rolling up the adjacent front-line positions as well.

Instead, the German support companies, unhampered by British artillery, were able to rush to the aid of their troops beside the crater. After fierce gunfire and a grenade fight, they then snuffed out the threat that the Royal Fusiliers posed to their entire front-line position.[18]

What was so disappointing from the British viewpoint was that the combination of the mine explosion and the dash of the 2nd Royal Fusiliers had so nearly defeated the Germans beside the Hawthorn Redoubt. Yet the British had ultimately failed due to their commander-in-chief's ill-judged plan. Ironically, by being too ambitious, Haig had made his plan self-defeating. By insisting on a plan that required the British gunners to shell the area to the rear of the German front-trench network, he had made it much harder to protect any incursions made within it. It was a criticism that was applicable to each of the penetrations into the German positions in the sectors covered by VII and VIII Corps (at Gommecourt and the Heidenkopf, as well as at Hawthorn Ridge – see Chapters 9 and 10).

To the south of the Royal Fusiliers, the 29th Division's right-hand unit, the 87th Brigade, had no more success in advancing through the machine-gunners' bullets than the Lancashire Fusiliers. The only difference was that for a while various reports suggested incorrectly that the right-hand battalion, the 1st Royal Inniskilling Fusiliers, might have crossed the German front line and even reached Beaumont Hamel itself. Flares shot up from the village led to similar questions being asked about incursions into Beaumont Hamel as had been asked concerning the supposed advance into Serre to the north (see Chapter 7, p. 72).[19]

It was these uncorroborated reports that persuaded the 29th Division's commander, Major-General Henry de Beauvoir de Lisle, to despatch yet another wave of soldiers, this time from his reserve brigade, the 88th Brigade, to see whether they could support the apparent breakthrough.[20] The advance by troops from the 1st Newfoundland Regiment, the only overseas infantry involved on 1 July, and the 1st Essex Regiment, was to target the area between the nose of Y Ravine (Point 89) and Point 03, the southern extremity of the 29th Division's front (see map 4).[21] Incredibly, given the intensity of the machine-gun fire that had greeted the first battalions advancing in this sector, no artillery to speak of was to be employed against the German gunners. The only cover for the renewed assault consisted of British machine-gun fire.[22]

The odds stacked against the attackers were increased still further after a last-minute conversation between Captain Arthur Raley, the Newfoundlanders' adjutant, and the brigade staff, as he recalled when interviewed about the debacle some years later:

We were told at first the two regiments would advance (the 1st Essex on the right and the Newfoundlanders on the left) . . . [Then] we were told to advance from where we were . . . We were in the third line . . . I actually phoned . . . Brigade Headquarters to ask whether we were to go alone, or with the people on our right. It was distinctly said we were to advance as soon as ready. So (at 9.15 a.m.) we went [forward without support] . . . I thought it was a very bad order!

[In] the field we advanced over, there was a gentle slope right down to the German line. There was no cover . . . Everybody was seen [by the Germans] all the way . . .

There was fairly long grass . . . That's probably the reason why I and the CO were alive. We . . . [went] over the top first . . . [The Germans] took no notice of us . . . When we got half way to the front line, we lay down . . . We could see everything going on around us. We had tufts of grass in front of us. Nothing else.[23]

It was from this position that Raley observed the German reaction to the Newfoundlanders' assault, which was to 'spray' the hillside with machine-gun bullets. In spite of that the Newfoundlanders carried on advancing. 'The only visible sign that the men knew they were under this terrible fire was that they all instinctively tucked their chins into an advanced shoulder, as they had so often done when fighting their way home against a blizzard in some little outpost in far away Newfoundland.'[24]

'[Some of] the men were carrying trench bridges, rolls of wire, [Bangalore] torpedoes. All sorts of things like that. [They] . . . weren't in any position to shoot . . . They simply were mowed down.'[25]

The German machine-gunners' task was made even easier because of the relatively small number of gaps left by British troops in their own wire. All the Germans had to do was to train their guns onto these gaps, through which the Newfoundlanders had to pass, to hose them with bullets, almost without exception.[26]

Ginger Byrne, a nineteen-year-old British soldier attached to the

Newfoundlanders for the day, was one of the few men advancing who reached the German wire without a scratch. But when the second man in his gun team 'went down like a log' shortly after the first had fallen, he realized it was time to take evasive action. 'The machine-gun bullets [made it] . . . like a hailstorm,' he recalled later. 'Ahead of me were two . . . dead . . . Newfoundland blokes. One on the left side, was lying well up to the German wire, [while] . . . the other, about twenty five yards to his right, was spreadeagled over the wire itself.' The only sensible option was to dive into the nearest shell hole, which Byrne did, remaining there all day until darkness enabled him to slip away.[27]

The Newfoundland battalion's Private Bert Ellis scribbled out his account of what he had witnessed while lying in hospital in Wandsworth, London, where he was taken to be treated for his wound. He had been hit in the right leg:

Our boys acted throughout as heroes. They went up on top singing, just as if they were going on a march, instead of facing death . . . It was like hell let loose . . . The machine-gun fire . . . mowed our men down like wheat before the scythe. No doubt you know what a noise the air hammer makes at the dock when they are working. Well, that's something like a machine gun sounds when in action. They played havoc with our men, and to make matters worse, they had what is called enfilading fire, which is the worst kind of fire to be under. You could almost see the bullets coming, they came so thick and fast.[28]

Another surviving Newfoundlander was the battalion's Private James McGrath. He started his account with words that might seem a statement of the obvious given all that happened to him: 'I shall never forget the beginning of the Somme offensive on July 1st 1916!' His account continued:

[When] we advanced to[wards] the German trenches, the machine-gun fire was something terrible. The Germans actually mowed us down like sheep.

I managed to get to their barbed wire, where I got the first shot. Then, [when I] went to jump into their trench, I got the second in the leg.

I lay in No Man's Land for fifteen hours, and then crawled a distance of a mile and a quarter. They fired on me again, this time fetching me in the left leg . . . So I waited for another hour, and moved again, only having the use of my left arm now.

As I was doing splendidly, nearing our own trench, they again fetched me, this time around the hip as I crawled on. I managed to get to our own line, which I saw was evacuated as our artillery was playing on their trenches. They retaliated, and kept me in a hole for another hour.

[Only] . . . then . . . was . . . I . . . rescued by Captain Windeler, who took me on his back to the dressing station, a distance of two miles. Well, thank God my wounds are all flesh wounds, and won't take long to heal up.[29]

Private McGrath appears to have been one of a select band who made it through the German wire. Although a few brave souls managed to progress far enough to lob grenades into the German front line, that was the limit of their advance. By the time the attack was called off, there was hardly a man standing. The Newfoundlanders ended up with more than 700 casualties out of the roughly 780 men who made the 'charge'.[30]

Afterwards, the eerily deserted landscape in No Man's Land, which earlier in the day had been teeming with advancing soldiers, brought home to at least one other survivor the scale of the disaster he had just witnessed. According to the aforementioned Private Bert Ellis:

When I was crawling back . . . which was 400 yards, I was all alone, and never met a [living] soul . . . Only dead! dead! Everywhere! The awful sight . . . made me so sick, that I . . . wonder[ed whether to] . . . go on, or stay there [with them] . . .

It wouldn't have been so bad. Only they turned the guns on us as we were trying to get back. What puzzles me most [is], how ever did I get back.

When the roll was called, only forty-three answered it, and out of that number 2 were from C Company.[31]

In some ways, both he and Private McGrath were lucky. During the afternoon Dudley Menaud-Lissenberg, confined to the same Royal Artillery observation post he had occupied since watching the first British troops go over the top at 7.30 that morning (see Chapter 1), saw what could happen to someone who was less fortunate: 'I watched a lone figure, a runner no doubt, coming back towards our lines from the far distant ridge, dropping every now and then into shell holes for cover. On reaching our barbed wire, he was about to jump into the trench, when a shell burst at his feet, and blew him sky high.'[32] It was as, Menaud-Lissenberg confirmed, 'a tragedy', one of many that day.

It was only after the 1st Essex Regiment had in its turn tried and failed to break the deadlock, at a cost of 230 additional casualties, that yet another assault was ordered for 12.30 p.m. (the one mentioned above in connection with the Lancashire Fusiliers).[33] It was supposed to be carried out in conjunction with a renewed attack by the 4th Division in the Heidenkopf sector. Twenty minutes beforehand the 88th Brigade's commander requested a postponement, which was granted. However, on being told that the 88th Brigade unit involved could not make it to the British front line in time for 12.45 p.m., the rearranged time, de Lisle, after consultation with Hunter-Weston, decided at long last to cut his losses and cancel all further attacks.[34] Given that the 29th Division's casualties had already reached the 5,000 mark, no one who knew the true facts could say it was a moment too soon.[35]

Indeed, the attacks might have been halted even sooner had the generals been near enough to the front line to see the suffering sanctioned under their name. Perhaps that explains why there is no official account of what the battlefield looked like after the last attack went in. But some of the participants were less squeamish. The twenty-three-year-old 2nd Lieutenant Arthur Stanford was so angered by what he had seen, while serving as an artillery liaison officer with the 2nd Battalion, the South Wales Borderers, the unit that had led the attack on the left of the 87th Brigade front, that he described the aftermath of the battle in the letter which he sent the next day to his father. 'Our men were lying in a row parallel to the trenches that they had come out of, mown down. Then those swines . . . [the] Huns fired on those unfortunate wounded men all day with machine guns and killed them all. If a man moved, he was [shot] . . . at once.'

Stanford, like so many of the 1 July survivors, only escaped by hiding in a shell hole until it was dark, and then racing back to the British front line. It was a sad homecoming. 'Out of the battalion there are 60 men left,' he wrote, adding sardonically that as far as the generals were concerned, 'this will constitute a small local repulse!'[36]

The loss or maiming of any man has a devastating effect on his family. However, because the Newfoundlanders came from such a small, tightly knit community, it affected them particularly severely, like those areas that fed into the Pals battalions. The family of William Knight, a motor mechanic who had enlisted as early as 1914 when he was twenty-two years old, must have suffered more than most.

The first of many separate casualty lists were sent to Newfoundland's Governor on 4 July. At that stage no one in St John's, Newfoundland's capital city, realized just how many of their regiment had been hit. Within days, however, the press woke up the population to the numbers affected. The lists were so long that families were not as a rule alerted privately, but had to endure the torment that was involved with going down to the local post office to see the casualty lists that had been pinned up there.

One can easily imagine the misery that a father or mother must have experienced when their loved one's name was spotted on the killed or missing lists in this manner. Even those posted as wounded must have raised terrible fears as to what that entailed: did it mean terrible burns or loss of limbs, or just a healable wound?

The Knight family had a different predicament. At a time when so many were mourning their injured or dead sons, they received no word about William. Eventually, his mother wrote to him in a bid to elicit just what had happened. The letter, written on 18 July, began:

Dear Will,
I received a card from you dated June 20th. I thought to get a letter, but I was disappointed. I know you are kept busy. A card is almost as good to let us know you keep well.

I was in great trouble after that battle. I was expecting to see your number . . . It was dreadful. Ten times worse than it really was, and it was bad enough. I thought of you when you told me always to remember no news [is] good news.

I didn't eat anything for days . . .

Poor Grandpa is like a fish out of water. He got the Post Office steps worn down going up to see the names.[37]

That same day William's grandfather, Warren, also decided to write. His letter started 'My dear Willie' and continued:

I am writing you these few lines to let you know that I got your letter of 18th of June in due time, and we were very glad to hear you were in good health when you wrote . . . I hope this will find the same now.

I see by it you were in the trenches when you wrote, and I hope you came out alright. But I see by the papers that you fought a big battle since then, and I hope to God you came through it alright. For it must have been an awful time. And if you got through, you must be one of the very lucky one[s]. I only hope you did. And if you did, we must thank God for it. If I can judge from the number of killed and wounded in the Casualties List[s] that have come in, they numbered up to now over 500, and are still coming in. But you are not in the number that have come in so far. And I hope and pray to God you won't be on it.

I note what you say . . . that the Battalion was making a name for itself . . . Well my son, if you were making a name for yourself when you wrote, you have [done] more than that since you wrote, for you have brought honour and glory to Newfoundlanders and Newfoundland . . .

Auntie . . . sends best love to you and hopes the war will soon be over, and that you will be home again once more safe and sound. And with the help of God you will. I must close now with love . . .

And may God bless you and watch over you . . .

Your loving Grandpa

Warren.[38]

There is no record of what happened within the Knight family immediately after the letters were sent. Perhaps Warren carried on 'wearing down' the steps at the Post Office, as he carried on searching for William's name on the casualty lists. And perhaps William's mother became more and more agitated over his inconsiderate failure to communicate. Or was the whole family left on tenterhooks, as they waited with bated breath for William's reply? Their wait was to be fruitless. On 26 July a letter from the Colonial Secretary was typed out and subsequently delivered to William's father Fred. It started with the words 'Dear Sir' and continued:

I regret to have to inform you that the Record Office for the First Newfoundland Regiment, London to-day reports that your son No. 290 Sergt. William B. Knight was killed in action on July 1st.

Yours sympathetically,

Colonial Secretary.

It must have been a terrible blow, although it may have taken some time to come to terms with the fact that William was never coming back. Some parents only did that after their son's personal effects were returned to them. If that was the case for the Knight family, then perhaps the letters William's mother and grandfather had written served some purpose after all. They were returned to their senders with the word 'Dead' written in red ink on the envelope.

There were, of course, others whose wait for news of their loved ones was even longer. Many had to wait five or six months before their terrible fears were confirmed. Eventually, most of them received letters which, although standardized, were full of such stirring patriotic sentiments that they fall into the category of historic documents. The terms of one such letter are here given in full:

Dear Sir,

For some time past, the Imperial Government have been making enquiries into those men of the First Newfoundland Regiment who have been reported missing since the action of 1st July. I very much regret to state, however, that from the correspondence which has taken place . . . it is evident that none of them are prisoners of war in Germany, and the authorities are reluctantly forced to the conclusion that all these gallant men . . . one of whom was very close to you, were killed in that fateful action on the 1st of July.

I desire to express to you on behalf of the Government, as well as myself, the sincerest sympathy in this time of sorrow. We feel the loss of our loved ones, but it will no doubt be some consolation to you to think that he, for whom you now mourn, willingly answered the call of King and Country, did his part nobly, and fell facing the foe, in defence of the principles of Righteousness, Truth and Liberty. Though he has laid down the earthly weapons of warfare, he now wears the Soldier's Crown of Victory, and his name will be inscribed upon the Glorious Roll of Honor, and be held in fragrant memory by all his fellow countrymen. When the victory is won, and Peace again reigns upon the earth, it will be a comforting thought to you that in this glorious achievement he bore no small part.

I trust that you may have the Grace and consolation of the Great Father of us all at this time.

With sincere sympathy,

Believe me to be

Your obedient servant

Colonial Secretary

9: Rattling the Cage

Heidenkopf, 1 July 1916

(See maps 2 and 4)

The scale of the disasters experienced by British forces opposite Serre and Beaumont Hamel made it hard to contemplate holding onto objectives seized in between these two villages. Yet that was what was asked of the British troops who on 1 July broke into the German position north of Beaumont Hamel and south of Serre. As noted in Chapter 6, this network of trenches was known to the Germans as the Heidenkopf, and to the British as the Quadrilateral, although this was strictly speaking the name of its most distinctive feature. This feature was a salient that stuck out westward towards the British line facing it (see map 4).

A more colourful German nickname for this feature was Löwenrücken (Lion's Back). This might have suggested to the unwary that it was a weak spot in the German defences, easier to capture than the lion's front, if such a place existed. In fact, it was bristling with danger as far as British attackers were concerned. Unbeknown to the British attack planners, hidden beneath the area to the west of the salient were the tips of four German tunnels packed with explosives, all ready to be set off at the push of a plunger.

As it transpired, the mines protecting the position were the least of the problems facing the attackers. The first British waves did not even target the area within the salient itself, which was protected by the explosives.[1] The biggest threat to progress during the first minutes of the assault was, as elsewhere on the Somme front, the danger posed by the German machine guns. As in the sectors to the north and south, no effective measures had been taken to destroy them. No sooner had the first British soldiers climbed over their parapets, minutes before zero hour, than the machine guns operated by the 121st Reserve Infantry Regiment's gunners burst into action.[2] This regiment, being the northernmost unit of the 26th Reserve Division, was the garrison in the Heidenkopf sector.

The machine-gunners' courage and efficiency were monitored admiringly by the regiment's Lieutenant Beck. He was the German officer who minutes before had been watching the British soldiers gloating at the damage being caused to the German trenches thanks to the efforts of their own weapons: the heavy guns operated by their artillery (see Chapter 6, p. 67). Peering through his periscope inside the armoured observation tower located behind the Heidenkopf, Beck noted approvingly that when the attack started the Germans were in the ascendancy: 'It was hard to miss the attackers since there were so many of them advancing together,' he reported. 'I watched as some machine guns cut through the waves of attackers like a piece of agricultural machinery.'[3]

The machine guns were only one of the weapons used to repel the attackers. There were also the so-called earth mortars, which fired enormous containers packed with glass as well as explosives into the enemy's ranks. As Lieutenant Beck appreciated, their effect could be even more destructive than they would otherwise have been when the detonators were set to go off some time after the missiles landed. 'At one point in the battle I saw a barrel-like shell flying through the air in a high curving arc and falling near a group of Englishmen,' Beck remembered, continuing:

The English soldiers, surprised by its arrival, were rooted to the spot, and one man even went over to take a closer look at it, and urged the others to do the same. No sooner had I started thinking about the diabolical consequences than I saw a huge black cloud go up into the air carrying with it the bodies of these men. One of them, a tall Scot, landed on one of the iron poles that had once held up our barbed wire. The pole went clean through his jaw, and from that moment his corpse stared at me through dead eyes.[4]

But all the weapons that the Germans employed so assiduously could not compensate for a fundamental error which they appear to have made. Firstly, the message that the mines might need to be exploded imminently did not reach the 'Pionier' (combat engineer) company responsible for blowing up the Heidenkopf mines quickly, so that its engineers and troops (collectively referred to hereinafter as pioneers) were not in position when the first waves of the attack approached. Secondly, it seems likely that the number of soldiers on either side of the minefield were kept to a minimum to lessen the lateral damage resulting from the mines' explosion.

That explains the following criticism concerning the use of such exploding mines, which was contained in the post-mortem report written by these pioneers after the fighting finished: 'If they are strong mines, they get in the way of secure defences. Because there is a fear that the stones thrown up by the explosion will fall back on the position, the trenches near to the minefield can only be manned after the detonation.'[5]

This comment, together with Lieutenant Beck's observation that British soldiers broke into the trenches supposedly protected by his regiment's 3rd Company, just to the south of the salient, raises the question. Was the initial breach in the German defences caused by a tactical error, possibly combined with a lucky shot which put out of action a machine gun that was intended to be covering the gap in their defences?

Whatever the contributing factors, the sparse evidence about the breach in the German defences does suggest that there was also some flair and gallantry involved on behalf of the British attackers. If the recollections of Sergeant-Major Percy Chappell of the 1st Battalion, the Somerset Light Infantry, are correct, the first wave, consisting of troops from his unit's sister battalion within the 4th Division's 11th Brigade, the 1st Rifle Brigade, were held up near the German wire, when his group of Somerset Light Infantry came up behind them. Another account describes how at this juncture the Rifle Brigade had to endure 'the most fearsome . . . rifle and machine gun fire'.[6] For a time there was a stand-off, Chappell reported, as the Germans and British threw hand grenades at each other. But then the officer in command all of a sudden shouted out 'Come on lads, let them have it!', whereupon the men of the Rifle Brigade charged forward, causing the German garrison in their front line to flee.[7]

The situation might have been brought under control quickly if German measures put in place for such an eventuality had not been foiled by the thick smoke that still shrouded this part of the front. 'I desperately fired off some red flares,' wrote Lieutenant Beck, 'the signal that called for the artillery to put down defensive fire which would prevent reinforcements reaching the enemy. But only a few guns responded.'[8]

The 1st Rifle Brigade were evidently not the only British battalion that benefited from the inadequacy of the German defences adjacent to the Heidenkopf salient. In the war diary for the 1st/8th Battalion, the Royal Warwickshire Regiment, the unit forming the first wave on the left of the Rifle Brigade, the 7.30 a.m. entry reads: 'Advance begins. Enemy first line reached and passed very quickly as also was the second. Only in one or two cases were any enemy seen in these two lines.'[9] This was another pointer backing up the theory that the Germans had thinned out their defences adjacent to the mined salient.

Not everyone in the British first wave was so lucky. The situation was

very different for those troops belonging to the 1st Battalion, the East
Lancashire Regiment, the 11th Brigade troops attacking to the south of
the salient, on the extreme right of the 4th Division. Those on the battalion's right could not even pass through the German barbed wire. It had not
been cut. Most of those from the battalion who did manage to enter the
German front line were either shot or captured.[10]

To make matters worse as far as the attackers were concerned, just as
they were doing on the southern side of the Gommecourt sector (see
Chapter 10, pp. 120–21), the German artillery combined with their machine-
gunners to sever the link between the British vanguard and supporting
troops. This was done by placing a wall of fire on No Man's Land.

One man who tried, and failed, to penetrate this barrier was the 1st East
Lancashires' intelligence officer, 2nd Lieutenant W. J. Page. Shortly after
zero hour, he attempted to follow the vanguard across No Man's Land.[11] 'It
was truly amazing that anyone could live in such devastating fire,' he wrote
in his after-action report.

There were many casualties. They included Lieutenant Newcombe, the
battalion's machine-gun officer. Within minutes of going over the top,
'Newky', who was coolly walking along in Page's wake, smoking a cigarette, was shot and killed. Shells and machine-gun bullets were claiming
their victims 'left right and centre,' Page reported:

Miraculously, I advanced through [all of] this until I came to the slightly sunken
road about midway in No Man's Land. Here I urged forward some men who were
trying to find shelter from the deadly fire, [although I can now see] they probably
had right on their side . . .

About eight minutes after Zero . . . [when] I was right [up] against the German
wire . . . I . . . [saw] a small group of enemy infantry standing on their parapet . . .
waving their caps on their wooden handled grenades . . . [and] shouting 'Come on
English!'. I . . . [emptied] my revolver into this group and as I did so, one of our
field guns . . . put their first shell right into the middle of them.

'That target was disposed of,' Page concluded, '[but] any [further] advance
was now impossible. Any movement . . . in No Man's Land brought a hail
of bullets.' Realizing that discretion was the better part of valour, he sought
refuge along with those close to him in one of a series of nearby shell holes.

Meanwhile the 1st Battalion, the Rifle Brigade, 11th Brigade's central unit,
was having more success. Although its right-hand company failed to breach

the defence line, some but by no means all of the left company had reached their first objective: the German front line. 'Most of us seemed to be knocked out,' the 1st Rifle Brigade's 2nd Lieutenant Glover reported afterwards to a more senior officer. But there was no time to count their losses just then. 'There were some Germans in the trench . . . and Sergeant Hall, Corporal Halls and myself started to bomb . . . [until they] cleared out to our right.'[12]

They then proceeded to advance to the third German line, and for a time to the fourth, with the 1st/8th Royal Warwicks coming up beside them on their left. These battalions were supported by men from their support battalions, the 1st Battalion, the Somerset Light Infantry, supporting the 1st Rifle Brigade, and the 1st/6th Battalion, the Royal Warwickshire Regiment, supporting the 1st/8th Royal Warwicks.

The 1st/8th Royal Warwicks' war diarist summarized their progress thus: 'At the third line, we were temporarily held up by machine gun fire. But [we] took it by rushes . . . We reached our objective about 35–40 minutes from Zero hour . . . and at once commenced consolidating and cleaning rifles.'

Their hold on the captured trench was weakened by their diminishing supply of hand grenades. 'Many times we were bombed from this position,' their war diarist recorded. 'We had to retire . . . line the parapet and hold on with machine [gun] and rifle fire. Parties were [then] detailed to collect as many bombs as could be found, both English and German, and when we had a good store, we again reached our objective.'[13]

Soon men from the 4th Division's supporting brigades had filled up the trench until it was if anything too full of men. As Glover put it, it was 'a . . . squash . . . everybody in the way of everybody else, [making] it extremely difficult to move or dig. I did try, but not very successfully to spread the 11th [Brigade] out to the right, and Captain Martin [of the 1st/8th Royal Warwicks] also tried to get the 10th and 12th [Brigades] to the left, but they were held back [by the Germans], and we couldn't get along the single trench [to help them].'

Glover described how this inability to move rapidly up and down the trench may have contributed to the first of many crises that occurred during that long hot day. 'Suddenly our right . . . [was] rushed by German bombers, and the men [in the area leading] up to our Battalion bombing squad rushed back to the left. The bombing squad was apparently cut off.'

It was a difficult moment. 'We were short of bombs,' Glover explained. 'And the Lewis guns were more or less out of action.' However, he somehow cobbled together a defence. 'All the bombs we had and could spare from the left were passed up, and with the help of a corporal, I managed to get together . . . four throwers . . . splendid fellows . . . who [helped us hang on to] . . . the trench.'

Even these 'splendid fellows' would not have been sufficient, however, if they had lacked support. 'There was another even finer,' Glover reported. It was a runner, who appears to have brought up supplies from the front German trench, where the various units supporting the vanguard were digging in. 'This runner made the trip between that trench and our own at least 20 times, bringing bombs and Lewis Gun ammunition. He did more than any single individual to keep things going.'

On one of these 'trips' the runner brought up a message from the commanding officer of the 2nd Seaforth Highlanders, instructing them to hold on as long as possible. Troops from the Seaforths, the only Scottish unit within the 4th Division's 10th Brigade, were one of the support units whose men had made it into the German front line. '[The] message from the Colonel of the Seaforths . . . [stated] he would send on [some more] bombs,' Glover explained. 'But for the runner, even that would have come too late. The throwers were dog tired and the Germans full of energy. By persuasion, we managed to get a team of about half a dozen who carried on manfully.'

Back near the site of the original break-in, Lieutenant Beck was feeling uneasy. The British advance had turned on those like him who were stationed behind the German front line. Before the British thrust forward, he had felt relatively secure in his armoured tower in between the first and second German trenches. After it, the tower felt more like a prison, especially when he heard English commands being shouted outside. 'The next moments would decide whether I lived or died,' Beck wrote later:

A . . . group of English soldiers marched up to my tower's entrance and shouted out: 'Are there any Germans in there?' When there was no reply, they threw in two hand grenades. They exploded, but only succeeded in destroying the wooden frame that acted as a barricade – as well as my hearing.

Shortly afterwards, a second group of English turned up, but they did not look twice at the tower since it looked as if it had already been dealt with.

1. and 2. *Top* The mass of earth, stones – and men – thrown into the air by the blowing up of the mine under Hawthorn Redoubt, near Beaumont Hamel, on 1 July 1916. It was the decision of Lieutenant-General Sir Aylmer Hunter-Weston (*top right*), VIII Corps' commander, to blow the mine ten minutes before zero hour that prepared the Germans for what was coming.

3. *Bottom* Lieutenant Geoffrey Malins (*left*), the cameraman who risked life and limb to film the explosion from just behind the British front line. His footage was seen by the millions who queued up to see the film of the Battle of the Somme.

4. *Above* Major-General Henry de Beauvoir de Lisle addresses some of the troops from the 1st Lancashire Fusiliers (29th Division) a couple of days before the attack.

5. *Below* Men from the 29th Division prepare for the attack on Beaumont Hamel at White City, the site of a group of dugouts hollowed out of a natural bank, near the front line.

6. and 7. Photographs of the 1st Lancashire Fusiliers taken from Malins' film: *above* they fix their bayonets, *below* they await zero hour in the sunken road halfway across No Man's Land.

8. and 9. *Left* General Sir Henry Rawlinson, the commander of the British 4th Army. *Right* General Sir Douglas Haig (*left*) with General Joseph Joffre, the irascible commander of the French Army, and David Lloyd George on the right.

10. Mametz in ruins after the British 4th Army captured the village on 1 July 1916.

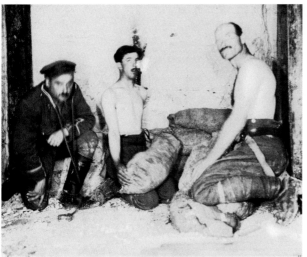

11. The enormous crater south of La Boisselle created by the explosion of another mine.

12. *Left* British miners with their listening equipment, seen in one of their mines.

13. and 14. *Left* Lieutenant Morris Bickersteth of the 15th West Yorkshire Regiment (the Leeds Pals), who died during the attack on Serre. *Right* Captain Billie Nevill of the 8th East Surreys, the instigator of the kicking of footballs across No Man's Land to encourage the men to advance, was killed during the advance towards Montauban.

15. and 16. *Left* Captain Charlie May, killed near Mametz, seen here with his wife, Maude, and their baby daughter, Pauline. *Right* Captain Alfred Bland, also killed near Mametz, with his wife, Violet (*inset*). Both officers were from the 22nd Manchester Regiment.

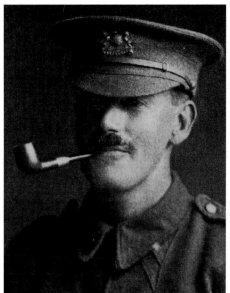

17. *Top left* Lieutenant Kenneth Macardle of the 17th Manchesters. He rallied his men when they were flagging south of Montauban during the 1 July 1916 attack and led them into the village that was captured.

18. *Top right* Sergeant Harry Tawney of the 22nd Manchesters was wounded after leading his men forward east of Mametz.

19. *Left* Sister Edith Appleton, who wrote an account of her experiences at the hospital at Étretat where some of the soldiers wounded on 1 July were taken.

20. British gunners prepare their 12-inch howitzer in Aveluy Wood.

21. A captured machine-gun post at Glatz Redoubt, which was one of the main obstacles to progress in the sector on 1 July 1916.

When he thought the coast was clear, Beck scuttled out and hid in a nearby shell hole, only to discover that there was a soldier standing guard just 10 metres away from where he had just fled. That discovery persuaded Beck that he, like the British soldiers who had taken refuge in No Man's Land, would probably have to wait until darkness fell before making good his escape.[14]

But even as Beck planned his exit, British fortunes, and 2nd Lieutenant Glover's in particular, changed once more. 'By way of precaution we built a barricade,' he reported, 'leaving about 35 yards of straight trench with a Lewis gun on top of a traverse, commanding it [while] . . . we held on to our original position.

'For a long time the Germans threw into [that] . . . stretch of trench and on[to] both parapets, but never showed up.'

Only when Glover's attention was distracted by the call of another officer sheltering in a dugout were the Germans able to rush forward without being spotted. They then, and as Glover reported it, 'drove our men out of the trench' and back to the 'base of the Quadrilateral'.[15]

It was probably during this headlong retreat to the German front line that one of the most dramatic actions of the whole operation took place. As the assault troops scurried back, those occupying the German front line, perhaps thinking that they had missed an order for a general retreat, began to flock back across No Man's Land to the British line. The whole position might have been surrendered, such was the panic engendered by the rush, had it not been for the twenty-four-year-old drummer Walter Ritchie, who, at considerable risk to life and limb, clambered up on the parapet and repeatedly sounded the charge on his bugle. It was that stirring sound, and the sight of him standing there so prominently in the midst of them, that stopped at least some of the retreating soldiers, and made it possible to restore order.[16]

Nevertheless the retreat from the third German line was a disappointment. The only saving grace as far as 2nd Lieutenant Glover was concerned was that there were more British troops inside the perimeter behind the German front line than he had ever dreamed possible. When he and his men arrived in the first German trench that ran along the base of the Heidenkopf salient, he was surprised to see that a substantial British presence had been built up and the position was being consolidated under the watchful gaze of Lieutenant-Colonel Hopkinson of the Seaforth Highlanders. Even the 10th Brigade's staff captain had put in an appearance. There were also between 100 and 200 other ranks.[17]

However, the hours they still had to spend in the German front line were now numbered. It had been decided that the British hold on the German trench network had become unsustainable, and should be terminated as soon as practicable. Hopkinson decided that the evacuation should be some time after dark when crossing No Man's Land would not be quite as dangerous as it was in broad daylight.

While all of this was going on, Lieutenant Beck had also made his move. Taking advantage of a moment when the British soldiers near his hiding place were distracted by an exchange of fire, he crawled out and slipped away to the rear. There he linked up with one of the units from his regiment's 3rd Battalion that was involved in the counter-attack. He accompanied them on the thrust that was supposed to capture the area around his armoured tower, only to find that some other Germans had arrived there first: 'The corpses of three dead English soldiers lay tangled up with some damaged machine guns and radio apparatus.'[18]

As darkness fell, the British soldiers marooned beside the German wire in No Man's Land were also liberated. But as the East Lancashire's Captain Page realized, the end of the day's fighting did not neatly bring to an end the British soldiers' torment. Although the night hid the wide expanse of No Man's Land that was littered with British bodies, 'the same awful scene' was only too evident for those like him and his brother officer, 2nd Lieutenant W. Daly, who passed through it on their way back to the British line.

Far from being an easy stroll back to home territory, the journey across No Man's Land was a nightmare. It was almost as disturbing as the attack. There were 'Very lights' shooting up in the air all around them, 'explosions of every kind', 'sudden bursts of machine guns' and 'salvos from guns which demanded rushes for cover to the nearest shell hole'. At the same time there was the knowledge that saving themselves meant abandoning their comrades. 'Some were tenderly placed in shell holes', although it was obvious they would not survive for long. But apart from that, all Page and his companion could do was to 'meander from one groaning figure to another, and give . . . [them] water . . . [or] a word of hope and cheer'.

By the time the two East Lancashire officers made it back to the British front line, they were exhausted. Nevertheless Page worked through the night, helping to bring in at least some of those whose positions he had memorized on the way back. However, when the first streaks of dawn lit up the dark sky and made further recovery of men too dangerous, even he had to call it a day. Page returned to the safety of the battalion's dugout in the support trench, where he was revived with a mug of tea.

'Of my feelings at that moment, it is very difficult to speak,' he wrote later. 'Tears and a lump in the throat sound very sentimental and effeminate. But we had lost so many friends and men we knew to be great in character . . . all for no purpose.'

The enormity of the disaster was brought home to Page when, on approaching the White City dugouts, he and Daly bumped into Brigadier-General Wilding, commander of the 10th Brigade who had also taken over command of the 11th Brigade. Its former commander, Brigadier-General Prowse, had been mortally wounded. On seeing Page and his brother officer, Wilding remarked rather tactlessly: 'What: officers of the East Lancashire Regiment? Why, I thought they were all killed.'[19]

But by that time the flood of bad news, and anxiety, had blunted all normal restraint and sensibility. The commanders in the field were not just dealing with isolated deaths. Their plans had to take into account the fact that there were thousands of casualties. They were dealing with an unprecedented catastrophe, and it was not over yet. Although the evacuation of the Heidenkopf salient had been successfully carried out by about 1 a.m. on the night of 1–2 July, there was still one company missing from the 10th Brigade.[20] This company from the 1st Battalion, the Royal Irish Fusiliers, had not received the notification that the occupation of the Heidenkopf must end, a decision that was made just after midnight, when it was finally acknowledged that all the reports about Serre being held by British troops were untrue.[21] The first three sets of runners sent to recover the Royal Irish Fusiliers did not even make it across No Man's Land. It was only during the morning of 2 July that a messenger finally made contact with them, enabling the last organized body of troops to vacate the German lines in the Heidenkopf sector at 11.15 a.m.[22]

They left behind them a scene of complete devastation. This was not just within the area at the tip of the salient, which was strewn with British and some German corpses, the result of the mines being exploded sometime after the attack started.[23] As another East Lancashire officer remarked, after being captured by the Germans the evening before, 'A broad stretch of . . . [No Man's Land] was coloured khaki by the British dead and wounded which carpeted the ground.'[24]

The large number of British casualties and the enforced evacuation confirmed the German victory, but in a way it was pyrrhic. According to

Lieutenant Beck, his surviving comrades in the 121st Reserve Regiment's 3rd Company were 'absolute wrecks'. There were only thirty-five of them. Three-quarters of the company had been killed. 'They sat in their dugout along with the survivors from other companies like lost orphans, too shattered to lift a finger. They had exhausted their powers of endurance.'[25]

At least they were tucked away from the destroyed positions. As Beck related: 'The trenches were full of horrific, gruesome sights. [In some places] 5 or 6 corpses were stacked up one on top of the other, friends mixed up with foes, their remains mutilated by the close combat which had surged to and fro.'[26]

His regiment's casualties were in excess of 500 for the first ten days of July, most of them incurred on 1 July.[27] But that was nothing compared with those suffered by the British. The losses of their 4th Division in this period were more than ten times that number, topping 5,900. The 11th Brigade alone lost over 3,200 men. All six battalions under its command had casualties in excess of 450 officers and men, with the highest losses approaching the 600 mark.[28]

In view of the numbers of men killed, wounded and missing, it is not surprising that the repercussions of the fighting were still being experienced for a long time after the end of the attack. According to Lieutenant Beck:

For days afterwards we could hear the cries for help and the groans of the English soldiers in No Man's Land. In spite of the efforts to recover them, only a few were brought in during the [first] night.

During the next few days, there was no more fighting on the battlefield. The English had learned their lesson. The front became deathly quiet, interrupted only now and then by an English soldier calling out from No Man's Land.

On the 4th day it poured with rain. That flushed a few more English soldiers out of the shell holes which filled up with water. We took them in as prisoners.[29]

However, it took ten days to restore some kind of order within the Heidenkopf position, according to the 121st Reserve Regiment's regimental history. Part of the clearing operation was solved when 150 German corpses were interred in a mass grave behind Feste Soden, a strongpoint to the east of the trenches taken by the British during the attack. But it was only on 11 July that the final British corpse was recovered from the area in No Man's Land just in front of the German front line. By that time the corpses removed were so high that in the words of the regimental history 'they contaminated the air'.[30]

The fact that the attack in the Heidenkopf sector resulted in so many deaths and so much suffering leads one to ask what its impact was on the Germans. A post-action report written by the commander of the 121st Reserve Regiment's 1st Battalion, the unit responsible for the northern portion of the sector, where the initial break-in had occurred, included the following admission: 'I wouldn't be able to hold my sector if I was not supported by the Regiment's 3rd Battalion.'[31] Another of his reports confirmed: 'The support of the 3rd Battalion and the assistance of the 11th Company of the 169th Regiment (the regiment responsible for the Serre front), was needed so badly that if it had not been for the aid from both these units, the sector would have been lost.'[32]

The German reliance on a unit that would have been used up on the Serre sector, had the advance there not been so comprehensively defeated, together with statements by soldiers in many of the British battalions which took part in the attack on the Heidenkopf sector, that they were beaten back by gunfire coming from both Serre and Beaumont Hamel, leads one to the conclusion that the German victories at these two villages stood the Heidenkopf defenders in good stead. Much of the success enjoyed by the Germans in the Heidenkopf sector can accurately be said to have been achieved thanks to their ascendancy opposite Serre and Beaumont Hamel.

After the 4th Division units were withdrawn from the front line, they were congratulated for attacking so strongly. That prompted the East Lancashire's Captain Page to conclude his report with the following critical verdict:

Divisional diaries may say that a certain very limited success was achieved, but from one who was in the midst of it . . . it may be glorious that many men die bravely in [a] vain endeavour, but many would have lived to accomplish . . . [great deeds] but for the ignorance . . . ill training and lack of thought of [our] general officers.[33]

10: Neither Fish Nor Fowl

Gommecourt, 1 July 1916

(See maps 2 and 3)

Of all the attacks carried out on 1 July 1916, arguably the most galling of all from the British point of view were the events at the northern tip of the British line, in the area surrounding Gommecourt. The attack here did not have to be anything more than a feint. It was a diversionary operation, intended to occupy the German garrison, so that its troops could not steal away only to reappear in time to blunt the main attack to the south.[1] It was also intended to prevent artillery behind Gommecourt being used against the British troops advancing towards Serre, the northernmost objective of the main attack being carried out by Rawlinson's 4th Army (see Chapter 7, p. 71).[2]

That explains why no serious attempt was made to conceal the preparations for the two-pronged assault in this northern sector.[3] As had been disclosed to the Germans by the captured miner Victor Wheat, there were to be separate attacks on Gommecourt's north-eastern and south-eastern flanks (see Chapter 5, pp. 60–61). They were to be carried out by the 46th and 56th Divisions respectively. If successful, the two arms of the pincer movement would meet east of the village, thereby cutting off the Gommecourt garrison from its line of communications.

The preparations were extensive. They even extended to the digging of advanced assault trenches. These were dug during the two nights between 22 and 24 June to the north-east of Gommecourt, taking the assault troops around 100–140 yards nearer to the Germans than they would have been in the pre-existing British front line.[4] South-east of the village, the night-time digging carried out between 26 and 28 June advanced the assault trench by no less than 350–400 yards. These digs nevertheless still left the northern division 250–300 yards and the southern division 300–400 yards of No Man's Land to cross during the planned assault.[5]

The desire to divert the enemy also explains why Lieutenant-General Thomas Snow, commander of VII Corps, whose two divisions were involved, proudly – or perhaps grimly – wrote to Haig four days before the attack: 'They know we are coming all right.'[6]

That would have been all very well if a token series of small-scale raids had been planned. Instead, Snow ordered his major-generals to make a full-blooded attack. In view of the catastrophe that ensued, it is not surprising that Snow's seemingly conspiratorial message to Haig, combined with his equally insensitive remarks following the tragedy (see below), led to the fifty-eight-year-old lieutenant-general being pilloried for sacrificing so many young lives. At least part of that criticism is unfair. Snow had in fact attempted to have the Gommecourt operations called off, warning his immediate superior, the fifty-five-year-old Lieutenant-General Edmund Allenby, the 3rd Army's commander, that the village was not a good place for a feint. Even before the attack, there were fears the area in and around the village had some of the strongest defences in the line, and this was one of the reasons why it was clear that if the British attack did not succeed, there would be difficulties disengaging without large casualties. Allenby brought these concerns to Haig's attention, but both Allenby and Snow fell into line after Haig demanded that the operation should go ahead in order to assist the main attack.[7]

Nevertheless, even though chained to this flawed operation, the two senior generals cannot totally escape censure for the way it was planned. Apart from anything else, sending the two divisions into battle with only eight heavy guns devoted to counter-battery work was a recipe for disaster, notwithstanding the twenty lighter guns also focused on silencing the German artillery. Snow and Allenby may not have been responsible for the restricted amount of artillery allocated to their sector, but if they believed its inadequacy would result in a death trap for the troops in their care, they were surely under a moral obligation to refuse to play any part in the attack. The fact that the commanders of these few guns were instructed by Snow and Allenby to focus more of their attention on the area being attacked by VIII Corps to the south, rather than on the German artillery dominating the area opposite Gommecourt, only added insult to injury and compounded the flaws in the operation.[8]

Because of the relatively free rein given to the German guns, it beggars belief that none of the generals could put his finger on the one factor which could have reduced the dangers being run: the need to shift sufficient men, grenades, machine guns and ammunition across No Man's Land before the German artillery made the area between the two enemies impassable.

After the fight for Gommecourt, which resulted in excess of 7,900 casualties, Lieutenant-Colonel Arthur Bates, commander of the 1st/5th London

Regiment (London Rifle Brigade), the 56th Division's leading left-hand assault battalion (see map 3), reproached the 169th Brigade's commander, Brigadier-General E. S. D'Ewes Coke, for failing to heed his warning along these lines: 'I was of the opinion . . . [which] I represented . . . to you as strongly as I felt I could . . . that it would be easier to try and get everyone across as soon as possible to be ready for any eventuality. And then if the widely expressed views that the enemy had no men or guns left to prevent us after the bombardment proved correct, the 4th Company could be used as "coolies" pure and simple.'[9]

It was the failure to heed the lieutenant-colonel's warning that was to play a critical role in what followed: the stranding of the division's vanguard in the German trenches, without sufficient ammunition to defend themselves, let alone to break through the enemy.

Given the disadvantages under which the whole concept of the operation laboured, the progress made by the attackers south-east of Gommecourt looked promising to begin with. That is not to say there were no difficulties. Private Arthur Schuman of the London Rifle Brigade, advancing across around 400 yards of No Man's Land, on the extreme left of the four battalions leading the assault, reported hearing machine guns crackling from every direction, and seeing men dropping all around him. On somehow managing to make it to the German wire, the 'entanglement', as he put it, had to be 'negotiated': 'There was only one opening . . . Not many of us got through,' he recalled. However, those who could pressed on, until they 'fell' into the first German trench. Schuman himself eventually ended up with a softer landing than he expected, which was welcome until he realized the 'cushion' turned out to be the remains of a dead German soldier.[10]

That first German trench was only a staging post. Over the next two hours favourable messages flowed back to the battalions' headquarters via runners, wounded soldiers and aircraft, stating that the assault troops were gradually moving forwards all along the line. By 10 a.m. the commanders monitoring the situation from the rear believed that all four of the 56th Division battalions who had led the advance, together with the other units who had gone over in support, had taken a portion of the third German trench.

However, that was the last good news of the day, as far as they were concerned. Shortly after 9.15 a.m. everything turned sour, as German artillery plastered No Man's Land with everything they had got. From that moment it was virtually impossible for any groups of men to cross over to the German lines. And instead of the much hoped-for messages that the next objectives had been reached, reports flooded into the battalions' headquarters describing the growing tragedy.

First came the reports that the battalions' support companies could not move forward because of the shelling. Then came the news that while making the attempt, they had been annihilated and had only a handful of men remaining. And finally came the haunting, desperate signals from the cut-off troops in the German lines, which were repeated time and again: 'SOS Bombs ... SOS Bombs ... SOS Bombs', signals that prompted more abortive rescue missions and more slaughter.[11]

It was not just German artillery that was imposing the blockade. One of the few British soldiers who survived the attempt to cross No Man's Land at this time spoke of the 'hail of bullets' that targeted his group each time they made a 30-yard dash to the next shell hole. The firing was so intense that they could not contemplate going directly across. These bullets killed both his companions and wounded him, before he could attain the safety of the German first line. As he later informed the parents of one of those hit, he could only save his own life and retrace his steps to the British lines by abandoning their son's and his companion's corpses where they had fallen.[12]

Then at around 12.30 p.m. German forces, perhaps realizing that the numbers of grenades being lobbed in their direction were lessening, counter-attacked and began pushing back the British forces, who were suddenly toothless due to the lack of grenades. Initially, they retired to the second trench.[13] But as the Germans surged forward, they withdrew to the first trench. At around 1.30 p.m. some were even spotted retreating across No Man's Land.[14]

All of a sudden the operation, which had started off being an out-and-out attack, was transformed into something akin to one of those great evacuations for which the British Army became famous during a later conflict. Those who looked back at the events at Gommecourt following the dark days of 1940 might have seen similarities with Britain's besieged army's rearguard actions in and around the French port of Dunkirk. But in this case, No Man's Land stood in for the Channel and the British front line for Ramsgate and Dover. In both cases perimeters were formed and held so that British troops could be evacuated.

As the Germans advanced, the 168th Brigade's battalions, on the 56th Division's right, gave up their bridgehead first. The retreat of its left unit, the 1st/12th Battalion, the London Regiment (the Rangers), was spotted from the brigade observation post at 3.10 p.m.[15] The grenades in the hands of the right unit, the 1st/14th Battalion, the London Regiment (London Scottish), ran out half an hour later, prompting the acting commanding officer, Captain H. C. Sparks, to sum up the situation in the following terms:

I am faced with this position. I have collected all bombs . . . from casualties. Every one has been used. Owing to the enemy's continued barrage fire, none can be brought to me. I am faced with three alternatives:
   a. to stay here with such of my men as are alive and be killed.
   b. to surrender to the enemy.
   c. to withdraw such of my men as I can.
   Either of the first two alternatives is distasteful to me. I propose to adopt the latter.

He then gave orders for as many of the wounded to be carried over No Man's Land as possible, with the remainder of his surviving men following immediately afterwards, while he and four men operated the Lewis gun that held back the enemy until the rest of the battalion who could get away had gone. Sparks and the four men then also departed, to earn plaudits from their commander for the cool way the captain had handled a very difficult situation.[16]

It is just possible that the 169th Brigade's units on the 56th Division's left might have gone back to their lines at about the same time had it not been for an unfortunate oversight. Given the fierceness of the fight, and the fact that the third German line was in fact a series of aligned but disconnected trenches separated from each other by huge mounds of earth, it is not surprising that some British troops never received the order to retire. That is what happened to one group serving with the London Rifle Brigade, the 169th Brigade's left unit. Its 2nd Lieutenant R. E. Petley and around forty men from the battalion's D Company were dug in at the extreme right of his battalion's sector of the German third line (Eck Trench, which, along with other trenches mentioned in this chapter, is shown on map 3), when at about 2 p.m. he realized they were all alone. Petley described the moment he found out in the following terms:

I . . . went along to the left to find Captain de Cologan but could find no trace of the rest of D Company nor C Company. I at once sent a message back to advanced headquarters asking for more bombs and men. I [subsequently] heard . . . that Captain de Cologan had passed the order to withdraw down to me before he left Eck, but as I did not receive it and as we were holding the Hun up on the right, I could see no reason for withdrawing without orders . . .

At 4 p.m. I sent the following to advanced headquarters.

'I sent a message to you about 2 hours ago to the effect that I am holding onto Eck with about 40 men including a dozen QVR [1st/9th Battalion, the London Regiment (Queen Victoria's Rifles) which had led the assault on the London Rifle Brigade's right] and one QWR [1st/16th Battalion, the London Regiment (Queen's Westminster Rifles) which had followed 169th Brigade's leading units into the German lines], and that I wanted more bombs. Quite out of touch to right and left. Have held off Germans on our left with barricade. It is quite "absurd" for us to lay here at night as we are.'

At 4.30 p.m. Sergeant Robinson appeared. He explained the situation, and brought me verbal orders to withdraw. I . . . told him to lead the party out . . . and . . . gave him the following message for Captain de Cologan: 'Sergeant Robinson brings me verbal orders to withdraw which of course reluctantly we must obey. Sergeant Robinson is bringing all the men down to you, and Sergeant Austin and I are trying to get Sergeant Olorenshaw. Should like some hot dinner when we get back!'[17]

Unfortunately, any thoughts of taking the wounded back with them had to be abandoned due to the fact that these members of the London Rifle Brigade were under fire. However, largely thanks to Petley and Sergeant Austin, who acted as the rearguard, most of those still standing made it back to the German first line (Fen and Ferret; see map 3), where they joined around sixty to seventy men already there. They did not arrive a minute too soon. Even as they retreated, Germans were advancing on three sides of the one remaining communication trench in their sector (Exe), which provided a relatively safe escape route.

It might have been better if they could have hung on in the German front line until dark. That would have enabled them to make a more leisurely retreat across No Man's Land. But at around 7.45 p.m., their supply of German grenades having dried up, the line suddenly broke following the order: 'Every man for himself.' And protected only by Petley, once again acting as the rearguard, accompanied by around a dozen men, the bulk of the last remaining British force in the German front line south-east of Gommecourt made a run for it pursued by Germans throwing grenades, and with bullets kicking up the soil all around them.[18] Sadly, the wounding and killing were not finished yet. 'Most of [my] . . . party were hit in No Man's Land,' Petley reported.[19]

The history books will mark down the 56th Division's attack as a failure. However, no one could complain that they had not put up a good show, and they might have fared a lot better had they not been asked to attack with one metaphorical hand tied behind their backs. Lieutenant-General Snow did not, at first at least, believe the same could be said about the 46th Division troops, under the command of Major-General Edward Montagu-Stuart-Wortley, who had simultaneously advanced towards Gommecourt from the north-west.

Three days later the shortcomings of Stuart-Wortley and his subordinates were exposed by a court of inquiry, which investigated amongst other things why it was that the division's 137th Brigade did not 'close with the enemy'.[20] One of the catalogue of errors identified was the decision to lay down a smokescreen over No Man's Land five minutes before the troops advanced.[21] Although it could be argued that the premature release of smoke shielded the first waves of the attack from the German guns, it also warned the defenders that the attack was about to begin. A better outcome might have resulted if the smoke had been delayed until the protective umbrellas provided by the British artillery lifted off the German front trenches, the lift being timed for the precise moment when the infantry were about to launch themselves over the German parapet.[22]

There was no similar justification for the chaos that was allowed to develop behind the British front line, even allowing for the increased difficulties of moving troops around because of the rainwater that had accumulated in the rear trenches. This was the result of the bad weather prior to the attack.

Given past experience, it should have been obvious that as soon as the German defenders saw the smoke floating towards them over No Man's Land, their artillery would shell the British front line, supports and communication trenches on which they had been registering their guns for months. Yet there was not even a plan to ensure that all the troops, reinforcements and supplies of bombs needed for the initial assault were clear of the British trenches before the German gunners could react.

If prior to the attack the support troops had been placed in assembly trenches near the advanced line, and ordered to move across the open in order of importance as soon as the smoke was released, there might not have been any difficulty. However, the organization of the support troops defied logic.

These troops, who were ordered to advance up communication trenches with their supplies of bombs, were placed behind the soldiers who were bound to find it hardest to move smartly up to the British front line: men burdened with huge bundles of barbed wire, steel poles, bombs, flares and other bulky impedimenta, whose movements were even more restricted than was originally anticipated because of the weather.[23] The pumps that had been used to extract most of the rainwater that had fallen during the preceding days had not been able to suck up the deep liquid mud that covered the bottom of the British trenches.[24]

The result was mayhem. Not only did the 'traffic jams' in the communication trenches make it impossible for the support troops to reach the advanced trenches and No Man's Land before they were raked by machine-gun fire. The almost solid mass of men moving up the congested communication trenches to the front could not be missed by the German gunners, who blasted the British lines with shrapnel and high explosive. A snapshot of the resulting 'horrors' is to be found in the following statement by Lieutenant Cyril Ashford, an intelligence officer in the 46th Division's southernmost brigade (137th Brigade):

During the action, I made several journeys through our trenches with messages from the Brigade Commander, and even without a burden, found it almost impossible to make progress. Casualties . . . were very heavy thanks to the intensity of the bombardment and the congestion, and [due] . . . to the fact that many men who fell . . . wounded [as well as] dead . . . disappeared beneath the mud. I stumbled over many bodies which were out of sight . . . [while] walking.[25]

Equally problematic was the astonishing failure to take into account updates concerning the state of the wire-cutting opposite the German front line. As late as 29 June, reports were being issued warning that hardly any of the wire had been cut separating 137th Brigade's right-hand unit, the 1st/6th Battalion, the South Staffordshire Regiment, from the Germans.[26] It is easy to understand how 18-pounder guns with their shells' low trajectory might have missed the wire in this position. It was protected by a dip in the ground to the north of the sunken Fonquevillers to Gommecourt road that marked the attack's right wing (see map 3).[27] What was harder to fathom was why Stuart-Wortley did not have a system in place to ensure everyone knew about the existing obstacle, so that evasive action could be taken.

As Snow concluded, when forwarding the court of inquiry transcript to General Allenby, there was 'no excuse' for the true situation not to have been known. Ordering the men to go on regardless was a dreadful mistake that was to have deadly consequences. It meant that the bulk of the 6th South Staffordshires' soldiers were allowed to wander blindly through the smoke into a mass of barbed wire, which in some places was 30–40 feet 'thick'. (That is, 30–40 feet separated the point in No Man's Land where British soldiers first encountered the wire, after advancing across No Man's Land from their trenches, from the point where these soldiers would emerge from the wire after cutting their way through it.) It goes without saying that once the wind blew the smoke away, soldiers attempting to cut their way through such wire were sitting ducks.

The tragic repercussions were only too evident to Lieutenant Cyril Ashford, the 137th Brigade's intelligence officer. His report included the following words: 'After the attack was abandoned, I examined the scene from the branches of a tall tree on the outskirts of Fonquevillers, and could see the dead and wounded like a high water mark close to the German wire.'[28]

The shortage of bombs and reinforcements on the far side of No Man's Land also ruined the advance made by the Sherwood Foresters within the 46th Division's left-hand brigade (139th Brigade) to the north. Some of the Foresters successfully entered the German front trench, and a few continued on into the second line, although the imprecise writing of the war diarists makes it hard to work out precisely how many. The history of the German 91st Reserve Regiment, which was holding part of the sector opposite the 46th Division, refers to the larger groups amounting to in excess of sixty men.[29]

Whatever the precise number, the few who survived all tell the same story: while they had grenades, they were able to dominate the area they had invaded, and to either kill or hold at bay any Germans they encountered. If swiftly supported, their thrusts might have become defendable bridgeheads, perhaps even a base for further exploitation, although their task was made more difficult owing to the failure by the men proceeding to the second German line having first omitted to clear the enemy out of their front-line dugouts. As a result, succeeding waves of British attackers had a fresh batch of defenders to contend with when approaching the first German line.

None of the British soldiers thrived in the German lines for long. Once their meagre supply of bombs ran out, they were as helpless as their comrades in the 56th Division who had run out of grenades to the south. Those who could had to withdraw, initially to shell holes in No Man's Land, and later that night to the British front line, from where they had started that morning.[30]

The experiences related by Corporal 'P. J.' Murphy give us a taste of what might have been achieved if only he and his group from the 1st/5th Battalion, the Sherwood Foresters, 139th Brigade's right-hand assault unit, had been properly supported:

My platoon spent the night in our front line. About 7.25 a.m. 2nd Lieutenant Barber gave . . . [the] order to fix bayonets. Smoke bombs were thrown by the Lincolns . . . Minutes later 2nd Lieutenant Barber gave us the order to advance. We all mounted the parapet by steps previously cut and proceeded to the advanced trench . . . [where] we stayed until 2nd Lieutenant Dornton gave the order to advance. As I advanced, I found that the men on my right were bearing to the right, so I doubled across to [tell] them to change their direction . . .

The smoke now became so dense that I lost touch with my platoon, but soon found 2nd Lieutenant Dornton, and accompanied him to the German wire. Here Captain Naylor, 2nd Lieutenant[s] Barber [and] . . . Cecil and . . . Private . . . Attenborough joined, and together we passed through the wire and into the German trench . . .

[There] we found about nine of the enemy in the bay we entered, five firing wildly from the fire platform, while the others were at the bottom of the trench. [They] bore the number 91 on [their] shoulder straps, wore respirators, but had no equipment on, and their bayonets were not fixed. Captain Naylor [who was] . . . leading, shot one of the Germans on the fire platform, whereupon the remainder dashed in the direction of a dugout situated under the parapet.

Dashing after them, I bayoneted the last two, while the remainder were shot . . . by [other members of] our party on the dugout steps.

Having cleared the bay, Captain Naylor ordered us onto the parados, ready to proceed to the second line, but having mounted, we found ourselves absolutely unsupported and dropped back into the trench. Corporal Harrison with two men now joined us. I directed him to proceed up the trench to the left. 2nd Lieutenant Cecil and myself, with Private Attenborough, went into the next bay on our right where we encountered an enemy bombing party. We held our ground until our bombs were exhausted when we withdrew to the bay which we [had] first entered . . .

A German ran up along the parados from the left. Captain Naylor shouted 'That man: shoot him!' But we were too late, for as we raised our rifles, the German dropped his bomb and jumped into the next bay. We were now subjected to bombing from both flanks, and having exhausted our own bombs, we 'replied' with [the] German[s'] 'potato mashers'. We held the bay while the store of bombs lasted ... [It was only after they ran out that] ... we were ... subjected to machine-gun fire and were compelled to retire.[31]

Not all the troops who had made it into German lines were so lucky. It was the awful realization that some of the 139th Brigade's Sherwood Foresters had not managed to escape which may have been behind what happened next. 'We heard them bombing for a considerable time before they were overcome,' Lieutenant Ashford reported later. '[But] it was impossible to reach them.'[32]

A prudent commander would have been prepared for the fact that the attack might not succeed. But possibly influenced by the morale-boosting propaganda which convinced nearly everyone that the attack would be a success, no provision had been made for providing a second veil of smoke should a second assault prove necessary. It was this failure to think ahead that was to prove fatal to the renewed attack ordered by Snow at 9.30 a.m.[33]

That is not to say there were not other contributory factors. The direct cause of the failure by troops lined up for the second attack even to leave their trenches appears to have been an error made by the officer in charge. Brigadier-General Bruce Williams, commander of the 46th Division's right-hand unit (137th Brigade), had delegated its organization to his brigade major, Richard Abadie. The major, who had been told by an officer from the 139th Brigade, the division's left-hand unit, that 139th Brigade would not attack unless smoke bombs were made available, appears to have issued an ambiguous order, or perhaps his clear order was misunderstood.

Abadie appears to have specified that the 137th Brigade units should advance 'smoke or no smoke', repeating the words of his commander, Brigadier-General Williams. Because of what he had been informed about the 139th Brigade's intentions, he realized that might mean the 137th Brigade's battalions would have to advance alone. But this was not made clear to his subordinates. Williams did not stop to think that the officers of the 137th Brigade's battalions in the front line, who had not been privy to his discussions, would wonder how to act if they suddenly discovered that the battalions on their left were not going to advance after all.

That is precisely what transpired. When at 3.30 p.m., the time for the advance, the officer in charge of the 137th Brigade's left-hand battalion was informed that the 139th Brigade's troops had not left their trenches – having further to advance they were supposed to move first – he decided he would ask for clearer instructions rather than ordering his men forward. The delay created a chain reaction. Because the senior officer in charge of the 1st/5th South Staffordshires, the southernmost 137th Brigade battalion, was wounded shortly before zero hour, the decision about whether it should advance was left in the hands of a very inexperienced eighteen-year-old. No one could blame him for not blowing the attack whistle when he saw that the troops on his left had not moved at zero hour.

As a result, the opportunity to make the attack, protected by the smoke and artillery laid on in the southern portion of the 46th Division's sector, was allowed to pass, without the German defences being retested. When he heard about the delay, the 137th Brigade's Brigadier-General Williams called off the advance.[34]

Whether or not that failure 'to close with the enemy', as VII Corps' Lieutenant-General Snow put it, was a blessing in disguise – in that it meant no more men were needlessly sacrificed – is open to question. It was obvious that another attack would have resulted in more lives lost or ruined. Even without the 3.30 p.m. attack, the 46th Division's casualties represented a substantial proportion of those who had gone over the top (approximately 50 per cent in at least two of the four assault battalions, the 1st/5th and 1st/7th Battalions, the Sherwood Foresters, suffering casualties of 415 and 445 men respectively).[35]

However, rather than questioning whether his own approach, and lack of supervision, had played a role in the catastrophe, Lieutenant-General Snow, prior to the convening of the court of inquiry, pinned at least part of the blame on Stuart-Wortley, accusing him of being responsible for the 46th Division's 'lack of offensive spirit'. In a critical letter sent to General Allenby the day after the attack, Snow recommended that the fifty-eight-year-old Stuart-Wortley, who could have been fitter – his legs were weakened by sciatica – should be replaced by 'a younger man'.[36] According to Snow, Stuart-Wortley was 'not of an age, neither has he the constitution, to allow him to be as much amongst his men in the front lines as is necessary to imbue all ranks with confidence and spirit'.[37]

At least some of these accusations, made at a time when Snow may well have felt his own job was on the line, were soon shown to be fallacious.

Evidence presented to the court of inquiry two days later exonerated Stuart-Wortley and his troops concerning the most hurtful charge laid against them: there was nothing to support the implication contained in Snow's remarks that the attack had failed because of the troops' cowardice.

Moreover, Snow, when forwarding the inquiry minutes to Allenby on 10 July, admitted that the 'outstanding' reason for the disaster was not Stuart-Wortley's mistakes, but rather 'the great distance between our trenches and those of the enemy'. His letter continued: 'Had the distance been 150 yards instead of [in some places] 350, the result would probably have been different: . . . We would have been able to keep our troops, after they had reached the enemy's trenches, supplied with grenades and rein-forcements'.[38] A month later, having survived in post, Snow's analysis also embraced the idea that the failure to make enough guns available for counter-battery work was critical.[39]

That was not enough to save Stuart-Wortley. In his 10 July letter, Snow insisted that there really was 'no excuse for the uncut state of the wire not being known', the checking having been 'badly arranged by the Division'. And 'disorganization . . . of the rear waves' should also have been prevented.[40] That being so, there probably was a reason for relieving Stuart-Wortley of his command and sending him home, which Haig duly did on the day of the inquiry.[41]

That said, one is bound to point out that ironically Stuart-Wortley's 'errors' may have saved lives. Because of the delays in the British trenches, fewer of his division's men were exposed to the murderous gunfire in and across No Man's Land than would otherwise have been the case. The 46th Division's casualties for the eight-day period up to and including 1 July were much lower than those of the 56th Division: almost 3,000 (including around 1,250 killed or missing) in the 46th Division, as against almost 5,000 (including around 2,000 killed or missing) in the 56th Division.[42] Yet the result achieved by both divisions was practically identical. Perhaps that only served to highlight the inadvisability of an operation whose principal objective could have been achieved just as effectively by an attack with far fewer casualties: if the British troops had taken all the steps they normally took prior to an imminent attack, but had in fact remained in their trenches, rather than advancing at zero hour, the effect would probably have been the same. The Germans would not have felt able to move their troops away from the sector in case the attack eventually did materialize.

However high feelings ran over the faulty attack plan and the way Stuart-Wortley was treated, Snow does deserve some credit for trying to ensure his troops were not demoralized. It was unfortunate therefore that when, on 4 July, he addressed some of the 56th Division's troops, Snow let slip that he was not in the least disappointed by their failure to hold on to the German lines they had taken. This was firstly because he had never really expected them to take the lines at all, and secondly because the operation was only a feint, designed to help the troops to the south. As should have been anticipated, many of the men he was speaking to were horrified by the admission that the operation, which had killed and maimed so many of their colleagues and friends, did not matter. It just reinforced their perception that the out-of-touch bunglers and butchers in command had little sensitivity when it came to the feelings of the common soldier.[43]

Given that the 600 casualties suffered by the 2nd Guard Reserve Division, the German unit responsible for the Gommecourt sector, were minuscule compared to those suffered by the British, the concluding message circulated by its commander, General Freiherr von Süsskind, was bound to be much sweeter than anything that could have been said by Snow. It included the following peroration: 'Though our losses are regrettable . . . the 1st July resulted in a complete victory for the 2nd Guard Reserve Division . . . The most westerly point of the German line on the Western Front remains . . . in our hands. Our brave troops will now resume our watch, confident that they will act with strength and tenacity to defeat any renewed attack made by the enemy, whenever it might come.'[44]

11: Achilles Heel

Schwaben Redoubt and Thiepval, 1 July 1916

(See maps 2 and 5)

On the heights overlooking the valley of the River Ancre, to the south of Beaumont Hamel and north of the village of Thiepval, lay one of the strongest – and one of the most important – positions defending the German front line: the fortified strongpoint known as Feste Schwaben (Schwaben Redoubt; see map 5).

This enormous complex, which contained trenches, dugouts and machine-gun emplacements, was located near the crest of the slope that ran down to the British front line in the north-eastern fringes of Thiepval Wood. Its frontage, which apparently spanned around 500 yards, enabled its garrison to protect the area behind the German trenches, some 300 yards lower down the slope in front of it. But because it also overlooked Thiepval, the next village to the south, as well as the German artillery positions north of the Ancre, it had a significance stretching far beyond its own front. Anyone approaching these places would have to contend with the guns at Feste Schwaben.

By the same token its location made it, in a way, a weak link in the German defences. The fact that it was set back from the German front line, on a flatter part of the slope than the incline further forward, made it impossible for its garrison to see the British emerging from their trenches directly in front of it. That meant the security of the Redoubt was reliant on the German front-line troops ahead of them, whose own position was vulnerable. Because of the cover given by foliage in Thiepval Wood, it was possible for British troops to approach their own front line without anyone on the German side of No Man's Land being any the wiser.

If the German front line in this sector was breached, and the Redoubt captured, the entire defensive system set up by the 26th Reserve Division would be jeopardized, amounting to a considerable breakthrough for the Allies. The division's regiments manned all three Thiepval sectors: Thiepval North, which included the area in front of and around the Redoubt; Thiepval Central, the area around the remains of Thiepval chateau, its church and the village itself; and Thiepval South, the area to the south of the village that included another lofty strongpoint known as the Leipzig Salient (see map 5). British gunners, once ensconced in the Redoubt, would also be able to see and hamper the operation of German artillery north of the Ancre, calling into question the viability of the positions north of the river that relied on these batteries for protection.

The British unit charged with the important task of taking Feste Schwaben, which was in effect the key to the whole German position north and south of the Ancre valley, was X Corps' 36th Division. It was better known to some as the Ulster Division, all of its battalions coming from the North of Ireland. That was in some respects an advantage. The Irish could be fierce, ruthless fighters, as anyone who had studied the internal conflict within Ireland could have pointed out. Also, although unblooded in battle, these recruits were not exactly novices. Many of the men in the 36th Division had received their first bout of military training within the Ulster Volunteer Force (UVF), an organization set up to resist the British government's desire to devolve powers to the Irish, encapsulated in its much-discussed Home Rule bill. The Protestants of Northern Ireland objected to the devolution of powers to the Irish, fearing that they, as the minority in a united Ireland, would receive unfavourable treatment. The training given to those in the UVF meant that at least some of the recruits had had similar experiences to those they would have had if they had joined the Territorial Army in England.

Many of them shared the same political beliefs, which was an added benefit. Ironically, resistance to the British government's Home Rule policy served to help its armed forces: the common goals pursued by the soldiers who enlisted via the UVF in the Northern Irish battalions of the British Army helped to establish a strong *esprit de corps* in such units. This was further strengthened because, as with the Pals battalions, many of the Irish recruits came from the same area.

The main political row between the British and the Protestants had been set aside for the duration of the war. But there were other difficulties. Many of the Irish troops who were used to the informality prevailing inside the UVF found it hard to accept the constraints imposed upon them by the less flexible British Army. This meant that in at least some of the units discipline was an exception rather than the rule.

The 36th Division's 9th Battalion, the Royal Irish Rifles, had not spent one day in France before a complaint was made about its troops' misbehaviour. Their commander was informed that the bar had been broken into during the boat trip from England to Boulogne, and some alcoholic drinks pilfered. The complaint was only put to one side after one of the officers paid for the drinks that had gone missing.[1] It was an inauspicious beginning to the French campaign. This would not be the last time that these courageous, but unruly, Irishmen would be diminished by their indiscipline and love of liquor.

They had not been long in France before this issue came to a head. Four of the 9th Battalion's NCOs failed to make it to a parade, because they had drunk too much French brandy and were out for the count in a local estaminet. That, combined with some minor looting by soldiers from other battalions within the same brigade, convinced Major-General Oliver Nugent, the 36th Division's fifty-five-year-old commander, that he had to further establish his authority or risk losing control altogether. He could not contemplate going into battle with such an 'undisciplined mob'. At a specially convened meeting, Nugent criticized the officers within the 107th Brigade, one of the three brigades under his command, for allowing their men to behave in a manner that reflected badly on his and their leadership. In an effort to lick the men into shape, and as a kind of punishment, the brigade was temporarily placed under the orders of a regular division, the 4th. It turned out to be a good solution, since this division was to be one of the first to enter the trenches, an area obviously free of the temptations on offer in the villages to the rear.[2]

However, it did not entirely solve the problem. During the period leading up to the 'Big Push', thirty-seven-year-old Major Frank Crozier, the Anglo-Irishman who became commanding officer of the 9th Royal Irish Rifles after the battalion's elderly colonel was struck down with pneumonia, had to deal with the fallout from a series of similar misdemeanours.[3] Given this background, it is perhaps no wonder that this man, described by his batman as a 'heavily built small gent' with a hot temper, decided he had to crack the whip a bit to stay ahead of his wayward charges. That made Crozier unpopular. He quickly acquired a reputation for being something of a martinet, and an exhibitionist. His subordinates did not like the way he sent patrols out into No Man's Land for no apparent purpose other than to show off.[4] And they didn't take kindly to a commander who interfered with their drinking habits.

They were too narrow-minded to realize there was method in his madness. Crozier had himself once been an unbridled drinker, and knew from personal experience the extent to which excessive amounts of alcohol impaired the performance of a soldier.[5] Discipline was clearly essential if a unit was going to be effective in a crisis. With that in mind, he had searched far and wide to find NCOs who, he hoped, could help to stamp out the indiscipline threatening to lessen his battalion's impact on the battlefield.[6] He hired the men he sought, but they never quite achieved what he wanted. Nevertheless, his drive for perfection combined with the rough unorthodoxy of the men serving under him prepared the battalion for what would be asked of it during the events that were to follow.

One of the first problems Crozier encountered revolved around the behaviour of his own orderly. This man was sent to serve with the battalion's front-line troops after getting drunk, only to be caught napping by a German patrol while in a listening post in No Man's Land. The German raiders took him prisoner, along with two other men from the battalion. Afterwards, the battalion's Captain George Gaffikin, a portly schoolmaster, who probably felt he should have made sure they were awake, assuaged his guilt by getting drunk in his turn. While under the influence, he ordered a junior officer to raid the German trenches in an attempt to recover the men who had been captured. The raid was only called off after Crozier found out what was afoot. He told Gaffikin that he would excuse his behaviour, but only if he promised never to drink again while on duty. The promise was duly made and kept.[7]

Another officer in Crozier's battalion had different vices. Although engaged to be married, he had slept with a local French girl and caught gonorrhoea. Crozier arranged for him to be given leave, so that he could seek help from a French doctor, rather than insisting that he should report the venereal disease to the British authorities, which would have led to his fiancée finding out.

But Crozier was less forgiving when the same officer lost his nerve during a German bombardment, and rushed to the rear without troubling to hide his flight from his men. In a later conflict he might have been given the benefit of the doubt, on the assumption he was suffering from shell shock. Crozier, however, branded his action cowardice in the face of the enemy, combined with desertion, and recommended he should be executed. Crozier demanded the same penalty for another ranker, Private James Crozier (no relation), who had deserted on a different occasion. The officer was eventually exonerated after his case was investigated by higher authorities, presumably because there really were mitigating circumstances. But for the private, there was to be no such clemency.

The way Crozier dealt with the desertion of the private, and its consequences, suggests that his judgement had been adversely affected by what he witnessed in the trenches. He had certainly seen more than his fair share of horrific sights. His memoirs are peppered with descriptions of innocent young men being buried, or vapourized in his presence, by the blasts from German high-explosive shells. It is quite likely it was this that sent him over the edge. Although he had decided to be strict with the recalcitrant Irishmen under his command, Crozier had for a time maintained his humanity. The Gaffikin incident showed he had a heart. At that point, he still retained the sense of proportion that tempered the enforcement of discipline with mercy.

The decision to recommend that his men should be executed changed all of that. Afterwards, there was no act too ghastly to contemplate. Crozier really had become as callous as his subordinates alleged.[8] The staging of the execution of the private, and the glee that accompanied its description in his memoirs, suggests that a moral vacuum had replaced his innate kindness. It was the ultimate irony: in the interests of defeating the barbarians, he was barbarically mistreating his own men.

The passages in Crozier's memoirs devoted to the execution reveal that it was carried out in two phases. They start with a description of proceedings on the day before the private was killed:

In the afternoon of [our] . . . first day out [of the line], we parade in [a] hollow square. The prisoner . . . is produced. Cap off, he is marched by the sergeant-major to the centre. The adjutant reads the name, number, charge, finding, sentence and confirmation by Sir Douglas Haig. [The prisoner] . . . stands erect. He does not flinch. Perhaps he is dazed. Who would not be? [He] . . . is marched away by the regimental police, while I, placing myself at the head of the Battalion, [but] behind the band, march back to [our] billets. The drums strike up. The men catch step.

Crozier's account went on to describe how early the next morning the condemned man was carried out into the snow. In an effort to make him insensible to what was about to take place, he had, with Crozier's approval, been given as much alcohol as he could consume during the night. Just in case that was insufficient, he was blindfolded, and trussed up with rope before being suspended from a hook attached to a stake driven into the ground in a back garden. 'He was hooked on like dead meat in a butcher's shop,' Crozier recalled. This occurred in the presence of the entire battalion, which had been lined up by Crozier out of sight but within earshot. Only he could observe both the battalion and the firing squad simultaneously, because he was standing on a mound near the wall, which shielded the bulk of the men from the unfolding events. In the meantime, the men in the firing squad had picked up their guns. They were not told which of the rifles were unloaded. That way, when they squeezed the trigger, they would not know whether they had killed the victim.

Just before the fatal shots were to be fired, Crozier theatrically called the men on the other side of the wall to attention. Then, the officer in charge of the firing squad lowered his handkerchief, and a volley of shots rang out. 'A ragged volley, it is true,' Crozier commented, 'yet a volley [nevertheless]. I see the medical officer examining the victim. He makes a sign. The subaltern strides forward. A single shot rings out. Life is . . . "extinct".' Private James Crozier is no more.[9] 'We march back to breakfast,' Crozier concluded, 'while . . . [some] men pay . . . [a] last tribute at the grave of an unfortunate comrade. This is war.'[10]

Although frustrated by the way his men repeatedly defied him, Crozier was well aware that his Irish troops also had many of the attributes of good soldiers. For example, he admired their physical prowess. His memoirs record how, shortly before the start of the great offensive, he came across some of his young men as they prepared to race across a pool situated to the rear of the front line. He agreed to give them starter's orders. 'They are all standing stark naked on the improvised springboard,' he wrote, savouring the moment:

How wonderful they look. Hard, muscular, fit, strong and supple . . . As they fix their eyes on me, and wait for the word 'go', I realize I am, thanks to circumstances, in the presence not only of boys versed in war, but men already known to women. I think, as I watch them ducking each other in the water, and playing like young seals I have so often seen up North, what a pity they are not married in order that they might plant their seed. Mankind has ordained that they . . . [might] shortly die. Alas, the weaklings and shirkers escape and breed like rabbits, while the strong suffer and are wiped out.[11]

Crozier realized there was a strong probability that they would all be wiped out after he had heard the trenchant views of Colonel Herbert Bernard, commander of the 10th Royal Irish Rifles. The two men had bumped into each other in Aveluy Wood (around half a mile south-west of the southern edge of Thiepval Wood, which contained the 36th Division's front line), while their men were assembling there during the night before the attack. Crozier and Bernard were in charge of two of the four battalions within the 107th Brigade, whose men had been ordered to exploit any breakthrough made by the 108th and 109th Brigades, the 36th Division units ordered to lead the attack on X Corps' front.[12]

The fifty-year-old Bernard, whose battalion was to advance on Crozier's right, was the voice of experience and reason as far as Crozier was concerned. One could see he had been around a long time just by looking at him: 'The Colonel's face is a study in parchment,' Crozier wrote in his autobiography. 'For the Indian sun had tanned and crinkled his skin, as is only possible after thirty-three years in the tropics.'[13]

Crozier's account reveals that while they were talking, Bernard let slip 'he is dubious of the success of the assault on Thiepval by the division on our right (32nd Division). "If that fails," he [Bernard] says, "where are we on the flank?"' They agreed that if, while advancing, they discovered that Thiepval was still in enemy hands, they would disobey the order to direct operations from the safety of their battalion headquarters. Instead, they would meet up in No Man's Land to agree on an alternative plan. And if only one of them made it past the front line, then this survivor was to command both battalions. Their agreement was passed on to the officers in both battalions.[14]

Bernard was too experienced to let anxiety upset his routine, and eventually decided he should get some rest. Crozier, who was too excited, threaded his way between the recumbent bodies of his men, most of whom were sleeping on the ground with their equipment piled up beside them. The majority of those who were awake were staring at the stars through the branches, probably wondering whether it was for the last time. Crozier talked to those he found to be awake, in lowered tones, offering them reassurance and encouragement, or what a student of Shakespeare's *Henry V* might have referred to as a 'little touch of Crozier in the night'.[15]

Crozier's account of his movements before the battle, like Shakespeare's description of King Henry's, is both stirring and tender. It describes how at the northern edge of Thiepval Wood he spied a dim light. 'Put that light out!' he hissed at the transgressor. 'Do you want to give the whole show away?' However, his voice softened when he learned it was a young private who was writing what he thought might be his last letter home. 'All right,'

Crozier said soothingly, when the young man apologized. 'No harm's done.' Then he added 'I expect you'll be all right.' But he took the letter so he could post it just in case.[16]

Crozier was not the only battalion commander within the 36th Division who could not sleep. Lieutenant-Colonel Francis Bowen, the thirty-seven-year-old commander of the 14th Battalion, the Royal Irish Rifles, part of the 109th Brigade, was also wandering about restlessly during the early hours of 1 July. At around 1 a.m., after his troops had filed into their assembly trenches behind the front line, which was situated in the north-eastern fringes of Thiepval Wood, he noted that the guns on both sides all of a sudden stopped firing. 'A lull seemed to settle over all the earth,' Bowen remembered, 'as if it were a mutual tightening up for the great struggle shortly to commence. A water hen called to its mate amidst the [nearby] reedy swamp, and a courageous nightingale made bold to treat us with a song.'[17]

The reining in of the guns gave him the opportunity to tell his company commanders, in a relatively peaceful atmosphere, what time they were going over. His battalion was one of two within the 109th Brigade, which was to follow the brigade's leading pair of battalions over the top. His men were to leave their assembly trenches behind the front line at 7.20 a.m., with a view to being ready to climb over the front-line parapet at zero hour (7.30). By then, troops from the brigade's two leading battalions, each spread out over a 250-yard front, would be lying out in No Man's Land as close as they could 'safely' get to the German front line, but no more than 150 yards away. All four battalions were to be ready to advance as soon as the artillery lifted off the German front trench at 7.30. Then they would advance a second time to take the second line, and then the third, in each case waiting for the wall of fire to lift.

The cessation of artillery fire aimed at the enemy's second and third lines was scheduled to take place at 7.48 and 8.48 a.m. respectively. The 108th Brigade's four battalions would be attempting to comply with a similar advance schedule on the left side of the division's front. The troops of the 107th Brigade, led by Crozier's and Bernard's men, were to follow in the footsteps of the 109th Brigade half an hour after zero hour, their job being to capture the fourth line as soon as the artillery lifted from it at 10.08 a.m.[18]

Lieutenant-Colonel Bowen's war diary records that both German and British soldiers had only a short respite from the deafening roar of the guns.

At around 3 a.m. 'the spell of comparative calm is broken by the enemy shelling the North end of Thiepval Wood,' Bowen recorded. 'The shells were falling all around [us] . . . The candles in the Battalion headquarters kept going out.'

The noise may explain why Bowen's war diary does not even mention one of the bravest acts performed by a man from his battalion that day. The lieutenant-colonel may never have heard the explosion that extinguished this hero's life. During the lead-up to the attack, a box of grenades was dropped onto the ground in one of the assembly trenches in Thiepval Wood. In the process, the pins from two grenades somehow became dislodged. The resulting explosions might have blown up everyone in the vicinity had it not been for the quick reaction of a twenty-year-old bomber called Billie McFadzean. Rather than seeking to save his own skin by attempting to run away, he flung himself in the opposite direction, landing on top of the grenades just before they exploded, thereby sacrificing his own life to save his comrades.

It was an almost unbelievably brave act, which deservedly earned McFadzean a posthumous Victoria Cross, the first to be won during the Battle of the Somme. However, it was to be just one of a series of such awards that were made in relation to the fighting that was to come, including no fewer than six VCs handed out to the soldiers, or their relatives, of X Corps, relating to acts of valour on 1 July 1916.[19]

Faced with similar circumstances, few men would have acted as Billie McFadzean did. Most soldiers found it hard enough steeling themselves to go over the top, even though there was a good chance they would not be killed. All sorts of strategies were employed to trick their minds into quiescence. Private Leslie Bell, a nineteen-year-old farmer's son serving in the 10th Battalion, the Royal Inniskilling Fusiliers, one of the pair of 109th Brigade units that were to be first over the parapet, has described his thoughts as he waited for zero hour:

[It] . . . was a lovely summer's morning. [When] the sun rose in the east, it was a very red colour. Someone said there was blood on the sun when [it] . . . appeared . . . [and] there would be more [spilt] . . . before [it] . . . would go down.

Some of the boys sat in the dawn [light] reading their bible[s]. Others [were] writing letters to their wives and girlfriends with a feeling that it would be the last they would ever write. Others were cleaning their rifles and bayonets, knowing that it was their only friend [that mattered once the attack started].

It is hard to know what the men's feelings were . . . Everyone was in a sort of daze . . . with the heavy gunfire. I myself . . . sad[ly] thought of home. At this . . . time, it would be milking time. The cows would be coming in from the meadows. And everything would be lovely and peaceful in . . . [our] village.[20]

His daydream was eventually interrupted. At 7.15 a.m. precisely the vanguard of his battalion climbed out of their trenches and, after emerging from the shelter provided by the Thiepval Wood trees, began the long climb up the incline leading towards the enemy. But this was just the first stage of the attack. As specified in his battalion's orders, the tramp up the hill was temporarily interrupted when they were within striking distance of the enemy positions (100 yards). At that point, Bell and his comrades obediently lay down and waited.

At first there was no reaction from the Germans. Most of them were holed up in their dugouts, listening for the sentries' cry that would tell them the artillery had lifted. They were still taking refuge there when, at 7.30 a.m., the buglers of the Royal Inniskilling Fusiliers in the British front line sounded the regimental call, followed by the advance, and simultaneously company and platoon leaders blew their whistles.[21] The war diarist of the 10th Royal Inniskilling Fusiliers was amazed by what happened next: 'Lines of men jumped up, and advanced at a steady march towards the enemy trenches. The spectacle of these lines of men moving forward with rifle[s] sloped, and the morning sun glinting on their fixed bayonets, keeping their alignment and distance as well as if on a ceremonial parade, unfaltering, unwavering, was not only impressive. It was extraordinary!'[22]

The simultaneous advance by the 9th Battalion, the Royal Inniskilling Fusiliers, on the right of the 10th Battalion, was watched by their commanding officer Lieutenant-Colonel Ambrose Ricardo, and his description of what he observed, laid out below, has become one of the most quoted passages about these first heart-stopping moments:

I stood on the parapet between the centre exits to wish them luck . . . They got going without delay. No fuss, no shouting, no running, everything solid and thorough, just like the men themselves. Here and there a boy would wave his hand to me as I shouted . . . to them through my megaphone. And all had . . . cheery face[s].

Most were carrying loads. Fancy advancing against heavy fire with a big roll of barbed wire on your shoulder![23]

The entry made by Lieutenant-Colonel Bowen in the war diary of the 14th
Royal Irish Rifles shows that he was equally impressed, at least initially:

The Brigade moved off as if on parade. Nothing finer in the way of an advance has
ever been seen . . . Alas, no sooner were [the 14th Royal Irish Rifles] . . . clear of
our own wire, [than] . . . the slow tat tat of the Hun machine guns from Thiepval
village and Beaumont Hamel caught the advance under a deadly cross fire.[24]

The following extract from the account by John Kennedy Hope, a private
in Bowen's battalion, underlines the extent to which the gunfire from his
unit's right flank transformed what minutes before had been the relatively
safe act of getting out of the trench into what can only be described as a
dicing with death:

A[n] . . . Inniskilling lying at the top [of the parapet] has got a bullet through his
steel hat. He rolls over into the trenches at my feet. He is an awful sight. His brain
is oozing out of the side of his head, and he is calling for his pal: . . . 'Billy Gray,
Billy Gray will you not come to me?' . . . He is the servant of an officer who is
lying in the [same] trench with a fractured thigh, and won't let anyone touch
him . . . He is bleeding badly . . . In a short time all is quiet. They die together.[25]

Not surprisingly, it was the troops of the 9th Royal Inniskilling Fusiliers,
advancing on the right, who were most vulnerable to the fire coming from
Thiepval. However, at least some of the men approaching the German
front line could consider themselves lucky. Whether due to what is often
referred to as the luck of the Irish or to expert shooting, the German
machine guns in and in front of the Schwaben Redoubt were hit by British
artillery, and most of their crews killed.[26] As a result, the Irishmen who
advanced in this sector of the front were spared having to advance through
the kind of murderous machine-gun fire that had been so devastating at the
northern end of the British attack. Their passage was eased still further by
the angle of the slope in front of this portion of the German front line: a
freakish rise in the ground made No Man's Land in front of it dead ground,
which could not be seen from the German trenches.[27]

Helped by this double dose of good fortune, large numbers of Irishmen
made it into the first pair of German trenches (both of which were designated as trench system 'A' on Ulster Division maps) before the garrison
could react. Then they moved on to the trench designated by the Ulster

Division as trench 'B', and even on to trench 'C' (these trench lines are marked on map 5).[28] In the process many of the German troops, who had constituted the garrison in the Schwaben Redoubt (part of trench 'B'), were either wounded, killed or taken prisoner.[29]

During this advance through the German lines only snapshots of what took place have been recorded. The account written by Hugh Stewart, a private in the 11th Battalion, the Royal Irish Rifles, the right-hand unit of the 36th Division's left-hand brigade (108th Brigade), has described how his group of attackers managed to prosper, even after their officer was killed by a shell. In this case it was their sergeant who took the initiative once they reached the first German trench, even though he had been wounded on the way over: 'The first bomb he threw [took] the door off a deep dugout. [He] flung . . . the next two . . . inside. He must have killed every German in it. We left him sitting just below the parapet with a grenade in each hand, ready for the next live German that came along.'[30]

Stewart went on to describe a more unconventional method of terror-izing the Germans whom they encountered in their trenches:

One soldier . . . made himself a special weapon . . . It was about half the length of a pick shaft, and on one end, he screwed a pear-shaped lump of cast iron. On the other, [there] was a leather thong which he kept tied around his waist. He used to parry a bayonet thrust with the rifle, and then swing this lump of cast iron upwards. No matter where it hit a man, it broke bones. He'd smash a man's wrist or hand. Then, when the rifle flew from the man's hands, he'd shoot him.[31]

Stewart was also looking quite fearsome as he and his comrades worked their way up the German communication trenches, if his own account is to be believed. 'I had a bayonet in one hand, and a revolver in the other,' he recalled. 'I used to shoe horses before I joined up, and had powerful . . . wrists . . . It was not a great hardship for me to fire one of them big heavy revolvers. They had a kick like a horse, but if you hit a man with a bullet from one of them, he gave no more trouble.'

However, it was only in the third trench that they encountered serious opposition. 'It was here that the real fighting started,' Stewart remembered. 'I had never killed a man with a bayonet before, and it sent shivers up and down my spine many's a night afterwards just thinking about it. It must have taken our lot about a quarter of an hour to clear a hundred yards or so of the trench . . . We took no prisoners . . . We cleared the trenches right down to the Mouquet Switch.'[32] (See map 5.)

In the meantime, Major Crozier had been preparing the 9th Royal Irish Rifles for their advance. The first danger encountered was on the causeways that bridged the portion of the River Ancre, running from north to south, separating Authuille Wood from Thiepval Wood. It would only have taken a group of well-directed shells, while the troops were on or near this crossing point, for the whole battalion to have been annihilated. Fortunately for Crozier and his men, their progress was masked by a mist, which rose up from the marshland around the river. The fact that British planes had absolute air supremacy over the whole Somme front gave them another layer of protection. Nevertheless, there were two near misses, as a brace of enemy shells splashed into the water just 20 yards away from where they were walking.

Their next ordeal involved waiting for the time when they were supposed to advance to the front line. It was an unnerving experience. Provoked first by the British shelling, and subsequently by the advance at 7.30 a.m., the German gunners had all guns blazing. One of their principal targets appears to have been to the rear of the British front line, just where Crozier and his men were resting. The only reason why the battalion of the 9th Royal Irish Rifles was not decimated was because its troops were sheltering behind a high bank, beside a track in Thiepval Wood known as Speyside. That made them 'immune' from the effects of the exploding shells, even though the missiles whizzing past overhead were only missing them 'by inches'. Their only consolation was that this level of fear was what many Germans in front-line dugouts had been forced to put up with for the previous seven days.

To buoy up their spirits, the men attempted to sing a song, but that was drowned out by the noise of the exploding shells. Terrorized by the German gunners, Crozier's whistle, the signal for the battalion to advance through Thiepval Wood to the front line, must in many ways have come as a blessed relief.

However, as Crozier confessed in his memoirs, while advancing he was stopped in his tracks by a horrific sight:

Through a gap in the trees . . . I see rows upon rows of British soldiers lying dead, dying and wounded in No Man's Land (in the area to the south attacked by the 32nd Division). Here and there, I see an officer urging on his followers.

Occasionally I see the[ir] hands thrown up, and then a body flop[ping] to the ground . . . [Shortly afterwards], I look southward from a different angle, and perceive heaped up masses of British corpses, suspended on the German wire in front of the Thiepval stronghold . . . The bursting shells and smoke make visibility poor . . . [But it is] enough to convince me [that] Thiepval is still held . . . Bernard was right.[33]

Crozier's account does not disclose how far he could see, nor for how long he looked. If he had been looking as far as the Thiepval South sector, and if he had watched for long enough, he might have seen the first episodes of a tragedy unfolding that developed into a veritable holocaust. The 17th Battalion, the Highland Light Infantry, supported by half of the 2nd Battalion, the King's Own Yorkshire Light Infantry, from the 32nd Division's right-hand brigade (the 97th Brigade), had managed to secure a foothold in the Leipzig Salient, the German strongpoint that jutted out towards the British line at Thiepval South's most southerly point (see map 5). However, any success that the battalion claimed was relatively insignificant, given that the soldiers had not been able to progress further than the German support line.[34]

That might not have mattered, if all the support troops needed to make a breakthrough could have followed. Unfortunately for the attackers, the Scottish troops' success had been achieved in completely different circumstances to those prevailing when the support troops attempted to cross No Man's Land. The 17th Highland Light Infantry troops, and those in the 2nd Battalion, the King's Own Yorkshire Light Infantry, who had followed closely in their wake, had crossed by creeping up to within 40 yards of the German front line under the protection of the artillery umbrella, at a time when most German machine-gunners were cowering in their dugouts. Once the British artillery lifted, and the German defenders were free to man their positions, they were able to make the approaches to the Salient more or less impassable.

That is certainly how it looked to the British troops who, after the Highland Light Infantry's initial incursion, sought to approach the Leipzig Salient bridgehead from the south-west. The German defenders gave no quarter to the troops within the 97th Brigade's 11th Battalion, the Border Regiment, who advanced from assembly trenches north of Authuille Wood at 8 a.m. Although some made it through the gunfire to join the Highland Light Infantry in the Salient, most were mowed down by machine-gun fire coming from their right, the portion of the German line not being attacked. Within a matter of minutes, almost 550 men from the Border Regiment were laid out behind the British front line and in No Man's Land.[35]

As if that was not bad enough, misadventure was turned into massacre by the rash decision not to provide a mechanism for halting the follow-up support units if the Border Regiment met stiff opposition. Even after the skittling over of so many young men from this regiment, there was no one to stop the 14th Brigade's 1st Battalion, the Dorsetshire Regiment, advancing from the same place.

The resulting mayhem, as the Dorsets emerged from the trees on the northern edge of Authuille Wood, still 100 yards behind the British front line, was described by their phlegmatic battalion war diarist thus: 'By the time half the Battalion had left the Wood, the end of Dumbarton Track (the track leading to the north of the Wood), and the ground up to our front line trench, was covered with our killed and wounded. Yet the men continued to jump up and advance over their fallen comrades as the word to go was given.' Only sixty-six of the Dorsets made it to the British front line, and only twenty-five of those were able to cross over to the German side of No Man's Land, to reinforce the Scottish troops and those from Yorkshire holding out there, a tiny return given the number in the battalion.[36] This battalion also ended up with a casualty count in excess of 500 men.[37]

The conveyor belt of battalions next saw the 14th Brigade's 19th Lancashire Fusiliers (3rd Salford Pals) advance from the Authuille Wood foliage, an act that ensured there would be more killing and maiming on the way to the British front line. Once again, as with the previous battalions, only a lucky few reached the bridgehead (the 19th Lancashire Fusiliers suffered over 275 casualties on 1 July).[38] The advance was only at long last called to a halt when an officer from the Lancashire Fusiliers took the initiative. He sent back a messenger to say that the British front-line position was too full of troops to house any more.[39]

At least those advancing into the Thiepval South sector had a bridgehead to show for all the casualties they had suffered. Those 32nd Division troops nearest to Lieutenant-Colonel Crozier and his battalion, as they advanced through Thiepval Wood – in the 96th Brigade, and on the 97th Brigade's left wing (see map 5) – fell without permanently capturing any terrain. Worse than that, the commander of X Corps, Lieutenant-General Sir Thomas Morland, became so fixated on misleading reports that the nearest battalion of all, the 15th Battalion, the Lancashire Fusiliers (1st Salford Pals), had managed to break through the German defences and reach the eastern edge of Thiepval village, that he deprived the 36th Division of the reinforcements which could have made a real difference (see Chapter 12, p. 153).

It has been hard to find any detailed witness statements describing the movements of the two leading assault battalions of the 96th Brigade, as they attempted to take Thiepval village. Instead, historians have had to fall back on impressionistic traces of their experiences in the surviving war diaries. There is for instance the war diarist of the 16th Battalion, the Northumberland Fusiliers (the Newcastle Commercials, 96th Brigade's right-hand assault battalion), who described how the German defenders taunted the attackers by climbing onto their parapets and waving at them to come nearer, so that they could be mowed down more easily.[40] Then there is the incident involving Alfred Lee Wood, a thirty-year-old captain in the 15th Lancashire Fusiliers, whose last words to one of his men on receiving a nasty gash on his head, and on being offered the chance to retire, were: 'No, I will get that machine-gunner.'[41] Wood did not succeed, although it took three shots to the head to fell him. He was one of the battalion's many casualties, which were approaching 475 on 1 July.[42]

Last, but not least, there is the letter that a captain in the 96th Brigade's follow-up battalion, the 16th Battalion, the Lancashire Fusiliers (2nd Salford Pals), wrote to the family of one of the missing private soldiers after the action. The captain stated that if he had been one of those left lying on the battlefield, he might well have lost his life when some of the more bloodthirsty Germans 'riddled . . . [those lying in No Man's Land] with bullets', which is what they did during the afternoon of 1 July.[43]

However, perhaps the best barometer of the terror that must surely have gripped the hearts of many, if not all, of the 96th Brigade soldiers who were ordered to attack Thiepval that day is the following account by 2nd Lieutenant Charles Marriot of the 16th Lancashire Fusiliers. At around 8 a.m. he was told he must clamber up the steepish slope from the eastern edge of Thiepval Wood to the stronghold known as Thiepval Fort, some 700 yards away up the hill. Afterwards he recalled what he witnessed, and felt, as he went on his way:

I . . . started to lead [my men] up a communication trench [behind our front line] . . . called Hamilton Avenue, or rather what was left of it. Gerry was plastering the whole sector with H. E. and already, it was less a trench than [a line of] shell holes and hummocks. Our scrambles over these were speeded [up] by the German machine-gunners, [up on the heights] above . . . [us].

[We saw some] gruesome sights as we struggled up to the front line. [I saw] hands, feet and shin bones [which] were protruding from the raw earth, stinking of high explosive. [I also saw] a smallish soldier, sitting in a shell hole, elbows on knees, a sandbag over his shoulders. I lifted it to see whether he [was] . . . alive, and [was shocked to find] he had no head. Further on, [I came across] a corporal, lying doubled up [on the ground]. Just in case anything could be done for him, I bent down to raise him a little, [only to find] his head was . . . [only] attached [to the rest of his body] by a bit of skin.

[When we reached the front trench, we found] it was so blown up and gouged by H. E., that only [sections] . . . of it remained . . . I was told that a badly wounded officer was lying in it, about twenty yards [away] . . . [To get to him, I had to climb] over a great blown-in block [of earth, with] bullets whizzing [past me, which sounded] like [buzzing] wasps . . . [He was] a tall . . . lieutenant, a Northumberland Fusilier, [who had been] shot through both knees, one wrist and one shoulder. The moment he [had] got up onto the parapet, the impact of the bullets [hitting him] had flung him backwards into the trench. I tried to bandage him up, and sent . . . for stretcher-bearers . . . [Then] I had to leave him . . .

We found others like him, shot straight back off the parapet. [A bullet had] drilled through the forehead of one [of them], a sergeant, [and] his brains [had] spread like hair over the back of his neck.

At last we were ready, and I was bracing myself . . . [to make] the hideous decision to go over the top . . . No Man's Land was covered with bodies, the whole of the 16th Northumberland Fusiliers seemed to be lying out there – when a sweating runner [arrived] with a message from the CO to stay put. My God, what a moment! . . . [The message meant] we were saved, in the nick of time.[44]

No wonder Lieutenant Marriot was relieved. By all accounts, Thiepval was unassailable that morning. As the British Official History put it, 'it was said, with some truth, that only bullet-proof soldiers could have taken Thiepval on this day'.[45]

12: An Opportunity Missed

Schwaben Redoubt and Thiepval, 1 July 1916

(See maps 2, 4 and 5)

As Lieutenant-Colonel Frank Crozier and his 9th Royal Irish Rifles came within sight of the British front line on the north-east fringes of Thiepval Wood, he realized that his battalion would suffer the same fate as those unfortunate men he had seen falling to the south (see Chapter 11, p. 144), unless something was done to neutralize the German artillery. The intensity of the shelling had transformed what was supposed to be a leisurely stroll over to the captured trenches into a suicide mission. But then a 'miracle' happened. As if by magic, the shelling abruptly ceased. Crozier noted his reaction in his autobiography:

Now's the chance, I think to myself. They must quicken pace and . . . get . . . across to the sunken road (around 100 yards from the British front line – see map 5), disengaging from each other, company by company.

I stand still and erect in the open, while each company passes. To each company commander, I give the amended order . . . George Gaffikin comes [past] . . . waving an orange handkerchief.

'Good-bye sir. Good luck!' he shouts to me en passant. 'Tell them I died a teetotaller. Put it on the stone if you find me.'

'Good luck George,' I say. 'But don't talk rot. Anyhow, you played the game!'

It was then, at this critical moment, that all the discipline and training imposed by Crozier came to fruition. Officers and men alike followed his barked-out instructions to the letter. They rapidly deployed in the sunken road so that when the German artillery started up again, targeting the edge of Thiepval Wood, most of the battalion were already out of harm's way.

But where were Colonel Bernard and his men of the 10th Royal Irish Rifles, who were supposed to be on Crozier's right? Crozier strode back into the interior of Thiepval Wood to find out, only to discover that the colonel had been killed by a shell during the advance. Bernard's men, who had congregated 300 yards behind the front line, were unwilling to move without orders from higher authority. That response incensed Crozier. He pulled out his revolver and threatened to shoot any man who refused to step forward. 'The words worked wonders,' Crozier reported later. The men he was threatening moved forward, and took their place in the sunken road alongside Crozier's battalion.[1]

The fact that the road was in a dip did not mean they were safe. Far from it. The sunken road was another prime target for the German artillery. Moreover, the German gunners were supported by those soldiers to the south who no longer had any attacks to ward off on their own front. The machine-gunners in and to the north of Thiepval, who had dispatched the front runners of the 32nd Division, only had to swivel round to their right if they wished to aim at the sunken road as well. That explains why it quickly became necessary for the men of the 9th and 10th Royal Irish Rifles sheltering in the sunken road to advance on the next stage of their journey. It was either that or risk being ripped to shreds.[2]

According to Crozier's servant, David Starrett:

Crozier doubled [over] to the sunken road . . . [On the way], he shouted: . . . 'Bernard has been killed!' . . . We reached our own men. They had taken what cover the place afforded. Crozier [had also] rallied what was left of the Tenth . . . [Then] he yelled: 'Sound the advance! Sound the advance, damn you!' The bugler's lips were dry. He had been wounded. His lungs were gone. A second later, he fell dead at [Crozier's] . . . feet. Hine cut the cord, and gave the bugle to someone who could play. [As he did so], Crozier was signalling his men on. He . . . fell into holes. His clothing was torn by bullets, but he himself was all right. Moving about as if on the parade ground, he again and again rallied his men.[3]

They advanced shortly after 8 a.m.[4] They were closely followed by the 107th Brigade's support unit, the 8th Battalion, the Royal Irish Rifles, or at least those of them who were not shot before they had cleared the parapet. The 8th Battalion's Tommy Ervine has described how he was queuing up for his turn to go over the top when one of the men climbing out in front of him stumbled back into the trench. He was just about to ask what was wrong when the man opened his mouth and blood came gushing out in spurts, each expulsion thrown up by another beat of his heart. The removal of his helmet explained why. He had a catastrophic head wound. There was nothing that could be done to stop him bleeding to death.[5]

Notwithstanding this and other losses, a number of soldiers from the 107th Brigade's battalions successfully crossed over into the previously captured German lines. By 10 a.m. at least some of the brigade's troops were ready to advance towards the trench referred to as 'D' on the Ulster Division maps (see map 5), but which the Germans would have called their second position. Shortly afterwards, about thirty-five of Crozier's men thrust forward into it, despite stiff opposition. They were reinforced there at about 11 a.m. by some men from the 8th Royal Irish Rifles.[6]

It is possible that some soldiers from these three units frightened the German artillery observers located in trench D's Feste Staufen (Stuff Redoubt), another strongpoint bridging the gap between Thiepval and Grandcourt to its north (see map 2). At any rate, some historians have quoted from the following account by Unteroffizier Felix Kircher of the 26th Reserve Field Artillery Regiment (without stating where they encountered it). Kircher claimed he was alarmed by the British vanguard's progress:

Suddenly . . . an observer shouted down the dugout steps in an amazed voice: 'Tommy is here. Come up!' We rushed up, and saw a lot of khaki-clothed men with flat steel helmets. They were the first Englishmen we had seen so near. [They were] running up and down in front of our barbed wire, searching for a breach . . . Most of them were young boys, about 20 years old, just like us.

We were in a desperate position. Being artillery observers, we had no weapons, and no ammunition. Each moment we expected a raid [backed] with hand grenades.

That is probably what would have transpired, had it not been for the barrage laid down by the German artillery, which scattered the British soldiers before they could act. 'We saw corpses whirling through the air,' Kircher reported. Then, as he watched, 'the survivors stormed back down the hill'.[7]

If Kircher's account is accurate, he had witnessed one of the critical phases of X Corps' attack. Even if not, what he described was certainly consistent with other testimony. The historian of the 8th Bavarian Reserve Regiment, when describing the German countermeasures, recorded that the artillery group Berta, whose guns were located behind the German second line, which ran from Feste Staufen to Grandcourt, burned all its most secret documents in a bid to keep them out of enemy hands.[8] And when Oberstleutnant Bram, commander of the 8th Bavarian Reserve Regiment, who had been ordered to mastermind the counter-attack, arrived at Feste Staufen at about 1 p.m., the sight of British soldiers patrolling near the wire in front of this line convinced him that he must hurry.[9]

It is almost painful to compare the snail-like pace of the British response to the opportunity that had opened up before them with the German reaction. Nobody could say that the British commanders were not given ample time to exploit their breakthrough. They were competing against German defenders who could hardly be said to have moved rapidly. This was partly because British artillery, guided by British planes with almost complete air supremacy, had created havoc within the German command structure.

The shelling had not only forced the local brigade commander, Lieutenant-General Friedrich von Auwärter of the 52nd Reserve Brigade, to shift his battle headquarters from Feste Zollern (Zollern Redoubt), yet another strongpoint in the German second line, to Courcelette. It had also cut telephone lines connecting the telephone exchange at Courcelette with other command posts in the German second line, one of the brigade's means of staying abreast of what was happening in the front line. It was 8.35 a.m. before Auwärter first heard that the Schwaben Redoubt's defences had been penetrated. Moreover, he only heard then after reading a message to that effect from the 26th Reserve Division, whom he was supposed to be keeping informed.[10]

Fifteen minutes later Auwärter learned that the enemy had reached Hansa Stellung (the name given to the portion of the trench, referred to as 'C' on the Ulster Division maps, that ran up to the southern bank of the Ancre), and the so-called artillery hollow, west of Grandcourt (see map 5).[11] Another hour had almost elapsed before he received an order from his divisional commander, Lieutenant-General Baron von Soden, instructing him to counter-attack. He was to act immediately using the troops already stationed in the German second position, even though that meant Auwärter would have to manage without assistance from one of the battalions being sent to help him.[12]

However, that was easier said than done. It was 10.20 a.m. before a message from Auwärter informed Bram that he was to lead the counter-attack with his 8th Bavarian Reserve Regiment. Yet more precious minutes then slipped past because Bram did not have a car. He had to walk all the way from Pys to Courcelette (around two miles as the crow flies) so that he could be briefed by Auwärter. They met at 11.15 a.m., after which there was another pause as Bram then had to walk on to Feste Staufen (another two miles as the crow flies), his command post for the attack. He arrived there at 1 p.m. It then took him an additional two hours to make the preparations for the counter-attack.

The right-hand group under his command was to attack Hansa Stellung, and the central group was to advance from Feste Staufen towards the Schwaben Redoubt. The third group could participate when it finally arrived.[13]

At least Bram was focusing on the correct objective. That was more than could be said for the man whose troops he was to come up against. Lieutenant-General Sir Thomas Morland, X Corps' fifty-year-old commander, could not get to grips with what was going on away from the 'observation tree' near Englebelmer, where he was attempting to track the events as they were unfolding through what he referred to in his diary as a 'big telescope'.[14]

Morland had started the day well enough. By 8.15 a.m. he had learned that troops from both of his attacking divisions had entered the German front line. Within half an hour of hearing this welcome news, he had instructed Major-General Edward Perceval, commander of the 49th Division, X Corps' reserve unit, to send a brigade to Thiepval Wood to await developments. The idea was that it would then be ready to support either the 36th or 32nd Division, depending on which had the greater need.[15]

However, when shortly afterwards Morland had the chance to use the 49th Division to help exploit the partial breakthrough made by the 36th Division's 108th and 109th Brigades, he not only baulked at committing his reserve troops so early in the battle, but he also attempted to countermand the standing order that required the 107th Brigade's assault troops to attack the German second position as soon as the artillery was lifted off it. It was an abrupt volte-face, given that just three-quarters of an hour earlier he had told Major-General Oliver Nugent, commander of the 36th (Ulster) Division, that the 107th Brigade's attack should go ahead in spite of the German gunfire coming from both flanks.[16] Such indecision was to be one of the hallmarks of Lieutenant-General Morland's leadership that day.

This first manifestation of a vacillating temperament did not, as it turned out, make a difference. The attack by the 107th Brigade proceeded anyway because the gunfire across No Man's Land meant it was impossible for runners carrying Morland's halt order to cross it in time.[17] Far more significant was his failure to analyse the situation logically, and to prioritize what was really important. It was to transform one of the most promising of all the British advances on 1 July into one of that day's many heroic defeats.

This is not to say that Morland had an easy task when it came to selecting his reserves strategy. He could have been criticized whichever way he turned. The argument in favour of backing the 32nd rather than the 36th Division was clear enough: if the reserves had been used to support the troops from the 36th Division's 107th Brigade, German gunfire from the flanks might have pinned them down, resulting in severe casualties for no gain. That risk would not have to be run if, before the 36th Division's renewed assault on the German second position, the reserves were used successfully to help the 32nd Division's 96th Brigade capture Thiepval, or at least the area to the north of the village, from where some of the worst enemy gunfire emanated.

Inconveniently for Morland, the argument for giving the reserves to the 36th Division was equally persuasive. When it came to contrasting the viability of his divisions' thrusts, it was clear that the 36th Division's assault was the stronger of the two. There was no question that the Irish troops had penetrated deep inside the German lines. Shortly before 10.30 a.m. X Corps received the 36th Division's message confirming that its troops were digging themselves in on the 'C' line.[18] If any further concrete proof was required, Morland only had to refer to the 10.30 a.m. situation report mentioned in X Corps' war diary, which told him that 500 German prisoners had already been passed back through the 36th Division's front line to the rear.[19]

The certainty that the 36th Division had made a partial breakthrough could be contrasted with the uncertainty concerning the depth of the 32nd Division's advance north of Thiepval. Even the 'excellent' image of the front as seen through Morland's large telescope could not tell him how successful the 32nd Division's thrust had been.[20] The most conclusive evidence that reached him suggested that not much had been achieved. The fact that Nugent had reported shortly after 8.30 a.m. that his 36th Division troops were being picked off by the 'deadly' machine-gun fire coming from Thiepval, and in particular from its chateau, on his troops' right, should have told Morland that the impact of the 32nd Division's advance towards and around the north of the village had not been great.[21]

The only evidence contradicting that conclusion was vague to say the least. It came in the form of two reports from artillery observers, which merely stated that some British troops had been spotted east of Thiepval.[22] Both of these reports were in the 32nd Division's hands before 11 a.m. Given that was all Morland had to go on during the morning and early afternoon of 1 July, it was no wonder that the only comments by X Corps' war diarist about the situation in the village were that it was 'not clear' and 'obscure'.[23]

Such an analysis might have prompted a more aggressive commander to give his limited reserves to the 36th Division, the more successful of the two claimants. That would certainly have appealed to the commander of the 32nd Division, Major-General Rycroft. When he was visited by Perceval at 12.30 p.m., Rycroft recommended that course of action, in the hope it would enable Thiepval to be assaulted from the north via the Mouquet Switch trench or the German second position (see map 5).[24]

But Morland was evidently no risk taker. Perhaps that was just part of his character. Or perhaps a more adventurist streak in his nature was reined in following the series of personal tragedies that had affected his life long before Germany even thought about invading France and Belgium. He had lost both his parents before he was six years old, making him an orphan, and then his thirty-three-year-old wife died in 1901, leaving him to care for their two young daughters.[25]

There is no proof that Morland consciously allowed these sharp knocks to affect the decisions he later made as a soldier, but it would have been surprising if they had not had some unacknowledged psychological effect. A general who has endured the grief brought on by such tragedies might well be more risk averse when it came to putting his men's lives on the line than one who has never suffered in this way.

Whether or not that is the key to understanding what ensued, Morland adopted a safety-first strategy: instead of taking what must have appeared at the time to be the more risky approach – which would have involved decisively handing over to Major-General Nugent all of 146th Brigade, the 49th Division unit he had sent to Thiepval Wood, with a view to exploiting the opportunity that had presented itself – Morland dithered. That ended up helping no one.

For the first three hours after X Corps was informed that the 36th Division's troops were digging in on the 'C' line, Morland indecisively sat on the fence and made no decisions relating to his reserves.[26] Then, after learning of the failure of the 32nd Division's follow-up attack on Thiepval at 1.50 a.m. – which had seen two companies of 16th Lancashire Fusiliers and 2nd Royal Inniskilling Fusiliers, both of the 96th Brigade, swatted away by the German gunners as easily as they had brushed aside the first attack by that brigade – he gave the 32nd Division first call on the majority of his 49th Division reserves. He was hoping that the 32nd Division's immediate success would benefit the 36th Division later.[27]

However logical such a strategy may have looked at the time to

Morland, it turned out to be hopelessly misguided. Shortly after 2.30 p.m.,
when Oberstleutnant Bram was already marshalling his forces for the
counter-attack towards Schwaben Redoubt, Morland was instructing
Major-General Perceval, commander of the 49th Division, that his 146th
Brigade must advance in the opposite direction to where it was really
needed: towards Thiepval.[28] The 36th Division had to make do with a
token battalion from the 148th Brigade, 146th Brigade's sister unit within
the 49th Division.[29]

Then, when the 146th Brigade's 4 p.m. attack towards Thiepval
was aborted after the leading troops were, predictably, scythed down by
German machine guns, Morland insisted that two of the 148th Brigade's
other battalions should be set aside to support the 32nd Division's 96th
Brigade in case they were needed for yet another advance on the same
target.[30]

Only after Morland learned during the middle of the afternoon that the
36th Division's troops were being forced to retreat did he abruptly change
tack, attempting to divide the available reinforcements between the two
attacking divisions more equitably. Unfortunately for him, by that stage
most of the support troops had already been committed to other parts of the
battlefield, making his attempt to rectify the situation next to impossible.

Morland's task was complicated by his inability to keep track of where
his reserves were located, as they were sent first to one side of the battlefield
and then to the other. As a result he was reduced to giving incredibly vague
orders, such as the one issued at 6.18 p.m., which can be boiled down as follows: if the 146th Brigade has a unit in the right position, let it make the
next attack on Thiepval. If not, then let 148th Brigade make the attack.[31]

In these circumstances it is not surprising to discover that the battalions on
the receiving end of all the orders and counter-orders flying around behind the
British front line were bemused — and delayed — by what they received. The
officers of one battalion, the 146th Brigade's 1st/7th West Yorkshire Regiment,
which had within the space of a couple of hours been ordered to participate in
two separate actions — at 4 p.m. attack Thiepval; afterwards, advance to the
edge of Thiepval Wood to hold the front line opposite Schwaben Redoubt —
were perplexed when they received yet another counter-order requiring them
to help out in Schwaben Redoubt itself.

It was given to these officers by the commanding officer of a 36th Division unit whom they happened to pass in Thiepval Wood on the way to
complying with the previous command. They would willingly have

complied with this counter-order immediately, had it not contradicted the previous command of their own brigadier. They remained in the dark until they had touched base with the headquarters of yet another 36th Division battalion, which had been copied in on an order stating that two 146th Brigade battalions were being ordered to reinforce the troops holding Schwaben Redoubt. Only then, at around 7.30 p.m., more than three hours after Morland's original order putting the brigade at the 36th Division's disposal, and more than eight hours after the division really needed support, were the brigade's troops finally released so that they could reinforce the British bridgehead.[32]

By that time, the situation in the vicinity of Schwaben Redoubt had completely changed. Whether or not Felix Kircher, the German artillery observer, had seen men belonging to the 8th or 9th Royal Irish Rifles, the men from these units were unable to remain for long in the captured portion of the German second position, such was the intensity of the fire coming from both flanks.

The firing from Beaucourt Redoubt, north of the River Ancre (see map 5), was another nail in the coffin for the attack to the south of the river. It suggested that the two 108th Brigade battalions which had advanced into German lines north of the Ancre, and which it was hoped would protect the right wing of the 29th Division as its troops moved past the Redoubt, had in the end been overcome.[33] That freed up another strongpoint, this time on the 36th Division's northern flank, from which German gunners could enfilade the stalled attackers.

The crucial moment, when a correct decision by Morland might have transformed the whole battle in the British troops' favour, was reached at around 11.30 a.m. It was about this time that the Irish survivors, who had reached the second German line (trench D) south of the Ancre were forced to retire to trenches B and C.[34] For the first time during the morning, the British attackers in the Schwaben Redoubt sector were on the back foot.

It was the British failure to maintain the momentum forwards that gave the Germans time and space to marshal their counter-attack. While Morland was spurning the chance to exploit the 107th Brigade's success, the commanders of the German 26th Reserve Division, the 52nd Reserve Brigade and the Bavarian 8th Reserve Regiment, slowly but surely put the necessary countermeasures in place. The first counter-attacks began shortly after 3 p.m. At first the German troops struggled to pierce the British advanced line, which curled around the eastern side of Schwaben Redoubt, but gradually, as more and more German forces were deployed, the 36th Division troops were pushed back. It was not so very different to what had happened on the southern side of Gommecourt (see Chapter 10, pp. 120–21).

The torment experienced by the Irish soldiers who had advanced to and in some cases beyond the German C line, only to be forced to retire, has been highlighted in some of the witness statements made by officers who, in the process, were captured. In one such report, Joseph Shannon, a twenty-five-year-old lieutenant in the 10th Royal Inniskilling Fusiliers, described what happened to him and his platoon, when he and his men retreated from the advanced trench they had been digging to the trench that appears to have been what the Irish referred to as the German C line:

It was while we were moving along this trench that a barrage of 5.9 inch shells burst . . . [nearby], killing [most of] . . . the men then in occupation. One of these shells bursting beside me, killed four men, while I sustained severe wounds in both legs from two . . . bullets. One . . . penetrated the right leg smashing the shin bone, and carrying away a portion of the tibia . . . I remained in this position with the mangled bodies of four men covering me for almost three quarters of an hour . . . [before two officers] relieved me.

Not surprisingly, considering the nature of Shannon's injuries, his would-be rescuers decided they could not carry him out of the danger area and left him where he was, after telling him they would come back with a stretcher. They did not return quickly enough. Before they reappeared, German counter-attacking troops arrived on the scene and he was taken prisoner.[35]

Perhaps Shannon could consider himself fortunate. Neither the Irish nor the Germans picked up John Berry, a twenty-seven-year-old accountant from Belfast serving in Lieutenant-Colonel Crozier's 9th Royal Irish Rifles. Berry was shot through the abdomen while advancing between the German C line and their second position. The bullet, which exited through his groin, severed a nerve and paralysed his right leg, leaving him marooned and deserted. That left him with no alternative but to try to help himself. 'I endeavoured to rejoin our troops in Thiepval Wood,' he wrote, 'but . . . could only crawl slowly. I crossed the enemy C line on [the] night of 2–3 July, and reached his B line near St Pierre Divion [at] about 7 p.m. on 4th July. I entered the trenches [there], but was unable to climb out through weakness. The enemy was then in possession of this line, and I was found some time later, and carried to his dressing station.'[36]

Meanwhile, those officers who could, had attempted to hold the Germans at bay by consolidating what remained of their C line. The troops on the left of the Irish line were led by the fifty-year-old Major Adam Jenkins of the 11th Battalion, the Royal Irish Rifles (the right-hand assault battalion in the 36th Division's left-hand brigade, the 108th Brigade); he must have been one of the oldest Irish soldiers, if not the oldest, in the German trenches on 1 July. In the following extract from a statement following his release from captivity, Jenkins described the measures that he and his men took:

The enemy third line was dug on our side of a sunken road . . . [Troops from] many different units began to crowd [into] . . . this road, among them being those of our people, who had advanced to the fourth enemy line and had been driven back. The road was very heavily shelled, causing numerous casualties. Being [the most] senior officer out of the Division, I at once withdrew all these troops from the road to the Schwaben Redoubt . . . The shelling [of the road] continued, but [because the road had been vacated, it] did little harm . . .

I sent several messages back asking for reinforcements, [consolidating] material and ammunition . . . [but] . . . no material ever reached me . . . This . . . made it . . . impossible . . . to consolidate as I . . . [w]ould have wished.

In my front . . . trench, I had a Lewis gun and about 60 rifles. In my centre trench I had a Stokes gun, a Vickers [machine] gun, and about 20 rifles, [and] in my . . . [support] trench I had a Lewis gun and about 40 rifles . . .

After very heavy shelling, the [German] counter-attack was launched . . . from my extreme left. The Stokes gun got the range at once, and as the enemy . . . [deployed] in close formation, he must have suffered very severely. After about six rounds from the Stokes gun the enemy retired.

We were [then] heavily shelled . . . again. Again they attempted [to] . . . advance, in larger numbers. [This time], they succeeded in getting farther forward. But the rifles and machine guns opened [up] on them, and drove them back a second time.

Again they shelled us, and again they attacked. [By now], my Vickers crew had all become casualties except [for] one man. I was assisting him with the gun when I was shot . . . by an enemy machine gun[ner].

The bullet that smacked into the right side of Jenkins' face, and passed over his palate before exiting one inch below the left molar bone, knocked him out cold, and probably convinced his men that he had been killed. When he finally came to, around twenty-four hours later, he could not see anything out of his left eye. But he could see enough out of his right eye to realize he was surrounded by Germans, his men having long since retreated.[37]

The retreat might have been expected to have made it easier to support the most advanced troops. However, the report filed from Schwaben Redoubt by Major Gaffikin of the 9th Royal Irish Rifles shortly after 3.30 p.m. stated:

We are in considerable difficulty . . . We are hanging on by our eyebrows . . . [We are] enfiladed by machine gun fire from the left, north of the Ancre, and are also getting quite a bad time from our right. It is impossible to do any work on top . . . We have practically no consolidating material. 6 balls of wire and no stakes. I do not think we shall be able to hold out tonight if we are attacked, as we can be taken from front to rear, unless Thiepval falls . . . The men are . . . exhausted . . . [They are] not fit to attack again . . . And both Lewis guns and machine guns are short of ammunition. We are [also] short of bombs.[38]

The situation of the Irish troops in and around the north-eastern edge of Thiepval Wood had also taken a turn for the worse. During the morning, the main anxiety was that Germans might attempt to seize the Irish front line while it was relatively sparsely guarded. During a moment of high tension some Germans who had been taken prisoner were so anxious to escape from the devastating fire laid down by their own guns that they sprinted across No Man's Land towards the British line, only to be bayoneted by the Irish support troops, who mistook them for counter-attackers in the heat of the moment.[39]

A second such incident occurred after another group of German soldiers was spotted moving towards the north-eastern edge of the Thiepval Wood. Lieutenant-Colonel Crozier, who rushed to take a look, saw 'an advancing crowd of field grey', and heard shouts from all around him that 'the Germans are on us!' A Lewis gun was deployed, whose operator proceeded to fire at what were believed to be the attacking hordes, until Crozier, who had been peering at them through his binoculars, suddenly shouted out: 'Cease fire, cease fire, for God's sake! . . . These men are prisoners surrendering, and some of our own wounded men are escorting them!'

It took some time for the gunfire to die down. Some of the men involved were from Colonel Bernard's battalion of the 10th Royal Irish Rifles. They had played their part in the failure to advance at the beginning of the attack, in what Crozier referred to as 'the shambles', and had lost their nerve. Such men felt that even captured Germans were fair game. '"After all, they are only Germans," I hear a youngster say,' Crozier reported. 'But I get the upper hand at last.'[40]

Ironically, the mass of prisoners surrendering, indicating the depth of the defeat suffered by the German garrison at the Schwaben Redoubt, also temporarily confused the German commanders, who believed they were watching their troops making a full-blooded counter-attack. That appears to be one reason why the German response to the Irish attack took so long to arrange, wrote the Bavarian 8th Reserve Regiment's historian.[41] However, by the end of the afternoon, the tables really had been turned. At that stage, it was not Germans who were seen fleeing the fighting arena; it was the Irish troops.

Lieutenant-Colonel Bowen of the 14th Royal Irish Rifles, who was running operations from his dugout in Thiepval Wood, was involved with one such incident, afterwards writing in his diary: 'I was aroused by a shout that the trench was full of men retiring . . . I stopped the rush in Elgin Avenue (the communication trench running through Thiepval Wood up to the front line) . . . [I] had to threaten with my revolver. It was a desperate scene. Shrapnel filled the air over us and the air was stiff with bullets, while [the] terror-stricken men rushed blindly on.'[42]

Crozier in his memoirs reported another truculent group, '[who say they are] damned if they are going to stay. [As far as they are concerned], it's all up.' He also recorded the consequences: 'A young sprinting subaltern heads them off. They push by him. He draws his revolver and threatens them. They take no notice. He fires. Down drops a British soldier at his feet. The effect is instantaneous. They turn back, [and go] to the assistance of their comrades.'[43]

But in spite of the injection of some new British battalions, the German counter-attack ground remorselessly on. After the Germans had dispatched some particularly stubborn Irish machine-gunners, who had been blocking the way into the south-eastern side of Schwaben Redoubt, at 7.45 p.m., it was only a matter of time before the way into the stronghold would be cleared.[44]

However, what finally convinced Major W. J. Peacocke of the 9th Royal Inniskilling Fusiliers, the most senior British officer in the German lines, that they would have to retire back to the original Irish front line was not the German thrust towards the Redoubt. It was the series of reports telling him that the Germans had retaken their front trench on the British flanks, thereby threatening to surround the remaining invaders. The Irish who were still holding on were ordered to hurry back to Thiepval Wood shortly after 11 p.m.[45]

One German who was amongst those gathered in the Redoubt has described the moment when he realized they had won: 'At about 11.30 p.m., those of us in Schwaben Redoubt could see thick lines of men moving in a broad front towards our front line . . . We wondered if they were German . . . Flares shot up in the neighbouring Thiepval sector enabled us to make out the shape of the helmets . . . We then realized it was the English who were retreating. [An officer] . . . ordered us to fire at them. The result was the enemy received a well-meant good-night greeting.'[46]

The German report does not record how many more men fell during that last desperate charge towards the Irish front line. All one can say, on the British side, is that the 36th Division's casualties incurred in the course of the attack were severe, the total approaching 5,500.[47] Its unit with the highest losses was the 11th Battalion, the Royal Inniskilling Fusiliers (approaching 600 casualties), which was the right-hand support battalion for the right-hand brigade (109th Brigade). That meant this battalion's troops not only had to endure the artillery barrage poured down onto No Man's Land after the initial few minutes of the attack, but they were also more exposed than any others to the raking machine-gun fire coming from Thiepval.[48]

The 36th Division's losses were by no means the end of it. Although its officers and men may have believed they had abandoned ship during the night of 1–2 July, some 49th Division men stayed on in the first German trench system, and were reinforced by more than 300 troops sent across No Man's Land to man the area between points A15 and A19 (south-west of the centre of the southern trench line within Schwaben Redoubt; see map 5) during the early afternoon of the next day.[49] They were only dislodged on 7 July, following an intense bombardment and a furious infantry attack. This increased the casualties sustained by the 49th Division's 148th Brigade to nearly 1,400, a tragic waste of life given that nothing valuable was gained through their extended stay in German lines.[50]

By way of contrast, the 2nd Battalion, the Manchester Regiment troops, part of 14th Brigade, which at 6 p.m. relieved the 32nd Division's assault battalions at the western end of the Leipzig Salient, ended up holding onto what turned out to be a permanent bridgehead in the German line. Thus this division's attack, which had not thrust nearly as deeply into the German defences as the Irish troops to the north, had eventually produced a more durable result.

Even this more limited incursion came at a price, the 32nd Division reporting casualties for 1–3 July in excess of 4,600.[51] Included within this figure were the grimmest statistics within the division, incurred by the 11th Border Regiment, whose casualties (as mentioned in Chapter 11) were approaching 550 officers and men.

It was probably the scale of suffering witnessed on the way to, and in, the German front line that provoked some of the cruellest retaliatory treatment of German prisoners recorded in a British war diary entry for 1 July. According to the war diarist of the 2nd Manchester Battalion: 'Considerable enjoyment was given to our troops by Lieutenant Robertson, who made the prisoners run across the open through their own artillery barrage. Upon reaching our line, these men were kept out of our dugouts by the sharp end of a bayonet.'[52]

Compared with the losses of X Corps, German casualties within the three Thiepval sectors were relatively low. The Bavarian 8th Reserve Regiment, whose troops spearheaded the counter-attack on Schwaben Redoubt, had 'just' 800 casualties during 1 and 3 July, the only days for which figures are specified in its regimental history, approximately a quarter being the men lost or captured during the Irish takeover of Schwaben Redoubt.[53] The 99th Reserve Regiment, which had held the remainder of the German front in the Thiepval North, Central and South sectors, suffered around 1,000 casualties on 1 July. This was a small number compared to those suffered by the British 32nd and 36th Divisions, but a high proportion of the men in the 99th Reserve's four battalions.[54]

Given that the units in the 36th Division were Pals battalions in all but name, it is no surprise to find that their communities back home were devastated. So numerous were the casualties that the British authorities did not always manage to warn all the families of deceased soldiers before the casualties were published in the local newspapers. As happened in St John's, Newfoundland, following the virtual annihilation of its battalion near Beaumont Hamel (see Chapter 8), those who could not read crowded around the newspaper cuttings containing the lists of casualties that had been pinned up in the windows of local newsagents, and asked friends and acquaintances whether they could see their relative's name listed. It was not uncommon for women or children to be seen running through the streets

of the afflicted Northern Irish towns or villages, with tears streaming down
their cheeks as they rushed home to tell their families the bad news they
had just heard.[55]

Just as poignant was the sight of notices printed in the newspapers
appealing for news of relatives who had been posted as missing. One such
notice filed in the *Belfast Evening Telegraph* read:

No news has been received regarding L'ce Corporal Walter Ferguson (14596)
YCVs since before the Big Push, and his relatives who reside at 2 Collingwood
Road Belfast are very anxious concerning him and would be grateful for any
information. In civil life he was a bookbinder . . .[56]

There was no follow-up report stating whether this missing corporal was
ever found, but there were very occasionally reports that those cited as having been killed had 'miraculously' come back from the dead. One notice in
the *Belfast Evening Telegraph*, which reported such an incident, stated:

Following the official report received by Mrs Geo Nesbitt, Richhill on Tuesday
stating that her son Pte Abner Nesbitt (RIF) had been killed in action on July 1st,
a wire has been received from a private hospital at Trowbridge Wilts notifying his
parents that Pte Nesbitt is lying wounded there.[57]

But it is likely that such notifications were few and far between. Much more
common were the heartfelt letters of condolence. A particularly touching
one filed in the Royal Ulster Museum reads:

Dear Friend Mary,
I saw in the newspaper that your brother has died of wounds in France. I am sorry
that one so dear to you is dead, and I want you to know how I feel about it. I said
a prayer and lit a candle for him at Mass on Sunday. You may think it will do him
no good, but it eased the burden I have in my heart for you. May God protect you
and all your family.
    Love Lizzie.[58]

13: Of Moles and Men

Ovillers, 1 July 1916

(See map 6)

If capturing lofty Schwaben Redoubt and Thiepval was the key that would help to unlock the German defences at the northern end of the German Somme line, then taking over the village of Ovillers, the gateway to the heights of Pozières, was surely one of the keys to the German 2nd Army's central core. An army commander standing on Hill number 160, the name used by German generals when referring to the heights, could see almost everything that was going on in the undulating landscape for miles around, as could his gunners.[1]

That may explain why Brigadier-General H. D. Tuson, commander of the 8th Division's 23rd Brigade, the III Corps unit entrusted with the task of capturing both of these strategically important villages, felt inspired to issue a stirring address to his troops before they went into action in front of Ovillers on 1 July. It started with the words:

In the coming great offensive, in which the British and French are fighting shoulder to shoulder against the common enemy, the 23rd Infantry Brigade has been selected, among many others, to be the first to break through the enemy's defences, and to capture the village of Pozières.

This is . . . the first step in what is hoped will prove to be a decisive and signal victory. Many divisions will pour through the gap opened for them by the Brigade.[2]

Tuson's brigade certainly had the most prestigious targets in the 8th Division, whose final objective for 1 July included as its northern wing the area just south-east of Mouquet Farm, and as its southern wing the area just south of the eastern outskirts of Pozières.[3] Because both Ovillers and Pozières lay just inside the right flank of the division, they naturally fell within the sphere of Tuson's 23rd Brigade, the division's right-hand unit.

However, with prestige came responsibility. As well as motivating his men, Tuson also appeared to be giving them a veiled warning when he added:

The enemy, with all his faults, is a brave fighter, and in all probability, the task set will prove no light one.

It is for us to show him that he has met more than his match at last, and that English men will not let his crimes against Europe and humanity go unpunished.[4]

This off-message admonition might have been blocked by Tuson's superiors had they seen it before it was circulated. The words clashed with the spirit of optimism that most British officers fighting on the Somme appear to have regarded as obligatory. Or perhaps the commanders of units within III Corps, such as the 8th Division's brigadiers, were given special dispensation to speak the unspeakable because of their leader's liberal nature.

The surviving correspondence of Lieutenant-General Sir William Pulteney, the fifty-five-year-old maverick commander of III Corps, suggests he was by far the most outspoken general at the top of the Army's hierarchy. Being a bachelor who evidently loved women, gossip and gardening, possibly in that order, it is not surprising to find his letters, even those written shortly before the big attack, laced with requests for news of high society, full of gardening tips, and dripping with sexual innuendo. When contacting Edith, Marchioness of Londonderry, an aristocratic confidante, on 22 June 1916, that is just a week before the original date for the big attack, he told her about the cold snap and the 'important' debate about whether he should revert to wearing his winter underwear, adding: 'I argued it was better to keep those parts cold so that they could fully appreciate the warmth of other parts when they got into them!!'[5] Pulteney went on to inform Edith that he had just returned to his headquarters following a recreational trip with a friend to Paris. 'We had a good time,' he assured her, 'but were hauled back on the Sunday night, so we had not much time to commit many atrocities.'[6]

His indiscretions were not restricted to his personal life. In the 29 June 1916 letter that Pulteney sent to Ettie, Lady Desborough, another friend to whom he wrote regularly, he revealed that because the enemy could 'get so deep down in this chalk, they are practically safe against the enormous shells' which his artillery was at that very moment throwing at them, two days before the great attack.[7] The letter is quoted to show that virtually no subject was off bounds as far as 'Putty', as he liked to call himself, was concerned. But it also suggests he knew full well that all the talk about the success of the attack being a formality was wishful thinking.

Or perhaps not. In the earlier letter to Edith Londonderry he had told her: 'My garden here is quite good . . . [but] the moles are an infernal nuisance. They burrow right through the flower beds, besides throwing up mighty mounds which deface the "gazon". However we have killed three in traps, and I beat all records by killing one in the open yesterday before he got back from his nocturnal visits. Bad luck being caught by an early bird like me, who knows the habits of those returning from other people's beds in the dawn!'[8]

This letter, written just days before the 'Big Push', raises the question as to whether Pulteney, a keen gardener, even when out in France with the BEF, felt that he and his artillery commander could catch the Germans out as easily as he had caught out the moles which dug up his lawn. If so, he was as guilty of being in denial as the rest of the optimists under his command.

Alfred Bundy, a lieutenant in the 23rd Brigade's 2nd Battalion, the Middlesex Regiment, quickly noticed the extraordinarily positive outlook prevailing when he entered the trenches opposite Ovillers for the first time, the day before the start of the battle, having just arrived at the front. That day's entry in his diary includes the words: 'We attack tomorrow, but it is freely stated there will be no resistance. Our drum fire has been going on for . . . days, and the German lines appear to have been pulverised. Surely nothing can live there.'[9]

His company commander, Captain Hunt, did not agree. He 'doesn't believe it will be so easy,' Bundy noted. Hunt was not alone in that. Captain Reginald Leetham, whose 2nd Battalion, the Rifle Brigade, was part of the 8th Division brigade (the 25th) that was to attack just north of the 23rd Brigade, had seen the consequences of being too overconfident. The evening after men from his battalion had raided the German trenches near Ovillers, during the bombardment before the 'Big Push', the German artillery had given the unit a good strafing. 'We had 8 men killed in one dugout,' Leetham noted in his diary for that day (26 June), 'and I saw the most horrible sight I have ever seen: two bodies without heads. Another only [had] the trunk left . . . But the thing that turned me up most was stepping round a corner to find a corpse with every stitch of clothing blown away.'

It appears to have been this scene, contrasted with the description of the undamaged German dugout entered in the course of the raid, which prompted Leetham to question in his diary the efficacy of the bombardment that was intended to soften up the enemy before the main attack:

[The raiders] . . . found the Boche front line so strongly occupied, it made one doubt whether all this bombardment was doing us much good. It was all a very fine exhibition of what our artillery could do, but what was the use of bombarding the Boche 30 feet below the level of the ground?

Our dugouts are wretched things with two to four feet of head cover and in the case of a direct hit the roof always gives way and buries the occupants. Not so the wily Hun!

Notwithstanding this scepticism, Leetham's notes are full of admiration for the spectacle of the bombardment. They describe how 'early on [during the bombardment], one observed [from the trenches] Pozières Church' with its 'great square tower', until 'later half of . . . [it] was knocked down'. He also 'saw the houses of Ovillers [being] destroyed' and 'flames of fires' in this and other villages 'lighting up the sky' at night.

'It was always a wonderful sight to see our shells bursting in every direction,' Leetham wrote. 'The first morning of the bombardment, the parapets of the trenches opposite were white with [the] chalk that had been thrown up [by the Germans] to make [them]. But towards the end of the week, they had been levelled to the ground, [and] all one saw were patches of brown earth. All the chalk had been blown away.'

While waiting by the assembly dugouts, about a mile from the front line, Leetham also found time on 30 June 1916 to appreciate nature, his senses sharpened no doubt by the realization that he might never see it again. During the night before the attack he wrote:

I stood outside. The weather had changed for the better . . . and I watched the most beautiful sunset behind the [nearby] wood. It was gloriously pink, which betokened a fine day for the morrow, the day of the battle.

After seeing the sunset, I tried to go to sleep, but it was again very cold, and I scarcely slept at all. I was up about three o'clock. It was just getting light, but the sky was [already] very beautiful [once again. It was] a wonderful sort of green where the previous night it had been pink.

According to Leetham, at about 4 a.m. the German artillery opened up 'in a more determined manner than they had ever done before, with the [obvious] intention of putting out of action as many of our batteries as possible'. As a result, when it became really light, 'the same places which the previous night had looked so lovely, with the sunset behind them, now . . . were almost obscured by clouds of white smoke that hung about in the still morning air'. Then, at 6.25 a.m., he registered that 'our hurricane bombardment commenced', which was the prelude to the infantry assault. 'It was . . . many times more intense than anything I had ever heard before, but I doubt that it killed many Boche!'[10]

Because Leetham's battalion was the 25th Brigade's reserve, he was not due to start advancing towards the front line until just after zero hour: 7.30 a.m. Consequently, he did not witness the moment when the attack began. However, Captain Alan Hanbury-Sparrow, an officer from the 2nd Battalion, the Royal Berkshire Regiment, one of 25th Brigade's assault units, who was acting as an observer for the artillery, has recorded his recollections.

At first he did not see very much. He was watching from his vantage point on a bank about 400 yards behind the front line, and during the initial stages of the attack a pall of red dust and smoke masked much of the action in No Man's Land from those attempting to track developments. Visibility was lessened still further by the mist that had descended over the battlefield by the time the 25th Brigade's assault battalions started their death-defying advance. The war diaries of the 25th and 23rd Brigades tell us that the troops in at least one of the 25th Brigade's assault battalions, along with those from at least one of the 23rd Brigade's assault battalions on their right, climbed out of their trenches shortly before zero hour, so that they were formed up, and on their way towards Ovillers, before the action began.[11]

This early move may have helped the first wave of the 2nd Battalion, the Devonshire Regiment, 23rd Brigade's left-hand unit, since they were within about 100 yards of the German front line before the advance proper began at 7.30 a.m. But it appears to have harmed the prospects of the battalion on its left. The war diarist for the 2nd Royal Berkshires, 25th Brigade's right-hand unit, states that German machine-gunners began to target their parapet well before zero hour, reacting to the 2nd Devons' advance at around 7.15 a.m.[12]

Captain Hanbury-Sparrow saw the advancing troops being swallowed up by the mist all right, and heard the first shots ring out from the German lines. But he came to the wrong conclusion about what had transpired. 'I thought . . . our front line [troops] had got into the [first] German trench,' he stated later, when asked about what he remembered of that day:

and so did the men that were with me . . . I reported . . . [this] to the Division, and I said: 'I'm going forward. I can't really see what is happening' . . . [But] I got a message to stay where I was, so I stayed . . . And then, presently, as . . . [the] barrage went forward . . . the air clear[ed], and I could see . . .

In the distance, I saw the barrage bounding on towards Pozières . . . In No Man's Land, [there were] heaps of dead, and [on the other side, there were the] Germans, almost standing up in their trenches . . . firing and sniping at those who had taken refuge in the shell holes . . . It was [an] . . . enormous disaster.[13]

The war diarist for the 2nd Devons put it slightly differently:

Immediately the troops advanced, the enemy opened a terrific machine gun fire from the front, and from both flanks, which mowed down our troops. This fire did not deter our men from continuing to advance, but only a very few reached the German lines alive. Some of these managed to effect an entry into the German lines, where they put up a determined fight against enormous odds, and were soon killed.

At first, and for some little time, owing to the mist and dust caused by our shell fire, it was difficult to realize exactly what had happened, although the heavy hostile machine gun fire told its own tale. The lines appeared at first sight to be intact. But it was soon made clear that the lines consisted only of dead or wounded, and that no-one was there to support the few who had got in, and to carry on with the advance.

The cause of this was eventually discovered. The 2nd Battalion, the West Yorkshire Regiment, the 23rd Brigade unit in support, had been caught by hostile machine gun and shell fire as soon as they advanced from their assembly trenches, and had been cut to pieces.[14]

A similar account could be given of the other assault battalions within the 8th Division, whether in the 70th Brigade on the division's left, the 25th Brigade in the centre, or the 23rd Brigade on the division's right. Around 200 men from the 2nd Battalion, the Middlesex Regiment, the 23rd Brigade unit on the Devons' right, for example, reached the German second line, only for those still standing to be whittled down to around a dozen by 9.15 a.m., when the remnants were forced to retire to shell holes in No Man's Land.[15]

They were the lucky ones, since as long as they were patient enough, they were able to return to the British front line after dark that night. The incidents witnessed in No Man's Land, and chronicled by the 2nd Middlesex's Lieutenant Bundy, were probably more representative of the experiences of the bulk of the battalion:

Went over the top ... after what seemed an interminable period of terrible apprehension ... The din was deafening, the fumes choking and [the] visibility limited, owing to the dust and clouds [of smoke] produced by exploding shells. It was a veritable inferno. I was 'momentarily' expecting to be blown to pieces.

My platoon continued to advance in good order without many casualties ... until we had reached nearly half way to the Boche front line. Suddenly however, an appalling rifle and machine gun fire opened [up on] ... us ... I shouted 'Down!', but most of those that were still not hit had already taken what cover they could ...

I dropped in[to] a shell hole ... [I] attempted to move ... but bullets were forming an impenetrable [barrier] ... and exposure of the head meant certain death. None of our men was visible. But pitiful groans and cries of pain ... came ... [from] all directions.

These desperate sounds left Bundy with a difficult dilemma. He had to decide whether to prioritize self-preservation or his desire to help his men. He took the only sensible option, and chose the former.[16]

In most of the Somme sectors, even those where there was the most appalling carnage, there were some troops who achieved something to be proud of. However, there were to be no British victors opposite Ovillers. Even the 2nd Battalion, the Lincolnshire Regiment, the 25th Brigade's left assault unit, who, following a fierce fight with the occupants, managed to seize a 200-yard stretch of the German front line, gradually saw their gains being eaten away by counter-attacks. First the 200 yards was reduced to 100 yards, following a German surge from the left, where there was a large gap between the Lincolns and the trenches held temporarily as a result of the 70th Brigade's incursion on 25th Brigade's left. Then the Lincolns were forced to retire to the German wire.

There they waited steadfastly, while their commanding officer, Lieutenant-Colonel Reginald Bastard, rushed back to their original front line to ask for directions from his brigadier. He agreed with Bastard that it was a lost cause, whereupon the lieutenant-colonel stole out into No Man's Land once again, and having reached his flock, shepherded them back to the position from whence they had started earlier that morning.[17]

This position was far from being the welcome refuge it had been when they had last seen it. The account by 2nd Lieutenant W. V. C. Lake of the 1st Royal Irish Rifles, the 25th Brigade's support unit that was supposed to be backing up the assault battalions, gives us an inkling as to why conditions in the front trench meant their assistance was not forthcoming. Many of the men in his platoon were shot down as soon as they attempted to climb over the parapet, and they fell back into the trench having been killed or wounded.

'Presently Captain Ross, our company commander came crawling along the trench quite oblivious of the groaning bodies that were under him,' Lake recalled. 'There was a glazed look on his face, which was streaming with blood, and in his mouth was a cigarette that would never light because of the blood on it. I said something as he passed, but he made no answer. He just continued on his way on all fours . . . I never saw him again.'

Perhaps something akin to the heavy explosion that went off just behind Lake shortly afterwards had something to do with that. 'I hunched my shoulders as a load of earth landed on my tin helmet,' he recalled. 'But alas, my runner had gone. He was blown to pieces. Nearby, another man lay bleeding from a nasty wound in his thigh. I went over to him . . . [But] I could see his femoral artery had been severed . . . First aid was of little use. I moistened his lips from my water bottle, and assured him he would soon be out of pain.' He soon was. He died with Lake watching over him.

'I became conscious then of a man making horrid noises with his mouth wide open,' Lake recalled. '[He sounded] like a trapped animal. My platoon sergeant was standing next to him, and fearing lest panic should spread, I said to him "Dump him on the jaw Sergeant." [The Sergeant] . . . was a heavy man with big biceps, and he dealt that man a punch which would have knocked out any boxer in the ring. But it made no difference. So stepping over to the man, I pointed down the trench and shouted . . . "Go!" [Whereupon] he turned and fled.'[18]

Meanwhile, Captain Leetham and a brother officer were trudging disconsolately up the communication trench with their 2nd Rifle Brigade platoons towards the front line, which Lake and his battalion should have long since vacated. 'We had realized something was wrong, for we were continually halted . . . The trench was evidently blocked [further on],' Leetham noted.

When they were about 500 yards from the front line, they realized why. They had come face to face with a crowd of panic-stricken wounded men, who were rushing back down the communication trench towards the dressing station. Their state of mind cannot have been helped by the sound of the machine-gun bullets that swished past them overhead. It was a sound which convinced Leetham that 'any doubt about the bombardment having driven the Boches out of their trenches was incorrect. One also realized that fellows in the open must be being mowed down like grass.'

About 300 yards further on, Leetham and his platoon branched off to the right, in a bid to find an emptier communication trench, leaving his brother officer to carry on with his platoon. As Leetham hurried his men forward, his mind was filled with foreboding after he heard the shrapnel bursting all around them. It was another indicator of conditions they would find in the front line.

His fears were increased when he came upon the first immobilized casualty he had seen that day. It was 'a man half buried in a shattered dugout,' Leetham recalled. He 'implored me to dig him out, but I could do nothing [for him] as my orders were [not to stop for anyone. I was] to hold the front line until I received orders to go over.'

However, nothing prepared Leetham for what he was to see when his men finally reached their destination and he was able to look over the top into No Man's Land: 'The first thing I saw in the space of a tennis court in front of me was the bodies of [about] 100 dead or severely wounded men lying in our own wire.' He could not even share the burden of what he had witnessed with another officer. Apart from his platoon, the portion of trench he was in was deserted. Leetham later found out that the company which had been ordered to hold the front line beside him had been unable to pass along their communication trench to the front line, because it was clogged up with wounded and dying men. His only consolation was in shooting across 300 yards of No Man's Land in the general direction of a German who was firing at some fleeing British soldiers. The German toppled over, so perhaps Leetham's frantic dash to the front had achieved something after all.[19]

No general likes to see his troops being decimated, as the 8th Division troops were, in front of Ovillers. But its commander, Major-General Hudson, must have at least felt partly vindicated by what had taken place. He had argued that the Ovillers attack should only go ahead if the attacks against the Leipzig Salient and La Boisselle had already succeeded, on the grounds that unquelled machine-gunners on these heights would be able to spray with bullets the troops advancing towards Ovillers, and in particular those advancing up the valleys on either side of the Ovillers spur.[20] That is precisely what had occurred.

Yet now Hudson was ordered to attack again at 5 p.m. He immediately informed III Corps' commander, Lieutenant-General Pulteney, that the attack could not succeed. It was quickly cancelled.

That was a wise decision. However, there were bitter recriminations about the foolish choices that had been made before the 7.30 a.m. assault. The 8th Division had suffered in excess of 5,100 casualties (including over 2,000 killed or missing) during the attack, and without making any gains whatsoever.[21] In contrast, the German casualties in the Ovillers sector were minimal when put alongside the British losses. The regimental history for the 26th Reserve Division's 180th Regiment states that the German regiment's losses on 1 July amounted to just 280 men.[22]

One of those most critical of the British attack was Brigadier-General J. H. W. Pollard, commander of the 25th Brigade. One suspects he might have sacked both Haig and Rawlinson for their naive tactics had he been in charge of the Army! What Pollard was complaining about was not just the dilution of the artillery barrage targeting the front system for being too ambitious, Haig's most heinous error (see Chapter 3, pp. 34–5), but also the artillery tactics that were the bedrock of all barrages put down by the British artillery on 1 July: the concept of a barrage that was lifted off the front system and then targeted the German rear positions according to a prearranged ('fixed') timetable. As Pollard put it:

A bombardment on some given line [in the rear] may be of value in damaging the enemy's defences, and preventing supports being sent up. But if the line in question is 1000 yards behind the line where our assaulting troops are being held up . . . the position is very far from satisfactory! To prevent reinforcements from reaching the enemy is of but minor value, if we are ourselves unable to maintain our hold upon the enemy's front line.

Owing to the difficulty which we experienced in getting the barrage brought back, my Brigade was practically deprived of the close artillery support which was at that time essential, as I reported by telephone, and those who had gained the enemy front line were unable to maintain their positions.[23]

A slightly less decorous critique of the British commanders who had 'masterminded' the Ovillers operation was included in the 13 July 1916 letter that the seventeen-year-old private, Cyril José, wrote to his sister Ivy, while he was recuperating in a Plymouth hospital after the attack. He had been shot through the chest while advancing towards Ovillers with the 2nd Devons:[24]

We were told it would be a walk-over. Our artillery had their machine guns and batteries all weighed off, and would splash them all out in the last few hours of the bombardment. Of course we might expect to be sniped at by a stray German naturally! We would advance, take [the] first, go on to village of Ovillers, then on to 3rd and 4th lines to [the] village of Pozières. If we met any opposition, we would dig in, and other regiments would come through us. Quite simp!

Well, we went over, after all the batteries and machine guns had been wiped out, though somehow, these batteries laid our trenches almost flat! . . .

Some people say you go absolutely mad. You don't. I've never felt so cool and matter of fact in my life. I was surprised. But I was still more surprised by the reception. You know what a hailstorm is. Well, that's about the chance one stood of dodging the bullets, shrapnel etc. Of course it must have been that stray sniper!

'Johnny', always considerate, ordered me to have a rest when I had got about 20 yards from his parapet. That was about 7.35 a.m. July 1st. I couldn't get back to our own lines until the next morning. I didn't eat anything, but lived on pulling off dead men's water bottles . . .

About 6 a.m. July 2nd, I began crawling back to our line. Old 'Johnny' sniped at me all the way back, but I dodged him by getting in shell holes etc and got back at last. I offered up a prayer of thanks when I dropped in our trench right by a chap [with a] . . . periscope, who had been watching me come in.[25]

Three days later in a letter to his mother, José graphically described how he coped with his wound while in No Man's Land: 'I couldn't bandage myself, but a chap pulled out my dressing and pulled open my coat. I held it to the wound, until it was soaked through, in about 2 minutes. Then I put the other on. When that got soaked, I chucked them both away, and let it go. When I got back in the trench my coat, cardigan and shirt were soaked through. Had to cut them off.'

He also did not stand on ceremony when it came to allocating blame for his ordeal:

Of course, some 'big bug' thought it a great idea to go over in broad daylight, instead of crawling up as near their parapet in the night under cover of the bombardment as poss, as usual, so that we could then dive in the trench with hardly any losses going across. Of course, Johnny wouldn't expect us then so much. I suppose they thought that if Johnny wouldn't expect us, he wouldn't see us. Certainly not! Result: Johnny spots us coming over the parapet and we have to go about 600 yards. What brains old Douglas must have.

Made me laugh when I read his despatch yesterday. 'I attacked . . .' Old women in England picturing Sir Doug in front of British waves, brandishing his sword [at] Johnny in [the] trenches. I'll get a job like that in the next war. Attack Johnny from 100 miles back! Still we can't all lead can we?[26]

14: Land of Hope and Glory

La Boisselle, 1 July 1916

(See maps 2 and 6)

It would have been fitting if the village of La Boisselle, which was incorporated into the German front-line system about three-quarters of a mile to the south of Ovillers, had been captured as a result of the explosion of a mine. It was one of the most intensively mined areas on the Western Front. In the months prior to the start of the great attack, first French, and then British, mining engineers had fought the Germans tooth and nail in an attempt to establish underground supremacy in the relatively narrow area that passed for No Man's Land to the west of the village.

Here, opposite a section of British front trenches referred to as 'the Glory Hole', the German front line stuck out towards their enemy in a long salient, so that at its blunted point a paltry 50 yards separated the two sides.

To the uninitiated, that might make it sound as though it was the ideal place to mount an attack. After all, the British generals involved at Gommecourt had tried to improve their chances by digging their assault trenches closer to the Germans (see Chapter 10, p. 118). However, here, the shape of the ground, disturbed by the many explosions that followed on from the extensive mining and undermining, and the closeness of the opposing lines at the tip of this salient, brought with it other problems for an attacker, which more than compensated for any apparent advantages.

For a start, No Man's Land opposite the German salient was no longer a smooth slope up which soldiers could rush unimpeded towards their goal. Due to the upheaval below, it was covered with huge mounds of white chalk and plunging holes, so that immediately west of La Boisselle itself the terrain resembled some ancient troglodyte settlement. These mounds and bumps made it hard for British gunners' observers to see the exact configuration of the German front line, even assuming the infamously inaccurate British guns could be relied upon to fire safely at a target that was so near to the British trenches.

But perhaps even more discouraging for the attackers were the consequences of the shape of the adjacent German front line, an important consideration given the habit of British generals to attack salients in a pincer movement from both sides. On either side of the La Boisselle salient, the German line curved backwards, that is, away from the British trenches, towards the east, forming what soldiers like to refer to as re-entrants (the concave opposite of a convex salient; see map 6). Not only did this mean that any British advance towards the trenches to the north and south of La Boisselle would involve having to cross under fire a No Man's Land that was up to 800 yards wide, but it was also a gift for any rapacious machine-gunner located in the salient itself. No group of British soldiers could approach the re-entrants without being enfiladed (shot at from the side) from the village of La Boisselle as they advanced, opening up the prospect that an entire platoon, company, or even battalion might be annihilated by one gun.

It was this nightmarish scenario that persuaded Captain Henry Hance, commander of the 179th Tunnelling Company, to recommend that a long tunnel should be excavated ending north-east of the tip of the salient under Y Sap, which doubled as a strongpoint (see map 6). He believed that if a giant mine could be exploded there, the lips of the resulting crater would act as a barrier to screen soldiers as they advanced towards the nearby re-entrant. Eventually his superiors agreed, and the race was on to see whether the mine could be dug in time for the offensive.

For similar reasons, in March 1916, Hance had been ordered to construct a second tunnel targeting a strongpoint, Schwaben Höhe, to the south of the village. This strongpoint was located at the tip of another salient in the German line that overlooked an even more pronounced re-entrant within the re-entrant mentioned above (see map 6). The second tunnel came to be known as the Lochnagar mine, taking its name from the nearby Lochnagar Street communication trench, behind the British front line.

We have already learned in relation to the Hawthorn Redoubt mine how important it was, when mining, not to alert the Germans (see Chapter 8, p. 94). Hance, writing after the mine was blown, has revealed the extraordinary lengths to which his miners went to keep the Lochnagar mine secret:

The work was . . . done 'in silence' (only whispering was permitted). A large number of bayonets were fitted with handles. The operator inserted the [bayonet] point in a crack in the face, or alongside a flint, of which there were any number in the chalk, [and] gave it a twist . . . [This] wrenched loose a piece of stone [or chalk] . . . which he caught with his other hand, and laid on the floor. If . . . he had to use greater force, another man . . . would catch the stone [or chalk] as it fell.

The men worked 'bare-footed' (in practice this would usually mean they took off their boots and padded around in socks or stockings). The floor of the gallery was carpeted with sandbags, and an officer was always present to preserve [the] 'silence'. As sandbags were filled with chalk, they were passed out along a line of men seated on the floor, and stacked against . . . [a] wall, ready for use later as tamping (material used to fill in the hole excavated, after the insertion of the explosives, so that the force of the blast made by the explosion did not escape down the part of the tunnel leading to its exit, but was focused on the area to be blown up).[1]

Discipline was doubtless buttressed because the men knew the risks they were running. A German tunnel was constructed under the Lochnagar mine. The German miners were frequently to be heard stumping up and down inside it, opening up the possibility that the Germans could blow up the British mine at any moment.[2]

Even if the British miners were not blown up, there was always the possibility they would suffocate if starved of oxygen. Such was the lack of breathable air in these long mines that it was often impossible to keep a candle burning except at the mine face, the only place where oxygen was pumped out of a hose.[3]

Captain Hugh Kerr, the engineer responsible for the Y Sap mine, was not going to let anyone connected with the 179th Tunnelling Company forget that traumatic day in September 1915, when carbon monoxide released following the blowing of a German mine near La Boisselle had killed a British miner. The miner was being lowered down the shaft after the explosion in order to investigate the damage. For some reason his breathing apparatus did not save him. The same deadly gas had also knocked out and hospitalized Kerr, even though he was still above ground.[4] It was dangerous work.

As with the Hawthorn Redoubt, speed was of the essence if the mines were to be ready in time for the 'Big Push', although in relation to the Lochnagar mine Hance's team had less to excavate. The work on the tunnel had been started by another tunnelling company in November 1915, only to be temporarily suspended when it was deployed elsewhere.[5] When the 179th Tunnelling Company took up the reins in March 1916, it only had to complete what had already been started. However, all the precautions slowed down the progress towards the German front line.

When the Lochnagar tunnel had been excavated forward for about 170 yards from the British front line, it was branched, with one arm, approximately 30 yards long, driven forward a little to the right, and the second arm, more or less the same length as the first, directed to the left. The digging was halted in mid-June, so that the two arms of the tunnel could be filled with explosives. Some 36,000 pounds of ammonal were packed into the tip of the left arm approximately 70 feet under the surface, and 24,000 pounds into the tip of the right arm, around 45 feet below the German trenches.

The same system was used to transport the explosives to the face of the mine as had been used to clear away the waste: men were lined up inside the tunnel, and the ammonal, safely wrapped up in waterproof bags, was passed down the line from man to man. Afterwards, with all the explosives in place, more than 100 yards of the tunnel was refilled with tamping.[6]

Meanwhile, the race was started to complete the much more extensive excavation necessary for the construction from scratch of the Y Sap mine. Here, the situation was complicated by the fact that the miners could not direct the tunnel straight towards their target from their existing works in front of La Boisselle. Instead, they had to drive it in a north-westerly direction for around 500 yards, before making a right-angled turn and proceeding in a north-easterly direction towards Y Sap (see map 6). In all they dug out over 1,000 yards of chalk.[7] It would not have been possible had the miners not been allocated around 600 men, who according to their commander 'worked like hell . . . humping sandbags out of the place'.[8] Eventually 40,000 pounds of ammonal was placed at the end of the mine, around 75 feet underground, and on 28 June 1916, after around 100 yards of the tunnel had been refilled with tamping, the Y Sap mine was also ready to be exploded.[9]

Lieutenant-General Sir William Pulteney, whose III Corps was responsible for the La Boisselle attack as well as that opposite Ovillers, wanted the mines to be exploded two minutes before zero hour on 1 July. That would have been all very well had it not interfered with the infantry, who, following the method of dealing with salients mentioned concerning the attack on Gommecourt (see Chapter 10, p. 118), had been ordered to attack La Boisselle from either side rather than head on. The interference displeased Lieutenant-Colonel Urmison of the 15th Battalion, the Royal Scots

Regiment, the 101st Brigade unit leading the assault on the extreme right of the 34th Division's attack. He did not like the order that required the leading unit on his left, stationed opposite the site of the mine in the Schwaben Höhe, to start advancing at zero hour from a position to his rear. Either Pulteney or the 34th Division's commander, Major-General Ingouville-Williams, or perhaps both, had ruled that the 101st Brigade's leading left-hand unit, the 10th Battalion, the Lincolnshire Regiment, had to start further back than the 15th Royal Scots, the leaders on the right, for fear that the debris thrown up by the mine would harm its advancing soldiers.[10]

Although Urmison protested, even going so far as to offer to swap places with the Lincolns, on the grounds that the existing plan would enable the German defenders in front of both units to act together in picking off the battalions one by one, the 101st Brigade's Brigadier-General R. C. Gore confessed that his hands were tied due to the decisions taken by his superiors.[11]

Gore was equally scathing about the decision that all three of the 34th Division's brigades should advance simultaneously. Although troops under the command of the division's support brigade, the 103rd Brigade, were to start some way back from the two leading brigades, which were to be stationed in the British front system, they were to advance down from the crest of the Tara and Usna Hills (behind the British front line in the La Boisselle sector) at zero hour, and would be exposed immediately to whatever artillery and machine-gun fire was provoked by the assault of the leading battalions.[12] If these troops suffered substantial losses, the 34th Division would have no reserve available to help it exploit any breakthrough.

Perhaps even more significant was the complaint raised by Lieutenant-Colonel G. R. V. Steward, commander of the 103rd Brigade's 27th Northumberland Fusiliers (the 4th Tyneside Irish) at a III Corps conference: he was concerned that of all the artillery available, none of the heavier guns or howitzers were going to target La Boiselle itself. Later, events would suggest that this was the most crucial point of all, but like so many concerns raised by battalion or brigade commanders, it was swept aside with a badly thought-through, complacent answer. In this case, Steward was informed that any German gunners in La Boiselle would be subdued by the heavy trench mortars, forgetting that these mortars were only to fire for the first twelve minutes after zero hour, whatever the opposition to the relatively small groups of British bombers detailed to take the village from the side or rear.[13]

So it was that the plan in the La Boisselle sector was waved through, not-withstanding all its faults, without substantial alteration. The 34th Division order issued on 15 June 1916 was the detailed embodiment of all those letters that had been passed between Haig and Rawlinson two months earlier. There would be an attack by one column, whose assault troops consisted of two battalions, to the north of the village, while to the south no fewer than three columns, each headed by a battalion and each backed up by support battalions, would attempt to take on the German forces there. The initial objectives would be the German front system, but that would only be a prelude to the main task allocated to the 34th Division, which was to go on to seize Contalmaison and the line leading from there up to Pozières. The northern flank of the division's final objective was just to the south of Pozières, and its southern flank was just to the south of the area south-east of Contalmaison.[14]

Two of the division's brigades, the 101st Brigade on its right and the 102nd Brigade on its left, would be responsible for the first two objectives, leaving the 103rd Brigade to make the final leap forward to Contalmaison.[15]

It is doubtful whether any of the misgivings voiced by the commanders of units at corps and brigade conferences were shared with the more junior officers of the 10th Lincolns, the 101st Brigade's leading left-hand assault unit, which was likely to be most affected by all of them. They certainly do not figure in the account by Major Walter Vignoles, the most detailed document compiled by an officer of that battalion available for public scru-tiny.[16] His account does, however, highlight other warning signs that were there for all to see before the great day.

Everyone in the 10th Lincolns knew about the botched raid on the enemy lines south of La Boisselle made by the 16th Royal Scots, a sister unit within the 101st Brigade, a couple of days earlier. Rather than the hoped-for result – the capture of German prisoners and a report confirming the front line was thinly held – the Royal Scots, as Vignoles put it, 'had a hot time', being met with determined resistance and machine-gun fire. The message taken from the raid could not have been more negative. 'The raid showed us that the trenches were heavily manned,' Vignoles recalled, 'and the bom-bardment had not knocked out the machine-guns.'[17]

In spite of this, Vignoles remarked that the men were strangely upbeat and confident that they were going to be successful. Or perhaps his account, without labouring the point, was intended by its author to make one of those universally true observations about humankind, whether at war or in peacetime: it is an unalterable characteristic of human nature that most men will refuse to believe that impending disasters will affect them.

'There was a kind of suppressed excitement running through all the men, as the time for the advance came nearer,' he wrote afterwards. 'I don't know why, for we all knew that there was a good chance of many of us being killed or wounded. But we were in good spirits, and they were not assumed either . . . I think the fact that at last we hoped to get to close quarters with the Boche, and defeat him accounted for it.'

Vignoles' account chronicles what the men did, as they waited for the mines to go off. They savoured their 'lighted pipes and cigarettes' and 'chatted and laughed'. In the heightened state of optimism encouraged by their superiors, they 'wondered whether the Boche would wait for us'. Another account, written by a private within the same battalion, records how some of the men, who were cooped up inside a dugout, raised their spirits with a rousing sing-song.[18]

While he and his men were waiting, Vignoles attempted to while away the time by sizing up the enemy trenches near the site of the mine they were to attack. 'I . . . could not see much,' he admitted afterwards. The German lines 'were veiled in a light mist, made worse no doubt by the smoke from the thousands of shells we were pumping into his lines.' The frustratingly lengthy period of enforced inactivity was brought to an end at 7.28 a.m. precisely. That was the moment when the two tunnelling company captains in charge of the La Boisselle mines pushed down their plungers, effectively firing the starting gun for the race to the German parapet.

Captain Hugh Kerr, situated in a dugout in a communication trench about 40 feet back from the British front line, described the moment when he pushed down the plunger for the Y Sap mine in the following terms:

When it came to the time, we just pooped the handle down. [John] Allen was with me in the dugout. Directly the handle went down, he nipped out the top to make sure it had gone off. It was well overcharged, and there wasn't much of a kick, and I said: 'Cor strike me pink, or something worse. It hasn't gone off! [By this time Allen] . . . was up on the top and said 'Cor, strike me. Hasn't it? Come up and have a look.' When I went out, there was still a helluva lot of smoke about. [It was] a wonderful sight![19]

Kerr might have been underwhelmed by the vibration through the ground set off by the blowing of his Y Sap mine, but for the men in the 10th

Lincolnshires, who saw or felt the mine nearest them go off, it was a welcome signal that their time had finally come.

Nevertheless the senior officers in the battalion, who were some way back from the British front line, were not as excited as their juniors further forward. Vignoles, who felt rather than saw the explosions, described them dismissively as 'three tremors of the earth'. His commanding officer, Major Kyme Cordeaux, likened the 'swaying' and 'rocking' ground to 'an earthquake'.[20] Other Lincolns appear to have been more impressed. Sergeant Dick Cammack, who was situated opposite the Lochnagar mine, recalled seeing how 'chalk flew about 100 yards into the air, and Germans with it . . . It came down all over us in powder, and made it difficult to see.'[21] Private Harry Baumber, who recorded that 'the trenches simply rocked like a boat', was amazed by what he witnessed. 'We seemed to be very close to it,' he wrote. 'We looked in awe as great pieces of earth as big as wagons . . . blasted skywards' along with what looked like 'a geyser of mud, chalk and flame'. The whole mass then seemed to 'hurtle and roll and then start to scream back all around us'.[22]

Simultaneously with the explosions, smoke bombs were thrown behind the British front line to the south of La Boisselle in the hope that the smoke would float over the minefield opposite the village, misleading the Germans into thinking that was to be the location of the impending attack.[23] It appeared to have the desired effect, for it was greeted with what the lieutenant in charge of smoke referred to as 'intense rifle and machine gun fire', alarmingly intense given all the promises that the German defences would be destroyed.

But it was only at zero hour, when the artillery barrage, which for the previous sixty-five minutes had been pulverizing the German trenches, lifted off the front line, that the advance proper got under way. As it did so, an 8th Division soldier to the north of La Boisselle witnessed a courageous act by a 34th Division piper that would not have been out of place centuries earlier during the Scottish victory over the English at the Battle of Bannockburn:

The Tyneside . . . [Scottish Brigade (the 102nd)] were on our right, and as their officers gave the signal to advance, I saw the piper . . . jump out of the trench and march straight over No Man's Land towards the German lines. The tremendous rattle of machine gun and rifle fire which the enemy at once opened on us . . . completely drowned the sound of his pipes. But it was obvious he was playing as though he would burst the bag, and just faintly through the din, we heard the mighty shout his comrades gave as they swarmed after him.

How he escaped death I can't understand, for the ground was literally ploughed up by the hail of bullets. But he seemed to bear a charmed life, and the last glimpse I had of him, as we too dashed out, showed him still marching erect, playing furiously, and quite regardless of the flying bullets and the men dropping all around him . . . [It was] the pluckiest thing I have ever saw.[24]

According to Private J. Elliot, who served in the same unit, the 20th Battalion, the Northumberland Fusiliers (1st Tyneside Scottish), which was leading the advance on the 34th Division's extreme left, the piper's uncle was not nearly as lucky: 'He was riddled with bullets, writhing and screaming. Another lad was just kneeling, his head thrown right back. Bullets were just slapping into him, knocking great bloody chunks off his body.'[25] He was far from being the only one to drop. Private Elliot believed that some of the Germans held their fire until his battalion were well on their way across No Man's Land. 'That way we would cop it if we came forward, and cop it just as bad if we tried to go back. We were just scythed down.'[26]

Given the ferocity of the German guns, it is a wonder that any of the 20th Northumberland Fusiliers reached the German trenches. Some even made it to the third line, according to the 102nd Brigade's war diary. However, they were unsupported, and it was not long before, as the brigade phrased it, those British troops in the German trenches were 'annihilated'.[27]

The attack by the two Tyneside Scottish units south of La Boisselle, representing the right arm of the pincer movement that was supposed to cut off the village, was met with equally determined opposition. Doctor Jim Fiddian, the medical officer with the 11th Suffolk Regiment (the 101st Brigade's left-hand support unit) reported their progress in the following terms:

From the back of my aid post, I could see to our left flank the men of our next brigade rise out of their lines of assembly trenches, and move speedily forward. Our artillery fire died away, [but] . . . a new noise arose: a perfectly hellish hail of machine gun bullets from the Boche, gradually swelling, as fresh guns came into action, [un]til it seemed a handkerchief thrown above the trench would have been riddled.

I [also] glanced at the lines of men on our [right] . . . as they passed over the wide depression that was the beginning of Sausage Valley. They were falling fast, [yet they were still] far from reaching even our own front line. I just had time to realize that there had been some miscalculation of the effect of our artillery fire on the Boche machine gunners [before I was called away as] casualties began to come in.[28]

The account by Major Cordeaux, the Lincolns' commanding officer, explains why:

The Battalion was immediately exposed to a heavy shell fire, shrapnel and HE (high explosive), and the most intense enfilade machine gun fire from La Boisselle and Heligoland Redoubt (marked on map 6). [Nevertheless, the Battalion] advanc[ed] . . . with the utmost steadiness and courage . . . The distance they were away from the German trenches, and the intensity of the fire did not allow of the possibility of rushing . . . the enemy line.[29]

The battalion's Private Harry Baumber recalled how, after climbing over the top, he found himself advancing:

behind a line of steadfast men walking grimly forward . . . wondering what was in store. We soon found out. I noticed men falling thick and fast about me, and all the time, [there was] a remorseless chatter of machine guns. It was akin to striding into a hail storm . . . All too soon, it was obvious Jerry was not being obliterated, his wire was not destroyed and we had been called upon to walk 800 yards across No Man's Land into Hell. [It was] a far cry from the walk-over we had been promised.

  Eventually . . . [the] enfilade machine gun fire [coming] from the flanks . . . [made it] a massacre, and although a few . . . struggled into his defences, we who were left [in No Man's Land] were simply pinned down where we lay. There was [certainly] no going forward, and at this time, no way of getting back to our lines. It was [a] . . . bloody shambles!

  If you moved an inch, it [provoked] a sweeping crackle of fire, and we survivors . . . realize[d] our only hope was to wait until dark.[30]

If testimony is needed to corroborate Baumber's recollections, it is perhaps best to fall back on the account by the German machine-gun company commander whose gunners were partly responsible for the massacre that had occurred. From his position in Zähringer Graben opposite the mouth of the Bécourt Mulde (Sausage Valley), he held back his troops until the time was just right:

Silently our machine-gunners and the infantry waited for the enemy to come nearer. Then, as he approached our trenches, the bullets fired by our machine-gunners and riflemen smashed like a hurricane into his bunched-up ranks. Some of our men climbed up onto our parapets and threw hand grenades at those attackers who were lying on the ground. In less than a minute, the battlefield seemed to be deserted.

However, it was not long before small groups, and subsequently whole units, began to retreat in the direction of Bécourt until it seemed all the attackers wanted to flood back to where they had started. They were hit by more gun fire emanating from our infantry and machine-gunners, and some of our men ran after the fleeing Englishmen so that they could capture them. Our guns carried on clattering for 2 hours before the fighting in the Bécourt Mulde died down.[31]

Meanwhile, completely insulated from the cataclysm that was unfolding in No Man's Land, the Lincolns' reserve company commanded by Major Vignoles, which had been stationed further to the rear, began its trek towards the front line. Their job was to carry forward ammunition and other supplies that would be needed by the assault companies if they were successful. They started off in blissful ignorance of the ghastly events unfolding further forward, their state of innocence being only gradually punctured by what they saw on the way.

'As we went along, we saw that the Boche had replied to our bombardment,' Vignoles recalled later. '. . . The trenches down which we were proceeding were broken in places, and a number of dead were lying about. From time to time, I looked over the parapet, and could see our men sweeping over No Man's Land and the enemy lines, although it was impossible to see how they were faring.'

Eventually, Vignoles' column of plodding men were stopped in their tracks by a long line of wounded who needed to pass quickly in the opposite direction. That was what prompted him to leave the security of the communication trench so that he could lead his men on top. Although by then, the first assault had been made, 'the noise was still terrific,' Vignoles noted:

Our guns were bombarding the enemy's rear lines, while the Boche was very heavily shelling our lines in front of La Boisselle to my left. The mist had lifted slightly, and the picture before me, combined with the uproar, gave me an impression which I am not likely to forget.

The ground fell from where I was [standing] into Sausage Valley, rising again beyond [to an area which was] covered with enemy trenches. No shells were falling on these, as our barrage had lifted, but dark green figures could be seen moving forward [towards them] on the right, while No Man's Land was littered with men, apparently lying down. [I did not] realize . . . at first . . . that these were all casualties, and that [those who] . . . had pushed on . . . [were all that] was left of the battalion. On my left, [the situation looked bleaker] . . . Huge shells . . . [fired by] . . . the enemy were bursting in the air . . .

[At] about 8.15 a.m . . . I thought we were held up on the left, but getting on moderately well on the right.

It was only then that Vignoles had his first taste of what the troops further forward had already encountered. 'The place where I was standing [became] . . . very lively,' he reported. 'I could hear the bullets cracking past me, and [I could] see the dust kicking up all round. I got the men out of the communication trench, and made them lie down. One or two were hit as they got out . . . I was just getting the last man out . . . when I heard [another] crack, and felt as if a red hot bar had been pushed through my hand. On looking down, I saw that I had been shot through four fingers . . . [and] I could see by the jet of blood that an artery had been cut.'

The presence of mind of his orderly, who quickly staunched the bleeding by placing a tourniquet around his arm, saved Major Vignoles' life. But it was clear that he could not continue.

As he gave his orders to his 2nd Lieutenant, J. H. Turnbull, who was about to take over, Vignoles scanned the area leading up to the British front line to see what was feasible. 'It did not look at all promising,' he concluded. 'Bullets were still kicking up the dust, and where we were supposed to advance, there was not a man to be seen behind the enemy's front line.' In the end, some of the men with their supplies made it across No Man's Land, coming to a halt to the right of the crater, whose lips protected them from the gunfire coming from La Boisselle. But just when they were hoping they were safe, as Turnbull described it, 'Goodness knows how many machine guns opened [up] on us.'[32] They had reached the limit of the advance. After being shot in the back, Turnbull had no option but to join the other wounded men who had congregated beside the crater with a view to escaping back to their own lines when darkness fell.

It was the dogged resistance of the German 110th Reserve Infantry Regiment, the 28th Reserve Division's right-hand unit, which ensured that

La Boisselle was not taken by the British on the first day of the attack. However, this did not mean that for the German garrison it had all been plain sailing. Although the village itself remained in German hands, a small permanent lodgement had been secured by around 200 British men in the area attacked by the 21st Northumberland Fusiliers (2nd Tyneside Scottish), supported by the 22nd Northumberland Fusiliers (3rd Tyneside Scottish) to its south. That is just to the left of where so many of the Lincolns and Suffolks had fallen.[33]

Although this British bridgehead in and behind the German front line represented a success of sorts for the attackers, the 34th Division could certainly not call it the much-desired breakthrough. The incursion by the 34th Division troops on their far right (initially by the 15th and 16th Royal Scots and subsequently by men from other battalions who joined them) was much more threatening for the Germans, although it would be some time before the full story of what happened was revealed. It is just possible that no one other than the participants would ever have understood what went wrong, had it not been for the determination of the 110th Reserve Regiment's Lieutenant Heine to ensure the truth came out. After being captured during the battle on 1 July, he was imprisoned in the Sutton Bonington prisoner-of-war camp near Nottingham. But he smuggled out his version of events on the British right by handing it in a rolled-up cigarette to a German prisoner who was about to be repatriated.

It explains the circumstances that enabled the 15th Royal Scots, with the 16th Royal Scots in support, to succeed, where so many other British units had failed. No one should say that the Royal Scots were given an easy pass over No Man's Land. There are many who will vouch for the terrifying wall of fire that was put down in front of their trenches. The following account by the Royal Scots' Private Frank Scott confirms that the ordeal his regiment had to endure was not so different from that experienced by all the other units in the division:

Crossing that ground . . . was pure hell owing to their machine-guns and shell fire. It was awful seeing . . . your chums go under, and not being able to do anything . . . [about it].

[However] some of us managed to get across all right . . . [We] found their front line absolutely battered to bits . . . [There were] . . . just . . . heaps [of] chalk, and hardly anybody in it. Those [who were] left, were so demoralised that they . . . surrendered right away.[34]

What made the difference between success and failure within the German lines once the Royal Scots arrived there is described in Lieutenant Heine's smuggled report. It starts by describing the difficulties that made it hard for his 2nd Company to put up a good fight. The basic problem was that the unit had not prepared the position for combat. The 2nd Company was brought forward at the last minute, because the British preliminary bombardment had killed and wounded so many German soldiers in the 8th Company that it was replacing.

Firstly, the soldiers in the trench occupied by Heine and his men could only see a short distance in front of them: a maximum of 40 metres, but in some places less than half as much. That was because just in front of their position the ground sloped down into what the British referred to as Sausage Valley, the large, long depression that the Germans called Bécourt Mulde (Bécourt Hollow). The area in front was dead ground where the British could approach without being seen.

A second problem was outlined in the report that one of his brother officers sent to Heine shortly before the attack. It contained alarming news: 'The neighbouring 111th Reserve Regiment company has vacated the 150 metre area leading up to the dividing line between the regiments . . . In the front trench there are only 4 or 5 groups of men . . . 9 or 10 groups have been pulled back into its second trench. They have also taken away the machine gun . . . that was previously guarding our sector. The machine gun held by [our left platoon] . . . is out of action.'

It was probably this simple oversight, this gap in the line, that was critical. But the following description of the attack, which Heine rolled up in his cigarette, suggests that he perhaps believed the British had come up with a new way of beating the Germans, and that it had to be brought to the attention of his commanders before a more dangerous breakthrough took place:

All of a sudden, the attackers emerged out of a Russian sap . . . just metres away from our trench, and proceeded to kill all the German defenders from the 2nd and 6th Companies before they could come out of their dugouts. They then collected what they needed out of the same sap, and used it to prepare the Pioneer Trench for defence . . . Those who were not consolidating, advanced along the Pioneer Trench towards the 2nd Position. No-one stood in their way.[35]

The only part of Heine's report which appears to be wrong relates to the claim that a Russian sap played a part in the breakthrough. British reports suggest that the only tunnel excavated south of La Boisselle prior to the attack, in addition to the Lochnagar mine, was designed to shelter British gunners who needed to be near the German trenches at and just before zero hour. Nowhere in the regular unit files is there a suggestion that a tunnel was used for the purpose suspected by Heine.[36]

Whether or not the Russian sap south of La Boisselle had any part to play in the initial breakthrough, what is certain is that a contingent of around 250 British soldiers consisting mainly of Royal Scots, but backed up by parties from various other 102nd and 103rd Brigade units, including the 11th Suffolks, and the 24th and 27th Northumberland Fusiliers (Tyneside Irish), had advanced up to Peake Trench, only to fall back to Wood Alley and Round Wood (see map 6). There were even reports that some of the 27th Northumberland Fusiliers reached Contalmaison, the 34th Division's second objective, before retiring to join the Royal Scots.[37]

A high proportion of those who managed to cross No Man's Land and to press on deep behind German lines were on the division's extreme right, thereby avoiding the worst of the gunfire emanating out of La Boisselle itself (the Royal Scots and 27th Northumberland Fusiliers all advanced on the division's right flank). This only went to highlight the high cost of ignoring the officer who had complained that not enough artillery was being devoted to quelling resistance in the village.

But there was to be an even more heinous 'crime' committed by those in command. No one who reads the correspondence written by Major Cordeaux, the 10th Lincolns' commanding officer, can feel anything but sympathy for the mental anguish he suffered in the course of 1 July. Yet he is said to have ordered one of the most senseless assaults in the course of that terrible day. The question is: was he forced to issue the order by his superiors? Although it was clear by the afternoon of 1 July that it was virtually impossible for a large group of men to cross No Man's Land opposite the Lochnagar crater, that was precisely where he apparently ordered the remnants of Vignoles' carrying company to go in the middle of the afternoon, acting in conjunction with men from the 18th Northumberland Fusiliers, the 34th Division's mining battalion. It was all part of the bid to take over the German front line which, in spite of the Royal Scots' progress behind it, was still held by their enemy.

According to Subaltern Bernard Anderson, the officer who in Vignoles' absence was to lead the attack, he informed Cordeaux that the Germans were still in their front line in force. But that only elicited the response that

divisional HQ 'was already aware of this menace'. The attack must nevertheless go ahead. At 3.20 p.m. Anderson led his men over the top, only for
the Lincolns leading the assault to be instantly mown down. The attack was
speedily abandoned.[38]

This was just one of a brace of attacks that took place at the behest or with
the knowledge of the 101st Brigade that afternoon, both ending with equally
tragic results. 2nd Lieutenant Andrew Wright, a survivor following the 11th
Suffolks' advance as the 10th Lincolns' support battalion that morning, has
pointed out that there were also more informally organized efforts:

Throughout the day, little rushes were attempted by survivors, many of whom
must already have been wounded. Occasionally, a man was seen running singly
till he fell. One particularly fine effort was directed by a dozen men against a point
in the German trenches known as the Heligoland Redoubt. They sprang suddenly, as it seemed, to life, and dashing forward at a sharp pace, only to be burned
to death by a discharge of flamethrowers, just as they breasted the parapet. This
was in the afternoon. The sight of their crumpled figures staggering back from the
tongues of flame and smoke, tearing hopelessly at their burning clothes, then falling one by one, was terrible.[39]

During the days that followed, the British troops slowly but surely established a hold over the whole sector. First blood went to the Royal Scots,
who took the German strongpoint Scots Redoubt on 2 July. Then it was
the turn of III Corps' third unit, the 19th Division, who finally took most
of La Boisselle the day afterwards.[40]

One of the German victims of this British dominance was the young
officer Aspirant Brachat. In the account he wrote after he was captured,
Brachat recorded his and his comrades' last free moments:

When the English approached our dugout, I yelled [at my men]: 'Get out! Face the
enemy.' I was standing by the entrance when I was wounded by hand grenades.
Our dugout caught fire. I stood between the English and the burning dugout
where the stocked-up ammunition had exploded. There was a lot of crying out
and screaming, as many of my dear comrades suffocated or were burned to death.
My only wish was to escape. I said a brief prayèr, then raced through the rapidly
increasing flames to reach the back exit. I was very surprised when I managed to
make it through the flames. How I did it, I still don't know. I rushed over my
comrades' corpses and climbed up the dugout stairs . . . An English officer pointed

his pistol at me. However before he could fire, he was shot by my brave comrade Förster. I put down my gun. I was surrounded by hundreds of Englishmen. I was captured.[41]

In some ways Brachat could consider himself fortunate. All the more so when he discovered that one of his captors was the French teenager who just a few years back had come to stay in his parents' home to learn German. Now he was using that German to translate for the British.

There were many British soldiers lying out in No Man's Land who would have given their eye teeth to be in Brachat's position. Their exact number was never recorded. However, the casualties for the 34th Division were probably in excess of 6,000, if figures supplied by some of the units are anything to go by. The 101st Brigade stated that they had lost over 2,200 men including more than 1,200 killed or missing,[42] while the 103rd Brigade reported casualties of just under 2,000 including 1,400 killed or missing.[43] The brigade major of the 34th Division's Royal Artillery, who walked over No Man's Land a few days after the battle, recalled seeing 'Line after line of dead men [who] lay where they had fallen.'[44]

It would have been bad enough if the wounded could have been brought into the British lines the same day. But as Dr Jim Fiddian, the 11th Suffolks' medical officer, confirmed, that was just not possible. Because there was still some fighting going on during 2 July, it was not safe to walk out between the enemy lines on that day. Then once the fighting stopped, the wounded in the British front line were collected and carted off to clearing stations and hospitals. It was only on the morning of 3 July that Fiddian was finally able to bring succour to those who needed it most: the wounded lying untended in No Man's Land.

The following extract from his account reveals the depths to which these poor men had sunk:

On first looking over the parapet [that morning], the whole ground seemed [to be] covered with dead men. But presently, a feeble cry of 'Stretcher bearer!' was raised, as some wounded man caught sight of me, and gradually the cry was taken up by scores of others.

[As I stepped forward, I could see] unwounded limbs were [being] waved in the air. [Then], shockingly, mutilated forms began to crawl grotesquely and infinitely slowly towards me . . . Never shall I forget that appalling sight . . . [which was] on our own battalion frontage.

[At first] it was still difficult to work with stretcher bearers . . . as sniping was [still] going on. But my orderly and I could get about carrying water in petrol tins . . .

One ghastly tragedy was marked out on the ground. There was a patch of burnt grass a few yards from the Boche wire, and from this, a trail of burned grass and shreds of burned clothing led back to where lay a scorched . . . naked body. I was glad I could not recognize it . . .

At least the burned was out of his misery. Fiddian almost wept as he flitted across the battlefield, endeavouring to provide short-term aid where he could, and reassuring everyone he spoke to that they would eventually be picked up.

Unfortunately, he was only able to relieve the pain being suffered by the first few men he came across. His tube of morphia tablets soon ran out. Thereafter he could only supply more primitive assistance. It was lucky there were lots of empty tins lying around that had been filled with water. Just about every man he spoke to wanted a drink before anything else.

But as Fiddian's account makes clear, some were too weak, or maimed, even to drink in a conventional manner:

[There was] a fellow sitting [in a] . . . sap, [with his] head . . . [leaning] forward. Blood and saliva [were] dropping from horrible wounds [on] . . . the lower part of [his] . . . face. [His] right arm [was] badly smashed, and [his] wounds [were] full of maggots . . .

He was dying for a drink, but could not drink from a cup or spoon on account of his shattered jaws, and he could not hold his head back or lie back because he immediately choked in either of these positions.

I was several minutes discovering a way of giving him a drink by tearing strips of a towel in his kit and pushing them, dripping wet upwards into his mouth on the point of a knife. His relief at the solution of the problem was expressed in [what in other circumstances would have been] a comic salute, and he finally went off, sitting bolt upright on a stretcher, again with [that same] comic salute.

There were so many casualties on the part of the front where he had been operating that Fiddian and his few stretcher-bearers would never have managed to clear the battlefield that night had he not had the bright idea of going to the divisional dressing station. There he met a sergeant in charge of fifty men who were all willing to help. Fiddian immediately escorted them all to the British front line, where as he put it: 'One of the Medical Officers of the Royal Scots with his bearers joined us, and [by working together], we [finally managed to get] . . . all the wounded away.'

Meanwhile the time had come for the 34th Division and all its units to be relieved, including those Royal Scots, Northumberland Fusiliers and Suffolks who had clung on around Scots Redoubt. 2nd Lieutenant Andrew Wright recalled many years later what he witnessed as survivors came back:

By 8 a.m. on the 4th (July) [Captain O. H.] Brown had brought his men back to Bécourt Wood. When they had rested a little, we marched them on to a camp . . . in the hills a mile west of Albert. Covered with the grime of the past three days, his torn sleeve revealing the same bandage that had been roughly fixed in No Man's Land, [Brown] . . . rode at their head, mounted on Eliza, a half-blind mare, the most obstinate and ungainly of the officers' chargers. Whenever he turned back to inspect the fours of his column, they cheered him loudly. Battalion Headquarters moved back independently, leaving the trenches at 11 a.m.

The last of the Suffolks to come away were the stretcher-bearers, who had been allowed to quit their tasks as they were finished, and to move back in couples in their own time. Some of them had stopped at the [Bécourt] château to pick roses from the garden walls, and, though it was not Minden day, had pinned them to their tunics which were fouled with blood.

15: Bull's Eye

Montauban, 1 July 1916

(See maps 2 and 8)

If there was one sector of the Somme battlefield about which Haig and Rawlinson really had information that justified their confidence, it was at the southern end of the German front line opposite Mametz and Montauban. Here they had experienced some good fortune. They had scored an intelligence coup. For who should walk over to their trench on 27 June but Arnold Fuchs and his friend Ernst Girndt, two deserters, fresh out of the German front line at Montauban, and willing to talk about it too.

As if to demonstrate that good fortune often arrives in pairs, another deserter turned himself in two days later. This time it was Oswald Lakemaker from the 109th Reserve Regiment's 1st Battalion with similar information about Mametz. The intelligence he provided, which was similar to that supplied by Fuchs and Girndt, could not have been clearer, even after being expressed in the strange language used in official intelligence reports. The report concerning Lakemaker started with the words 'Our bombardment, prisoner states to have been very effective', and continued:

He describes the front line trench as consisting of a line of shell holes. Four dugouts in his platoon had collapsed . . . There was one good dugout in his Zug (platoon) in which about forty-five of them crowded during the bombardment. The entrance was twice blown in – they dug their way out . . . He said he had heard it was even worse behind than in the front line . . .[1]

The report painted an even more negative picture concerning the state of mind of Lakemaker's platoon:

Prisoner states morale is badly shaken . . . Prisoner says most of the men are longing for the attack to come. They remained in their dugouts during the [recent] gas attack in the hope that if we attacked they would be captured.

The writer of the intelligence report added that, according to Lakemaker:

The men of the 109th Reserve Regiment complained at having to leave the deep dugouts that they had constructed in the Ovillers sector, and live in the less well built ones in their present line, which they say are not fit to resist the artillery fire.[2]

Nevertheless, Lakemaker's interrogation revealed there was a weak point in the German line. The question was: should Rawlinson alter his master plan to take advantage of it?

And if he decided he should, could he? Time was short. Even if this evidence had reached Rawlinson the same morning (29 June), he only had forty-eight hours to react to it before zero hour. Also, before even considering changing the focus of the British attack, the 4th Army would have to take a view on whether Lakemaker could be trusted. After all, he had defected voluntarily. He had not fallen into British hands by accident. Was he a German plant, an agent provocateur, who was helping to set up a trap? Or could what he was saying be taken at face value? Was he just another vulnerable human being whose frailty had meant that carrying on in the trenches was just too much for him to bear?

That was certainly a question which exercised the minds of the British intelligence officers. When writing the report about Arnold Fuchs and Ernst Girndt, who claimed they had defected from the 12th Division's 62nd Regiment after their dugout had caved in with them inside, their case handler had commented: 'Prisoner statements seem accurate, the only suspicious feature being that they should have been able to desert in daylight with no interference from their own side. They explained this by saying that our bombardment was too intense to permit : . . anyone [to] fire . . : at them from their own side.'[3]

The intelligence officer appeared to have no such reservations about Lakemaker, possibly because his age and profession made him sound a safer bet. He was thirty-one years old, and was, as the intelligence officer put it, 'an educated man'. He had worked in an optician's shop before joining up. Lakemaker had also given the intelligence officer a convincing reason for defecting: he became desperate when, because of the shelling, no food or water could be supplied to the men in the front line; deserting was one way of putting an end to his torment.[4]

Given the importance of the message that Lakemaker and the two 62nd Regiment deserters had entrusted to the officers who had interrogated them, it is disturbing to see how this vital piece of intelligence was misinterpreted. In line with the positive thinking pervading the minds of many

British officers at that time, a positive gloss was put on the deserters' testimony when referring to it in the 4th Army Intelligence Summary. Rather than conceding that the intelligence was not necessarily relevant to other sectors, a much more general thesis was taken from it. The final intelligence summary issued before the start of the battle contained the following staggeringly over-optimistic conclusion: 'It is apparent that our artillery fire has been most effective. Most of the dugouts in the German front line have been blown in or blocked up.'[5]

The lack of rigour applied by the writer of the intelligence summary in coming up with that deduction is alarming. First, it unjustifiably extrapolated the few isolated reports on specific areas to produce a general picture of the whole front. Second, it totally ignored the evidence that contradicted the chosen thesis. Had not Lakemaker expressly indicated that the stronger dugouts in Ovillers might be more bombproof than the more flimsy versions in front of Mametz? Furthermore, the writer makes no reference to additional evidence supplied by prisoners from the Fricourt sector, which suggested that their dugouts were also still in good working order.[6]

One can only assume that the intelligence officer's judgement was swayed by a misinterpretation of the evidence supplied by a fourth German prisoner, from the Thiepval sector, who had reported that some of the entrances to the dugouts in his area had been 'blocked' by the bombardment. A closer reading of the evidence suggested that while the entrances may have caved in, the dugouts themselves had survived, making the superficial damage reversible.[7]

Whatever the reason, the intelligence officers' failure to interpret the facts correctly appears to have had disastrous consequences. The advice which Haig and Rawlinson should have been given was that there were proven weaknesses in the southern part of the front. This should have encouraged them firstly to concentrate a large proportion of their reserves there, and secondly to give instructions to the commanders of XIII and XV Corps to be ready to exploit the likely breakthrough in this sector.

Instead, Haig and Rawlinson were given to understand that the dugouts had been destroyed all along the front, leading them to conclude, as they did: why not attack everywhere in that case with more or less equal force?

The only saving grace was that, at least opposite Mametz and Montauban, the villages dominating the German front line after its sharp turn towards the east (see map 2), there really were grounds for the optimistic forecasts handed down by the officers to the troops.

It is unlikely that such grounds were explained to the cooks, or those who, on the evening before the battle, had to feed the 7th Division troops waiting south of Mametz, at the western end of this west-to-east stretch of the front line. Private A. R. Brennan of the 7th Division's 2nd Royal Irish Regiment noticed that 'rations and rum issues were plentiful that evening'. At the time he was grateful. Only later did he wonder whether 'we were being fattened for the slaughter. Some of us may have guessed it, but few could have thought that the Somme was to call for such a ghastly toll in human lives.'

Brennan's own fears about the next day, when his battalion and his brigade (the 22nd Brigade) were to play supporting roles in the second phase of the 7th Division's attack, appear to have diminished with the magnificent array of artillery that he saw in action from the safety of the British back trenches:

On the . . . 30th [of June], we moved into trenches on a ridge overlooking Happy Valley, just in front of a battery of eighteen pounders. Down below, the Valley presented an animated scene. Thousands of troops . . . were assembled together for what all thought was to be the big breakthrough . . .

On the other side of the Valley, a seemingly endless supply of big guns, wheel to wheel almost, sent out a continuous chain of projectiles towards the trenches of the long suffering Boche. They had a splendidly sheltered position, which the enemy would have found difficult to locate even if his artillery had been active. As it was, it seemed we had completely silenced him, and our job on the morrow promised to be an easy walk-over.[8]

That evidently was a sentiment shared by at least one of the officers, whose 30th Division unit, the 18th Battalion, the King's (Liverpool) Regiment, occupied part of the front line at the eastern end of this west-east stretch of trench, south of Montauban. When he had attempted to calm the nerves of Private James Deary prior to the assault – which as already mentioned had previously been scheduled to take place two days earlier – the officer had told him: 'Deary, all we shall have to do tomorrow is to go over the top, and collect the helmets.'[9]

Such optimism only began to dissipate in some quarters just before the attack was about to begin. Zero hour (7.30 a.m. here, as elsewhere, north of the Somme) was still two minutes away when Lance Corporal Edward Fisher, whose 18th Division support unit (10th Battalion, the Essex

Regiment) had started advancing from behind the centre of this west-east
stretch of trench, discovered that it was not going to be that simple:

After walking about twenty yards, I looked left to see if my men were keeping a
straight line, [and] . . . saw a sight I shall never forget: [what looked like] a giant
fountain rising [above the lines of men in front of me] about a hundred yards
[ahead] . . . It rose [higher and higher, until it was] nearly as high as Nelson's Column . . . [before it] slowly toppled over . . . [As it fell], huge slabs of earth and
chalk [came] thudding down, some with flames attached, on to the troops
[underneath].[10]

The eruption of almost biblical proportions, which Fisher had seen rise up
from the ground, was the result of British miners blowing up another of
their mines, this time packed with a 'mere' 5,000 pounds of explosives,
which had been placed under the German salient at Casino Point (see map
8). It was one of a series of mines exploded along the southern end of
the German front line shortly before zero hour. However, it appears to
have been the only one whose blast injured British soldiers as a result of a
mistake. Brigadier-General H. W. Higginson, commander of the 18th
Division's 53rd Brigade, whose men were injured by the rubble thrown up
by the explosion, alleged that the plunger on the mine had been pushed
down one minute later than planned (at 7.28 rather than 7.27 a.m.), imply-
ing that this was the reason why the detonation had wounded so many of
his men.

The explosion was evidently even more disruptive for the Germans.
According to Higginson, 'one machine gun which had been firing from
Casino Point was seen to go up in the air, and was afterwards found in No
Man's Land. [A] considerable number of dead Huns were also seen lying
round the crater.'[11] But it was the mayhem within the surrounding trenches,
as much as the devastation at the blast's epicentre, which was to be most
helpful to the attackers. As the stunned German defenders attempted to
gather their wits, the troops in the 53rd Brigade's leading battalions rushed
into the front trench, and after quelling any opposition, moved on, only
coming to a halt when faced with stiff opposition in and around
Pommiers Redoubt, 400 yards to the north of the captured Pommiers
Trench (see map 8).[12]

A British artillery observer who was tracking the troops' progress so
that he could relay it back to the gunners further back has described what

he witnessed as the advance along the rest of this east-west stretch of trench line started:

The 1st of July opened with a glorious though very misty morning. Dense belts of fog were hanging in the valleys (where the British front line was situated), and only the tops of the hills were to be seen (Montauban was on the ridge to the north of the British line) . . . Until 7.15 a.m. observation was practically impossible owing to the eddies of mist, rising smoke, flashing of bursting shells, and all one could see was the blurred outline of some miles of what appeared to be volcanoes in eruption.

At 7.20 a.m. rows of steel helmets and the glitter of bayonets were to be seen all along the front line. At 7.25 a.m., the scaling ladders having been placed in position, a steady stream of men flowed over the parapet, and waited in the tall grass till all were there, and then formed up. At 7.30 a.m . . . they were off, the mist lifting just enough to show the long line of divisions attacking. On our right, the French 39th Division. In front of us our 30th Division. On our left the 18th.

The line advanced steadily, scarcely meeting any opposition in the first three lines of trenches . . .

After the mist lifted, the light for observing was perfect. I had of course my own glass, and also a 7 foot monster recently arrived from the Lady Roberts' Telescope Fund, and every detail showed up with the utmost accuracy. There was no Hun shelling, and gradually [our] people emerged from their tunnels and sat on top of their shafts, till it felt quite like [being in] a point to point crowd.[13]

That may have been what it felt like from behind the junction point between the French and British Armies (see map 8). But elsewhere there were German pockets of resistance that at times threatened to be insuperable. Such pockets were the inevitable consequence of the German propaganda which informed troops that anyone captured would be shot.

Although the 'propaganda' was exaggerated, and hundreds of German prisoners were taken in the course of the assault, it is sad to have to confirm that it was not completely without foundation. Recalling the events leading up to the battle, Sydney Fuller, a private in the 8th Suffolk Regiment, which was the reserve 53rd Brigade Battalion available to exploit the blowing up of the Casino Point mine, wrote: 'The CO had us parade in the afternoon (on 30 June) when he gave us a short serious address, the main thing he impressed on us being: "Kill all you can, and don't take any prisoners."'[14]

Another British soldier who was fired up by an equally bloodthirsty exhortation was Albert Andrews, a twenty-five-year-old private in the 19th Manchesters (4th Manchester Pals), the right-hand leading battalion within the 30th Division's left-hand brigade (21st Brigade; see map 8). His account of the reception they received from the Germans as they advanced over the 400 yards of No Man's Land separating them goes some way to explaining why he and his fellow Mancunians embraced such an uncivilized command:

As we travelled along . . . Fritz let us have it with shrapnel, machine guns and rifles . . . Our lads kept falling . . . and about half way across, the second wave catches up with the first to fill these gaps up. About 100 yards from the German trench our officer turned and said 'Up a bit on the left!' Then pitched forwards. That was the last order he ever gave . . .

I jumped into the German trench, what was left of it . . . near a dugout . . . In the doorway there was a big barrel. As soon as I jumped in, a German leapt from behind the barrel. But I was already on guard and . . . had my bayonet on his chest. He was trembling . . . with his hands above his head [and was] saying something to me which I did not understand . . .

I pointed to his belt and bayonet. He took these off, and his hat . . . as well, emptied his pockets and offered the lot to me.

Just then one of my mates was coming up the trench. 'Get out of the way, Andy. Leave him to me! I'll give him one to himself!' He meant he would throw a bomb at him which would have blown him to pieces.

[The German soldier] . . . was on his knees in front of me now . . . pleading . . . 'He's an old man,' I said . . . He looked sixty. At the finish, I pointed my thumb to our lines . . . He jumped up, and with his hands above his head, ran out of our trench towards our lines, calling out all the time . . .

We both [then] bombed the dugout, and turned round to go along the trench when three [more] . . . Germans came running towards us with their hands up . . . We both fired, and two fell, my mate saying as he let go: 'That's for my Brother in the Dardanelles. And as he fired again and the third German fell 'That's for my winter in the trenches. We walked up to them and one of them moved. My mate kicked him and pushed his bayonet into him. That finished him . . .

This kind of thing was going on all along the line, no Germans being spared. We hadn't exactly been told 'No prisoners,' but we were given to understand that was what was wanted. The same kind of thing happened at the second German trench and the third.

Then we waited outside Glatz Redoubt, all our guns being turned on this ring of trenches . . . [Then] we got the order 'Charge!', and away we went at the double, killing all that stayed there. A good many retreated towards Montauban, and we opened fire on them [too].[15]

It was still only 8.30 a.m. But that was more or less the limit of the 19th Manchesters' assault. (It was to push forward a relatively short distance later in the day.) It was eventually supported by its sister battalion within the 21st Brigade, 18th King's (Liverpool), which largely due to a German machine-gunner concealed on its left, suffered around 500 casualties before coming up on the 19th Manchesters' left, and the 89th Brigade, whose line sloped away from being level on the right, down Dublin Trench (see map 8).[16] It is a measure of the extent to which the British artillery and infantry dominated the Germans on the extreme right of the 4th Army's attack, that the casualties suffered by the two battalions in the 89th Brigade were in both cases fewer than 150; this must be a record for units advancing such distances on 1 July 1916.[17]

But for the 30th Division's third brigade, 90th Brigade, Glatz Redoubt and the adjacent trench to the west was just a beginning. Its two leading battalions, the 16th and 17th Manchesters, left the original British front line at 8.30 a.m. with the expectation they would advance into Montauban itself, passing through the 19th Manchesters on the way.

This was the fulfilment of XIII Corps' plan plotted by its commander Lieutenant-General Walter Congreve. It required his corps' 30th and 18th Divisions to advance to the north, north-west and east of Montauban, so that his troops would link up with those of XV Corps to the north-west of that village, and with the French to its south-east. In order to accomplish the latter purpose, the extreme right wing of the advance was to be halted some distance to the south of the village, so that the link with Britain's French ally could be made south of Bernafay Wood at the southern end of Dublin Trench (see map 8).[18]

One of those participating in the 90th Brigade's thrust was Kenneth Macardle, a twenty-six-year-old 2nd Lieutenant in the 17th Manchesters. His account starts by recording his excitement the night before when he learned for the first time that he was going to be allowed to join in. 'Oh blessed Adjutant Macdonald,' he wrote excitedly in his diary during the evening of 30 June, adding:

Tonight's the night. Tomorrow is der Tag . . . Only four officers per company go over. Yet although I missed all the wonderful training the others had, I am to go in with the company.

The others have done it over and over again. [They have] stormed the trenches, taken Montauban . . . a dozen times down by Picquigny where it was all marked out with flags. And shallow trenches exactly to scale. They know every house, as it was before we bombarded the village with 12 inch shells. They know every yard. Where every man is to go. They have passed most of it on to me.

On the way up from Etinehem (around four miles south-east of Albert) to Cambridge Copse (about half a mile north-west of Maricourt), where they were to enter the assembly trenches, Macardle found himself walking beside 'young' Victor Godfrey of the 2nd Royal Scots Fusiliers, which would be the Manchesters' support battalion the next day. They had worked together in the spring. 'We had a lot to talk about,' Macardle affirmed. 'He was a very good looking young man. We talked a lot about a girl six years older than himself whom he wanted to marry.'

But eventually such thoughts about the future and marital bliss had to be put to one side, so that he could concentrate on the present. First of all Macardle had to endure what he referred to as a 'comfortless' cold, sleepless night in the assembly trenches. 'They were very crowded and there was no room to sit', let alone lie down, he recalled. Then there was the long slow dawning of the new day.[19] And finally, at 6.25 a.m., the intense artillery barrage started, as it did all the way along the Somme front, making it hard for a man to think of anything except when it would lift off the front German trenches so that the long-awaited assault could begin?

Macardle went on to describe his battalion's advance from the original British front line in the following terms:

A Company [started] . . . in front. Next came a carrying party of Scots. And then our company (B Company). We were one and a quarter miles from Montauban, and between us and that heavily wooded village, every inch of ground was churned up and pitted with shell holes.

It was impossible even to locate the enemy's front line. His second was a great irregular ditch, all craters and newly turned earth.

But Macardle's great test would only start at about 10 a.m. when after passing through the 89th Brigade units, the 17th Manchesters were due to charge into the village from the area north of Glatz Redoubt. They had been held up at the Redoubt by the British artillery, which only lifted onto trenches north of Montauban at that time.

'At last it was time to go,' Macardle recalled:

I looked at A Company, [expecting] to see them rise. But the seconds ticked on, [and nothing happened]. I found a[n A Company] sergeant, and shouting in his ear, asked where were his officers. 'All gone Sir!' he shouted back.

[But] then I saw Wain . . . the last of A Company's officers, his face haggard with pain, one leg covered with blood. His voice, full of sobs . . . he shouted: 'Get up you bastards! Blast your souls! Get up!' When I waved to him, he smiled, and dropped [to the ground], knowing it was no longer up to him. We of B Company took over.

As Macardle and the survivors from both companies rose to their feet to make their great rush forward, they faced machine-gun and rifle fire coming from their left. But once they reached their objective, there was little if any opposition. There was not much left of the village. All that remained was what Macardle referred to as a 'monstrous heap of rubble', stinking of rotting corpses. Everywhere he looked there were 'dead and dying Germans, some with terrible wounds'. Those who were unharmed because they had taken refuge in their dugouts were only too glad to surrender. As Macardle put it, they then 'went streaming back to Maricourt, unguarded, holding their arms up and calling "Mercy Kamerad". They had thrown away their . . . equipment and were utterly demoralised.'

After the capture of Montauban, the 90th Brigade battalions advanced to Montauban Alley north of the village, with a view to holding the heights against the inevitable counter-attack. They had achieved all their objectives and it was only 11 a.m. Just as important was the fact that although the casualties could not be described as light, they had been kept within reasonable bounds by the standards of 1 July 1916. Around 330 men were killed, wounded or missing in Macardle's battalion, while 90th Brigade's total casualties were under 1,200.[20]

Although parts of the 18th Division (the unit whipped into shape by Ivor Maxse, the major-general whose training methods were to become a byword for all that was slick and effective in the British Army) had made equally fast inroads into the German lines – its left-hand brigade, 54th Brigade, reached Pommiers Trench before 8 a.m. – there were hold-ups elsewhere.[21] The worst of these were in Maxse's easternmost brigade, 55th Brigade, which was supposed to be protecting the 30th Division's left flank (see map 8). In fact it was the delayed advance by this brigade's right-hand unit, the 8th East Surreys, which had left the way open for a German machine-gunner, in a strongpoint known as the Warren, to cut down a substantial proportion of the 18th King's (Liverpool), 30th Division's left-hand battalion.

The cause of the problem was not the 8th East Surreys, whose Captain Billie Nevill had famously arranged for two footballs to be kicked across No Man's Land in an effort to strengthen the resolve of his men. The East Surreys and another 55th Brigade battalion, the 7th Queen's Royal Regiment (West Surrey), were held up because the 7th Buffs, their sister company within 55th Brigade, had not been able to clear the area near the Montauban–Carnoy road where there was an occupied minefield (see map 8). The logjam was only cleared when, following the 30th Division's thrust to Glatz Redoubt and towards Montauban, the Germans holding up the 55th Brigade troops decided to retreat, fearful that their lines of communication to the north were about to be severed. But it was after 5 p.m. before the Queen's Royal Regiment, and the other 18th Division troops, were lined up along Montauban Alley to the west of the 30th Division units, thereby enabling the two divisions to hold the position securely.[22]

At a time when the 55th Brigade hold-up was threatening to delay the whole operation beyond the end of the first day, the commander of the 18th Division's reserve unit, the 8th Suffolks, was ordered to position his troops just behind the original British front line in case additional troops were needed to resolve the crisis. As it turned out, the hold-up was cleared without their assistance, and during the afternoon they proceeded into a nearby assembly trench. But there, the regiment's Sydney Fuller saw a sight that made his blood run cold:

Several of our men were lying in it, killed by the enemy's shells. In one place, a man was kneeling, as if in prayer, his hands covering his face. Lying in the trench behind him was another man, face downwards, half buried in the earth thrown into the trench by the shells. A short distance away, another man was sitting on the fire step, buried to the knees, and looking as if he had suddenly turned to stone.

A little further along the trench, I stepped on something, and looking down, I saw a piece of a man's backbone, and pieces of flesh strewn about the trench. Hanging down from the parapet in the corner of the traverse, was a mass of entrails, already swarming with flies. And so on, here and there along the trench, wherever the enemy's shells had dropped in.[23]

The grotesque human remains that had taken Fuller's breath away were a salutary reminder of the damage the German artillery could wreak if they were not dominated and subdued with massive firepower. A lot of space has been devoted in this chapter to the infantry's successes. But none of it would have been possible had it not been for the British, and French, artillery. Without giving precise details of the extent to which French batteries helped out in the XIII Corps' sector, the British official history asserts that in the areas covered by Congreve's corps and the French XX Corps, on XIII Corps' right, the British and French batteries outnumbered the Germans 'nearly four to one . . . and during the 1st July it practically destroyed its opponents, so that there was almost a complete absence of artillery reply'.[24]

Set against this background it comes as no surprise to discover that the French – whose artillery had destroyed German dugouts just as effectively in their sectors north and south of the Somme as the British did in the Montauban and Mametz sectors – should have fared so well on 1 July. The French XX Corps, whose two divisions, the 39th and 11th Divisions, assaulted the German trenches north of the Somme immediately on the British right at the same zero hour (7.30 a.m.), achieved all of its objectives, including taking the village of Curlu. Meanwhile the two French corps south of the Somme, which surprised the Germans by attacking at 9.30 a.m., were equally successful, capturing Dompierre and Becquincourt (see map 9). The combined number of prisoners captured by the French was in excess of 4,000.[25]

Interestingly, given the state of the German defences after all this pummelling by the British and French artillery, the British casualties in the Montauban sector were still relatively high: over 3,000 for each of XIII Corps' assaulting divisions, with 30th Division's total including about 825 killed or missing, and 18th Division's total including about 950 killed or missing.[26]

It is only the German casualty statistics that are more predictable. Their 6th Bavarian Reserve Regiment, which was one of the German units operating in the Montauban sector and in the sector attacked by the French north of the Somme, suffered casualties of at least 2,000 officers and men, although there is one source who claims that of the regiment's 3,500 men only 500 were left standing at the end of the battle.[27]

These are just the statistics. What about the facts on the ground? The contrast between the hurricane bombardment that had produced the horrific scene spotted by Fuller and the relative peace and quiet that had descended over the battlefield by the time he witnessed it, could not have been more dramatic. 'The enemy's guns were by now quite quiet and only . . . comparative[ly] few of ours were firing,' Fuller reported. It was a testament to the unchallenged superiority that British forces had achieved on this part of the front. The question now was: could Rawlinson exploit it?

16: The Attack

Mametz and Fricourt, 1 July 1916

(See maps 2 and 7)

After all the torments endured by British soldiers in the front line, it seems ever so slightly unfair that it is the contents of the pages written by the war poets which for most of us are our main source of information about life in the trenches during World War 1. That being said, it is no surprise to find at least one of these poets in place so he could write up his experiences on the first day of the Battle of the Somme.

Siegfried Sassoon was a twenty-nine-year-old 2nd Lieutenant in the 1st Battalion, the Royal Welch Fusiliers, a 7th Division unit, when the great day arrived. His battalion was stationed in the support trenches to the south-west of Mametz during the first Somme attack. Although it was destined not to participate in the first phase of the 'Big Push', Sassoon nevertheless claims he played a minor role in ensuring the attacks by his brigade, 22nd Brigade, went as smoothly as could be expected.

Because he was one of the most intelligent spectators at the beginning of the great attack, it is no surprise to learn that Sassoon was not entirely convinced by all the claims that the initial assault would be plain sailing. But in his first entry on the lead-up to the battle, he recalls feeling strangely, irrationally reassured by what was written in his unit's orders:

Seventh Division Battle Plan didn't look aggressively unpleasant on paper as I transcribed it into my notebook. Rose Trench, Orchard Alley, Apple Alley and Willow Avenue were among the first objectives in our sector, and my mind very properly insisted on their gentler associations. Nevertheless, this topographical Arcadia was to be seized, cleared and occupied when the historic moment arrived . . . There wasn't going to be any mistake about it this time. We decided, with quite a glow of excitement, that the Fourth Army was going to fairly wipe the floor with the Boches.[1]

Although he and his battalion were not going to play a direct role in the German defeat, Sassoon nevertheless wanted to do something that would make a difference. While waiting for the fighting to start, he decided that his very small contribution would involve his increasing the size of the gaps in the British wire by using the wire cutters he had purchased from the Army and Navy Stores in London. 'Any fool could foresee what happened when troops got bunched up as they left their trench for a daylight attack,' he wrote.[2] Widening the gaps in the wire would hopefully lessen the chance of that happening to the men in the 20th Manchesters (the sister battalion within the 22nd Brigade), who had been given the thankless task of going over the top and up the slope in No Man's Land the next day, with a view to capturing Sunken Road Trench (see map 7).

With that in mind, during the early morning of 30 June, Sassoon clambered out of the front-line trench, followed by an assistant, crept out through the long grass and lying on his stomach, made a start. It involved 'shearing savagely at the tangles which had bewildered us in the dark, but which were now [in daylight] at our mercy'. It was all the more exciting because he had not asked his company commander for permission to complete the task they had started the night before. 'It was rather like going out to weed a neglected garden after being warned there might be a tiger among the gooseberry bushes,' Sassoon commented.

Fortunately for Sassoon, and his assistant, the tiger never materialized, and after being called in by his company commander who had eventually seen what he was doing, the two men crawled back to the front trench without a shot being fired at them. 'It had been great fun,' Sassoon remarked, flourishing his wire cutters.[3]

Whether or not Sassoon really did make the impact he claimed, his account of the moments leading up to the assault certainly helps set the scene for the attack itself. It starts with the preamble: 'On July the first, the weather, after an early morning mist, was of the kind commonly called heavenly.' It then goes on to describe what he experienced in the assembly trench dugout, where he and his company commander had taken refuge prior to the attack: 'The air vibrated, and the earth rocked and shuddered. Through the sustained uproar the tap and uproar of machine guns could be identified. But . . . no retaliation came our way, until a few 5.9 shells shook the roof of our dugout.' All the while both Sassoon and his commander 'sat speechless, deafened and stupefied by the seismic state of affairs', and when the commander lit a cigarette, 'the match flame staggered crazily'.[4]

However, for the most vivid account of what it was like to be in the attack itself the best source is the 22nd Manchesters' Sergeant Harry Tawney, the thirty-five-year-old economic history lecturer, who now had to step up to the plate and pass muster as warrior and leader. It has been suggested before that this Manchester battalion might have a crucial part to play, situated as it was on the 7th Division's right wing. The reason why its role was so important was that the success of the whole plan devised by XV Corps' commander, Lieutenant-General Horne, relied on the 22nd Manchesters' objective being taken.

Horne had devised his plan with the express intention of bypassing the strongly held village of Fricourt west of Mametz, at least during the first stage of the attack. Instead of assaulting Fricourt head on, a tactic similar to that devised for Gommecourt (see Chapter 10, p. 118) had been proposed: attacks were to be launched on the northern flank of the village by XV Corps' 21st Division and on the eastern flank of Mametz by the 7th Division, with a view to joining forces behind Fricourt's back.

That was where the Manchesters, and the 2nd Battalion, the Queen's Royal Regiment (West Surrey), came in. They were the battalions that would help to form the right arm of this pincer movement. After circling round the eastern side of Mametz, they or the other units in their brigade and division would, it was hoped, end up holding not just Danzig Alley and Fritz Trench, north-east of Mametz, but they would go on to establish contact with the left arm of the pincer at Bottom Wood (see map 7).[5]

But before the attack started, the battalions had to be assembled. According to Harry Tawney, the 22nd Manchesters' assembly routine began during the evening of 30 June, when shortly before their 9.30 p.m. departure from the Bois de Tailles, those who wanted to were blessed by a 'priest':

The priest stood in the door of the wooden shanty. The communicants stood and knelt in ranks outside. One guessed at the familiar words through the rattling of rifle bolts, the bursts of song, and occasional laughter from the other men, as they put their equipment together outside their little bivouacs, bushes bent till they met, and covered with tarpaulins, or smoked happily in an unwonted freedom from fatigues.

An hour later we fell in on the edge of the wood, and after the roll was called by companies, moved off. It was a perfect evening, and the immense overwhelming tranquillity of sky and down uniting . . . millions of enemies and allies in its solemn unavoidable embrace dwarfed into insignificance the wrath of man and his feverish . . . [destructive] . . . energy. One forgot the object for which we were marching to the trenches. One felt as though one were on the verge of some new and tremendous discovery. And the soft cheering of the knots of men who turned

out to watch us pass seemed like the last faint hail of landsmen to explorers bound
for unknown seas.

Then the heat struck us and at the first halt we flung ourselves down panting
like dogs.

It normally took the men around forty minutes to march from the wood,
the Bois de Tailles, to the front line. The Manchesters' section was just to
the south-east of Bulgar Point, this being the spot where they had lost
all those officers at the beginning of June (see Chapter 4, p. 38). However,
on this occasion, they were held up every ten or twenty yards by what
Tawney referred to as a 'wretched machine gun section' who apparently
had not yet learned how to carry their 'beastly instruments'. Two hours
passed before they reached their bit of trench.

More delays occurred even after they arrived. There were too many men
for the available trench space; somehow they had to be crushed in. And that
in its turn led to another difficulty. Tawney had to force his way up and
down the trench to check everyone was in the right place. It was well after
midnight before the men could rest.[6] As for Tawney himself, he snuggled
up in a cubbyhole in the trench wall, and pretended to be asleep when an
officer asked him to move so he could climb in as well. 'This is a holiday,
and out of school we're all equal,' Tawney thought, but did not say, pleased
at having the chance to apply his left-wing principles to the Army.

He didn't rest for long, fearful the men would think he was shirking.
Eventually the new day dawned, and soon the intense bombardment that
preceded all the attacks on 1 July was unleashed on the German trenches
opposite the 7th Division's front as well.

When, six days previously, Tawney had watched the bombardment
of the German trenches from a distance, he had not been impressed (see
Chapter 4, p. 50). But being more or less in the thick of it was a very different matter, as his euphoric description bears witness:

It was a glorious morning, and as though there were some mysterious sympathy
between the wonders of the ear and eye, the bewildering tumult seemed to grow
more insistent with the growing brilliance of the atmosphere and the intenser blue
of the July sky. The sound was different not only in magnitude, but in quality
from anything known to me.

It was not a succession of explosions, or a continuous roar. I at least never heard
either a gun or a bursting shell. It was not a noise; it was a symphony. It did not

move. It hung over us. It was as though the air were full of a vast agonized passion, bursting now into groans and sighs, now into shrill screams, and pitiful wimpers, shuddering beneath terrible blows, torn by unearthly whips, vibrating with the solemn pulse of enormous wings.

And the supernatural tumult did not pass in this direction or that. It did not begin, intensify, decline and end. It was poised in the air, a stationary panorama of sound, a condition of the atmosphere . . . It seemed one had only to lift one's eyes to be appalled by the writhing of the tormented element above one, that a hand raised ever so little above the level of the trench would be sucked away into a whirlpool, revolving with cruel and incredible velocity over infinite depths.

And this feeling, while it filled one with awe, filled one also with triumphant exultation, the exultation of struggling against a storm in mountains, or watching the irresistible course of a swift and destructive river.

Although stunned by this wall of sound, Tawney somehow managed to carry on as normal:

One was intent on practical details, wiping the trench dirt off the bolt of one's rifle, reminding the men of what each was to do, and when the message went round 'Five minutes to go!', seeing that all bayonets were fixed.

At 7.30 we went up the ladders, doubled through the gaps in the wire and lay down waiting for the line to form up on each side of us. When it was ready, we went forward not doubling, but at a walk. For we had 900 yards of rough ground to the trench, which was our first objective, and about fifteen hundred to a further trench where we were to wait for orders.

It was during this advance that Tawney was to undergo a kind of metamorphosis. Even as late as the evening before, he had still been more a civilian than a soldier. He had been exasperated once again by the inefficiency of the Army. It did not even know how to train troops to move up a trench without long delays. However, as he moved into enemy territory, the warrior lurking somewhere deep inside him began to loosen the bonds that had restrained this side of his character for so long.

The first stage of this change occurred within seconds of his advance into No Man's Land:

I hadn't gone ten yards before I felt a load fall from me . . . I had been worried by the thought 'Suppose one should lose one's head and get other men cut up.

Suppose one's legs should take fright and refuse to move.' Now I knew it was all right. I shouldn't be frightened, and I shouldn't lose my head. Imagine the joy of that discovery! I felt quite happy and self-possessed. It wasn't courage. That I imagine is the quality of facing danger which one knows to be danger, of making one's spirit triumph over the bestial desire to live in this body. But I knew that I was in no danger. I knew I shouldn't be hurt . . .

And all the time . . . one was shouting the sort of thing that NCOs do shout, and no one attends to. 'Keep your extension!' 'Don't bunch!' 'Keep up on the left!' . . .

We crossed three lines that had once been trenches, and tumbled into the fourth, our first objective. 'If it's all like this, it's a cake walk' said a little man beside me . . .

But it was not all going to be like this, and the torment to which Tawney was exposed, as he sought to manage the bloodshed behind enemy lines, led to a second shift in his feelings, as his innate sensitivity was overridden by a degree of callousness:

On the parados lay a wounded man . . . shot, to judge by the blood on his tunic, through the loins or stomach. I went to him and he grunted, as if to say 'I am in terrible pain. You must do something for me . . .' I hate touching wounded men . . . One hurts them so much, and there's so little to be done. I tried without much success to ease his equipment, and then thought of getting him into the trench. But it was crowded with men, and there was no place to put him. So I left him.

He grunted again angrily [this time], and looked at me with hatred as well as pain in his eyes. It was horrible! It was as though he cursed me for being alive and strong when he was in torture.

I tried to forget him, by snatching a spade from one of the men and working fiercely on the parapet. But one's mind wasn't in it. It was over there, there where they were waiting for us . . .

When I looked round, I saw the men staring stupidly, like calves smelling blood, at two figures. One was doubled up over his stomach, hugging himself and frowning. The other was holding his hand out and looking at it with a puzzled expression. It was covered with blood. The fingers . . . were blown off. And he seemed to be saying: ' . . . This is a funny kind of thing to have for a hand.' But our orders not to be held up by attending to the wounded were strict. So I'm thankful to say there was no question what to do for them.

But it was the events that occurred during the second phase of the advance which were to bring about the most extreme change of all: the transformation of a civilized professorial type into what Tawney himself referred to as a 'palaeolithic savage', who once blooded quickly rediscovered the excitement of the hunt, the joy that could be gained from killing, an emotion that he had not experienced since he had last fired his catapult as a child, and his shotgun as a young man.

What made the change so unexpected was that Tawney had started off this second phase wondering whether the delayed resumption of their advance would result in the Germans being able to shoot at him:

It was time to make for our next objective. In fact . . . we were three minutes overdue. Not . . . a trifle. The artillery were to lift from the next trench at the hour fixed for us to go forward. Our delay meant that the Germans had a chance of reoccupying it, supposing them to have gone to earth under the bombardment.

Anyway, when we'd topped a little fold in the ground, we walked straight into a zone of machine gun fire. The whole line dropped like one man, some dead and wounded, the rest taking instinctively to such cover as the ground offered . . .

For the moment, the sight of the Germans drove everything else out of my head . . . [They made] an easy target . . . Some of them . . . knelt – one for a moment even stood – on top of their parapet to shoot . . . [They were] . . . not much more than a hundred yards of us . . . One couldn't miss them. Every man I fired at dropped . . . except one . . . Him, the boldest of the lot, I missed more than once. I was puzzled and angry . . . Not that I wanted to hurt him, or anyone else. It was [the] missing I hated.

Many soldiers have talked about the red mist that descends over their normal sensibilities when in the midst of battle. That has its uses, for it helps to banish fear. But when the mist lifts and the soldier has to come face to face with the consequences of all the shooting, that has to be the most painful moment of all. This was the stage Tawney was at after seeing off the enemy north of Bulgar Alley–Bucket Trench, where he and his men appear to have become marooned (see map 7):

When the Germans got back into their trench, I stopped firing, and looked about me. Just in front of me lay a boy, who had been my batman till I sacked him for slackness. I had cursed him the day before for being drunk. He lay quite flat and might have been resting, except for a big ragged hole at the base of his skull where a bullet had come out.

His closest friend, also a bit of a scallywag, was dead beside him. Next to me, a man was trying with grimy hands to dab a field dressing on to the back of a lance corporal, shot it seemed through the chest, who was clutching his knees and rocking to and fro . . . My platoon officer lay on his back. His face and hands were as white as marble. His lungs were labouring like a bellows worked by machinery. But his soul was [already] gone.

'Is there any chance for us, sergeant?' a man whispered. I said it would be all right. The [Queen's] would be coming through us in an hour and we would go forward with them. All the same, it looked as if they wouldn't find much except corpses.

Some might say it is to Tawney's credit that he did not disappear into a shell hole and wait to be rescued by the support battalion that was bound to advance sooner or later. Others might respond he was in shock, and as a result misguided. Whichever description suits him best, he decided he had to find out how many men were left, and who was on their right and left.

The man he sent to find out who was on the right did not prosper. No sooner had he left the security of his shell hole than a report came back to tell Tawney: 'He's hit.'

'That hurt me,' Tawney remarked. 'It was as if I'd condemned him to death.' He resolved to crawl out to see whether the battalion's left-hand company could be located. 'The officer, a [mere] boy was – no blame to him – at the end of his tether. He protested, but in the end let me go.'

'Of course [with the benefit of hindsight] it was idiotic,' Tawney subsequently conceded. 'If our company had lost half or more of its strength, why should [the left-hand] company have fared any better?':

Anyway, as I crawled back, first straight back and then off to my right, everything seemed peaceful enough. One couldn't believe that the air a foot or two above one's head was deadly . . .

Then I saw a knot of men lying down away to the right. I didn't realize they were dead or wounded and waved to them, [calling out]: 'Reinforce!' When they didn't move, I knelt up and waved again.

I don't know what most men feel like when they're wounded. What I felt was that I had been hit by a tremendous iron hammer swung by a giant of inconceivable strength, and then twisted with a sickening sort of wrench, so that my head and back banged on the ground, and my feet struggled as though they didn't belong to me. For a second or two, my breath wouldn't come. I thought . . . this is death, and hoped it wouldn't take too long.

I tried to turn on my side, but the pain when I moved was like a knife, and stopped me dead. There was nothing to do but lie on my back. After a few minutes, two men in my platoon crawled back past me . . . They saw me . . . but . . . didn't stop . . . I could have cried at their being so cruel. It's being cut off from human beings that's as bad as anything when one's copped it badly. And when a lad wriggled up to me, and asked 'What's up, Sergeant?' I loved him. I said 'Not dying I think, but pretty bad.' . . . He wriggled on. What else could he do?

I raised my knees to ease my pain in my stomach, and at once bullets came over. So I put them down. Not that I much minded dying now . . . By a merciful arrangement, when one's half dead, the extra plunge does not seem very terrible . . .

It was very hot . . . I began to shout feebly for stretcher bearers . . . Of course, it was . . . cowardly. They couldn't hear me and if they could, they oughtn't to have come. It was asking them to commit suicide. But I'd lost my self-respect.

Tawney's next memory was a nice one:

It was a lovely evening, and a man stood beside me. I caught him by his ankle in terror lest he should vanish. In answer to his shouts . . . a doctor came and looked at me. Then, promising to return in a minute, they went off to attend to someone else. That was the worst moment I had. I thought they were deceiving me. That they were leaving me for good. A man badly knocked out feels as though the world had spun him off into a desert of unpeopled space . . . The sense of abandonment goes near to break his heart. I did so want to be spoken kindly to, and I began to whimper, partly to myself and partly out loud.

But they came back, and directly the doctor spoke to his orderly, I knew he was one of the best men I had ever met . . . He listened like an angel while I told him a confused non-sensical yarn about being hit in the back by a nose cap . . . He said I had been shot with a rifle bullet through the chest and abdomen, and gave me morphia . . . There was nothing more he could do. No stretcher bearers were at hand, so it was out of the question to get me in that night.

But after I had felt that divine compassion flow over me, I didn't care. I was like a dog kicked and bullied by everyone that's at last found a kind master.[7]

Tawney's account does not stretch to describing his removal from the battlefield, but he was eventually carried in, and survived to tell the tale.

Nearly 350 men from the 22nd Manchesters battalion were either killed or missing, their total casualties being in excess of 470.[8]

The sacrifice of so many young men was not entirely in vain. Benefiting from the Manchesters' initial thrust, the support unit, the 2nd Queen's Royal Regiment (West Surrey), was eventually able to join them in Bucket Trench, before moving on to seize the 91st Brigade's first objective, Danzig Alley. The 2nd Queen's ended the day the master of Fritz Trench, to the north-east of Mametz, linked up with the leading left-hand 91st Brigade battalion, the 1st South Staffordshires. This battalion not only captured Mametz itself but also held the northern end of the long line of trenches running down from north of Mametz, round its western side, ending up in the German front line south-west of the village. (This line is shown in map 7.) It was finally secured thanks to assistance from battalions in the 7th Division's third brigade, 22nd Brigade.[9]

The attacks by the 21st Division brigades north of Fricourt also had mixed fortunes. On the one hand, its northern brigade, 64th Brigade, ended the day with a bridgehead running from the German front line to Crucifix Trench, linked up with the Royal Scots in Scots Redoubt (see map 7; see also Chapter 14, p. 192). On the other hand, some of the units under its command suffered disastrous losses. Some of the worst disasters affected units within the 50th Brigade, which had been 'borrowed' from the 17th Division. For example, the 10th West Yorkshires, who were supposed to advance past the northern side of Fricourt, in the process neutralizing guns that might enfilade the two 21st Division brigades attacking further north, had the unhappy distinction of suffering no fewer than 710 casualties on 1 July. They were victims of the failure by the commanders of XV Corps and the division to provide covering artillery fire on an ongoing basis in the areas not being attacked, because of the decision not to assault Fricourt head-on during the first phase. The mines that were exploded in the area around the German Tambour provided insufficient protection.[10]

The repercussions from the failure of that attack were felt when a head-on assault on Fricourt's strongest defences was ordered notwithstanding the fact that the attack by the 10th West Yorkshires, which was supposed to first make the village more vulnerable, had failed. Brigadier-General W. J. T. Glasgow of the 50th Brigade objected, but was overruled, with the result that the ill-fated attack by the 7th Green Howards went ahead at 2.30 p.m. Many of the attackers were predictably mown down, as the battalion lost over 350 men within three minutes, more than would have been the case if the preliminary artillery barrage had not missed the wire in front of the position. That left the attackers with just a few gaps in the wire through which they could penetrate, always a godsend to the defending machine-gunners.[11]

It was the second disaster of the day for the 7th Green Howards. At 7.45 that morning the battalion's Major Kent had inexplicably ordered his company to advance towards Fricourt, even though he should have known that no advance was to be made until the 10th West Yorkshires had done their job of attacking in order to make the village more vulnerable. The men of the 7th Green Howards were scythed down by a single machine gun just as quickly as their colleagues were in the later attack. When Lieutenant-Colonel Ronald Fife, their commanding officer, heard what had happened, his first reaction was to accuse Kent of going 'mad'.[12] It is possible that Kent, who was also wounded, did have a moment of madness. However, probably no one outside his family and friends will ever know, since Kent never explained on the record why he had given such a premature order.

The crumbling state of the front-line system defences in the Mametz sector might have led one to expect that in capturing them and the village itself, the casualties would be relatively slight. As it turned out, they were more or less the same as those suffered in capturing Montauban: the 7th Division's casualties for the day were approaching 3,400, including over 1,000 killed or missing. The 21st Division's were higher for a lesser gain (this was predictable given that its defences had not been dented prior to the attack): in excess of 4,200. This included nearly 1,300 killed or missing. The casualties of 50th Brigade were in excess of 1,100, including around 600 killed or missing.[13]

These British losses were of little comfort to those Germans who feared that now that Mametz and Montauban had fallen, they would be targeted next. Sergeant Karl Eisler of the Feldartillerie Regiment 29 was shocked to learn that he and his gunners based in and around Contalmaison were not to be reinforced: 'We shuddered when we learned there were to be no reinforcements,' he recalled later:

It made us feel very bitter. Why were they not reinforcing us? Were we to be sacrificed as our reward for all we had done. We could still have held on if we had been sent new troops. As it was, we barely had any troops protecting us.

The gentlemen at our headquarters had driven off into the night in their cars because they were worried there would be a breakthrough.[14]

Eisler might have felt less resentful if he had known the extent of the German losses. The 109th Reserve Regiment, which was responsible for the Mametz sector, had suffered casualties in excess of 2,100, a low figure compared with British losses, but large for the Germans, who had fewer men involved in the battle.[15]

Even these shocking statistics could not prevent another German from feeling hard done by. Colonel Leibrock was the commander of the 6th Bavarian Reserve Infantry Regiment, the unit responsible for the Montauban sector. Ever since his arrival at the sector headquarters south of Bernafay Wood, at 4 a.m. on 1 July, his life had been a nightmare.

He was greeted with the 'welcome' news that the headquarters had no telephone link with most of the companies in the front-line positions. And there was no point asking the commander of the 12th Division whether the headquarters could be moved. He had already said no. Then, in the middle of the morning, an English soldier arrived at the dugout and asked Leibrock to surrender. He told Leibrock he might as well, given that the 109th Reserve Infantry Regiment, responsible for the Mametz sector, had already thrown in the towel.

This news threw Leibrock into a lather. But he was not going to surrender to one man without some corroboration that what he was saying was correct. In the meantime he took the Englishman as his prisoner.

Events took a turn for the worse when an aeroplane began circling overhead. That prompted Leibrock to send a courier to the telephone centre in Bernafay Wood to ask for a plane to see it off. Before the courier could return, the dugout was surrounded by English soldiers. Leibrock asked the one company he was in touch with by telephone to come quickly to save him. But its commander said that would be impossible. If he came, his own position would be taken.

Eventually after a firefight, Leibrock surrendered, only to learn that the English wanted to shoot a German officer, possibly him. Luckily a British doctor intervened, and he was taken into captivity.[16]

There was no such lucky escape for three of the four 22nd Manchester officers whose letters have been featured in this book (see Chapter 4, p. 38). Captains Alfred Bland and Charlie May, and Lieutenant William Gomersall, all died during the attack. We only know a bit about the circumstances surrounding Charlie May's wounds, because of a letter that his batman Arthur Bunting wrote to his wife Effie. It mentions that he was in the German trenches, and then continues: 'I had just turned the corner of the trench when I heard the shell burst, and Captain called to me. I nursed him best I could, and tied his limbs together with my puttees, poor fellow, and while I was with him Dear I said my prayers over and over again, for it looked a thousand to one on us both being blown to pieces, and no cover to get under. It was just a case of awaiting your turn next please, but it didn't come and here we are . . .'[17]

On 11 July, Maude May wrote to Bunting to ask him some questions. She wanted to know exactly what had happened to her husband on the battlefield: 'During those three hours you sat with my husband, did he suffer? Was he conscious? Where were his wounds? Did he say any words at all that you could distinguish? Tell me everything . . .'

Later in the month, Maude replied to a letter Bunting must have written to her about her husband's personal effects:

Thank you for seeing to the Captain's packing. Everything has reached me quite in order. The heart-breaking task of packing the Valise and touching his clothes etc seemed to bring home to me more than ever this dreadful calamity. I don't know how I'll get through life without him . . . Can there be anything in life for me again?

The photographs in the leather case of Baby and me, and the Captain's pocket book. Was he carrying those with him when he was struck? Was he carrying his haversack? And the cap that came home. Was that the one he was wearing at the time?

I shall worry you with all these questions, but these details mean so much to me. When I see you, I want to hear every detail about my beloved, from the time the attack started, until the time he passed away. You are to spare me nothing Bunting! Oh, how I long for a chat with you.

17: Repercussions

The Somme, Picardy and London, 1–4 July

(See maps 1 and 2)

No soldier who was in Picardy on 1 July 1916 ever forgot where he was when the great attack started. Dick Read of the 8th Leicestershire Regiment remembered that he spent the day at La Cauchie, half a mile north-west of Gommecourt.

From there, he heard the gunfire rising to a climax shortly before 7.30 a.m. and this told him that his pals in the 46th Division had started their attack. But as the day progressed and the firing died down, he wondered what had happened. Was it quiet because the German defenders had been defeated, or was it the British who had been knocked out?

The account that Read wrote records the rumours that were rife:

[The British] . . . had broken through . . . [They] had been held up . . . They were going over again shortly . . . [They] had been wiped out . . .

Then [at] about 9 p.m., in the gathering dusk, we saw some transport limbers in the distance. As they approached . . . by signs on the limbers, we saw they were South Staffords. The drivers looked spick and span in violent contrast to what we could now see was a mass of about eighty men . . . They looked dishevelled, dirty, hollow-eyed, and grime-streaked, their sandbag-covered tin hats chalky, muddy, dusty. Every now and then, the step broke and they seemed to march anyhow, with heads bent, either looking straight before them, or at the ground . . .

We sensed somehow that these men had seen hell . . . [But] none of us dared ask the question, until one of us shouted: 'How d' you go on mates?' . . . [None of them] took the slightest notice, save a corporal carrying three rifles, who was bringing up the rear . . . He half turned, and indicating the weary straggling figures before him, shrugged expressively, [and said]: 'General f . . . up in command again,' and he went on. Then he turned again, [and added]: 'Back where they f . . . well started.'[1]

Similar scenes were played out in many of the villages that stood in the midst of the unspoilt landscape behind the front. Lieutenant Edgar Lord of the 15th Lancashire Fusiliers was waiting anxiously in Bouzincourt (about a mile to the north-west of Albert) for news of his battalion, who had been fighting with the 32nd Division at Thiepval, when he saw 'hundreds of men with wounds of every description' coming down the dusty road towards him:

A few of the worst cases came . . . in the ambulances. [But they] were in very . . . [short] supply . . . [Others came in] carts, wagons, lorries, limbers, water tanks and any [other] vehicles which [could] . . . give a lift. [They] were crammed to the utmost.

The walking cases were choked with dust. [They were] staggering along between the limbers, sometimes helping each other [by] forming human crutches. Most of them [were] wearing blood-stained bandages, and many [wore] . . . improvised splints.

The remnants of Lord's own battalion only made it back three days later. There were just three officers and thirty-seven men out of twenty-six officers and around six hundred men who had gone into battle: 'What a sight this small band presented when we met them. [They had] weary, haggard and drawn faces, exhausted bodies and legs that almost could not carry their burden . . . Their thoughts were too tragic for words. All had lost many friends . . . and as I marched along with them . . . I felt like a warder escorting a condemned prisoner. The band joined us, and as it played "Keep the Home Fire Burning, Till the boys come home", I nearly wept.'

However, that was only one of several painful obligations that this young man carried out over the next days. First he had to write to the mother of his friend Ivan Doncaster to tell her she might never see him again. A private had been brought in, after lying for three days in No Man's Land. He claimed he had seen Ivan being shot in the head ten yards from the German wire. As the man's mind was wandering, it was difficult to know whether his story was reliable. But Lord passed it on to Ivan's family anyway. Then he had to salvage the equipment that was scattered in the trenches. Finally, he had to help bury the dead. As Lord recalled, when he wrote up his experiences later: 'Corpses lay everywhere, and the stench from the decaying bodies was very unpleasant.' The corpses could also be disturbing:

A blackened hand protruding from the ground was gruesome to say the least. One night, I was detailed with a dozen men, to bury some of our dead near our new front line. As some of them had been doing this the night before, they were feeling sick and groggy, so I ordered them to dig holes in the ground and make wooden crosses whilst I went with a . . . gunner to handle the corpses.

It was a ghastly job . . . [which involved] feeling for their identity disks and effects . . . in the dark . . . Most of them were bloated having been killed some days earlier . . .

One man whom we handled had lost both feet, and the hand wearing his identity disk had been so badly smashed, that the disk was mixed with the putrefying flesh. After a vain attempt to recover it, we interred him as unknown.[2]

There were many such tasks. Some turned the survivors' stomachs. Chaplain Halet, who was attached to the 4th Division, has described how he had to take a few deep breaths when he saw what was going on outside the field ambulance, where he was helping out on 2 July. 'I came past an incineration burning steadily. Around it, lay in great heaps, thousands of blood soaked bandages, and several stretchers in an indescribable condition. The men were feeding the incineration methodically, imperturbably. [But] the sight and smell of it nearly made me sick.'

It was strange that it was this experience which pushed him to the edge, given all the other sights and smells he had taken in his stride at the field ambulance since arriving in France. As he said: 'I have seen [some] awful sights. Men broken and shattered beyond recognition, limbs torn and mangled, faces half blown away. I have seen blood flow in streams.'

That was par for the course for a field ambulance, which was the institution in the medical chain between the advanced dressing station, the medical unit nearest to the front line, and the casualty clearing station, located further back than the field ambulance. In field ambulances, as the Reverend Halet affirmed, you expected to see a man 'caked with yellow mud' so that 'the very outline of his puttees disappear in it'. According to Halet, the typical patient will have 'a drooping head', and he will be 'wincing every few moments'. His uniform will probably be 'torn, sometimes literally burned by shell fire, sometimes soaked through and dripping with blood'. He will be 'unkempt, unshaven, blood spattered: a wreck'.

It was clear that he found the patients' mental suffering more disturbing than anything:

I have seen officers and men absolutely unscathed in the body, but with that queer staring look in their eyes, which means [they have] shell shock . . . In [many] . . .

of their faces, [I] have seen the look of men who have gazed upon death very closely, and much worse . . .

Hell can't be much worse than what we've been through . . . a private . . . said to me, who had been blown into the air and then buried by a shell. And I believed him . . . for I have seen it on his face and on all their faces.[3]

It seems that it took around forty-eight hours after 1 July for wounded men like those cared for by Halet to reach the hospitals set up to give them longer-term care. Sister Edith Appleton, a thirty-nine-year-old nurse at General Hospital No. 1 in Étretat (about 12 miles north of Le Havre), recorded her first contact with soldiers from the Somme in her diary entry for 4 July:

Wounded. Hundreds upon hundreds, on stretchers, being carried, walking, all covered from head to foot in well caked mud. The rush and buzz of ambulances and motor buses is the only thing I can remember of yesterday outside my wards. Inside . . . we had horrible bad wounds in numbers, some crawling with maggots, some stinking . . . with gangrene.

One poor lad had both eyes shot through, and there they were, all smashed and mixed up with the eyelashes. He was quite calm . . . [but] very tired. He said: 'Shall I need an operation? I can't see anything.' Poor boy, he never will.

Three men died in the train, and two only just reached hospital before they went west too. Three were completely dumb.

Edith Appleton noted that her hospital took over 1,000 wounded soldiers on 4 July, and her 6 July diary entry highlighted what the surge in demand for hospital places meant for admission procedures:

In ordinary times, we get a telegram from Abbeville saying a train with so many on board has left, and is coming to us. Then they stopped giving numbers, [and] just said full train. Now not even a telegram comes. But the full trains do!

Yesterday, in addition to our 1,300 beds, we took over the lounge of a large restaurant, the orderlies' barracks, the ambulance garage, the Casino front, and part of the officers' mess.[4]

It seems that the call on beds was so acute that the nurses in some hospitals were not even alerted when the first batch of Somme wounded were sent to them. At least that was the experience of Marjorie Beeton, a granddaughter of the famous cook, at the No. 2 British Red Cross Hospital in Rouen. Included in her diary for 3 July is the following note:

[I] was washing up breakfast things [at] 10 a.m. when [the] convoy whistle blew. On looking out, [I] saw the most pathetic procession struggling up the drive, about 30 [of the] weariest looking men, mud coated tatters of clothing and grimly stained bandages covering their mutilated limbs. Some were limping, and others bent nearly double with the painful weight of smashed up arms.

[I] thought first of all they were a party of tommies, but when they got closer, one could see they were officers. There must have been an unprecedented call on the ambulances if they had to send officers on foot.

Whereas the first patients sent to Étretat appeared to include in particular those wounded at Gommecourt (Edith Appleton was told her hospital was 'serving the division that has acted as a draw to save the other divisions'), the Rouen hospital seems to have particularly included officers from the 34th Division, who as mentioned in Chapter 14 had been in action at La Boisselle. Her subsequent diary entries refer to Major Morton from the 34th Division, whose unit had lost men near the Lochnagar Crater on 1 July: 'He was in with both legs wounded, one very badly,' she recalled, adding: 'This poor man had lain out on the field for 48 hours before being picked up. He was deliberately fired on by the Germans.'

She also named a Captain Bellamy, who appears to have been an officer with the 34th Division's 10th Lincolns. According to Beeton, 'his spine is hopelessly injured. [He is] paralysed below the waist. [He is] such a fine looking man; most cheery and plucky.'

Marjorie Beeton, a Voluntary Aid Nurse, was clearly shocked by the injuries her patients had to endure. Later in the month she wrote: 'The whole place resounds with terrible groans and reeks of foul dressings. Ugh!' Then on another day she noted: 'I'm getting very Shavian in my ideas on surgery. Why torture the poor thing when they know he was bound to die in a day or two.'[5]

Those caring for the wounded had by necessity to move centre stage after 1 July. It is interesting also to see how subsequent events affected those who were, fortunately for them, still on the fringes.

The 'Big Push' had made Nancy Peto, wife of Basil Peto, a Conservative Member of Parliament, very agitated. Although it was unlikely the Germans would harm her directly in her London townhouse, she was nevertheless vulnerable because her sons were soldiers in France. That prompted her to write the following entry in her diary for 4 July:

It is now 11 p.m. and as I pulled my bedroom curtains apart to open the window still wider, having turned off the electric light first of all – police precautions – I see five or six powerful searchlights throwing great beams of light across the sky. Not having thought about Zeppelins and their attendant horrors for some time, this reminder strikes a fresh chill upon one's heart. How much it has to bear and suffer! How it jumps and throbs at every little unexpected sound, at some sudden association with those darling boys, and above all the strain that is put upon it when one hears the 'rat-tat' on the front door which means nothing else but a telegram.

The shaking hand that undoes those awkward folds after withdrawing it from the envelope, the hasty look at the signature first, while one's heart seems to cease to beat. The reaction on finding it is but a message on politics, or an acceptance or refusal of some invitation. The sigh of relief, the inward prayer, the return to one's occupation, only to suffer every detail all over again the next time a telegram comes.[6]

The events of 1 July appear to have aroused at least one of the British Expeditionary Force soldiers not involved in the first round of fighting. Perhaps realizing that his time was coming, and that he had better make the most of every day he had left, on 1 July thirty-eight-year-old Brigadier-General Llewelyn Price Davies sent Eileen, his wife, the following romantic note, the first of a series of such letters, which were doubtless intended to spice up their marriage during their enforced separation: 'I have a nice cool attic, and [if only she were here] Baby could rest on the bed whilst I worked, like we used to do so often in the old days. Then Baby would be naughty and interrupt, and have to be smacked and kissed.' Marginally changing tack, he added: 'Of course, I knew you wanted your present. You see, when Baby says she wants something, or something is wearing out, I just make a note of it in my head, and of course Baby must have nice undies because that's half the fun!!'

Two days later he wrote another letter, this time reproaching his wife: 'You never said what the present was like when you tried it on. Were you a sweet Baby? Darling I dreamed last night I was walking with you in a crowded [room] . . . I kissed you. Such a nice kiss too.' He went on in a subsequent letter to mention that 'Violet' had written to him describing her

underclothes. 'I told her she must show them to us some day,' he informed
his wife. That, however, must have been too much for Eileen to stomach,
because a few days later, after his wife had banned him from seeing Violet
unless she was 'decent', Price Davies wrote back: 'Tell Violet I have a jeal-
ous wife and so cannot see her little trousies. I am quite disappointed. It
could have been such fun!!!'

On receiving this, his wife relented, and wrote to tell him he could see
Violet in her 'trousies' as long as they looked at them together. At this Price
Davies remonstrated: 'That's what I meant: that we should both see Violet's
trousies. You didn't think I wanted to see them alone did you?! She is a
wicked woman and you never know what might happen!!'[7]

Meanwhile, in France, the 10th Lincolns' Lieutenant-Colonel Kyme
Cordeaux, having survived the La Boisselle attack, wrote to tell his family
what his views were on all the comments in the press following the 1 July
attack: 'How wild the papers at home make me with their casualties "very
slight". My God the British public are fools!' Warming to his theme, he followed this up in a subsequent letter: 'The papers and people at home seem
to have taken leave of their senses, and talk as if the whole German Army
was crumpled up. Remember all advances made are up to the present but a
short distance in depth here and there, and progress is slow, and our casualties have necessarily been very heavy.'[8]

For his part, General Sir Douglas Haig certainly was not happy with the
way the advance had panned out in the northern part of the line. In his
diary note for 1 July he wrote: 'I am inclined to believe from further reports
that few of VIII Corps (Hunter-Weston's unit) left their trenches!! . . . The
VIII Corps seems to want looking after.'[9]

Lieutenant-General Hunter-Weston would probably have agreed with
that statement. During the middle of the afternoon on 1 July he wrote to
his wife Grace admitting 'We have not attained the success we hoped
for . . . The result of the day's fighting up to the present, 3 p.m., has been
disappointing.'[10]

However, writing the next day to General Sir William Robertson, Chief
of the Imperial General Staff, he pointed out that he had not been given
sufficient ammunition to do the job properly. Hunter-Weston stated that he
had used 1⅓ shells per yard of front attacked, whereas what he needed were
10 shells per yard. This implied that Rawlinson and Haig had hugely overestimated the amount of front that could be quelled with the ammunition
and guns at their disposal. He could not have been more correct.

Whatever his faults, Hunter-Weston had put his finger not just on the problem in his own sector, but on the problem for the whole attack with the exception of the southern end of the line. If adequate guns and ammunition had been laid on for the selected fronts, not only could corps commanders such as Hunter-Weston have applied a strong enough barrage to confine most of the German machine-gunners to their dugouts until they were overrun, but the British corps commanders might have felt at liberty to devote a large proportion of their heavy artillery to counter-battery work.

As it was, Hunter-Weston in particular did not ring-fence the artillery that would concentrate exclusively on counter-battery work, and not enough counter-battery work was done on his front. This was one reason why VIII Corps' performance on 1 July was found wanting. Whereas XIII Corps, which set aside a large chunk of its batteries for counter-battery work, thrived.[11] XIII Corps' performance was also boosted because French batteries helped out by firing at targets in its sector.

These points are arguably the key to understanding what went wrong on 1 July. Nevertheless, not wishing his views about their errors to get back to Rawlinson and Haig, Hunter-Weston added a rider to the complaint he made to Robertson: 'The latter is for your ear alone. It is inadvisable to give currency to such unpleasant and dangerous facts.'[12]

Sadly, confiding in Britain's top general did not have the desired effect. Ultimately, Hunter-Weston's fate lay in Haig's hands, and he evidently did not rate Hunter-Weston highly. After VIII Corps, along with X Corps, was sidelined, being transferred from the 4th Army to Lieutenant-General Sir Hubert Gough's Reserve Army on 3 July, it and its commander were given their marching orders on 19 July. They were to be moved as a job lot to the Ypres sector, never to participate in the Battle of the Somme again.

It was a humiliating fall from grace. Although Hunter-Weston was glad to be parting company with Gough, whom he astutely adjudged to be impetuous and over-optimistic, he had to admit it was galling that club gossips would assume he had been 'stellenbosched'.[13]

Even if we were not to accept Hunter-Weston's claim that he was just being rested, one would be bound to point out that he would not be the first senior officer on the Somme to be 'ungummed'. Nor would he be the last. The hiring and firing was not restricted to the British side of No Man's Land. The most high-profile German officer to be sacked from his post in the aftermath of the great attack was General Paul Grünert, the chief of staff to the commander of the German 2nd Army, General Fritz von Below.

Grünert had given the German General von Pannewitz, commander of the XVII Corps, permission to retreat, south of the Somme, following the success of the French attack on 1 July. This displeased the German Commander-in-Chief, General Erich von Falkenhayn, who decided Grünert must pay the price for retreating when he should have been urging his men to regain their lost positions even if it meant fighting to the last man.

The German Prince Rupprecht, who, as we have seen, was no admirer of von Falkenhayn, believed that Grünert was being punished unfairly. Commenting in the entries in his diary written after the big attack, Rupprecht confirmed that Grünert had warned von Falkenhayn again and again that German forces were stretched too thinly over the Somme front. Now Grünert was being made accountable for von Falkenhayn's failure to take the warnings seriously.

Rupprecht also accused von Falkenhayn of using Grünert's dismissal to undermine General von Below, another injustice according to the Prussian prince. Everyone assumed that von Below had known about Grünert's decision, so that criticizing Grünert was also an implicit rebuke aimed at von Below. Grünert's dismissal was only the first step. Just over two weeks later the number of troops under von Below's command was drastically reduced.

Whilst he would remain in charge of German forces fighting north of the Somme, albeit in a unit referred to as the 1st Army, the troops south of the Somme, in the 2nd Army, were henceforth to be commanded by General Max von Gallwitz. The sting in the tail, as far as the sixty-two-year-old von Below was concerned, was that the sixty-four-year-old von Gallwitz was also given command of the group consisting of the two armies. Von Below was naturally upset. It was an astonishing way of rewarding a general who deserved to be congratulated rather than reprimanded. He had won a victory of sorts against all the odds. With a fraction of the resources available to the British, he had somehow managed to hold a line, even if it was in places further back than where it had been when the offensive started.[14] Of course no one can say that a general smarting under such unjust treatment suffered as much as a soldier wounded in the front line. However, for all the talk that the men at the top had it easy on the Somme, no one could say a general treated like von Below had been given his just deserts.

18: Can't See the Wood for the Trees

Mametz Wood, 2–12 July 1916

(See maps 2 and 10)

Unexpectedly, one of the safest places on the battlefield during the early morning of 2 July was the British front line opposite the village of Fricourt. Here, near the spot in No Man's Land where his battalion, the 7th Green Howards, had lost so many men the previous day, Lieutenant-Colonel Ronald Fife came to the conclusion that there was going to be no more fighting over Fricourt. 'There was no fire coming from [the] enemy trenches, and I formed the opinion they had gone back,' he recalled.

Acting on his recommendation, Brigadier-General Fell, whose 51st Brigade had relieved the 50th Brigade, immediately requested that all British shelling of Fricourt should cease so that patrols could reconnoitre. No sooner had it been arranged than Fife determined to conduct his own preliminary investigation:

I then walked down the road to Fricourt. Where the road crosses our front trenches, I saw a man . . . I told him that I was going to see if any of my men were still lying wounded in front and asked him to come with me, which he did. We followed [the] line of advance of A and D Companies, and found the dead lying very thick on the ground . . . [There were] no wounded . . . [I] sent the man back with a message . . . [for Lieutenant-]Colonel Forrest [commander of the 7th] Lincolnshire Regiment saying that I was going into Fricourt . . . and should be glad of a small escort. The man did not return, and after waiting a quarter of an hour, I walked into the German trenches.

They were much battered, and a good many dead were lying in them . . . Coming to a very deep dugout I shouted down, 'Komm heraus!' . . . There was no reply. I then climbed onto the parapet again and saw my messenger returning. He brought a message from Colonel Forrest . . . saying that the Lincolns were going to attack . . .

I sat down and waited, and soon after saw the Lincolns coming out of their trenches in attack formation . . . Not a shot was fired at them . . . As they advanced . . . through Fricourt . . . batches of the enemy emerged from dugouts and surrendered.[1]

The annexation of Fricourt so early on 2 July took to three the tally of villages captured and secured by British troops as a direct result of the 1 July attack. There was no serious German attempt to take back Mametz, and German counter-attacks towards Montauban were repulsed during the night of 1–2 July. Bernafay Wood (about 500 yards east of Montauban) was taken with minimal casualties on 3 July.

German attempts to shore up their defences gave the British forces scope to push forward their front lines, particularly in the southern part of the front where they had been so successful. By the time Haig met with the French General Joffre on 3 July to plan their next move, Rawlinson's troops within XV Corps' 7th Division were already approaching the landmark that was likely to be the next significant barrier to progress: Mametz Wood. Progress had also been made in III Corps' sector: a 19th Division brigade had seized the Heligoland strongpoint (Sausage Redoubt) that had dominated the area south of La Boisselle, and had entered, without fully capturing, the village of La Boisselle itself. It was finally taken over by British forces on 4 July.[2] Only the village of Ovillers, and the villages to the north of it, proved capable of prolonged resistance, as was confirmed by the German resistance on 3 July. All British efforts to force their way into Ovillers and Thiepval were blocked by the intrepid defenders.[3]

The ease with which British forces had moved north from their bridgehead in the south, and the difficulties they encountered when attempting to thrust eastwards from the centre of the British line towards Pozières, made it very clear to Haig where he should push next: from south to north. However, while that was obviously the way to cause maximum damage to the Germans, it also threatened to upset the fragile alliance with the French.

The diverging views of the Allies spilled over at the meeting between the two countries' top generals that had been convened for a 3 p.m. start at Château Val Vion, Haig's headquarters in Beauquesne (some 12 miles north-east of Amiens, and about 13 miles from the German front line).

The problem was that the French, intoxicated by their, and the British, success in the south, had failed to take into account the fact that there had been a virtual massacre of British troops in the centre and north. Notwithstanding this, Joffre wanted Haig to persevere with the attack on what the French General liked to refer to as 'Thiepval Hill'. Haig responded by stating that he wanted to attack Longueval from the south, and asked whether the French could help by advancing towards Guillemont. In his diary Haig described Joffre's reaction: 'At this, General Joffre exploded in a fit of rage . . . His breast heaved and his face flushed . . . He could not approve of it. He ordered me to attack Thiepval and Pozières. If I attacked Longueval I would be beaten . . . etc., etc.'

When Haig calmly replied that he did not have to obey Joffre's 'orders' because the British Army's ultimate master was its government, the French leader eventually stopped trying to change his British counterpart's mind and merely indicated his disagreement.[4]

After the French had departed, Haig turned his attention to working out the best way to make the attack on the Longueval sector of the German second line come to fruition. He gave Rawlinson the benefit of his deliberations the very next day. 'I impressed on him the importance of getting Trônes Wood to cover [our] right flank, and Mametz Wood . . . to cover the left flank of our attack against the Longueval front.'[5]

At the time few realized what 'getting' a wood entailed. If they had, perhaps Mametz Wood would have been seized before it, and the trenches covering it, were occupied by the enemy. Once defended, the wood became a formidable obstacle. A fit adult in peacetime conditions might have expected to be able to walk through it, using the ride (lane) which ran through the trees from the wood's north-eastern edge to its south-eastern edge, going more or less down its centre, in about 15 to 20 minutes. In peacetime, the same adult would have taken even less time to walk from one side of the wood to the other, using one of the two rides that crossed it from east to west. But passing through the wood was quite another matter once it was protected by a group of determined defenders armed with guns.

Mametz Wood, which contained a mixture of mature oak, beech and birch trees, interspersed with thick undergrowth, consisting principally of hawthorn and briar, was the ideal place for a group of soldiers, planning to ambush an advancing enemy. There were countless places where the defenders could hide. The wood was all the harder for attackers, unable to use its rides, to navigate because of what some might say was its indescribably irregular shape. It did not take much distraction for a soldier to lose his sense of direction once amongst the trees. If he was pinned down by gunfire, hours could pass trying to sort that problem out. The wood, although not huge, stretched over a substantial area. It was just under a mile long, in other words from its north-east edge to the southernmost point, and it was just over 1,000 yards wide at its widest point from east to west.

That being the case, and given all the lives that were to be lost and reputations ruined in connection with the fighting over this mass of woodland, it is frustrating to learn that British forces did not take it during the middle of the afternoon of 3 July. Patrols had reported that at that time Mametz Wood and Quadrangle Trench, one of the trenches snaking around the south-westerly approaches to the wood, were empty, so there was nothing to stop British troops entering the wood.

There was a gap in the layers of German defences that had protected Mametz Wood, caused by the surrender of hundreds of German troops. They had surrendered earlier that day after being cornered in two other woods, Shelter and Bottom Woods (see maps 6 and 7). These two woods had been taken by those British troops in the 17th and 21st Divisions who had advanced from Fricourt, and from the area to its north, after the village had been captured.

However, it was 5 p.m. on 3 July before XV Corps' commander, Lieutenant-General Horne, permitted his 7th Division to go for Mametz Wood, and the advance of the troops ordered to take it was delayed after a guide went astray. Before the next morning, patrols were reporting that there were Germans in both Quadrangle Trench and Wood Trench, which protected Mametz Wood from the south, as well as in the wood itself. British troops had missed their chance.[6]

2nd Lieutenant Siegfried Sassoon has described the part he claimed that he played in the course of the first British attempt to unpick the newly set-up German defences.[7] During the night of 4–5 July troops from his battalion, the 1st Royal Welch Fusiliers, as well as from two other units on its left, had managed to overcome the German garrison facing them in Quadrangle Trench. However, the 2nd Royal Irish Regiment, the fourth battalion in the attack, on the Fusiliers' right, had been repulsed before they could reach Wood Trench. Sassoon says he led the patrol that was sent to the western end of Quadrangle Trench with a view to crossing over the intervening valley to reach the western end of Wood Trench.

Whether or not it was literally true, the following extract from Sassoon's account certainly gives us a sense of what it was like to be in Quadrangle Trench that night:

It was about 500 yards across the open to the newly captured Quadrangle Trench . . . To the right I found young Fernby . . . He told me that no one knew what had happened on our right . . . We went along the trench that was less than waist deep . . . In some places it was only a foot deep, and . . . men were lying wounded and killed by sniping . . . Kendle who had been trying to [help] a badly wounded man . . . joined me and we continued mostly on all fours along the dwindling trench . . . We came to a bombing post . . . I took a bag of bombs and crawled another sixty . . . yards with Kendle close behind me.

The trench became a shallow groove and ended where the ground overlooked a little valley along which there was a light railway line . . . From the other side . . . came an occasional rifle shot, and a helmet bobbed up for a moment. 'I'll just have a shot at him,' Kendle said, wriggling away from the crumbling bank that gave us cover . . . I remember seeing him push his . . . tin hat back from his forehead and then raise himself a few inches to take aim. After firing once he looked at us with a . . . smile. A second later he fell sideways. A blotchy mark showed where the bullet had hit him just above the eyes.

The circumstances being what they were, I had no justification for being either shocked or astonished. But after blank awareness that he was killed, all feelings . . . contracted to a single intention: to settle that sniper on the other side of the valley.

If I had stopped to think I should not have gone at all. As it was . . . I . . . abruptly informed Fernby that I was going to find out who was there, and set off at a downhill double . . . I was . . . out of breath as I trotted up the opposite slope. Just before I arrived at the top I slowed up and threw my two bombs. Then I rushed at the bank vaguely expecting some sort of scuffle . . . Quite unexpectedly I found myself looking down into a . . . trench with a great many Germans in it. Fortunately for me they were already retreating. It had not occurred to them they were being attacked by a single fool. And Fernby with presence of mind which probably saved me had covered my advance by traversing the top of the trench with his Lewis gun.[8]

Whether or not Sassoon's courageous charge really did clear a section of Wood Trench, the Royal Irish Regiment troops had by that stage already returned to their starting position. Therefore, they were not in a position to take advantage of any breach in the line that Sassoon's mad dash may have created.

In any case the Sassoon account only covers a preliminary action. For a window into the first attack on Mametz Wood itself, we have to fall back on the recollections of Llewelyn Wyn Griffith, a twenty-five-year-old captain in the 15th Royal Welch Fusiliers, who had recently been transferred to the staff of the 38th (Welsh) Division's 115th Brigade. As such, he had privileged access to the views of its brigadier-general, Horatio Evans.

According to Wyn Griffith, Brigadier-General Evans was one of the few

officers in the British Army who was totally irreproachable. He was everything that Wyn Griffith's previous brigadier was not. When serving in the
15th Royal Fusiliers, Wyn Griffith had come under the jurisdiction of that
battalion's Brigadier-General Llewelyn Price Davies, commander of the
38th Division's 113th Brigade. This was the same Price Davies who on
1 July, the day after his thirty-eighth birthday, tormented his wife Eileen
about her and her friend's underwear (see Chapter 17).

Perhaps it was this interest in women's apparel that led to Price Davies
being referred to as Jane or Mary behind his back. Or perhaps it was his
boyish face, his prim way of speaking, and his meticulous obsession with
the relatively unimportant domestic economies of trench life. Heaven help
a soldier who left an empty tin lying at the bottom of a trench after he had
eaten his fill, or one who did not ensure that the height of the parapet above
the firestep was no more than the four feet six inches mentioned in the
regulations. If it was even as little as a few inches out, Price Davies would
be on to it like a bloodhound, using his wooden staff cut to exactly that
length to measure any deviation. Even his legendary bravery was a curse.
He may have won a Victoria Cross and a DSO, but he did not use his courage sensibly. Like so many of the over-promoted heroes who dominated the
senior officer corps during the Battle of the Somme, he could not wait to
escape from the constraints of his dugout so that he could once again experience the thrill of the battlefield. He would willingly expose himself to
danger while doing the rounds of the units under his command, and would
expect those with whom he was conversing to follow suit.[9]

Brigadier-General Horatio Evans was cut from a totally different cloth.
Having already reached his mid-fifties by the time he commanded 115th
Brigade during the Battle of the Somme, he was past the stage of hungering
for the re-creation of past glories. Nor was he in the business of pointing out
trivial infractions. The one time Evans reprimanded Wyn Griffith was
after the young captain had pretended he knew how to ride so that he could
keep up with his new master. 'Good Lord, you might have broken your
neck. Don't do things like that again,' he scolded Wyn Griffith.[10] Evans
regarded it as his duty to protect those under his command from themselves
as well as from the Germans, a universally admired characteristic in any
other setting than the World War I trenches. It was typical of the man that
he was prepared to stick up for this high-minded principle even though he
knew it might well be his undoing.

The first time this principle was tested in front of Wyn Griffith was on

6 July. That was when Evans received the order from the 38th Division's commander, Major-General Ivor Philipps, telling him to attack Mametz Wood. The attack was to take place the next morning. The troops of 115th Brigade were to wait behind the crest of a fold in the landscape north of Caterpillar Wood (east of Mametz Wood) until the time came for the attack, which would be at 8 a.m. on 7 July, or at 8.30 a.m. if a preliminary night-time attack by 17th Division on the other side of the wood was unsuccessful. The 17th Division was to advance again towards Mametz Wood at the same time as Brigadier-General Evans' men.

The problem was not just that the attack by Evans' brigade was going to be made in the full light of day, rather than at dawn when troops might be protected by the darkness when crossing No Man's Land. Evans had understood Philipps' order to mean he must attack with two battalions abreast of each other, rather than what he had recommended to Philipps' staff officer when they had reconnoitred the battlefield before the attack started. The reconnoitring had told him that a battalion which hugged the northern edge of Caterpillar Wood as it advanced towards Mametz Wood would be hidden from German gunners in the German second position and in the two woods, Flatiron and Sabot Copses, south of that position. However, a battalion that advanced to the north of the first battalion would be visible. By insisting on having a second battalion attack on the right of the first battalion, Major-General Philipps was condemning it to heavy casualties.

But did he actually insist on this? The 38th Division's Order 36 on 6 July 1916 in fact contained nothing expressly instructing that two battalions should attack abreast of each other. That raises the question: did Philipps or a member of his staff instruct Brigadier-General Evans verbally that two battalions abreast was what they wanted? Or was Evans so exhausted that he misunderstood what was meant by the written instruction that there should be 'two battalions in position in Caterpillar Wood'? We may never know the answer to this question about the order which was to have such tragic consequences.

The allocation of blame does not affect the outcome. Evans believed that he had been taken for a mug, that his name had been used to put in place tactics with which he disagreed.[11] Wyn Griffith later described the reaction of Brigadier-General Evans. He was:

cursing . . . his orders. He said that only a mad man could have issued them. He called the Divisional Staff a lot of plumbers, herring gutted at that. He argued . . .

and asked for some control over the artillery . . . but got nothing. We are not allowed to attack at dawn. We must wait for the show at Contalmaison . . . Why shouldn't both attacks be made at the same time? It would spread out the German fire.[12]

Before the attack started, Brigadier-General Evans moved his headquarters to one of the dugouts in Pommiers Redoubt, the strongpoint captured on 1 July. From there, 1,000 yards south of Mametz Wood, Wyn Griffith was able to hear the different bombardments as the day's attacks were launched. First there was the thunderous sound of the attack going in at Contalmaison, which was visible on a hill until that was concealed by the thick smoke. Then at 8 a.m. the artillery barrage on Mametz Wood started up. Minutes later the telephone line linking the 115th Brigade's headquarters with the 16th Welch Regiment and the 11th South Wales Borderers, the two assault battalions, went dead, severed by the German shelling. At a stroke this cut off Evans, and Wyn Griffith, from his men.

The news of what had happened only filtered back to Pommiers Redoubt between 9 and 10 a.m. after a staff officer was sent up to find out. It was not good. For some unexplained reason, the smokescreen that was supposed to have been laid on had not materialized. This meant that anyone who advanced beyond the crest that had shielded the men before zero hour was a sitting duck for the German gunners in the copses to the north, as well as in their second line to the north, not to mention the Germans in Mametz Wood itself. The advance had stalled 200 yards away from 115th Brigade's first objective, the eastern edge of the wood.

There might have been some hope if a renewed artillery barrage could have been organized to coincide with another dash forwards. But as Wyn Griffith pointed out, even that was beyond the bunglers higher up the hierarchy:

[At 10.25 a.m.] a message arrived from the Division. In twenty minutes time the artillery would begin another bombardment of the edge of the Wood, and under cover of this we were to renew the attack in twenty minutes.[13] [But what was the good of that?]. We were a thousand yards away from the battalions with no telephone communication. There were maps at Divisional Headquarters. They knew where we were. They knew where the battalions were and they knew that our lines were cut. A simple sum in arithmetic [would have told them that we could not pass on the information to the battalions in time.]

Our operation was isolated . . . So there was complete freedom of choice as to time. With all the hours of the clock to choose from some mastermind must needs select the only hour to be avoided.[14]

More bad news seeped back to the Pommiers Redoubt, which was not helped by the deployment of the 10th South Wales Borderers, the third of the brigade's battalions.

Then shortly after 4 p.m., as if the division was intentionally taunting Brigadier-General Evans and his men, yet another message arrived. Once again it announced, at what effectively was the last minute, that yet another artillery bombardment was to be laid down at 4.30 p.m. for a 5 p.m. attack. In fact, the unit's war diaries suggest that the badly thought-out timing of both artillery barrages, at 10.45 a.m. as well as at 4.30 p.m., was selected by Horne's XV Corps.[15]

This time Evans meant to be on hand, that is if the advance utilizing the 17th Royal Welch Fusiliers, the fourth of his battalions, could be arranged in time. With Wyn Griffith in tow, he immediately set out for the gully north of Caterpillar Wood, where he knew his men were congregating. It was an arduous journey through the mud, made worse by the appalling weather. But that was not the dominating event of the afternoon. Wyn Griffith would never forget the moment when his brigadier confided in him for the first time. They were in the gully north of Caterpillar Wood where the survivors were congregating. Evans was clearly in a torment.

'This is sheer lunacy,' said the [Brigadier-]General. 'I've tried all day to stop it. We could creep up to the edge of the Wood by night and rush it in the morning, but they won't listen to me. It breaks my heart . . .'

'If I could get you through on the telephone, would you talk to them again?' I asked.

'Of course I would, but all the wires are cut, and there is no time to go back.'

'I know of a telephone to an Artillery Group . . . They might get you through to the division,' I answered.

'Find out at once . . .,' he replied.

They were in luck. A telephone line could be linked to the division. Minutes later Wyn Griffith was sitting in a trench in Caterpillar Wood while Evans argued his case down the receiver. There was opposition to what he was recommending. He wanted to close down the attack. But eventually, as he put down the phone, Wyn Griffith registered that he had won.

The botched operation had cost the two assault battalions in excess of 400 casualties.[16] But that was nothing compared with the slaughter that could have occurred had the operation not been terminated when it was. 'Well it saved the lives of . . . hundreds of men,' Evans remarked sometime later, as he and Wyn Griffith sat together once they were back in Pommiers Redoubt. Evans continued:

'But it has put an end to me.'
'Why do you say that?'
'I spoke my mind about the whole business. You heard me. They wanted us to press on at all costs, talked about determination, and suggested that I didn't realize the importance of the operation. As good as told me that I was tired and didn't want to tackle the job. Difficult to judge on the spot, they said. As if the whole trouble hadn't arisen because someone found it so easy to judge when he was six miles away and had never seen the country and couldn't read a map.
'You mark my word. They'll send me home for this. They want butchers not brigadiers. They'll remember now that I told them before we began that the attack could not succeed unless the machine guns were masked. I shall be in England in a month.'[17]

The 17th Division's attempts to capture Quadrangle Support Trench that day were equally unsuccessful. In at least one case the reason for failure was the same. Lieutenant-General Horne and his staff appeared to have no idea how long it took to move around the battlefield. That led to their attempt to squeeze another attack in at 8 a.m. that morning, 7 July, between the pre-liminary attack at 2 a.m. and the main attack at 8.30 a.m., not stopping to think that it might be difficult for the assault troops to make it to the British front line in time. Partly because the 12th Manchesters arrived after the British artillery barrage had lifted off the German front-line trenches, their casualties soared. They were in excess of 550, a tragic loss of life given that taking Quadrangle Support Trench was only a preliminary to the main objective: Mametz Wood itself.[18]

An even more fundamental argument against the series of attacks mounted on Quadrangle Support Trench was provided by fifty-eight-year-old Major-General Ivor Pilcher of 17th Division to the XV Corps' staff officer who was briefing him about one such operation: 'I said that when

Contalmaison fell, Quadrangle Support would fall of itself. And that as long as Contalmaison was in the hands of the enemy, Quadrangle Support was no use as it was both commanded by and enfiladed from Contalmaison.' But his opposition to the XV Corps' strategy was dismissed out of hand, possibly with the belief that, like Brigadier-General Evans, Pilcher was not to be trusted.[19]

Without there being an independent inquiry into who was really responsible for all the frustrated attempts to take Mametz Wood, and its covering trenches, both 17th Division's Major-General Pilcher and 38th Division's Major-General Phillips were sent back to England before the next big attack. However, Pilcher at least ended up being vindicated after a fashion. The Quadrangle Support Trench was taken by 17th Division forces after Contalmaison had been taken during the afternoon of 10 July, just as he predicted.[20]

Eventually, the simpler strategy of just advancing through Mametz Wood from south to north turned out to be the way to crack this particular nut. That strategy, put into effect at 4.15 a.m. on 10 July, had seen the troops in 38th Division's 113th and 114th Brigades advance to the northern of the two east-west running cross rides in the wood, before being halted.

That was where the Welshmen had reached before Brigadier-General Evans was ordered to take over the whole force inside Mametz Wood on 11 July. Shortly after he had moved into the wood, word came back that his brigade-major had been wounded, and would Wyn Griffith come up to help.

It was only as Wyn Griffith walked up the wood's main ride that he realized the depths to which the men fighting amongst its trees and thick undergrowth had sunk. He saw that:

Equipment, ammunition, rolls of barbed wire, tins of food, gas helmets and rifles were lying about everywhere. There were more corpses than [living] men. But there were worse sights than corpses. Limbs and [legless and armless] trunks, here and there a detached head, forming splashes of red against the green leaves and as in advertisement of the horror of our way of life and death and of our crucifixion of youth, one tree held in its branches a leg with its torn flesh hanging down over a spray of leaf.[21]

Eventually, near where the second crossride cut through the central ride, Wyn Griffith stumbled upon Brigadier-General Evans' headquarters. It consisted of the beginning of a trench and the odd shell hole. There were no dugouts to hide away in out here. As he was watching, a runner brought in a message for the brigadier. Wyn Griffith described Evans' face hardening as he took in what was being asked of them. Rather than just holding the line, some 300 yards back from the north of Mametz Wood, they were being told to advance and take the rest of the wood once and for all.

Evans wanted to take the remaining German garrison by surprise, using the bayonet rather than the shell to subdue them on this occasion. But just a quarter of an hour before zero hour, or at 3 p.m., British shells came shrieking overhead, landing hundreds of yards to the north of the headquarters.

Their arrival stirred up the men in the clearing where they were gathered, as urgent steps were taken to send a bevy of runners through Mametz Wood to tell the division to desist. Little did the men who fired those guns realize the danger they were creating for their own side. German gunners reacted and began in their turn to carpet the area behind the assembled Welshmen with shells, creating a huge risk for those who had to leave the wood by its southern exit.

'The Brigadier sat on a tree-trunk,' Wyn Griffith recalled. 'This is the end of everything,' Evans muttered. 'Sheer stupidity . . . What good can a barrage do in a wood like this?'[22]

The British shelling continued for around forty-five minutes. Then just as suddenly as it had started, it finally came to an end, making it possible for the battalions in Mametz Wood to advance as they had been ordered. Only the brigade's 11th South Wales Borderers, the right-hand battalion, made it to the northern edge of the wood. The other battalions, advancing on its left, found that the north of the wood was too strongly garrisoned, and they were repulsed. That left the South Wales Borderers on a limb and they decided they needed to retire too.[23]

But there was a price to pay even for that temporary advance. 'It was nearing dusk when Taylor (the signaller, who was also in charge of the runners) came up to me,' Wyn Griffith recalled. '"I've got bad news," he said.'

It was about Watcyn, Wyn Griffith's younger brother. He was one of the runners who had taken the messages through the German shells to the division. He had delivered his message but had been hit on the way back. Wyn Griffith's reaction is recorded in his memoirs:

'My God he's lying out there now Taylor!'
'No old man. He's gone.'
'Yes, yes, he's gone.'

So I had sent him to his death bearing a message from my own hand in an endeavour to save other men's brothers.

Somehow life had to carry on. There were 'more orders to draft, situation reports to send out, demands for more bombs, enemy trench mortars to be shelled into silence, machine guns wanted by everybody. The [Brigadier-] General put his hand on my shoulder. It began to grow dark. An order came from the Division to say that we would be relieved that night.'[24]

The relief of the whole division by the 21st Division was accomplished by 9 a.m. the next morning (12 July).[25] And then, miraculously, the Germans decided that they could not maintain their grip on the northern portion of Mametz Wood after all. They just melted away, moving back to their second line where they could fight on with renewed vigour.[26] As for the 38th Division, it would be some time before they were back in good shape. They had sustained 3,250 casualties.[27]

A few days later Wyn Griffith was preparing for the move to another sector when his eye was arrested by an affecting sight:

It was early in the morning of a fine day in July . . . Against this background of freshness and purity a slow moving worm of dingy yellow twisted itself round the corner made by a jutting shoulder of the downland. The battalions of the brigade were marching along the road [but] it was clear there was a lack of spine. No ring of feet . . . slack knees and frequent hitching of packs, a doddering rise and fall of heads, and much leaning forward . . . This loss of quality in a unit marching away from the Somme battlefield was made more evident by the rising memory of the sturdy column which swung its way down the hedge-bound lanes in the early mornings of the end of June a bare fortnight past singing and laughing in the happiness of relief from the fetters of the trenches of Flanders. Today the silence was unbroken save by the shuffling of feet and the clanking of equipment.[28]

19: Big Bang

Bazentin-Longueval Ridge, 14 July 1916

(See maps 2 and 11)

British successes at the southern end of the Somme line encouraged Haig to dream of sunlit pastures where there would no longer be any Germans opposing him. The process that he hoped might lead to this happy ending was what he liked to refer to as German 'demoralization'.

'Signs of serious demoralization in the ranks of many of the enemy's units have been evident as a result of our successes during the last few days,' Haig wrote in the letter he sent to the Chief of the Imperial General Staff, Sir William Robertson, on 9 July 1916. He added: 'In the enemy's present condition, demoralization might spread quickly.'[1]

Haig's hopes can only have been raised by what the French had achieved on his right. Although they had not pressed forward north of the Somme, preferring to bide their time until they had cleared Germans out of Favière Wood (half a mile north-east of Maricourt), they had nevertheless captured Hem (around 1½ miles south-east of Curlu). South of the Somme their progress was even more encouraging than the British advances around Montauban: already by the end of the day on 4 July the French had pierced the German second position at Herbécourt and Assevillers and had reached Flaucourt and Belloy (see map 11), and by 9 July they had another scalp: Biaches.

Perhaps most encouraging of all was the German termination of their Verdun offensive on 11 July, with a view to making available more units to defend the Somme front. Thus one of the principal aims of the Somme attack had been achieved.

However, it was not just the Germans who were feeling the pinch. The enormous losses that his own army had sustained during the first day of the battle had lowered morale on Haig's side of No Man's Land as well. This came to his notice after a number of the men from the 11th Border Regiment, a unit which had sustained in excess of 500 casualties on 1 July, stated that they were too sick to participate in an attack that was planned for the night of 10 July.

Eventually Captain G. A. C. Palmer, the relatively junior officer placed

in command following the death of their original lieutenant-colonel, recommended that the regiment's doctor, Lieutenant G. N. Kirkwood, should
be asked whether he believed the men were fit for duty. Kirkwood thought
they were not and he wrote out a note to be sent to the 97th Brigade's brigadier suggesting that all the men called on for the attack should be excused
on the grounds that 'few if any are not suffering from some degree of shell
shock'.[2]

A message came back from the 97th Brigade ruling that the attack must
nevertheless go ahead. But when the officers attempted to lead the men to
the front line, some of those men lost contact with the column leaders. As a
result the attack was called off.

This horrified the Reserve Army's commander Lieutenant-General
Hubert Gough, who had been given control of the units at the north end of
the line. In his letter to the commander of X Corps, he stated that the men's
conduct in his view 'merits the extreme penalty' and bemoaned the fact
that there was not enough evidence for the men to be court-martialled.

As for the doctor, Lieutenant Kirkwood, Gough reckoned he should be
dismissed since if allowed to carry on, he would be 'a source of danger' to
the service.[3] Haig disagreed with Gough's hard-line penalty, and ruled that
the doctor should be pardoned on the grounds that Captain Palmer was the
culprit. He was to have a black mark written on his confidential records,
even though at the time he had himself been suffering from shell shock.[4]

Such 'demoralization' of his own men was just one of the unpalatable
consequences for Haig of 1 July. Another was his diminished authority.
Until 1 July he had powers matching those of a dictator once the Cabinet
had given him carte blanche to attack the Germans. He could more or less
do anything he wanted on the battlefield. The gigantic butcher's bill on
1 July changed all that. No longer could Haig assume that all of his generals
would back his strategy. Even Rawlinson appears to have realized that now
he had the chance to spread his wings.

The first manifestation of this new-found freedom related to the next
attack both men wanted to carry out targeting the German second position
between Bazentin-le-Petit and Longueval. Rawlinson's preference was to
make the attack from the south with troops from two corps as soon as they
were ready, and to conceal their move over No Man's Land by advancing at
night.

Haig stated that he was against the advance of 'large masses in night
operations especially with inexperienced staff officers and young troops'.[5]

Instead he ordered Rawlinson to make a two-part advance in daylight. The corps nearest to the German second position (Henry Horne's XV Corps) was to attack first, aiming at taking Bazentin-le-Petit Wood and Bazentin-le-Grand Wood. Only after the capture of that objective was Horne to advance towards Longueval to the east, while Walter Congreve's XIII Corps would simultaneously advance on Longueval from the south.[6]

If Haig had proposed this plan before 1 July, it is possible that it might have been accepted. But after 1 July his generals were not going to rubber-stamp a strategy that they could see was flawed. Horne objected to it on the grounds that if his XV Corps attacked without support, all the German guns could be used against it. Whereas if XV Corps and XIII Corps attacked simultaneously, German firepower would be split between them.

The fact that even Horne, who had nearly always supported Haig's tactics, was prepared to protest, may well have been critical in making Haig think again. Or perhaps it was merely because the operation was being put back a day from 13 July to 14 July, which would give XIII Corps sufficient time to construct the assembly trenches requested by Haig on the slopes leading up to Longueval. Haig might also have been persuaded to change his mind by Rawlinson's 11 July letter, which tempered the refusal to immediately accept Haig's diktat with a promise that Rawlinson would still do his best even if Haig eventually refused to back the night-attack plan.[7] Whatever the reason, when Rawlinson asked Haig again whether he would agree to the night attack, he consented.[8]

One of the conditions stipulated by Haig in return for sanctioning the night attack was the capture of Trônes Wood, so that the advancing troops' right flank would be protected. This appeared to be in hand on 11 July when negotiations about which plan to accept were coming to a conclusion. The 30th Division seemed to have captured the wood just in time after several previous attempts had failed. However, the next day the Germans returned to the wood with a vengeance, and the decision to replace the 30th Division with fresh 18th Division units did not make the hoped-for difference. The first attack by the 18th Division at 7 p.m. on 13 July fared no better than most of the earlier attempts. Given that the assault on the German second position was scheduled to take place at 3.25 the following morning, time was fast running out.

One can therefore understand the anxiety that must have been running through the mind of Lieutenant-General Congreve, the XIII Corps commander, when at 12.40 a.m. on 14 July he rang the 18th Division's Major-General Ivor Maxse to ask him what he proposed to do about it. Maxse's response was that he would hand the task over to the 54th Brigade's Herbert Shoubridge, the brigadier-general who controlled the 18th Division unit which had enjoyed the most clear-cut success on 1 July.

The officer chosen to lead this vital mission could not have been better qualified for the job. Not only did Lieutenant-Colonel Frank Maxwell, the forty-four-year-old commander of the 12th Middlesex Regiment, have nerves of steel – he had already won one Victoria Cross – but he was also a considerate and charismatic leader. It was an unusual combination. In one of the many letters he wrote to his wife, Maxwell told her that unlike most men he was not at all put out if another man's blood was sprayed all over him – apart for being 'sorry for the victim's poor mother or wife . . . Happily I possess a temperament that seems immune from nerves or shocks to the system . . . And for this there is much to be thankful for even if it does mean there may be something good missing.'[9]

His cool head was to come in useful in Trônes Wood. When Maxwell was briefed, he had been given to understand that some of the British troops inside the wood had reached the northern apex (the wood was shaped a bit like a triangle with a more or less flat bottom in the south-west and the apex in the north). However, when he questioned those he encountered, Maxwell concluded that the troops had lost their bearings after entering the wood, and had presumed the eastern side was the north.

He resolved to line up the 12th Middlesex and 6th Northamptonshire soldiers placed under his command along the base of the 'triangle', so that they could sweep through Trônes Wood without missing any of the lurking enemy. 'Nerves were very highly strung,' he recalled. 'To counteract this, I ordered every man to fire as he advanced . . . This . . . had the desired effect and the advance continued much more steadily and in better order.'

It also appeared to frighten the Germans who were concealed in the undergrowth. Maxwell saw many Germans running out of Trônes Wood as they heard his line approaching. After he and seventy of his men had dealt with the strongpoint on the west of the wood, they eventually reached the wood's northernmost point. In the nick of time the job was done.[10]

Nothing was to be left to chance for the main attack. The crucial question that had to be solved was: how to move the assault battalions for each of the two corps hundreds of yards across No Man's Land and position them around 500 yards away from the German trenches without being seen or heard, all of the moving to be done in the dark? Overall, the XIII Corps battalions had to move around 1,200 yards from their start position (the north-west corner of Bernafay Wood to Marlboro Wood) to their objective (Delville Wood–Longueval–Bazentin-le-Grand); whereas the XV Corps battalions only had to move 300–600 yards from their start position (Marlboro Wood–north of Mametz Wood) to their objective (Bazentin-le-Grand Wood–Bazentin-le-Petit Wood and village, and the cemetery 500 yards away).[11]

The solution to the problem posed was to employ one of two devices: either an easily findable landmark such as a road could be used to mark the direction of the move towards the German line, and then tapes running at right angles from the road could be pegged down, behind which the men could assemble. If there was no road or other landmark, then a tape leading from the British line towards the German trench on a particular bearing could be used instead, and tapes running at right angles to the main tape would then mark the line of assembly. Using this system, the men were all in position well before zero hour, thereby giving themselves the chance to creep even closer before the artillery lifted off the German front line.[12]

As well as finding a way of assembling the troops without the Germans noticing, Rawlinson realized that the artillery deficit had to be sorted. For the first time since the war started, there really were enough guns and ammunition not only to cut through what some quaintly called the German 'obstacle' – the wiring that had obstructed so many men two weeks earlier – but also to obliterate the German front trenches and force those in dugouts to remain underground while the British forces approached.

Whereas on 1 July there had been approximately 1,500 guns to cover around 25,000 yards of front, on 14 July there were about 1,000 guns for 6,000 yards. If the number of guns seems less, that is because the German front attacked was now smaller, about 25 per cent of the area assaulted by the 4th Army on the opening day of the battle. The critical statistics were the number of yards of front for each gun, and the amount and weight of ammunition expended for each yard of front. If the above figures are used, the number of yards of front per gun was 16 yards on 1 July and 6 yards on 14 July. In other words, gun to yardage ratio was almost three times as favourable on 14 July as it was on 1 July.[13]

Equally important was the speed at which the shells were fired. The final intense shelling was originally going to last for half an hour. However, the

9th Division's gunners pointed out that their infantry, who were to lie out in No Man's Land until the artillery lifted off the front trenches, could end up being knocked out by the German retaliatory barrage, if the intense bombardment went on that long. As a result of this intervention, it was agreed that the intense firing by British guns should only last five minutes.[14] Those interested in artillery statistics might question why, as it turned out, the British shelling was so much more effective on 14 July than it had been on 1 July. Although the number of guns per yard of front was much greater on 14 July, the extra number of shells fired per yard of front on 14 July as compared with 1 July was not nearly as pronounced. (The number of shells fired on 1 July was 1,627,824. If we accept the rough figure for the length of front given in the British official history, in other words 25,000 yards, that means the number of shells expended per yard was about sixty-five. The number of shells fired on 14 July was 491,804. If we assume the front shelled was 6,000 yards, as specified in the British official history, the number of shells fired per yard was around eighty-one, that is, around 25 per cent more than on 1 July.) The answer is possibly that in some circumstances, firing a lot of shells very quickly at an enemy was more scary for him – and more likely to confine him to his dugout – than if the same number of shells were fired over a longer period.

Certainly Neil Fraser-Tytler, the Royal Artillery observer, was impressed when at 3.20 a.m. so many guns began firing simultaneously. Afterwards he wrote: 'It was a stupendous spectacle! The darkness lit up by thousands of gun flashes. The flicker of countless bursting shells along the northern skyline, followed a few minutes later by a succession of frantic SOS rockets and the glare of burning Hun ammunition dumps.'[15]

The French were also impressed. When General Maurice Balfourier, the commander of the French XX Corps, advised the British general Archibald Montgomery-Massingberd not to go ahead with the night attack, Montgomery-Massingberd famously retorted: 'Tell General Balfourier with my compliments that if we are not on the Longueval ridge at 8 tomorrow morning, I will eat my hat.' That morning, the British met all expectations, and having established themselves on the ridge, a French liaison officer rang through to General Balfourier and told him: 'Ils ont osé; ils ont réussi' ('They dared to have a go; they succeeded'). Balfourier is said to have replied: 'Alors le Général Montgomery ne mange pas son châpeau' ('So General Montgomery isn't going to eat his hat').

But most important of all, the Germans were stunned by the firepower put together by the British gunners, which took troops from all four of the British assault divisions, the 7th and 21st of XV Corps and the 3rd and 9th of XIII Corps, onto the ridge. The features captured included Bazentin-le-Grand and Bazentin-le-Grand Wood, Bazentin-le-Petit and Bazentin-le-Petit Wood. Some of the British divisions had an easier job than others. For example, there was a difficulty because of uncut wire on the front attacked by the 3rd Division's 8th Brigade. It was only finessed when some troops went round the side of the obstacle and then, having reached the German trenches, bombed down them until they arrived at the area opposite the uncut wire. By way of contrast, the 7th Division's 20th Brigade troops captured all of their objectives at the exact time scheduled in their orders.

That did not mean the Germans were comprehensively defeated along the whole 6,000 yards attacked. For example, although the British grabbed a foothold in the southern half of Longueval, they could not eject the Germans from the northern portion of the village. Also, although some British troops entered the southern part of Delville Wood, come 15 July it certainly could not be said that the wood was under British control.

Surprisingly, given how proud the British were of what they achieved on 14 July, there are remarkably few interesting or vivid accounts of what transpired after they attacked. However, we get a feel for the kind of to-ing and fro-ing that went on in the Longueval sector of the ridge that day, and afterwards, from the following letter written by Major John Bates, a doctor with the 8th Black Watch, the 26th Brigade unit within the 9th Division, which was on the extreme right of the British attack:

During that first morning after we attacked I was in a trench when a [shell] . . . burst exactly over my head. My servant, a yard on one side of me, was wounded, and my orderly, a yard the other side was killed outright. I then jumped into a shell hole to attend to two fellows wounded. I went back to the trench 20 yards away for some gauze, and while I was getting it, an enormous shell landed in the hole I had just left and blew the two wounded men to bits and killed my corporal who I had left there.

I then selected a house for my dressing station. While I was there, the house next to it was blown to smithereens by one enormous shell and smothered the patients with brick dust so that we looked like millers. And five minutes afterwards the house opposite caught fire and was burned down and we had to clear out . . .

At one spot I chose for a dressing station, the only Red Cross flag I could hang up was a piece of German white shirt, with 2 pieces of bandages soaked in blood pinned across it, the whole tied onto a German bayonet on a rifle which I stuck in a tree outside . . .

On the last day I was completely surrounded by Germans but they never spotted me as I was in a dugout with 3 patients . . . During the 7 hour bombardment before, a shell had blown in the entrance, so it didn't look like a dugout at all, just a heap of ruins.

Our fellows did a magnificent charge, cleared the village of the enemy and I was just able to escape but on hands and knees as the Hun by that time had got a machine gun in the church 100 yards away and had spotted us trying to get away.

All three patients could walk so we got them away all right.[16]

Major-General William Furse, commander of the 9th Division, might have had to reconcile himself to the prospect of a long war of attrition for the unconquered parts of Longueval. Major-General Campbell, commander of the 21st Division, may have had similar difficulties in clearing the north-west corner of Bazentin-le-Petit Wood. (Resistance there carried on until 7 p.m., and even then there was an unsubdued German machine-gunner nearby.) But that did not constrain the commanders of the units within the inner brigades of each corps (XIII Corps' 3rd Division and XV Corps' 7th Division) who wanted to exploit their success. By 10 a.m. opposition had melted away from their respective sectors due to the strength of their initial thrusts. Officers from the 3rd Division wandered northwards to High Wood without seeing any evidence of German troops or trenches.

However, neither of these divisions was permitted to use up their spare unused brigades in making a further advance. Lieutenant-General Horne of XV Corps had already decided to let the available cavalry make the first move from the new front line.

The 2nd Indian Cavalry Division had been ordered to advance from its place of assembly near Morlancourt (four miles south of Albert) at 7.40 a.m. It only moved at 8.20 a.m., and such were the difficulties of riding horses through a slippery landscape pitted with shell holes that the advance guard, the Secunderabad Cavalry Brigade, only reached the valley south of Montauban at noon. It was then held back by XIII Corps in the hope that Longueval would be captured before the advance guard was let loose.

At 3.30 p.m. General Horne received an erroneous report stating that all of Longueval was finally in British hands. This prompted him to order the

7th Division to advance to High Wood at 5.15 p.m., and he asked XIII Corps to permit the cavalry to cover its right flank.

In the end it was the 7th Division's 91st Brigade that held up the advance. But by 6.45 p.m. both it and the cavalry were in place east of Bazentin-le-Petit cemetery, making it possible to advance towards High Wood at around 7 p.m. The 91st Brigade troops found few Germans in the southern part of the wood. The north part was another matter, however, and the brigade did not attempt to push past the Switch Line that cuts through the northern part in an east-west direction.[17]

The sight of the lines of mounted horsemen heading for Sabot Copse, and subsequently to the rendez-vous with the 7th Division infantry, boosted the morale of all British soldiers who saw them. One of them, the chaplain Pat Leonard, attached to the 3rd Division's 76th Brigade, recalled how:

During the evening we stopped our work (digging in following that day's advance) to watch the most inspiring spectacle of the War. Down over the ridge behind us came the cavalry in long lines. First came fierce-looking Indians, their turbans streaming behind them as they cantered past, some with lances with points agleam, others armed with carbines and machine guns. Behind came our English cavalry, and behind them again more Indians until we thought they would never end.

Across the valley they cantered and up the other side until just behind the crest they halted, and formed up into their troops and squadrons. Soon after the last of them had passed the crest, we heard the German machine guns tapping out their stream of death.[18]

Lest readers fear that means they came to a sticky end, I have quoted the details of what ensued over the crest from the 7th Dragoon Guards' history:

As the two leading squadrons broke into a gallop and deployed they [had come] . . . under machine-gun fire from both flanks. But this did surprisingly little damage.

All B Squadron had their lances unslung. The rest drew their swords . . . After a couple of hundred yards (Lieutenant) Pope and his troop reached a steep bank beyond which lay a field of standing corn . . . Leaping up the bank they wheeled to the right, levelled lances and charged some machine-gunners taking cover in ... shell holes. About 15 of the enemy were speared ... thirty-two surrendered. Others fled.

The fire was now intense, and as it would have been suicide to continue, the rest of the Regiment dismounted under the cover of the bank, and came into action with rifles and Hotchkiss guns.

Meanwhile 2nd Lieutenant Pope, seeing some of his men wounded in the cornfield, bravely rode out three times under fire and brought in two of them across his saddle.

Lieutenant Hartley led his machine-gun section out to a flank, but before he could come into action, the gun horse was killed, and he himself was mortally wounded while trying to extricate the gun.

The 7th Dragoon Guards ended the day with twenty-four men and thirty-eight horses on their casualty list. That was a trifle compared with the casualties sustained by the four British infantry divisions who had reached the German 2nd position that day. Figures quoted in the British official history suggest they were around the 9,000 mark.[19]

It was not as bad as Pat Leonard may have feared when he had heard the machine guns start up. But given that so much store had been set on the cavalry breaking the deadlock once and for all, its failure to dominate the battlefield meant that 14 July, which had started so promisingly, had a disappointing ending.

20: Surrounded

Delville Wood, 15–20 July 1916

(See maps 2 and 12)

The biggest disappointment about the night-time attack on 14 July from the British point of view was its failure to make serious inroads into Delville Wood. The chain of reasons explaining why the wood's capture was so important are inscribed in Haig's diary: it would have been unreasonable to expect the French to advance on Maurepas, its next objective to the south of the British line, if the 4th Army had not first neutralized the German position at Falfemont Farm. And before that could take place, Ginchy and Guillemont had to be taken care of, operations which in their turn would be simplified if Delville Wood was taken.[1]

It was against this background that a message was sent down to the commanders in the front line during the evening of 14 July and the early hours of 15 July. This stated that Longueval, and Delville Wood, had to be captured 'urgently' and 'at all costs'.[2] The job was given to the 1st South African Brigade.

Two South African battalions, the 2nd Natal & Orange Free State Infantry Regiment and the 3rd Transvaal and Rhodesia Regiment, were ordered to advance through the southern part of Longueval into the wood at 5 a.m. on 15 July.[3] The conditions they encountered were recorded in the memoirs of Dudley Meredith, a twenty-year-old private serving with the 3rd South African Battalion's C Company, in the following terms:

As we marched up the road to Longueval (they had spent the night in a trench north of Montauban) . . . the dawn began to break . . . It was dark and quiet . . . Longueval . . . [consisted of] smoking heaps of bricks and shell holes filled with water, but we could [still] see what had [once] been the main street . . . Numbers of dead 'Scotties' were lying about, [and] . . . a little way down the street was a large number of dead Germans, most of them horribly mutilated.

Stunned by a sight which led to the realization that such carnage might strike them at any minute, the South Africans turned towards the east, only to have their breath taken away by what Meredith referred to as the 'great beauty' of Delville Wood. At that point, 'the Wood had not been shelled much,' Meredith recalled, 'and the stately trees and leafy undergrowth in the hazy dawn of a midsummer morning had such a peaceful look. Except for the quiet tramp of men . . . all was still.' He went on:

A short distance into the Wood, we came to a shallow trench, barely waist deep, manned by Cameron Highlanders. This trench, known as Buchanan Street, marked the 'spearhead' of the advance . . . the previous day . . . We deployed in front of it and [then] silently waited the order to advance . . . Our orders were to take the [southern half of] the Wood and dig ourselves in along the outer edge.

Soon after we moved off, our company wheeled to the right, and before long, we found ourselves at the [southern] edge . . . Three or four hundred yards across the fields was a ruined factory (Waterlot Farm) . . . [and] on the skyline, we could see figures moving about . . . For half an hour, there was much . . . argument as to whether they were French or German . . . Word was sent down the line after a while that they were Germans, and we were to [open] fire. The hot fire we were [in our turn] subjected to was convincing proof, if it were needed, that this was indeed the enemy.

Meredith's report confirms that even before receiving this confirmation, C Company had not been idle:

We had been digging ourselves in with our entrenching tools, and the whizzing . . . bullets made us set to [it] with redoubled vigour . . . [But] trying to dig in the hard clay . . . [in between the] matted tree roots . . . was very slow work. Most of us, after several hours . . . had only a shallow shelter not more than eighteen inches deep. The result was [that] our casualties were very heavy: . . . five out of the six . . . C Company . . . officers were wounded by the time we had been in the Wood two hours.[4]

One of the C Company casualties to whom Meredith was referring was Private Bert Nock. He has described how during the period when no one peering out of Delville Wood was sure whether the soldiers in the surrounding countryside were Germans, his lieutenant sent one of the men to silence a machine gun that was firing on their left. The lieutenant feared they might be shooting at their allies, the French. 'But it continued,' Nock reported, 'so he told me to "go and tell that bloody gunner to stop"':

I got up, and . . . [walking] a yard or two inside the Wood . . . I found . . . [its] edge . . . turned fairly sharply to the rear of our position (see map 12) . . . I continued in line with the edge . . . [Then] to my surprise, and horror, I realized there was not a single living soul in sight, and that half a dozen or so of our fellows were lying dead.

Standing behind a tree about three inches in diameter, I pushed aside a small branch and peeped out. I then spotted a machine gun nearly buried in the ground about a third of the distance from the enemy trench and cleverly camouflaged. At that instant, two shots were fired [by the gun], and I fell to my knees . . . My right arm . . . felt funny, and when I tried to move . . . it swung round in a circle from just above my elbow . . . I felt no pain as the nerve had been severed.

Fortunately for Nock, help was at hand from a South African machine-gun post inside Delville Wood. After he had been patched up and had asked a gunner to inform the lieutenant what had happened, he found himself wandering back to Longueval, and from there towards the rear. There was no guarantee that he would make it. By this time, having realized that troops were in the wood, German gunners were raining their shells down both on it and on and around Longueval. The German artillery also targeted the sunken road leading from Longueval back to Montauban, the route that most of the injured men had to pass in order to access expert medical help. Whatever the reasoning behind the tactics of the German artillery, their effect could not have been crueller. It meant that the defenceless wounded, who could be forgiven for being grateful that they had made it out of the maelstrom, were being sucked into the battle again just when they thought they had escaped.

Nock's account describes what he witnessed when on the way to the rear he crossed over to the other side of this sunken road to walk around a recently created crater:

As I was crossing over, I heard a voice calling for help. I looked down and saw a fellow at the bottom [of the crater who had] obviously [been] blinded [and who had] lost a leg . . . [He was] trying to climb [out] . . . I had to look away. Otherwise I would have fallen in . . .

[On] the other side of the crater . . . I could see [other] wounded men making their way back . . . The one . . . in front of me was a member of the 4th Regiment, South African Scottish . . . A shell landed right beside him, and . . . when I reached the spot, [all I could see of him was] . . . his kilt and legs sticking out from the side of the . . . road.[5]

Perhaps the dead man was one of the lucky ones. Nock himself made it back to a hospital in London where he narrowly avoided having his injured arm amputated. But for every one South African soldier saved, there were many others who had to endure hours of agony before being put out of their misery. A runner who visited the aid post in Longueval and was overwhelmed by the stink of iodine, blood and cordite, was surprised how men with 'ghastly' injuries clung on to life. He cited the example of men who had been disembowelled but who nevertheless asked for cigarettes and water.[6]

At least they could speak and drink. Such pleasures were denied to those with serious facial injuries. Private Alf Mandy, a South African in the 2nd Battalion, whose jaw had been shot away by a German sniper during the third day of the Delville Wood siege, was fortunate not to be executed by a British officer when he was apprehended in the dark on the way to the dressing station. Because of his wound, Mandy could not talk, leading the officer to suspect he was a German up to no good. His life was only spared thanks to the officer's subordinates who arrived and helped to identify him in the nick of time.

That was just the beginning of his post-action ordeal. The doctors and nurses at the dressing stations and hospital he passed through could not work out how to feed him. 'They had no feeding cups and could do nothing for me during the two days I was in the hospital [in Corbie],' Mandy reported. A solution was only worked out after he was put on a barge that was to transport him up the Somme to Abbeville:

As soon as I could attract the attention of a nurse, I showed [her] my notebook which stated I had not drunk anything for three days. She came back with a feeding cup, but even that did not quite solve my difficulty. Nor did a normal sized rubber tube fitted onto the spout. Fortunately she found a very narrow tube and I whittled it down to a point and gradually worked it down my throat past the obstruction. The nurse then fitted the cup onto the tube and [was consequently able to pour] . . . liquid down my throat. In that way I was able to slake my terrible thirst and get some liquid foods into my stomach.[7]

Casualties during the morning of 15 July were not confined to the 3rd South African Battalion's C Company (Meredith's and Nock's unit). The other

South African units on the edge of Delville Wood were equally exposed. It was flanked on its left by the 3rd South Africans' A, B and D Companies in that order (see map 12). And as soon as the wood south of Princes Street had been taken over, the 2nd South African Battalion advanced to the fringes of the wood encircling the northern half.

By 2.40 p.m. the perimeter of Delville Wood was entirely under the control of the South African troops, except for the north-west side which abutted onto the northern half of Longueval, still in German hands. It was accepted that a separate operation would be needed to clear the machine guns holding this north-west side. That being the case, the 2nd South African Battalion dug in on Strand Street, a trench set back to the east of the north-west perimeter. As can be seen on map 12, Strand Street ran from the north of the wood to its junction with Princes Street in the centre.[8]

Theoretically, the troops in Delville Wood were controlled from the headquarters in the Buchanan Street and Princes Street trenches. However, the reality was somewhat different: because of the shelling, there were long periods when troops on the fringes were cut off from the nerve centre.

German infantry made its first of many attempts to wrest the wood from the South Africans by advancing towards its north-east perimeter during the afternoon of 15 July. They were repulsed, although not before the 2nd Battalion had suffered heavy losses. But it was the South Africans' attempts to capture the north-west part of the wood that led to some of the fiercest fighting.

Their first attempt was made by a South African battalion and a Scottish battalion at 10 a.m. on 16 July. The South Africans' 1st Cape Province Regiment advanced from Princes Street northwards within the wood alongside the 11th Royal Scots (9th Division's 27th Brigade), whose troops advanced in the open. Neither made much headway, being pinned down by heavy machine-gun fire. Some indication of its intensity is to be found in the following extracts of the post-action account written by Arthur Craig, a lieutenant serving in the 1st South African Battalion's B Company:

I got hit twice in the left shoulder . . . I dropped . . . short of the German trench. Most of my men . . . had [also] fallen . . . Seventy-five yards away . . . machine guns were blazing at me . . . While lying on the ground, my tunic was torn to shreds by machine-gun bullets, [and] my equipment cut to pieces . . . Then [Private William] Faulds climbed the barricade (which separated the South African trench from the German trench at right angles to it) and crawled towards me. He was accompanied by . . . [two other men]. It took them twenty-five minutes to drag me [from where I was lying] over the barricade. They pulled me by my left leg. One of my rescuers was badly [wounded] . . . It was a miracle any of us got out alive.[9]

After the fighting had petered out in the north-west corner of Delville Wood, the commander of the South Africans' 1st Battalion, Lieutenant-Colonel Frederick Dawson, informed Brigadier-General Tim Lukin of the South African Brigade that his men were 'exhausted' and needed to be relieved soon. This was passed on to Major-General Bill Furse of the 9th Division. But instead of being told he could replace the tired troops, Lukin was sent an order at 10.30 p.m. on 16 July instructing him to prepare the men in the north-west corner of the wood for another attack that was to go in at 2 a.m. the following morning. The delay was to give the South African and Scottish troops time to vacate the north-west section of the wood, so that the German garrison there and in the northern half of Longueval could be softened up by the artillery.

Predictably perhaps, given the state of the men, it was another failure.[10] That did not stop Rawlinson writing in his diary entry for 17 July: 'I was much annoyed this morning to find that my orders of last night for the enemy to be turned out of the northern end of Longueval had not been carried out by the 9th Division. I spoke to Congreve (XIII Corps' commander) severely [and] conveyed to him the Commander-in-Chief's displeasure, and told him to pass it on to Bill Furse (9th Division's commander). I am seriously considering whether the 9th Division should be sent away.'[11]

Perhaps if he had seen the messages coming in from the surviving officers on the wood's eastern perimeter, Rawlinson might have done just that. At 5.50 p.m. on 16 July, Captain Richard Medlicott, who, as commander of the 3rd South African Battalion's B Company, was responsible for part of the area south of Princes Street (see map 12), reported to the battalion's commander, Lieutenant-Colonel Edward Thackeray: 'The enemy are sending up reinforcements to the extent of several hundreds and are going into trenches east and north east of Princes Street. These Huns are coming from Ginchy . . . I have done my best to cheer the men up . . . [They] are really shaken and [the] officer commanding A Company (which was south of Medlicott's company) reports that his men are in a bad way.'[12]

Ten minutes later, Lieutenant Owen Thomas of A Company explained why: 'Many rifles are hit and many are temporarily out of action with mud and dirt being blown over them. Actual strength of Company now in line . . . 81.'[13] By the time Thomas sent in his report the following morning, A Company had lost another ten men due to the German shelling. 'The Vickers machine gun has been put out of action and the gun withdrawn,' he reported. 'Nothing has been heard or seen of 3 Division. I was given to understand they were attacking at dawn. My Company has been so depleted and the remaining few are now so exhausted, that I do not consider we could put up an effective resistance if the enemy were to attack.'[14]

One report filed by a South African soldier serving with the headquarters of the 2nd South African Battalion, located in the vicinity of the junction of Buchanan and Princes Street, described the effect of the ferocious German response to the South African and British shelling in the following terms: 'That night (16–17 July) . . . we were shelled unceasingly. The foliage of the trees disappeared rapidly, and by the morning . . . only bare stumps remained . . . We could see through to the open country in every direction.'[15]

That should have made the relative calm and disappearance of the German forces from the hotly contested north-western section of Delville Wood during the night all the more suspicious. Attempts had been made to probe the German defences to the west of Strand Street with a view to joining up with the 3rd Division's 76th Brigade troops who at 3.45 a.m. on 18 July had advanced from the west into the coveted northern half of Longueval, and into the orchard beyond. However, instead of being met with the expected resistance, the South Africans in their 1st Battalion discovered the enemy had moved out of the wood altogether.[16]

If the absence of any opposition during the early hours of 18 July had not put the South Africans on their guard, they were soon brought back to reality with a bump as the German artillery began to fire at the wood with a vengeance at 8.30 a.m.[17] The wood's perimeter, as well as the north-western section, were at the epicentre of the bombardment. Private Ernest Solomon, who was with the 3rd South African Battalion's A Company, in the south-east corner, recalled in his memoirs:

The 18th was ushered into being with a shock so fierce . . . that nature [itself] groaned under the strain . . . The German gunners seem[ed] . . . to open the very floodgates of their resources, [and] launched upon us an attack that reached a pitch of violence and intensity the like of which we had never before experienced.

The air was filled with the shrieks of shells that rained upon us unceasingly. The atmosphere seemed to be rent asunder by the endless succession of terrific explosions. Sand and stones [were] hurled up ... [and] showered over us clattering onto our steel helmets. The earth shook. Trees crashed over ... [It was a] raging inferno.

Solomon's account does not shrink from describing the feeling of helplessness he and his comrades all felt, as they crouched in their foxholes, forbidden to put an end to their trials by attacking their tormentors. It details the 'queer little cry' made by the man in the hole a few yards away from his during their first day in the Delville Wood, which told Solomon that his neighbour had been shot. When he turned to look, the man was lying 'still on his face' before being pronounced dead by the summoned stretcher-bearer. There was no need for such a pronouncement for another man who 'was cut clean in half by a shell', or for the man who 'just disappeared ... Whether he was buried or just blown to pieces was never [discovered] ...'

Solomon's list of maimings goes on and on:

Two well-known Johannesburg footballers lay with broken legs. One died. The other today wears an artificial limb. One man whose singing had so often delighted us at camp concerts lay in a shell hole, his face calm, his body bearing no outward sign of mutilation. They said he had been killed by concussion. Another young fellow had both his legs blown off ...

At intervals along the line, great cavities marked the spots where shells had pitched clean onto shelters and blown their occupants to eternity. Men were put out of action singly and in bunches. One Lewis gun team was wiped out to a man. All around in and out of shell holes, in and out of their one-time shelters, lay the dead bodies of men.

That was all on the first day. As if that was not bad enough, their own artillery shelled them on the second day. 'One gun ... had been misdirected' and it took several runners carrying messages before the firing was stopped, 'but not before it had killed several of our men'.

As each hour passed, the trees, which at least gave the men the illusion that they were sheltered, were swept aside. 'Bushes and small trees were torn up, large trees uprooted. Many a grand monarch of the wood, lifted from its roots and projected forward was seen to crash through the branches of other trees and settle down full length [on the ground]. Others borne up by neighbourly branches rested in that position like so many tired giants.'

To cap it all, on the second day in Delville Wood, they also had to withstand the rain that at times 'came down in torrents', soaking them. But as Solomon explained: 'The three previous days, eventful and trying as they had been, were to the 18th, as is the calm to the storm it precedes.'

Yet somehow, notwithstanding the fresh spate of killings and woundings, the survivors on the eastern fringes of the wood hung on, Solomon reported. 'Major Jackson was killed . . . Our only remaining company officer [was] wounded . . . One man's shelter was completely covered in. With feverish haste, he was dug out. Nose, ears, mouth and eyes full of sand . . . [He was] trembl[ing] . . . like a leaf . . . He had been unable to move a muscle beneath the weight . . . that covered him, and thought . . . that his last moments had come.'[18]

While the men on the east of the wood were being pounded, similar treatment that was being applied to those in the north-west section forced the 76th Brigade's troops to retire. This had a knock-on effect: the arrival of Germans on the west side of the wood eventually meant the 1st South African Battalion's rearguard had to retreat back to Strand Street where they had started earlier that morning.[19]

The heavy casualties in that battalion (approaching 630 for the days spent in Delville Wood) may explain the paucity of the information concerning its last stand. The sparse entries in the war diary certainly make clear that the battalion was pushed to the limit. At around 8 a.m. its commander, Lieutenant-Colonel Dawson, who was in charge of all forces in the wood, had sent fifty reinforcements to bolster the battalion's defences, only for three of the party to return shortly after midday to report that just twelve men of the battalion were still standing. Dawson's plan to send 150 more men to replace them had to be aborted on account of the intense German artillery fire.[20]

The only aid that reached the beleaguered garrison in the north-west of Delville Wood came thanks to the efforts of junior officers who acted on their own initiative. One such reinforcement was organized by 2nd Lieutenant Errol Tatham, a twenty-four-year-old solicitor during peacetime, who because of the high casualty rate in his unit, the 2nd South African Battalion, had been roped in to act as the adjutant. The testimony describing his movements during that hectic afternoon gives us an insight into conditions in the front line and the support trench, which is denied us by the usual sources.

Tatham evidently did not relish being tied down in the headquarters trenches in and around Buchanan Street and Princes Street at a time when the men who had previously served under him in his battalion's B Company were faced with an existential threat, alongside the remnants of the 1st Battalion, in Strand Street. At around 3 p.m. on 18 July he handed over the adjutant's haversack to the battalion orderly room sergeant and went up to the front line. When Tatham first arrived in Strand Street, the troops there were being directed by the 1st Battalion's Major Edward Burges, who told him that he desperately needed more hands on deck. Tatham went away and came back with the few men he could find, only to discover that during his absence Burges had been mortally wounded.[21] That meant Tatham had to take over the command. His spell as leader did not last long.

'I saw him lying in the [Strand Street] trench wounded in the shoulder,' Private William Poole of the 2nd South African Battalion reported later:

He had the wound dressed. After lying there for a time . . . I saw him get up [and I saw him] encouraging the men and giving orders. He was . . . the only officer left. He was evidently in great pain, but continued encouraging the men for about half an hour. He then lay down for about five minutes, looking very pale. [Having regained his strength] he . . . got up and left the trench . . . I wanted to go with him . . . to the dressing station . . . because I could see he was very weak, [but] he said I was not to [come] . . . [I] was to stay behind and help to hold the trench as there were so few men left.[22]

Tatham's decision to stagger back to Buchanan Street was made not a minute too soon. Even as he approached the headquarters trench and climbed onto the pile of sandbags that protected the shell hole where a stretcher-bearer, William Helfrich, was sheltering with a casualty from the intense shelling, the two sides were exchanging gunfire. 'The Germans were advancing, and there was heavy machine-gun and rifle fire going on . . . [when] Lieutenant Tatham [all of a sudden] appeared on the parapet above us,' Helfrich reported:

He had his . . . arm in a sling . . . I told him to jump down quickly as . . . [the Germans] were firing at him. He . . . swayed forward as if he were going to fall, and I said: 'Don't fall on this man as he has a fractured leg', indicating the case on the stretcher. Just then, he pitched forward, and I just touched him so that he fell clear of the stretcher.

He . . . sat up and said, 'Look at this' . . . [moving his arm, which had been shot away above and below the elbow]. 'The b[astards] . . . are using [exploding] bullets.' I . . . took off his tunic and started to put a tourniquet on his arm. 'Don't trouble about me,' he said, 'I'm finished.'

'No [you're not],' I said. 'They will amputate your arm and you will be . . . [fine].' 'No [I won't],' he . . . said. 'There are other wounds.' . . . [He] told me to look at his chest. I opened his shirt and saw that his right breast had been shot away . . . He [also] had a bullet wound through the left side of his chest just above the heart.

He then asked, 'What would happen if I took off the tourniquet?' I told him he would bleed to death. He implored me to loosen it . . .

'No sir, I . . . [can]not,' I replied . . . He asked me if I had any morphia . . . I told him I [did not have any] . . .

Just then the casualty . . . on the stretcher called me . . . After attending to him, I returned to the Lieutenant and found he had loosened the tourniquet with his teeth . . . He was . . . practically unconscious . . . murmuring: 'Rain . . . beautiful rain . . . lovely rain.' I raised his head . . . [and cradled it in my arms, but it was to no avail] . . . A few minutes [later], he passed away.[23]

Shortly afterwards, the Germans overran the South African defences protecting the shelter where Tatham had died, temporarily taking Helfrich prisoner (he later escaped) and surging forward to the south of Delville Wood on either side of Buchanan Street. It took a charge by men from the 7th Seaforth Highlanders and 8th Black Watch (26th Brigade) to send them scurrying back to the centre of the wood. Incredibly, the South Africans in Buchanan Street itself, who later that evening were reinforced with just over 100 men, managed to hold on, repulsing any attempts by the Germans passing on either side of them to capture them.

No one could complain that those in charge had not been warned what was coming. At 1.50 p.m. Lieutenant-Colonel Edward Thackeray had sent the following situation report to Brigadier-General Lukin: 'Over three hours intensive bombardment of trenches on north-west, northern and eastern sides. We have suffered terribly. Many have no garrison left. In others the few left have been forced to retire. Such men as are falling back, I am detaining in support trench, Buchanan Street, and will endeavour to hold that line.'[24]

Given that Lukin had turned down the chance of relieving his men during the night of 17–18 July, on the grounds that it would interrupt preparations for the overnight counter-attack, such desperate words must have cut him to the quick. Whether or not he was to blame, Lukin had made a miscalculation. Now it was too late to rescue his men. Relief during such intense shelling was unthinkable.[25]

Extreme measures were certainly required if those on the perimeter of Delville Wood were to have even a fighting chance. Private Frank Marillier, a Lewis gunner, who had been supporting the infantry on the wood's north-east fringes, has described how he escaped. 'Our lives were saved when a very brave officer, Captain Hoptroff (of the 2nd South African Battalion's D Company) made his way to our position. He wasted no time. "Get out! Get out!" he said, and was almost immediately hit by a bullet . . . [He] was killed outright.' But those two words had been enough to save the gunners' lives, and they raced back through the wood to join the seventy-odd men clustered around Thackeray's headquarters in Buchanan Street.[26]

It is unclear who gave Captain Hoptroff the order to call in his men. Perhaps he used his own initiative. The South Africans in most of the other units guarding the east and south-east of Delville Wood were less fortunate. Some, like Private John Lawson's platoon (15th platoon in the 3rd South African Battalion's D Company), which was holding the perimeter facing east (see map 12), did not even have any NCOs left, let alone officers. Cut off as they were from all contact with the battalion headquarters by the terrible shelling, Lawson and his friend Private Breytenbach realized that 'it was now everyone for himself'. Only a wound or death could release them from their torment, made worse by the unnaturally dark conditions that had depressed them since the morning:

It was as if night forever refused to give way to day. A drizzling rain was falling in an atmosphere unstirred by a breath of wind . . . Intense shell fire had again commenced . . . Smoke and gases clung to and polluted the air, making a canopy impervious to light. What a contrast was this . . . morning to the morning . . . when we first entered what was a beautiful sylvan scene, but [which was] now everywhere a dreary waste.

Midday came, and with it a meal eaten under this filthy pall. During the whole of this day No Man's Land was enveloped in this semi-darkness, making it impossible to see anything but blurred outlines.

Our little party had to wait in their cramped condition of tortured suspense till nearly 3 p.m. for the only relief we now looked for, the relief afforded by the excitement of . . . desperate fighting against great odds. The enemy now launched an attack in overwhelming numbers amid the continued roar of the artillery. Once more they found us ready, this small party of utterly worn-out men, shaking off their slumbers to stand up in their shallow trench and face [up to them] . . . As the Huns came on, they were mowed down. Every shot must have told. Our rifles smoked and became unbearably hot. But though the end seemed near, it was not yet.

When the Huns wavered and broke, they were reinforced and came on again. We again prevailed and drove them back . . . Once more they had failed, [although] the lip of our trench told more plainly than words . . . how near they were to not failing.

[But] exhaustion now did what shell fire and counter-attacks had failed to do, and we collapsed in our trench spent in body and . . . spirit. The task we had been set had been too great for us. What happened during the next two hours or so, I do not know. Numbed in all my senses, I gazed vacantly into space . . . [until] I was rudely awakened by [yet another] shell which exploded just over me.

The shell that wounded John Lawson and killed his friend Breytenbach may have set them free. But before he followed the by now well-worn track through the barrage that was still barking over Delville Wood towards Longueval, Lawson spoke to one of just six men who were still on guard. 'I aroused some of the young, brave, worn-out sleepers, and told one of them that I had been badly hit, and was going to try and walk out. He . . . asked me what he was to do. I said there was nothing to do except carry on, as the orders of Saturday morning (15 July) had not been countermanded.'[27]

Given the chaos caused by the German thrust to the south, it seems almost incredible that those few officers who were still in place continued to send messages back to the Buchanan Street headquarters. At some point during the late afternoon, the following message sent by Lieutenant Owen Thomas, still commanding the 3rd South African Battalion's A Company, would have confirmed Lieutenant-Colonel Thackeray's worst fears:

I am now the only officer left in A Company. Our Lewis gun crew have been blown up. Can you send another crew? I have wounded men lying all along my front, [but] . . . have no stretchers . . . They are dying for want of treatment, my field dressings being all used up. Can you obtain stretcher-bearers? Urgent! . . . It is impossible to spare men to take wounded away . . . I consider the position is now untenable . . . My breastworks . . . [are] all blown in . . . and my front is now very lightly held with many gaps. Most of the men here are suffering from shell shock . . . To save the rest of the men it will be necessary to withdraw.[28]

This message appears to have been sent shortly before A Company was overrun. Ernest Solomon has recorded what he witnessed as the events that afternoon reached their climax on A Company's front:

Every gun ceased firing with a startling abruptness. [There was] a brief blessed . . . silence, and then the sentries' 'Here they come' brought every man to his feet to meet the coming attack . . . But we could not stem the tide of the advancing infantry . . . They came at our flanks, thus cutting us off from the rear.

Some men from (the 3rd South African Battalion's) C Company ran up [to us]. 'The Germans are in the Wood behind . . .' they said. And there they were, sure enough.

It was the beginning of the end for the unit, which once had called itself A Company, but which now consisted of fewer than thirty men.[29]

C Company, south of A Company on the perimeter, had also been surrounded, and its few survivors captured or killed. Shortly before he surrendered, Dudley Meredith, who had survived to see the lovely wood transformed into a killing field, was horrified by what the Germans had done to the last of the officers in the position: 'Lieutenant Barton,' he reported, was 'lying kicking in his death agonies' on the ground beside him. 'I was alone in the trench.'[30] Meredith really had fought to the last man.

This meant that after all the steadfast endurance exhibited by the South Africans, their only positions remaining by the end of 18 July were those held by Thackeray and his men in Buchanan Street, a few men on the south side of Delville Wood's perimeter, and the remnants of B and D Company on the eastern perimeter, which unbeknown to Thackeray hung on until early the next morning.

It is heartbreaking to hear how near this small pocket of South Africans on the extreme eastern side of Delville Wood came to being relieved. Major-General Bill Furse of the 9th Division wanted the entire South African Brigade to be relieved during the night of 18–19 July. But although some of its unengaged units were sent to the rear that night, those on the eastern and south-eastern fringes of the wood were left to their fate, because he had been led to believe they had been overrun.

Notwithstanding this misconception, they might nevertheless have been saved. On the evening of 18 July, Furse had ordered 26th Brigade's commander to use a fresh battalion that had been made available to retake the portion of Delville Wood south of Princes Street during the night. Such an action would, if successful, have resulted in the rescue of the surviving South Africans. However, the scheduled assault was eventually called off because it was thought that troops who did not know the ground over which they were attacking would get lost in the dark.

Even then, there was hope that something could have been done for the South Africans. If only the attack scheduled for the morning of 19 July had gone in at 6.15 a.m., as originally planned, they might have been relieved. Unfortunately for the men waiting on the eastern fringes of Delville Wood, the allocated British troops from 53rd Brigade, led by the 8th Norfolks, only began their advance through the southern half of the wood at 7.15 a.m., their late start preventing them from benefiting from the curtain of artillery fire that preceded their forward thrust. The advance petered out before the edges of the wood could be reached. A subsequent attempt to drive forwards north of Princes Street was also halted by German gunfire.[31]

In the meantime, the remnants of the 3rd South Africans' D Company, holding the position on Delville Wood's eastern fringes either side of Princes Street, had been whittled down still further. The South Africans had demonstrated a true 'backs to the wall never give in' attitude. One platoon ended up with thirteen men, before it was finally reduced to just seven. According to one of them, their spirits ever since they had taken up their positions were maintained by the 'gallantry and cheeriness' of Lieutenant Francis Somerset, who 'insisted on our shaving and tidying ourselves, saying that a corpse looked bad enough without our making ourselves look worse than we needed when our time came'.[32]

As a result of his encouragement, the men carried on fighting to the last, deepening their trench and conserving ammunition so that they would be able to withstand the next assault. These few men, fighting alongside other platoons of similar strength, managed to withstand the German attacks on 18 July, sometimes repelling assaults from both front and back simultaneously. Eventually the Germans backed off, unable to quell the South Africans' machine guns. But then the gunners who had previously been supporting the South Africans, shelled them, not realizing they were still there. That prompted Lieutenant Somerset to attempt to lead his men out. In the process he was, as one witness put it, 'shot through the forehead . . . He died instantly.'[33]

Undaunted, Captain Richard Medlicott, the officer in charge of the 3rd South Africans' B Company, just to the south of Somerset's men, was as he later reported, 'determined to hold on'. His company sent up rockets, waved the platoon flag at an aeroplane that flew low overhead, and just hoped the promised counter-attack by the British would materialize the next morning. It never reached him. Half an hour after the British 53rd Brigade troops finally advanced eastwards during the morning of 19 July, the Germans cut in from the north, catching Medlicott and his gunners, as well as the men in D Company to their north, without the ammunition they would have needed to carry on.[34] Those who did not die in the fighting were taken prisoner with the exception of one machine-gunner, who was summarily executed by his German captor, and another who, perhaps fearing a similar fate, blew his brains out with Lieutenant Somerset's pistol.[35]

The torment that these men must have experienced, psychologically as well as physically, can explain such extreme behaviour. But if their powers of endurance were tested, one wonders how the men under Lieutenant-Colonel Thackeray's command, still holding out in Buchanan Street, managed to remain at their posts. Having repulsed three German attacks during the night of 18–19 July, the last one by firing at the enemy who had been creeping up on them from both front and back, they were 'just about finished', as Thackeray admitted in a message sent to the sergeant-major commanding the remnants of the 2nd South African Battalion's C Company, the other pocket of resistance, on the southern edge of Delville Wood.

'Thank God our fellows have held on to the finish,' Thackeray wrote, adding: 'They have had a terrible time . . . The . . . majority have gone under. Am hoping [for] relief today early.' His hopes that he and his men were to be relieved quickly were, however, to be dashed. At 1.15 p.m. his message to Brigadier-General Lukin included the following words:

There is some hold up [concerning] . . . our relief . . . This relief is most important in view of enemy's close proximity, some 100 yards. They snipe continually and have machine guns both on [our] west and east . . . So far the SAI have held on, but I feel the strain is becoming too much.

Our heavy artillery shelled our . . . trench [for] some two hours and . . . injured . . . and buried several [of] our men . . . Enemy's fire . . . killed two officers and many men . . . I cannot evacuate my wounded, or bury my dead on account of snipers. Four men have been hit helping one casualty. As I have now only Lieutenant Phillips and one or two NCOs, I do not feel we can hold the trench in the face of any determined attack . . . Will you manage . . . [our] relief as soon as possible.

But not only was Thackeray not relieved that night, he was still wondering when he was to be released from his stand twenty-four hours after his last message to Lukin. At 1 p.m. on 20 July he contacted Lukin again: 'Urgent. My men are on their last legs. I cannot keep some of them awake. They drop with their rifles in their hands, and sleep in spite of [the] heavy shelling. We are expecting an attack. Even that cannot keep some of them from dropping down . . . Please relieve these men today without fail, as I fear they have come to the end of their endurance.'

The delay in carrying out the relief probably increased because the 9th Division was itself relieved of responsibility for the front during the night of 19–20 July. Another contributing factor was the failure of a second counter-attack, this time carried out by troops under the 3rd Division's 76th Brigade during the early morning of 20 July.[36] It was only at 4.15 p.m. on 20 July that the commander of the 53rd Brigade finally sent Thackeray a message confirming he would be relieved, and that same evening the two officers with him and 140 other ranks stumbled exhausted out of Delville Wood.[37]

Given the ferocity of the German attacks on 18 July, even the survival of that small band of men had to be considered miraculous. However, there was no escaping the conclusion that the South African Brigade, which had gone into battle on 14 July with around 3,150 men, had been decimated for no gain. Any territory taken on or after 14 July had subsequently been lost. At the end of the fighting on 20 July, there were only 720 men from the South African Brigade still standing. Some 77 per cent of the brigade's fighting strength on 14 July had been lost by 20 July, a casualty rate comparable to the worst of the losses on 1 July, albeit over a longer period. One battalion, the 3rd South African, emerged from Delville Wood with just over 100 men out of around 875 who went in five days earlier.[38]

The large numbers of dead in such a relatively small area prompted a British soldier who was in action in Delville Wood the following month to write: 'I never remember having seen so many dead in so small a stretch of ground. In one of the rides they lay five and six deep.'[39] That comment was made after the summer heat had accelerated the decay of the corpses and poisoned the air with the stink of rotting flesh.

On 20 July some of the men whose decaying remains would one day offend the nostrils of that writer were still alive, if only just. A German who visited Delville Wood that day noted in his diary: 'The Wood was a wasteland of shattered trees, charred and burning stumps, craters thick with mud ... blood and corpses. [There were] corpses everywhere. In places they were piled four deep. Worst of all was the lowing of the wounded. It sounded like a cattle ring at a spring fair.'[40]

21: Repulsed

Pozières, 15 July 1916

(See maps 2, 6 and 14)

When Rawlinson wrote down his objectives for the first day of the Battle of the Somme, there was one village that he was particularly keen to see on the list: Pozières.[1] Therefore, after being buoyed up by all the congratulations which flowed in after the attack on 14 July, it must have been a sobering thought to realize, fifteen days after the battle started, that this much sought-after site had not even been attacked, let alone taken.[2]

He hoped that 15 July would change all that. III Corps, which had been excluded from the attack the day before, apart from snatching a couple of small features on the extreme left wing,[3] had ordered no fewer than three divisions to converge on the village. The 1st Division was to try and approach it by advancing north-westwards up the German second position from the western edge of Bazentin-le-Petit Wood. The 25th Division was to send patrols in from the west. But most important of all, the 34th Division's 112th Brigade was to mount the day's only direct attacks on Pozières from the south.[4] This represented a change from the original plan, which had envisaged making the principal thrust towards Pozières from the west after capturing Ovillers (see Chapter 13). After countless attacks, Ovillers only fell to the troops from X Corps on 16 July.[5]

Elated as he was by the success on 14 July, Rawlinson appears to have been confident as he signed off on III Corps' multi-division assault that within hours he would have secured another important scalp.[6] Little did he realize that when Pozières was attacked, British forces would be embarking on one of those marathons which was going to make the Somme a byword for slow dogged advances against well dug-in defences.

What Rawlinson and Lieutenant-General Sir Hubert Gough, who, as commander of the Reserve Army would subsequently assume responsibility for the front, did not appear to appreciate was that conquering Pozières did not just involve a straightforward attack on the village. The Germans had erected defences with many layers. First there were the trenches to the south, buttressed by the blockhouse to the west of the village. Then there was the fortification of houses within Pozières itself. Even after breaking through these works, there were then arguably the toughest obstacles of all: the double line of trenches constituting the German second position to the east of the village, which defended its most important feature: the so-called Pozières heights, topped by the village's windmill, from where it was possible to look down on the Somme landscape for miles around.

Although a lot has been written about some of the attacks on Pozières, little is known about what happened there on 15 July apart from the fact that there were two separate assaults, the first commencing at 9.20 a.m. and the second at 6 p.m. They only merit one paragraph in the British official history. The first attack ended with 112th Brigade's four battalions reaching a trench line around 200–300 yards south of the village. A little extra detail is available about the second attack thanks to an account written by Rupert Whiteman, who as a twenty-five-year-old lance corporal in the 10th Royal Fusiliers participated in it. This second attack, combined with Whiteman's experiences shortly beforehand, was enough to turn this eager young man, who had come to the Somme excited by the thought that being in a battle would be a great adventure, into someone who loathed everything associated with war and fighting.

The 10th Royal Fusiliers were not involved on the first day of the battle. They only reached the Somme sector on 7 July 1916, arriving at Albert in what Whiteman described as 'drenching rain'. Along with the rest of the battalion, he spent his first night sheltering under tarpaulin sheets held up two feet above the ground on wooden stakes. His enthusiasm undampened by the primitive conditions, the next day he was almost envious of the men who were given the battalion's first assignment, which involved burying British soldiers. As he confessed in his account, Whiteman had a 'morbid fascination' concerning the dead. Moreover, if he had been offered the chance to go home at this point, he would have rejected the opportunity: 'I am glad not to remain behind just when the excitement starts,' he noted, adding, 'I feel it is good to be going up' on learning that the battalion was to go into the front-line trenches. Even when during the move to the front, he spied human forms lying huddled in the grass through the twilight gloom, he remained enchanted at the 'prospect of seeing and experiencing new things'.

This positive attitude was all to change more quickly than Whiteman anticipated. No sooner did he hear the sound of machine-gun bullets whizzing over his head as the battalion walked towards the trenches on 9 July than he began to wish he was elsewhere.

But it was his spell leading a burial party on 10 July, near where the road from La Boisselle to Contalmaison meets the road leading down Sausage valley, which really put him off. It was a 'nauseating job,' Whiteman recalled. The corpses stank, and he along with the other members of the party could only bear to be near them if they smoked while they worked. The 'things', who had once been men, were rotting after being left out too long in the hot sun. There was 'no removing of private papers or identity disks, no respectful arranging of limbs . . . They are not sons of Mothers to us,' Whiteman admitted. They were 'just things . . . without personality . . . carrion to be removed from sight in the shortest possible time.'

No wonder the burial party all suffered from what Whiteman referred to as 'acute nausea'. The first body he tried to lift onto the trench board, which doubled as a stretcher, had been trodden into the thick mud and had to be 'loosened' with a pick. It was the first of many. The sergeant in charge instructed them to put the British corpses in one hole, and the Germans in another. The last corpse was 'fat' and 'green faced', and when it 'burst asunder' on the board that was being used as a stretcher, Whiteman's men downed tools and rushed off vomiting.

And that was just the beginning of the day. Afterwards Whiteman had to endure the horror of being summoned to go over the top, only for the advance to be halted before the men in his unit saw any Germans. Then, before the day ended, the blast from a German shell hurled him along with seven other men into the same hole where they had buried the corpses that morning, and buried him in turn. He later recalled how he felt in the 'confined space . . . under a great mass of earth . . . breathing [in] warm suffocating fumes of High Explosive' with those 'strange things under me, warm and terribly soft'. He was in a 'mad fury' as he clawed at the earth, screaming, struggling to free himself from what can only be described as hell beneath the earth.

Whiteman was eventually dug out by the other men in the trench who had seen what had happened. But then he had to endure a 'terrible night' of shell shock, which involved him 'trembling . . . from head to foot' and wincing every time a shell landed in the vicinity. The one respite was when his friend Cecil Porter sat down beside him, perhaps discerning that, as Whiteman put it, 'I could sit down and cry like a child' at any minute. He only returned to something approximating his normal self when the sun came up the next morning, dispersing the terrors that had turned the previous night into a seemingly endless nightmare.

All of this occurred before he had done any fighting. During the morning of 15 July, Whiteman learned they were to attack northwards towards Pozières, taking care to stay between the Contalmaison–Pozières road and the Bailiff Wood–Pozières road (see maps 2, 6 and 14).

As they moved forward towards the village, Pozières looked inviting. Whiteman's account records what he witnessed as he approached it from the south: 'We can see some ¾ of a mile away a clump of green trees on another ridge. We are told they are the apple trees surrounding our objective. The intervening country seems . . . pleasant with patches of coarse grass and fewer shell holes [than further back].'

This was a welcome change from the landscape they had passed through on the way from the original British front line. There, Whiteman noted, 'the surrounding country, normally [corn] . . . fields looks barren, dusty and scorched, devoid of greenery . . . [The] uniform drab colour of pulverised earth broken up by shell holes' is the dominant image that was impressed not just on his mind's eye but on the memories of all who saw it.

The greenery surrounding Pozières contrasted dramatically with all they had seen beforehand. 'We have much to be thankful for,' Whiteman wrote. '[The] weather is glorious . . . But for the machine-gun bullets, we should select such a day for a picnic.'

But the bullets were to spoil any hopes he had of making this a day for celebration. One of the first men in Whiteman's platoon to be shot was a favourite of his. Cecil Porter had sat with him on the night when he thought his nerve was going after he had been buried by the German shell. Seconds before Porter was shot, Whiteman had instructed him to 'Keep distance!'

'All right Whitie,' Porter had replied, and then 'stopped, threw his rifle in the air . . . fell on his face, and lay still . . . I am not allowed to stop and help him,' Whiteman commented.

As if the bullets were not enough, Whiteman's men discovered the German wire had only small gaps in it. The only way to penetrate it was to pass through the gaps that had apparently been left intentionally. Whether or not that was the case, according to Whiteman they were 'death traps . . . ideal targets for the gunner since there is no other way to get beyond the wire . . . and then into the village'.

'I can see a gap directly ahead wide enough to allow three or four men to pass abreast,' Whiteman remembered, 'and to this I run as in a dream. I find the ground in and around the gap carpeted with dead and wounded.' But even that did not stop him. Like a man possessed, he ran on, treading on wounded and dead alike in the scramble to pass through the gap quickly enough to avoid being shot.

He would have dived into the trench he came across a few yards past the wire, were it not for the fact that it was full of those 10th Royal Fusiliers who had beaten him to it. His only option was to lie flat on the ground so that the trench parados hid him from the German machine-gunners. From there, as Whiteman noted, he looked back to where he had come from: 'I see . . . three dead men hanging in the entanglements like half-filled khaki chaff sacks with arms trying to reach the ground. On the far side of the . . . wire . . . which is about 10 feet thick and 4 feet high on . . . average . . . there [are] . . . many bundles in the grass: those who attempted to crawl through . . . [but failed].'

Looking ahead, he saw that a man called Steadman was moving his legs into a position so that he could spring to his feet and race for the nearby trench:

I called to him: 'Don't be a fool Steadman!', but it was no use. He was up and racing . . . the ten paces to the trench. He found it packed with men, so [he] sat on the edge ready to slip in. Too late. They got him through the head, and he lay [on the ground], until someone pulled him in by [his] . . . feet.

An officer somehow managed to crawl down the line, rolling over and over, anything to avoid exposing himself to the machine-gunners. He told Whiteman that at zero hour, 6 p.m., a red rocket would be fired from the British rear. That would be the signal telling them the British shelling would lift off the front trenches so that they could make their final dash to the German front line. The officer then crawled away to remind the other men.

If Whiteman had waited for the rockets, he would never have advanced. As is recorded in the battalion war diary: 'An attempt was made to fire the two rockets from Brigade Headquarters. Unfortunately owing to these being damp, this was not successful, the result being that some of the troops advanced to the attack and others waited for the signal.' Even for these troops it seems 'two or three precious minutes were lost', which permitted the German machine-gunners to send out an even more impenetrable wall of metal than had been used to halt the attack that morning.[7]

That did not stop Whiteman making the attempt to rush forward, following the lead of the men who emerged from the trench. 'A few minutes earlier, there was no sign of life . . . in the forward area,' he wrote. 'But now as if by magic, the space between the trench and the "wood" is alive with khaki figures racing towards the . . . [trees].'

'Once more I am disembodied and without fear,' Whiteman remembered. 'Everything seems strange and unreal. The sight of men being mowed down in front and beside me, the shots and cries of the wounded, the persistent harsh rattle of . . . machine guns aimed in my direction does not affect me.'

He only came to his senses after making it to the orchard south of Pozières. There, he watched aghast at the treatment a German machine-gunner meted out to the British Lewis team sitting behind them. The machine-gunner:

riddles the No. 1 who nearly falls on me. No. 2 then mans the gun but he only lasts a few minutes. [He is] soon followed by No. 3, hit through the head in both cases. That leaves the officer. It is suicide to man the gun in that position. But he thinks otherwise. He arranges himself behind the gun, looses off a few dozen rounds when he gets two bullets through the neck, sits up, looks at me in amazement clutching his neck, then topples over on to the other three.

Eventually, the order to retire was given, at which all those who could do so retreated to the trench from which they had sprung at 6 p.m. They included Whiteman, who lived to immortalize the exploits of the men in his battalion. At first he feared that only thirty-two men from his battalion had survived. That was the number of men who answered the first roll call after the advance. Subsequently it transpired that his battalion's casualties 'only' numbered around 250, fewer than those of three of the other battalions in the brigade. The whole brigade had sustained casualties in excess of 1,400 men, including over 340 killed and wounded.[8]

If the brigade had taken Pozières, this level of casualties might have led to the operations that day being regarded as a success. The problem was that Pozières' defences had barely been dented. Many more attacks would have to be mounted and lives lost before it and the heights behind it were finally captured.

22: A Terrible Mistake

Fromelles: Part 1, 13–19 July 1916

(See map 13)

Ever since Haig had discovered during the lead-up to 1 July that his forces would have 'considerable numerical superiority' over the Germans, he had become obsessed with the need to keep it that way.[1] So when, shortly before the 14 July attack, he learned that the enemy had recently transferred nine battalions from the Lens–Lille sector to the Somme, Haig wracked his brains trying to come up with a strategy that would cut off that source of reinforcements.[2]

Accordingly, he latched onto the idea of authorizing an operation targeting the German front-line system in the area overlooked by Aubers and Fromelles, about six miles south-west of Armentières and ten miles west of Lille. The first plan was to make it a mere display of force, fierce enough to convince the Germans that they must not risk taking their troops away from the sector, however bad the situation became on the Somme, but static enough to ensure there would be minimal British casualties.

However, it was quickly converted into a fully fledged attack with some elements of a mere display of force still attached to it.[3] The problem was that in striving to accommodate these two conflicting concepts, each was compromised, until it became clear that neither purpose would be accomplished satisfactorily. It was similar to what happened on 1 July at Gommecourt.

The operation at Fromelles was to represent a kind of watershed for another reason. It was the first time that Australian forces had been involved in a major action on the Western Front. The 5th Australian Division, part of 2 ANZAC (Australian and New Zealand Army Corps), was the Australian unit involved in the Fromelles battle. But within days of the 5th Division's attack, the 1st Australian Division, part of 1 ANZAC, started to play a leading role on the Somme itself. It was to be supported there by the two other 1 ANZAC divisions, the 2nd and 4th Australian Divisions.

By all accounts, most of the Australians who came over to fight in France were tanned, fit and strong. Some were well-seasoned fighters, having survived the Gallipoli campaign. However, the majority had never fought in a pitched battle before, and consequently were prone to make mistakes that more experienced soldiers might have avoided. Their inexperience was to be a significant factor both at Fromelles and at the Somme.

Although Fromelles has come to be identified with the 5th Australian Division, the 4,200-yard front being attacked was split more or less equally between the British 61st Division, part of the 1st Army's XI Corps, which was to attack on the right (western) half of the sector, and the 5th Australian Division, which was responsible for the left (eastern) half. The British and the Australians had to overcome similar obstacles.

Even before the Fromelles battle started, it was easy to see how mixing attack and mere display within one action was going to create difficulties. One part of the attack order devised by Lieutenant-General Sir Richard Haking, commander of XI Corps, who was to lead the operation, was contained in a section that came under the heading 'Mankilling'. It required the artillery to lift their barrage from the German front line onto the enemy's support trenches and beyond, the normal action when an attack was about to be made. However, rather than only doing this once just before the infantry advanced, Haking wanted the barrage to return to the German front line shortly after lifting off it. The lifting off was just a ploy to tempt the Germans to emerge from their dugouts, whereupon the artillery barrage was to return to the front line with the object of killing as many Germans as possible. It was to be repeated on several occasions.

In an attempt to deceive the Germans still further, the order stated that each 'lift' was to be accompanied by the following action: 'During each of the lifts . . . the infantry in the trenches will show their bayonets over the parapet, dummy heads and shoulders will be shown over the parapet, officers will blow their whistles and shout orders, in order to induce the enemy to man his parapets.'[4]

It was an ideal piece of trickery if one wanted to make the enemy believe that an attack was imminent, but it might be considered suicidal if adopted prior to an actual attack, where secrecy about the timing of the assault was crucial. Not that secrecy was at a premium prior to the start of the Fromelles attack. 2nd Lieutenant Waldo Zander, a Jewish warehouseman from Sydney, serving in the 30th Battalion, the unit in the 8th Australian Brigade that was to support its assault battalions on the extreme left of the attack, recalled after the battle how confused he had been by the mixed messages he and his men were given before the attack started. On the one hand he had been told 'Secrecy must be strictly observed'. On the other hand he noted:

In every estaminet in the neighbourhood, there was nothing else to be heard but the 'stunt'. Even the 'mamoiselles' asked us when it was coming off. Artillery began to move up and dig themselves in, while the roads near the entrances of the avenues assumed a more crowded appearance. Dumps sprang up here and there, and every time one went up the communication trenches, one passed men carrying ammunition and 'plum puddings' (another name for the mortar bombs on sticks also known as toffee apples). The Boche couldn't have helped seeing all these preparations, for his planes were over often enough.[5]

This was just one of the characteristics that the Fromelles attack had in common with the Gommecourt disaster. Equally problematic was the distance separating the opposing front lines. The Australian Brigadier-General Harold 'Pompey' Elliott, commander of the 15th Australian Brigade, evidently did not trust the Australian gunners to neutralize the Germans facing him. This explains why he was so upset at being asked to send his men across the 400 yards of No Man's Land opposite his sector, just to the left of the central Sugar Loaf salient in the German front line that dominated the area between the opposing trenches.

When the opportunity presented itself to complain, Elliott bypassed his commanding officer, Major-General James McCay, and instead buttonholed Colonel H. C. L. Howard, a visiting staff officer from GHQ, to make sure he understood what was being asked of the Australians. When Elliott pointed out that his brigade was being asked to cross an area which was twice the maximum yardage recommended in the pamphlet issued to all officers who served in France (200 yards), Howard agreed the attack would end up being a 'bloody holocaust'.[6]

After the attack, Elliott criticized Major-General McCay for not having protested to Haking about the plan.[7] Elliott evidently believed that McCay put personal pride ahead of what was good for his men. There is certainly evidence suggesting that McCay's judgement may have been swayed by his desire to lead the first Australian division into battle. Lieutenant-Colonel Walter Cass, the commander of McCay's 54th Battalion, who was to play such a pivotal role during the Fromelles attack, recalls how McCay could not wait to order him to mount a raid on the German trenches within hours of their arriving in the Fromelles sector. It was only called off after McCay heard about the part they were to play in the Fromelles attack.[8]

Notwithstanding McCay's failure to object, Elliott's complaint via Colonel Howard appears to have had some effect. Haig's 15 July acceptance of Haking's plan to begin the attack on 17 July had the following condition scrawled on the bottom of it: it was only to go ahead if 'an adequate supply of guns and ammunition for counter-battery work' was provided.[9]

Elliott's comments may also have prompted Haig's intervention, discussed during the 16 July meeting attended by GHQ's Deputy Chief of the General Staff, Major-General Richard Butler, and Generals Monro and Plumer, commanders of the 1st and 2nd Armies respectively: Haig only wanted the attack to be made if there was sufficient artillery to both capture and hold the German trenches. According to Butler, there was now no necessity for the attack to go ahead the following day.[10] However, far from seizing the chance to take a step back, Haking told the generals gathered around the conference table that he was 'satisfied' with the resources allocated, the ammunition was 'ample', and he was 'confident' the operation would be a success.

That afternoon, as if the fates were straining to persuade the generals to abort the operation, it rained so heavily that Butler returned to the 1st Army's headquarters at Chocques to tell Monro's staff that the operation should be postponed or even cancelled if the weather made that desirable. But Haking once again turned down the chance to cancel, preferring to postpone the operation.[11] It was only after Haking had written to Monro telling him of yet another postponement because of the weather on 17 July that the 1st Army's commander finally decided that the operation should be called off.

However, when Monro informed GHQ, the Commander-in-Chief's staff replied that Haig would like the operation to go ahead after all, weather permitting, unless resources were inadequate.[12] Given that Haking had already stated that he was satisfied with the resources, it would have been hard for him now to claim the reverse. So it was that the third chance to cancel this hybrid operation was allowed to pass. Haking eventually decreed that it should commence at 6 p.m. on 19 July after a seven-hour softening-up bombardment.

His decision reeked of complacency. Given that the events of 1 July had demonstrated just three weeks earlier the likely consequence of advancing across a wide stretch of No Man's Land in broad daylight, Haking's decision seems perverse – that is, unless he reckoned the Germans would be terrorized by his artillery. But would they?

Haking's supporters could correctly claim that he was not responsible for deciding on the number of guns and the amount of ammunition that were made available for the attack. But he was responsible for deciding the size of the front he could attack with the artillery supplied. He had initially been told he could attack with three divisions supported by the guns from two other divisions. When the number of guns was scaled down, he reduced the width of his attack so that it covered a smaller area, 4,200 yards, and the number of divisions involved in the attack were reduced from three to two.[13]

As mentioned in Chapter 3, General Rawlinson's artillery adviser had warned him that one heavy howitzer per 100 yards of trench would be required if German defences were to be obliterated. Yet Haking seems to have been proposing an attack using between twenty-eight and thirty-four heavy howitzers over 4,200 yards, which amounted to one heavy howitzer per 150 yards or per 123 yards, depending on which figure one accepts.[14] And that was only taking into account the German front line. The figure was substantially lower than the adviser's suggested gun-per-yard ratio if the German second line was also taken into account.

Neither these flaws nor the generals' prevarications were known to the troops who were to do the attacking. Those who had heard the statement that Haking wanted to be read to all the units involved went into battle with the following words ringing in their ears:

When everything is ready, our guns consisting of some 300 pieces of all descriptions . . . will commence an intense bombardment of the enemy's front system of trenches . . . When we have cut all the wire, destroyed all the enemy machine-gun emplacements, knocked down most of his parapets, killed a large proportion of the enemy, and thoroughly frightened the remainder, our infantry will assault, capture and hold the enemy's support line along the enemy's whole front.[15]

At around 10 o'clock on the morning of the attack (19 July), an hour before the beginning of the main softening-up bombardment, Brigadier-General Elliott of the 15th Australian Brigade started writing what, given the concerns he had mentioned to Colonel Howard, might be described as a deceptively optimistic letter to his 'Dear little wifie':

I am writing this in the morning, and about 6 o'clock this evening we will start a battle. Nothing like what is going on down on the Somme, but in other wars, it would be a very considerable battle indeed. I have taken every precaution that I can think of to help my boys along, and I am now awaiting the signal which will launch so many of my boys to their death. They are all eagerly awaiting the signal and we hope to so pound the enemy's trenches that we won't have much loss at all. Yesterday, our artillery hit up his trenches quite a lot and he was very quiet last night compared to what he was previously. I think he had had a bellyfull. And what he got yesterday won't be the least compared with what he will commence to get in about an hour's time and will continue to get until about 6 o'clock tonight.

Then our boys will dash across with the bayonet, and we hope to gain quite a good bit of the first line. No-one doubts we will succeed in taking it. The trouble they all seem to say will be to hold it when we have it won. I am going up to watch the assault from our front line. I can't stay away back here. If mischance comes, I can only say: God bless and keep you, my dear little true wife and helpmate, and may our little sweet pets comfort you always. I seem to be confident, more so this time than before, that I will be all right. Perhaps your own faith in this belief is helping me . . .

My will is in the safe in the office marked with my name . . .'[16]

Like many of the soldiers going into battle for the first time, Private Henry Williams, one of the 'boys' in Elliott's brigade, had written what he realized might be his last letter two days earlier. It was addressed to his 'Dear Mother', and it continued:

The time is near at hand for a great offensive, and should I fall, I shall be proud to know I did so in the cause of righteousness . . . and . . . justice . . . which is honourable in the sight of God and mankind. This is a great blow to you, but cheer up, for I am sure it is only for a short time, till we meet again in the new land . . . God bless you till we meet again.[17]

These were just words. For many of the Australians in the 5th Division, who had never been in a battle before let alone one against such a sophisticated foe as the Germans, a true understanding of what they were getting into was only properly registered when the German guns began targeting them. 'It was all right for about ten minutes,' 2nd Lieutenant Zander of the 30th Battalion recalled as his unit moved up to the east side of the support line. 'Then the Bosch opened up, as it seemed to us, especially at us. The 5.9s . . . came in pairs. Some were over . . . but a few found their mark, and our faces grew sad as we saw some of our pals going away on stretchers, endeavouring to not show the agony they were suffering from their wounds.'

As 6 p.m. approached, Zander and the carrying parties from his battalion moved to the front line, which had recently been vacated by the 8th Brigade's assault battalions. 'Dead seemed to be everywhere,' he reported:

One man had got a hit from a shell, and half his face was blown away. He lay across the duckboard track, blocking it. A sergeant stepped forward and shifted him to one side, while another person covered the dead man's face with a blood-stained tunic lying near[by]. It all seemed so terrible to us . . . but we were not used to the sight of dead [men] then.

Further along the line, a dump of ammunition was alight, and as the flames got a further grip, the cartridges started to explode. Their sharp, staccato explosions could be heard clearly against the dull crashes of the heavy shells bursting nearby. We passed this dump and reached our position.

As it turned out, hitting the dump was to be a mixed blessing for the Germans. The smoke drifted across No Man's Land, and would eventually act as a protective veil for the exposed Australian soldiers, who had to carry supplies across to their comrades on the German line. Meanwhile the dull red glow left behind after the flames died down guided many a lost man who had to cross back to the Australian front line during the night.[18]

Zander and his comrades in the 30th Battalion, a support unit, would have to cross and recross No Man's Land several times that night. For notwithstanding all the flaws inherent in Haking's plan, men from the assaulting battalions on the left of the attack (see map 13) were able to make it across to the German front line in spite of everything. There they met remarkably little opposition, at least in the short term. They were helped by the relatively short distance they had to cross – fewer than 200 yards, rather than the 400 yards facing battalions in the 15th Australian Brigade on their right – and their distance from the Sugar Loaf salient that stuck out into No Man's Land to the right of 15th Brigade meant they were to some extent cushioned by not being the first to attract the attention of the German gunners whose machine guns enfiladed the area between the opposing front lines.

The leading waves of Australian troops on the left had all climbed over their parapets shortly before 6 p.m. After successfully crossing their side of No Man's Land, they went to ground near the German wire, before charging into the German lines as soon as the barrage pulverizing the parapet in front of them had lifted. They were relieved to discover that their artillery, for all its inexperience, had more or less destroyed the German front-line defences.

In his after-action report Lieutenant-Colonel Fred Toll, commander of the 8th Australian Brigade's 31st Battalion, the brigade's right-hand unit, wrote:

'On arrival [in the German front line], we found great devastation had taken place by our gunfire, and many of the enemy were lying dead or dying in their dugouts and emplacements. It was found that underground works contained many Germans, who were at once bombed and killed.'[19] Another Australian soldier confirmed that at least some of the Germans in the front line who were begging for mercy were met with 'cold Australian steel'.[20]

However, Toll's men had paid a high price. German shellfire on the British front line was so heavy just before the attack that officers and men alike wondered whether their enemy had been forewarned. Losses were further increased by Australian artillery, which for a time had rained shells on their own front line.

Francis Law, one of Toll's sergeants, who was amongst those who reached the German front line, described the consequences of losing so many men:

Recognizing the futility of advance [toward the German second line] across open ground . . . and no officer being in the vicinity (our loss of officers was very heavy . . .), I held up the advance, ordering the men (about 100 in number) to return to the German [front-line] trench . . .

Just then an officer came over waving his revolver . . . shouting: 'Go on boys''. They went and with a hearty 'Damn' with trimmings, I went also.[21]

Toll's report describes how 'the remainder swept on with the intention of capturing the second and third trenches in the first line system . . . We went on and on, but no trace could be found of the same. It [soon became] . . . evident that the information supplied as to enemy defences . . . [was] incorrect . . . The "trenches" shown on aerial photos were nothing but ditches full of water, along which [there] were straight lines of trees.'[22]

Toll's men dug in about 400 yards behind the German front line, while their commanding officer advanced another 150 yards, only stopping after seeing a German strongpoint protected by 5-foot-high barbed wire straight ahead. That told him they had already gone far enough, and he and his staff retired to build up the defences in the original German front line, in case his advanced line of troops needed to retire during the night. Toll's advanced line, which had been greeted by intense enemy shelling, eventually moved back about 100 yards nearer to the front line. There the 31st Battalion entered a ditch that was also occupied on their left by the 32nd Battalion, a sister battalion in the 8th Australian Brigade, and on their right by the 14th Australian Brigade's 54th Battalion.[23]

Toll's report summed up the challenge facing his unit thus:

Very few of our men were available for the (defence) of the enemy's first line . . . [However] all men available . . . were . . . ordered to strengthen [the] parados by transferring [sand]bags from [our] 'rear' to [our] 'front', and [by] throwing up dirt, using entrenching tools and [the] few shovels in hand. Picks, shovels and sandbags were in urgent demand, but where thousands [of sandbags] were required, hundreds only were available . . . It was a heartbreaking job, attempting to block the various openings in the trenches with the material at hand, but the men performed miracles cheerfully [although] . . . we were under shell and machine-gun fire . . . all the time.

Nevertheless, at 7.25 p.m. Toll felt confident enough to send the following message to his brigadier, Edwin Tivey: 'Can hold enemy's first line if reinforcements are sent over urgently. Send men with picks and shovels, extra ammunition for machine guns, and men.'[24]

Observers monitoring the initial progress of the British 182nd Brigade's 2nd/7th Royal Warwickshire Regiment, the 61st Division unit on the extreme right of the attack, can be forgiven for being equally optimistic. At 5.31 p.m. precisely, the two assault companies began to move out through the 'sally ports' that had been opened up in the British parapet, and deployed in a ditch just in front of it. Then, at 5.50 p.m., they set out on their perilous journey across No Man's Land, advancing in four waves. Like the Australians on the extreme left, they reached the area around 40 yards in front of the German trenches before the artillery barrage lifted. That was the signal for them to charge the German front line, if that was an accurate way of describing the 'almost obliterated' trenches full of German corpses.[25]

They arrived just in time to greet the surviving German troops, who were emerging from the deep dugouts where they had taken refuge from British shells. No resistance was offered, although the Germans might have been more combative had they known their fate. Directed by British soldiers' hand signals to make their way across No Man's Land, many were shot by the men left behind in the British trenches, who thought the Germans were staging a counter-attack.

At the same time, some of the British troops attempted to expand the area they had captured by filing along the German front line to right and left, while some of the remaining men advanced to their objective, the German support line. Their initial success was recorded by an observation officer reporting to the right-hand artillery group, who, at 6.05 p.m., sent a message stating 'Infantry are in.'[26] This was confirmed by the following message sent at 6.15 p.m. by Captain Donaldson of the 2nd/7th Royal War-wicks: 'About 20 men hold enemy support line. It is being shelled.'

But they were the last words recorded from these brave men, who had spearheaded the British attack. Within minutes of Donaldson's message reaching Battalion HQ, another message came in from Major Welch located in the signalling post in the original British front line. According to Welch, the enemy were closing in from both sides: 'Pickelhaubes' had been seen moving in on the British troops from their left, and were about to cut off the men in the support line from troops in the German front line who had by this time been reinforced by a third company. At 7.05 p.m. this message was followed by another one from Welch. It contained just three ominous words: 'Bombers cut off.'

Just over an hour later, the remnants of the battalion were ordered to retire. After all the bloodshed, none of the ground won was to be retained. At 9.45 p.m. the following terse message from the battalion's Lieutenant Crosbie summed up how initial triumph had been transformed into a disaster: 'Germans have manned their front line, and those who went over first are no more.' The only men who made it back from the German lines were from the reinforcement company whose troops had failed to link up with the Warwicks in the German support line.

The situation was even bleaker on the left of the 2nd/7th Royal War-wicks. The troops in the four battalions to its left were either too far from the German front line when the artillery barrage lifted, so that they were cut down by the German machine-gunners who won the race to the para-pet, or they were shot while passing through sally ports in their parapet. Only an insignificant number of men from two of the battalions are believed to have made it into the German front trenches.[27]

It is more complicated to describe the progress of the 61st Division's left-hand unit, the 2nd/1st Buckinghamshire Battalion, whose job it was to capture the most important feature in the German line, the salient known as the Sugar Loaf. This battalion had been weakened long before the 19 July attack. A German shell had hit a gas canister on 18 July, resulting in the loss of seventy-eight men. Also before the 19 July assault approximately one hundred others were casualties, the victims of German shelling.

As a result, the attacking companies had been reduced to 120 men by the time they emerged from the Rhonda sap, a communication trench that stuck out from the British line opposite the Sugar Loaf. There was to be no attempt at stealth. Instead they charged the Sugar Loaf strongpoint with a cheer. Witnesses saw some men climb onto the German parapet, but that was the last direct sighting.[28]

Nevertheless, for some time afterwards, there was hope inside British headquarters that they really had broken through where so many attacks had failed before. At 6.23 a.m. an artillery observer reported '184 Brigade in', only to be contradicted by a report at 6.51 a.m.: 'Germans holding their parapet strongly all along. No sign of our people.'[29] But for some reason that report appears to have been disregarded by the commanders higher up the hierarchy, who, for the best part of an hour, permitted their wishful thinking to hold sway over the content of the most recent report.

There was similar confusion over the fate of Brigadier-General Elliott's 15th Australian Brigade, whose 59th and 60th Battalions had sent their men over their parapets at 5.45 a.m.[30] At first, the long distance separating them from the enemy appeared to be helping them. Initial reports at 6.02 a.m. stated that although there was enemy gunfire, it was 'not very hot'.[31] Shortly before 6.30 a.m. Elliott sent a report to General McCay, containing the words: 'Attack appears to be successful. Practical cessation of enemy musketry.'[32]

Imagine Elliott's disappointment, therefore, when just minutes later he was forced to send General McCay a message confirming his worst fears concerning his right-hand unit: '59th Battalion held up half way across No Man's Land. Heavy casualties.'[33] Whether or not the 184th Brigade on their right had managed to penetrate the German defences in the Sugar Loaf stronghold, they had not quelled the Sugar Loaf machine-gunners, who had sprayed the area to their right with bullets. There were devastating consequences. Around thirty-five minutes later another message from Elliott confirmed there had been no improvement: 'The trenches are full of the enemy, and every man who rises is shot down.'[34]

It was only later that Elliott, who was himself nearly hit on several occasions, discovered the full details of the appalling ordeal endured by his men.

He mentioned some of what he had learned in his subsequent correspondence. For example, he recalled how Lieutenant Andrew Morrow, a man
whom he had known since he was 'a wee chap', had:

led his men on magnificently until . . . a piece of shell struck him in the face, and
crushed it in fearfully. His men carried him out, and I was hopeful he would live,
though he would have been badly disfigured and he was [a] very handsome lad.
But he died next day from shock . . .

(Lieutenant) Wally Vaile was shot through both ankles and his arm was all
smashed up. Morrow died in the ambulance, and Vaile got as far as Calais. It was
the exposure and loss of blood that killed Morrow and him. Yet, when they were
carried in, both were so brave and bright, not a word of pain or complaint. Vaile
never seemed to think of himself, but only of (Lieutenant) Jack Bowden. He wanted
him brought in, but in his bravery, Jack Bowden had pushed far out to the enemy's
trenches, and in spite of many efforts the boys could not get his body in.[35]

These men were far from being the only officers put out of action. Another
officer, who insisted on joining 'the charge' in spite of being hit in the throat
earlier in the day, was 'blown to pieces by a shell', and the commander of
the 59th Battalion was so shocked by his experiences that he had to be
relieved by Major Bert Layh, his number two. Fortunately Layh was safe,
Elliott wrote to his wife, but only just: 'A large shell burst and blew him
into a deep hole full of mud and water and half drowned or smothered him,
and it was only with the greatest difficulty that he got out.'[36]

The news that the 59th Battalion had been held up might have prompted
some commanders to have called off the attack. The arguments in favour of
doing so became all the stronger after Brigadier-General Carter announced
at 7.35 p.m. that the advance of his 184th Brigade, which made up the other
half of the central section of the attack, had been unsuccessful.[37] The previous reports that the 2nd/1st Buckinghamshire Battalion were in the Sugar
Loaf were dismissed as 'doubtful'. This admission that should have
told McCay, and Haking once it had filtered up to him, that the Anglo-
Australian force had failed to capture the key to the success of the whole
enterprise.

Instead, perhaps fired up by reports that Elliott's 60th Battalion had
made it into the German lines to the left of the 59th Battalion's sector,
McCay sanctioned the use of the third 15th Australian Brigade battalion,
58th Battalion, in the attack, hoping that such reinforcement would help

the 59th Battalion to make it into the German front trenches.[38] Shortly afterwards, at 7.52 p.m., the 184th Brigade's commander, Brigadier-General Carter, sent Elliott a message that was to highlight yet another fatal flaw in Haking's plan. It stated: 'Am attacking [again] at 9 p.m. Can your right Bn co-operate?'[39] This prompted Elliott to order the 58th Battalion to attack the 59th Battalion's objective at the same time.

If Haking had ensured that XI Corps and all its brigades and divisions had liaison officers in each other's headquarters, this message from Carter might not have resulted in the problematic consequences. However, those liaison officers were lacking, even though Haking had ordered that the central attack on the Sugar Loaf strongpoint and its surrounding area should be conducted by two divisions; this decision made it quite likely that unexpected events might crop up that would require swift communication between the different units. So when at around 8.20 p.m. Haking telephoned Major-General Colin Mackenzie, the 61st Division's commander, and ordered him to cancel his 9 p.m. attack and withdraw all his troops to their original starting point with a view to preparing for another assault the next day, Elliott was none the wiser.[40]

This continued to be the case despite the 61st Division sending the following message to the 5th Australian Division at 8.30 p.m.: 'Under instructions from Corps Commander, am withdrawing from captured enemy trenches after dark.'[41] Either McCay did not see the message or he did not understand its significance: even if he had read the message, he would not have realized how important it was to relay it to Elliott unless he had also seen Carter's message asking for Elliott's support. If McCay had not seen Carter's message, despite Elliott's claim that it was sent to the 15th Australian Brigade via the 5th Australian Division, then McCay would not have known that Elliott might have committed himself to an attack which would be doomed without the participation of Carter's brigade.[42]

There is a third possibility. It is also possible that McCay had not understood the 61st Division's message; its wording was ambiguous in that it could have meant that the 184th Brigade was withdrawing to the original front line so that it could attack again.

Whatever the explanation, McCay did not appear to have realized anything had gone wrong until around 9.10 p.m. That was when Elliott's message describing the 58th Battalion's advance to support the 61st Division's 'attack' reached the 5th Australian Division, just minutes after a message from XI Corps arrived stating that the 61st Division had been ordered not to attack.[43] There is no record of McCay's reaction when he received Elliott's message. Whether or not he regarded himself as the culprit for not having informed Elliott, McCay was probably horrified. Nevertheless it was 9.37 p.m., more than seventy minutes after Carter's attack was cancelled, before Elliott was finally informed that the 61st Division's 9 p.m. attack had been called off.[44]

It was too late. At 9 p.m. troops from Elliott's 58th Battalion had advanced towards the German lines at the very same point where the 59th Battalion had been pinned down three hours earlier. Only this time there was no simultaneous advance opposite the German stronghold to divert the Sugar Loaf's machine-gunners and infantry.

The Australian official historian described it as 'one of the bravest, most hopeless assaults ever undertaken by the Australian Imperial Force'.[45] When the order to attack was given:

they went forward . . . carrying with them a number of survivors of the 59th, until, when they were two-thirds of the way across No Man's Land, there was opened from the salient a fire of machine guns so severe that the line was shattered . . . The survivors obtained slight cover in a ditch. As they lay there with the terrifying din of machine-gun bullets cracking overhead (its commander Major Hutchinson), apparently in an endeavour to lift the wave farther, went on alone and fell riddled by bullets close to the German wire. The two companies of the 58th which made the attack were practically annihilated.

Because of the numbers of casualties, there is no record of the men's torment. The best evidence of their progress was the macabre sight recorded by an Australian who visited the battlefield after the 1918 Armistice. 'We found No Man's Land full of our dead. In the narrow sector west of the Laies River and east of the Sugar Loaf salient, the skulls and bones and torn uniforms were lying about everywhere. I found a bit of Australian kit lying fifty yards from the corner of the salient, and the bones of an Australian officer and several men within 100 yards of it.'[46]

It is likely that at least some of these remains were the last traces of those men who attacked with the 58th Battalion. These were men whose deaths were clearly the result of Haking's bungling, whether or not some, or all, of the other generals involved, including McCay, Carter, Elliott and Mackenzie, bear some responsibility as well.

23: Sacrifice of the Australians

Fromelles: Part 2, 19–24 July 1916

(See map 13)

If the failings at Fromelles had been confined to flaws in the attack plan, casualties might have been kept to a manageable level. What increased them dramatically was the failure by the responsible generals to appreciate when the game was up, and when to cut and run.

With the benefit of hindsight, the time for abandoning the Fromelles attack and ordering a return to the Australians' original front line appears to have been reached shortly after 9 p.m. on 19 July, following the disastrous advance by the 58th Battalion. By that stage, not only had the troops constituting the spearhead of Lieutenant-General Haking's force been routed, but an attempt to thrust forward again had failed as well.

However, in a battle where communication via telephone lines connecting the generals with the men doing the fighting was spasmodic at best, and where more often than not, those in charge had to wait for messages to be delivered by runners or pigeons, there were bound to be delays that in today's fast-moving world we would consider unacceptable. Poor communications were at the root of the generals' insistence that they should strengthen the Australians' position established east of the Sugar Loaf rather than seek to withdraw them from danger.

Fresh impetus was given to efforts to reinforce the Australians in the perimeter, as evidenced by the flurry of activity at Haking's and McCay's headquarters, after a report came in stating that at 9.10 p.m. on 19 July an aircraft crew had spotted flares being fired from the Sugar Loaf.[1] This naturally led the staff at the headquarters of the 5th Australian Division and XI Corps to wonder whether the 184th Brigade's attack had succeeded after all. It was the second time that questions had been asked about the progress of the 2nd/1st Buckinghamshire Battalion in the Sugar Loaf, and reacting to it like a wounded bull, Lieutenant-General Haking resolved to go on the offensive again. The Sugar Loaf was to be attacked that night, and the rest of the front in the morning. It was with this in mind that Haking's staff officer, Brigadier Anderson, visited McCay's headquarters to tell him at

10.10 p.m. that it was of 'the greatest importance' that his troops should maintain their hold on the perimeter to the left of the attack.[2]

That was easier said than done, as Waldo Zander and his comrades in the 30th Battalion, the 8th Australian Brigade's support company, could have told him. The following extract from Zander's report of his experiences that night reveals all too starkly what could befall those who attempted to cross No Man's Land with a view to bringing supplies to troops in the perimeter:

The Hun sent some incendiary shells over, and these set alight . . . anything they came in contact with when they burst, their flickering flames throwing a ghostly light over the dead and debris lying about. One poor wretch, who had his arm blown off by a shell, was crawling painfully across No Man's Land endeavouring to reach shelter and aid, when one of these diabolical incendiary shells burst nearby, splintering him with its burning contents. By the light made by a bursting shell, he was seen to be frantically trying to smother the flames that were eating into his very flesh, tearing up handfuls of mud and earth in his endeavour and agony. His screams could be heard for a second or two – then [there was] silence . . . We passed his body the next morning, one side cruelly charred and burned.[3]

Zander's conclusion that No Man's Land was unsafe has been corroborated by a report written by Captain Barbour of the 30th Battalion. In it, Barbour described how before going over the top, he sought advice from a superior officer on where was the safest place to cross No Man's Land:

Major Purser was greatly distressed at the time, informing me his company . . . had been cut up going across on the left where I met him and were unable to advance far, all the officers being killed or wounded . . . On account of the heavy firing, none of the wounded could be reached until after dark.

[Nevertheless, he] . . . personally conducted me to a position where he thought we had a better chance of getting across. I immediately gave necessary instructions to my platoon, and moved over the breastworks, soon meeting with casualties . . . [caused by] rifle and MG fire. A shell also landed on the leading section causing losses, amongst the casualties being Private Ross, my batman, who had a limb blown off.

Several of us were stunned, and thrown into a shell hole. On recovering, we pressed forward, passing large numbers of killed and wounded (the latter we had instructions not to assist, so as to avoid delay), and then entered the German trench, as directed, on the left.[4]

If those descriptions of the perils of crossing No Man's Land would not have been enough to persuade the generals that the Australians' hold on their perimeter was unsustainable in the long term, they might have been convinced that was the case had they questioned Barbour on what he witnessed in, and behind, the German front line. To his surprise, when he and his men finally clambered into the German trench, they found it littered with corpses, most of them German, but there was not a living soldier in sight.

Incredibly, after all that had been learned by British forces on 1 July about the dangers of not securing the German front line so that soldiers advancing beyond it were not fired at from behind or cut off from their line of communications, no one had thought to check that this basic lesson had been taken on board by the Australians. It was not the other rankers who were blameworthy. They were just obeying orders. Major-General McCay's instructions to his brigades had expressly stipulated that as soon as the enemy in the front line had been quelled, the troops were to drop everything and advance to the limits of the perimeter.[5]

Realizing that the deserted, eerie scene might be replaced by one crawling with fighting troops at any moment, Barbour instructed his men to dig in and collect any ammunition they could find with a view to building up a dump, while he moved up the nearest communication trench to see what was happening further forward. He ended up standing in the ditch where some 32nd Battalion troops were struggling to hold on despite being fired at by the Germans.

It was then that Barbour was surprised for a second time. The troops in this advanced position were so widely spaced out that Captain A. R. White, who was in command on the left of the perimeter, had no idea who was holding the line on his right. As far as Barbour could tell, there was a gap between White's men and the next group of Australian soldiers, through which a determined German attack would be able to thrust whenever it wanted.

Barbour's account records what he did next:

I worked [my way] towards the right where firing was also going on with the object of finding connection there. After some time, I came across some more members of . . . [the] 32nd Battalion and later [other] elements of the 8th Brigade, intermingled, occupying a position somewhat similar to the conditions prevailing on the left. I . . . finally met an officer . . . Captain [Charles] Mills (. . . [of the] 31st Battalion). This officer explained he had only a few men left, but would hold on . . .

The whole of the line I inspected, especially on the left, was very exposed, being enfiladed and continuously swept with rifle and machine-gun fire. Casualties [were] very frequent, unfortunately the wounded falling into the water [in the ditch]. The [German] artillery also had the range to a yard. The water itself was no great physical discomfort [to those who were not hit], but the ammunition got muddy and the rifles clogged badly . . .

Owing to the mud choking their rifles, many of the men kept 3 or 4 rifles in reserve by collecting those of the casualties . . . An enormous amount of sandbagging . . . was necessary to form a parapet, which was difficult under the prevailing conditions and shortage of materials.

Although Barbour was able to report back to Captain White, thereby enabling White to make arrangements to cover the gap between him and Captain Mills' group, the cover must have been very thin. Furthermore, filling in the gap on White's right did not mean the perimeter was secure. If Barbour had probed further to the right, he would have seen that on Mills' right, there was another wide gap, on the other side of which the equally depleted troops of the 14th Australian Brigade's 54th Battalion were situated, occupying a drain to which they had retired after a 600-yard foray to their front.[6]

Their orders emanated from their commander, Lieutenant-Colonel Cass, who had selected a German dugout in a trench just behind the original German front line as his headquarters.[7] It was a far cry from what was being endured on the advanced line, containing as it did electric lights and two beds. The walls were papered, and even decorated with gold moulding similar to picture-frame moulding. 'It had [a] table, armchair, [and] heating stove,' Cass recalled later.

From this relatively sheltered spot, he attempted to mastermind all movements within the perimeter held by the 14th and 8th Brigades. The messages he sent, and those that came into his HQ from the advanced line, tell us a lot about how Cass went about cheering up his men as well as about the difficulties they were having to endure, details to which Generals McCay and Haking might have been privy had they thought of employing a liaison officer to fill them in on the situation in the front line.[8]

At 9.15 p.m. on 19 July, using terminology that we would find offensive today, but which was apparently par for the course within the predominantly white Australian Infantry Force of 1916, Cass sent the following stirring words to his officers in the advanced line: 'Tell the men how splendid[ly] they have done and to hang on like death to a nigger.' This was followed by an exhortation to 'work hard and make your position strong, for we shall be counter-attacked tonight. We must not lose one yard of the ground we have taken, and for the honour of the 54th and the Brigade, hang on. What we have, we hold and never let a German come into our line except as prisoner. You have my entire confidence.'

The messages coming back to him were intended to be optimistic, but had they been relayed to the generals, they might have found them disturbing rather than encouraging. Lieutenant Harris reported from the advanced line: 'We are linked on [the] right with [the] 53rd . . . Must get sandbags and shovels. Engineers have sent for pump. We are in water to our waists in some places! Have about 450 men. If material comes can make a "fair" position.'

At 12.55 a.m. Harris reported '53rd have asked for reinforcements to put where they link up with us. I have sent them about 50 men. Can't spare another man from our firing line . . . Still going strong. Cigarettes and matches at a premium.' He then added fifty minutes later: 'We now have bullet-proof parapet 5 to 9 feet high all along our line.' Harris did not say how the men were going to manage if the Germans shelled the parapet before counter-attacking.

While Lieutenant Harris and Captain White were doing what they could to secure their brigades' fronts at one side of the battlefield, the doctors and stretcher-bearers to their rear, on the other side of No Man's Land, were endeavouring to keep up with the large numbers of wounded men produced by the fighting. Each of the brigades had its own 'field ambulance', a unit whose key personnel were doctors, stretcher-bearers and ambulance drivers. Each field ambulance operated out of its own 'main dressing station' a few miles back from the front line. The field ambulances also manned one or more 'advanced dressing stations', which they set up nearer to the front. The theory was that the regimental stretcher-bearers would carry their wounded to their regimental aid posts, and the field ambulance's bearers would then move the wounded men to the nearest advanced dressing station from where they would be taken by ambulance to the main dressing station. Other ambulances would convey the more serious cases to a casualty clearing station.

But on 19 July the unexpectedly high casualties, including amongst the regimental stretcher-bearers who in at least one case advanced with and were shot up behind the assaulting battalions, meant that the rule book stating what was supposed to happen had to be quickly torn up.[9] Stretcher-bearers belonging to one field ambulance were moved around the rear end of the battlefield like pawns around a chessboard, filling in wherever they were most needed.

Private Langford Colley-Priest, who nominally belonged to the 8th Field Ambulance, was moved to another field ambulance's advanced dressing station before the pre-battle bombardment had even commenced. The first casualty he mentioned in his diary was suffering from shell shock two hours before the start of the attack: He 'is sitting by my side, poor devil. His whole body is shaking. One would think he was shivering from the cold. His nerves must be shattered.'[10] Colley-Priest's own attempt to put a brave face on it cannot have been helped when a number of German shells landed 200 yards away. 'Too close to be pleasant,' he commented with commendable understatement.

But the stretcher-bearers were cheered up when, at around 10 p.m. on 19 July, positive news reached the advanced dressing stations: the Australians had taken two lines of German trenches. 'They are into the 4th line . . . Complete system of German trenches taken and being held at all costs . . . Some are through into the village of Fromelles.'[11] This optimistic view of the fighting was reinforced by what Colley-Priest observed next: 'A small batch of German prisoners just been marched by. About a dozen were brought into our dressing station to have their wounds dressed.'

Around four hours passed before Colley-Priest received the first hint that the attack had not proceeded as smoothly as was at first represented. '2 a.m. Orders to move off to the trenches to do our bit,' he recorded. 'All very anxious to be in the "strafe".' To this he subsequently added the telling comment: 'If only we knew!' Unblooded, misinformed, and naively over-optimistic, Colley-Priest certainly had no idea what was awaiting him, nor what were the unexpected circumstances requiring him to be ferried to another unit's advanced dressing station.

When he arrived, Colley-Priest was immediately instructed to make his way down one of the communication trenches designed to protect the troops as they advanced to the front line from the rear. 'I went down with a chap who knew the run of the trenches,' he recalled. 'He gave me a warning when we were approaching any dangerous spot. Here, we had to crouch down, and run like blazes. The bullets from machine guns were whistling over our heads. About half way down . . . we passed a dead chap who was hanging halfway over the parapet. A number of dangerous points were passed before we reached the firing line.'

It was only then that he realized the scale of the disaster, as the following brief summary of his impressions, scribbled into Colley-Priest's diary after the event, bears witness: 'The sight that I looked on here I will never forget. Good God, it was terrible! Dead Australians lying about. Had to pick our way over them to reach our wounded men who signalled to us. In some places, the dead were piled four and five deep. The trench was almost battered down by shrapnel.'

Encumbered as he was by having to carry one end of a stretcher, weighed down with the body weight of one of the wounded men he and his colleague had collected, it is not surprising to learn that the trip back up the narrow communication trench was even harder than the way down. 'In some places there was barely room for a stretcher to pass,' Colley-Priest noted. It did not help that the ground was uneven. The first journey back to the field ambulance took an energy-sapping two hours. 'In one part of this terrible journey, I tripped and fell over the stretcher. [After that] I was very nervous in case I should hurt the poor fellow again, who had a very serious wound. My whole body was trembling. [I] was forced to sit down and rest for about 15 minutes. I could not possibly go on [straightaway]. I must have kept about 20 stretcher cases waiting, but they all knew what was wrong.' Fortunately he eventually made it back to the dressing station without further mishap.

However, while Colley-Priest was enduring his baptism by fire in and behind the original Australian front line, those in the advanced line on the other side of No Man's Land had even more reason to feel anxious. At 2.05 a.m. on 20 July the 54th Battalion's Lieutenant Hirst sent a message to Lieutenant-Colonel Cass containing the following words: 'Flares are going up almost in rear of our right about the old German trench. I heard that the 53rd are not joined up with the 15th Brigade, or any other battalion.'[12]

It was this message, and the facts on the ground that lay behind it, which underlined the folly of leaving the 8th and 14th Australian Brigades treading water, literally as well as metaphorically, in German lines. One reason why the Australian commanders were so slow to react to the worsening situation was their unshakeable optimism. Never have the descriptive words 'they were in denial' been more apt. Although there had been no definite news about the 15th Brigade's 60th Battalion after its initial advance towards the area to the east of the Sugar Loaf, a belief had been fostered that no news, apart from optimistic statements by wounded soldiers from an unspecified battalion, meant good news.

One major factor behind this fallacious thinking may have been a report at 6.40 a.m. by a forward artillery observer claiming to have observed Australian infantry in the German trenches behind the 59th Battalion's first objective, just to the east of the junction of the River Laies with the German front line.[13] Given that at more or less the same time a clear message had informed the 15th Brigade that its 59th Battalion was held up in No Man's Land, it is perhaps understandable that some individuals might have supposed this sighting was of 60th Battalion soldiers, as they had advanced on the left of 59th Battalion.[14] But after that initial sighting, there appears to have been no hard evidence that the 60th Battalion was still, or had ever been, in the German trenches. And yet report after report went up the Australian hierarchy including the assumption that the 60th Battalion had been successful.[15]

It was only at midnight on 19–20 July that the 15th Brigade sent a conclusive report to General McCay: 'Following message from [the 58th Battalion's] Major Denehy indicates that the attack of this Brigade has completely failed. Such men of the 60th as actually reached the enemy's trench being killed or captured. The two companies of 58th mown down when close [to] enemy's trench. Very few came back.'[16] It prompted a speedy response from McCay, who rang up XI Corps to ask whether he should now withdraw his 8th and 14th Brigades from the German lines, only to be told they must hang on.[17] Lieutenant-General Haking was still hoping the 184th Brigade would attack the Sugar Loaf that night.

It is at this point that critics of Haking could with justification query his judgement once again. He now had all the information that was needed about the first attack to make an informed decision. If he had had the sense to set up a liaison network between his corps and the front-line units, Haking would not only have realized how dangerous it was to maintain the Australians in the perimeter, but he would also have known that the 184th Brigade attack he had ordered was out of the question.

Because he had not organized such a structure, Haking was constantly being surprised by, and reacting to, events on the ground, rather than anticipating them and being prepared for all eventualities. He only knew for certain that the night attack would have to be cancelled after

Brigadier-General Carter, commander of 184th Brigade, reported at 3 a.m. on 20 July that German guns had so damaged his communication trenches that it would be impossible for his fresh battalion to make it to the Australian front line before daylight.[18]

Even then, Haking was all for making another attack later in the day. In order to leave open the remote possibility that another daylight attack would succeed where the previous one had failed, even though there was now no chance of taking the Germans by surprise, the Australians were expected to hold their line for a few more critical hours.

That was more easily said than done. Cass was still counting on the 60th Battalion to protect his right when at 2.40 a.m. he sent the following message to Colonel Harold Pope, his brigade's commander: 'Can you give me any information on the position on my right? Enemy gunfire is coming from my right rear and taking me in reverse. Is the right of 53 Bn secure?'[19]

The moment when Cass's question was answered has been described by Major Cowey, one of the 55th Battalion officers who, as darkness fell, had followed his unit's troops across No Man's Land with a view to reinforcing the 14th Australian Brigade's assault battalions:

Word came back for more bombs and bombers for Lieutenant Matthews (on the right in the advanced line), and Lieutenant-Colonel (D. M.) McConaghy (Cowey's commander operating from a dugout near Cass) ordered me to go . . . to the assistance of this officer . . . I decided to get forward from the right, after traversing the German original front line . . . I . . . proceeded on my way preceded by two men, all the time passing men who were hurrying in the opposite direction . . . [They] warned us not to go further . . .

When the two men who were with me turned a certain traverse, I heard a cry of 'Hands oop!' . . . followed by the explosion of a bomb. I waited for some sign of what had happened, did not observe any . . . [then] concluded that [it was] the Germans, [who] had accounted for my two men and [who, if not stopped], would continue along the trench.[20]

Cowey swiftly reported back to Lieutenant-Colonels McConaghy and Cass.

If the Australians had only been threatened from one side, it is possible they might have been able to hold on. But while the Germans were putting them under pressure on their right, the Australians were also fighting a losing battle on their left. Captain Charles Mills of the 8th Brigade's 31st

Battalion witnessed the genesis of the developing crisis from his vantage point 150 yards to the south of the Germans' original front line, while chatting to the 32nd Battalion's Captain White near the junction of their respective front lines: 'Standing near White was a very "windy" sergeant of the 32nd who, while we were talking, was hysterically shouting . . . "We must all get back, or we will all be killed!" and I had occasion to speak to him rather rudely.'[21]

Minutes later Mills had to eat his words after they saw a group of Germans emerging from their base in Delangre Farm, south-east of the 32nd Battalion's position. White assured Mills he would cut them off, but his good intentions were undermined when he saw another group of Germans clambering over the communication trench to his rear. That was the beginning of the end as far as White was concerned. He and his men tried to drive out these infiltrators, and only when, hampered by the lack of hand grenades, he concluded that it was impossible, did he order the survivors in his battalion to retire to the original Australian front line.[22]

At more or less the same time, the Australian position on the right side of the perimeter began to deteriorate, the growing crisis being reflected in a series of increasingly desperate messages that Lieutenant-Colonel Cass fired off to his brigadier. At 3.20 a.m. on 20 July, Cass reported to Colonel Pope: 'Position is serious.' The reason? 'We have no grenades, and enemy is preparing to attack. If the right breaks, I shall have a very difficult job to hold on. Will you send help and grenades at once.'[23] Five minutes later Cass updated Pope: 'Position very serious.' There had been a major development: '53rd are retiring. Enemy behind them, and in their old front line . . . within 100 yds of my right . . . Use guns on position . . . Urgent!'

The message that Cass sent to Pope at 4.20 a.m. began with the words 'Position almost desperate!' before concluding: 'Have temporarily checked the enemy. But . . . 53rd have . . . lost confidence and will not . . . stand their ground. Some appear to be breaking across No Man's Land. If they give way to my right rear, I must withdraw, or be surrounded.'

Whether or not Cass's messages all reached the 14th Brigade's HQ, by about 5 p.m. Pope, realizing that his men could not hold out much longer, alerted the staff at the 5th Australian Division. At first, he was palmed off with the mantra that the 14th Brigade must continue to hold the line. But when Pope rang again, having discovered that most of the 8th Brigade had retired to the Australian original front line, an urgent phone call was put through to McCay, who was in conference with the 1st Army commander,

General Monro. It was Monro who finally decided to call off the whole Fromelles operation and give the 14th Brigade permission to withdraw.[24]

But on account of the communication problem, that decision was far from being the end of it. Before he could react, Cass had to wait for a runner to deliver Pope's message. Although Pope had already confirmed that the 8th Brigade had retired, and that Cass could expect to be released as well during the coming night, the message sent to Cass at 5.15 a.m., and received around an hour and a quarter later, insisted: 'Do not retire until you receive word.'[25] In the meantime, the existential struggle within the shrinking perimeter carried on.

Next to break were the remnants of the 8th Brigade's 31st Battalion, whose troops were still holding the advanced line, as well as the original German front line behind them. When the battalion's remaining position in the advanced line was attacked from both sides at around 5.30 a.m. on 20 July, some of the men ran for their lives, ignoring attempts by their commanding officer, at the point of a revolver, to stop their flight to the original Australian front line.[26] The 31st Battalion's commander, Lieutenant-Colonel Toll, then reluctantly followed his remaining men across No Man's Land.

Because the 8th Brigade's retirement was, in the words of Toll, 'a shambles', it is hard to work out exactly when each group of its men left the German lines. At some point during the brigade's retreat, possibly before the final panic-stricken rush back from the advanced line, Waldo Zander of the 30th Battalion, who had not left the original German front line since reaching it the previous evening, realized it was time for him to depart as well. His account describes his final moments in the German position:

We saw some machine gunners running back towards us, and setting up their guns in the old Boche line. We asked them the reason, and were told they had received orders to fall back, take up a defensive position and cover the coming retirement of the chaps in front.

Gradually the people in front began to dribble back . . . We could see the Hun advancing, and now his barrage came down on the part of the line where we were. At the same, the enemy began to bomb in from the flanks, and there was nothing . . . for us to [do] . . . but . . . to fall back, and regain our original line. This was done slowly, while others covered their retirement with Lewis guns as they made their way across No Man's Land.

One Lewis gun crew on the Brigade's extreme right flank stuck to it to the last, and after all the rest had fallen back, they could still be heard firing. We could see the Boche working along the trench on both their flanks towards them, but they still stuck to their post, and the gun kept firing. [Eventually], we saw some stick bombs [being] thrown into their little stronghold, then [there was] silence.[27]

Despite the disappearance of the 8th Brigade, one of the reasons why the Germans on the left did not break through the Australian defences was the inspiring example set by Captain Norman Gibbins of the 55th Battalion. Whereas Cass controlled the main movements of troops within the 14th Brigade's section of the perimeter, from his underground dugout in the German front line Gibbins cheered on the men above ground. His contribution was not restricted to one sector. Wherever there was a crisis, he managed to make his presence felt.

Although his principal task was on the left wing of the 14th Brigade's area, Gibbins also spent time in the advanced line, and he instigated the building of a barrier that bridged a gap in the defences protecting the original German front-line trench. But it was his heroic last-ditch counter-attack, the second of such ventures, to repel the German infiltration from the left side of the original German trench, that was never forgotten by those who saw it. According to one witness: 'His head was then bandaged by a white cloth, and he was clearly visible for a distance of thirty to forty yards. He went across the top of the trenches in full view of everyone, his men scrambling closely after him.'[28]

Gibbins was assisted by Sergeant-Major Francis Law and eight other men from the 8th Brigade's 31st Battalion, whose position in the original German front line had insulated them from the frenzied attacks and counter-attacks on the extreme left. Law was ordered by Gibbins to fill the lacuna created by his comrades' departure. With that in mind, Law and his eight men had moved to a position in the original German front line that was 150 yards to the left of a fortified manned 'outwork' – a bank of sandbags built up under orders from Gibbins. As this outwork ran 40 yards to the south of a destroyed portion of the original German front line, it protected Law's new position from attacks from the south. As he later recalled, there was now no one between his band of eight men and the Germans:

We attempted to seize the crown of the higher ground a further 100 yards to our left, but discovered a strong party of the enemy in possession. A furious grenade fight now took place, the enemy making five successive attempts to storm along the trench. But each in turn was met and defeated. During a lull in the fighting, Captain Gibbins came up to see what all the clatter was about, and was just in time to help in repulsing another attack.[29]

Given the fine line between defiant defence and humiliating envelopment, it is interesting to learn that Cass, whose nearest 54th Battalion troops were around 300 yards to the right of Law's position, appears to have had little say on what was being done on the extreme left. The message he sent to the 14th Brigade at 6.15 a.m. on 20 July, as he basked in the relative calm following yet another heroic counter-attack, this one being on the right, led by another 55th Battalion officer, Lieutenant Denoon, contained none of the growing sense of panic detected in his previous communications: 'Position much easier and improved . . . Is 8th Brigade retiring, as I have just seen a message to that effect?'[30]

Twenty-five minutes later, having at last received Pope's warning that the 14th Brigade might be ordered to retire at any minute, Cass ordered his Lewis machine-gun section to start sending their guns back to the original Australian front line.[31] But as the minutes ticked past with no sign of the final decision to withdraw, there was mounting anxiety in Cass's dugout, as evidenced by the message he sent to Pope at 7.20 a.m. It included the words: 'No order to withdraw yet.'[32]

Cass's anxiety was matched by the alarm evident in Major-General McCay's headquarters. At 7.45 p.m., after hearing that none of the eight runners who had been sent across No Man's Land to tell Cass to evacuate had returned to confirm the message had been delivered, McCay wanted an aircraft to drop a copy of the message into the perimeter. His proposal was only rejected after representatives of the Royal Flying Corps pointed out that the message might just as easily be picked up by a German as an Australian.[33]

Unbeknown to McCay, one of the eight runners who had set off at 7 a.m. on 20 July eventually did make it to the original German front line, at 7.50 a.m., whereupon he handed Cass the following order: 'All 14th Bde troops withdraw from German lines.'[34]

The order was long overdue, and one could sympathize with Cass, and all the men still in the garrison, who felt that they had been hung out to dry. The same applies to all those families who lost loved ones during the period after midnight, that is after McCay informed Haking that the right side of the perimeter was unprotected. No one could blame Generals Haking and Monro for the time it had taken to get the runner across No Man's

Land in daylight. But they were responsible for allowing hours of darkness to slip past after Haking received McCay's aforementioned message, when it would have been possible to summon the boys back more quickly. It was entirely due to their failure to act that the lives of all those in the perimeter came to depend on the slim chance that a runner would make it through the German gunfire.

It was fitting that this fatally flawed operation should terminate with yet another costly mistake. This time the error came about because of a misunderstanding within the perimeter. When Cass was told to prepare to evacuate, he requested Lieutenant-Colonel McConaghy of the 55th Battalion to ensure that the battalion company in the German original front line should act as the rearguard under the command of Captain Gibbins, who at the time was holding the left side of the perimeter with another company. However, the message that was passed from McConaghy to Gibbins appears to have been garbled, so that Gibbins believed it was not just him who was being asked to retire to the original German front line, but the whole of the company he was commanding.

This set in train an explosive chain reaction: the Germans, who until that point had been held at bay by Gibbins's men, burst forward over the now undefended Australian left, at a stroke cutting off the thirty-odd Australians still in the advanced line from their line of escape. This prompted those Australians to charge through the Germans, killing or wounding any of them who stood in their path.[35]

The Australian accounts do not record how many casualties resulted from this latest disaster. But they do record that it set in motion a hastily hatched evacuation of the German lines, with most of the Australians from the three battalions still inside the perimeter crawling back to the original Australian front line via a shallow sap that had been hollowed out across No Man's Land during the previous night.

Some could not bring themselves to take their turn in the sap. Many were shot as they attempted to race across No Man's Land. There was also to be a tragic end as far as Captain Gibbins was concerned. Rather than waiting patiently in the queue that had built up in the sap, after a well-aimed shell wounded some of the men in front of him, he and some men climbed out, and made a run for the Australian parapet. As he reached the top, Gibbins turned his head sharply, as if he wanted to check there was no one else who needed his assistance. As it transpired, this was one good deed too many. At that precise moment a bullet struck him in the head, and down he fell, another victim of the failure to retreat when it was relatively safe.[36]

Those wounded Australians who did make it back to their original front line may have hoped that they would be rushed to the rear and given immediate medical attention. If that was their expectation they were to be disappointed. There were so many men lying untended in the Australian front line, when first the 31st Battalion's commander, Lieutenant-Colonel Toll, and then Lieutenant-Colonel Cass reached it, that they both hurried back to their brigade headquarters to request assistance; in Toll's case, he had requested an artillery bombardment to quieten the German guns, whose shells were mercilessly pummelling the Australian front line.[37] Hugh Knyvett, a twenty-nine-year-old corporal in the 15th Brigade's 57th Battalion, later reported: 'The sight of those trenches that next morning (20 July) are burned into my brain . . . If you had gathered the stock of a thousand butcher shops, cut it into small pieces, and strewn it about, it would give you a faint conception of the shambles that those trenches were.'[38]

It is no wonder emergency assistance was called in. Sergeant Reginald Gray of the 2nd New Zealand Field Ambulance has described the role he played after he was taken, along with two medical officers and around forty stretcher-bearers, at about 10 a.m. on 20 July to the Advanced Dressing Station that was to deal with the wounded on the extreme left of the Australian front line.[39] Gray reported his movements thus:

We reached the Aid Post, a battered brick farmhouse . . . named Eaton Hall, and here our two officers remained with some Australian officers . . . They sent us (Gray and another sergeant), and their stretcher-bearers, to report to the medical officers up in the support trenches. The communication trench is about 100 yards from this place, and we were soon in it, ducking where shells had blown the parapet in and dodging holes in the duckboard. It was a gloomy procession that passed us, men broken in the fight, some crying, others clutching at us, and begging us to help the men still out in No Man's Land. A general passed. He was broken hearted. His brigade had been decimated. He said just as he was passing 'Give us your best boys. God knows we need it.'

The sight of the remnant of the Australian bearers [un]nerved us . . . They were done . . . The sight at the first trench beggars any description . . . Dead and wounded were everywhere, in every imaginable state of awfulness. Great shell holes had torn the ground, and rifles, bombs, ammunition, rations, all the impedimenta of an army, [were] littered . . . behind the parapet . . .

One of the Australians standing by a periscope told me he had his rifle drawn on a German outside the enemy trench, and was pulling the trigger when he saw him drag one of our men from the wire into their trench. I looked through the periscope. There in front was . . . the German front line . . . The horrors of No Man's Land were visible too. Wounded were still out . . .

Every man in our squad would have gone for them had there been a remote chance of getting over the parapet . . . [However], to show a part of the body would have meant certain death . . . Water bottles were thrown over . . . The men who got in told us they were dying for just that . . . The only thing [we could do] was wait for nightfall.[40]

Corporal Knyvett, who as part of the 57th Battalion was holding the right side of the Australian front line, ventured into No Man's Land the next night (20–21 July). He later reported what he saw:

There were men . . . with legs off, and arms hanging by a (piece of) skin, and men sightless with half their face gone, with bowels exposed, and every kind of unmentionable wounds . . .

We had organized parties of rescue, but we still had practically no stretchers, and . . . most of the men had to be carried in on our backs . . . One of the most [unselfish] actions . . . was by a sergeant. We found a man on the German barbed wire, who was so badly wounded that, when we tried to pick him up . . . it almost seemed we'd pull him apart. The blood was gushing from his mouth . . . He begged us to put him out of his misery . . . But the sergeant threw himself down on the ground and made of his body a human sledge. Others joined us and we put the wounded man on his back and dragged them [both] . . . across . . . No Man's Land . . . So anxious were we to get to safety that we did not notice the condition of the man underneath, until we got into our trenches. Then it was hard to see which was the worst wounded of the two.

One lad who looked about fifteen called to me . . . Both his legs were broken . . . He was one of those overgrown lads, who had added a couple of years in declaring his age to get into the Army. But the circumstances brought out his youth, and he clung to me as though I was his father . . . He was the only one who did not say 'Take the other fellow first'.[41]

Notwithstanding the best efforts of Knyvett and his fellow rescuers, there were still many wounded men lying in No Man's Land when the new day dawned (21 July). One of these missing men was a Captain Mortimer, who was said to be lying wounded near the parapet. Sergeant Billy Miles, who, as part of the 8th Brigade's 29th Battalion, was holding the left section of the Australian line, has described what happened to Mortimer after he volunteered to bring him in:

I . . . was given a Red Cross badge for my arm, and over I went, landing in a shell hole . . . I asked two or three wounded men if they had seen Captain Mortimer, but could not find him . . . I jumped . . . into another shell hole . . . and heard someone call out from the German lines. Looking over, I saw a man beckoning to me . . . I walked slowly towards him, stopping . . . to pick up a pair of field glasses. I stopped at the edge of his wire, and the following conversation took place:

Fritz: What are you supposed to be doing?

I replied: Tending wounded men, giving them a drink and cutting their equipment off, so they will be more comfortable till we can get them in.

He said: You may be laying wires. This is not the 'usages' of war.

I replied: Oh yes it is. The Red Cross is always allowed to work unmolested.

[He said]: What did you pick up just now?

[I replied]: A pair of field glasses.

[He said]: It might have been a bomb.

[I replied]: I'll show you . . .

But he said: Don't put your hand in your pocket. Put your hands above your head.

I did so, and stood . . . for some time, while he spoke through a field telephone to his . . . headquarters. Then . . . [he] put his telephone down . . . [and] . . . said . . .:

What rank are you?

[I replied]: Only a private, Sir.

He said: Well, I want you to go back to your lines, and ask an officer to come over here, and we will have a parliament, and see if we arrange about collecting the wounded. Will you come back, and let me know what they say?

Sergeant Miles said he would, and walked back to his line, where it was agreed that the 29th Battalion's Major Murdoch would go with Miles to discuss the terms of a truce. Before they went over, a placard, consisting of newspaper pasted on a board with red cushion material stuck on top to form a red cross, was waved from side to side above the parapet to attract the Germans' attention.

Back at the German wire, Murdoch was told that the Australians could pick up the wounded on their half of No Man's Land, leaving the Germans to do the same on their side. But the arrangement could only go ahead if, after discussing it with his superiors, Murdoch agreed to be blindfolded and kept as a hostage in the German lines until the truce was concluded.[42]

Murdoch and Miles were then sent back to the Australian lines, but not before a single shot, fired by an Australian, who evidently had not been apprised of the delicate negotiations, underlined the risk Murdoch would be running if the deal went ahead. Unfortunately for the wounded men, Major-General McCay refused to allow the truce to go ahead, a decision for which he has been unjustly vilified. McCay was only obeying orders. Even if he had wanted to allow the truce to go ahead, General Monro's refusal to sanction it would have overruled him.[43]

That said, most of the Germans in the front line appear to have been more merciful than their superiors, allowing Australian stretcher-bearers to pick up wounded and dead alike as long as they did not show themselves too prominently.[44] However, there were a substantial number of exceptions, according to the following extract from a letter that Brigadier-General Elliott sent to his wife on 24 July:

A lot of our poor wounded have been lying out and slowly perishing between the lines. We have rescued . . . hundreds of them, but had to stop owing to the German fire. There was one poor fellow lying close to the German trenches. Our watchers saw a German come out as though he was going to help the poor chap. But instead, he deliberately put a bomb against him and blew him up . . . There is still one poor fellow out there alive after four days. Isn't it dreadful; no food or water . . . Fortunately the days are cool, but we cannot go to him for the Germans shoot whenever we attempt to get across to him. He was feebly waving a white handkerchief this morning.[45]

The fate of this man is unknown, but it seems likely he was left to starve or bleed to death. Perhaps he would have preferred the fate of the blinded defenceless soldier seen walking round in circles, falling and walking round in circles again opposite the Sugar Loaf. He was eventually put out of his misery by a German bullet.[46]

What is known are the numbers of Australian and British casualties: in excess of 5,300 Australian and 1,400 British.[47] Even these figures conceal the extremity of the disaster in the crucial central sector of the attack where the Australian 59th and 60th Battalions suffered casualties of around 675 and

740 respectively, and whose 20 July post-action roll calls could only muster four officers and ninety other ranks, and four officers and sixty-one other ranks, respectively.[48]

These high casualties did not appear to bother Lieutenant-General Haking. On the same day that Elliott was complaining to his wife about the cruelties of war, Haking was sending the following shockingly callous and complacent words to General Monro: 'Briefly speaking, the artillery preparation was adequate. There were sufficient guns and sufficient ammunition. The wire was properly cut, and the assaulting battalions had a clear run into the enemy's trenches.' However, Haking claimed that although the Australians had 'attacked in the most gallant manner', they 'were not sufficiently trained to consolidate the ground gained', in particular on their left. As for the 61st Division, 'they were not sufficiently imbued with the offensive spirit . . . With two trained divisions, the position would have been a gift after the artillery bombardment . . . I think the attack has done both divisions a great deal of good.'[49]

Haking's verdict was certainly not shared by all the commanders involved in the Fromelles attack. The journalist Charles Bean, who later wrote the *Official History of Australia in the War of 1914–1918*, provided interesting insights into the views of the three Australian brigade commanders after he visited their headquarters on 20 July. 'Old Elliott was dead asleep,' he recorded, 'but McCay came in and woke him up. When Elliott came out, I felt almost as if I were in the presence of a man who had just lost his wife. He looked down and could hardly speak. He was clearly terribly depressed and overwrought.'

'McCay was also anxious,' Bean stated, and blamed the British for his disastrous order to send in the 58th Battalion's two companies. 'The British [mistakenly] reported . . . that they had captured the cap of the salient,' McCay explained. However, 'Colonel Pope of 14 Brigade rather disgusted me by the boastful way he talked,' Bean noted. 'I think he had been refreshing himself after the strain. "Well, we were the only brigade who didn't come back till we were told to," Pope said with meaning. He was rather contemptuous about Elliott and the 15th Brigade.'[50]

Pope may have been on a high when he saw Bean, but later that afternoon McCay stated that Pope was 'incapable of comprehending or doing anything', shorthand for accusing him of being drunk, and he relieved him of his brigade just as he was about to be made a brigadier.[51] Pope's dismissal was the final irony: the one man whose unit had excelled during the

Fromelles debacle was being fired, whereas those whose orders had condemned hundreds of men to years of agony and misery after suffering life-changing wounds were allowed to carry on, their positions undisturbed despite their reputations being blemished.

Pope was not the only brigade commander to lose his job over the Fromelles debacle. Brigadier Carlton of the 184th Brigade was also sent home, making him in the eyes of some a convenient scapegoat for the failure to capture the Sugar Loaf. In the eyes of others, Carlton deserved to be sacked because he had shown himself to be as impractical as some of the more senior generals. On previous occasions he had not endeared himself to his subordinates when they were ordered to carry gas canisters to the front over impassable ground, and when he had blurted out instructions about a planned raid in a public place. Now, Carlton's inability to think through the consequences of his actions had cost men's lives: he had unforgivably failed to ensure that Elliott was warned once his renewed attack on the Sugar Loaf was called off. Lieutenant-Colonel Williams, commander of the 2nd/1st Buckinghamshire Regiment, who, from his position in the front line could see that the many casualties made the renewed attack ordered by Carter unfeasible, was also deprived of his command.[52]

In spite of all the torments endured, reputations ruined and jobs lost in the course of the attack, it is just possible that it might on balance have been justified if its principal aim, stopping the flow of German reinforcements to the Somme, had been achieved. But even that was compromised by Lieutenant-General Haking's foolish decision to permit the object of the attack to be explained in written – and verbal – orders that were circulated.[53] The Germans seized a copy, probably finding it in the pocket of one of the men they captured or killed. It was for them a significant discovery. Once they had read it, they could react to the fighting on the Somme as if the Fromelles attack had never happened.

24: The Charge

Pozières, 18–23 July 1916

(See maps 2 and 14)

The day after the 17 July 1916 postponement of the attack featuring the 5th Australian Division opposite Fromelles, their fellow countrymen in the 1st Australian Division, one of the units that the Fromelles attack was designed to protect, were 'booked' for their first attack on the Somme. 'I want you to go into the line and attack Pozières tomorrow night,' Reserve Army General Sir Hubert Gough told Major-General Harold Walker, the 1st Australian Division's commander.[1]

This impetuous command was given even before Lieutenant-General Sir William Birdwood, commander of 1 ANZAC (1st Australian and New Zealand Army Corps), who was supposed to be Walker's direct superior, had reached his Somme headquarters at Contay, let alone had a chance to comment on what was planned for one of his divisions. Not that anyone on the 1 ANZAC staff would have been that surprised by what Gough was asking. It was consistent with his reputation as a thruster, a commander in a hurry who did not believe in slowing down the pace of his units' attacks if the only motive was to comply with army conventions.

Gough had started the war as a brigadier in the cavalry before rising within the space of two years to be first the youngest lieutenant-general in the British Army and subsequently an army commander. He was still just forty-five years old when the Battle of the Somme began. He had not reached these dizzy heights by playing a long game.

His desire to be a mover and shaker had only been increased by his wartime experiences.[2] During 1915, Gough had shown his superiors that he knew how to break through the German front line, doing it first as a major-general in charge of a division at Festubert, and then as a lieutenant-general commanding a corps at Loos. Such was the optimism in some of the military circles of the day, both he and those higher up the Army hierarchy believed that the only reason why his troops at Loos had not made a clean break through the second line as well was because the then Commander-in-Chief in France, Field Marshal Sir John French, had not made the reserves, or enough hand grenades, available in time. It was no wonder that

Gough regarded 'consolidation', a concept so keenly espoused by many World War I commanders, as a dirty word, unless it was combined with speedy exploitation of any breach in the enemy lines.

The failure to ensure his commanders had the wherewithal to exploit their initial successes quickly had cost Field Marshal French his job, but the perception that this alone had deprived Gough of the glory that should have been his had helped to catapult him up to the next step in his meteoric career. Haig evidently had had his potential in mind when he entrusted Gough and his Reserve Army with the task of exploiting any breakthrough that might have been achieved by Rawlinson's 4th Army.

Through no fault of his own, Gough's Reserve Army had not had the opportunity to bare its teeth on or immediately after 1 July. But sixteen days later, he finally had his chance to shine. On 18 July, Haig decided that Rawlinson could not focus on the push eastwards towards Guillemont and Ginchy, actions that Haig realized had to be taken on before the French would agree to attack at Maurepas, if the 4th Army also had to attack Pozières.[3]

However, there was one caveat attached to his handing over Pozières to Gough. On 20 July, just hours after hearing of the Australian disaster at Fromelles, Haig wrote in his diary: 'The reality of the fighting and the shelling seems to have been somewhat greater than many had expected!', adding: 'I . . . saw Gen. Gough at Toutencourt (HQ Reserve Army) . . . I told him to go into all details (concerning his Pozières attack plan) carefully as 1st Aust. Div. had not been engaged before and possibly overlooked the difficulties of this kind of fighting.'[4] Events would show this was a warning that Haig might have enforced more persistently had he been a hands-on Commander-in-Chief, or a better judge of character.

If only Haig had been privy to what went on in Gough's headquarters, he might have realized that he could not just wash his hands of Pozières after handing down general instructions. Gough's ill thought-out instructions to General Walker, admittedly given before Haig's warning, were hardly what he would have expected, given the Australians' inexperience.

Nor was the response from Gough's subordinates: ironically, given Haig's anxiety about the Australians' lack of attention to detail, it was the thirty-nine-year-old 1 ANZAC Chief of Staff, Brigadier-General Cyril Brudenell White, who by pointing out the logistical difficulties helped convince Gough that an immediate attack was impractical.[5] The line south of Pozières, reached by previous British attacks, was too far away from the

German front line if GHQ's advice being handed out to commanders was to be complied with. As noted in Chapter 22, asking troops to advance more than 200 yards across No Man's Land was believed to be disadvantageous. It would take time to dig closer jumping-off positions. The attack was duly put back to the night of 21–22 July and subsequently to the night of 22–23 July.[6]

That meant it could be made on the same night as the general attack planned by Rawlinson's 4th Army. Orders issued by Rawlinson on 21 and 22 July meant that his three remaining corps would be attacking German lines at Guillemont, Delville Wood, Longueval, High Wood and the Switch Line, which ran through the northern end of High Wood as well as to the east and west at both sides of the wood. The westernmost target of the 4th Army was to be an attack on Munster Alley (see map 14).[7] Gough hoped that X Corps' 48th Division would cover the Australians' left. The written order he issued on 21 July envisaged this division taking the trenches leading into the west side of Pozières, leaving the Australians free to attack the village from the south.[8]

Whatever their shortcomings when it came to battlefield experience, at least against first-class opposition, no one could complain about the Australian soldiers' morale. The diary of events compiled by Captain John Harris, a thirty-seven-year-old schoolmaster before becoming an officer in the 3rd Battalion of the 1st Australian Division's 1st Brigade, recorded how 'the sitting-down tactics' adopted ever since they had been shipped to France in March 1916 had 'almost worn out the patience' of his troops. They were 'spoiling for a fight . . . There were few who did not experience . . . relief when the colonel announced to a full meeting of officers: "Gentlemen our period of training is over."'[9]

His account went on to describe their journey south from Bailleul, near Armentières, followed by a series of marches culminating in the troops' arrival at Warloy-Baillon on 16 July, a British base just six miles west of the original 1 July front line.[10]

'Goodbye Flanders, with its swampy meadows intersected with numerous ditches,' Harris wrote in his account:

its people, always rather dour and suspicious of soldiers . . . A night's railway journey brought us to another France . . . where the people were gayer and more hospitable. They flocked out into the street to gaze at 'Les Australiens' . . . The Australians were new to them.

The country too was very different: rolling chalk downs covered with close cropped grass and showing great white sears where trenches had been made either for exercise or for strong points well in the rear of the line . . . The cornfields were a blaze of glory with the gold of the wheat, the yellow of the charlock (wild mustard), the scarlet and blue of the poppies and cornflowers. For a week we marched through perfect summer weather . . . though the dust of the hot white roads and the blazing sun overhead diminished our appreciation of the country's great natural beauty.

Some observers stared at the Australians as they would have done if they had come across an exotic species imported from a faraway land. The observers included Paul Maze, a French artist attached to the Reserve Army, who had been instructed by Gough to make drawings of the German front line. In the following extract from his memoirs, Maze describes the moment when while standing on a hill near Toutencourt, he set eyes on the Australians – and heard them – for the first time:

I was chatting to [a] . . . peasant who had stopped [ploughing] to mop his brow, when both our heads turned towards the sound of a brass band in the valley below. As we listened, the sun, as though by magic, suddenly came out and lifted the mist like a curtain. There, on the road below, were columns and columns of Australian regiments moving like long snakes. I waited until the sound of their tramping feet came up the hill. They passed, swaying under the weight of their swaying haversacks, and singing tunes which for months afterwards were to be heard wherever they went. Endlessly, battalion after battalion went by, impressing me with the fine physique of the men, all tanned by the Gallipoli sun.[11]

Harris's account goes on to describe the 'strenuous preparations' during their three-day stay at Warloy for the ordeal that lay ahead. These preparations included reverting to battle order:

All packs, officers' valises, and blankets had to be stored. (Floppy Australian) hats were collected, as henceforth the steel helmet alone was to be worn. Officers must wear service jackets and equipment differing in no way from their men. Square patches of pink cloth were sewn on the back of the jacket just under the collar to enable the artillery and other observers to distinguish our men.

Here, for the first time, we heard the sound of a heavy barrage . . . The whole horizon was lit by one broad pulsating glare. It was not altogether comforting to think that in a few days we would be in the middle of it.

The unit war diaries state that the 1st Australian Division's assault battalions moved towards the front during the afternoon of 19 July. Without exception, they all passed through the town of Albert. It acted as a kind of filter separating the relatively peaceful conditions to the west of the town from the turmoil to the east where everybody was on a war footing.

It is hard to find an Australian soldier's diary that does not replicate Harris's memory of:

this small town, which will always be remembered by those who fought in the Battle of the Somme . . . Its only feature of interest is its great battered brick church, surmounted by a large gilded statue of the Virgin holding aloft the Child. This statue has been displaced by a shell, but the metal base has held it from falling, and now the statue hangs head downwards right over the street, almost in the attitude of one diving. The French . . . have a prophecy that when the statue falls, the War will end.

Whatever its significance to the religious and superstitious, many of the passing Australians referred to the statue irreverently as 'Fanny Durack', the well-known Australian swimmer who had won a gold medal at the 1912 Olympic Games. Paul Maze, who passed the statue several times, as he went to and from the front line, came up with a darker interpretation. He thought the Virgin was making 'a despairing gesture, as though she was throwing the child into the battle'.[12]

Albert during the late afternoon of 19 July must have been packed with troops. Harris recalls the 'clattering' over the cobbled streets as 'roaring streams of traffic and troops . . . guns, water carts, travelling kitchens, strings of horses, motor cars and lorries' competed to pass through. His battalion eventually made it out the other side: 'Just outside the town, we halted, moved off the road into the grass and had our tea. The mounted officers sent back their horses and, as the darkness came on, we sat down, and waited patiently for the guides who were to lead us to the trenches we were to occupy.'

At this point Harris's account, like Maze's, becomes tinged with foreboding:

After the precautions always observed in the North to avoid observation, the apparent carelessness of detection was most marked. Beside the main road, were masses of troops . . . There were open camps everywhere with roaring bivouac fires, surrounded by groups of men, [and] there were guns everywhere . . . And though some . . . shells were bursting about 300 yards away, no sort of precautions were taken to disperse the troops, [or] . . . to hide . . . the camps, or even in many cases, to camouflage the guns.

But the critical comments within Harris's account were atypical. Apcar de Vine, an NCO in the 1st Australian Brigade's 4th Battalion, whose troops paused at more or less the same spot, noted: 'The . . . roads are simply packed with troops moving towards or from the forward area . . . Many English regiments pass us who have been relieved from the front . . . They have been very successful and are all singing as they march along, every man wearing a German helmet.'[13]

De Vine's more optimistic tone was perhaps influenced by what happened next. As his diary explains, his first night east of Albert, although far from comfortable, was spent in a rear area, where he was unlikely to be called upon to do any fighting:

After an hour's rest, we march on to the old front line. We are now at La Boisselle . . . It is not long before we are all covered in white chalk . . . Very many dead are lying about, buried in the wreckage of their trenches, and blown up by the mines . . .

We eventually settle down for the night . . . in a captured German trench. Very heavy shelling is going on by the guns in front of us . . . Fritz is throwing . . . tear shells into his old front line . . . making the air . . . heavy with the smell of gas. Both of my eyes have become inflamed. We all feel it a good deal . . . I get absolutely no sleep during the night. The whole earth is trembling under the shock of bursting shells and firing cannons.

Harris's account makes it clear that his battalion's next resting place had far more dangerous projectiles to contend with:

At last our guides arrived, and we set off in single file . . . for the trenches. It was not quite dark . . . and we could see enough to pick our way after leaving the road, and to discern some of our surroundings. As we went on, the grass became rarer and the shell holes more numerous . . . A faint sickly smell came to our nostrils to remind us we were passing over the ground captured from the Germans during the first attack of July 1st. The pace was very slow to enable our guide to get his bearings, and, in spite of their training and light loads, the men were . . . exhausted when at last the trench was reached.

About twenty minutes before we reached our destination, a series of loud explosions were seen and heard on our left front. Our guide cheered us up by remarking '. . . They're getting crumped again.' Crumps are 5.9 inch HE (heavy explosive) shells, and as we were relieving [the company being shelled], we had an exciting night to look forward to.

We found the trench to be deep and strong, and well traversed, but there was no shelter of any kind . . . except for holes scraped in the forward face . . . At Company headquarters . . . I found the Company commander . . . and formally took over the trench stores . . . [which] consisted of a few picks and shovels, and an eighth of a jar of rum. He told me his company had only been there 24 hours, but had had a bad time, as the Bosch crumped the position day and night. It was about half a mile behind the front line, with one trench between us and the front line . . .

Our trench was fortunately quite dry, but rather unpleasant, owing to the fact that two bodies had been imperfectly buried in it, and the ground both to front and rear was strewn with unburied dead . . . One of our first duties was to send out a burying party . . . to collect the identity disks and to bury the bodies nearest to the trench.

Sure enough the crumps came along with great regularity, but we were very fortunate, as many were duds, and during the three days we were there, only five actually fell in the trench, two of these one night, when all the Company was out on a working party. However, the frequent explosions, and the impossibility of lying down properly, made sleep at night almost out of the question. [While] overcoats, our last remaining luxury, had to be done up in bundles and sent away.

Luxuries of a different kind were being sifted to the rear. In a letter to his mother, Lieutenant Art Smith, an artillery officer in the 3rd Field Artillery Brigade, mentioned some of the items he found near the La Boisselle mine craters:

In [the] huge dugouts, one finds furniture, beds, electric light fittings, lamps . . . [and] crockery . . . all apparently left in a hurry . . . In one dugout I found such things as a splendid carpet on the floor . . . walls papered with . . . pretty wallpaper, bedsteads . . . glass panelled doors, cupboards stacked with appetizing eatables, and . . . unmistakeable signs of the dugout being used by at least one woman. One article left behind was a lady's motor coat . . . [and there was also a lady's] veil and . . . glove.[14]

But as Smith confided to his mother, there was also a sinister side to trench sightseeing:

Evidence that the German casualties were heavy [during the 1 July attack] is plainly borne out by the . . . number of graves in shell craters, and also in other places not quite so suitable. Bodies have been tossed hurriedly into [these] craters and covered by a few inches of soil. In the trenches, where it was too risky to get out to bury the dead, they have just been buried in the parapets, or on the trench floor where they lay, by throwing a few spadefuls of earth over them. This is not . . . a success, as after a few days, when one treads on one of these spots, it sinks uncannily and bulges out a few feet further on.

But terrible as these nightmarish scenes were, the trauma experienced by those who saw them could not compare with the torment endured by those who witnessed their own comrades being maimed and mutilated. The following entry in the diary written by Athol Dunlop, a private in the 1st Australian Division's 1st Light Mortar Company, describes his bewildered shock when his unit suffered its first casualties while resting beside the Chalk Pit, an area several hundred yards behind the front line, which had been deemed safe enough to accommodate a dressing station:

After resting for a couple of hours, we started getting our ammunition ready. Then came our first horror. A huge howitzer shell burst in our midst, killing seven and wounding five, [leaving] some with their legs off, [and] some with arms [off] . . . All that was left of one poor [man] was his boots. I had just moved away from the spot, so [I] only got covered with dust. Never will I forget the cries of those poor chaps.[15]

It was all the more heartbreaking because the main operation had not yet started. The same could be said for losses incurred in the course of the preliminary Australian action in the Pozières sector on the night of 21–22 July. The main attack, scheduled for the next night, was to contain a conventional frontal attack on the three trenches ringing the southern edge of Pozières. But if they were to safeguard their right flank, the Australians also had to bomb up the parallel pair of trenches on their right, which ran more or less at right angles to these three lines.

On 1 July these latter trenches, referred to on maps as OG1 and OG2 (Old German trenches 1 and 2), had constituted part of the German second position. Their parapets faced the original British front line to the west. But after it subsequently became clear that the main threat was coming from the south, their defences had been adapted so that they represented a substantial obstacle to attackers approaching from the south as well.

It would have been ideal if OG1 and OG2 could have been captured at the same time as the three trenches ringing the south of Pozières. However, that was most unlikely. Troops advancing over open ground to the west of OG1 would probably advance much faster than those confined to a narrow trench with manned strongpoints built into it. The only practical alternative appeared to be to try to neutralize them in advance. That is why arrangements were made to target the two trenches at 2.30 a.m. on 22 July. They were to be captured up to OG1's junction with Pozières Trench, the German front line, and up to OG2's nearby junction with Munster Alley (see map 14).

The plan could not have been more simple. Trench mortars and artillery were to keep the German troops' heads down, thereby enabling the assault troops, consisting of 100 men supplied by the 3rd Australian Brigade's 9th Battalion, to rush the strongpoints protecting the trenches.[16] However, for some unexplained reason, the attack was a shambles from start to finish. Inadequate provision of mortar shells did not help. Nor did the fact that the paltry fourteen shells available were fired more than half an hour before the attack. But what sealed its fate was the complete absence of any support from the artillery.

Predictably the attack failed. Germans behind the OG1 strongpoint attacked, deluged the Australians with a hail of hand grenades backed up by machine-gun fire, isolating those soldiers who managed to approach near enough to threaten their stronghold. Philip Browne, a twenty-one-year-old sergeant, did his best to supply these men with the hand grenades they needed if they were to advance further, but he was hit, making him one of forty-five casualties incurred before the attacks on both OG1 and OG2 were abandoned.

It made for an inauspicious start to the Australian campaign. However, good could have come out of it if lessons had been learned. The debacle should have warned the Australians' commanders that while superior physical strength, and courage, might have been sufficient at Gallipoli where the enemy were the Turks, these characteristics were no substitute for organized planning when facing up to sophisticated German opposition.

The attack also highlighted the long-lasting pain and suffering that were

22. Lieutenant-Colonel Frank Crozier, the commander of the 9th Royal Irish Rifles, during the 1 July 1916 attack north of Thiepval. His servant described him as a 'heavily built small gent' with a hot temper.

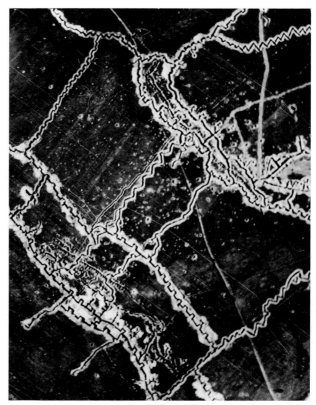

23. An aerial photograph of the trench system within Schwaben Redoubt (*upper right*). The firing line and support trench are lower left. Four communication trenches link them with the rear.

24. *Below* The Border Regiment rests in dugouts and trenches in Thiepval Wood.

25. *Above* A soldier fires a Lewis gun, near Ovillers.

26. *Below* Wearing anti-gas hoods, a two-man team with their Vickers machine gun, near Ovillers.

27. *Above* A soldier fills a Mills bomb, near Thiepval.

28. *Below* A 15-inch howitzer is loaded in Englebelmer Wood.

29. and 30. *Left* An early attack on Trônes Wood. It was finally captured during the night of 13–14 July, when British troops led by Lieutenant-Colonel Frank Maxwell VC (*right*) drove out the last remaining Germans.

31. Delville Wood as it was following the battles in it: just a few trees standing with no foliage.

32. Longueval after it had been pulverized by British and German shells during the conflict.

33. Australian prisoners following the fighting at Fromelles on 19–20 July 1916.

34., 35. and 36. *Above left* Major-General James McCay, the commander of the 5th Australian Division, who some have blamed for the disaster at Fromelles. *Above right* Lieutenant-Colonel Walter Cass, the commander of the 54th Australian Battalion at Fromelles. *Below* Brigadier-General Harold 'Pompey' Elliott, the commander of the Australian 15th Brigade at Fromelles.

37., 38. and 39. *Top* Pozières village as it was before the war, with the Albert to Bapaume road running through it. *Centre* The Chalk Pit south of Pozières, one of the landmarks passed by all soldiers on the way to the front at Pozières. *Bottom* The remains of 'Gibraltar', the fortified tower that was designed to protect Pozières against attacks coming from the west.

40. An Australian soldier, wearing a German pickelhaube helmet, celebrates the capture of the village on 23 July 1916 with a shave.

41. The remains of the 'OG' (Old German) line near Pozières.

the likely consequence of such inattention to detail, not just in the immediate aftermath of the attack, on the Somme, but also in Australia, for years to come.

Sergeant Browne's was a case in point. Although his Red Cross wounded and missing file suggests he was buried in a shell hole the next day, his remains were never seen again.[17] Furthermore, his long-suffering parents, James and Jessie Browne, back in Queensland, never received a clear explanation as to how he died despite years of correspondence with the Australian authorities.

The problem was that there were conflicting reports. The most convincing account, filed by a J. R. Childs, stated that 'he volunteered to carry bombs up to the front line. I was just behind him [in] No Man's Land when a whiz-bang caught him and killed him.' But given that his account was contradicted by other letters, there was to be no closure.

The most positive feedback that Sergeant Browne's parents received came from a soldier who had not even seen their son's courageous act. It included the patriotic words: 'Deeply as we all regretted his loss, there is not one of us but envies him so glorious a death in his country's service, and I cannot say how proud I am to have been his friend. May we all do our duty as well and [as] honourably.'[18] This probably voiced sentiments with which most of the soldiers fighting on the Somme would have agreed, particularly if they had been asked before becoming involved in combat, but it was little consolation for Browne's parents, who had seen their son effectively swallowed up, without having the opportunity to draw a line under their loss by being told the nature of his death, or where he was interred.

Different mistakes were to be made before, during and after the main attack on the German trenches to the left of the OG lines. It was eventually scheduled to start at 12.30 a.m. on 23 July. Given that a long, hard late-night fight was in prospect, it might have been sensible to have spared the assault troops the exhausting task of digging the jumping-off trenches halfway across No Man's Land during the night of 21–22 July. Captain John Harris's men were out digging in the dark until 3 a.m. Their lack of discipline during the charge the next day, and Harris's subsequent mental breakdown, lead one to question whether their exhaustion was in part to blame.

Bringing the assault troops up to the front line long before they were due to go over the top was also a questionable decision. The following note from Captain Harris's account shows that he appreciated the risks they had all been running: 'I found, as I thought, that some careless fellow had kicked over a rubbish tin and strewn its contents along the trench. On closer examination it was perceived that a couple of shells had pitched right in the trench.'

The failure to set up a fail-safe system for getting his troops into the correct positions before they proceeded to assembly trenches represented another challenge for the inexperienced Aussies. If asked, Harris might well have said that starting his pre-attack reorganization at 6 p.m. on 22 July was too early. It turned out to be none too soon. His company was ultimately going to advance in two separate 'waves' from one jumping-off trench. In order to ensure that each wave was spread along the whole front allocated to his company, it was necessary to intersperse the platoons in wave one with the platoons in wave two within the jumping-off trench (i.e. a wave-one platoon on the left of the trench should have a wave-two platoon on its right, and that wave-two platoon should have a wave-one platoon on its right, and so on).

It was easy to see how this could be achieved in theory, but it was harder to organize in practice within the confines of the very narrow trench they occupied to the rear of the front line. Their reorganization was delayed still further by the arrival of a shell that killed one man and wounded five. It was only at 8 p.m. that Harris and his men were finally able to start their march towards the front line.

'A small foretaste of the future in store [for us] was provided by three shrapnel shells which burst right over the head of the column,' Harris reported. 'Fortunately, they burst very high, and though the pellets rattled down like hail all round, no-one was hit.' However, as he feared, further difficulties lay ahead:

Some inspired idiot, probably a traffic control man, broke into the middle of the long string of men . . . and led them away to the right, behind another brigade sector, whence they were only recovered after [a] long search. As they tumbled into the trench in any old place when they arrived, the whole process of sorting out and arranging afresh had to be undertaken [all over again . . . This] rearrangement was considerably enlivened by the activity of the German machine-guns and whiz bangs!

Thanks to the 'help', Harris and his men were only finally able to settle down and prepare themselves for what was coming minutes before the attack was due to begin.

Paul Maze's account suggests that he arrived in one of the assembly trenches well before Harris's men, where he was overwhelmed by the look of the bronzed Australians with whom he was to go over the top. 'The rays of the vanishing sun were glowing on rows of scarlet faces. With shirt sleeves rolled up, showing their big forearms, the men were busy having tea or cleaning their rifles, sliding the breech up and down in a significant way. They certainly looked fit, these Anzacs.'[19]

The Anzacs included the twenty-five-year-old Lance Corporal Douglas Horton, like Harris, a schoolmaster in civilian life. His account gives an insight into conditions in the jumping-off trench just in front of the one occupied by Harris.[20] Horton's unit, the 1st Battalion, was located on the right side of the 1st Australian Brigade's 800-yard-wide sector.[21] Its troops were to go over the top first, their objectives being the German front line, Pozières Trench, and their second line, just beyond the railway (see map 14). Once that was captured, Harris and his 3rd Battalion were to leapfrog over them to take the third objective, the south-east side of the main road running from Albert to Bapaume: 1st Australian Brigade's 2nd Battalion was to attack on the 1st Battalion's left, and 3rd Australian Brigade's battalions (9th on the right and 11th on the left) were to mirror the 1st and 2nd Battalions' progress on the east (right) side of the Australians' attack.

In his account, Horton mentioned the growing suspense during the last hour before the attack: 'It would be impossible to give one's thoughts during that hour. They ranged over everything.' But they almost certainly included one overriding question which had been preying on Horton's mind since that morning:

Would we be alive and able to enjoy the sun on the morrow, [or] would we be in hospital minus limbs or suffering from wounds? These thoughts would persist, but they were not the subjects of conversations. Each man knew that his comrade had such thoughts, but each man knew he was expected to behave as though such a thought had never come within the sphere of his consciousness. . . . We all [felt] bound to cover such thoughts with a cloak.

It would . . . be wrong in my case . . . to say I did not feel nervous, but it was not a nervousness which caused hesitation when the [time] to move came, but rather just the nervousness that comes to anyone who has the gift of imagination.

At 23 minutes past 12, the word was passed along: 'Five minutes to go'. Three minutes later 'Two minutes to go. Prepare to move.' And then, as our barrage crashed down on the enemy trenches, the order came: 'Move!' . . . A few seconds [later] . . . we were all out in No Man's Land. We walked about 15 yards and then lay down.

Harris, watching from one of the assembly trenches behind Horton's, recorded the impact of the bombardment in the following terms: 'The rearrangement of the Company in the assembly trench was only just completed and reported to Battalion Headquarters, when our bombardment opened, and all hell let loose. The German first line was marked by an almost continuous wall of fire, with shrapnel bursting overhead, and Heavy Explosive all along the line of the trench.'[22]

Lieutenant Keith McConnel, who was commanding one of the assault platoons in Horton's battalion, described the bombardment thus: 'There were 2,000 odd guns engaged. And the barrage was like one sheet of flame, and sounded like one long-drawn deafening roar.'[23]

Paul Maze, embedded with an undisclosed assault unit, recorded: 'Suddenly a crash fell like a thunderbolt and the earth shuddered. Hundreds of guns had opened fire . . . Shells came shrieking and burst over Pozières where now tongues of flames were rising, glaring on lines of waiting men, mesmerized by this unprecedented burst of sound.'[24]

The intense barrage on the German front line may have made a deep impression on those watching, but it only lasted two minutes before leaping forward to the second line, which was the objective for Horton's D Company. By then, the German guns were replying in kind. But their fire came too late to obstruct the first wave of the 1st Battalion's troops, who rushed forward to seize Pozières Trench, with Horton and his men following closely in their wake. Afterwards, Horton reported that:

the memory of the stunt is a blur. It . . . calls up a picture of a terrific thunderstorm on a pitch dark night. One can recall the flashes lighting the sky, and just a few of the events that happened.

Here, one heard a chap calling for assistance and, knowing it was contrary to orders, one saw a boy walk over and bind up the wounded man. In another place [in Pozières Trench] the Germans had been caught in [their] dugout and a Mills [bomb] had accounted for them. Here, several had been bayoneted, whilst lying round [was] the evidence of the intensity of our barrage.

In one place I saw a German, rifle to shoulder, finger crooked round the trigger, standing in the trench, but without the slightest movement. On walking up to him, I ascertained he had been killed by concussion and left standing where he was when the shell burst. There was no wound. Apparently the shell had landed close by, his heart had given one last jump and then forever stood still . . . I [also] passed an Australian and a German, each transfixed by the other's bayonet . . .

In the lightning flashes one caught glimpses of phantom figures, some with rifles at the slope, some with them at the high port, head[s] held high in the air, striding through the hell that surrounded them. So must the hero who freed the Walkyrie have strode through the ring of burning flame that surrounded her.

The noise overhead, apart from the bursting of innumerable shells, [resembled] the swish of the wings of countless thousands of birds flying above. So closely did the shells seem to move, so great was the weight of metal passing in either direction that one . . . wondered why one barrage did not crash into the other.

What were a man's thoughts as he walked through this hell let loose on earth? His mind was free from fear. He simply went on, not troubling about the risk, bent on getting to grips with the enemy. There were times when a shell, landing perhaps a few feet away, brought him up suddenly with a jerk, but after that, he went on again . . .

There was little fighting [in the German front line]. The barrage had been too severe.

Harris recalled it as 'a shallow ditch of linked up shell holes . . . which was dotted with groups of men, some cheering wildly, some singing, and some roaring.'

The second line was even less of an obstacle. According to Horton, it had been 'completely obliterated by the . . . shell fire'. One of the few officers who had not been hit had to show them where to dig in amongst the trees that surrounded them. 'Just a few yards ahead on the edge of the wood was a battery of 5.9's, and lying between us and the guns was one of the gunners.'

Horton made it to his objective without a scratch. 2nd Lieutenant Lewis Blackmore, the officer commanding the right-hand platoon in the first wave of Horton's D Company, was not so fortunate. According to Lieutenant Keith McConnel, who was in charge of the left platoon in the first wave, 'ten minutes before we moved out [of the supports to move up to] the front trenches, two . . . shells landed in our trench, where Blackmore's platoon were [waiting], and cleaned out half his platoon in [one] go, killing eight and settling the others. For this reason, Blackmore had to "change over", and at the last minute take charge of . . . 13 platoon, who had not had the job explained to them. It was a vile bit of luck.'[25]

It could have jeopardized the whole attack, as McConnel realized, when during the advance he noticed that Blackmore's men were cutting across the line of his platoon's advance, rather than making for what was supposed to be their portion of the second German line. 'I thought for a moment the show was all up,' McConnel wrote in his diary:

However, I found Blackmore, and screeched into his ear what was wrong, and somehow he got them back again to the right. Poor old chap. It was the last thing he did in this world. He and his sergeant were both shot through the head before they got to the first German line.

I thought we would never reach that line, and when we did, we found that B Company (the company advancing in front of his) . . . had made a mistake at the fork road (which branched across their front) and had left about 70 yards of trench untaken . . . [Fortunately] there were only a few Germans in it, and we finished them off.

He and his men then set out in search of the tramline, which was located just in front of the second line and parallel to it. If they reached it before 1 a.m., they would be just in time to take advantage of the cover provided by the barrage that was scheduled to lift to the third objective half an hour after zero.

However, on the way, the problem that had bedevilled Blackmore's and B Company's advance began to affect McConnel's own unit. They were bunching to the left, leaving a gap on the right, which was all the wider because Blackmore's men were nowhere to be seen. 'I didn't know what in the hell to do at first,' he wrote, 'but finally I got ahead and gesticulated wildly at them, shouting: "Come on 1st Battalion!", and then: "Spread out to the right!"' Thanks to this intervention, they reached the tramline at three minutes to one. 'That was where we got it properly though,' McConnel reported:

The Huns landed an inflammatory shell right in amongst us . . . A small red-hot piece bored its way into my left leg, and it lit up the whole show . . . Then everything seemed to open up on us. I was just getting up to get the men across the line, when a shell burst just behind me, and I knew immediately my right leg was broken . . . Thank God I had enough guts left to hold my watch up to the light and give the lads the yell to rush just on the tick of one o'clock.

Shortly afterwards, McConnel remembers seeing Harris's 3rd Battalion rushing past, on their way to take the third objective alongside the Albert to Bapaume road, where by 4 a.m. they were dug in. It was a feat matched on Harris's right and left except in the OG lines.

Delays in OG1 and OG2 were not for want of trying. Although held up by a German strongpoint just to the north of the junction between Pozières Trench and OG1, the Germans having abandoned the position they had fought so hard to retain on 22 July, it was taken just before 1 a.m. John Leak, a private in the 9th Australian Battalion, dashed forward without orders, flung himself into the position and finished off the three Germans holding it. When his officer reached the scene, he found Leak wiping the blood off his bayonet with his felt hat [which, contrary to orders, he had retained]. It was an act of great bravery that deservedly won Leak a Victoria Cross.[26]

But it did not enable the Australians to proceed any further up the OG lines. German guns had made progress up OG2 impossible, and even the position, won thanks to Leak's heroism in OG1, was lost after a German counter-attack pushed the Australians around 150 yards south of the junction of OG1 and Pozières Trench. This ground was only wrested back after another remarkable piece of Australian heroism, this time by bombers and 'bayonet men' acting under the command of the 10th Australian Battalion's Lieutenant Arthur Blackburn, who was also subsequently rewarded with a Victoria Cross.

Blackburn subsequently described what he did as:

the biggest bastard of a job I have ever struck. Our heavies in the preliminary bombardment had knocked part of [OG1] . . . out of existence, and Fritz could see into stretches of it from his second line (OG2). About every twenty yards, the trench would be obliterated for three or four yards, and you would have to expose yourself to get any further. Of course as soon as Fritz found that we were attacking it, he got machine guns and snipers trained onto the gaps and this made it most unhealthy. In addition to this, his dugouts in the trench I was attacking were 30–40 feet deep and he was fighting like fury to keep it.

The climax in this tiny corner of the battlefield occurred after Blackburn crawled up to the junction of OG1 with the Pozières Trench, only to find he had been cut off from the remainder of his troops by a German machine-gunner who was firing from OG2, south-east of where he was lying. 'For a few moments, it looked as if we were cut off,' he wrote:

But on moving to the left flank [up another trench], I discovered a ruined tunnel. On crawling down this [tunnel], I began digging on the other side of it. It was blocked up with fallen earth. I was afraid this might . . . [lead to] an enemy position, but on calling out, I was much relieved to ascertain that it was the 9th Battalion firing line [in Pozières Trench, captured during the main attack] . . .

I had very soon established a passage wide enough to crawl through. Captain Chambers, of the 9th Battalion, [then] immediately sent men and tools forward through this tunnel to my assistance, and we consolidated the position. I [had] started at 5 in the morning and by two in the afternoon I had cleared [up to Pozières Trench] . . . I was relieved then as I was just about collapsing.

The survivors among the men who had been supporting Blackburn were also close to collapse. During the operation fourteen of the attackers had been killed.[27]

The failure of the troops on the right, in OG1 and OG2, to match the extent of the advance in the centre and on the left, did not inhibit the Australian troops' celebration just to the south of Pozières. But closer analysis of how the victory had been achieved might have muted their crowing somewhat. If Captain Harris's experience is anything to go by, mistakes were made by the men in his 3rd Battalion which, like those described by Lieutenant McConnel, could have wiped out all the gains against more committed opposition.

As had happened during the advance made by the 1st Battalion, the troops had failed to obey explicit instructions to spread out across their front. This meant that by the time Harris caught up with them near the south-east side of the Albert to Bapaume road, the majority of his D Company, which was supposed to be on the right of the Battalion's C Company, had ended up on its left.

Given the limited number of Germans opposing them in the immediate aftermath of the charge, that was easily sorted out. The fact that many of the 'diggers' in D Company's second wave had, in their excitement, cast aside their picks and shovels to free themselves up for the fight, was less easily accommodated, according to Harris. It left them 'bitterly regretting' their folly when, on arriving at the third objective, they found they were reduced to hacking away the earth to make a trench with inadequate entrenching tools.

For all the talk of capturing the third German line, there was no trench to take at what was grandly, but misleadingly, called the third objective. Worse still, keenness to kill Germans had encouraged some of Harris's men to advance to the third line prior to the barrage being lifted. Before they could do any damage to the enemy, half a dozen men and an officer from the 3rd Battalion had needlessly lost their lives.

But arguably the most telling result of the Australian failure to organize their troops properly was the fact that the 3rd Australian Brigade unit, which was supposed to capture the third objective on D Company's right, did not reach its position until several hours later. It was subsequently discovered that the company in question had been delayed in a communication trench to the rear by troops who had missed a turning and had doubled back into the path of the battalion which had been following them on the way to the front.[28] Such unnecessary snarl-ups were to become a recurring feature of Australian attempts to conduct orderly attacks during their time on the Somme.

The fact that the chaos resulting from such examples of disorganization was self-inflicted and avoidable made them all the more demoralizing. Although they were not the direct responsibility of senior commanders such as Gough, one cannot help wondering whether he had taken Haig's warning that he should monitor the Australians' preparations carefully. And one cannot help questioning whether Haig's own policy of delegation was too extreme, and whether it should have been tempered, concerning Pozières as much as Fromelles, by a system of checks and balances which could have ensured that he was quickly informed if sensible measures were not being taken.

Whether or not ordinary Australian soldiers registered their commanders' shortcomings, it is hard to find any giving voice to criticism during 23 July.

Captain John Harris has described how his men in the 3rd Battalion's D Company had by 6 a.m. dug so hard that their trench was deep enough for them to stand up in it. 'Except for a few sentry groups, the men exhausted by their strenuous work and lack of sleep were allowed to rest. Huddled up in strange contorted attitudes in the trench, or stretched out in shell holes to the rear, they slept in all the discomfort and danger, as if they were in their feather beds.' While they rested, some of those who remained on duty made use of the armchairs that Harris's batman had found in a nearby ruined house and placed in a large shell hole behind the widened area of their trench which was the company's headquarters.

Harris recalled: 'We made a real[ly] good breakfast of "bully", bread and jam, and tea, and shortly afterwards the Colonel arrived to inspect the new front line. It was a warm still July morning. The war seemed to have receded into the distance, except for a few shells in front from our own barrage.'

25: An Eye for an Eye

Pozières, 23–26 July 1916

(See maps 2 and 14)

Given that British troops had attempted to capture Pozières on several occasions before 23 July, and given that the Australians had, it seemed, broken the back of the Pozières defences at their first attempt, it is hardly surprising that men and commanders alike were cock-a-hoop. The fact that they had been victorious in spite of their mistakes perhaps led some of them to believe they were invincible.

Euphoria about their achievements was all the more pronounced amongst those out of the front line who had heard the outcome of the 4th Army's 23 July general attack. Pozières, which had been attacked by the Reserve Army rather than the 4th Army, was the only major success of the day. Not one of the principal landmarks aimed at by the 4th Army's III, XV and XIII Corps (see Chapter 24) on 23 July had been captured. Guillemont, Delville Wood, Longueval, High Wood, the Switch Line and Munster Alley would all have to be attacked on another day.[1]

However, writing with the benefit of hindsight, Lance Corporal Douglas Horton poured scorn on his and his mates' naivety which led them to hope that they had the Germans beaten:

In the fullness of our conceit and the depth of our ignorance, [we] congratulated ourselves on the wonderful success we had made [of our attack], and we were not alone in saying that the magnitude of the victory was out of all proportion to the number of casualties.

We were young and had much to learn. The next sixty hours taught [us] quite a lot about attacks, and the aftermath thereof . . .

All day . . . we . . . felt elated by our success . . . We lay on the parados of the trench basking in the sun. Here, half a dozen would be sitting down having a meal. The iron rations were in great demand. All day there [was] too much movement in and around the trench. To us it signified nothing. But the enemy were making full use of the powers of observation, and we were to pay the full price of our recklessness on the morrow and on the days that followed.[2]

Such repentance did not appear to be called for that night. The first German counter-attack, at 5.30 p.m. on 23 July, targeting the Australians' vulnerable right flank, between the Albert to Bapaume road and the tramway south of it, had been easily repulsed. Superficially at least, it seemed as though the Australians had the Germans on the run.

But if the celebrating Australians had paused to think, they might have come up with a very different view of the situation in which they found themselves. For example, would they have repulsed the first German counter-attack so easily if the Australian defences had been softened up first by artillery? What the counter-attack did do was to highlight the swelling boil on the Australian right that had not been lanced. The line held by the right-hand Australian battalion was bent back, so that it faced the Germans in the uncaptured portion of the OG lines, rather than lining up with the other battalions along the Albert to Bapaume road. The 9th Battalion on the right had not been as successful as those units on the left of the attack. This alone made it clear that the whole Australian position was vulnerable to a stronger assault from that quarter.[3]

Of more immediate concern were the dugouts inside Pozières itself, which despite claims by some that the village had already been taken, were evidently still full of Germans. Because of this, the task of clearing the village was in some ways more dangerous than the charge constituting the main attack itself. The febrile atmosphere that still existed as a result of the continuing German resistance helps one to understand, if not to excuse, the cruel treatment the Australians meted out to their prisoners.

Lieutenant Elmer Laing of the 3rd Australian Brigade's 12th Battalion, a farmer from Western Australia, was probably used to shooting vermin on his farm. Perhaps he regarded Germans as being no more deserving of consideration. When at 8 p.m. on 23 July he was ordered to clear the remaining Germans out of Pozières, the 8th Battalion having already moved to its north-eastern edge, Laing decided in advance that he would show 'no mercy for snipers'. He had been provoked. Not only had his battalion lost several men to German sharpshooters during the day, but shortly before his platoon advanced, the man standing next to him suddenly collapsed after being shot in the head.

The following extract from Laing's letter to his 'Dad and Mum', in which he described the incident, certainly gives the impression that he felt he was justified in behaving ruthlessly in return. 'The men had great sport chucking bombs down any hole they saw,' he wrote:

The Huns [who] saw our chaps coming with bayonets fixed [either] cleared, or tried to surrender. But it was too late [for that]! . . . One Hun fired three times at me, and missed me each time. Then, one of my men got him. Another, in a well fitted-up wireless station, tried to give himself up as soon as he saw our chaps on top of him. 'Come out you bastard!' yelled one of our men. I heard him, rushed back from the right, shouting at the chap to shoot the swine, or I would. So he got him. Altogether we 'got' six killed and eighteen out of the dugouts.[4]

The eighteen owed their reprieve to the fact that they were found in what Laing referred to 'as a great piece of work about 25 feet underground fitted up as a hospital with plenty of bandages etc.' Far from resenting them for their comfortable hiding place, Laing described it as 'the only thing I shall ever bless the Germans for. It was the saving of us and our wounded. It was beautifully built up with wood, and had two entrances with a third one blown in.'

That did not stop Laing cracking a joke at the expense of the German prisoners, perhaps reacting to what he took to be the spurious claim by their commanding officer that as a German he had a very English-sounding name. 'There was a captain there who told me his name was Ponsonby Lyons, and that he was commandant of Pozières. I told him he was [once the commandant], but that Captain Vowles (Laing's company commander) would be pleased to relieve him [of that heavy burden]. We [then] had them all escorted to the rear. And very pleased they were to get away. As one chap said, he did not wish to be there when the [German] bombardment started.'[5]

Whether or not they reached the rear safely is open to question. Corporal Archibald Barwick of the 1st Battalion, who had remarked on 'how fierce and ferocious the boys are once they taste blood', mentioned in his diary the treatment handed out to fifteen German Red Cross prisoners. 'They were marched down and searched. 13 of them were found to be carrying daggers and revolvers. They [were] promptly put against a wall and finished.'[6]

This is not to say that compassion was lacking amongst some of the victors at Pozières. Lieutenant James Aitken, whose 11th Battalion captured a stretch of Pozières Trench to the right of Captain Harris's 3rd Battalion, wrote in his next letter addressed to 'Mother dear' how 'great' it was to see the Germans crying out for mercy. 'They got it too, sometimes! In our first trench [where] bodies were everywhere . . . twisted into all shapes, one

German was buried alive . . . My attention was drawn to him. I said to the man [who had asked me what he should do]: "You can shoot him, or dig him out. Please yourself" . . . I'm pleased to say he dug him out, and I sent him away with the other prisoners.'[7]

Another man with moral scruples was Fred Callaway, a twenty-five-year-old company sergeant-major serving in the 2nd Australian Battalion, which had attacked on the left flank of the 1st Australian Brigade. In his after-action letter home Callaway described the fate of eight Germans whom he, his commanding officer and a lance corporal flushed out of yet another dugout:

I threw a bomb [into it], and they came up whining 'Mercy Kamerad, mercy'. Needless to say, we soon kicked 'em into line.

There was one of them with a big red cross on each arm. He clung to me, crying for mercy. I felt beneath his coat, and got a dagger and a beautiful revolver off of him. I pointed to his red cross, and then to the revolver. He only cried. I lifted my revolver to shoot the swine . . . [whereupon] he fell down, and grabbed my knees crying out for mercy. I hadn't the heart to shoot him in cold blood . . . [though] he deserved it. Any red cross man bearing arms is liable to be shot on sight.

Callaway justified his impulse to commit a war crime by adding: 'The Hun individually is a coward . . . [He is also] cunning. If you go at him with the bayonet, he will scream for mercy. Spare him, take him prisoner, and he will come behind you and stick you, or shoot you in the back. Our lads know this, and they take no chances. I saw some awful cold-blooded acts, but you can't blame the men. They must protect themselves.'[8]

Perhaps Callaway had heard the rumour about the 2nd Australian Battalion's popular Lieutenant Walter Host. He had captured some Germans in a Pozières dugout. According to a report in his Red Cross file, 'His men wanted to finish them off, but the Lieutenant stopped them. Thereupon a severely wounded German picked up a bayonet and ran him through the body.'[9] This version of events was disputed by other Australian soldiers, who claimed that Lieutenant Host had been killed by a shell while escorting German prisoners to the rear whom he had captured and spared.[10] Whatever the true cause of death, the clear message was that killing prisoners was a lot less risky than capturing them.

After all this bloodletting, the German occupants of the imposing concrete blockhouse located near the south-west corner of the village, a building referred to by the Australians as 'Gibraltar', could count themselves fortunate to be on the receiving end of a party of ten led by the 2nd Battalion's 2nd Lieutenant Walter Waterhouse, a devout Christian. In his account this twenty-eight-year-old Methodist, who described himself as a university 'demonstrator' on his Army enlistment papers, described how the blockhouse was captured:

At the entrance, we got a German, and quickly had him with his hands up . . . Then I called for any others to come out. In single file, there streamed up the concrete steps 2 officers and 25 men . . . With the corporal, I then went downstairs with [an] electric torch . . . in one hand and [a] revolver in the other . . . On the first floor down, were 3 machine guns and 27 boxes of belt ammunition together with automatic pistols, rifles, ranging equipment, field glasses, [and] plenty of rations and beer . . . It was rightly termed a stronghold . . .

Leading down from the first flight, was a second flight of stone steps, and here, we found a room used as officers' quarters in which [there] was a wounded captain and his soldier servant . . . From these quarters, there led off a long passage-way fitted up with bunks for the men, and here, [there] were dozens of Mauser rifles and bandoliers of ammunition. Turning a corner at the end of the passage, we found another cellar passage at right angles, and at the end of it, saw a German sergeant and two . . . privates. We rushed them and quickly had them with their hands up. The sergeant seemed inclined to draw his pistol, but my revolver [held up] under his nose brought him to his senses.[11]

Waterhouse's approach may have saved the lives of some of the Germans in the Gibraltar blockhouse, but he was too late to rescue all of them. When Lieutenant John Stevenson, an engineer with 1st Field Company, visited the blockhouse for the first time later that day, he found what he referred to as 'a strange sight': 'Two little Persian kittens were enjoying a breakfast of human brains. The top of a German's head had been sliced off and was lying beside him like a bowl specially set down for the cats.'[12]

As Lance Corporal Douglas Horton's account makes clear, when 24 July dawned, the prospects were nothing if not rosy from the viewpoint of the surviving Australians in Pozières: '[It] was an ideal July summer day. The blue sky above and the sun's warm rays called for a day of pleasure.'

Unfortunately for Horton, he would shortly discover it was a fool's paradise:

We [certainly] do recall that day. [However, it was] not because of the pleasure we had, but because of the hours of untold agony that we endured . . .

Towards morning . . . I must have dozed a bit, for my first recollection of the . . . day was a couple of shells landing over the trench. This was [just] the beginning. The shelling never stopped. Hour after hour, shells fired from the enemy batteries fell within a few yards of the trench, or on the trench itself. I have been in many bombardments, but always hold the opinion that the . . . bombardment of Pozières was the worst I was ever called upon to suffer. Why? Because of the precision of the shellfire. Few shells . . . went astray. Only on about two occasions was there what one would call a barrage put down on us. But for the sixty hours, from [the] morning, till the time we were relieved, the shellfire was sustained, unbroken. Shells of small calibre were not much in evidence. By far the greater part of the shellfire was 5.9's or larger shells, and these fell with unbroken regularity throughout the following hours within a few yards of their target . . .

It was while sitting in the trench that I saw what I considered the gamest fellow of the war . . . A shell landed . . . amongst four men. They were shattered and buried. We dug them out. [But only] one man came out alive. His leg was broken, his hands and arm shattered, and his head was burnt . . . [However,] it was impossible to take him from the trench [while the shellfire continued]. The way back was impassible. The communication sap had ceased to exist . . . We did what we could for him, little as it was. We laid him on the bottom of the trench and obtained a stretcher. We bandaged him as well as possible . . . Then he had to wait . . .

What that means, will be apparent from the following . . . I had lost my pipe about an hour previously, and on orders being given to deepen the trench, I found it buried 18 inches [under the surface] in the bottom of the trench. This boy . . . had to lie and allow all this debris to fall on his poor broken body . . . At times, it was impossible for him to stifle a groan, but . . . he at once apologized . . . for . . . being unable to stand the pain without a sound.[13]

Horton's account does not relate whether this brave man survived. Descriptions of conditions at the dressing stations and aid posts to the rear suggest that lying on a stretcher there was almost as perilous as being in the front line. Lance Corporal Roger Morgan, attached to the 2nd Australian Battalion from the 1st Field Ambulance, reported: 'Our dugout seems right in the barrage line . . . Shells are falling all round this place. Stretcher bearers have not returned in sufficient numbers to clear. In the aid post the scene was terrible. Outside it was worse. We have to dress wounds out in the open [by the] roadside, or in trenches. Many were hit, unable to move. Others were buried alive.'[14]

The abbreviated diary note written by Albert Coates, a medical orderly with the 7th Australian Battalion, refers to an equally grisly scene he witnessed at the 11th Australian Battalion's aid post further to the east:

At 4.30 a.m. [on 23 July], the Medical Officer and I move to the support lines . . . Arrive in support lines at 7.30 a.m., and wait two hours for orders . . . We stop in the 11th Battalion dressing station to make plans for the evacuation of our wounded. I leave the dressing station in search of a company officer. Return and find the dressing station shelled. All wounded lying there are killed. The 11th Battalion Medical Officer seriously and our own Medical Officer badly wounded. What a sight! Mangled remains on the stretchers.[15]

Given the treatment meted out to the dressing stations hundreds of yards behind the new front line, it is not surprising to learn that the men in 'the supports', in between the Chalk Pit (see map 14) and the Albert to Bapaume road, were equally exposed. Private Athol Dunlop, whose trench mortars had remained in their original position in the supports to guard against a German counter-attack, has recorded what he had to endure: 'Going down to the chalk pits for rations and water was a most risky job . . . The road was being shelled the whole way.' There were dead men all along the track. 'On Tuesday afternoon (25 July), a huge shell burst on our parapet killing our sergeant and two other men, besides burying three others. I managed to rescue two of these latter, and another chap got the other man out. He was badly smashed about. I was extremely lucky, as I was next to the sergeant, but only got buried to the waist with loose earth.'[16]

It is interesting to see what types of men could endure the remorseless bone-shaking shelling for longest. According to the 3rd Battalion's Captain John Harris, 'The men who had growled [whilst] in comfortable billets, and [who] only worked under pressure at good safe jobs well in the rear, were happy as sandboys now [they were in the front line], and actually worked as if they enjoyed it.' As for the Irishman in the company, who never stopped talking, he showed an 'absolute indifference to danger'. When a bullet or piece of shrapnel hit his helmet, he amused those around him by stopping his chatter only to ask: 'Ours or theirs?'

Conversely Harris, who could not have been more dutiful and courageous before, during and after the attack, gradually felt his moral and physical strength ebbing away. His account suggests that stopping for breakfast and then relaxing in the armchairs which his batman had looted from the ruins shortly after the main attack paradoxically helped to tip him over the edge. It was as if the rest and recreation lowered his guard: 'I can vividly remember the intense difficulty of keeping awake, and trying to take in further instructions,' he reported when writing of this period. But it was only after yet another sleepless night, during which he and his men were expecting an attack at any minute, that Harris recalled feeling 'dazed' after a series of shells landed 'too close to be pleasant'.

At 7 p.m. on 24 July his colonel sent him back to the battalion's headquarters in Pozières Trench. 'Battalion Headquarters was ... a deep German dugout opening towards the front,' Harris remembered, adding, 'My further interest in proceedings terminated next morning when I arrived at the top of the dugout, and was met by the explosion of a whiz bang which ... hit the top of the parapet, killed a man who had just stepped out of the dugout in front of me, and knocked me down to the bottom of the steps with the dead man on top of me.'[17]

As his personal file makes clear, Harris, through no fault of his own, had had a mental breakdown, and was suffering from shell shock. This was apparently just as likely to strike down fit, tanned, muscular Aussies as any other soldiers, although intuition might make us wonder whether sensitive poets, and imaginative schoolmasters such as Harris, might have been even more susceptible to it.

The reports that Lieutenant-Colonel Iven Mackay, the thirty-four-year-old commanding officer of the 4th Australian Battalion, sent back to Brigadier-General Neville Smyth of the 1st Australian Brigade between midday and 2 p.m. on 24 July, shows that Harris was far from being the only soldier wavering under the onslaught. One such message read:

About 4 enemy guns (5.9") are firing on the line held by us (on the left of the Australian line, with troops on the extreme left being on the north-west side of the Albert to Bapaume road, and the remainder around fifty to seventy yards to the south of the road's south-east side).

[There is] no particular system of shelling ... The guns do not follow [the] line of the trench ... but drop shells here and there promiscuously ... at a steady rate ... The trenches are being blown in at frequent intervals, and are already seriously blocked. The only work being conducted is digging work to excavate casualties ... Casualties in 2 companies holding this line were for previous 6 hours . . . about 100 . . . It appears that this . . . shelling, following on strenuous digging, has left some of the men rather shaken.[18]

Given that casualties were mounting by the hour even without any offensive operations being launched, it obviously made sense to try advancing to where the Germans guns were firing from with a view to neutralizing them as quickly as possible. That being the case, no one could criticize General Gough of the Reserve Army for giving the 1st Australian Division an order during the early afternoon of 24 July stating that attacks should be made towards the east and north.[19] It was the way the attacks were organized that invited censure.

One might have hoped that following the 'boxing in' of some of the assault troops prior to the advance on 23 July ('boxing in' meaning that troops wanting to advance were unable to do so because other troops obstructed their path towards the Australian front line), lessons would have been learned which could have stopped it happening again. However, it is all the more disappointing to discover that the same problem manifested itself during the lead-up to the first frontal attack on the OG lines, from west to east, which was scheduled for 2 a.m. on 25 July.

A very precise arrangement had been made that was designed to prevent any such obstruction: this permitted the assault company from the 7th Australian Battalion, which had furthest to go to reach its jumping-off point at the northernmost end of the sector being attacked, between the Albert to Bapaume road and the railway to the south, to leave its trench first, at midnight on the night of 24–25 July. It was to be followed by the 5th Australian Battalion's two companies, which were to attack south of the 7th Battalion.

However, the organization of the 3rd Australian Brigade, which had been given control of the two battalions for the attack, was so lax that compliance with the arrangement was not enforced. The 5th Battalion companies arrived prematurely at the point in the trench from where they had to file out, and they then proceeded first. This delayed the 7th Battalion to such an extent that its company arrived at the jumping-off positions ten minutes after the Australian artillery, following an intense two-minute barrage, had lifted from the German front line.[20] To compound the problem, 7th Battalion's support company was misdirected and ended up in Pozières.[21]

Perhaps even that would not have mattered had one of the most important lessons from Fromelles been taken on board. The Fromelles attack would at least have had some chance of succeeding if the troops which took the German front line had remained in that trench to ward off any counter-attacks from the flanks. The same might be said of the attack on 25 July. But after the 5th Battalion had seized the shallow remnants of OG1, from which most of the Germans had already retreated, the Australian first wave swept on to take OG2, leaving OG1 more or less exposed to attacks from the north.

In a mirror image of what had happened at Fromelles, the first sign that warned the Australians in OG2 that they risked being surrounded was a flare shooting up on their left rear. This was followed by a counter-attack by the Germans down OG1 from north to south that almost succeeded in cutting off the Australians from their base, including the 10th Australian Battalion troops who had captured a German post on the communication trench just to the north of Munster Alley. They were only saved by the decision of the 5th Battalion's commander to retire swiftly to OG1 where, after what the Australian official historian referred to as 'one of the most desperate bomb fights in the history of the AIF', the Australians ended up holding most of the OG1 line between its junction with Pozières Trench and the railway. This was a relatively small dividend for an attack that had ended up costing the 5th Battalion more than 450 casualties.[22]

If anything, the blunder leading up to the sister attack scheduled for 3.45 a.m. on 25 July, following an intense fifteen-minute barrage, was potentially even more disastrous. The 1st Australian Division had mistakenly issued an order specifying that the attack of its 1st Brigade towards the north should take place at 3.45 a.m. on 26 July instead of on 25 July. An attempt to rectify the error by issuing a new order containing the correct date was frustrated after the order went astray. The result was that Brigadier-General Smyth of the 1st Australian Brigade only discovered at 11.55 p.m. on 24 July that he was supposed to be attacking just under four hours later, and his 4th Battalion only began its advance up K Trench (running northwards up the western side of Pozières) at 3.55 a.m., ten minutes after the artillery barrage had lifted.[23]

Fortunately, the opposition encountered by the 4th Battalion in K Trench evaporated after the 8th Battalion, also acting under the 1st Australian Brigade, advanced northwards on the east of the trench, ending up north of the Pozières cemetery, and this so terrified the German garrison in K Trench that they ran for their lives.[24] That does not mean the mistake in timing did not have some undesirable consequences.

Lieutenant-Colonel Owen Howell Price described the repercussions for his 3rd Battalion, which was not warned in advance about the attack, in the following terms:

At 03.45 [a.m. on 25 July], I received orders of an attack being made by the 8th Battalion . . . which I was to support with three companies. When the [German] heavy artillery began, my trenches were full of men, but I could not move them back because of the attack proceeding. I was quite unaware of the situation and, receiving no word from the 8th Battalion, I went forward to reconnoitre the position . . .

I decided to push forward one company [only], but when I returned to my trenches, I found they were quite untenable. A Company had been practically wiped out . . . As the artillery were going over the first line at the time, I decided to move forward closer up to the 8th Battalion line. As soon as this movement commenced, the enemy artillery shortened range, and we were obliged to pass through a terrific barrage of high explosive . . . A great number of men were buried.[25]

Nevertheless, thanks to the injection of additional troops from the 6th Australian Battalion into the new front line, the advance ended up being a success, at least measured by the amount of ground taken.[26] After the move, there was a continuous line running round the north, west and south of Pozières, the only failure to establish a line beyond the village being on the eastern side.

The men whose lives were put at risk by the advance, however, might have viewed the situation differently. The 4th Battalion's Lieutenant-Colonel Mackay, reporting what he had witnessed on 25 July, wrote:

I have been along the whole of the captured trench to where we link up with the 8th Battalion. Shelling throughout the day has been . . . continuous, and the Germans have guns which can enfilade many portions of the trench, with the result that it has been badly knocked about and in many places filled in. The men are endeavouring to clear out the trench, but they are by this time very tired, and cannot keep pace with the trench destruction of the artillery. Casualties are numerous and it is extremely difficult to get them away owing to the continuous shellfire, and the scarcity and weariness of the stretcher bearers.[27]

Unbeknown to the Australians, the German shelling was intended to soften them up before the counter-attack scheduled for 25 July at 4.30 p.m.

However, because every movement by a German unit led to its being shelled by the guns supporting the 1st Australian Division's infantry, the attack, and a subsequent assault planned for 8.30 p.m., had to be called off, thereby ending any hopes the Germans had of recapturing Pozières.[28]

That night, the majority of the troops within the 1st and 3rd Australian Brigades were at last relieved by those in the 1st Australian Division's 2nd Brigade and the 2nd Australian Division's 5th Brigade. But with no means of knowing that the Germans had written off Pozières, the replacement troops had to remain at their posts and grit their teeth. The bombardment on 26 July was, if anything, to prove even more intense than the day before.

There was no attempt by the Australians to conduct offensive operations north of the Albert to Bapaume road on 26 July, although during the night there had been another effort to attack the OG lines between the road and the railway to its south. On this occasion the assault was condemned to failure because of the misguided decision not to cover the attackers' advance with artillery, and thereby to attempt to surprise the defenders, together with the fact that the assault troops were given neither enough time to reconnoitre the terrain nor enough grenades to support those who did make it into OG1.[29]

After his troops in the front line north-east of Pozières had been withstanding the shelling for the best part of a day, Lieutenant-Colonel Gordon Bennett of the 6th Australian Battalion reported at 4.05 a.m.: 'My men are being unmercifully shelled. They cannot hold on if attack is launched. The firing line and my headquarters are being plastered with heavy guns, and the town is being swept with shrapnel. I myself am OK but the front line is being buried.'[30]

A few hours later, with the German rate of fire appearing to reach a climax, Lieutenant-Colonel Carl Jess, commanding officer of the 7th Australian Battalion, some of whose troops were in K Trench, sent his brigadier an even more desperate message from the Gibraltar blockhouse stating: 'Enemy have been consistently shelling our lines throughout the day. Has been impossible to construct adequate trenches owing to the pulped nature of the ground . . . Men are so dazed that they are incapable of digging or fighting. Consider relief imperative as we could not resist attack if this is the preparation for it.'[31]

Then, seizing the telephone, which still linked Pozières with the 2nd Australian Brigade, Jess recommended that the only way to forestall the counter-attack, given that visibility was so reduced, was to fire with all available guns at the German front line. This message shocked Brigadier-General John Forsyth of the 2nd Brigade, who replied: 'Men must and will fight if necessary. All artillery now turned on against bombardment.' Jess responded: 'No movement by officers or men in shelled areas to retire has been made. Men have stuck to crater hole . . . No-one will move in a rearward direction. Messages were sent to enable headquarters in rear to realize the seriousness of the position.'[32]

It appears to have been Jess's plea that eventually persuaded General Gough to sanction the saturation of the German lines with gunfire from the Reserve Army's heaviest guns. Shortly after 10.30 p.m. the German gunfire, after three days of terrorizing the Australians, finally subsided.[33] The improved state of affairs was immediately reflected in the messages sent back by the troops in Pozières, one brief communication from the 7th Australian Battalion's Lieutenant Fred Hoad speaking volumes: 'Situation much improved, artillery fire having diminished. Men tired but cheery.'[34] That night the 2nd Australian Division at long last relieved the remaining units of the 1st Australian Division.

But it was a much-depleted force that passed through Albert on the way to the rear. The 1st Australian Division had suffered 5,285 casualties in the course of capturing Pozières, and everyone knew there were more casualties to come if the crest of the slope to the east of the village was to be overcome as well.[35]

Such statistics were not disclosed to the other ranks, even if an estimate had by that stage been computed. However, as Private Bowman's diary entry for 27 July recorded concerning his 9th Australian Battalion's stay at Warloy Baillon, twelve miles west of Pozières: 'One can form a fair idea what our casualties were. In our section, [the] scouts, 28 men went into Pozières . . . There are [only] six of us here now.' He added: 'Nearly every man here has a German forage cap or spiked helmet or some other German souvenir. The reaction is remarkable after being through that hell. Nearly everyone chatters or laughs loudly. It is really forced, but it is far better than sitting down and brooding on what we have been through.'[36]

But Bowman's reaction was by no means universal. Ted Rule of the 14th Battalion (4th Australian Division), whose unit would eventually follow the 2nd Australian Division into the line, wrote down his impressions of the traumatized troops in his memoirs thus:

The 1st Division . . . came back through Warloy one morning fairly early, having spent the night around Albert and Senlis. Although we knew it [had been] . . . stiff fighting, we had our eyes opened when we saw these men march by . . . They looked like men who had been in hell. Almost without exception, each man looked drawn and haggard, and so dazed they appeared to be walking in a dream . . . Their eyes looked glassy and starey. Quite a few were silly . . . These were the only noisy ones in the crowd. Their appearance before they had a night's sleep and clean up must have been twice as ill as when we saw them. We noticed they had lost a lot of men. Some companies seemed to have been nearly wiped out . . . In all my experience I've never seen men more shaken than these.[37]

26: The Check

Pozières Heights, 29 July 1916

(See maps 2 and 14)

The arrival of a fresh Australian division in Pozières was not without its disadvantages. The 2nd Australian Division's troops themselves may not have been appreciably inferior to those in the 1st Australian Division, but there was a question mark hanging over its fifty-two-year-old commander, Major-General Gordon Legge.

Some of the doubts in British minds may have been prompted not so much by his accent, but by the direct way he spoke about the causes he championed. Unlike General Walker, the 1st Australian Division's commander, Legge was an Australian, albeit a naturalized one. He had been born in England and had emigrated to Australia, with his parents, aged fifteen. Nevertheless his adopted nationality made him a rarity. The only other Australian major-general on the Western Front during 1916 was James McCay, commander of the 5th Australian Division.

No one doubted that Legge could handle the administrative and logistical sides of running a division. Unusually for an Australian officer, he had gone to university, a training that helped his rapid promotion to all the top jobs in the Australian Army. However, there were doubts concerning his ability to plan an attack. Although he had led a division at Gallipoli, he had yet to handle a large-scale offensive.[1] Those who were prejudiced against Australian military leaders in general may have believed they had even more right to be wary concerning Legge, after the mistakes General McCay had made, or was perceived to have made, at Fromelles.

What particularly alarmed Legge's British staff officers was his propensity to propose all sorts of impractical ideas. These views were masked while he was working alongside a rigorous chief of staff, but they could not be discounted on the Somme, where he was saddled with a chief of staff who had a similar reputation.[2]

The concern that Legge would not be up to the job was made more acute because of his tendency sometimes to rub fellow officers up the wrong way. General Birdwood, the commander of 1 ANZAC, defended the decision to appoint General Walker rather than Legge as the temporary head of the corps in April 1916, stating in a letter to Australia's governor-general: 'He (Legge) does not have the full confidence of those serving under him, while Walker most distinctly does.'[3]

Perhaps Legge's subordinates thought he was too forceful, or too cocky. If so, they would have been in good company. It was a view held by at least some of the British officers with whom he served when working as the Australian representative on the Imperial General Staff between 1912 and 1914. His imaginative ideas, and the brash way he put them across, clashed with the British officers' more orthodox, understated approach, even when Legge's analysis produced the better solution to the problem being considered. This was not altogether surprising. Before becoming a soldier, Legge had trained as a barrister, so he knew how to put together an unassailable case.

The British contingent in France probably felt he was attacking them when he refused to hold his tongue on the issue that obsessed him over any other: the need to have more Australian units commanded by Australians. Birdwood was one British officer who found Legge a trial. One practice that irked the fifty-year-old commander of 1 ANZAC more than any other was when Legge would complain to the Australian Minister of Defence if anything was going wrong instead of yielding to the views of his superior officers. Birdwood was almost as scathing about Legge's garrulousness, remarking to one colleague: 'How he can talk!' After the Australians departed from the Somme, Birdwood confided to the Australian Governor-General: 'When they came and told me that Legge was ill, and could not speak because of a sore throat, I could imagine no more terrible affliction for him, and [thought] that that would probably be the punishment meted out to him on the Day of Judgement.'

Notwithstanding these defects, Birdwood tried to give Legge what he wanted. Legge was permitted to name the day and the time of day when he would like to mount the next Australian attack. It had to target the heights east of Pozières, as well as the ridge to the north of the village. In response, Legge came up with an impractical plan, which involved an advance during the night of 28–29 July with remarkably little preparation. Nevertheless, the 1 ANZAC commander and his chief of staff, Brigadier-General Brudenell White, waved it through without reservation.[4]

That was not very clever of them. Legge's order to his division, issued at 5 a.m. on 28 July, would not permit the jumping-off trenches, half dug on the night of 27–28 July, to be completed. Although the Australian troops would have some protection, because they would be advancing at night, the result was that they were destined to face a long march (between 400 and 600 yards depending where they were advancing) across No Man's Land. Although that had not proved an obstacle to the attack made by Rawlinson's 4th Army on 14 July, it was always possible that assault would remain a one-off success. The Germans were now on the lookout for enemy attacks made at night. If they spotted the troops by the light of a flare as they left their trenches, then the Australians would be faced with exactly the kind of situation that had confronted British troops on 1 July, and Australian troops on 19 July at Fromelles: too far to go while under fire.[5]

The artillery arrangements were equally worrying. They prompted Haig to make the following entry in his diary during the evening of 28 July:

Gen. Birch (his artillery adviser) . . . reported that the Australians had at the last moment said that they would attack without artillery support and 'they did not believe that machine-gun fire could do them much harm!' Birch at once saw General Gough, commander of the Reserve Army, who arranged that the original artillery programme should be carried out. The Australians are splendid fellows, but very ignorant!

The problem was that even the original programme was sparse, to say the least, containing as it did just one minute of intense firing on the front line, followed by ten minutes on the second line. After that, the artillery would fire their guns over the heads of the Germans who were most likely to stop the advance in its tracks.[6]

Given the plan's evident flaws, it is tempting to enquire what it was that persuaded Birdwood and White to accept it. Had they not acted decisively to snuff out Gough's premature plan for the first attack on Pozières? What made this time so different? Afterwards, Legge complained that Gough repeatedly urged him to hurry up.[7] Perhaps Birdwood was being pressurized as well. Or was it that Birdwood and White had been browbeaten by Legge into believing that the Australian government would not be very happy if they did not allow the one Australian divisional general on the Somme to have his way? Legge had certainly badgered White about the need to promote Australians to senior positions.[8] Perhaps that, in combination with Legge's garrulousness, had led to a moment of weakness.

But there was another reason that could just as easily have been used – and perhaps was used – to justify the hastily cobbled-together plan. Although

German shelling eventually died down during the night of 26–27 July, on the morning of 27 July it started up again. It then reached such a level of intensity that it became apparent the 2nd Australian Division would be likely to lose more men if it just stayed in its trenches than it would during a moderately well-planned attack.

The strain that this shelling imposed on those at the receiving end of it has been well documented by Aubrey Wiltshire. He was a twenty-five-year-old captain in the 6th Australian Brigade's 22nd Battalion, the 2nd Australian Division unit that had moved up to relieve the 1st Australian Division's 6th Battalion during the night of 26–27 July. In the following extract from his account, he described how they coped:

At 5.30 p.m. (26 July), we marched through Albert . . . A great artillery battle was in progress . . . Eventually two guides reported, and we commenced . . . [our] advance in single file . . . It was pitch dark and shells were bursting . . . every-where . . . Presently, we reached an awful area, a tangled mass of . . . 30 foot . . . deep pits . . . with girders, bricks and other sharp things sticking up. One would . . . tumble into one of these, and then would commence the painful ascent streaming [with] sweat . . . It was some time before we realized that . . . [this] area [had] once [been] the village of Pozières . . .

The 'village' had been uprooted, and not a vestige of it remains, except a few bricks and beams at the bottom of these pits made by high explosive . . . The place resembles a filthy rubbish heap. Equipment, rifles, Lewis gun magazines . . . and a thousand other things litter the ground. Stinking corpses lie [everywhere]. There a man . . . all shrivelled up . . . with his face blown off. Here a . . . lad with his leg lying beside him. [One] . . . chap was leaning against a tree with a . . . trickle of blood on his face and no other apparent injury [except that he was] bloated with gas . . . [We were] crawling and walking over this filth with the reek of putrefaction in our nostrils.[9]

Notwithstanding the obstacles in their path, Wiltshire's battalion made it to its position in the front line and support areas north of Pozières, as did the 6th Australian Brigade's 24th Battalion whose twenty-eight-year-old private, Arthur Clifford, also kept a diary. According to Clifford: 'It was 2 a.m. (27 July) before we got into the line . . . As soon as we got into our positions, we got to work to deepen the trench, which in a lot of places was only 18 inches deep . . . We worked like niggers, and by daylight, had it down to about 3 feet six inches.'

However, as Clifford's account bore witness, that was not deep enough: 'Lieutenant (Alan) Kerr and Corporal Jaggers were blown up [by] . . . the first shell to fall on us. Nothing of Lieutenant Kerr was ever found.' Clifford went on to chronicle how the Germans 'kept up a withering fire for the next 36 hours', adding 'By evening half my company had gone.'[10]

Wiltshire's account reveals that his company fared no better:

[Most of] our dead were lying . . . where they had been thrown, over the parados. The trenches were so narrow, this was the only way to deal with a dead . . . man . . . In the firing line, we saw a hand sticking out [of the bottom of the trench]. It belonged to the body of an Australian, who had about an inch of dirt on him . . . Everyone was trampling over him.

[I] arranged for the collection of all Australians . . . After dark they were to be put in shell holes and buried. The German bodies were built into the parapet to stop the bullets.

Our guns had superiority during the morning (of 27 July) . . . but in the afternoon the Germans did what they liked with us . . . The air was full of explosions and smoke . . . Working forward, [they] pitted every inch of ground up to our [parapet. Then] the parapet [itself] was blown about, and Sergeant Scott was buried . . . We dug him out, little the worse [for wear], while their snipers potted at us through the breach . . .

Sutherland was also buried. The shock made him [behave] like a baby. I made him lie down and covered him up. [By this time], the fellows were all getting a bit rattled, so I walked along [the trench] . . . joked and asked questions . . . [That] left them all cheerful.

[At] about 3 [p.m.], I was sitting on the firestep . . . when a shell came right through [the parapet], and burst . . . I felt a tremendous weight fall on my left leg, above the knee, and, [when I came to my senses, I noticed I was] covered with blood . . . The air was full of groans and cries . . . Poor Newton, who was next to me, lay [in] a mangled dead mass on the floor [of the trench. Another man] was writhing, terribly injured, but alive. Adair's leg and arm were [hit] . . . causing him terrible agony. Sergeant Scott [who] had [had] his hip blown away . . . was [also] in great pain. King [had] had his hand blown off. On pulling down my trousers, I found my leg was covered in blood from a wound three inches above the knee. [I] fastened on a field dressing . . .

The shells [kept blowing] the trench in on the dead and wounded . . . The groans and cries, [combined with the] constant crash[ing of the shells], made a hell of the place . . . I . . . ordered all the sentries back . . . to their posts to watch for any signs of [an] attack, and supervised the carrying out of the worst cases. I was lying right in the 'gangway', and they could not help treading on my wounded leg as they passed . . . [I passed out.]

When I came to, [Lieutenant Edwin] Bazeley was bending over me. Just then another shell burst over us, and a splinter caught my other foot . . . Another piece wounded Bazeley, passing clean through his shoulder. There was a [great] . . . deal of blood. [Our men] . . . carried us out on waterproof sheets, as the worst cases had gone on the stretchers. The men could only carry us a few yards at a time . . . [They] ran from shell hole to shell hole. It was a dreadfully rough path. Rotten corpses were lying everywhere. One was on a stretcher, so my men tipped it off and dumped me and the waterproof on top of its loathsome dampness.

Both Wiltshire and Bazeley eventually made it back to the safety of the casualty clearing station. But as Clifford reported in his diary, his ordeal continued until that evening, when he and around twenty other men from his battalion were sent to replenish their supply of hand grenades from Sausage Valley: 'The communication trench being so open, it was a job for us to find any cover . . . Fenotti . . . was running across the open ground in front of me, when a shell landed under his feet . . . Only his head and shoulders were left behind . . . [The rest of us] . . . got back safely.'

As he recorded, on the way Clifford saw some horrific sights along the road leading to Pozières from the advanced dressing station:

It is nicknamed Dead Man's Road because both sides of . . . [it] are lined with dead Tommies and Australians. It is awful to see the way their bodies are mangled about, but the worst part is to see the gun teams driving over the bodies of the dead, and the wheels of the wagons crushing them up.

In the support trenches of the 22nd Battalion, we had to walk over dead men, and occasionally bits of men . . . half buried . . . Everywhere, there were blackened [corpses, . . . some] torn, [and some] whole.[11]

But as Clifford explained, it was the shelling once he returned to the front line that unnerved him most of all: 'We sat there in K Trench hour after hour, waiting to be killed or buried by the collapsing banks . . . The shock of the explosion of these shells is terrific. Dirt, stones, and pieces of metal were falling on us . . . and all we could do was crowd against the sides of the trench, while the earth-shaking explosives fell fast around us . . . [Some] men were buried alive . . . [and] dug out, only to be buried again.'[12]

The casualties suffered by the 24th Battalion during 27 July are not specified in its war diary, but they are unlikely to have been fewer than the 173
men lost by the 22nd Battalion, whose casualties included Captain Wiltshire.[13] Even these statistics were misleading. They did not cover those men
who, although still on their feet, were so shocked and dazed by lack of sleep
and the shelling that they were in no fit state to lead the assault on the ridge
north of Pozières. The same applies to the 5th Australian Brigade's 19th
Battalion, located on the east side of the village, whose reported casualties
were approaching 350 men, as well as the other battalions in that brigade,
who had suffered substantial losses during 26–27 July while supporting the
unsuccessful attempts of British troops to capture Munster Alley.[14]

That being the case, it is easy to see why General Legge wanted to bring
up fresh troops for his big attack, scheduled to take place at 12.15 a.m. during the night of 28–29 July. In his attack order issued at 5 a.m. on 28 July, he
specified that his 7th Australian Brigade should take centre stage, with the
5th and 6th Brigades relegated to the right and left flanks respectively.[15]
However, the decision upset the 6th Brigade's outspoken forty-three-year-
old commander, Brigadier-General John Gellibrand, who wondered how
the 7th Brigade's three battalions, without any prior knowledge of the area,
apart from that gleaned by their commanders from a last-minute survey,
could hope to compete with well dug-in German defenders. His pessimistic
expectations concerning the attack (reminiscent of the views of Brigadier-
General Harold Elliott of the 15th Australian Brigade prior to Fromelles)
were only intensified by reports that some of the 7th Brigade's staff were
inefficient.[16]

Nevertheless, again like Elliott prior to the Fromelles attack, Gellibrand
swallowed his misgivings, convinced by the message contained in the following words which he had read out to his troops before they went into the
line: 'It has been said that when you go out, twenty-five per cent of you
will be killed. You will be killed if you go forward. You will be killed if
you go back. It is better to be killed going forward!'[17]

Notwithstanding Gellibrand's reservations, the key role in the attack
towards the east was to be taken by the 7th Australian Brigade's 28th
Battalion, which was to advance towards the OG lines just to the north
of the Albert to Bapaume road. Before the attack order was issued, its
troops spent the night in trenches near Sausage Valley. Ernest Norgard, one
of its young privates, recalled afterwards: 'Sleep was impossible because of
the artillery, and [because] . . . of an awful stench, [the reason for] . . .

which none of us could account. So we put in long hours thinking of home ... As daylight dawned (on 28 July) ... being naturally anxious to explore our surroundings, we set out right away. Quite close to where we slept, [we found some] dead Germans. [They were] everywhere ... It was the most awful sight I had [ever] seen.' His account continued: 'At three o'clock our platoon commander ... assembled the platoon and addressed us with: "Well lads, we are going over the top. We go over tonight."'[18]

At 6 p.m. on 28 July the men making up the 28th Australian Battalion moved towards their jumping-off positions, in a shallow depression on the northern side of the junction of the railway and the Albert to Pozières road (see map 14). By the time they advanced, which they did fourteen minutes before the beginning of the intense softening-up barrage scheduled to start at 12.14 a.m., they could have had no illusions about the challenge they were facing. They had seen what the shelling had done to the men of the 19th Battalion they had passed on the way in. According to the 28th Battalion's Francis Mauger:

Most of them were broken ... [They were] big strong fellows, [but they] shook like leaves. Some of them just sat staring straight in front of them taking no notice of anything, while others talked hysterically ... the topic [being] ... the terrible effects of the great shells. Their nerves had completely given way. Most of them had been buried [by the shells' explosions] ... God knows how many of their mates they had seen blown to bits.[19]

Mauger's foreboding appears to have been shared by many of the soldiers in the 6th Australian Brigade, whose 23rd Battalion was to spearhead the advance to the north, its objective being the ridge north of Pozières' cemetery. Their anxieties can only have intensified with the rumours that greeted them as they approached the front. When Victor Graham, a nineteen-year-old motor mechanic serving with the brigade's 21st Battalion, asked some French civilians whom he encountered west of Albert what was making the air smell so bad, he received the chilling response: 'Boo coo Australie fini Pozières.'[20]

After the battle, the 23rd Battalion's Private Fred Hocking, an eighteen-year-old clerk from Melbourne, would write to his 'Dear old Father' about what he had witnessed. In his letter one of his most vivid memories was of how the 1st Australian Division veterans had put the wind up those going into the line by telling them: '"Oh don't worry, you'll all get skittled. In a charge up there, the first wave gets cut down to the last man." That heartened us up,' he wrote, 'since we knew that . . . our platoon was in the first wave.'

However, by the time Hocking and his battalion arrived in the reserve lines, south of Pozières, all his worst fears had been miraculously swept away: 'As I looked over to Pozières, where the shells were bursting thick and heavy, I felt as if I didn't care what happened. My senses were numbed,' he informed his father. That did not stop Hocking responding to his major's comment 'There'll be very few men in the [German] trenches, if any', with a sceptical 'Not arf, as the cockneys say.'

Hocking's letter to his father suggests that he was much more impressed by the pre-attack artillery barrage ordered up by Legge than Haig had been: 'As a quarter past twelve approached, the bombardment swelled . . . to unbelievable proportions. The ground rocked and reeled under the terrific rain of shells, as [our] guns belched out on the German position. It was like the climax of a thunderstorm [in] . . . hell. Suddenly the order came: '"First wave get ready. Fix bayonets. Advance!"'

While the front-line troops were surging forwards, the tension grew in the 6th Australian Brigade's Headquarters a long way to the rear. It was monitored by Charles Bean, the Australian journalist embedded with his country's forces.[21] The scribbled notes in his notebook set the scene for the disaster that was about to unfold in the following terms:

I came up for this, the first big attack by the 2nd Australian Division, to Gellibrand's HQ in Sausage Valley. All the brigades' [headquarters] are very far back [from the front line], quite close together in deep German dugouts. I am writing this in Gelly's bedroom, 20 feet under the ground [which] . . . some German commander had turned into something like a well-upholstered railway compartment. [In the room there are] dark wooden battens, stone-coloured wallpaper, electric light fittings, [and] a bunk on which Gelly is now lying. He is very seedy. The telephone by his bed leads to the 7th Brigade.

The first timed entry in Bean's account, recorded at 12.14 a.m., confirmed that at least the artillery was on schedule: '1 minute intense bombardment. Never heard anything quite like it.' But it also contained the disturbing observation: 'A fair amount of m.g. fire in several places before this started.' This suggested that in spite of all the talk about needing to take the enemy unawares, the Germans had seen the Australians coming.

Bean's account goes on to describe how his eyes nevertheless searched the night sky for signs of the attack's success. He knew that if it proceeded according to plan, the red German flares, which had soared up into the sky over the Pozières heights at the beginning of the attack, would gradually peter out. But as his chronicle reveals, although the number of flares diminished at first, they obstinately failed to subside completely: 'At 12.55 a.m.,' he wrote, 'Flares still going . . . I can hear a[n] m.g. [7th Australian Brigade's Brigadier-General John] Paton has rung up asking if this does not seem to Gellibrand curious. Also, he wants to know why they have no news.'

Unfortunately, Gellibrand had no easy answer, either then or for the next two hours, as Bean's chronicle of the flares' progress bore witness:

1.35 [a.m.] Flares still being thrown up constantly . . .
2.25 [a.m.] Still red lights over Pozières . . .
Gelly . . . cool as ice, obviously had battle on his mind, but slept between whiles.

It was only at 3.15 a.m., three hours after the start of the attack, that there finally arrived the first messages from the front which Paton had been craving. The news they contained could hardly have been worse. The message from Lieutenant-Colonel Jas Walker, commanding officer of Paton's 25th Battalion (the unit on the left of 28th Battalion), which had taken about an hour to be couriered from battalion headquarters, stated:

Captain [John] Nix has come in wounded and reports as follows: 'Jumping off point was left at midnight, and we proceeded to 300 yards of enemy's front line. Rifle and machine-gun fire was opened on them here about 7 or 8 minutes past midnight. The artillery fire up to 14 minutes past 12 was not heavy enough to keep the enemy down. The first objective was reached without very much trouble or many casualties. This line was very shallow. Only about 3 feet deep, and caused some confusion at whether it was the real objective or not.

The next waves pushed on towards [the] second objective, and were met with very heavy machine-gun fire, which caused a great number of casualties. The waves approached to within about 5 yards of second objective when, in addition to machine-gun fire, a considerable number of bombs were thrown. Captain Nix tried to reorganize this line to assault second objective, but had not sufficient men left, as they were being shot down fast, so the order to fall back on to first objective was given. On reaching first objective again, he had no men left at all, and had to come back to position held by 6th Brigade. Captain Nix thinks the best part of company are casualties ... about 120 [men] ... Captain Nix thinks the other companies fared about the same.'[22]

Subsequent reports concerning the advance by units on either side of Captain Nix's were, if anything, even more damning as far as Legge's planning was concerned. On the far right, south of the Albert to Bapaume road, German machine-gunners had spotted the 5th Brigade's troops more than an hour before zero hour, and had pinned down the advance before it started.[23]

The situation on Nix's immediate right, just to the north of the road, had much graver consequences: the 28th Battalion troops had reached the German wire in front of OG1, only to find it had not been touched by the artillery, leaving them as sitting ducks for the German gunners. Here there was slaughter on a scale not seen on the Somme since 1 July, one report describing how because 'the German wire remained intact', the 28th Battalion men 'could go neither forward nor back. They tore at the barbed wire with their hands, searching for openings' as German machine guns and artillery swept them aside.

Such was the ferocity of the German shooting that there were few witnesses able afterwards to report in detail on what occurred. The only traces today are in the Red Cross Wounded and Missing files, which contain letters from the surviving soldiers designed to help families discover what had happened to their loved ones. One such letter describes the heroism of the 28th Battalion's Lieutenant Paddy Bell, who, perhaps fired up with the excitement of the charge, or perhaps because he was a spirited Irishman who preferred to go down fighting, jumped onto the unresisting wire still clutching his revolver and shouted: 'We'll gallop through this!'[24] One of the last recorded sightings of this courageous twenty-six-year-old officer stated that after he was 'shot through the forehead', his corpse, which like another of his brother officers was 'terribly lacerated, almost in shreds', was left hanging on the wire. It was an undignified end for a man described by one of his subordinates as 'a bonzer officer, one of the best', who was 'very popular with the men'.[25]

Another witness was moved to write: '... it was an awful sight to see our poor ... [men] hanging lifelessly on the wire entanglements ... and it was sickening to hear ... our chaps' ... moans and groans'.[26] Such horrific sights, which must surely have even surpassed the pessimistic expectations of those who had seen the shell-shocked troops on the way in, prompted

Francis Mauger to conclude: the Germans put down 'a perfect barrier' of machine-gun bullets and bombs 'all along the wire . . . In about fifteen minutes the 28th had ceased to exist . . . We never had a chance.'[27]

Fortunately for the Australians participating in the advance towards the north, the artillery had done a better job of cutting the wire in front of the German trenches to the north of the Pozières cemetery. In the following extracts from his account, Fred Hocking does not even mention the wire as constituting an obstacle, when he and his comrades in the 23rd Battalion advanced towards the German front line:

On and on we went. It seemed miles. The bullets whistled past me, and men were falling everywhere. But I took no more notice of them than [I would if I had been] . . . in another world. Out of the 200 who started in the first wave, only about 40 were now left. Our major was ahead roaring out 'Come on 23rd!', although we didn't need any telling, for we were barging along as fast as our loads would let us.

All of a sudden we saw the Germans. [It was] my first chance to get at them . . . The few of us who were left bolted on. We felt equal to attacking a [whole] battalion . . . They waited until we were within about 20 yards of them. Then they threw [their] . . . bombs at us. They went off in a wall of flame a few yards in front [of us. But] still we ran on. Young Macdonald, who was with me, roared out unmentionable . . . [swear words]. He was as mad as a tiger, [and as he ran], he shook his head like a great dog.

'Right,' I said. 'Stick the bayonet into them. Take no prisoners!' But the Germans ran like rabbits . . . across to their other trench. [At that moment], my greatest desire was to kill one [of them]. The dozen of us that were left set [out] after them. Then, biff! I was lying on the ground. [In a way I was lucky. I heard] the machine guns . . . crackling . . . Thousands of bullets were screeching just above me. Had I been up[right], I should certainly have been riddled.

I'd like to have a talk to those people who say that bullets didn't hurt when they hit . . . I lay on the ground . . . and literally bit the dust . . . After that, it seemed to go red hot. The machine guns having slackened a little, I looked at my leg. Little spurts of [blood] . . . were coming out of it . . . I'm done, I thought. But I undid my puttee, and [then] wound it round tightly, and . . . started to make a bold bid for it . . . As soon as I started to crawl, my leg started to give me what for, with the rough jerks I had to give it. I'd gone what must have been about 100 yards . . . when I found one of our sergeants in a shell hole . . . We hailed each other with delight, and started off afresh . . . It's marvellous what a man will do when [his] life is at stake. We at last reached the trench where the remainder of our battalion had dug in.[28]

Hocking eventually made it back to the casualty clearing station in the rear (ending up in England), but not before the 23rd Battalion was forced to give up around two-thirds of its hard-won second objective.[29] Although the 7th Brigade's 26th Battalion, on the 23rd Battalion's right, temporarily captured and held its portion of OG1, its officers ordered the men to retire after seeing that Captain John Nix and the 25th Battalion, on their right, had been forced to fall back to their starting position. That made it impossible for the 23rd Battalion to hold on to the right side of the ridge it had captured, exposed as it was to gunfire from OG1.[30] But the left side of the ridge, north of the Pozières cemetery, was held, making it the only success story of the night, a poor return for the loss of so many men: approaching 1,500 casualties, including more than 450 from the 28th Battalion.[31]

Amongst those listed as missing from the 28th Battalion was Noel Sainsbury, a twenty-year-old private. Several months were to elapse before his father William, who ran an agricultural auctioneers and produce sales business in Perth, heard convincing proof that his son had died. William Sainsbury received a letter from Wisbey Sinclair, a captured Australian soldier, who confirmed that Lance Corporal George Bruce-Drayton, another prisoner of war from the 28th Battalion, had seen Noel lying dead in the German trenches. Accompanying the letter was a YMCA ticket retrieved from Noel's pockets.[32]

It is unclear whether Noel's father and his mother, Georgina, ever discovered the true circumstances of their son's death, which appear to be contained in Bruce-Drayton's statement in Noel Sainsbury's Red Cross file. According to Bruce-Drayton, Noel 'was a Lewis gunner, [who] was captured a few minutes before me. He was wounded in the right leg and [was] sitting in the trench when I came in. A German officer, who could speak English, cross-questioned him, and said: "I will soon finish you." . . . Then [the German] shot him twice in the head and chest saying, "That's what I do to English swine."'[33] Probably, and some might say thankfully, Noel's parents were never shown the evidence of their son's traumatic last moments. If not, perhaps they were comforted by the verdict of Wisbey Sinclair, their correspondent in the German prison camp, whose letter contained the following more soothing words: 'It is comforting to know he died with his comrades in a good cause.'[34]

There was to be no such closure for the parents of the thirty-year-old Lieutenant Goldthorp Raws, who mysteriously disappeared during the 23rd Battalion's attack on the ridge north of the Pozières cemetery. A court of inquiry, which heard evidence from two witnesses on 12 August 1916, concluded that '. . . there is not sufficient evidence forthcoming to show the definite fate' of this officer, who was therefore officially classed as one of the missing.[35] Before coming to this conclusion, the court heard from the 23rd Battalion's Private John McGuire, who stated:

I was a member of C Company . . . and on the night in question was in the first wave of the attack. We were mixed up with . . . units of the 7th Brigade . . . Sometime during the attack, I distinctly heard Mr Raws' voice urging the men keep their line . . . We advanced right over Brind's Road which was our [2nd] objective (see map 16) for a distance of about 150 yards. Just about here I saw Mr Raws in the light of a German flare. The word was then passed that we had gone too far, and that the road was further back. With a lot of others, I immediately went back to the road, and started to dig in. I asked the men about me if Mr Raws had come back, but they could not tell me. When I last saw Mr Raws, he must have been within 50 or 100 yards of the [next line of] German trenches in front of us.[36]

Private McGuire's evidence, which suggested that Lieutenant Raws might have been abandoned behind the German lines, was contradicted by the following report from the 23rd Battalion's Lance Corporal James Alliston, who had mentioned the missing officer to a doctor in a casualty clearing station: 'He appeared . . . to know Mr Raws personally, and said that Mr Raws had passed through his hands with wounds in the head, and had been sent on.'[37]

This evidence provided the backdrop to the extraordinary correspondence between Alec, Goldthorp Raws' older brother, who happened to be serving in the same battalion, and their family back in Australia. In the first letter of the series written to Lennon, their older brother, on 3 August, Alec broke the news about 'Goldy' in the following terms:

Goldy is 'gone': quite probably taken prisoner and all right. If killed, he could not have died in agony, because our stretcher bearers were out in No Man's Land that same night, and then the next day, and he couldn't have been missed. I was out searching for him myself the next night, and the German flares made it all as bright as day . . . He may have been taken away wounded by the brigade on our left.[38]

Five days later Alec wrote to his sister:

Goldy . . . is either dead, [a] prisoner, or wounded in the head, so that he is more or less blinded (an extra detail he must have been given by James Alliston, the witness at the court of inquiry that Alec attended) . . . I shall tell Father and Mother that he has been wounded, but will recover . . . and that I don't know where he is yet.[39]

That was followed by a letter to his brother-in-law confirming: 'I've told Mother and Father he is wounded, but that I don't know his whereabouts. I had to tell them something.'[40]

By 16 August the 'white' subterfuge was wearing thin, prompting Alec to write to his sister: 'If he is posted as missing by the time you get this, it will mean he has not been traced to any hospital . . . I write of him as still alive, but it must be admitted that hope ebbs.'[41]

It was only on 19 August that he finally came clean with his father, telling him: 'There is no further news of Goldy . . . If he has not been found by the time you receive this, he will have been posted as missing. In fact he is already posted as such . . . I would advise you to place no great hope on Goldy turning up as a prisoner, unless he is notified as such, because though the chance is there, it would be foolish to cling feverishly to what would probably prove a groundless hope in the end.'[42]

The precise circumstances behind Goldthorp Raws' disappearance will probably never be known. But just over a month later the most likely explanation was noted down in his Red Cross file following an interview with the 23rd Battalion's Corporal William Begley. Although Begley had become deaf, and could only speak in a whisper, the result of shell shock and concussion, he was able to convey the following facts to his interviewer: 'While we were charging across at Pozières, Lieutenant Raws was about 20 yards from me. I saw a shell land near where he was, but never saw him after. That is the last I saw of him. [I] think he was blown to pieces.'[43]

It seems to be this report, together with the corroborating account of a second soldier, which finally persuaded the authorities in January 1918, about sixteen months after the action on the ridge north of Pozières, to confirm they were satisfied that Goldthorp Raws had been killed in action.[44] Only then could his family abandon the campaign they had waged to prove that he had died, thereby enabling them to wind up his estate and move on with their lives. Delays such as this highlighted the cruelty of war, not just to the soldiers, but also to those left behind.

The mid-August 1916 realization that his beloved brother had probably been killed provoked a strong reaction in Alec Raws, who until then had been very patriotic, leading him to conclude one letter to his older brother: 'I honestly believe Goldy, and many other officers, were murdered on [that] night . . . by the incompetence, callousness and personal vanity of those high in authority . . . I am so bitter, and the facts are so palpable, that it must be said.'[45]

27: On Parole

Guillemont, 30 July 1916

(See maps 2 and 15)

There are many reasons why attacks on the Somme were unsuccessful. As we have seen, it was sometimes because the German barbed wire was not cut. Sometimes there was not enough artillery. Sometimes the attack started too far back. But when it came to holding a post-mortem on why the village of Guillemont was not captured on 30 July 1916, there is a case for saying all of these failings, and more, were applicable.

Guillemont was to be one of the most important targets, if not the most important, for the general attack mounted by the 4th Army in combination with the French, on 30 July. As on 23 July when the last general attack had been made, villages, trenches and woods were to be attacked all along the 4th Army's front, with the added bonus that this time the French were to participate as well. They were to attempt to take Maurepas, south of the 4th Army's line, while Rawlinson's 4th Army went for Falfemont Farm, Guillemont, Delville Wood, Longueval, the Switch Line, Wood Lane (the trench connecting Delville Wood to High Wood) and Munster Alley.[1]

Guillemont was such a vital part of this mix because it was Haig's way of linking up with the French. If the village were once captured, the French were much more likely to be able to advance alongside the British on the north side of the Somme River. Haig believed that the two allies represented a much more formidable force when advancing side by side than when their attacks diverged in different directions.

However, if Rawlinson meant to help his master achieve his aim, he certainly had a funny way of going about it. Wasn't it GHQ policy that battalions should start no more than 200 yards away from their first objective (see Chapter 22, p. 280)? Yet here he was, permitting an attack where the 30th Division's 90th Brigade battalions that were to attack Guillemont and its surroundings had to cross no less than 700 yards of No Man's Land. That was the least of it: The troops within 30th Division's 89th Brigade, who were advancing to the south, had an additional 750 yards to travel before they reached their objective.[2]

Admittedly, such distances had not ruined Rawlinson's chances on 14 July (see Chapter 19). But that was a night attack. This advance on Guillemont was to be made in daylight; the start time had been changed from 4 a.m. when it was dark to 4.45 a.m. when it was light, to please the French. Attacking in daylight brought few benefits for the 30th Division troops who were going to attack Guillemont. Because the wire protecting the German position was on a reverse slope, British artillery observers could not see whether it had been cut. Nor could it be viewed from the air. On the morning of the attack there was a thick mist.[3]

We know that the wire was no longer an obstacle immediately to the east of the village because a detailed report was made about the 2nd Royal Scots Fusiliers, the one British unit which ventured inside Guillemont on the day of the attack (30 July). This report by that battalion's company quartermaster, Sergeant A. E. Borland, describes how his D Company passed straight through where the wire had been. It also contains an account of the critical moment when, after entering the village, Borland discovered they were in serious trouble.

His report appears to suggest that their advance into the village was more or less unopposed. Once inside, they had consolidated in a partly filled-in trench, with tree stumps growing out of it, that ran through the village. A crater behind it served as D Company's headquarters. Protection from being rushed while they were settling in was provided by two Lewis gunners, who were sent forward to act as a screen in front of the trench. They did not arrive a minute too soon, writes Borland. 'The covering party . . . reported that the Germans were gathering in front, and in some old ruins about eighty yards to the left front.'[4] That was only to be expected. But then a message arrived that caused consternation: 'Sergeant Bowman who had charge of the left patrol . . . came in and reported that he could not find any trace of the [18th] Manchesters (who were supposed to be protecting their left).'

The Royal Scots Fusiliers' Lieutenant Murray told Bowman to retrace his steps and when he found the Manchesters, he was to tell them to 'Hurry up!' This Bowman duly did, and he returned around forty minutes later to confirm he had found the Manchesters near the German wire. On being told that the Royal Scots Fusiliers were in the village, he had said he would join them there, and shortly afterwards a captain and about twenty men from the 18th Manchester Battalion joined them in the trench. The new intake took the party to around 200 men, enough to hold the line for a while, but not enough to resist a determined counter-attack. This was all the more worrying since they had seen a group of Germans moving round their left flank, evidently preparing to counter-attack them from the side or rear. The Fusiliers countered by swinging their left wing around towards the left so that it was facing the would-be German infiltrators.

On seeing what was coming Lieutenant Murray said he would go back to Battalion HQ, which was in a tunnel east of Trônes Wood, to seek reinforcements. He left the Manchesters' captain in charge, being the only officer available. The Royal Scots Fusiliers' 2nd Lieutenant Small, who had not seen action before, was beyond helping. 'It was his first time in action,' Borland explained, 'and his nerves would not allow him to move from the shell hole, or take any part in the [coming] fight.' But according to Borland, Lieutenant Small was not the only man amongst the defenders who had cold feet:

[Lieutenant] Murray had [barely] disappeared before the Captain called me over and told me 'We must retire.' I pointed out to him that our position was quite good, that [Lieutenant] . . . Murray would be back with ammunition and reinforcements long before the counter-attack and that if his battalion came up as he assured us [it would], there wouldn't even be a counter-attack.

The upshot was that the Fusiliers and the Manchesters stayed where they were. But when Murray had been away about forty-five minutes, Borland admits even he began to fear the worst:

At 9.15 [a.m.] I called in the covering party and Lewis guns, as they were being enfiladed . . . I was afraid to leave them out any longer in case I should not be able to get them in later . . .

I then asked the Captain if he would send a message back to Battalion HQ, as I feared [Lieutenant] . . . Murray had been knocked out. He replied: 'I can't address your Commanding Officer; send it yourself.' I therefore wrote the message saying that our position was likely to become untenable, that ammunition and reinforcements were essential at once, that I was utterly unable to cope with it myself, as the left flank was entirely open, but that I could with luck hold on half an hour or so.

Before the message was sent, the Manchesters' captain once again said that they should all retire. Borland's account contains his response:

I replied: 'It's up to you then to give the order.'

He said: 'I don't belong to the RSF, so I can't give the order.'

I answered: 'I do belong to the RSF, and I'll never give that order.'

His account describes the action he took, as the Germans, who by this time were firing at anyone who showed themselves above the trench parapet, closed in:

About 10 o'clock (a.m.) one Lewis gun was knocked out . . . 'I called to the other gun[ner] to come . . . and take its place as that . . . position was the best in the trench. The gunner . . . was killed as he ran [to do my bidding], but another gunner crawled out under murderous fire, retrieved the gun and got it into action.

[However] the loss of the gun crippled us. The German fire became [even more] intense. So, although I knew it was only a forlorn hope, I asked [Lieutenant] . . . Small if he would try to get back to HQ, [with a view to] bring[ing] relief. He immediately assented . . . and started off [moving to the rear], bobbing from one shell hole to another in a wonderfully cool way. The Germans concentrated all their fire on him, but as long as I could see him, he kept bobbing on.

Shortly afterwards Borland was distracted by another piece of bad news. About a dozen men from the battalion's C Company had come into the trench from the rear. They informed Borland that their Company had been more or less wiped out, including their commander and company sergeant-major, who had both been killed. Sure enough, when he peered out of the trench, he saw that Germans were now advancing towards their rear. Until that point he had been lying on the lip of the shell hole using the parados of the trench as a rifle rest. It was a relatively safe position since his head was concealed from the Germans by a tree and its foliage. But this new development changed all that. The sight of the approaching Germans meant the game was up. While the Manchesters' captain ran off shouting 'Retire!', Borland endeavoured to direct the men towards the platoon of A Company away to their right (south):

The men were . . . out of the trench, and [they were] bunching . . . They were [being] shot down like sheep. I shouted to them to get back into the trench, and [then] to move along towards A Company. About twenty of them did so . . . I ran along the parados and . . . reached A Company [too] . . . But . . . the Germans . . . seemed to be everywhere. I jumped into a shell hole, and [had] just managed to bury my haversack which contained . . . important documents and maps, when three Germans . . . [leaped] on top of me, [and] stripped me of my equipment . . . I was a prisoner.

It was a humiliating end to a courageous last stand. Looking on the bright side, Borland was extremely fortunate to survive. The other side of the coin revealed a bleaker picture: the failure to capture Guillemont was not just down to bad luck. The preparation of the attack against the village and the strongpoints that supported it had not been carried out carefully.

The British force that entered Guillemont had been too weak, and its formation too full of holes for it to be able to repulse counter-attacks. The gap between the Royal Scots Fusiliers' companies on the east of the village and its companies on the west side appears to be one reason why the Germans were victorious. They never had to engage all units in the battalion simultaneously. The British vulnerability as a result was exacerbated by its artillery's shortcomings. It did not cut the wire in front of a significant portion of the German position north of Guillemont's quarry (see map 15).[5] Furthermore the artillery did not manage to quell the machine-gunners operating out of Guillemont's railway station as well as in the quarry.[6] As a consequence German gunners within these strongpoints were able to repulse attacks launched by the 2nd Division's 5th Brigade (towards the station) and 90th Brigade's 18th Manchesters (towards the quarry), and were able to act as bases for the men sent to harass any British forces entering the village centre.[7]

The repercussions for the 2nd Royal Scots Fusiliers, the spearhead of the whole operation, make grim reading. The battalion sustained no fewer than 650 casualties, including in excess of 550 killed or missing, the total figure for the battalion amounting to almost 50 per cent of the casualties for the whole of the 90th Brigade, which came to around 1,400.[8]

Their attack had not been helped by equally significant failings to the south of the village, where no unit even approached Falfemont Farm, the principal objective there; the only landmark captured by 30th Division's 89th Brigade was the German strongpoint within Maltz Horn Farm (see map 15).[9] Not that the French fared any better; they failed to take their main target for the day, Maurepas.

The one 'highlight' within the subsidiary attacks made by the 4th Army that evening, at 6.10 p.m., was the capture of one half of a German position known uninspiringly as Intermediate Trench, to the west of High Wood.

There was to be no great leap forward which would stun the world and convince the public that their commander-in-chief's tactics were proving successful.[10] That being the case, it is not surprising that there was disquiet in London about the lack of progress as the first month of the conflict came to an end. However, rather than being played out in public or in the newspapers (as would be the case today), protests were merely voiced by politicians to other politicians.

The following extract from the 1 August 1916 memorandum that Winston Churchill had circulated within the Cabinet raised the fundamental question: would Haig and Rawlinson ever break through?

The month that has passed has enabled the enemy to make whatever preparations behind his original lines he may think necessary . . . A very powerful . . . artillery has . . . been assembled against us, and this will greatly aggravate the difficulties of further advance.

Nor are we making for any point of strategic . . . consequence . . . What are Péronne and Bapaume, even if we were likely to take them?[11]

Churchill's question was batted away by the War Committee. But even without the benefit of hindsight, it is hard to see why the politicians did not take advantage of the head of steam that was building up against Haig's Somme adventure. If he really was not going to break through on the Somme, would it not have been better if he had started a new attack elsewhere, where there was a chance of taking the Germans by surprise? Sir William Robertson, the Chief of the Imperial General Staff, evidently thought they should at least address this question when he wrote to Haig on 29 July: 'The Powers that be are beginning to get a little uneasy in regard to the situation. In general, what is bothering them is the probability that we may soon have to face a bill of 2 to 300,000 casualties with no very great gains additional to the present. It is thought that the primary aim – relief of Verdun – has to some extent been achieved.'[12]

Haig was upset to find that he was being audited by the man whom he expected to defend him against political interference. But in his reply he gave Robertson what was needed to disarm his critics: Firstly, he was not going to sanction any attacks that were not well prepared and likely to succeed. Secondly, carrying on as he was, chipping steadily away at the German defences, would be likely to pay dividends in the long run. According to Haig, a lot had been achieved already. As well as taking the heat out of the German actions at Verdun and against the Russians, the Germans had 'used up' no fewer than thirty divisions on the Somme in just one month, compared with thirty-five in five months at Verdun. At that rate 'in another 6 weeks, the enemy should be hard put . . . to find men.' Furthermore Haig believed that 'the maintenance of a steady offensive pressure will result eventually in his complete overthrow'. As for the price, 'losses in July's fighting totalled about 120,000 more than they would have been had we not attacked'. Haig felt that such a figure, which was small relative to the losses being experienced by all the countries involved in the conflict, should not be the reason for terminating the offensive.[13] The members of the War Committee evidently agreed. They liked what they heard when Robertson read Haig's letter to them. That enabled Robertson to write back to Haig assuring him he had the government's support.[14]

Whether he would have had the support of the public if they had known the true facts is another matter. In such circumstances women, and in particular those women who saw at first hand the harshest consequences of the war of attrition to which Haig had become wedded, might have sent any government packing who backed him had they only had the right to vote.

Sister Edith Appleton, who was still in the General Hospital Number 1 in Étretat at the end of July, was one of the nurses who saw the wounded men at their most vulnerable. One wonders how she would have voted after she had finished caring for James Lennox, the twenty-four-year-old private in the 12th Royal Irish Rifles. During the battle north of Thiepval on 1 July he had been wounded. A bullet or a piece of shrapnel had become lodged in his diaphragm, a wound that condemned him to a slow, agonizing death.

At first the soldier whom Edith Appleton referred to as her 'poor little chest boy' had a painful internal abscess. Then his temperature shot up to 104 degrees as the iron bullet or shrapnel poisoned him. That prompted Edith to 'wish him well away, where he will only know about happy things'. For one glorious day, however, he appeared to be getting a shade better. His temperature came down. But even then, as Edith recorded in her diary, 'he . . . does not look right and has such a quick pulse. I think he will die quite soon.'

No such luck. James Lennox was doomed not to escape so easily, and two weeks after she wrote wishing he could pass away, she was called upon to write to his fiancée, and to his mother who had written to Edith asking whether her son could write to her. There was no question of him doing the writing for himself. He was so weak it was even hard for him to turn his head. 'I . . . wanted him to tell me his own words,' Edith recalled when she wrote up that day's diary entry:

But all he said was 'I don't know what there is you could say.' I knew his mother was his greatest anxiety, and so wrote: 'I am no stronger at all. But I have tried my hardest to take all my food and medicine, and to get well.'

He said: 'Yes, say that I wanted her to know just that.'

Edith finished her note about him in her diary with the words: 'I don't think he'll be detained longer than this week, and hope not for his sake.' But Lennox confounded all her expectations, and it was only on 23 August that he finally passed away, prompting Edith to write in her diary: 'Never have I seen such a slow painful death! It was as if the boy were chained to Earth for punishment. Towards the end it was agony for him to draw his little gasping breaths. And I felt I must clasp my hand over his nose and mouth, and quench the flickering flame. I am very glad for the boy to be away.'[15]

28: Second Time Lucky

Pozières Heights, 29 July–4 August 1916

(See maps 2 and 14)

On 29 July 1916, the very day when Sir William Robertson was writing to warn Haig that questions were being asked about the slow progress in France, the British Commander-in-Chief was already taking steps to ensure that at least one of his commanders would 'buck up'. It was the tactics employed by the Australian Major-General Legge that had irked him into action. In Haig's diary note for that day he described what he had done about it: 'After lunch I visited HQ Reserve Army, and impressed on (General) Gough (commander of the Reserve Army) and his SGSO that they must supervise more closely the plans of the Anzac Corps. Some of their divisional generals are so ignorant, and like so many colonials, so conceited, that they cannot be trusted. I then went on to the HQ Anzacs at Contay.'

There, Haig sternly dressed down 1 ANZAC's commander, Lieutenant-General Sir William Birdwood, and his chief of staff Brigadier-General Cyril Brudenell White, for not having supervised Legge, a man whom he took to be a 'buck stick' (a braggart) without any of the knowledge that might have supported his decisions. Then, taking them over to the map, the better to illustrate the elementary mistakes that had been made, Haig warned them with reference to their successes in Gallipoli: 'You are not now fighting "Bashi Bazouks". This is a serious scientific war and you are up against the most serious scientific nation in the world.' Curtly swatting away White's attempt to interrupt him, he interjected: 'Listen to what I am saying young man. I am giving you the benefit of my experience', before going on to explain what they should do next time.

Above all else, Haig believed they must insist on a thorough softening-up operation by the artillery and the digging of assembly trenches not more than 200 yards away from the German front line before they attacked again. As the meeting drew to a close, White, ignoring a warning shake of the head from one of Haig's staff, said: 'I can't let you go sir without responding.' He then proceeded to point out some of the mitigating factors, which included his judgement that whatever the impression given by Legge's mannerisms, he had certainly not undertaken the attack in a light-hearted spirit, and would now take on board all Haig's suggestions. Haig, whose account of the meeting showed that he appreciated White's willingness to take the criticism on the chin, replied: 'I dare say you are right young man.'[1]

Following the visit, the repeat attack on OG1 and OG2, which that morning had been scheduled for the night of 30–31 July, was quietly postponed to allow time for the assembly trenches, advocated by Haig, to be dug.[2] Given that 1 ANZAC's artillery adviser had told Birdwood and White that the necessary shelling of the German wire and trenches could be completed in a day if that was required, the speed at which the assembly trenches could be dug became critical.[3] Legge hoped that the digging could be completed in time for the attack to go ahead on 2 August.[4] In the event that it could, a programme of artillery firing was agreed upon which would fit in with that date.[5]

The first serious attempt to have the trenches dug, during the night of 31 July–1 August, was obstructed by the German artillery. It was reacting to the ill-advised decision to include spells of very intense shelling within the preliminary bombardment at a time when the 7th Australian Brigade's troops would be out digging. As a result, virtually no work was done on the 7th Brigade's front during the night. That prompted Legge's chief of staff on 1 August to instruct the brigade's commander Brigadier-General Paton:

This trench to be dug tonight is most important . . . I do not think your officers . . . realized it last night. I would like you to put a senior officer in charge tonight to see the thing through. We may have to put up with some casualties, but all the ranks should know that the work is to save our men in the attack . . . The 6th Brigade got half of their line down last night and expect to finish it tonight. Will you give this your personal attention?[6]

When, notwithstanding their forecasts, neither 6th nor 7th Brigade was able to complete their assembly trenches during the night of 1–2 August, White took it upon himself to visit all three brigades to find out the true situation. Legge, optimistic as ever, had told the Reserve Army staff that the trenches would be finished during the night of 2–3 August, so that the attack could go ahead on the evening of 3 August.[7] The Reserve Army staff officers were most put out when White begged to differ. They cited Legge's forecast, at which White retorted: 'Well, you can order them to do it if you like, and of course they will do it.' But he then went on to tell them what still needed to be done. They quickly backed down and the attack was scheduled for the night of 4 August, at 9.15 p.m., a time when it would be daylight as the assault began, but dark before German artillery had a chance to register their guns on the captured trenches.[8] None of the brigadiers wanted to risk compromising the attack on account of their troops losing their way because they could not see.[9]

As on 29 July, the attack would be led by three of the 7th Brigade's battalions, only this time it would be the 27th Battalion just to the north of the Albert to Bapaume road, with the 25th Battalion on its left, and the 26th Battalion on the 25th's left.

The 6th Brigade's 22nd Battalion would be on the extreme left, and the 5th Brigade's 20th Battalion on the extreme right of the attack south of the Albert to Bapaume road. The 5th Brigade's 18th Battalion would be on the 20th Battalion's left, with its own left side positioned beside the road.[10]

The reaction by the BEF's top generals to the postponement underlined their ignorance concerning the front line. That night Haig wrote in his diary that he had met General Gough, commander of the Reserve Army, while out riding. 'He (Gough) said [the] Australian Corps had again put off their attack. I thought the cause was due to the ignorance of the 2nd Australian Division's staff and that the GOC (General Officer Commanding) Legge was not much good. He (Gough) had called for his (Legge's) reasons in writing as to why this delay had occurred.'

Legge would subsequently defend himself by saying he had always stated that his forecasts were based on the understanding that the conditions in No Man's Land made the digging feasible.[11] That does not entirely exonerate him. His estimates were unrealistic, and he had failed to set up a system that would ensure he received accurate intelligence about the diggers' progress. His superiors might have looked on him more indulgently if he had placed liaison officers with the digging battalions so that they could have physically checked out what they were told. Or, at the very least, they could have talked to the officers in charge of the digging, for example the 23rd Australian Battalion's Lieutenant Alec Raws.

Alec Raws, whose brother Lieutenant Goldthorp Raws had gone missing during the 29 July attack, was one of two junior officers in charge of the 23rd Battalion's assembly trench-digging party. He appears to have been on duty during the night of 31 July–1 August.[12] He and Lieutenant Lionel Short had taken over from the battalion's Captain Frederick Ward, who had been mortally wounded earlier that night. As Raws recalled, in a letter

that he subsequently wrote to his sister, their problems started long before
they reached the site where the trenches had to be dug:

The first night [when] I went right up to the front line, [we] . . . had to march for
three miles under shellfire, go out into No Man's Land in front of the German
trenches, and dig a narrow trench to be used to jump off from in another assault. I
was posted . . . to bring up the rear and prevent straggling. We went in single file
along communication trenches. We were shelled all the way up, but got absolute
hell when passing through a particularly heavy curtain of fire which the enemy
was [laying] . . . on a ruined village (Pozières) . . .

In the midst of this barrage, our line was held up. I went up from the rear and
found that . . . about half of us . . . had been cut off . . . from the rest of the battalion and were lost. I would gladly have shot myself, for I had not the slightest idea
where our lines, or the enemy's, were, and the shells were coming at us from . . .
three directions.

We lay down terror-stricken along a bank. The shelling was awful. I took a
long drink of neat whiskey, and [then] went up and down the bank trying to find
a man who could tell [me] where we were. Eventually I found one. He led me
along a broken track and we found a trench. He said he was sure it led to our lines.
So we went back and got the men. It was hard to make them move. They were so
badly broken. [But in the end] we found our way to the right spot out in No Man's
Land. I was so happy that I did not care at all for the danger . . . [although] we
were being shot at all the time . . . I [had been told] that if we did not finish the job
before daylight, a new assault planned for the next night would fail . . . We had to
drive the men by every means. And dig ourselves. The wounded and killed had to
be thrown on one side. I refused to let any sound man help a wounded man.

Just before daybreak, an engineer officer, who was hopelessly rattled, ordered
us to go, [although] the trench was not finished. I took it on myself to insist on the
men staying, saying that any man who stopped digging would be shot. We dug
on, and finished amid a tornado of bursting shells. All the time . . . the enemy
flares were making the whole area almost as light as day. We got away as best we
could.

I was again in the rear going back . . . [Once] again, we were cut off and lost. I
was buried twice . . . with dead and dying. The ground was covered with bodies
in all stages of decay and mutilation . . . I would, after struggling free from the
earth, pick up a body . . . and try to lift him out with me, [only] to find him a
decayed corpse. I pulled a head off [one man], and was covered with blood. The
horror was indescribable.

In the dim misty light of dawn, I collected about 50 men and sent them off . . . on the right track for home. Two brave fellows stayed behind and helped me with the only unburied wounded man we . . . [found] . . . We got down to the first dressing station. There, I met another of our men, who was certain that his cobber was lying wounded in that barrage of fire. I would have given my immortal soul to get out of it. But I simply had to go back with him and a stretcher-bearer. We spent two hours in that devastated village searching . . . But all [the men] we found were dead. The sights I saw during that search, and the smell can, I know, never be exceeded by anything else the war may show me.[13]

If only Legge had appointed a liaison officer to sift through testimony such as this and to report back to him during the morning of 1 August, he would have saved himself from a lot of the criticism that came his way because he was believed to be out of touch.

Alec Raws' other correspondence, which tracks his transformation from eager patriot to bitter would-be whistleblower, contained additional lessons. One of the most important was that if the brigadiers persisted in driving their men forward without any restraint, then even those who evaded the German shells might end up as nervous wrecks, in no fit state to conduct further operations, let alone return to normal civilian life after the fighting had finished.

Just two weeks earlier, the prospect of being in a real-life battle had seemed so exciting. Raws had then written to his brother-in-law: 'I am quite excited, Norman, because I go out tonight to the fighting line . . . Tomorrow I shall be in the midst of it all . . . There is something rather humorous in the situation . . . John Alexander Raws, who cannot [bear to] tread upon a worm, who has never struck a human being except in fun, who cannot read of the bravery of others at the front without tears welling [up] . . . I go forth tomorrow to kill and maim!'[14]

Yet after losing a brother, and two of his best friends, and going to hell and back on the front line, all that *joie de vivre* had evaporated.[15] In one indignant letter Raws told Lennon, his older brother:

I boil to see the war through in order . . . to expose some things the Australian public never dream of . . . Towards the end, it was useless to call for volunteers. The men were done . . . [and] they were also bitter. They knew that the more they did, the more they were called on to do. It seems impossible to think that I did . . . say most dreadful things to broken men to shake them into activity . . . I remember cursing a man as a shirker, and roughly shaking him, [only] to find him stiff in death.[16]

On 4 August, just hours before he had to lead his men up towards the front prior to the long-awaited attack, Raws wrote to a friend:

I go over in an attack on the German trenches tonight . . . My battalion has been in it for eight days . . . [Only] one third of it is left . . . We are lousy, stinking, ragged, unshaven, [and] sleepless. Even when we're back a bit, we can't sleep for our own guns. I have one puttee, a dead man's helmet, another dead man's gas protector, [and yet another] . . . dead man's bayonet. My tunic is rotten with other men's blood and partly splattered with a comrade's brains . . .

The great horror of many of us is the fear of being lost with troops at night on the battlefield . . . I have kept my nerve so far. The . . . difficulty is to keep it. The bravest of all often lose it. Courage does not count here. It is all nerve. Once that goes, one becomes a gibbering maniac . . . The sad part is that one can see no end of this. If we live tonight, we have to go through tomorrow night and next week and next month.[17]

Alec Raws' luck was to hold during that night's attack. At least he survived. But not before he had experienced a reprise of his worst nightmare, becoming lost at the head of a column of troops in Pozières. In yet another letter to his brother Lennon, he wrote: 'I had to drive men who were . . . blocking the way . . . in . . . [a] trench . . . ahead of us . . . with my revolver.'[18] Such blockages, which had become a feature of the 1st Australian Division's attacks, were to be just as much of a distraction for Legge's 2nd Australian Division. As a result of one such blockage, caused by the 7th Australian Brigade's 26th Battalion unexpectedly filing into a communication trench that was supposed to be reserved for the 6th Australian Brigade's 22nd Battalion, the greater part of the 22nd Battalion, the assaulting unit on the extreme left of the attack, did not reach its assembly trench until almost half an hour after zero hour.[19]

The account by the 22nd Battalion's Keith Anderson, a twenty-four-year-old sergeant who found his way barred, gives a hint of the desperation experienced by the men. Having waited patiently for the big moment, they found that poor staff work by their superiors was jeopardizing their plans, and their lives. In his account Anderson wrote:

4 August 1916: Tonight is the night of our charge. We have little time to think of what lies in front. But are busy receiving instructions and equipping.

[Shortly after] . . . 5 o'clock, we are ready to proceed to Pozières and slowly wind our way . . . in single file . . . up Sausage Gully . . . We are not long unmolested. Our movement is observed by two German aeroplanes, and the head of the gully is shelled. We turn off at a communication trench and work our way up to Pozières. We are caught in a very heavy barrage (the German reaction to the intense preliminary bombardment by the Australian heavy artillery between 5 and 6 p.m.), but get fair shelter in the trench, which however 'terminates', and it is necessary for us to get [out of the 'terminated' trench] into the open.[20] [However] we are held up [in another stretch of trench] and find it almost impossible to go forward. Men are getting wounded and there is little prospect of our reaching our assembly trenches by [the] schedule[d] time . . . The case is now desperate and word comes through to push on at all cost. Leaving the trench, we dash through Pozières down a sunken road and up K Trench. We [eventually] reach our assembly trench, but not without many casualties.

If OG1's left-hand section had been strongly held by its German garrison, this delay, which meant missing the protection of the three-minute barrage on the German front line, might have ruined not just 22nd Battalion's prospects of seizing its objectives, but also the remainder of the attack on its right. Its absence on the left would have enabled the Germans to spray their gunfire down OG1 and OG2, decimating the 7th Australian Brigade's battalions and simultaneously cutting them off from their lines of communication to the rear.

There was to be a fine line between success and failure. As Lieutenant Anderson's account bears witness, he personally found himself isolated and entangled in the remnants of the German barbed wire after the first wave of which he and his men formed a part was finally ordered to advance. But his account goes on to describe the heart-stopping moment when looming defeat was transformed into victory: 'There is a rousing cheer, and looking up, I see the 2nd wave coming up in grand style . . . Jumping up, I rush into the German trench which is hardly recognizable. We meet with little opposition, but capture some forty odd prisoners.'[21]

However, as described by 2nd Lieutenant Robert Blanchard, the one surviving officer of the 22nd Battalion company leading the second wave's charge, the limited opposition in OG1 and OG2 did not mean that German defences were toothless. A machine gun had been overlooked to the left of the trenches attacked, and there was always the possibility a soldier would be hit by a German shell:

I saw Major [Murdoch] Mackay (the officer who had led them past the blockage on the way to the assembly trench) killed. And as I turned round to tell (2nd Lieutenant Leslie) Pritchard . . . [who] was about 30 yards behind me . . . [that] he was now in charge of the Company, I saw him bowled over . . . I fear he must have been killed, as an officer from another battalion . . . gave me a detailed description of a lieutenant, whose body he had seen lying out in the same place two days later . . . I was the only officer who came out [unscathed] . . . out of the six of us.[22]

Although OG2 was taken as well, matching a similar success by 5th Australian Brigade troops on the extreme south of the attack, between the Albert to Bapaume road and the railway, and by the 26th Battalion of the 7th Australian Brigade that attacked just to the south of the 22nd Battalion, there was no cause for unrestrained celebration. The fallen twenty-four-year-old 2nd Lieutenant Pritchard and his brother officers were just some of the 22nd Battalion's casualties, which were approaching 300 by the end of the day, a much higher number than might have been expected in the circumstances had it not been for the easily avoidable mix-up on the way to the line.[23]

At least they had something to show for it. Frank Corney, a twenty-one-year-old lieutenant in the 26th Battalion, recorded in a letter to his mother his amazement at the scale of their conquest: 'I shall never forget the scene before us, and on our flanks, when daylight came. Germans were popping up from shell holes just in front of us, holding their hands, and coming in to be taken prisoners. There were not so many in our sector, but on our right they were coming in by the dozens. (Some 500 prisoners were taken by the 7th Australian Brigade, according to its after-action report.)[24] In the distance, we could see the enemy artillery and some infantry scampering for their lives over the hills [until they were] . . . out of sight.'[25]

It is perhaps not surprising that German defiance in the face of the attack was patchy at best, given the demoralized content of the correspondence found in some of the German prisoners' pockets. One soldier in the 18th Reserve Division's 84th Reserve Regiment had written on 2 August:

For heaven's sake send a food parcel. One cannot [get anything decent to] eat and there's nothing to drink . . . I cannot give you any more details, apart from the fact that the fighting around Pozières can best be summed up in one [or two] word[s. It's hell!] For what's happening here is like nothing else on earth. There are heaps of corpses, a horrible stench and wire lying amongst pieces of dead men. The 84th [Reserve] Regiment has lost at least two thirds of its strength . . . We're now 600 yards back. Tomorrow we go back again to the front line. We are desperate! No time for more . . .[26]

Another German soldier in the same regiment wrote on the same day: 'We went into the line with 180 men. Now we're down to 30. The whole battalion only has around 200 men left. Now we are being reinforced with another 40 to 50 men. Ready for more slaughter. The best solution would be to get a minor wound . . .'[27]

One of the captured German officers from the 17th Reserve Division's 162nd Regiment, who appeared to assume there had been a more significant breakthrough than had actually taken place, asked his captors: 'Are you in Courcelette?'[28]

The falling morale in the German front line does not appear to have infected their machine-gunners whose ceaseless shooting punished any mistakes by the Australians. The 26th Battalion's progress had created a second problem. Once again it could have been avoided. After all the attack postponements prior to 4 August, in order to make sure the assembly trenches had been completed, when the 26th Battalion troops came to deploy opposite their portion of the front, they discovered that their stretch of assembly trench had not been dug. As a result, they occupied the assembly trenches that were supposed to be held by the 25th Battalion, the assaulting unit on their right. This measure set off a chain of events that was to have extremely undesirable consequences as far as the 7th Australian Brigade's units were concerned.

The 25th Battalion's troops, unable to proceed into their portion of the assembly trench, found themselves cooped up in Sydney Street, the communication trench that led back from the assembly trench to the rear, and this in its turn delayed some of the troops in the 27th Battalion, the unit ordered to attack on the 25th Battalion's right. Fortunately, aided by the fact that the deployment was carried out in daylight, most of the troops could be hurried into position just before the attack commenced. Only the 27th Battalion's fourth wave 'suffered severely' because of the difficulty encountered, being pinned down by German artillery as its men advanced from the support trenches, which it would have vacated earlier had there not been this snarl-up.[29]

One of its casualties was the officer leading the company forward, the forty-two-year-old Major Trevor Cunningham, who consequently could not prevent the survivors drifting away from their planned advance line. This exacerbated the problem caused by the yawning gap between the 27th Battalion troops who had made it into OG1, and those in the 25th and 26th Battalions, who perhaps disoriented on account of their last-minute assembly, strayed to the left of their allocated targets in OG1 and OG2.

As for Major Cunningham, his name was included on the missing list, one of the 7th Australian Brigade's 942 casualties on 4–5 August.[30] According to the battalion's adjutant, Cunningham's batman, who was with his master as they advanced, was partly buried by a shell. 'When the smoke cleared away, he could not see anything of Major Cunningham. [The Major's] . . . broken . . . glasses were found a few days later . . . I am afraid he was killed and [then] probably buried by shellfire.'[31] Although his death was officially registered at the end of September 1916, his family had to wait no fewer than nineteen years before his remains were finally dug up, along with his identity disk, rank badges and one gold cufflink with his initials 'T.R.C.' engraved on it.[32]

Notwithstanding these Australian misadventures, Germans in all the 7th Australian Brigade sectors of OG1 and OG2 were routed sooner or later. Some were cornered in their dugouts before they could climb out on the lifting of the three-minute burst of intense shelling on OG1 commencing at 9.15 p.m. Others surrendered or fled to the rear following the intense ten-minute shelling of OG2. However, thanks to the dislocation within the Australian ranks caused by the initial failure to complete the digging of the assembly trenches, for a time the fate of the stretch of OG1 south of 'the Elbow' (see map 14) hung in the balance.

It was supposed to have been captured by the 25th and 27th Battalions. But for several crucial hours it was guarded by just four Australian machine guns, making it vulnerable to a counter-attack. Also the 27th Battalion's sector of OG2 was temporarily abandoned by the Australians, once it was realized that the trench had been more or less obliterated by their heavy artillery and that the diverted troops from the fourth wave were not available to dig a replacement. The Australian presence in the vulnerable portion of OG1 was only reinforced, and the 27th Battalion's section of OG2 and the ruin of the windmill beyond (see map 14) were only finally captured, after the first of several German counter-attacks was repulsed shortly before dawn on 5 August.[33] It was only then that General Legge could legitimately claim to have taken all the planned objectives.

That did not mean there had not been serious errors on his watch. In the wake of over a thousand casualties sustained during the operation, there must have been some parents who wondered whether their son's injury might have been prevented by better management at the top. One particularly heartbreaking case involved the 22nd Battalion's Lance Corporal William Hatcher, who was just twenty years old. A gaping hole in his stomach caused by a shell splinter or bullet had left his young life hanging by a thread by the time he reached the 3rd Casualty Clearing Station in Puchevillers (about ten miles north-east of Amiens).

He was watched over there by a Sister M. Aitken, who at his request wrote to his parents, Thomas and Eliza, back in Victoria shortly after his death on 7 August. Her letter started with the words: 'I have the worst possible news for you', before going on to describe how he had been admitted to her hospital the previous day, having been severely wounded in the abdomen, only for his condition to gradually deteriorate. 'He . . . passed away peacefully this morning at 10.30,' she noted. 'My heart ached for you so far away from your loved one. Rest assured we did what we could for him. He had a nice comfortable bed, and every attention from us all. We did our best, but the issue was in God's hands.'[34]

It would be nice to think that Sister Aitken's warm letter reached the Hatchers before the formulaic notification dated 31 August from the Base Records Office in Australia. It included the words: 'I regret to advise you that no. 739 Private W. L. Hatcher, 22nd Battalion, has been reported wounded, the nature of which is not yet known here. It is not stated as being serious, and in the absence of further reports, it is to be assumed that all wounded are progressing satisfactorily.'

The formal notification that unfortunately the wound had been more serious than anticipated and that William had died of his wounds was only finally drafted on 15 January 1917, which would have been a painfully long delay for his parents had it not been for Sister Aitken's intervention.[35]

29: Counter-Attack

Pozières Heights, 5–7 August 1916

(See maps 2 and 14)

During the morning of 5 August 1916, General Gough, commander of the Reserve Army, had the following message sent to the 2nd Australian Division's headquarters. 'Warm congratulations on the complete success of last night's operations which have inflicted a severe defeat on the enemy . . .'[1]

However, tacked on to the bottom of the version relayed to the division's brigades was the admonition from General Legge: 'GOC (General Officer Commanding) . . . wishes to impress on commanding officers the necessity for holding what we have'. Whatever criticism could be levelled at Legge for what had happened during his division's first attempt to take the Pozières heights, now that they had been taken, he could not be accused of not warning his brigadiers that they should be prepared for all eventualities.

Legge was right to be concerned. For his part, General Fritz von Below, commander of the German 1st Army, circulated the following order to his commanders:

The Pozières Plateau . . . must be recovered whatever the cost. If it were to remain in British hands, it would give them a big advantage. Attacks will be made by waves 80 yards apart. Troops who reach the plateau must hold on until reinforced, however many men are lost. Any officer or soldier who fails to resist to the death on ground captured will be court-martialled immediately.[2]

However, the realization that the battle for the Pozières heights might shortly begin again left Legge facing a dilemma. If he 'played safe' by packing OG1 and OG2 with troops, he ran the risk of their being decimated once the almost inevitable bombardment started. On the other hand, if he reduced the number of soldiers in the front line, it would give the German infantry the opportunity to recapture what they had just lost. It was the impossible attempt to square this circle that was to turn at least two of the Australian battalion commanders against their own leaders.

Interestingly, both of them came from the Leane family. One of them, Lieutenant-Colonel Raymond Leane, the thirty-eight-year-old commanding officer of the 4th Australian Division's 48th Battalion, had achieved such notoriety within Australia for his daring exploits at Gallipoli that the official historian rated him 'the most famous fighting commander in the A.I.F. (Australian Imperial Force)'.[3] He was supported by his brother Ben, who acted as his adjutant at Pozières. But it was their older brother, Major Allan Leane, the forty-four-year-old commander of the 7th Australian Brigade's 28th Battalion, who was the first in the family who felt the need to temper the Army's insistence on obedience with what he felt was right.

This conflict was to come to the fore in relation to the portion of the OG lines just to the north of the Albert to Bapaume Road that was supposed to have been grabbed by the 27th Battalion. It was Allan Leane's 28th Battalion which had stepped into the breach, and had driven away the first German counter-attack on the newly captured heights, and which had rushed forward to occupy the part of OG2 that 27th Battalion had felt obliged to abandon (see Chapter 28).[4]

At 6.18 a.m. on 5 August, Allan Leane was able to report to Brigadier-General Paton of the 7th Australian Brigade that his men had more or less secured the 27th Battalion's objectives. Given the tenuous nature of their occupation, Leane must have been surprised to receive Paton's 7 a.m. message telling him: 'If situation permits, and there is now no counter-attack, your two companies should . . . [be] withdrawn from OG1 and OG2 to our original front line.'[5]

It was an instruction backed by Legge, who had warned Paton: 'It is possible that the counter-attacks are intended by enemy to cause you to keep men in [the] front line while they shell you.'[6] However, at 8 a.m. Allan Leane replied: 'Situation does not permit of any withdrawal. Three companies of 28th are in front line and are urgently required there', a response that was repeated after German artillery started pounding OG2 for the first time since it was captured, a prelude to the renewed shelling of the entire area occupied by the Australians.[7] Leane only deigned to comply with the repeated order to 'thin out' the line shortly after midday, following the receipt of a direct order telling him to hold the trenches with Lewis guns and a minimum number of men.[8]

As if disobedience by one brother was not enough for one day, Allan's brother Ray, whose 48th Battalion was part of the 4th Australian Division's 12th Australian Brigade that had been temporarily placed under

Legge's command, also refused to obey his brigadier's orders.[9] He had been told he must take over the 27th Battalion's 600-yard front in the OG lines running from the Albert to Bapaume road up to the Elbow during the night of 5–6 August. He did not mind doing that. But as the following extract from his after-action account reveals, Ray Leane believed he had good reason to deploy his men as he thought best, after he had done a 'recce', without interference from those who had never set foot anywhere near the front line:

This front being unknown to me, I decided to take my adjutant (twenty-seven-year-old Captain Ben Leane, his younger brother), and company commanders to reconnoitre the ground before taking over . . . No [guide] . . . could be secured [beyond the Gibraltar blockhouse], so I decided to push on without one . . .

[At] the Cemetery . . . I was informed it was not wise to expose ourselves, since we were in full view of the Hun position. We [nevertheless] had a good look . . . and were returning, when a . . . battery opened [up] on us. Needless to say, we all got as close to the ground as possible! [Although] the trench in which we were located was full of dead . . . we were forced to remain in this position for nearly an hour. We were buried with earth several times. It was not a pleasant experience, and the effect of it caused two [of the] company commanders to be useless from then on. Both were evacuated with shell shock.[10]

Their shock is perhaps better understood after reading the fuller version of their ordeal in the shallow communication trench that Ben Leane sent to Phyllis, his wife back in Australia:

Our dead and the German dead were lying thick in it, still unburied. We must have shown our heads over the top, for very soon we heard a shell coming our way. We ducked just in time to miss it. From then onwards they peppered the trench, following us as we ran. At length we had to give up and crawl, and I can assure you now, it was no pleasant job to crawl over the top of bodies that had been dead for some days.

Shell after shell burst [a]round us, and at last there was a tremendous crash, and I felt the ground closing in on top of me. A big clod shoved my head into the bottom of the trench and I began to think the debris was never going to stop falling and I should be buried after a while. However I managed to wriggle out, and then I found that the side of the trench had been blown right in and had buried Ray and Roberts as well.[11]

Somehow they dug themselves out and made it back to where they had started. Ray Leane's account goes on to explain how in spite of all the risks he had taken to inform himself about the front line, army protocol meant that when it came to organizing his men, his hands were tied:

On my return to Tara Hill [my] orders were issued for the relief of the 27th Battalion . . . and a copy [was] sent to the Brigade. I had . . . [discovered] that there were no trenches worthy of the name forward of Tramway Trench (see map 14). Although . . . OG1 and OG2 existed in name . . . [they] were really [just] a mass of shell holes. It appeared to me that I could hold the ground more safely . . . by employing my strength in depth. I therefore decided to place two companies forward of Pozières [in the OG lines] with supports in Tramway Trench. The other two companies I placed in reserve at the Chalk Pit (south of Pozières) . . .

The Brigade Commander [Duncan Glasfurd] sent for me and informed me that he was not satisfied with my dispositions and ordered me to have the whole battalion in the forward positions . . . I told him I considered it a needless waste of men on account of the heavy shelling [and the absence of effective] cover.

We [nevertheless] moved off shortly after, and on my way forward I received a written instruction from the Brigade Commander confirming his previous order . . . I was now faced with . . . [a] problem. If I obeyed orders, I [feared] . . . that the men would be shot to pieces, and would be unable to withstand the counter-attack when it came . . . If I disobeyed the order and lost the ridge, my career [in the Army] . . . would be over. I decided to take the risk . . . [concerning] one company and placed it in the Chalk Pit . . . I placed [our] support [company in] Tramway Trench.

The move into the position was . . . [terrifying. There was] heavy shelling over the whole area . . . I lost over [100[12] men even] . . . before the trenches were reached.[13]

More were lost during the night. When Ray Leane, once again accompanied by his brother Ben, went to inspect the line the next morning (6 August), he reported there were 'dead and wounded everywhere'. Ben's description was more specific: 'The "trench" was simply an indescribable chaos of shell holes. The ground everywhere [had been] . . . pulverized [until] the whole area [was] of the consistency of ploughed ground to the depth of . . . six feet.'

After taking a look at 'the promised land' of Courcelette and Martin-puich, green and inviting after the desolation of Pozières, down in the valley beyond the crest on which they were standing, the brothers returned to their headquarters in Tramway Trench. Ben Leane later informed his wife:

Shells rain down like hailstones, exploding everywhere, changing regular lines of trenches into an unimaginable [series] of craters, men are thrown bodily into the air, others are torn asunder, others again receive great gaping wounds, and scores go down with such severe shell shock, that they are worse than useless. I have seen men trembling in every limb, weeping like babies, cowering at every explosion.[14]

It is no wonder that those men who had been holding the line were close to breaking point. On 5 August, Brigadier-General Paton of the 7th Australian Brigade had backed his plea to have his troops relieved by messaging Legge that 'the men are much shaken and exhausted, and [they are] losing heavily thanks to the incessant . . . enemy shell fire'.[15]

Lieutenant Alec Raws, whose 23rd Battalion had advanced on the extreme left flank of the 4 August attack, later described his torment, and his exhilaration, at being released from his supporting role in the following words, addressed to his surviving brother:

You say you hope[d] . . . the strain . . . had not been too great for me . . . It . . . was really bad. Only the men you would have trusted and believed in before [going into the line have] proved equal to it. One or two of my friends stood [up to it] splendidly . . . But many other fine men broke . . . Everyone called it shell shock. But [real] shell shock is very rare. What ninety per cent [of broken men] get is justifiable funk due to the collapse of . . . self-control.

I felt fearful that my nerves . . . [were] going [on] . . . the . . . last morning (6 August). I had [kept] . . . going with far more responsibility than was right for one so inexperienced for two days and two nights, [managing] for hours without another officer even to consult, and with my men utterly broken, shelled to pieces . . . After stand to at daybreak (on 6 August), I quietly curled up in a little funk hole in the front trench. I could just get my head and shoulders in, and my legs [were] all bent up across the trench which was only 18 inches wide. And I fell asleep for a blessed hour.

When I awakened, I was all right, and our relieving troops, glorious to see, were filing in . . . [Then] the barrage miraculously lifted behind us as we moved out. It had been a nightmare . . . to the last; . . . exhausted as we were, we did not see how we could get through [it] . . . We almost cried for joy, and would have leaped and laughed with happiness had our feet not dragged so heavily.[16]

But for every man who came out, another would have to go in. One of those ordered to march up to the front during the evening of 6 August was Ted Rule, a sergeant in the 4th Australian Brigade's 14th Battalion, another 4th Australian Division unit temporarily under Legge's control, which was to hold the line just to the north of Ray Leane's 48th Battalion. Sergeant Rule found what he observed as he moved up deeply disturbing. While waiting in a communication trench south of Pozières for some walking wounded to pass, he was transfixed by the sight of a shell-shocked soldier. 'He . . . [was] the picture of terror . . . trembling from head to foot,' Sergeant Rule recalled.

But that was nothing compared with the sensations that Rule experienced once he came closer to Pozières. While passing up a sunken road, he wondered why 'in this road we walked on, what seemed to be mud rose again like india rubber'. It was only when he came across a partly blown-in trench nearer to the front that he realized: 'Dead men were lying [in] . . . it. Some were partly buried with just an arm or a leg sticking out . . . It was here I came to know what that spongy feeling underfoot meant. It was the first time I had scrambled over dead [men] . . . I was . . . horrified.'

His state of mind was hardly improved by the answer to a question he put to one of the 28th Battalion soldiers he was relieving, about what he should do with the blanket he was carrying. 'His answer was that we would be damned lucky if we ever used a blanket again,' Rule remembered. Ray Leane, 28th Battalion's commander, gave an even more worrying reply when Rule, who had been left stranded in the supports without orders, asked what he should do: 'Get up to the front and help your mates. You'll be attacked tonight,' Leane told Rule.

After stumbling in the dark over more bodies and trenches, Rule appears to have ended up in Tramway Trench, the front line before the 4 August attack and now the support line for the troops in OG1. There he quickly found out what had transformed the soldier he had seen on the way in into a gibbering wreck: the roaring and crashing of the never-ending succession of shells searching for their trench, the clods of earth that thumped into their bodies, and every now and then the desperate shouts for help and the mad rush to dig out yet another soldier who had been buried after the explosion of a shell. Or in Sergeant Rule's words, it was:

one huge nightmare. . . . We sat huddled in the bottom of the trench resting against each other's knees . . . showered [again and again] with falling earth from the [shell] bursts. We tried to be cheerful, but the jokes were very feeble.

[Then], just as the first peep of dawn came into the sky, it struck me that . . . the shells were falling farther back. I was the first . . . in our bay to notice it.

A few minutes later Rule, peering through his binoculars, saw what he described as 'one of the queerest sights I have ever seen'. A line of Australians on the crest ahead, each man apparently locked in mortal combat with a German, as if fighting his own war, the ensemble being a melée of men fighting, shooting and some even on their knees as if praying for their lives. It was only later, after the fighting had died down, and a long line of German prisoners had been escorted past them to the rear, that he discovered what had happened.[17]

Concealed by the early morning mist on 7 August, the Germans had advanced at about 4.15 a.m. just to the south of the Elbow in the OG Lines, passing through the thin line of machine-gunners who were supposed to be holding them at bay, their advance enabling them to attack the 48th Battalion's left-hand platoon from the rear. After the garrison in OG1 had exhausted their supply of hand grenades and suffered several casualties, the young lieutenant left in charge, fearing that if he fought on they would all be massacred, surrendered.

If the Germans had quickly exploited their breakthrough, they might have cut through the sparse Australian defences and attempted to retake Pozières as well as its ridge. Their rapid advance had certainly alarmed Ray Leane. Although he was thankful that his refusal to obey his brigadier had enabled him the night before to replace the companies which had been decimated with fresh troops, and although he had sent his support company forward from Tramline Trench, for some time he had no idea what would transpire. According to the battalion's medical officer, his commanding officer did not plan to give in even if a whole German division appeared through the mist: 'Leane fixed a bayonet to a rifle, filled his pockets with bombs, and remarked calmly the bastards would never take him alive.'[18]

The fact that he was never put to the test was the result of the prompt action of another equally intrepid Australian officer: the 14th Battalion's Lieutenant Bert Jacka VC, who had been sheltering from the shelling in a dugout just to the north of where the Germans broke through. One report covering his action that morning suggests that the breakthrough might have been partly his fault. It stated that he had sent the five Lewis guns which had been under his command back to the rear because he felt he had enough infantry to hold the position without them.[19] Whether or not that report is accurate, what Jacka did to rectify the situation can only be characterized as heroic.

The *Official History of Australia in the War* describes how he reacted in the following terms:

Lieutenant Jacka had gone up at dawn to the trench [from the dugout] and found the bombardment still falling heavily. He had not long returned to the underground chamber when his men . . . were roused by a deafening explosion at the foot of the stairs. The attacking Germans had reached the dugout entrance and had rolled a bomb down the shaft. Two revolver shots were immediately heard. Jacka had fired at the German bomber up the stairway. At once he rushed up, followed by his men . . . [stumbling] over two of their groaning mates who had been maimed by the bomb. The enemy had swept past and could be seen in large numbers between this dugout and . . . Pozières. Jacka immediately decided to line up all the sound men he could find, seven or eight in number, and to dash through the enemy back to Pozières.

His men had hardly been drawn up when he saw the column of the 48th Battalion's prisoners and their escort returning towards them. He let them come to within thirty yards, and then jumped out of the back of the trench and charged. About half the German guards threw down their rifles, but the rest opened fire, and every man of Jacka's small party was hit with rifle bullets . . . The captured men of the 48th also broke away, some of them seizing the rifles of their guard, while the remainder of the guard tried to shoot them down.

It was the resulting melée, swelled by the arrival on the scene of more Australian troops from both north, south and west, that Sergeant Rule had seen. Jacka was in the thick of it, and in the course of the fighting he received a wound from which he nearly died. However, the fighting that he had instigated eventually ended in the way he desired, the Germans in their turn surrendering. The verdict of the Australian Official Historian could not have been more laudatory: 'Jacka's counter-attack, which . . . led to this result, stands as the most dramatic and effective act of audacity in the history of the A.I.F.'[20]

The petering-out of the German counter-offensive, which left the Australians holding ninety-one prisoners, turned out to be the last serious effort by the Germans to recapture either Pozières or its heights.[21] In the eyes of some, the repulsing of the counter-attacks was no cause for further congratulations. Critics of General Gough, 1 ANZAC and General Legge might suggest that it was their tactics which had acted as an open invitation to the Germans to make the counter-attack in the first place. In the eyes of such critics the way the generals conducted themselves earned them another black mark against their names, to add to those already chalked up after the abortive attack during the night of 28–29 August. There was certainly a significant human cost: the 2nd Australian Division's casualties soared to in excess of 6,800, and that was excluding those within the units borrowed from the 4th Australian Division.[22] Ray Leane's 48th Battalion had lost almost 600 men during its two days in the line, whereas the 45th Battalion, its sister battalion in the 12th Australian Brigade, had lost almost 340 men.[23]

These generals' supporters might respond that the tactics leading up to the counter-attack could hardly be faulted, given the additional casualties that must have been suffered if OG1 and OG2 had been packed with troops on 5–7 August. Whoever is right, what is beyond doubt is that after all the ups and downs, the Australians had won a great victory, and in the words of the war diarist employed by one of the units in the 7th Australian Brigade: 'the two [OG] lines captured [and held] brought the [strategically important] Pozières Ridge into [the] possession of the British [once and for all]'.[24]

30: The Back Door

Mouquet Farm, 7–15 August 1916

(See maps 2 and 16)

After struggling to harness the mercurial but unreliable Major-General Legge, the generals in charge of the Reserve Army and 1 ANZAC could be excused for breathing a sigh of relief when he departed from the battlefield to be replaced by the much more conservative commander of the 4th Australian Division, the fifty-six-year-old Major-General Sir Herbert Cox. He took over command of the Australian front-line sector on the Somme during the morning of 7 August.[1]

One important point in his favour, from his superiors' point of view, was that although he had spent much of his career in the Indian Army, unlike Legge he was English, and consequently did not feel he had to use his elbows to make his voice heard. There was no danger that Cox would need to curry favour by exaggerating what could be achieved. The downside was that he could hardly be called inspiring. John Monash, who was to become Australia's most famous general, was certainly no fan. Monash served under Cox at Gallipoli, and described him as 'one of those crochety, livery, old Indian officers, whom the climate had dried and shrivelled up into a bag of nerves'. However, Cox had other strengths. He made up for his lack of charisma by being a stickler for detail, and for discipline.[2]

Not surprisingly, that did not endear him to at least some of the Australians who had to serve under him. It only accentuated the clash of cultures that occurred when men from such different backgrounds were thrown together. On the one hand there were Cox and his British staff who wanted everything to be carried out just as it was in the British Army. On the other hand there were the Australians who agreed that discipline was necessary on the battlefield, but who could not see the point of all the superficial rules and regulations that seemed so important to British officers.

The debate over which uniform to wear was a case in point. The distinctive Australian tunic was no longer being manufactured. Yet most of the Australians refused to wear the British version, even though that meant they often looked down at heel in the shabby uniforms they could not replace without compromising their desire to dress the Australian way. That was in marked contrast to the British officers who, according to Charles Bean, the Australian journalist embedded with his country's forces, 'were apt to carry the regard for dress . . . to the most vicious extreme'.[3] Bean put the different attitudes down to the different cultures: the Australian refusal to dress up sprang from the fact that 'the whole tendency is against being neat . . . Public opinion is against great care being devoted to a man's personal appearance, as being unessential and is all in favour of whatever is essential.'[4]

There was a similar clash concerning the way officers related to other ranks. Australian officers thought nothing of entertaining an NCO for dinner, yet this was regarded as out of the question by most of their opposite numbers in the British Army.[5] As Bean pointed out: 'the Englishman . . . is afraid of his officer [and] stands in awe of him as an acknowledged superior being of a different class. But the Australian does not stand in that sort of awe of his officer, because [they are all] . . . of the same class.'[6]

Australian officers were constantly on the lookout for talent amongst NCOs and in the ranks so that they could be offered commissions. This would have been anathema to Major-General Cox, for whom the impossibility of ignoring class barriers must have been reinforced by his postings in India, a society where the different classes and castes did not mix. He could not conceive how anyone might think that working-class men could discipline university graduates and businessmen.[7]

This hidebound attitude, if not held in check, could lead to unpleasant incidents. Before going into the line, the 23rd Battalion's Lieutenant Alec Raws was harshly reprimanded by a British officer on horseback who took him for a private. This prompted Raws to write to his brother telling him that some of the British officers 'address us as if we are low-born dogs'. According to Raws, the British officer in question, who had understandably not seen the star on his shoulder, the only sign that could have told him Raws was an officer, 'nearly rode over me . . . and then asked me why the Devil I didn't get out of the way . . . I asked him why the Hell I should get out of the way and also whether there was not enough f. . . . . . road for him without having to ride over me.' This seemingly insolent reply apparently made the British officer apoplectic – he furiously threatened to take Raws to the nearest guard tent – and the altercation was only terminated after Raws finally admitted he was an officer too. '[On hearing this],' Raws continued, 'he looked me over and raised his eyebrows . . . and said "Oh, an Australian. Of course." And as he rode off I heard him [mutter something which included the word]: "Impossible!"'[8]

A related bone of contention concerned the Australian soldiers' refusal to salute their officers. 'It goes against our grain to make these fine fellows salute us when they somehow feel it demeans them to do so,' Raws told his brother.[9] This clearly irritated the British. To such an extent that in the middle of the struggle at Pozières, a message from General Gough was handed to the commanding officers of the 2nd and 4th Battalions informing them that their men were not saluting his car when it passed, although the general's flag was prominently displayed on the bonnet, and concluding: 'This practice must cease.'[10]

It is against this general background that one must view Major-General Cox's exasperation with his Australian charges. It boiled over after he observed their casual marching during their move to the Somme on 13 July. His severely critical verdict, recorded in the 4th Australian Division war diary, states:

The march discipline of the infantry marching in could scarcely be worse. The day was cool and cloudy, the march from 10 to 15 miles only . . . There may have been some excuse for men being sore-footed, as a large number of the Australian-made boots are very bad and required renewing. But there was no excuse for the manner in which men fell out without permission and straggled just as they pleased for miles in some cases behind their units. They sat on carts, or put their rifles or kits on them without permission and were generally ill-disciplined.[11]

Cox could not be blamed for being worried by what he saw. The 14th Battalion's Sergeant Ted Rule confirmed that: 'Hard as we were, we had men lying out along the roads for miles, too exhausted to go farther.'[12] This prompted the circulation of an order the very next day that started with the words 'The march discipline of the troops of the Division yesterday was very indifferent', and went on to list the worst misdemeanours. 'Men . . . were allowed to straggle in twos and threes behind their units', 'transport was covered with the rifles and equipment of men who looked perfectly fit', 'men were sitting on the wagons', and 'the Divisional order as to not smoking between halts was generally neglected'. The remedy was as follows:

The General Officer Commanding is well aware that this will not be cured until officers make their men feel that to fall out while still being able to struggle on is a disgrace . . . But, as it seems to him officers are not aware of what goes on behind their units, he directs that . . . the officer commanding . . . will ride in [the] rear of his unit for the second half of every march . . . Men who fall out without permission . . . are to receive exemplary punishment . . . Officers . . . will take the name of every man who falls out . . . All such men will be paraded next day and medically inspected. If passed fit, they will be given two hours marching drill in full marching order daily till the next move their unit makes.[13]

Unfortunately for Cox, this did not have the desired effect. On 27 July a confidential memorandum was circulated to the battalion officers in the 4th Australian Division with an instruction that it be shown to all of their officers. It pointed out that 'it is wearisome to re-iterate the precautions to be taken and rules to be enforced in orders to maintain efficient march discipline. These have been laid down time after time. If officers cannot loyally do their duty to their men and to their commanding officers, they will be removed for incompetency.'[14]

However, if Cox hoped that mere words could tame the Australians, he was to be sadly mistaken. The 51st Battalion's Captain Thomas Louch has described the spectacle he witnessed two days later:

At Halloy-(lès-Pernois, 11 miles north-west of Amiens), we trained strenuously for the forthcoming battle . . . All went well until our last day there, July 28, when the 11th Battalion came back from . . . Pozières . . . and went into billets in the adjoining village of Berteaucourt-les-Dames. All the ex-11th [Battalion] men of the 51st Battalion went over to see their former mates, and after a convivial evening, returned home, many very much the worse for wear.

The next morning [when] we set out for Hérissart (11 miles to the south-east as the crow flies), it was very hot and there was a very long haul uphill . . . In their intoxicated condition, some of the men were incapable of keeping up with the march and fell out. The march discipline was appalling. This would not have mattered . . . had not the 4th Divisional commander . . . and Brigadier-General [Thomas] Glasgow (of the 13th Australian Brigade) chosen that morning to take up a position on the road to watch the Battalion on the march. Not knowing that they were to be there, the Battalion straggled past . . . The Brigadier and Lieutenant-Colonel (Arthur) Ross, [our commanding officer] were mortified.[15]

The episode was recorded in the 4th Australian Division's war diary in the following terms: 'The Brigadier reported that 310 men fell out with permission, 46 without. Sore feet was probably not the only cause for this, as last night the 1st Australian Division passed through and halted at some of the billets of this brigade . . . There were many meetings of old friends at estaminets and a good deal of liquor [was] consumed.'[16]

The division's war diary does not disclose whether or not Major-General Cox ever did persuade his Australians to march as smartly as their British counterparts. Regardless, both he and his Australians soon had more important matters to deal with after receiving 1 ANZAC's 7 August order to advance towards the north. It was to be the first of a series of attacks that represented the second stage of the plan to cut off Thiepval's lines of communication, capturing Pozières being the first stage. This new step-by-step approach would, it was hoped, eventually force German troops in Thiepval either to flee or surrender before they were surrounded. Alternatively, it would pave the way for the Reserve Army to attack Thiepval from the rear.[17]

The first major obstacle that had to be swept away by this northward move was another formidable German stronghold, contained in the trenches and cellars of a ruined property called La Ferme du Mouquet (Mouquet Farm). However, before it could be attacked, the three German positions to its south had to be taken, action that would be facilitated if, as planned, the British II Corps advanced simultaneously on the Australians' left.

The speed of the advance, and the direction of travel, was to be constrained by Haig's new-found zeal to only attack after careful preparation. This followed on from his recent exchange of letters with Sir William Robertson, Chief of the Imperial General Staff, about the growing concern in London over the high level of casualties despite the failure to break through the German lines. Haig's 2 August 1916 instruction to his army commanders, Gough and Rawlinson, written by Lieutenant-General Kiggell, Chief of the General Staff, made it clear that it was designed to free up resources for the part of the front which had to be mastered first – the areas in and around Guillemont, Ginchy and Falfemont Farm – so that the British could link up with the French. All serious attacks planned for the areas to the north-west, opposite III and XV Corps, were, for the moment at least, to be suspended. But Haig's instruction was also provoked, one suspects, by the desire not to upset 'the powers that be' in London.

Meanwhile, as the following extract from the 2 August order demonstrates, Gough, north of Pozières, and Rawlinson, while advancing towards the east, were supposed to perform a precarious, and some might say impossible, balancing act, giving equal weight to conflicting demands:

The operations . . . are to be carried out with as little expenditure of fresh troops and of munitions as circumstances permit . . . But in each attack undertaken a sufficient force must be employed to make success as certain as possible . . . Economy of men and munitions is to be sought for not by employing insufficient force for the object in view, but by a careful selection of objectives.[18]

Park Lane (the eastward extension of Ration Trench, also known as 5th Avenue; see map 16) was the first of the barriers that the Australians had to take if they were to progress northwards, After being pulverized by the artillery, most of it fell into the hands of the 15th Australian Battalion, part of the 4th Australian Division's 4th Australian Brigade, at the first attempt during the night of 8–9 August. The only reason why Park Lane had to be abandoned, and then retaken with even less bloodshed the following night, was because the British 12th Division's advance on their left was thwarted during the first attack. That meant the Australian troops were vulnerable to being attacked from their left.[19]

There were plans to carry on with similar small advances during the build-up to the next planned leap forward, but the second of these was foiled on 11 August by intense German shelling. As on 7 August, the counter-attacks were repulsed, but in a virtual repeat of the problems experienced by Ray Leane's 48th Australian Battalion (see Chapter 29), the troops employed by the 4th Australian Brigade's 16th Battalion were decimated – the battalion sustained over 400 casualties – and had to be relieved.[20] So much for limited attacks resulting in the 'economy of men and munitions', as requested by Haig.

The using up of the 4th Australian Brigade's resources explains why – as had happened with disastrous results prior to the 2nd Australian Division's 28–29 August attack on the OG lines – a unit without previous experience of the sector, the 13th Australian Brigade's 50th Battalion, was rushed up to the front line for the 4th Australian Brigade's next advance. It was scheduled for 10.30 p.m. on 12 August, its objective being the second barrier in front of Mouquet Farm, the eastward extension of Skyline Trench (see map 16).

It is hard to find precise details about this important step in the closing in on Thiepval. But in a letter written by the 50th Battalion's twenty-one-year-old Captain Harold Armitage, a trainee teacher before he joined the Army, he at least gives us some idea:

Since last writing to you, I have been to hell, and have had the luck to get back again . . . We left Albert on 12th August in the morning . . . Little did we think

that a few hours' time would see us over the top and well into a Hun's trench . . .
When we arrived at the support trenches, we got orders to go into some trenches
north-west of Pozières, and . . . [that night] we had to hop out and at them.

We set out for the jumping off place (Park Avenue), and got along very
well until half a mile from the front. And then we got iron foundries, Essen,
Krupp and Hartz Mountains thrown at us. The Huns knew the exact location of
the communication trench (one of theirs) and lobbed into a length of about 100
yards a shell every ten yards every five seconds. That is what the 50th got through
before starting work. The trench was absolutely smashed and we lost a fair number of men.

Our next trouble was to keep alive in the front trench . . . and for four and a
half hours, the Huns simply poured shells onto us . . . Then it began. 'It' was our
artillery preparation. Talk about a wall of bursting flame. We had to take about
[750] . . . yards of Hun trench and that [750] . . . yards had three minutes of awful
bombardment, a sheet of flame the whole length representing the burning shells.[21]
The dust from the explosions and the intense glare cast an orange glow over the
proceedings. While this was going on, we sneaked up to about 50 yards from the
objective. It was a weird sight. Our boys steadily advancing against a background
of solid golden flame. And the noise! It was terrific!

The artillery lifted back 50 yards . . . Then came the supreme moment of the
lot: 'Righto, Charge!' and with a sounding of whistles, we jumped up and charged
like blue hell across those few yards. My word the boys travelled! No cheering,
bayonets carried at high port . . . [until] we reached the trenches, or what was left
of them. We found only about 42 live men. The rest were 'knocked out'. Beresford
soon bombed these into the 'Kamerad!' attitude, but we only took five unwounded
prisoners.

Then work started. We had to dig in, almost a new line of trench. My word the
boys did dig. And we had a very decent line before dawn.[22]

But while Captain Armitage, whose C Company was on the right of the
attack, believed that his battalion and 13th Battalion on his left had been
successful, the position on the ground on the left was far from secure. This
appears to have been a direct result of the rushed preparations for the
advance, a state of affairs that was supposed to have been abandoned following Haig's 2 August instruction. Orders defining the objective had not
reached at least one of the left-wing platoons before the attack.[23]

As the following extract from 50th Battalion's twenty-one-year-old
Captain Jim Churchill-Smith demonstrates, there was a potentially fatal

350-yard gap between the battalion's B Company, which was on Armitage's left, and the battalion's extreme left wing:

Captain Hancock having been wounded . . . I was sent for, and left Albert at 9.30 a.m. on the morning of the 13th . . . As there were no communication trenches dug to the new front line . . . I was compelled to run the gauntlet across [what until the attack had been] No Man's Land to the . . . [captured position]. I got across safely and jumped into C Company's trench (Captain Armitage's position) . . . my way to the left passing through [first] C Company, and [then] B Company. I walked through a quarry (see map 16), which I believe was full of Germans. [I] had hardly got there, when a flare went up, and I at once saw I was nearly in . . . German lines . . . [I] turned back and called out: '50th Battalion Australians! Where are you?' . . . [I] heard a reply: 'Here we are. Come on.' I . . . made for the direction of the voices, and got into a trench held by Sergeant Mills and about twenty [of our] men . . . about twenty 'Derby' recruits . . . [from a British battalion] and 4 Lewis and 1 Vickers machine guns.

At about 10.30 p.m. the Germans attacked [the British] on my left, and forced them to retire [from most of Skyline Trench, also known as 6th Avenue, much of which had been captured at the same time as the Australians were making their 12 August attack] thus leaving me absolutely isolated. The Germans then bombed down the trench towards my position and killed [some] . . . of my men. Fortunately the Germans stopped . . . when about twenty yards from my position, and so we were all saved . . . There is little doubt they could have 'settled' the small number I had with me as I had very few bombs.[24]

The position of Churchill-Smith would have been weakened still further had he not dissuaded the British recruits from abandoning the post by threatening to shoot with his revolver any who tried to depart.[25]

While he awaited a reply to the message asking for instructions, which he sent to his battalion's headquarters the next morning (14 August), plans were being hatched to launch yet another attack that night. Its object was not only to relieve his post. The idea was it would, if successful, see the 13th Australian Brigade's 51st Battalion start the process of encircling Mouquet Farm by seizing the German line, Fabeck Graben, to its northeast (see map 16).

The 4th Australian Division's 13th Brigade had taken control of the northern portion of Major-General Cox's front the previous afternoon.[26] Its arrival appeared to coincide with a hoped-for uplift in British fortunes.

Although most of Skyline Trench had been taken back by the Germans, as mentioned above, Munster Alley had finally been captured at the same time as 4th Australian Brigade's advance on 12 August, thanks to III Corps' 15th (Scottish) Division's thrust along it, assisted by Australian bombers and machine-gunners.[27] Now there was the prospect of a significant advance in the bid to encircle Thiepval. Churchill-Smith records how 'relieved' he felt when he learned that the attack, featuring the 13th Australian Brigade's 51st and 50th Battalions on the flanks and the 13th Battalion, 'borrowed' from the 4th Australian Brigade, in the centre, was scheduled for 10 p.m. that night.

However, the reaction of other officers to the order for the attack, issued by the 13th Brigade at 5 p.m. on 14 August, could not have been more different.[28] In response to the vicious German shelling that had tormented the Australians for much of the day, the intensity of the German shooting having been sparked off by the capture of a British document stating that the impending attack on Mouquet Farm was part of the campaign to isolate Thiepval, the 50th Battalion's B Company sent the following message at 7.55 p.m. to its commanding officer: 'We cannot move. We have few tools, few bombs, no water, and the men are badly shaken [by the shelling]. At present we are digging a number out. I have too few men to take up the frontage and after consulting the [other] company commanders, have decided to remain fast.'[29]

Not surprisingly, this upset the commander of the 13th Battalion, who was supposed to advance on the right of 50th Battalion, while Lieutenant-Colonel Arthur Ross, whose 51st Battalion was to attack on the far right, echoed the views of the company commanders of 50th Battalion when he sent the following stark message to Brigadier-General Glasgow of the 13th Australian Brigade: '. . . 13th CO (commanding officer) thinks, and it is my genuine, (not [because I am] depressed) opinion, that it would be a mistake to press the offensive further in this salient. We are heavily shelled from due East right round to North West, and the communications are simply awful.'[30] It seems that the 13th Battalion was no better off, as Captain Harry Mount, its officer in charge on the front line, reported shortly before the attack: 'C Company rattled and only have 35 men.'[31]

The surviving documents do not disclose whether the parlous state of the troops' situation in the front line, and their commanders' morale, were shared with Major-General Cox before zero hour. His own morale must have been dented by the news that the Germans had recaptured Skyline

Trench on his right. Whether or not Cox was made aware of the dire situation and the commanders' declining morale, there was to be no reprieve for the men in the trenches. The source of the protest, 50th Battalion, appears to have been told that whatever their difficulties, they had to attack come what may. The battalion's Captain Harold Armitage described in his letter home what happened next:

On the 14th, he (the Germans) gave us seven hours of perfect 'inferno'. What a time we had! Few of us thought we'd get through that day . . . That night we were sent out on a very difficult stunt. We had to go out to the left and advance to dig in on the skyline (north of the quarry shown on the map, but south to south-west of Mouquet Farm with the battalion's left wing supporting Churchill-Smith's post further to the south-west). By this time we'd lost about two thirds of our men, we'd had no sleep . . . and the men were dead tired . . . We got out OK and forward into position on the objective, but Fritz spotted us and made our lives precarious with machine guns and shells . . . [Five officers were] wounded . . . I tried to get the men dug in, but after 30 minutes of hell, and vain endeavour with open flanks, I gave the word to get back to our line. I lost 43 men in a very short hour!

Churchill-Smith could not escape so easily. His ordeal at the reinforced post, which was to continue for another twenty-four hours, was made worse by demands from his own side: 'Next morning (15th) an aeroplane came overhead and called for us to show our position, which we did by sending up a green flare. But I am afraid the enemy saw where it came from as, immediately after, they set up a tremendous artillery enfilade fire which they kept going all day, causing many casualties. During the afternoon . . . [the British] company evacuated their position . . . [in] the trench owing to the heavy shelling . . . This made me isolated once more.'[32]

The torment that he, and those lying wounded in his post, must have endured is highlighted by what happened to Victor Dridan, a lieutenant in his early twenties in Churchill-Smith's battalion, who was wounded while on the way to reinforce the post. According to one witness at the post, Dridan had 'part of his right arm shot away. All the bone was gone between the elbow and the shoulder. The arm was strapped up [and] . . . it stopped bleeding . . . [though] it was not bandaged. He was in our trench from [about] midnight (during the night of 14–15 August) till about midday (15 August) . . . when he was [finally] carried away by a stretcher party.'[33]

Another witness's conflicting testimony stated that the arm was 'shattered . . . from the elbow to the wrist', thereby enabling him to apply a tourniquet above the elbow.[34] Whatever the exact nature of the mutilation, all witnesses agreed that Dridan, having been wounded, had to remain in the trench for much longer than was advisable. In the words of one of the witnesses, 'he could not be moved that night because of the British and German barrage fire'.[35] As if that was not enough, after he was taken away, a German shell exploded near the stretcher-bearing party on the long journey to the rear, killing one bearer, wounding another and terrifying Dridan who, notwithstanding his terrible injury, jumped up and ran for cover. In spite of the shock he must have experienced in this latest incident, he successfully made it back to the field ambulance operating at Warloy-Baillon, only to die shortly after his arm was amputated.[36]

Churchill-Smith and his men somehow held on at their post until they were relieved at 10.30 p.m. on 15 August. But there was no matching success story on 50th Battalion's right, an outcome that did not bode well for Major-General Cox's reputation. He had ignored Brigadier-General Brudenell White's recommendation that because the 1,200-yard-wide objective was a substantial distance (around 400 yards) from the pre-attack Australian front line, the 51st and 13th Battalions should advance to Fabeck Graben in two stages.[37]

Rather than adopting White's safety-first approach, which appeared to be in line with Haig's 2 August order to General Gough, Cox (like Legge for the attack on 28–29 July) had elected to take a relatively distant objective in one giant leap. He was not allowing time for deep assembly and communication trenches to be dug near the objective, which would conceal the men before zero hour.[38]

Although jumping-off trenches were dug, they do not appear to have been anything like those dug prior to the successful attack of 4–5 August, nor were they within the maximum distance (200 yards) recommended by GHQ.[39] The result was that the outcome of the central and right side of the 14 August attack was similar to what had occurred when there was an equivalent lack of preparation on 28–29 July. German machine-gunners appear to have spotted the 51st Battalion's troops on the extreme right as they deployed in No Man's Land, and their fire stopped the Australians in their tracks.

This had a knock-on effect. Although the 51st Battalion's left company reached the German trench, it was forced to retire after finding its left and right flanks were unsupported by other units. The same applied to the 13th Battalion, which had reached the German trench in the centre only to find it had to retire because it was unsupported on both sides.[40]

That evening the 51st Battalion's Lieutenant-Colonel Arthur Ross sent Brigadier-General Glasgow of the 13th Australian Brigade what amounted to a blistering critique of the plan hatched by Major-General Cox. Only it was couched in the polite language that generations of British officers are brought up and trained to use when making a complaint. Ross like Glasgow was British:

The intense barrage [on and in front of the objective] was of only 5 minutes' duration.[41] The objective is in some places almost 300 yards from my starting parallel and for such a distance, I suggest that a prolonged bombardment of say 20 minutes is necessary! The deployment start was made in good order . . . [However] the barrage . . . appeared to be 'over' as the enemy machine guns fired throughout . . . though I hate blaming artillery.[42]

Probably without realizing it, Ross had refuted the report exculpating the attack planners that Glasgow sent to Cox. The latter report stated that the reason for the enemy's quick reaction to the advance was that the 'enemy either anticipated our attack or was preparing an attack himself'.[43] It glossed over the fact that the planning was flawed.

As had happened during Legge's earlier check, there were tragic consequences, albeit on a smaller scale. The 13th Battalion came out of it relatively well; its casualties for the operations on 12 and 14 August were approaching 150.[44] However, casualties for the 50th Battalion were in excess of 400 for the two operations, while those from the 51st Battalion amounted to more than 300 for its single attempt to advance.[45]

One of those 300 was the twenty-five-year-old 2nd Lieutenant Oscar Chilvers, a bank clerk before the war, who eventually ended up in the 51st Battalion's A Company. This was the unit on the extreme right of the attack that had been held up by machine guns before it could reach the German trenches. According to one witness: 'Lieutenant Chilvers was wounded in the thigh in the charge. [He was] in No Man's Land about 150 yards from the German trench. He was able to walk but seemed to have lost heart and refused help to return to our lines. He remained sitting where he was.'[46] Another witness added: 'A [search] party went out the next morning to get in wounded. He was still out there [then], and could not be got in because of a shortage of stretcher-bearers. He could stand up, but lost his nerve and would not face getting in himself. That night again he was searched for, but could not be found. Shells were bursting all over the place. He must have been blown up by one of these.'[47]

Chilvers appears to be another example of those most unfortunate cases: condemned to be injured by the incompetence of his leaders and then swallowed up by the hungry battlefield so that his parents had to endure all the heartache of grieving for a son who for months was posted as missing. It was only in April 1917 that a court of inquiry ruled that he had been killed in action, a certificate of death being issued in July of that year. Only then could probate be secured by his mother Elenor and his sister Lucy, the executrixes of his estate.[48]

Unlike Legge, Major-General Cox was not to be given – in the short term at least – the opportunity for a second crack at the objective he had failed to capture. Cox's front-line units were relieved during the night of 15–16 August and the following morning, enabling him to hand over the front to Major-General Harold Walker, commander of the incoming 1st Australian Division, at 5 p.m. on 16 August.[49]

The 4th Australian Division's departure from the front was not intended as an implicit rebuke for a job not completed satisfactorily. There were other reasons for ringing the changes: apart from anything else, the division's casualties were already in excess of 4,750. Also, the amount of time that each division could spend in the line was restricted because of the desire to fit each of them in for a second 'tour' before they were loaded onto the trains heading north. These trains had already been booked for the last week of the month and the first half of September.[50] The 1st Australian Division was already scheduled to replace Cox's division before the result of the 14 August attack was known.[51]

However, that raises the question: how can it be fair that after Cox had failed to mount a sensible attack, there were no protests from on high, a marked contrast compared with what had transpired after Legge's setback on 28–29 July? There might be no simple answer other than that, unlike Legge, Cox had not made himself unpopular by challenging the status quo, a dangerous activity in a conservative institution such as the Army. The payback was that he would be protected for his one-off mistake. It was perhaps another manifestation of the hierarchy of misdemeanours that could be committed on the Western Front. It seems that causing hundreds of casualties inadvertently was a less heinous crime than rocking the boat.

31: Butchers

High Wood, 18 August 1916

(See maps 2 and 17)

Generals during World War I, particularly those who commanded troops on the Somme, have frequently been accused of being butchers, another way of saying they needlessly threw their men's lives away. Either that or when planning their attacks they did not consider the number of men likely to be killed or maimed as a result of their poorly thought-out plans.

In fact, it is not so surprising that generals, exposed to the level of killing which took place on the Somme, should have quickly become inured to the violence. What is sad is that no efforts appear to have been spent endeavouring to ensure there was some way of counterbalancing this trend. One wonders whether the propensity of the generals to treat their troops as if they were mere statistics might have been tempered somewhat if they had simultaneously been 'brainwashed' in the other direction. What would have happened if, for example, they had been force-fed a daily diet of some of the touching stories about the men they led – men like twenty-seven-year-old Alan Lloyd for instance?

Alan Lloyd was a lieutenant in the Royal Field Artillery (C Battery, 78th Brigade), whose eighteen-pounder guns were responsible for cutting the wire protecting the German trenches. Like thousands of other officers and men serving in the BEF, he was just an ordinary young man who had been sucked into an historic event. By the time he arrived on the Somme, after the initial 1 July thrust, he had a wife, Margot, and they had a young son called David. It is clear from his correspondence that they maintained a loving household. But what makes his letters to Margot stand out is their playful intimacy and passion, maintained in spite of his absence, in spite of everything.

In his first letters Alan attempted to reassure his wife that he was happy, and most importantly, safe, while at the same time being careful not to disclose more than was permitted by the censorship rules. 'We've been very busy lately,' he wrote on 6 July, 'and you can well guess why, because you were quite right in your little surmise. What a smart little wife for a dull Hub! We are . . . flourishing, and not having a bad time at all. It's great sport, advancing over the Hun trenches, and I hope it will continue. It's also much more comfortable, because the Hun has to take back his heavy guns and has only small stuff against us.'[1]

A week later he wrote to Margot:

Is small wife happy . . . because Hub is, and there's no reason why small wife should be anxious, because we're quite all right and enjoying ourselves though we have plenty of fighting . . . at present. We are doing quite well . . . and we are gradually pushing the Hun back. I don't think he likes it very much. He's bombarded all day and . . . night, and . . . gets blue Hell . . .

Don't worry belovedest little angel, all is going quite well, and Hub takes ever such care.[2]

But at the same time as he was telling her not to go overboard with fears for his safety, Alan was refusing to rein in his own feelings for her. The letter he sent on 19 July made it abundantly clear he found her irresistible, even at a distance. It began with the words 'Beloved little angel wife' and continued:

How is my little wife . . . Is she behaving herself . . . and not getting into any mischief, nor doing anything she shouldn't? Because Hub will come to her with a big stick . . . and give her this hard if she is a trial to anybody!

Hubbins is very well . . . He . . . dreams of his little wife, and gets very pash! Isn't he bad? Do you love him very much? . . . If so, why don't you send him some choccies.[3]

Three days later, in another letter wherein he was at pains to stress he was billeted well to the rear of the guns behind the front line, Alan informed Margot that nevertheless 'The noise of the guns was quite noticeable, and even at times rather trying. But your husband sleeps through it all like a top and wishes he could hug . . . his petite wife . . . and get "close" to her! Do you know what he means by this? He is a bad 'un when he thinks of your lovely little soft cuddlesome self with nothing on . . .'[4]

But Margot, it seems, only learned about the safe side of her husband's life at the front. In another letter, which appears to have been sent to a relation or friend the day before the romantic letter to Margot, Alan Lloyd admitted he had been 'FOO (Forward Observation Officer) several times, once in the big attack on his 2nd line, which was very successful. On this

occasion I was right up with the infantry and got a machine-gun bullet
through my tunic on the right elbow. It tore the shirt and vest [but] . . .
never touched the skin.'[5] None of this was mentioned to Margot. Instead he
wrote to her on 1 August about her holiday in Salterton, Devon: 'I wish
your hub was there too. What a time we'd have . . . We'd bathe together in
the briney, and do all sorts of funny things.'[6]

On 3 August, as if he knew his time was running out, Lloyd wrote no
fewer than three letters, including what turned out to be the last letter to
his wife. In it, he asked whether she would have wanted him with her in
Devon, whether their son David was well, before finishing with 'Hub has
had some lovely parcels from his little spouse. She is a darling.'[7] Perhaps the
'choccies' he had requested were among them. If so, one can only hope he
had a chance to savour them. The very next morning the forward observation post where he was located was hit by a shell, and he was killed.

On 5 August one of Lloyd's pals from the same brigade wrote to Margot
to tell her what had been gleaned from the reports of those who had been
with him: 'Poor old Alan was very badly hit,' Lieutenant Arthur Impey
informed her:

He never had a dog's chance, and died in about 20 minutes.

He was quite conscious, and asked if he was badly hit. They told him no.

He seemed quite happy, and in no pain . . . [He] said he would be all right soon.
He never knew what was really the matter, and died without knowing what was
happening.[8]

To the best of my knowledge no one has ever alleged that any of the commanders under whom Alan Lloyd served were directly responsible for his
death. But if they had known the details, and seen the correspondence
between this man and his wife, as well as samples of the correspondence
between thousands of other young couples who had been tragically affected
in the same way, one wonders whether the decisions they made and the
events that ensued might have turned out differently. There were several
sites on the Somme where the tactics employed might not have been what
they were had the men's welfare been paramount. Pozières, Delville Wood
and Guillemont are just three of the best-known locations where thousands
of lives were lost or ruined in the course of multiple badly planned attacks.
To that infamous list must be added another: High Wood.

This mass of trees, whose ominous dark outline showed up on maps as a diamond-shaped obstacle separating the German second position captured on 14 July from the third position that Haig wanted to assault in the next leap forward, had already been attacked four times before Alan Lloyd's death. So many corpses were littered between the roots of its trees and in the surrounding countryside that the whole area ended up epitomizing the horrific nature of the Somme experience. One witness who had been there noted how:

in the undergrowth of the wood, and in the standing corn which covered the entire area, lay the dead of many different regiments. The result was that, owing to the scorching summer weather, the troops in the line lived in an atmosphere of pollution and in a positive torment of bluebottle flies. In one sap in particular, as one moved along it, the flies rose in such clouds that their buzzing sounded as the noise of a threshing machine. In this sap, sentries could only tolerate the conditions by standing with their handkerchiefs tied over their mouths and nostrils.[9]

Another witness pointed out how 'in the . . . heat the air is fouled with innumerable dead so lightly covered that in unsuspected though extensive places one's tread disturbing the surface uncovers them, or swarms of maggots show what one is seated near'.[10]

According to a soldier from the 2nd Royal Welch Fusiliers, the corpses he saw just inside High Wood when his battalion was holding the line there in the latter half of July were not even buried: 'Some parts of the parapet had been built up with dead men, and here and there arms and legs were protruding. In one bay . . . the heads of two men could be seen. Their teeth were showing so that they seemed to be grinning horribly down at us.'[11] It is upsetting to learn that such hellish violence might never have occurred had the senior commanders responsible for attacking the wood only proceeded more carefully. And that is not just another reference to the missed opportunity on 14 July. On 20 July the 2nd Royal Welch Fusiliers, from 33rd Division's 19th Brigade, swept through the wood and for a glorious moment held most if not all of it, including its coveted western point.[12]

This point, which overlooked the terrain to the west of the wood, was never lost by British forces as a result of anything the Germans did. The divisional order to abandon it reached the battalion well before the German counter-attack, and the shelling, which eventually persuaded the Fusiliers they must withdraw to the south of the wood. It was later discovered, according to one of the participants, that a mistake had been made by the staff at General Horne's XV Corps, who should have been encouraging the division to reinforce the Royal Welch Fusiliers so that they could hold on to what they had captured, rather than telling them to retire from it.[13]

On the same day another lesson was learned that should have had an impact on future attacks. The troops of the 7th Division's 20th Brigade had tried and failed to take the trench known as Wood Lane, which ran from High Wood's eastern point to Delville Wood. This prompted the brigade's commander, Brigadier-General Deverell, to advise the 7th Division's General Watts that, in his view, Wood Lane could not be taken while High Wood and the Switch Trench, which ran through the north of the wood and to west and east either side of it, were in enemy hands.[14]

But this advice was completely ignored, with the result that a series of abortive attacks were mounted on Wood Lane – and the linked High Wood – over the coming weeks. One man who had reason to rue the failure to learn from past mistakes was the machine-gunner Private Arthur Russell of the 98th Brigade's Machine Gun Company, another 33rd Division unit. On 18 August, the day when there were attempts to advance all along the 4th Army's front, he and his gun team had been ordered to support the attack by the 4th King's (Liverpool) Regiment on Wood Lane. It was part of an operation led by three of the 98th Brigade's battalions, and it also targeted High Wood itself. But given that nothing significant had changed since 20 July, it is not surprising that the 98th Brigade fared no better than its predecessor the 20th Brigade.

Afterwards, Russell described the consequences for him and his six-man gun team as they entered the sap running forward into No Man's Land from the front-line trench:

A terrific explosion blew me off my feet. Earth and sandbags cascaded down and the sides of the trench caved in on top of me. Stunned and dazed, I dragged myself out of the tumbled debris . . . Two yards in front of me, the gunner who had been carrying the tripod lay face down in the bottom of the trench, with a large gory gash across the small of his back . . . He was groaning . . .

I saw another gunner on his knees, a great wound at the back of his neck from which blood was spurting freely. His head had gone forward, and his steel helmet held suspended by its strap was hanging down below his face. It was full of blood and overflowing. He was dead.[15]

So were two of the other members of the gun team. Although Russell and the only other survivor in his team were able to retire to the rear, there was no escaping the fact that the attack itself was yet another disaster. While some of the 98th Brigade troops entered the German trench inside the wood, and others penetrated the front-line defences in Wood Lane, none were able to hold out against the machine-gun fire coming from areas occupied by the German defenders. Consequently, in the end, all the 98th Brigade troops who could move had to retire to the positions from where they had started.[16] It was one of many disappointments that day. There were successes by British forces in the Intermediate Trench to the west of High Wood, and north of Guillemont, but the prime target, the village of Guillemont itself, remained in German hands.[17]

The fact that Rawlinson's 4th Army was making so little progress where it really mattered, and that Haig had decided to attack the German third position – running from Morval to Le Sars – from bases including Guillemont and High Wood, eventually provoked Haig to read the riot act to Rawlinson. In the following letter the Chief of the General Staff, Lieutenant-General Launcelot Kiggell, confirming what Haig had discussed with Rawlinson, told the 4th Army's commander in no uncertain terms that there had to be an improvement, or else. Concerning Guillemont, he wrote:

The only conclusion that can be drawn from the repeated failure of attacks on Guillemont is that something is wanting in the methods employed.

The next attack must be thoroughly prepared for, in accordance with the principles which have been successful in previous attacks, and which are, or should be, known to commanders of all ranks.

Kiggell went on to stress that notwithstanding the previous instruction that 'economy of men and munitions is to be sought', Haig wanted Rawlinson to use sufficient force 'to beat down all opposition'. He also hoped Rawlinson would allow 'the necessary time for preparation' so that subordinate commanders could study what they had to do, and pass on instructions to their men. At the same time, when working out the date of the next attack, which should be a general one, Rawlinson was to bear in mind Haig's demand that 'not a moment must be lost in carrying it out'.

However, it was what Kiggell wrote about the need for generals to play a more proactive role that highlighted Haig's dissatisfaction with Rawlinson's methods to date:

In actual execution of plans, when control by higher commanders is impossible, subordinates on the spot must use their own initiative . . . But in preparation, close supervision by higher commanders . . . is their duty . . .

It appears to the Commander-in-Chief that some misconception exists in the Army as to the object and limitation of the principle of the initiative of subordinates, and it is essential that this misconception should be corrected at once.[18]

It is ironic that just four days after Haig had instructed Rawlinson to behave less like the proverbial butcher, one of Rawlinson's subordinate commanders was permitted to punish one of his brigadiers for seeking to stand up for the men in his brigade.

The brigadier in question was the forty-nine-year-old Frederick Carleton, whose 98th Brigade had made the doomed High Wood and Wood Lane attack on 18 August. He reckoned that a subsequent instruction given to him by his immediate superior, the 33rd Division's Major-General Herman Landon, requiring the 98th Brigade troops to dig a new fire trench to cover a gap in the British line, was overloading his men. They were already struggling to deal with the digging required on their existing front without being given extra urgent tasks by the division. Given the circumstances, Carleton politely, but firmly, asked Landon on 27 August whether he would think again before demanding that 98th Brigade comply with his instruction.

If this had been the first time Carleton had questioned one of Landon's instructions, it is possible that the major-general would have had a civilized discussion with his brigadier and reached a compromise solution. But papers filed in the Imperial War Museum suggest that Carleton had transgressed on a previous occasion. He had questioned an order asking him to make just the kind of last-minute attack that Haig was now discouraging. Carleton had a good reason for pointing out the order was impractical. Within the space of three hours he would have had to rush his troops five miles over congested roads to reach the assembly point in time. This might have proved impossible. On that previous occasion Landon's staff officer, who had presented the order to Carleton, had backed down, but not before making it clear he believed Carleton was being obstructive.

This time Landon was not going to take any more nonsense. On 28 August he fired off a letter to his superior, XV Corps' General Horne, saying he was sacking Carleton for allegedly failing to comply with his instructions relating to the new trench: 'Present conditions . . . require characteristics in a brigadier which are not possessed by General Carleton, i.e.

[someone who has] quick practical methods of command, and a cheerful outlook which will communicate itself to the troops.'

Carleton, who was told to hand over his command to another brigadier immediately, was devastated, as can be seen from the following words he included in the letter he sent to his wife: 'Darling . . . I am going . . . to give you the shock of your life. I have I fear been stellenbosched . . . We were ordered to do something which was a physical impossibility. We did our best and failed, human endurance having reached its limits. I have been sacrificed to the ambitions of an unscrupulous general but thank God I've done nothing to reproach myself with.'[19] It is not clear whether Carleton was impugning Landon or Horne when he referred to the 'unscrupulous general'. Perhaps both were in his sights. Landon had told Carleton it was Horne who was pressing him to have the trench dug so that it was complete before the next attack.

Whatever the correct attribution of responsibility for this incident, one is bound to say that it is Horne who comes out worst from what happened in and around High Wood in July and August. His failure to take on board the advice given by Brigadier-General Deverell of the 20th Brigade meant that he never got a grip on which parts of the German defences had to be obliterated to make the other parts vulnerable. It was similar to the problem that had surfaced during the attacks on Contalmaison and the western side of Mametz Wood (see Chapter 18).

On that occasion Major-General Pilcher was relieved of his command for having the temerity to point out the flaws running through Horne's strategy. Now, at High Wood, Horne was losing another committed officer, by trying to force his troops to work faster than human endurance could bear.

32: The Human Factor

Mouquet Farm, 17–23 August 1916

(See maps 2 and 16)

If only Haig had given the same attention to the capture of Mouquet Farm as he had devoted to the second attempt to push forward to Pozières Ridge, the resulting success might have disarmed his harshest critics. They were understandably frustrated by the slow progress he was making, and more and more concerned at the growing casualty list.

In fairness to Haig, Mouquet Farm was not the most important of targets from a strategic point of view at this stage. It was understandable that he should want to focus his attention on the 4th Army's moves towards the eastern part of the Somme sector so that his troops could move forward with the French. But that raises another fundamental question: if Haig could not give the Mouquet Farm operations enough resources and attention, should he not have suspended them until he had time to direct them properly? As it was, the attacks on Mouquet Farm, and the surrounding trenches, represented the worst of all possible worlds. Because of the attempt to keep the number of participating troops to a minimum as Haig had instructed, the attacks failed again and again, thereby pushing up the number of casualties rather than reducing them.

The next two attacks by Major-General Harold Walker's 1st Australian Division, which took over the front from the 4th Australian Division on 16 August, are cases in point.[1] He was not helped by having troops under his command who, if not exactly mutinous, were unenthusiastic to say the least. That was evident from their reactions when General Birdwood first broke the news to the men that their services were needed once again. When he told them 'I have some wonderful news, beautiful news. We will be in action in a few days', the men did not conceal their displeasure. 'You old bastard!' was the considered response of more than one of them.[2]

You could not blame them. If it was possible, the conditions they would be called on to endure were to be even worse than before. Private Eric Moorhead, a soldier from the 5th Australian Battalion who was involved in improving the trenches before the next attack towards the east, characterized them as:

indescribable. On the shell-torn ground lay . . . innumerable . . . decaying corpses, stinking and ghastly. From some of them gases were issuing, sometimes through the mouth as if [they were still] alive. Fragments of humanity were everywhere. Here a leg, clad in Australian trousers, protruded from the ground. There a German's hand, and heads crawling with maggots, half eaten away, [stuck out] . . . from the side of the sap. You sat on the side of the trench to find you were sitting on a . . . corpse's stomach, and trod on the floor of the sap to find the same. Equipment, rifles, bombs, everything conceivable [were strewn all over] . . . the saps, and everywhere [there] were stinking masses of flesh that had once been living men.[3]

Faced with such sights, some of the men, who had been traumatized by their first tour in the trenches, did not have the physical or psychological strength to take any more of the torment that was part and parcel of a day in the front line. Private Moorhead was probably expressing commonly held sentiments when, on 17 August, he admitted in his account: 'You would not have called us heroes if you had seen us, quivering at the knees and smoking cigarettes to keep the nerves up.' Moorhead apparently believed that some of his officers were equally unimpressed by the announcement that they would soon be participating in another attack. As he subsequently recalled: 'To get the Battalion declared unfit, many of us were practically ordered to parade sick.'[4]

Charles Bean, the Australian journalist, was so shocked by what he witnessed on the way from Pozières to Mouquet Farm that he recorded his impressions in his notebook. According to Bean, the ditch that passed for a trench 'started about 3 feet deep, but it rapidly became shallower (because it had been) . . . broken into by shell after shell'. The cost of expecting men to use such an inadequate channel was only too evident. There were 'bits of' dead soldiers everywhere. Here some 'dead men's legs', there 'a shoulder', and over there 'a half-buried body which stuck out of the tumbled red soil' like the half-submerged hull of a sunk ship. 'The bodies [were] in all sorts of decay. Some eaten away to the skull. [Others] blackened . . . [their] dried black skin drawn back from [their] teeth, [and their] eyelids dried thick and flattened, like those of a mummy'. It was only when the trench, which had gradually grown even shallower, was eventually replaced by a series of shell holes that the corpses disappeared too, probably because they were 'buried somewhere below'.[5]

The fact that many of the injuries seen by Bean resulted from the incompetence of the men's leaders made them hard for him to stomach. On 18 August, while troops from the British 98th Brigade were being point-lessly sacrificed south of High Wood (Haig had specially requested that the Reserve Army should make its advance coincide with the next 4th Army attack,[6] mentioned in Chapter 31), those in the 1st Australian Brigade's 3rd Battalion were suffering in a similar cause. They had been told they must take the area halfway to Fabeck Graben, the same objective that the troops of Major-General Cox's 4th Australian Division had failed to capture in their last assault on 14 August (see Chapter 30). But their advance was sty-mied by the Australians' own artillery, which fired on, and just in front of, the trench of the attacking 3rd Battalion. Meanwhile, the 2nd Australian Brigade's simultaneous inability to progress east of the OG lines was the result of another error: they were not given the artillery plan in time, and therefore could not schedule their advance to ensure they reached the enemy parapets before the Germans.

These reverses, caused by human errors, overshadowed the 4th Austra-lian Battalion's minuscule advance towards Mouquet Farm. The one concrete dividend earned by the move northwards, which led to almost 350 casualties, was not the taking of a village, farm or trench, but the capture of a strategically insignificant position referred to as Point 55 (see map 16).[7]

Lieutenant-Colonel Iven Mackay, the 4th Battalion's tough, unsympa-thetic commander, believed his men could have done much better. In the course of a pep talk after the action, he urged them to be braver next time. The battalion could not achieve its objectives if men scampered back to the rear at the slightest excuse, he said, adding: 'A man is not wounded if his face is splashed with dust, or if a small clod hits his back.' He also supported the sentence handed down to a lance corporal who had deserted before the attack: to suffer death by shooting. It was commuted to fifteen years' penal servitude because, thankfully, the Australians would not permit their volunteers to be executed.[8]

No such pep talk was required for the troops of the Reserve Army's British II Corps, who advanced northwards on 18 August until they were in line with those in Skyline Trench. By midday on 19 August the front line of the British troops coming up to the west of the Australians stretched westwards along Skyline Trench to the original German front line north-east of the Nab.[9]

Charles Bean, who evidently felt that the fault lay not with the

Australian troops but with their commander, wrote sarcastically of the role played by the head of the Reserve Army, General Gough, in the following terms: 'It has pleased the wonderful commander Gough . . . to express some sort of displeasure at the failure of the . . . attack into which he hurried us . . . I believe he had the cheek to tell General Walker that he ought to go up to Pozières to see things for himself before the next attack.' Warming to his theme, the entry in Bean's diary continues: 'How can a division in its second go, after the hardest fight which . . . troops [fighting for the British] have ever had, be expected to be as fresh and as good as before they went through the experience when it has lost 50%, and is filled up with 30% of recruits with 20% not filled up at all?'[10]

Worse was to follow three days later. Major-General Walker, following in Cox's footsteps, rejected the advice of Brigadier-General Brudenell White to restrict the advance to a few hundred yards.[11] Walker insisted that although his 3rd Australian Brigade battalions were depleted and the men exhausted, they could lift themselves just enough to take Fabeck Graben itself. But like Cox before him, he had miscalculated.

The attack plan that Walker came up with was as flawed as Major-General Legge's prior to the 28–29 July attack on Pozières Ridge. The movement into position in daylight so that the attack could start at 6 p.m., combined with the failure to dig communication trenches which could conceal the troops' assembly, condemned the 10th Australian Battalion to intense shelling for an hour before the advance even started. As a result it lost more than 120 men to the German guns before zero hour.

By the time the whistles blew and the men of the 10th Australian Battalion moved forward, the German machine-gunners on the Australians' right were already waiting for them, firing through the ineffective artillery barrage. Although the left of the battalion made it into Fabeck Graben, its right was halted by the machine-gun fire. That meant the way was open for the Germans to make an encircling movement around the Australians' right flank. This might not have been so disastrous had there not been yet another mistake, on their left flank. The 11th Battalion, which was supposed to be covering the left of the 10th Battalion, did not reach the front line in time to advance at zero hour. It was yet another example of an Australian unit failing to make it into the attack position in time. In order to avoid being cut off as a result, by 10 p.m. all the Australians in Fabeck Graben who could still run or walk had retired to the line from where the battalion had started.[12]

During the early morning of 22 August, before news of the attack's failure had filtered back to the rear, Charles Bean moved up to the 10th Battalion's headquarters with a view to finding out what had occurred. The notes he made in his diary, recording what he witnessed on the way to the headquarters, highlighted the devastating cost of supporting the troops in the front line:

One poor chap had had his tunic and shirt torn [so that what remained of his torso was] bare . . . You looked down past the white skin of the chest to his back bone. His whole body had been ripped open. He was bent back almost double as if he had taken strychnine . . . Another had his skull broken, just like an eggshell. Another lay peacefully like a wax figure on whom the dust has long settled. Others that we came across . . . might have been living men lying on the floor of the trench.[13]

However, what shocked Bean more than anything was not the tragic loss of life, or the failure to bury the dead, but the discovery that Major Redberg, the 10th Battalion's acting commanding officer, had fallen asleep without waiting to find out how his battalion had fared. Was it because Redberg was irresponsible, or was this just another example of an exhausted burned-out soldier being asked to do too much? Bean feared it was the former, but suspected that it might also be the latter.[14]

It is impossible to know how many of the battalion would have fallen if the plan had been well thought out. All that is certain is that over half of those who had attacked (336 out of 650) became casualties.[15] The dead included David Badger, a twenty-year-old sergeant. The following words extracted from the last letter he wrote to his parents were heartbreakingly idealistic given the errors that may well have contributed to his demise. 'When you see this, I'll be dead. Don't worry . . . Try to think I did the only possible thing, as I tell you I would do it again if I had the chance. Send someone else in my place.'[16] Badger's Red Cross file suggests that he might have been one of the NCOs who led the 10th Battalion's men into the enemy's trenches.[17] All the officers were either killed or wounded just before or in the course of the attack, except for one who was wounded shortly after making it into Fabeck Graben.[18]

It was unfortunate that one of the wounded officers, thirty-two-year-old 2nd Lieutenant Herbert Crowle, was so small. If he had been taller than the 5 foot 5 inches recorded on his enlistment papers, the machine-gun bullets that hit him in the upper thigh might have had a less devastating effect. He might have avoided injury altogether had he been in General Cox's 4th Australian Division, where there was less enthusiasm for promoting NCOs. Crowle, who only became an officer shortly before the attack, may have been targeted by the German machine-gunners anxious to wipe out the leaders of the assault before anyone else.

In spite of the severity of Crowle's wound, stretcher-bearers managed to pick him up, and he was eventually taken to the 3rd Casualty Clearing Station in Puchevillers. There, a surgeon attempted to cut out the dead tissue from his buttocks that had become infected and gangrenous. It soon became clear, however, that the operation had not been successful, prompting Crowle on 24 August to write warning his wife Beatrice in Adelaide:

You must be prepared for the worst to happen any day. It is no use trying to hide things. I am in terrible agony. Had I been brought in straight away, I had a hope. But now gas gangrene has set in, and it is so bad, the doctor could not save it (the leg) by taking it off, as it has gone too far, and the only hope is that the salts they have put in may drain the gangrene. Otherwise there is no hope. Tomorrow I shall know the worst, as the dressing was to be left on for three days, and tomorrow is the third day. It smells rotten . . . I am very sorry dear, but still, you will be provided for . . . I am easy on that score.

Mercifully perhaps, Herbert Crowle died the next day.[19]

Fortunately for the men in the 12th Australian Battalion on the left of Crowle's 10th Battalion, and for their relatives back home, its 21 August objective was consistent with the spirit, if not the letter, of Brigadier-General Brudenell White's recommendation: a manageable advance to the German trench just to the south-east of Mouquet Farm.[20] Thanks to accurate shooting by the artillery, the trench was duly taken and held, the operation only being marred by yet another example of indiscipline on the part of Australian troops: some of the men, tempted perhaps by the sight of fleeing Germans taking refuge in the farm, could not resist entering its precincts so that they could chase them.

They would not be the last Australians on the Mouquet Farm front to advance too far without sufficient support, or without permission from their headquarters. On this occasion, unnecessary injuries were incurred because some men became the victims of their own guns. Their sacrifice was particularly galling, because no permanent lodgement in the farm was achieved. After the first rush of blood had carried them forward, the survivors quickly realized that their presence in the farm was unsustainable, and they slunk back to join their comrades on the battalion's objective.

According to the Red Cross files, twenty-one-year-old 2nd Lieutenant Alfred Hearps was one of the officers who entered Mouquet Farm. His batman Private Bean (no relation to the journalist Charles Bean) reported that he had been with Hearps after his master had been hit in the neck by a shell fragment which paralyzed him. Bean loyally waited beside Lieutenant Hearps for half an hour, long after the rest of the Australian troops had departed, only scurrying back to the Australian front line after Hearps asked him to go in order to seek help. When this brave man eventually made it back to the Australian front line, Lieutenant Roper, the officer in command, remarked that 'God only knew' how he had escaped from the farm, which was by this time once more in German hands. But he refused to countenance risking the lives of stretcher-bearers to bring Hearps in, his hard-hearted, but sensible, decision being influenced perhaps by Bean's observation that no man could hope to survive such a severe wound.

Lieutenant Roper certainly could not have anticipated the eleven months of torment that his decision would inflict upon Hearps' relatives at home. Hearps' identity disk was subsequently handed in to the 12th Battalion by another unit, whose troops also reached the farm. But there was no accompanying report available stating that his corpse had been seen. As a result, Hearps was registered as one of the missing, a verdict which was not challenged by the inconclusive evidence sent to his mother, Eva, by the Red Cross. That pricked her to write back in February 1917, pleading for them to help her find out the truth concerning her 'beloved son', adding: 'I am heartbroken concerning my son's fate [all the more so because] everything is so indefinite. I really don't know what to think or what to do. Surely if his disc has been returned and his body identified, the Defence should notify me. Will you please let me know exactly what you think. The suspense is getting more than I can bear!'

Eva Hearps' heartless correspondent at the Base Records department at the Ministry of Defence was not impressed by what the Red Cross had sent her, telling her that the evidence, which for the most part consisted of soldiers stating that others had seen Hearps' corpse, was not 'sufficiently authentic' given that it was only 'hearsay'. It took three more months for a court of inquiry to be convened to consider his case. Even when it finally confirmed that Alfred had indeed been killed in action, Eva Hearps did not find out because she had separated from her husband and moved out of the marital home where official correspondence concerning her son was being sent.

If the deterioration of their relationship was on account of the grief caused by their son's disappearance, it would not have been the first time that a family tragedy had driven a couple apart. But Eva's case was particularly poignant. Because she was not still living at the address where the notification of death was sent, her agony was prolonged, and her angst exacerbated. Her unsettled state of mind cannot have been helped by the letter she received from the battalion chaplain stating that her son had been killed, at a time when she believed the Department of Defence was still denying that her son had been killed in action. The whole saga of whether Alfred was dead or alive was only cleared up after her husband eventually deigned to visit her in Sydney in August 1917 to tell her the bad news.

But that was not the end of it. Eva's departure from the marital home effectively cut her off from the right to see, let alone possess, her son's personal effects, which her husband jealously kept from her. It was not until 1920 that Eva Hearps was able to inform the authorities that the battle between herself and her husband had ended after the woman she referred to as '"the individual" who had shared her life with him' had the 'audacity' to write stating that her husband had passed away in his turn. It was too late by then for Eva to claim her son's camera, clothes and books, although as she said: 'I would have given anything for my dear boy's things that were returned. I would have treasured them.' But now all she wanted was a photograph of her son's grave, which she had been notified was near Mouquet Farm.[21]

I have made much of Eva Hearps' trials and tribulations in an effort to highlight the anguish that so many mothers of Somme casualties had to endure. But she was of course far from being the only parent of a 12th Battalion soldier to suffer from the generals' decision to creep forward to Mouquet Farm. In spite of the unambitious extent of the advance, almost 100 of the 242 casualties within the 12th Battalion were recorded as having being killed or missing during its final tour in the Somme trenches.[22]

The 12th Battalion's surviving officers and other ranks who had secured the salient a short distance to the south-east of Mouquet Farm (see map 16) were to be relieved during the evening of 22 August. That same day two more victims were added to the list. As German shells rained down on the support lines and communication trenches in an effort to disrupt the assembly of the fresh troops who were being brought up to the front, yet another missile homed in on its target. This missile hit the 6 foot 2 inch Tasmanian cricketer Lieutenant Leo Butler of the 12th Battalion, ripping off his left leg below the knee, injuring his right foot, and killing the man standing beside him. They had been on their way to the front line so that they could hold it until the new troops arrived. Such a severe injury, sustained at a time when it was impossible to be rushed back to the doctors at the nearest casualty clearing station because of the shelling, might have meant oblivion for most soldiers. But because thirty-three-year-old Leo Butler was the first cousin of the journalist Charles Bean, Leo's fate was investigated and subsequently immortalized by his cousin's prose. Within days of hearing that Leo had been wounded, Bean contacted the battalion and asked his cousin's comrades about how Leo had been treated.

They told him that a series of tourniquets managed to staunch the worst of the bleeding. Leo Butler's second bit of 'luck' was to be hit near a muscular corporal, who had the strength and the courage to carry him on his back 150 yards away from the unprotected danger point where he had been wounded. Stretcher-bearers summoned from his company's headquarters bore Leo a bit further on the way towards greater safety, but the shelling made it too dangerous to carry him further to the rear. Consequently, Leo had to spend his first night after the injury in his company commander's dugout, his pain eased by the doctor who visited him there.

The next morning, the shelling having abated somewhat, Leo was carried around two miles to the place where the horse-drawn ambulances were waiting. That was followed by another one-mile journey to the dressing station, where his bandages were checked. From there, a motor ambulance transported him to the 'hospital' at Warloy, where he had a third piece of 'good fortune'. A friend who was working in the casualty clearing station, and who did not recognize him at first, happened to look at the ticket attached to Leo's person, and realized that this Lieutenant Butler was his lifelong friend Leo.[23] This can only have meant Leo received preferential treatment.

Whether or not that helped him to be processed more quickly, Leo eventually ended up at Puchevillers, where he was strong enough for a surgeon to think it worthwhile to take the drastic step of amputating what was left of the left leg stump as well as two toes from his right foot. Because he made it through the operation, it was hoped that Leo would survive, although because the circulation had been damaged in his right leg, there was a fear it would have had to be amputated as well. Unfortunately, or perhaps one should say fortunately, such hopes were dashed, and at 11 p.m. that night, 23 August, Leo passed away.

According to Charles Bean's Hardyesque description of the bucolic backdrop to Leo Butler's final resting place, which he sent to Leo's parents, the funeral service in the small cemetery at Puchevillers, studded with wooden crosses, was a modest affair, attended by him and five other friends and acquaintances:

The grave is in the corner of a wheat field overlooking . . . wide undulating beautiful country, far away from the guns, with rows of great trees topping the distant hills and the peaceful country between. A country cart track wanders down past it. As the service was proceeding, the rough wooden coffin clearly covering the frame of a splendid man (for it was bigger . . . than most soldiers' coffins) lying there under the Union Jack, the sun shining on the wheat fields and three aeroplanes wheeling through the sky near the aerodrome, two French farming people came by, a middle-aged woman in a Holland dress carrying some sort of big pewter can on her arm, and a man over the middle age with his scythe fresh from the mowing. The man took off his cap and leaned on his scythe and the woman stood there in the road while the chaplain read. Then I saw her going away, dabbing her eyes, and the man went too to his work.[24]

Charles Bean's poetic account must have been a great comfort to Leo Butler's father and mother, referred to by all within the family as 'Uncle Ted' and 'Aunt Amy', since it is frequently mentioned as such in letters, including those sent out to Charles Bean and his brother at the front. Letters from Charles Bean's mother, at least one of which was written beside the drawing-room window in the family's house in Hobart, overlooking 'the river where yachts and a few small fishing boats pass every now and then', also mentioned the outpouring of support in the form of letters of condolence from 'children, old people, middle-aged men, labourers, [from the] Salvation Army [and the] Golf Club'.[25] It almost felt as if 'all Hobart is sharing his parents' loss, rich and poor, old and young'.[26] In the short term at least, Uncle Ted, who it was feared would break down on hearing the dreadful news, told Charles Bean's mother, just ten days after Leo's death, that 'I have . . . such a feeling of peace today. [I am] quite happy. I feel almost ashamed of myself. I think Leo must be near me.'[27]

Aunt Amy on the other hand wrote to Charles's brother Jack admitting that she had been 'very sad and down' as Leo 'was just the whole world to us'. Uncle Ted, who regarded Leo as 'the apple of his eye', had always hoped he would eventually take over from him in the office. 'Now he will have to go on to the end.' And gone too were their hopes that Leo would be there 'to comfort the one who was left' when one of them died. And yet once Amy heard the details of his terrible wounds, she would not have had it any different. 'It would have been terrible for Leo, and he of all people so full of life and energy, to be such a cripple and so maimed. I am sure he would only have wished to live for our sakes.'[28]

As for Charles Bean, he commemorated the memory of his cousin in his notebook in the following terms:

So Leo, the finest specimen of manhood in Hobart, the big genial kindly chap, who used always to come and meet us at the boat when she arrived, and see us off when we sailed, who was always in one's mind a man of the open air – the tennis court, the cricket pitch – is gone. He was never quite suited for the family office, a hard man to find the best profession for, splendid generous chap though he was. But he found it as a soldier . . . He was a born leader. Men jumped at him at once . . . He was not the sharp rattling type of soldier, imposing though he was. He spoke in a gentle, even quiet tone . . . He did not shout at his men at any time. He was a . . . perfect gentleman from the top of his curly head to the soles of his great boots.

His death marked a turning point in the way Charles Bean viewed not only the Mouquet Farm offensive, but also the entire war. It prompted him to write 'When we saw his coffin . . . laid in the ground . . . I couldn't help wondering whether it was worth it, whether there is anything gained in this war that justifies such sacrifices'.[29]

That was a sentiment which must have crossed the minds of the Reverend John Raws and his son Lennon after they heard that Alec Raws had also died on 23 August. Just over an hour before Leo Butler's death, Alec had been hit by a German shell while on the way with men from the 23rd Australian Battalion to the front line at Mouquet Farm. The battalion was one of the 2nd Australian Division units that was relieving the 1st Australian Division on the northern front.

The first inkling the Raws family had that something was wrong was six days later when John Raws received an official telegram stating that Alec's brother Goldy (Goldthorp) was missing. Cruelly, the postal service had not yet delivered the series of letters Alec had written in an attempt to minimize his parents' anxiety and grief on hearing about their younger son. Lennon later wrote in his diary: 'When we received word about Goldy, I felt that Alec had gone too. Otherwise he would have been sure to have sent a cable to his parents.'

However, Lennon could not have been more upset when weeks later a colleague burst into his office to confirm his worst fears: Alec had been killed in action. 'The thought of what it meant to mother and father, and a great love and pity for the two boys, swallowed up so suddenly in the black gulf of war, overwhelmed me, and I burst into tears,' he wrote in his diary. He immediately took the train to Adelaide so that he could be with his family. His father met him at the station. 'He was wonderfully brave,' Lennon recorded, 'although occasionally he would break down. Mother had to keep calm to help him, but we sorrowed even more for her, because she could not find relief in tears.'

Lennon only stayed a few days, but in that time he managed to distil from the family's grief a sense of the unity that many other mourning families must have experienced as they came together to celebrate young lives lost. 'It was one of those beautifully sacred times which come through sorrow,' he recalled later. 'Helen (his sister) was over as well, and we were united for the time being by a common bond, which is too often broken by the friction of ordinary life.'[30] They had to wait another fifteen months before they had the opportunity to draw a similar line under Goldy's life, that being the time it took for him to be declared killed in action.[31]

33: Shell-Shocked

Mouquet Farm, 28 August–8 September 1916

(See maps 2 and 16)

One might have expected that the series of ignominious defeats in front of Mouquet Farm would have told the commanders of the Australian troops that their methodology was all wrong. However, when Major-General Cox, hardened by his previous experiences earlier in the month, returned to the Mouquet Farm front with his 4th Australian Division on 28 August for their last week on the Somme, he brushed aside the 'innovation' suggested by Brigadier-General Brudenell White, the 1 ANZAC commander's chief of staff.[1] White had suggested that Cox should use a larger force when attacking the farm than had been used hitherto.

White's suggestion was not entirely born of desperation. He had observed that all the previous attacks on the farm, and the trenches around it, including two equally unsuccessful attacks made by Major-General Legge's 2nd Australian Division, had been made by just two or three battalions. This frugal use of units had been encouraged by the Reserve Army's General Gough, who, ever since the dreadful shelling of his troops in Pozières, had castigated any commander who put too many men into the front line. But sometimes even the highest-flying generals make errors of judgement: if it meant that there were not enough troops to mop up the German front line after the leading troops had burst into and passed beyond it, then extra manpower had to be provided.

That was all the more important when considering a location such as Mouquet Farm, where the front system did not just consist of conventional trenches. The ruined farm appears to have contained a collection of linked-up tunnels whose entrances were dotted around it. Arguably it would take more Australian troops to stand guard over all of these openings than would have been required to clear a conventional trench system.

After Cox's division, featuring just two and a half battalions, had made yet another abortive attempt to take the farm and the neighbouring Fabeck Graben on 29 August, White confided in the embedded journalist Charles Bean, telling him he had proposed Cox should use at least three battalions, adding: 'I wish I had been strong and asked for it to be done by a whole brigade!' This prompted Bean, still bitterly resentful of the generals whose strategy had deprived him of his beloved cousin Leo Butler, to write in his diary:

It's all very well for army generals to sit with their maps and to talk about attacking with patrols . . . The General (Gough) is apt to push a division at a place like Pozières, and then talk of the 'unnecessary loss of life' being due to the divisional commander using a 'quite unnecessary number of troops: My dear chap, to take one of these lightly held positions, you don't want great depth in the attack. You don't want a host of men swarming over the place to be shelled to hell next day. Quite a light line will do it.' But . . . unless we . . . swarm into every part, we . . . [will] find our thin line in parts of the trench[es] only, the enemy knowing the alleys through which to attack us . . . us knowing nothing at all. To take a position which the Germans consider as important as this one, you need your men to be swarming over it after the attack like flies![2]

After losing more than 500 men in the course of his attack on 29 August, Cox finally acquiesced. For the last operation his division would make before following the other Australian divisions to the north, he would use the whole of his 13th Australian Brigade.[3] Like previous attacks by the 1st and 4th Australian Divisions, it would consist of thrusts targeting Mouquet Farm and Fabeck Graben. But this time the brigadier in charge, Brigadier-General Glasgow, would have access to all his men: if all went well, his 49th Battalion would take Fabeck Graben on the right, 51st Battalion would dig in north of the farm on the left, with 52nd Battalion filling in between. The fourth battalion, 50th Battalion, would be deployed in Park Lane to the rear, but would be ready to reinforce the assault units should the need arise. The attack was to be made on 3 September, thereby complying with Haig's order that Gough's next operation would be on the same day as the next general attack being made by Rawlinson's 4th Army and the French.[4]

Ironically, the nerves of the troops in the reserve unit were tested first. In the case of at least one officer, they were found to be wanting. The account written by twenty-two-year-old Pat Auld, a sensitive lieutenant in the 50th Battalion, makes it clear that there was no single event that caused his nerve to fail him. It was an accumulation of one horrific event after another that gradually ground down his resilience until he was no longer the master of his own actions. According to Auld, what he could justifiably have described as the beginning of his descent into hell began during the evening before the 3 September attack. He had been ordered to deepen Park Lane Trench, where he and his men were to be stationed at zero hour:

The men dug in silence as if their lives depended on it, as indeed they did. At the end of an hour, while going along the line supervising the work, the sound of a man's voice raised unduly brought me to the spot. As the strictest silence had been enjoined, I rebuked him sharply and demanded an explanation. He had thrown down his tools and stood crying: 'A dead man! A dead man! His spade had unearthed a decomposed body which smelt vile.

I told him that unless he got to work and dislodged it quickly, he would be dead himself in a few short hours. To give him confidence I jumped [down] into the . . . trench, and tugged at a protruding arm [only for it to come] . . . away in my hand[s], separating from the rest of the body at the shoulder. This grisly relic was thrown over the parapet, where in due course, and piece by piece, the whole body followed it, to be finally followed by the earth dug from the trench.

It was to be the first of several such incidents that occurred during the night. But Auld and his men did not stop their work, which was helped along by the Very lights shot up into the air by the enemy. Their 'pale flickering glow helped to dispel the blackness' in which they were working. By 5.10 a.m. on 3 September, the hour of the attack, Lieutenant Auld and his men felt they were as ready as they ever would be for what was to come. He remembered the start of the pre-attack bombardment in the following terms:

Suddenly, without warning, as the faint grey streaks of dawn began to appear, a crescendo of noise broke . . . the silence and 'the heaviest artillery barrage the world had ever seen' began. What a sight! For a few moments I stood on the parados of the . . . trench, and watched this tornado of steel and high explosive thundering down upon Mouquet Farm.

How could anything live in that inferno? Smoke, dust, glare, a thousand flashes of light bursting in momentary brightness . . . accompanied by gangrenous earth erupting . . . like a thousand devils dancing in satanic glee. But above all noise, noise, noise! Intense vibration, reverberation, a hideous orchestra of death that filled the human soul with misery and fear . . . [Then] almost imperceptibly, after what seemed an eternity of pandemonium, the barrage lifted and fell again on a new line further forward . . . The attack had begun.

It was only then that the German artillery retaliated, targeting Park Lane as well as the area between it and the front line. It was accurate to call this a 'softening-up' barrage. As Lieutenant Auld noted, each blast diminished his ability to exercise self-control. And there were lots of explosions:

Shell after shell exploded just in front of or just behind the trench, sending over us showers of earth which came hurtling down on our steel helmets as we crouched fearfully against the forward wall. In several places landslides had occurred blocking free movement along the trench and rendering that portion of it useless for protection.

To sit inactive under intensive shell fire for hours is one of the worst features of modern warfare . . . The sight of your comrades . . . being killed and wounded puts a strain upon you that calls for the highest degree of self-control. The temptation to bolt becomes very strong and has to be resisted in every possible way. Any action is better than the dreadful suspense of waiting your turn to be slaughtered or hideously maimed. But no action is possible, and you just sit on hoping against hope that your name is not inscribed on any shell and with a horrible dread that it is.

Several men had already been wounded, and the stretcher-bearers were in the process of carrying them away when the inevitable happened and a shell landed near where Auld was crouching. 'Recovering from the concussion of the explosion, I noticed that the man next to me, Farrer, had been hit. His head had fallen forward on his chest, and he lay huddled and twitching. A shrapnel pellet had . . . entered [his] head above the left temple, smashing the skull, portions of which I could see protruding amidst the blood which gushed out and trickled scarlet down his face.'

But there was no time for sentimentality, Auld reported. 'I had no doubt that he was dead, and obeying the rule that no dead body must be left amongst the living, I ordered the sergeant to heave him over the parapet', where he would have to lie alongside the body parts that had been extracted from the trench a few hours earlier. Imagine Auld's surprise, therefore, when a few minutes later he saw the same man sitting up semi-conscious in the trench with a bandage round his head. The sergeant had discovered he was still breathing, and by disobeying Auld's instructions had saved his life. The necessity for such a last-minute reprieve on account of his own callousness horrified Auld. But he barely had time to catch his breath after shouting in the revived man's ear that he would have to go back to the rear under his own steam, before he was called away to deal with the next crisis.

In the midst of all the mayhem and noise he had been daydreaming. In his mind's eye, he had been transported back to a peaceful, even idyllic, scene that took place most Sundays when he was back home in the south of Australia. He was imagining he was sipping a cold sparkling beer under the old walnut tree after a civilized game of tennis, when his thoughts were interrupted by another deafening explosion. A German shell had landed in the next bay, caving in the sides of the trench and burying all the men who had been in or near its path. 'What a moment before had been a trench was now a reeking smoking mound of putrid soil, literally a living tomb,' Auld reported.

The realization that there were living men under what had amounted to an avalanche of earth prompted frantic digging efforts by those in the vicinity, efforts which became more urgent and frenetic the deeper they probed. The first man they uncovered was 'shaken and dazed' but otherwise unhurt. The second was choking and fighting for breath, his face a deep purple. The third was bleeding and unconscious, only just alive. Before they could extricate the last victim, whose purple skin and matted hair had been glimpsed at the bottom of the excavated hole, Auld caught sight of an ominous black speck in the sky. He quickly realized it was another shell speeding towards them. Seconds later there was a gigantic explosion, the force of which sent him flying through the air before depositing him in the next bay.

It took some time for Auld to come to his senses. When he did, his first thought was of the buried man, who might yet be rescued if he moved quickly. However, as he stumbled round the corner, the sight that met his eyes appalled him. The man who had been digging beside him was still more or less upright, supported as he was by the parados. But as Auld recorded, 'The whole of the left side of his body from the shoulder downward was almost completely severed . . . Another . . . [man's] head had been completely cut off . . . The trunk lay crushed and bloody nearby.' Two of the men who had helped dig out the men buried by the first shell had been buried in their turn. Other men were now searching for them.

It was this nightmarish scene, coming so quickly after the other traumatic events he had witnessed, that finally brought Auld's psychological defences crashing down. 'Something seemed to snap in my brain and I felt my self-control going,' he confessed later. 'That purply black neck and matted hair . . . that rolling head staring at me with its sightless eyes. I could not stay and face it. I . . . [had to] get away . . . Staggering along the trench,

I began to laugh, and the sound brought me face to face with madness. No, by God, I . . . [would] not go mad. I crouched in the trench hands to my face and . . . by [making] a conscious effort returned to at least a degree of sanity and self-control.'

He was helped by the reappearance of his company commander Major Herbert who, oblivious to Auld's psychological torment, ordered him, shortly after 9.30 a.m., to prepare the company for action. According to Herbert, the assault troops in the left-hand battalion, the 51st Battalion, were no longer in contact with their commander. It was feared they had all been killed or captured. That meant there was a gap in the front line, and Auld's company had to fill it.[5]

The 5.10 a.m. advance by the 51st Battalion, on the left wing of the attack, through Mouquet Farm had started so promisingly. After two whole companies had passed through the farm, they reached the objective 200 yards to its north, leaving a third company to occupy the farm itself. For half an hour it looked as if the adoption of Brigadier-General White's suggestion to use more troops was paying off. Messages sent before 8 a.m. back to Lieutenant-Colonel Arthur Ross in the 51st Battalion and the brigade headquarters dugout near the Pozières cemetery all confirmed that Mouquet Farm had finally been taken. Shortly afterwards, however, Bert Clifford, the twenty-six-year-old lieutenant in charge of one of the assault groups north of the farm, saw a sight that must have chilled him to the bone: it was a party of around thirty men from the 52nd Battalion, on whom he had been relying to protect his right flank, scurrying to the rear pursued by Germans.

If he had been a more senior, or faint-hearted, officer, Clifford might have realized that this made his own position untenable, and ordered a retreat there and then. But being a farmer from Western Australia, he appears to have been a steadfast character, and when the twenty-one-year-old Lieutenant Francis Bailey, an even more inexperienced officer holding the new front line alongside him, assured him that their orders were to hold on 'at all costs', he decided to do as they had been told. Their decision to stay was supported by Captain Howard Williams, the officer in charge in Mouquet Farm, who sent them fifty of his men while curving round his own right to hold the Germans on his right at bay.

However, the German pressure on their right was made all the more dangerous given that it was matched by gunfire from their left and rear. At 8.30 a.m. Clifford's scribbled note to headquarters included the following desperate situation report: 'Being hard pressed. Enemy bombing up our trench from both ends. Strong point on our left rear has not been cleared, as they are sniping in our rear . . . Can a party be organised to clear strong-point? If not, it will go hard with us. Only have about 30 men with me. No sign of a communication trench to us from farm as yet. Lost trace of the 52nd. Believe we have gone too far.'

It was to be Clifford's last message. Captain Williams, whose own com-munications between Mouquet Farm and HQ were cut off shortly afterwards, fought on until he was down to what amounted to the strength of a platoon, just two officers and thirty men out of the 200 with which he had started, before finally deciding at 9.30 a.m. he could wait no longer, abandoning Clifford and his men to their fate. For those who might suggest that Williams did not wait long enough, there is evidence to suggest he waited too long. As he retired a sniper killed him, drilling a bullet through his forehead.[6]

By all accounts, Clifford, Bailey and their men fought to a bloody finish. While still in his advanced line, Bailey ordered another officer accompanied by a private to return to Mouquet Farm to seek out a machine gun, only for both men to be shot by a German machine-gunner, while sheltering in a shell hole during their retreat.[7] Then Bailey, who already had head and shoulder wounds, was shot in the head again, this time fatally. He was last seen lying as if about to fire another shot at the enemy in a shell hole.[8] As for Clifford, who led his troops nobly until the very end, he was shot in the head and killed seconds before the Germans moved in to capture the wounded survivors.[9] But their heroic refusal to retire or surrender served no useful purpose, apart from highlighting a lesson that had been restrain-ing the whole offensive ever since the first potential breakthrough at Montauban on 1 July: it might be tempting to make a deep thrust after breaking through the German front-line defences, but it was very risky, as the Germans who cut in from the flanks north of Mouquet Farm had demonstrated.[10]

The gap in the Australian front line that Lieutenant Pat Auld's company had to fill was not, however, solely the result of these dramatic events in and around Mouquet Farm. There had been problems in the centre of the attack as well. Although the 49th Australian Battalion had successfully cap-tured the portion of Fabeck Graben on the extreme right (see map 16), its left had been repulsed, and the 52nd Australian Battalion had fared even worse. It had advanced sufficiently so that part of one of its companies was in touch with the 49th Battalion, albeit from a base some way behind the latter's front line, but on its left there was a large expanse of trench that the 52nd Battalion had not been able to subdue in the initial advance. It was to guard against a German counter-attack through this yawning opening that Auld and his men, led by their company commander Major Herbert, were ordered to march, to what Brigadier-General Glasgow hoped could still be called the Australian front line.

They set out from Park Lane at 10.30 a.m., shortly after Mouquet Farm had been retaken by the Germans. But long before they reached their goal, Auld, who was bringing up the rear, realized that they had become separated from Major Herbert and the men in front. Because he was unsure of the way, Auld and the thirty to forty men with him had to tramp all the way back to battalion headquarters in order to obtain directions, no easy task for these shocked, exhausted men, wet through with perspiration and parched with thirst on account of their prior attempt to keep up with the fast pace set by their company leader.

But once safely ensconced in the battalion dugout, Auld realized he was losing control of himself once again:

The air of the dugout was warm and heavy, and acted as a soporific on my tired and bewildered mind . . . I almost fell asleep on the steps of the dugout as I sat vaguely and unsatisfactorily attempting to answer . . . Colonel [Salisbury's] questions. I noticed them (the Colonel and his adjutant) exchange glances, and realized stupidly that I was making a fool of myself. But nothing seemed to matter. All my soul craved for was sleep and relief from this hell on earth, and my mind began to soar deliciously . . . as if I was an Eastern mystic in a trance.

Coming from a long way off the Colonel's voice broke in sharply. How many men have you got with you? Confusedly I began to mumble something in reply . . . [He interrupted], and with anger in his voice he shouted: 'Have you got 4 or 40?' It was the best thing he could have done. The anger rising within me to meet his brought me back to reality, and I snapped back: '40!'

'Very well then,' the Colonel replied, and proceeded to issue the necessary instructions.

Twenty minutes later, led this time by a guide, Auld started out up the communication trench leading towards the front line once again, his men ducking and weaving every time a shell burst nearby. It was to be another terrifying journey: 'In the course of a few yards we had to walk over two dead bodies lying lengthways in the trench,' Auld reported. 'One [was] stark naked with bulging eyes [and had] . . . blood oozing from . . . nose, ears and mouth . . . The other had a gaping wound in his side . . . His clothes were torn to shreds . . . I felt sick as my boot met soft unresisting human flesh.'

The route to the front ended with them having to race down the forward slope of a hill, in full view of the German front line, in an attempt to avoid casualties. Given it was daylight they had to be thankful only a few men were hit. Then there was another rise before they descended again to the valley containing the quarry. It was here that they found the dugout occupied by Major Herbert. Although pleased to see that Auld and his men had not been hit as he feared, the major did not stand on ceremony. Auld was to take over the command of the battalion front line, which ran from a point in front of the quarry to a strongpoint on its right. From there he was to probe the gap to the right to see whether he could make contact with the 52nd Battalion.

The realization that he had to pass through an unprotected landscape into which the German artillery was pumping shrapnel and high explosive filled Auld with dread. But he had to do it and his account describes how, after finding two volunteers, they finally set out from the strongpoint on their right. 'Bent double . . . with my revolver in hand, cocked ready for instant use, the three of us crept cautiously [forwards],' Auld wrote, '. . . cringing at the groan and crash of heavy shells, crouching . . . to escape the flying steel of high explosive, peering through the gaps and round the mounds of shattered trenches.'

They were pulled up short by a sharp bend in the trench. Leaving his men behind, Auld stepped forward to reconnoitre:

What I saw as I peered along that trench has burned into my soul. It was literally a trench of death . . . without a bay or bend . . . for 30 or 40 yards. The dead bodies of Australian soldiers lay in profusion in all sorts of attitudes, just as they had died . . . Some were obviously freshly killed, while others had been dead for 2 or 3 days. [They were] swollen and black, putrid and stinking, under the hot sun and the myriads of flies . . . We looked over the parapet, and amidst the shell holes and tortured ground, saw more and yet more bodies in the familiar Australian uniform. Horror, fear and anger mingled in a surging passion of hate against the perpetrators of this misery and I shook my fist in impotent rage [at] . . . the Germans who . . . were the sole cause of this outrage against civilization and humanity.

But pity for the dead soon turned to fear for their own safety as yet another shell exploded nearby, forcing them to take cover from the resulting shower of earth. Trembling and dazed, they started to walk on again, until it gradually dawned on all of them that they were lost once more. Moreover, they could not simply retrace their steps to find their bearings, since the constant shelling had completely altered the look of the terrain they had just crossed.

It was only when they saw a couple of German stretcher-bearers walking towards them that they realized they must have strayed into German lines. They beat a hasty retreat in the opposite direction. Eventually, 'deafened by the noise of high explosive, half blinded by flying soil . . . suffocated by the acrid fumes of bursting shells and sickened almost beyond endurance by the appalling stench of putrefying bodies', they ended up back at the strongpoint from where they had started. They were still there when later that afternoon, as if by a miracle, another man from the 50th Battalion climbed over the parapet, claiming he had come from the 52nd Battalion. Too relieved to complain about all their needless suffering, the news was conveyed back to their brigade, and within a matter of hours a series of posts had been manned linking the 50th and 52nd Battalions.

All would have been well had a gunner from their left rear not decided, shortly after dusk, to fire his weapon in their direction. Auld's account describes the sheer terror the resumption of the shelling engendered in the front line:

The long drawn moaning sound of the [first] shell's approach and the terrific force of its explosion sent cold shivers up and down our spines. Our sleepy minds struggling to retain consciousness suddenly became acutely and agonizingly aware that each succeeding shell was falling closer to the . . . remains of our trench. A cold sweat poured out of my shivering body and stark fear and anguish tore at my soul.

For the second time that day I began to lose control. Crouching in abject terror, we listened to the harsh screeching groan of the [next] fast approaching monster of death. Every nerve was taut and tense and quivered as we steeled ourselves to resist the convulsion of the descending horror. With a roar and concussion, transcending in volume and intensity any previous or subsequent experience, the huge steel projectile hit the ground and exploded within a few yards of the strongpost. The earth rocked and broke and the sides of the trench collapsed in several places. Lumps of earth and showers of loose war blasted soil poured down upon us like hail . . . Stunned and choking from the vile fumes of the exploded lyddite, I staggered down the battered trench, my enfeebled mind and will desperately intent on escaping . . .

All sense of duty and loyalty to my men had gone. I felt I could no longer face up to the appalling conditions which were so violently abhorrent to the deepest instincts of the human soul. The primitive instinct of self-preservation held complete sway. My one desire was to reach the quarry dugout and tell Major Herbert that I could not go on. But as I approached the dugout, the enormity of my action in deserting my post began slowly to impinge itself on my muddled brain. At the entrance to the dugout I hesitated, and from the outer darkness saw again the interior dimly lit by candles and filled with silent depressed men. Major Herbert sat at the table, with the light full on his face. He looked straight at me but showed no sign of recognition.

In that instant I recognized that one step forward meant disgrace and the stigma of cowardice for the rest of my life. Cowardice in the face of the enemy, the worst sin a soldier can commit. I drew back further into the gloom and fought the greatest battle of the war – for me. It lasted but a few minutes. Gradually self-control returned, conquering the demoralizing fear that had nearly been my undoing. I turned and slowly climbed out of the quarry and made my way back into the trench.

In the meantime the remnants of the 52nd Battalion, the unit that Auld and his men had sought with such tenacity, had been enduring a trial every bit as testing. A substantial proportion of its casualties were suffered during the initial attack, in the course of which most of three of its companies either failed to take their objective, or were repulsed after overrunning it. The battalion's only enduring success was largely thanks to a pair of its officers who happened to be brothers. Because they stood out from the battalion both in terms of stature as well as in terms of brave deeds, they were differentiated by nicknames: Lieutenant Duncan Maxwell, aged twenty-four, who was 6 foot 3 inches tall, was known as 'Little', whereas twenty-eight-year-old Lieutenant Arthur Maxwell, who at 6 foot 5 inches towered over his comrades, including his younger brother, was known as 'Big'.

If it had not been for Big Maxwell, it is doubtful whether the one company that did succeed would have made it to the German front line. Because of the failure to reconnoitre before the attack, the company was facing the wrong way until Big Maxwell, the battalion's intelligence officer, put them right. But it was Little Maxwell whose action saved the day once the action started. When the company's charismatic leader, Captain Charles Littler, was wounded just short of the German trenches, the assaulting troops faltered until Little Maxwell seized Littler's stick, and waving it in the air, led the charge into an abandoned section of the German firing line. After the link-up with the 49th Australian Battalion had been effected, Little Maxwell then proceeded, with the eighty-one men from his own battalion who had joined him in the captured trench, to erect barricades on the west side of the garrison to hold back Germans who he was sure would do anything they could to eject the Australians.[11]

However, although an attempt by German infantry to seize the trench was made and resisted, the greatest challenge came from the German artillery. During the afternoon of 4 September, after the headquarters of both 1 ANZAC and Major-General Cox's 4th Australian Division had been relieved by the Canadian Corps and its 1st Canadian Division respectively, German shelling threatened to drive Little Maxwell and his men out of their trench. The shelling first wiped out most of the men holding 150 yards of the position nearest the left barricade, who by this time included many of the 250 men from the 13th Canadian Battalion sent up to reinforce the Australians. Then, after Little Maxwell backed by five Australians and Canadians manned a barricade a short distance to the east of the area that had been bombarded, a shell smashed into them, killing or wounding all of them except Little. His combative spirit dented but not extinguished, he retired another 20 yards, ready to resist the expected counter-attack on his own, and only when it did not materialize was he able to move back into the piece of trench he had just vacated.

Given that the shelling left him with fewer than fifty men, Little Maxwell could have been excused for retiring at this juncture, but determined to finish the job he had started, he sent a message back to his commander that included the words 'Will try to hold on where I am' until the relieving forces arrived. He then proceeded to do just that. He personally lay out in the dark with another man ahead of the rest of the garrison to ensure that the remains of the barricade that had most recently been targeted would be retained. And when during that night, 4–5 September, men from the 16th Canadian Battalion arrived, he escorted them to the site of the original barricades. It was almost entirely due to his leadership that the Canadians south-west of the captured portion of Fabeck Graben were in a position to link up with the units holding the left side of the front south of Mouquet Farm on 5 September (see map 16)[12] That must have made it all the more galling for Little Maxwell to learn later, after the 3rd Canadian Brigade finally relieved the 13th Australian Brigade on 5 September, that not only had the attempt to capture Thiepval by the back door before the planned mid-September thrust been abandoned by order of Haig, but that the Canadians on 8 September had lost the one important gain made and held thanks to his support: the captured portion of Fabeck Graben.[13]

But there were compensations. In the course of the general attack on 3 September, the 4th Army at long last captured Guillemont – or to put it more accurately, the 4th Army captured the mixture of wood splinters and rubble on the land that had once contained the village.[14] Most, if not all, of the structures that had once stood within the village had long since been pulverized by the artillery of both sides. The French had also enjoyed their own successes. North of the Somme they had taken Cléry and Le Forest. South of the Somme they had captured Soyécourt and Chilly (see map 9).[15]

That sudden change of plan must have pained those who had lost their sons and husbands even more. The 52nd Australian Battalion had suffered 450 casualties during the fighting around Mouquet Farm, the highest of all the units in the 13th Australian Brigade, whose four battalions had sustained casualties approaching 1,350.[16] The 52nd Battalion's losses included twenty-six-year-old Lieutenant Len Wadsley, whose family had a fruit farm in Tasmania. He appears to have been one of the unfortunate men who, as part of the battalion's C Company, raced over their objective without realizing it and suffered the consequences as they tried to return. According to one witness in his Red Cross file, 'A friend of mine . . . saw him with his head blown off lying near the German parapet.'[17]

What makes Wadsley's death so poignant is not so much the way he died, horrific though it was, but rather the fact that the Somme snuffed out such a friendly, trusting character whose optimistic, patriotic, 'glass half full' letters, preserved for posterity by his family, act as a memorial not only to him, but also to thousands of others like him cut off in their prime. Most of the letters were addressed to his widowed father and three sisters, who all lived together at Pendennis, the family's fruit farm. Despite all the hardships he was enduring, Len invariably maintained the same jaunty, cheerful tone in his correspondence, which probably reflected his everyday personality. The letters commenced long before he left Australia. Like so many young soldiers who abandoned their families so that they could join the Army, he realized his family would not be pleased at his decision to abandon them: 'Now Dad. Don't be downhearted. It's up to me to go if I can do any good,' he wrote to his father, Wright, on learning that he was to be sent overseas sooner than they had all expected, adding 'I have every confidence in coming through all right.'

Although obviously excited by what he witnessed as he moved away from his provincial roots, Len's letters were full of what he was missing at home. While training in Melbourne, he wrote about the Victorian apples – 'not a patch on Tassy's, no flavour hardly' – and the cherries, strawberries and other fruits – 'plentiful, but none come up to those at Pendennis'. And when he missed the visit of his brother Ted's fiancée to the farm, he wrote to her saying: 'I don't know whether to congratulate you or not, because if you knew Ted as I do, all you would want would be sympathy! . . . I wish I had been at home to give you a right royal welcome and to rub your face with raspberries and thus inaugurate you as one of the family.'

But a darker side emerged once Len landed in France. The day before the 3 September attack, he told a sergeant in his platoon that he feared he would not come out of it alive, and Len wrote a moving last letter that he asked another soldier to post to his family if he did not come back. One can easily imagine the tears they must have cried as they read the words he had hoped would help them deal with his passing. It started with a characteristic 'Dear Everybody At Home' and continued:

If you receive this, I will by then have passed to the Great Beyond. We are just preparing to go in on a fairly large stunt which may be the end of a good many of us, and I may be one of the number . . . Well, I leave myself in the hands of the Almighty and trust him absolutely. You may depend on it, I've done my job and you'll have no need to be ashamed of me. I would have liked to have got back again, but 'twas not meant that I should. Never mind, girls, there'll be someone else to take my place.

Goodbye Dad. Goodbye girls. Let the rest of the family know I think of you all and hope to meet you all again later on. 'Tis rotten having to write this, but c'est la guerre. One thing we know: Fritz has a much worse time than we do. I guess there'll be great rejoicing when it's all over. We are all thoroughly sick of it. Well, goodbye again to you all. From your son and bro. Len.[18]

Wright Wadsley and the girls had lost their dear Len. But at least Len had left behind seven siblings. It is hard to imagine how Benjamin and Eliza Potter in South Australia felt after hearing that four of their sons had

participated in the 52nd Battalion attack on 3 September, and that afterwards three of them were missing. Ralph, the surviving son, returned to
the area east of Mouquet Farm in March 1917, only to find his missing
brother Edward's decomposed remains lying beside his gas helmet with
some letters and the identity disk inside it.[19] Shortly afterwards Benjamin
and Eliza were told that their other two sons had also been killed in action.
The surviving son, who was wounded a few days after finding his brother's
corpse, then wrote to the Australian authorities to ask whether he might be
excused further service: his parents were both unwell and he was the only
son left who could support them. He was duly discharged on compassion-
ate grounds, his story foreshadowing the plot of a famous film made years
later about the surviving brother in the American Army in World War II.[20]

The deaths of Len Wadsley and the three Potter boys epitomize the
needless sacrifice that was made on the Somme as a whole. It had taken the
Australians no fewer than ten attacks to move forward from Pozières to
where they were after the 3 September attack. And even though soldiers
such as Lieutenant Duncan Maxwell could congratulate themselves on
holding trenches taken and retained thanks to individual acts of valour, the
truth was that further attacks aiming to exploit the capture of the part of
Fabeck Graben taken on 3 September would have been too predictable to
have had a realistic chance of breaking through.

The same could perhaps be said about so many of the attacks made in the
course of the Somme offensive, and perhaps even about the offensive itself
after the first great attack had failed to break through. Once that had happened, Haig should arguably have abandoned the attack on the Somme and
attacked elsewhere. But just as during the many attempted advances towards
Mouquet Farm and Fabeck Graben, there was always another permutation
to try, so, when deciding whether to carry on with the Somme offensive,
there was always another reason to carry on, just in case victory lay around
the next corner.

34: Last Throw of the Dice

Ginchy, 9 September 1916

(See maps 2 and 15)

Even while Haig's troops were struggling to fathom how to winkle the Germans out of the villages and wooded areas that he had told them stood in the way of his next great offensive, planned for the middle of September, he tempted fate by asking Rawlinson, and Gough, to submit their plans for what he hoped would be the long-awaited breakthrough. As usual this was relayed by Lieutenant-General Sir Launcelot Kiggell, the Chief of the General Staff. On 19 August 1916, Kiggell informed the commander of the 4th Army and the Reserve Army in a letter that Haig would like to see their suggestions within the next nine days.[1]

Three days before setting this deadline, Kiggell had given Rawlinson and Gough some good news. They may have had difficulty breaking through in the past, but this time there would be a new dimension to their attack. The 'tanks' that had been talked about so much were finally coming on-stream. The first batch were scheduled to arrive in France over 'the next few weeks', Kiggell told them.[2] 'The plans of attack should state in detail how it is proposed to employ the tanks,' he stressed pointedly at the end of his 19 August letter, in an apparent attempt to warn Rawlinson and Gough that Haig expected a lot of them.

In spite of all the talk about them, these 'tanks' were an unknown quantity in August 1916. Nothing like them had ever been seen on a battlefield before. In his 19 August letter Kiggell described them as 'Heavy Section armoured cars', but then felt the need to enclose with it a kind of manual that was a potted guide as to what the tanks were and what they could do. They were evidently massive, weighing no less than 28 tons. The male versions carried two 6-pounder and four Hotchkiss guns, while the females carried five Vickers machine guns and one Hotchkiss gun. Both versions were big enough to require a crew of seven. That made the tanks more like moving fortresses than conventional vehicles. The fact that they moved around on caterpillar tracks rather than normal wheels differentiated them still further from normal vehicles.

According to this manual, 'the chief attributes of the tank are its power of crossing obstacles, its fire power, its momentum and its invulnerability against shrapnel and small arms fire. Its chief weakness is its liability to be knocked out by artillery or heavy trench mortars.' It was anticipated there would be between fifty and sixty tanks available on the Somme front by 15 September. Given that Haig thought they might be game changers, and might panic demoralized Germans into surrendering, one suspects that he awaited the 4th Army's plan in particular with bated breath. In the first instance, Rawlinson was to be given double the number of tanks that were being made available to the Reserve Army.

If so, he was once again to be disappointed. Haig had given Rawlinson to understand that he wanted him to target the German third position stretching from Morval in the south to Le Sars to the north. But Rawlinson, predictably, in the letter he sent to Haig on 28 August, pointed out the logistical difficulties of taking the three trench 'systems' necessary to reach the point indicated by his commander-in-chief.

The first German trench system, which ran from Combles to Martinpuich via Bouleaux Wood, Flers and High Wood, and which would only be some 200 to 600 yards from where the 4th Army's front line was likely to be by mid-September, was quite manageable given the appropriate troops and artillery, with or without tanks. What was more difficult to work out was how tanks would improve the 4th Army's chances against the second and third trench systems.

The second German trench system, which ran from south of Flers to Le Sars via Eaucourt l'Abbaye, only protected part of the German front. It branched off the first system near Flers, and was 3,000 yards north of the first system by the time both systems reached the Albert–Bapaume road. The third system, which ran in front of Morval to Butte de Warlencourt, a 50-foot-high prehistoric burial mound, via Lesboeufs and Gueudecourt, was around 1,500 yards behind the second system, and parallel to it.

If it were not for the tanks, both the second and third systems would be 'out of the question', Rawlinson told Haig in a letter dispatched to Kiggell. The second system was too far from the first system, and the third system was out of range of the British guns. However, the arrival of the tanks left him facing a dilemma. It was possible that the tanks might be successful against the second and third systems. In that case, he would have thrown away the chance to make a quick breakthrough if he did not back them up with artillery and infantry. Rawlinson continued: 'On the other hand, we may by expecting too much of the tanks, and be tempted to undertake an operation which is beyond our power, and . . . this might cause very heavy losses. Moreover if the attack failed [and a tank was captured], the secret of the tanks would be given away once and for all.' That being the case, he was in favour of taking the trench systems one by one over a number of days.[3]

Given Haig's negative reaction to Rawlinson's step-by-step approach before 1 July, it will come as no surprise to learn that he rejected what Rawlinson proposed for mid-September. Giving voice to this in his diary entry for 29 August, Haig wrote: 'In my opinion he is not making enough of the situation with the deterioration and all round loss of morale of the enemy troops. I think we should make our attack as strong and as violent as possible, and plan to go as far as possible.'[4]

Writing back to Rawlinson on 31 August, again using Kiggell as conduit, Haig insisted that the attack had to be 'planned as a decisive operation'. Never had circumstances been more in their favour. Not only did they have their new secret weapon, the tanks, to help them. They also had fresh divisions to do the attacking, and they were helped by the fact that German morale was plummeting, making them less keen to stand and fight. Assuming that the 4th Army could take both Bouleaux Wood and Ginchy before the attack started, Haig felt that Rawlinson should try during the first day of the offensive to seize at the very least the eastern wing of the German third position. This meant that on that critical first day Rawlinson must target the line running from Morval to Flers, via Lesboeufs and Gueudecourt. If he broke through there, then the line running from Morval to Bapaume via Le Transloy could be held as a flank guard, giving the cavalry plus available infantry the chance to march north-westwards, mopping up the surviving German defences that could not be overwhelmed from the west.[5]

If this discussion had taken place just after 1 July, at a time when Haig's star appeared to be on the wane, it is possible that Rawlinson might have stood his ground and argued against what he was being asked to do contrary to his better judgement. However, now that his own star had reached the lowest point it had ever occupied since the victorious 14 July, Rawlinson can be forgiven for agreeing to do anything, within reason, to pacify his master. Given that Haig had been complaining about his tactics concerning Guillemont (see Chapter 31), Rawlinson may have wondered whether it would soon be his turn to be '*stellenbosched*'.

In Rawlinson's diary entry for 30 August he described the reasoning that persuaded him to go along with Haig: 'The Chief is anxious to have a gamble . . . If we succeed, it may bring the Boche to terms. If we fail, we have all the winter to recuperate . . . A success would have a great effect around the world. It is worth risking.'[6] That decided, on 31 August he wrote back to Haig, again through Kiggell, beginning his letter by supinely stating 'I understand that the plan I submitted . . . was not . . . sufficiently ambitious', and terminating it by agreeing to attack all the villages Haig had specified on the first day of the big offensive.[7]

Ironically, at the very moment when Rawlinson felt that his own position was coming under threat because of the stout defence put up by the Germans with relatively few divisions and restricted ammunition, Erich von Falkenhayn finally lost his job as the German Chief of the General Staff. He was replaced on 29 August by Field Marshal von Hindenburg, with General Ludendorff acting as First Quartermaster-General.

This change was long overdue according to Prince Rupprecht, who had, until just days before the changeover, been the commander of the German 6th Army. Henceforth Rupprecht was to be in charge of the group of armies that oversaw the German 1st and 2nd Armies, the units directly responsible for the fighting on the Somme.[8] As such, he would be in a position to corroborate Haig's declaration that German soldiers' morale and fighting capacity were being gradually degraded. However, Rupprecht would also be able to appreciate how the new German commanders eventually eased the plight of the unit commanders on the Somme by permitting them to make tactical withdrawals, and by proactively discussing with them their need for reinforcements and ammunition.

But that was all in the future. There was nothing that the appointments of Hindenburg, Ludendorff and Rupprecht could do to thwart the inexorable progress eastwards of the British forces. Delville Wood finally fell into British hands on 27 August, and as we have seen Guillemont and Wedge Wood (south-east of Guillemont) followed suit on 3 September. The much sought-after Falfemont Farm went the same way, being captured by the British on the night of 4–5 September. Meanwhile the French captured Cléry and Le Forest, as well as Soyécourt and Chilly in the south. By 9 September the only outstanding site Haig particularly wanted to take before the start of the mid-September offensive was Ginchy. That was not for want of trying. The village defences had been penetrated on several occasions beforehand, only for the garrison to drive out the invaders.

Curiously for such an important strategic target, there are few detailed accounts that describe how the village fell, which it did when it was attacked by the 16th (Irish) Division on 9 September at 4.45 p.m. The most lively of the accounts appears in a letter sent to his aunt Maggie by 2nd Lieutenant Arthur Young of the 7th Royal Irish Fusiliers, a 49th Brigade unit assigned to the 16th Division's 48th Brigade. The letter started off by setting the scene:

Try and picture in your mind's eye a fairly broad valley running more or less north and south. You must imagine that the Germans are somewhere over the further, or eastern, crest. You are looking across the valley from the ruins of Guillemont. About half right the further crest rises to a height crowned by a mass of wreckage and tangled trees. Well, that is Ginchy. It was like being near the foot of [Hampstead Heath's] Parliament Hill, with the village on top.

The unit's immediate surroundings were equally well described: they were in a shallow trench that stank of rotting corpses. The bodies had been buried when the parapet gave way on being hit. 'The smell turned us sick,' Young admitted. It was already the afternoon of 9 September before he heard they were going to be sent over the top to support the Royal Irish Rifles. 'I was dismayed,' he confessed, explaining that he already knew what that meant because he had been in a previous advance. They arrived in the front line at 4.45 p.m. just in time to see a sight that thrilled him no end:

Between the outer fringe of Ginchy and the front line of our own trenches is No Man's Land, a wilderness of pits so close together that you could ride astraddle the partitions between any two of them. As you look half right obliquely along No Man's Land you behold a great host of . . . coated men rise out of the earth and surge forward and upward in a torrent.

We joined in on the left . . . By this time we were all wildly excited. Our shouts and yells must have struck terror into the Huns who were firing their machine guns down the slope. But there was no wavering in the Irish host. We advanced at a steady walking pace. That numbing dread had now left me . . . I was intoxicated with the glory of it all.

Then he saw the screen of shells sweeping towards their front. 'I knew it was a case of now or never, and stumbled on feverishly. We managed to get through the barrage in the nick of time, for it closed behind us, and after that we had no shells to fear in front of us.' That did not mean there was no German shelling. 'One [shell] landed in the midst of a bunch of men about seventy yards away on my right. I have a most vivid recollection of seeing a tremendous burst of clay and earth go shooting up into the air – and even parts of human bodies, and that when the smoke cleared there was nothing left.'

They reached Ginchy. But then they had to clamber over fallen trees, beams and mounds of brick and rubble, ignoring the crackling of rifle fire that greeted them, only hearing the cheering of the Irishmen as they pushed forward. At last they saw some Germans. Young's account continued: 'They were in a trench . . . Some had their hands up. Others were kneeling and holding their arms out to us. Still others were running up and down the trench distractedly as if they didn't know which way to go. But as we got closer they went down on their knees too.' After penetrating the German front line, Young's unit found themselves on a plateau, surrounded by a wood. From here he could see Germans fleeing over the distant ridge, with Irishmen in hot pursuit.

Young also witnessed other Germans being captured in a sunken road that ran eastwards out of the village:

They were very frightened and huddled together with hands upraised. They began to empty their pockets, and handed out souvenirs, watches, compasses, cigars and even wanted to shake hands with us.

I got a handful of cigars off a dead Boche and smoked them . . . Also a tin of cigarettes. Poor devil . . . his chocolates also came in handy. He must have been a cheery soul when living, for he had a photograph of himself in his pocket in a group with his wife and children, and the picture made him look a jolly old sport, [a far cry from what I had in front of me:] . . . Here he was dead with both his legs missing.

However, of all the action that Young saw that day as Ginchy was captured once and for all, perhaps the strongest memory was of the way the Irish treated their prisoners:

Not one of these Huns, some of whom had been engaged in slaughtering our men up to the very last moment, was killed . . . When you remember that . . . our men were worked up to a frenzy of excitement, this crowning act of mercy to their foes is surely to their eternal credit.

In fact kindness and compassion for the wounded is about the one decent thing I have seen in war.[9]

It is good to hear Lieutenant Young's positive analysis of the Irish troops' behaviour at Ginchy. But given other testimony that is less flattering to Allied soldiers in this regard, one wonders whether he was just being naive, or whether he had just chanced upon an area where good treatment of prisoners was an important consideration. A lot of that would go out of the window in the wake of the great attack that was to follow.

But then a lot was sacrificed in order to make the next attack a success. Given the pressure that was building up against Haig because of the minuscule progress on the Somme battlefield since 14 July, it was not unnatural that he should want to include everything in his armoury in order to improve his chances. That meant using the tanks that after a long gestation period were just becoming available should he want to deploy them.

Haig's attitude is clear in a letter that he sent to the Chief of the Imperial General Staff, Sir William Robertson, on 22 August: It would be 'folly' not 'to use every means at my disposal in what is likely to be the crowning effort of this year,' he wrote.[10] But that was not the opinion of all those tank experts and enthusiasts whose jobs did not depend on showing short-term gains on the Somme. Lieutenant-Colonel Ernest Swinton, the man who had come up with the original idea for the tanks, and who had done as much as anyone to transform the theoretical concept of a tank into reality, was strongly in favour of waiting until a mass of tanks could be used in one action.[11]

That being the case it is surprising that no politician appears to have sought to rein in Haig. Arguably the decision on whether to use the tanks on the Somme should have been taken by the British government. Just as it would be unthinkable today for the head of the Army to be given control over the nuclear deterrent, so the government in 1916 should at least have had their say on a new weapon that could have saved the lives of hundreds of thousands of men.

A last-ditch effort to change Haig's mind about using tanks was made by Sir Maurice Hankey, secretary of the War Committee.[12] On 7 September he tried over dinner to change the minds of Haig's senior staff officers at GHQ in France. He pointed out that the 'caterpillars', as he called them, were not designed for a slow-moving battle like the Somme where the numerous craters stopped them from changing direction or advancing quickly. Tanks would be best employed en masse on a new battlefield where there were no obstacles and where they could exploit the fact that the enemy was not equipped to resist them.

But by that stage, with many of the tanks already in France, and with just days to go before the planned offensive, it was next to impossible to find anyone who would even think of such a negative step. After that dinner, the idea of persuading anyone to save the tanks for the future was dropped.

35: Bloodlust

Flers, 15 September 1916

(See map 17)

Some of the 'fresh' troops whom Haig and Rawlinson were relying on to spearhead their mid-September offensive had come to France all the way from New Zealand. On the way the New Zealanders, like the Australians, had participated in the Gallipoli campaign. But it was while supporting British interests in Egypt before and after Gallipoli that they sustained losses from an unexpected source: women.

The problem was that men who were a long way away from home naturally gravitated to where they could find a release for their pent-up sexual desires. That was what made the red-light district in Cairo so enticing. There, for a knock-down price the men were able to have sex with a different prostitute each night without anyone at home being any the wiser. But there was a catch. During 1914–16 the Cairo red-light district was one of the filthiest of places on earth. It was a breeding ground for parasites and infection.

That is why Major-General Alexander Godley, commander of the New Zealand Expeditionary Force, warned Colonel James Allen, the New Zealand Minister of Defence, when New Zealand troops first arrived in Egypt: 'The only trouble I foresee is venereal. I am afraid we are bound to lose about 10 per cent of the men through it. The women here are all full of it . . . There is a great deal of syphilis and gonorrhea.'[1]

He was right to be concerned. Ettie Rout, a New Zealander who attempted to shame her government into addressing the issue rather than sweeping it under the carpet, was informed that in March 1916, the month before the New Zealand Division was shipped to France, there were no fewer than 10,000 New Zealanders in Egypt suffering from VD.[2]

This problem was not just restricted to the troops in Cairo. Leave in London, which was also crawling with prostitutes, could be just as hazardous, if data collected by New Zealand's director of medical services was accurate. He told his Minister of Defence that during 1916–17 the admissions of Australasian soldiers to hospitals in London because of venereal diseases amounted to more than 18 per cent of those soldiers who visited the city.[3]

All sorts of measures were taken to try to cut the incidence of the disease. They included marching the men through the Cairo red-light district during daylight hours so that the soldiers could see what the women they had been consorting with really looked like. Another measure was supplying the men with a calomel-based ointment together with instructions that it should be applied to the penis before sexual intercourse. Unfortunately, as the assistant director of New Zealand's Medical Service reported, the prostitutes would not allow the men to use the ointment because it 'blistered them', adding that the ointment was instead used for other purposes: 'Natives found [it] very useful for curing the lice in their hair.' The failure to come up with an effective policy could have undermined New Zealand's foreign policy. The outraged official representing the National Committee of New Zealand's YMCA wrote to New Zealand's Commissioner in Egypt warning that if 'the truth were known . . . voluntary recruiting throughout the Dominion would stop dead'.

The VD figures only improved after the New Zealand Expeditionary Force was sent to France in April 1916. That was not because paid-for sex was all of a sudden off the agenda. It was just that there were other more sophisticated ways of giving soldiers thrills. That at least was the verdict of Sergeant John Russell, a New Zealander who had worked for the Bank of New Zealand before enlisting. After being shipped to France, he sampled the night life in Boulogne, and left behind the following account of the entertainment on offer at a back-street estaminet:

Right on time, a trio of shapely flappers skipped on stage in scanty attire that left nothing to the imagination above the waist . . . At the end of a snappy tumbling turn, they lined up as though to wait for the applause to subside before making their exit . . . But when it showed no sign of abating, and it became obvious that the boys were in the mood for still greater thrills, the trio tossed off their tiny G-strings and proceeded to give a demonstration of poise and agility in a series of graceful slow motion evolutions that beside highlighting their turbulent 'topsies' in all their spectacular splendour, gave liberal prominence to their less glamorous but even more fascinating fannies . . . [which had been shaved] either for the sake of uniformity or as a routine refinement. It gave their bodies an all over sleek and well groomed look that was amazingly good for the morale of war weary troops.

The girls climaxed their act in an unhurried and informal line up 'as is', in which their major attractions were displayed in a natural perspective in a big way, before eventually moving off stage. At . . . [this] point my mate agreed that another little drink wouldn't do us any harm before we wove our way back to

barracks . . . [It had been] an exciting, but quite wholesome, evening's fun, compared with which, our somewhat similar after dark experiences in Cairo had been
very crude and unsavory, and no more stimulating than a cup of cold tea or a
dangle parade [a parade where the soldiers pulled down their trousers so that the
medical officer could inspect their penises to check they did not have VD].[4]

It should be stressed that these statistics and this story are not intended to
suggest that New Zealanders were any more sex-obsessed than the soldiers
of any other nation. Nor did it affect their ability to show their mettle as
soldiers. After they finally took to the battlefield of the Somme, it quickly
became clear they had deployed some of the best units in France. A similar
caution should be mentioned concerning their bloodletting (see below). A
careful reading of all the relevant chapters in this book will show that units
from many of the countries profiled at times indulged in similar activities.

The New Zealanders were not involved in the early stages of the 'Big
Push'. It was only in the second half of August 1916 that the New Zealand
Division, commanded by New Zealander Major-General Andrew Russell,
were extracted from the relatively quiet backwaters surrounding Armentières and sent down south. Their first stop saw them occupying a group of
villages near Abbeville, and it was here that they received the first hint of
what was to be expected of them.

Lindsay Inglis, a twenty-two-year-old captain in the 3rd New Zealand Rifle
Brigade's 1st Battalion, is a good sounding board when it comes to analysing
what was right and wrong about what they were told to do. He had been a
trainee lawyer before joining the New Zealand Expeditionary Force, and
would one day rise to the top of the military hierarchy, ending his career as a
major-general. After World War II he became the president of a military court
in occupied Germany. Writing after World War I, Inglis wondered whether the
first stripping away of the New Zealanders' moral code and values took place
during a series of lectures. These were given to their troops by a huge red-headed
Scottish major, who visited the New Zealand Division units at the end of
August in order to tell them how to behave when they encountered their first
Germans.[5] The lectures evidently made a great impression, the major's bloodthirsty exhortations being vividly recorded in several soldiers' diaries. According
to Inglis, the lecture he attended included the following clear-cut message:

We don't want prisoners. We have to feed prisoners. What we have to do is to kill
Huns. The only good Hun is a dead Hun.

The Hun will shoot or throw bombs at you and your mates till you get within reach of him with your bayonet. Then, like the dirty snivelling coward he is, he will put up his hands and squeal, 'Kamerad!' That's your chance to stick him in the soft part of the belly where the bayonet goes in easily and comes out quickly.

If he runs away, go for his kidneys. It's a sure spot where the bayonet goes in and comes out like cutting cheese.[6]

There was also an attempt to characterize Germans as obsequious waiters who, in peacetime, made themselves as servile as possible in the hope they would be given a big tip.[7] The implication was that if the Germans were given half a chance during the approaching battles, they would use similar acting skills to catch the New Zealanders off their guard so that they could kill them. That was another reason to shoot first and ask questions later. And if following hand-to-hand fighting, the rifle attached to the bayonet was dropped, New Zealanders were told they should take a fork out of their tunic pockets and stab their adversary in the throat – 'a fitting end for a dirty German waiter!'

Not surprisingly, given the major's colourful language, quotations from these lectures were 'bandied about for a time' by the men who heard them, Inglis reported. But future events would suggest that these lectures may have been the factor which indoctrinated the New Zealanders into believing that the Germans could be dispatched with impunity. 'It would be interesting to know to what extent . . . [these lectures were] responsible for deeds of the kind which even in war amount to nothing less than brutal murder,' Inglis wrote in his memoirs, adding 'We were astonished that it should have been officially sanctioned.'[8]

The same could have been said about the barbaric treatment meted out to Private Frank Hughes of the 2nd Canterbury battalion. He was shot on 25 August by firing squad following a court martial, for deserting his post in the Armentières sector. Whilst it was not Hughes's first such offence, and one can see that if his misdemeanour went unpunished, others might have followed his example, there is a lurking suspicion that even during such a fiercely contested conflict a twenty-first-century court martial might have punished him less severely. More effort would have been expended in digging up mitigating circumstances.

The way his mother back in Wellington, New Zealand, found out about how her son had been treated was certainly unedifying. She received a

42. Brigadier-General John Gellibrand (wearing the soft hat), the commander of the 6th Australian Brigade, and some of his officers eating breakfast in Sausage Valley. Gellibrand had his headquarters here during the doomed attack on the night of 28–29 July 1916.

43. Lieutenant Albert Jacka VC of the 14th Australian Battalion, whose response on 7 August when the Germans attacked the Australian positions east of Pozières was described by the official historian as 'the most dramatic and effective act of audacity in the history of the A.I.F.'

44. Three 8-inch howitzers support the Allied advance from Fricourt.

45. British troops repair the road leading from Montauban to Guillemont, described in the official history as 'straight, desolate and swept by fire'.

46. and 47. Mouquet Farm before it was destroyed; and the site where Mouquet Farm had once stood before it was destroyed by gunfire.

48. Australian journalist Charles Bean (*second from left*) standing between Duncan and Arthur Maxwell (nicknamed 'Little' and 'Big' respectively), who as Lieutenants feature in chapter 33. Bean's cousin Angus Butler is on the right.

49. Lieutenant Leo Butler, another of Charles Bean's cousins, who was serving in the 12th Australian Battalion when he was hit. He later died in hospital.

50. Alec Raws (*left*) was well known for the many letters he wrote home describing the horrific conditions on the front line before he died. He is seen here standing beside his brother Goldy, who was also killed, and his father (*right*).

51. Dead Germans, following the British capture of Guillemont on 3 September 1916.

52. *Left* British soldiers occupy a trench that ran between some trees in the captured village of Ginchy.

53. and 54. *Left* New Zealand reinforcements march through Wellington: this is where their big adventure started. *Right* New Zealanders from an Auckland battalion in the German Switch Trench following its capture on 15 September 1916.

55. British soldiers congregating around a Mark 1 tank. It was used as a headquarters after being disabled during the fighting west of Flers on 15 September 1916.

56. *Top* A Canadian soldier stands on top of the Sugar Factory south of Courcelette, which was captured by Canadian forces on 15 September 1916.

57. and 58. *Left* Canadian wounded en route to a dressing station after the fighting in and around Courcelette in September 1916. *Below* Although some Canadians had been told to execute their prisoners, the observance of such an edict was far from universal if this photograph is anything to go by. Here, Canadians feed their prisoners.

59. In Hyde Park, King George V pins a Victoria Cross on to Captain Archie White's jacket, the reward for his acts of conspicuous gallantry during the fighting at Feste Staufen.

60. to 62. *Left* Private Howard Kippenberger, who fought courageously during the 1st Canterbury's capture of Gird Trench on 27 September 1916. *Centre* 2nd Lieutenant Alexander Aitken led the New Zealand 1st Otago Battalion into battle on 27 September 1916. *Right* Lieutenant-Colonel Bernard Freyberg, who rallied the men in the Hood Battalion (Royal Naval Division) when German gunfire threatened to thwart their advance into Beaucourt on 13 November 1916. For this, Freyberg, who had been been wounded, was awarded the Victoria Cross.

63. *Above* The Somme was famous for its terrible conditions. Here men from the Middlesex Regiment tramp through the mud as they leave the Somme.

64. *Centre* A sodden grave of an unknown soldier amidst the mud at Thiepval symbolizes the awful terrain at the end of the battle.

65. *Below* The end of the line. One of the last structures left standing at Beaumont Hamel: the remains of its railway station, the village where the battle started at 7.20 a.m. on 1 July 1916.

letter from James Allen, New Zealand's Defence Minister, stating that 'H' Hughes had been executed. This prompted her to write back stating that the minister must have made a mistake, since her son's initial was 'F' for Frank. She ended her letter on a tragically optimistic note, stating 'I still believe my son to be living', a phrase that caused much hand-wringing in the Defence Ministry.[9] Eventually, a new letter was drafted by James Allen, stating that unfortunately her son Frank was the soldier who had been executed and ending 'I deeply deplore this matter and sympathise with you in your son's tragic end.'[10] One can only imagine how Mrs Hughes might have greeted such a hollow message, given that it was her son's own government which had permitted him to be punished in this way. In contrast, the Australians did not permit any of their soldiers to be executed.

On 2 September, the day before the last Australian attack at Mouquet Farm, the New Zealand Division departed from the Abbeville area with a view to entering the fray.[11] The thought that they were about to go into action excited many of the men who had had enough of forced marches and the other monotonous training exercises they had to endure. First of all they heard the distant boom of the guns as they entered Allonville, north-east of Amiens. Then they noticed the enormous amount of military traffic using the main road.[12] The closer they came to Albert, the more aware they became of the vast enterprise they were joining. One side of the straight Amiens to Albert road was dominated by the fresh soldiers marching towards the battlefields in choking clouds of chalky dust thrown up by the men's boots. On the other side, the exhausted soldiers who had already fought were stumbling away from the fighting. They were only separated by a seemingly endless stream of double-banked motor lorries that rumbled over the cobbles in the centre of the road. 'The ceaseless traffic [was] supplying the furnace with fuel and carrying out the waste,' Captain Inglis commented. 'Shells, food, guns and men [were] moving in. Empty lorries, salvage, tired men on their feet and broken men in ambulance[s were] coming out.'[13]

Captain Inglis has described the night he and his men spent at Dernancourt, south of Albert, and their camping site the following night near Fricourt, as being lit up by the gun flashes that were continuously going off in a great arc around them, and by the Very lights which shot up into the air all along the front line before falling and fading. These, Inglis noticed, contrasted with the smaller 'twinkling lights that covered the slopes and valleys about us and marked the peaceful bivouacs of thousands massed ready to feed the furnace in the next thrust'.

One of these thousands was Cuthbert Free, a captain in the 2nd Canterbury Battalion, who was camping nearby in Fricourt Wood with his unit. He encapsulated the New Zealanders' optimistic, carefree attitude in the letter he wrote to his fiancée on 10 September. It started with the words 'Most wonderfully contented tonight' and continued:

We are bivouacked in what is officially styled a wood, but which to our eyes is a small plantation . . . We have our own camp fire, big, bright and cheerful. On it we've cooked our dinner. Round it we've smoked our pipes and yarned our yarns, and by and by, we will turn to bunk in our little bundles of hazel branches, and sleep with our toes in the fire which the sentry will keep glowing until breakfast time. We've had a glass of port all round from the bottle Tonkin has been hoarding . . . Upton has played Elgar, Liszt and Dvorak on his tin whistle. We've sung sentimental ditties . . . more or less [in] harmony, and the mantle of Epicureus clothes us with golden peace whereof the flickering of the fire is symbolical.[14]

While many of the New Zealanders in his unit might have been experiencing a similar feeling of well-being, it is unlikely that Inglis would have shared it given his movements the day before. On 9 September he had accompanied a group of officers who wanted to reconnoitre the front line that they would soon be occupying. As they set out from Pommiers Redoubt, their view had been obstructed by the mixture of morning mist and cordite smoke, which concealed the 'brown ridges streaked with white, where thrown up chalk marked the trench lines'. They could, however, see their immediate surroundings. Not that that was anything to write home about. As Inglis remarked, 'nothing' in the envelope of the landscape through which they passed 'had survived'. What had once been villages were now 'brick-covered mounds'. Woods were sparse and ragged remains of their former glory. 'There was no green. Only charred brown earth and white chalk.'

According to Inglis, the front line, Tea Trench, which had been held by British troops until the New Zealanders relieved them, was if anything even grimmer:

To the reek of explosives which filled the air farther back among the guns was added the stench of corpses which lay about everywhere on and in the earth, tilled down by shells. Dead of both sides, swollen and sodden, [in] mud-stained grey and khaki uniforms, were tossed in all attitudes among the earth of the parapets and heaved out behind the crumbling ditches that passed for trenches. Pale, discoloured hands and limbs, stiff feet and swollen buttocks projected grotesquely from the soil.

Obscene disintegrated things lay about in the worst parts. Here and there the bottom of a trench would quiver hastily as one stepped on a corpse trampled under the mud. Fat, green flies, too bloated to fly, crawled adhesively on one's face and hands. Rotting clothing and equipment lay about. Among it all, listless, blear-eyed, unshaven men huddled in small groups . . . Some were asleep. Most watched us stupidly. The whole effect was of stagnant putrid inactivity . . . The sights, the smells, the aspect of the limp miserable garrison, and the haze which hung over all and shut out the sun, did not combine to make the prospect of coming into this place a pleasing one.[15]

Nevertheless, the New Zealanders were by no means despondent. Shortly before their move from the area around Abbeville to the front line, some of them were told about the tanks. On 1 September, Lieutenant-Colonel Bert Hart of the 1st Wellington Battalion had been one of around a hundred generals and commanding officers who, along with the Prince of Wales, watched a special display featuring what he referred to as an 'armoured machine-gun machine'. Hart had witnessed five of the 'huge steel contraptions' being let loose on mock-ups of the trench system attacked by the British on 1 July, proving they could carry their crew of nine with four machine guns through fences, over trenches, and up banks 8 feet high. It was in Hart's opinion an 'extraordinary engineering feat'.[16]

By 8 September some of the 'contraptions' had reached Dernancourt, a mile south of Albert. That was where Captain Inglis saw on the railway lines 'a long train of flat trucks with great hump-backed tarpaulin-covered loads', each guarded by a sentry.[17] It was his first sighting of the mysterious new weapon that was rumoured to be on the way to the Somme to assist their advance. The machines, initially referred to by many soldiers as 'caterpillars' and latterly as 'tanks', were finally unveiled to all the troops on 13 September as they moved up towards the front line ready for the offensive.

Some believed the tanks would 'put the fear of God into the Huns'.[18] Others were more circumspect. Alexander Aitken, a twenty-two-year-old 2nd lieutenant in the 1st Otago Battalion, reported his first impressions in his memoirs: the tanks looked like giant toads basking in the sun. He could see their potential, but was disappointed when during another demonstration in a hollow behind the lines, one of the machines fell on its side and lay there while its track furthest from the ground spun around helplessly. 'It was too easy to visualize what effect such a mishap might cause two days hence,' he commented.[19]

During the build-up to the great attack, the process of desensitization continued. While the shooting of Frank Hughes may have played a part in this, the gruesome sights that the New Zealanders saw after they moved up to the front probably quickened the process. One of those affected was Claude Burley, a twenty-seven-year-old private in the 2nd Wellington Battalion, who as a soldier was forced to bed down with men he managed back in the sawmill where he worked in peacetime. He was horrified when, on 13 September, shortly after his battalion occupied Check and Carlton trenches, behind the Somme front line, a grenade went off in Corporal Cliff Curran's hands that blew him and Private Tommy Mooney to smithereens just yards away from where Burley was standing.[20] 'Only a few minutes before you were laughing and joking with the boys,' Burley wrote in a letter home after his first action, 'and then there they lay, what remained of their lifeless bodies, just a heap of mangled flesh and blood . . . Can you imagine. Pieces of hands . . . limbs and brains scattered about you.' At the time it was, as he put it, 'horrible'.

But then, Burley confessed, after getting worked up into such a state, gradually the terrible sights and tragic losses became so commonplace that 'you take no notice of it . . . and it is only when you get away from it, that . . . you . . . realize . . . that all the boys have been either killed or wounded. They just seem to pass away from your presence out there, and you do not notice they have gone till you have a muster and roll call.'[21]

In his letter home Burley described how he had himself only escaped being blown up, along with Corporal Curran and Private Mooney, because he had found the remains of a German Bible in the trench that they had been deepening. It had once belonged to one of the dead Germans extracted from the soil. Burley had been about to join Curran and Mooney in the next bay when, attracted by a passage in the book he had found, he stopped to read it. That was the only reason why he was not standing beside them when the grenade exploded. It could be said that the gruesome discovery had saved his life. That was putting the best gloss on having to dig where so many dead men were buried.

Burley described the discovery of more of these decayed corpses in the course of digging assembly and communication trenches in front of their front line on 14 September, the day before the next great attack, as 'sicken-ing . . . My stomach heaved all the time with all the smells and sights,' he wrote, 'and I was mighty glad when we were finished and went back in comparative safety [to] . . . the old trench we were living in (in or near to Carlton Trench).'[22]

Further to the rear, repeated exposure to harrowing sights also influ-enced thirty-two-year-old Sergeant Arthur Rhind, a bank clerk before he enlisted, who worked in a similar capacity for the New Zealand Division. Frustrated by being confined to the division's headquarters, when he was finally permitted out in the field he resolved to make the most of it. He described his day out to inspect the line held by the Germans on 1 July as if he was writing up a good day's sightseeing. One entry on 13 September, just two days before the New Zealand Division's first attack, began: 'Have just returned from a most interesting trip.' Rhind went on to chronicle how he visited Fricourt, and King George's Hill nearby, which was 'like a bee-hive from holes made by our artillery'. It had a cross at the top to mark the place where men from the 20th Manchesters had fallen. As for La Boisselle, it was 'just as if the village had been blown off the face of the map'. From another hill overlooking Mametz Wood he could see the shells landing in the German trenches and 'theirs' on 'ours', which inspired him to conclude, 'The whole sight was wonderful . . . We had a great view for miles around.' Nothing could spoil what for him was an exciting excursion. Not even the more macabre specimens he and his guide encountered after descending the thirty-five steps leading into one of the German dugouts he had admired so enthusiastically. The German corpse that he came across with 'half his body blown away', and the dead German 'with a bayonet hole through his stomach', were all part and parcel of the trench experience even though, as Rhind recorded, this particular corpse was 'pretty high'.[23]

Rhind was far from being the only New Zealander doing the tour of the German trenches on 12–13 September. After also visiting King George's Hill, twenty-three-year-old Lance Corporal George Hulme, another Aucklander, saw equally grisly sights in the dugout he visited. 'Lying across a bed was a Hun officer, whose heart was gouged [a]round. Also his eyes and cheek . . . [had been] removed by a bayonet. Our . . . fellows, who had [had] the nerve to enter such a death trap, must have got the Huns first and [must have] then . . . [gone] mad and [given] the Huns what they deserved.'[24]

Not every New Zealander had time for sightseeing, however. Leslie Kenney, a twenty-five-year-old telegraphist attached to the New Zealand

Division's signal company, spent the day on 12 September installing telephone cables in the reserve trenches near Bazentin-le-Petit. In the process he was deafened by the phalanx of guns that had already started the softening-up process leading to the attack. According to Kenney, there were hundreds of guns lined up just behind where he was working, crammed together, wheel to wheel, in line after line 'until one lost count'. They were firing incessantly, he reported, 'jumping, jolting, roaring as if possessed', tormenting those like Kenney working in their vicinity with 'the stinging hot blasts of flame and half-burned cordite' which curled back into the infantry's trenches. The din made by the guns was enhanced by the shouts of their commanders through megaphones, which had to be used if they were to make themselves heard. This produced a cacophony of sound which was so overwhelming that, as Kenney observed, 'the senses gradually become numb. A peculiar ringing in the ears sets in, and the individual proceeds about his task with a feeling of unreality as if acting in some sort of . . . waking dream.'[25]

Perhaps that partly explains the matter-of-fact way in which Kenney, and other diarists, described what they witnessed while going about their work. As he moved about a landscape that in places was so pitted with shell holes it would have been hard to draw a circle five feet in diameter without touching one of them, Kenney recorded in his mind's eye the devastation wreaked by the guns he had seen firing. It was not just the woods that were 'blackened shell-torn tree trunks devoid of all foliage', but there were also the heaps of rubbish and discarded war material strewn over large areas which had once been picturesque villages. While on the way to supply telephone cables for the New Zealanders' reserve trenches on 13 September, Kenney entered a German dugout that must have impressed even his numbed brain. It still contained the remains of its previous enemy occupant. A shell had made a large hole nearby. 'The force of this explosion had evidently caught this man standing in front of his dugout, for his skull was on the roof, and the rest of his body, in the mud-soaked rags of what had once been a uniform, lay sprawled inside on the floor.'

The destruction wreaked by the guns of both sides between the support trenches and the front line where Kenney was laying cables on 14 September was even more extreme. As he pointed out, there were mangled enemy corpses 'everywhere'. His diary also mentioned the 'walls of trenches, broken and spattered with human remains, discarded equipment, blood-stained and filthy with mud, broken rifles, rusty bayonets, clothing of every description, and all the indescribable wreckage of war reeking with that awful putrefying smell of carrion flesh'.

On the way back to his unit's base at Pommiers Redoubt, Kenney noticed the 'gorgeously coloured sunset', an incongruous setting for all the death and destruction to which he had been exposed during the day. He also spotted at Green Dump 'twenty motor-driven armoured tractors', each one 'shaped like a flat torpedo' resembling 'a small battleship lying on its side', which he was told were to lead the advance the next day.

Because Kenney would not be accompanying the tanks, his ordeal was over as soon as he reached Pommiers Redoubt. But as he fell asleep, undisturbed by the guns going off all around him, the trial for the soldiers making up the assault battalions who were to advance at 6.20 a.m. the next day was only just beginning. An account written by Private William Wilson, a twenty-five-year-old farmer serving in the 2nd Battalion of the 3rd New Zealand Rifle Brigade, referred to his and his comrades' state of mind the evening before the attack: 'We are as brave as lions now, but when death cuts loose in the morning, will we have the guts to face it?'[26] Whether or not his comrades felt the same way, they all put on a cheery face as they fell in at Fricourt Wood ready for their move to the assembly trenches. Then they marched northwards, fortified by the strains of the band that had been brought up to play them on their way.

The journey to the front line was a test of nerves in itself. After passing through Mametz Wood, the New Zealanders had to run the gauntlet of the German guns as they followed the main track through a valley that the enemy artillery were pounding relentlessly. The marching soldiers saw that there had been many victims. Wilson's account states that dead horses and mules lay all along the cobbled road, some of them only partly buried. Alongside were countless smashed wagons. But it was the reaction to the graves marked by primitive crosses, and half dug up and desecrated by shells and horse-drawn limbers, that he found most remarkable. 'I saw bodies lying unearthed,' he recorded, 'but although thousands pass by daily, nobody takes much notice of these sights.'

Wilson was impressed enough by what he saw, however, just before he left the valley to enter the communication trenches leading to the front line to mention it in his account: 'The ground was . . . freshly torn up and six horses were lying dead with their harness still on. Their bodies were frightfully torn. A big shell must have landed on them, as the limber was also "matchwood". A little to one side of the road, were two new graves containing the bodies of the drivers.' After clambering through communication trenches, Wilson's platoon eventually made it to their assembly trenches north of the Longueval to Bazentin-le-Grand road at around 10.30 p.m. on 14 September.[27] It was a cold night, but their attempts to dig funk holes in the side of the trench where they had to wait for some eight hours were terminated abruptly after they found they were 'unearthing something in a uniform'. The bad smell told them it was yet another decomposing corpse, another factor which made Wilson and his comrades long for the waiting to end so that they could rush forward.

They were not in the foremost assembly trench. The assembly trenches nearest to the Germans were occupied by the 2nd New Zealand Brigade's 2nd Auckland Battalion on the right and the 2nd Otago Battalion on the left. It would be down to them to ensure that the attack began on the right foot.[28] They would not be advancing alone. The assaulting troops from XV Corps' British 41st Division would be on their immediate right, with troops from the third of the corps' divisions, the British 14th Division, on the right of 41st Division. XIV Corps would be attacking on XV Corps' right. There was also to be support on the New Zealanders' left supplied by the British troops in III Corps, while III Corps' left was in its turn to be supported by the Reserve Army's Canadian Corps.

The 2nd New Zealand Brigade's advance represented only the first of the attack's four separate stages. At 6.20 a.m. on 15 September this brigade was to make the initial advance to the north with a view to taking Crest Trench, around 150 yards up the slope from its battalions' assembly trenches, before going on approximately 450 yards to capture 950 yards of Switch Trench on the same ridge (see map 17 for all trenches in this paragraph).[29] At 7.20 a.m. the 3rd New Zealand Rifle Brigade's 4th Battalion was to advance to take the next line of German trenches, around 1,000 yards further north down the other side of the ridge.[30] Then at 8.20 a.m. the 3rd New Zealand Rifle Brigade's 2nd and 3rd Battalions were to advance north of Flers, paving the way for the brigade's 1st Battalion to seize Grove Alley, the final objective, shortly after 10.50 a.m.[31]

The times for the first two of these stages were even more important than had been the case hitherto, since the attackers were to be protected by a 'creeping' barrage. Shells were to rain down just ahead of the advancing New Zealanders, shielding them from any Germans who might be lying in wait in front of the trench being attacked, as the New Zealanders crept forward in the approach to the German trenches.[32]

If the four tanks allocated to the New Zealanders' front had materialized in the front line so that their advance could have preceded the infantry, the attack might have proceeded more smoothly. However, five minutes before the advance was due to begin, news reached the 3rd New Zealand Rifle Brigade that one of the tanks was out of action and the remaining three would be late.[33] At 6.20 a.m. when the 2nd New Zealand Brigade's battalions moved forward, they did so without the support of the giant 'caterpillars' from which so much was expected. This had a significant effect on the progress of the 2nd Otago and Auckland Battalions. The former was particularly vulnerable, being exposed for that much longer in No Man's Land, where the men were picked off by the Germans to their left who were still holding out in High Wood.

One of the attackers on the right was George Tuck, a twenty-two-year-old carpenter serving in the 2nd Auckland Battalion, who had risen through the ranks to become a 2nd lieutenant. He has recorded the critical moment, following the lifting of the barrage from Switch Trench, when he saw the lines of men ahead of him stop 20 yards out to throw grenades at the German defenders. Leaderless, because of the number of their NCOs killed or wounded during the advance, they were cowed by the grenades the Germans were throwing at them. They may also have been demoralized by the thinning out of their lines, the consequence of having hugged the creeping barrage too closely. 'I scream again and again: "Don't stop!"' Tuck reported. He realized 'the Germans had at that moment a glorious opportunity to repel the assault'.

But they would have needed to make an impression quickly for, as Tuck later described it, the massed line of attackers eager to pounce on their tormentors was 'like nothing more than a great ocean wave raising itself and seeming to hesitate'. Straining to seize the initiative, he forced himself onwards and managed to walk down Switch Trench's battered parapet into the midst of their foe. 'On my right and left I see some others do the same,' Tuck remembered:

Then the great wave breaks over the trench. A terrible scene ensues. I don't use the bayonet. One man recoils from me against another. They both drop to the one shot. I turn about and get the nearest to me. Then the next. All this in a few moments.

Then our men flood the trench . . . It was not a fight. It was swift vengeance . . . The Germans in that trench were from two to three inches taller than our men.

[But] . . . our men had suffered in the advance . . . As soon as they entered, the Hun wanted to surrender. I do not blame our men that they would make them fight [and] . . . die, or not fight and die anyhow.

According to Tuck, the initial assault was followed by frenetic activity. While one of his men ran along the trench screaming 'Come on you bastards. This is man's work. [You are] not killing women and children [now]!' others 'dug' the surviving Germans out of their dugouts, whereupon most of them were despatched.[34]

The scale of the killing following the surrender of the German garrison is partially glossed over by the ambiguous wording in Brigadier-General William Braithwaite's report on how his battalions' prisoners were treated: 'Only two Red Cross men and two wounded were left alive in the Crest Trench', and in Switch Trench 'the only prisoners taken were four German officers,' he reported. The report filed by the 2nd Auckland Battalion's Lieutenant-Colonel Charles Brown was more forthright: 'No prisoners except wounded were taken by this battalion, as at this stage, it was impossible to do so without delaying the operation.'[35]

Perhaps guessing what was about to happen, some members of the Switch Trench garrison decided discretion was the better part of valour, and ran for their lives. Many of the Germans were mowed down by a Lewis gun that was quickly mounted on the trench parados.[36] Those who were not hit were pursued by New Zealanders, whose lust for blood was too inflamed to stop in the objective they had been set. One such hothead was twenty-one-year-old Walter Graham, a clerk in a loan company before he enlisted, who ended up in the 2nd Battalion the Otago Regiment, the unit on the left. The following extract from his after-action report explained that the rush of blood to his head came after the German defenders had terrified him:

Our platoon went over in the second wave, and I could see the Germans' heads above the trench firing at us when we got halfway across. Even when we joined the first wave, I could see that our ranks were pretty thin . . . While we were lying down waiting for the rush, Fritz was rattling away with his machine guns . . . For a few seconds he ripped up the ground about a yard in front of me. It gave me a bit of a fright, and I wasted no time in wriggling back a few yards. I also yelled out to the man on my left to get back, but when I looked at his face, I saw that he was dead. When we stood up and started to run, their fire slackened off . . . and soon stopped altogether. Half of them put their hands up . . . and some took to their heels . . .

We all wanted to get at them with the bayonet, but some of us were faster than others . . . I jumped into the Hun trench and found it was so deep I couldn't climb out at the other side. So I pulled [what looked like] a dead Hun into a sitting position at the side of the trench, stood on his shoulders and managed to climb out. When I think of it now, it was a horrible thing to do, and I am not quite sure if he was dead or not . . . I did not notice . . . in the excitement of the moment. I was chasing [a] fellow and almost had him. But [then] I . . . found [it] was not . . . safe, as the fellows behind were firing. So I lay down, took steady aim, and shot him.

[Then] another poor beggar came stumbling towards me [as if he wanted to surrender. He had] a shower of bullets flying around him. I knew that if I let him come too near me, I would stand a good chance of getting hit . . . so I gave him a bullet in the chest when he was about 15 yards from me.[37]

As Tuck and his men dug a new trench around 60 yards past the trench they had just captured, a measure designed to help them escape the worst of the shelling that was bound to follow, the 4th Battalion of the 3rd New Zealand Brigade passed through them heading for the next objective, which they also took at around 7.50 a.m.[38]

That opened the way for the second piece of leapfrogging, with the 3rd New Zealand Rifle Brigade's 2nd Battalion on the right and its 3rd Battalion on the left advancing at 8.20 a.m. to attack Flers Trench and Flers Support Trench.[39] Private William Wilson has chronicled how the men in his 2nd Battalion section were temporarily held up by a 'nest' of German machine-gunners, who proceeded to mow down the advancing New Zealanders. He survived by taking cover in a shell hole, only emerging after he saw that around twelve of his comrades had crawled around to the left and taken the strongpost from the side. But it is Wilson's description of what happened next that is so chilling:

The Huns . . . never tried to escape, but threw up their 'paws' and . . . above the roar of the battle we could . . . hear [their cry]. 'Mercy, Kamerad, mercy!' But they had done too much damage with their two machine guns . . . Their cry for mercy was never heeded. As I was making for the scene, I saw the bayonet used for the first time. God it was frightful! But it was all over in a few seconds. Fully a dozen Germans were [left] lying in their death throes. Some of the Huns tried to run but they were quickly dropped.

One of our officers rushed forward [to prevent] . . . any more slaughter. He had to . . . threaten our men with his revolver to keep them off.

But as the following extract from Wilson's account demonstrates, he was too late to prevent the cold-blooded execution of one of the captured Germans: 'As I arrived . . . a German was on his knees with his hands above his head [begging for] mercy. A young chap . . . walked up to him, gazed at him a few seconds, and then deliberately at three yards' distance pushed out his rifle and blew the Hun's head practically off.'[40]

Wilson only accompanied his comrades for long enough to help them take their portion of the next trench. It was empty, the Germans having fled. He was wounded in the leg before they reached their final objective north of Flers. However, Captain Inglis remained on the scene, and he was able to describe the final action of the day. His account mentions the successful use of a tank, which at around 10.30 a.m. finally reached the place where the 3rd New Zealand Rifle Brigade's 3rd Battalion was held up in front of Flers Trench. The tank broke through the wire obstructing their advance.[41] Inglis's account also describes his decision to attack his company's allotted portion of Grove Alley, the final objective for that day, which was designed to protect the New Zealanders, and troops from XV Corps' other two divisions, against any German incursion from the north-west (see map 18). That entailed his company's left advancing around 600 yards north of Flers, with its right going a further 200 yards, the extra distance on the right being the result of the line classed as the objective facing the north-west.[42]

The XV Corps' other divisions needed protecting because they had also had a relatively successful day, even if they had not broken through to their final objective. The 41st Division's battalions, on the New Zealanders' immediate right, eventually reached the line just north of Flers, which represented the third of their four objectives. The 14th Division's performance was more patchy. While its left battalion reached Bull's Road, the third objective, north-east of Flers, its right battalion halted just south of the road.[43]

Inglis's account is also to be commended for the way it frankly owns up to the mistakes he made. The most costly error occurred after the 450-yard stretch of Grove Alley they were targeting had been captured, which happened around 11 a.m.[44] As at Switch Trench, when it came to the tipping point, the German garrison of Grove Alley consisting of around 200 men had not been willing to stand and fight. Instead they had bolted. That alone explained the success of Inglis's relatively small force. Had it been held up on the grassy flat plateau over which it rushed forward, the force would have been annihilated by the gunfire coming from the higher ground north of Grove Alley, if not from the Alley itself.

But the occupation of the Alley created a different problem for the New Zealanders. Seeing that Germans were advancing down the gulley surrounding Glebe Street, to the right rear of the 120 men in Grove Alley, Inglis sent a message to the officer in charge of the newly taken position, telling him to peel off with a platoon to secure the area behind their right flank. 'Watching [the messenger] anxiously, I saw . . . [him] reach the trench,' Inglis reported. However, to Inglis's 'amazement', when the officer walked back with about twenty men, they were followed by all the other troops in Grove Alley, thereby vacating the trench they had just captured.

Inglis somehow managed to stop them retiring back to Flers itself, and considered attempting to retake the Alley. He only decided against this idea after it became clear that with only two other officers near him, it would not be practical to form them up again in the midst of the German artillery barrage that had descended on the plateau. This was all the more upsetting because Inglis rightly concluded he was to blame for the Alley's loss. He should have ensured that the men who were to remain in Grove Alley had been warned about the retirement on their right flank before any movement was attempted. That being said, the New Zealanders had not done so badly. They had advanced almost a mile and a half during the day, which in the static war of 1916 was something of a record.

The other mistake had been made as his men advanced through the northern streets of Flers, prior to the assault on Grove Alley. When Inglis pointed his rifle down a dugout they were passing, a bespectacled German with a beard who was standing on the steps shouted out: 'Nicht schliessen! One wound[ed]!' Inglis passed on, but one of his men, whom Inglis described as 'harder hearted', was less merciful and lobbed a couple of Mills grenades into the dugout. It was an act that snuffed out any opposition that might have been brewing there. But it was arguably one more war crime to add to all those that had gone before. Nevertheless, Inglis subsequently admitted his decision had been unwise since, had it not been overridden, it would have left his men a hostage to fortune. No one could tell whether these Germans, left at liberty in their rear, might have attacked his men later.[45]

The fear that the New Zealanders might be surprised by German troops left behind in Flers was later shown to be justified after Private Burley and his comrades in the 2nd Wellington Battalion were attacked while passing through Flers later that night. By then Flers was no longer the village it had once been. Burley's letter, written from the United Kingdom after he had been wounded and repatriated, describes how when passing a jumble of 'broken-down brick buildings . . . fallen trees . . . wreckage of all sorts [and] . . . hundreds of dead Huns', they were targeted by a hidden German machine-gunner who claimed several scalps.[46]

What remained of Burley's platoon scoured the area for the culprits, but only managed to capture four out of approximately thirty who had been hiding. 'These four were searched and relieved of anything which we wanted in the way of souvenirs,' Burley stated:

I claimed a helmet . . . [a] belt and some postcards . . . Then we were ordered to send them back . . . But we were all so mad at them killing six of our mates and the Sergeant that we 'ended' them with our bayonets.

I [still] have the helmet and have managed to keep it with the cards etc. in the hospital with me, but I had a job to hang on to them. I was ordered to hand them in, but here I am with them . . . in my locker. Lady Courtis who visits here to represent the NZ contingent association in South Wales offered me five pounds for them but I would not part with [them] . . .[47]

So it was that the ripples made by the 'No Prisoners' lecture, delivered with such relish at the end of August, spread out not only to Flers but also back to the United Kingdom. Civilized ladies wishing to bask in the success of their young men queued up to purchase trophies of their 'heroism' on the battlefield, thus creating a market for goods taken by nefarious means. The women eventually realized the scale of the sacrifice entailed in securing a place like Flers: the New Zealand Division's casualties on 15 September, which amounted to in excess of 1,900, could not be concealed forever.[48] But in the short term at least, only those women whose loved ones' correspondence openly admitted how their pre-war decency had been swept aside by the fighting, realized the full cost of going to war.

Even the New Zealanders' officers may not have realized the scale of the problem. Captain Inglis, who steadfastly believed that most of his men were incapable of committing deeds on the battlefield which were tantamount to murder, witnessed a scene suggesting that at least some of them might be. While he and his men were carrying out the wounded men they had found lying stranded at the aid post to the rear of Abbey Road during the morning of 17 September, he overheard one of the carriers, who had just discovered that the soldier on his stretcher was German, saying 'Rob the bastard and stick a bayonet through him.'

Before Inglis could know for certain whether the suggestion that their charge should be murdered was sincere, he intervened, and the German in question was then carried to the dressing station.[49] But given the other evidence of war crimes by New Zealanders that has been cited, there is a possibility that what Inglis had witnessed was just the tip of a sinister iceberg, which meant that no German prisoner taken into captivity by New Zealanders could be sure he would survive to tell the tale.

36: The Caterpillars

High Wood, Courcelette, the Quadrilateral, 15 September 1916

(See map 17)

During the days leading up to zero hour on 15 September, while XV Corps, and its New Zealand Division, were still preparing for the great leap forward described in the last chapter, British and Canadian troops in XIV and III Corps and the Canadian Corps made their final preparations for the big attack. Some of the preparations were left until the last moment. Two days before the great day, there were still some British troops who had never heard of tanks, let alone knew what they themselves were about to do. After the attack, Sergeant Harold Horne of the 1st/6th Battalion the Northumberland Fusiliers, part of the 50th Division, which had been ordered to advance towards Martinpuich (north-west of High Wood) on 15 September, noted: 'On our way up to the trenches, we passed groups of large objects concealed under camouflage netting, but in the dark could not see what they were.' Only once he and his companions were in position for the attack, were they let into the tank 'secret'. They were ordered to fill in their trench at each of the tanks' allotted crossing places.[1]

Gunners were likewise told on 14 September to 'keep away from fixed lanes where "tanks" are going to attack'. Douglas Pegler, the battery sergeant-major who recorded this order in his diary, added: 'Lord knows what "tanks" are. Some sort of armoured cars I hear.'[2]

The night before the attack, the tanks had to be escorted to their assembly positions behind the infantry's front line. Rifleman W. J. Gray of the 1st/9th Battalion the London Regiment (Queen Victoria's Rifles) was asked to do the honours for the three tanks that were to support the 56th Division, the unit which on 15 September was to attack on the 4th Army's southern flank (see map 17 for details of where British divisions were going to attack). The 56th Division was in the sector now controlled by Lieutenant-General Earl of Cavan's XIV Corps. (He and his corps had taken over the command of the sector from Lieutenant-General Congreve's XIII Corps on 17 August after Congreve had to return to England because of ill health.)[3] Progress was painfully slow, because of the care that had to be taken when selecting a pathway that ran between the many shell holes.

This was only alleviated somewhat after the tank officer in command suggested a possible solution. 'I think we should get on much better if you had my torch and walked five or six yards in front of the leading tank, picking out the most suitable ground for the tank to take', he told Gray. Rifleman Gray was happy to do that while not too close to the enemy, but as they approached his battalion headquarters, he decided to switch the torch off, only switching it on again from time to time. On seeing this, the tank officer alighted and asked what was the matter. When Gray explained, the officer was sympathetic, but insisted 'they were very late, and as they must get the tanks up at any cost, they must take the risk'. Gray was even more perturbed when told he must escort one of the tanks to just behind the front line, all the more so when the German artillery strafed them en route. But they eventually arrived at the appointed place in one piece, and Gray was able to switch off the torch once and for all, commenting 'My job was over for which I was profoundly thankful.'[4]

Gray's reservations concerning the tanks he escorted highlights the difficulties that all the tank commanders faced. All British troops wished them well, and hoped that the tank would turn out to be the weapon which would finally break the deadlock. However, they did not want tanks anywhere near their positions for fear that they, or their unit, would be targeted by the German gunners trying to hit the tanks. The tank commanders' tasks were made harder because of the way they were treated and trained. Lieutenant Basil Henriques, the twenty-five-year-old commander of the only tank to reach the Quadrilateral strongpoint between Ginchy and Morval, the sector targeted by XIV Corps' 6th Division, has described the challenges he faced as a result (see map 17).

Incredibly, Henriques and his crew had only worked together in a tank on one occasion before they were shipped to France. They had never had a chance to try out the guns in the tank allocated to them before going into action. Nor had they ever fired any guns on a tank that was moving. They had never practised manoeuvring the tank over countryside that they had not reconnoitred previously. Nor had they been trained to drive the tank with the front flaps closed so that they could only see where they were going through small slits covered with glass prisms or by peering through their periscopes.

Equally worrying was the failure of Henriques' commanders to give him clear written instructions prior to or on the day of the attack. He knew he was supposed to reach the German front line just before the infantry. But no one had told him the time he should advance into No Man's Land in

order to comply with that schedule. The failure to supply Henriques and
the other tank commanders with equipment to facilitate communication
with their tank crews was another obstacle. The noise inside the tank made
it virtually impossible to converse with other members of the crew. Henriques had to resort to tapping crew members on the shoulder with a stick
whenever he wanted to attract their attention.[5]

The infantry who were to be supported by the tanks had no inkling of
these and many other failings. That was very unfair given the treatment of
tank commanders and crew during the 15 September attack. During the
operation no artillery would be fired within zones leading up to the first
objective where the tanks were supposed to advance. These tank lanes were
100 yards wide for each tank.[6] They made sense from the tank crews' point
of view, but they represented death traps if the tanks did not successfully
make it to the German front line. In such a situation the British infantry
would have to advance towards German riflemen and machine-gunners
who had not been fired on by British or Canadian guns.

This would be even harder to bear given that after much experimenta-
tion during the previous attacks on the Somme, an artillery system had
been evolved which was designed to help the attacking infantry get into the
German trenches. The new system was designed to catch any German
machine-gunners who were either in front of, or behind, the main trench
lines. It was known as the 'creeping' barrage, and as the name suggested, it
involved the barrage creeping forward gradually over the area leading up
to each trench line. It was often combined with a simultaneous second barrage that remained fixed on the trench under attack. Both barrages would
lift off the trench line at a specified moment, and if infantrymen were to
derive the maximum benefit from it, they had to be ready to leap into the
trench in question at that precise moment.

Any thoughts of the dangers arising from the introduction of the
artillery-free tank zones appear to have been far from the minds of most
British soldiers when shortly before zero hour they saw – and heard – tanks
approaching. The Northumberland Fusiliers' Sergeant Horne recalled
hearing the 'hum of machinery' coming up behind his trench. He was
amazed by what appeared: several 'great toad-like things with caterpillar
tracks' and with guns sticking out in several directions. One of these monstrous apparitions forged past him, utilizing the 'bridge' he had helped to
construct by filling in that part of the trench. Then it disappeared into the
morning mist, lumbering across No Man's Land towards the Germans.[7]

Whether Sergeant Horne or any British infantrymen ever fully appreciated the enormous courage required to penetrate – in what was essentially a slow-moving, albeit armed, metal box – behind enemy lines, in some cases unsupported by any British forces, is open to question. Lieutenant Henriques' report on his own experiences underlines the torment he personally endured on 15 September. It started with the breakdown of the two tanks that were supposed to accompany his tank into battle, and the panic-stricken discovery shortly before midnight on 14–15 September that his own tank was low on petrol. Not only that: new stocks of petrol that should have been delivered to a local dump were not there. Henriques' section commander dashed back to collect the necessary fuel, and only reappeared shortly before 4 a.m. on 15 September. Only after his tank had been filled up were Henriques and his crew able to drive it to the starting point behind the British front line.

On the way, the tank had to be driven down a sunken road that was covered with the bodies of dead Germans. That involved driving over their corpses, which already stank even before they were squashed by the tank's tracks. However, the tank reached the front line in good time for the 6.20 a.m. attack, arriving at around 5.30 a.m. Ten minutes later Henriques ordered his driver to advance to the German front line, enabling him to approach the area occupied by the Quadrilateral before the 6th Division troops made their bid to join him there.

Although Henriques and his crew claim they did manage to destroy one or two machine-gun positions, what they achieved was not enough to save the infantry. Some of the 6th Division troops were cut down by German gunfire as they advanced. Others were not able to make it past the German wire that had not been cut.[8] The infantry's chances of making it into the German line were further reduced by the apparent inability of the British artillery to target the Quadrilateral. Their maps did not correctly show where the strongpoint was situated. The British artillery also failed to act on an order issued by XIV Corps telling them that two of the three tank lanes left for the tanks should be replaced by normal shelling activity.[9]

The appearance of Henriques' tank prompted a violent reaction from the German machine-gunners in and around the Quadrilateral. Henriques later described the effects on him and his crew inside the tank:

A smash against the [visor] flap in front caused splinters to come in and the blood to pour down my face. Another minute and my driver got the same. Then our prism glass broke to pieces. Then another smash – I think it must have been a bomb – right in my face. The next one wounded my driver so badly that he had to stop. By this time I could see nothing at all. All my prisms (covering slits in the tank's armour) were broken. And one periscope [was broken too] . . . It was impossible to look through the other. On turning round I saw my gunners lying on the floor. I couldn't make out why, and yelled to them to fire. I could see absolutely nothing. The only thing to do was to open the front flap slightly, and peep through. Eventually this got hit and the enemy could fire in on us at close range.[10]

But perhaps the most alarming development of all was the realization that the bullets fired at the bulging sponsons, the metalwork fastened to the side of the tank to support the guns, were penetrating into the tank's interior. That was the reason why the gunners had abandoned their guns and had laid down on the floor. A combination of these factors convinced Henriques that they might all be killed, or the tank might be captured if he hung around behind the German lines any longer. With that in mind, he very reluctantly ordered the crew to take the tank back to base.

It was a decision that was to haunt him for months after the tank made it back to the British line. After getting back, Henriques had what we would now refer to as a mental breakdown. It is believed that this was partly sparked off by the conditions in the tank during the attack. The belief that he had been a coward also appears to have played its part. Some have speculated that there was a third reason as well: Henriques' grief caused by the death of one of the tank commanders in his section, whose tank was damaged before the attack.

The tank commander in question was the twenty-year-old Lieutenant George Macpherson. The two men had struck up a close friendship. Whether it was anything more than that is impossible to say from publicly available evidence. However, one study has suggested that Henriques might have been attracted to his younger companion. He certainly wrote about Macpherson in glowing terms, describing him as 'tall with . . . blue eyes . . . and an almost girlish complexion'. Whatever their exact relationship, there is no doubt that Henriques was very fond of Macpherson. As a result he would have been devastated when it was alleged that Macpherson had not only been killed later that day after his tank had been repaired and deployed for a subsequent attack, but that he had committed suicide and left behind a suicide note stating: 'My God. I've been a coward.'[11] Doubts have been expressed as to whether this allegation that he committed suicide holds water. But the fact that the allegation was made may have had something to do with Henriques' subsequent depression.

As has been suggested by Basil Henriques' critique, many mistakes were made concerning the first use of tanks. But perhaps the most foolish error of all, in relation to their use on 15 September 1916, was the decision by III Corps' Lieutenant-General Pulteney to use four of the seven tanks that were allotted to him in High Wood. It was a move that not only ignored the wishes of Major-General Charles Barter, commander of the 47th Division, who had been entrusted with the capture of the wood; it also defied common sense. It was obvious that the crew of a shut-down tank would be hard pressed to find its way through a mass of trees, and even if a tank did make it through the wood, the noise that would be made by creating a pathway through the trees would be sufficient to warn any Germans in the vicinity of what was coming. The fact that the use of tanks would make it impossible to shell the wood was another important factor that should have been considered.

The consequence of Pulteney's decision was that for the first hours of the attack, the 47th Division troops inside the wood had to battle with the German garrison, and as a result incurred unnecessary losses.[12] The contrast between the progress made by a 47th Division unit outside High Wood with the lack of progress inside the wood is neatly highlighted in an account written by Vernon Wilkinson, a nineteen-year-old private in the 1st/15th Battalion, the London Regiment (Civil Service Rifles). Although most of the battalion fought inside the wood, his company ended up advancing just outside its eastern edge. As a result his moves were for the most part conducted under the protective umbrella of a barrage laid on by the British artillery.

The conditions he witnessed were shocking even before the whistles blew to indicate the latest batch of fighting had started. At the same time they seemed to symbolize the crossover between the new world and the old world. As his battalion marched up from Delville Wood to High Wood, Wilkinson saw numerous dead horses, some so badly hit that half their insides were lying out covered with swarms of flies. Their plight, and their suggestion of a bygone age, could be contrasted with the new high-tech weapons, the 'caterpillars', one of which they passed on the way to the front line.

Wilkinson's account records how after his unit arrived in the trench on the southern edge of High Wood, they were perturbed to see the corpses of some of the trench's previous occupants; they were lying on the parados above them where they had been thrown so as to get them out of the trench. Wilkinson's subsequent comments in his account suggest that he intended to take some Germans with him if they ever killed him: 'We attempted a little breakfast in the early hours, but the jam tasted of paraffin, so we gave it up. A substantial rum ration however soon satisfied us. There was actually some rum to spare as some of the lads would not participate . . . They wished to have all their senses about them when the great time came. Others were quite merry. Personally I . . . consumed plenty to make me feel like killing Jerry.'

At 6.20 a.m. (zero hour) they clambered over the top of the parapet, only to be met with 'a murderous machine-gun fire'. It was obvious from what Wilkinson noted about the British artillery that he was not in one of the tank lanes. 'The bark of our 18 pounders was heard above everything else. The shells . . . seemed to . . . skim over our heads.' However, that appeared to have no effect on the German machine-gunners. 'Young Reader fell . . . with a groan . . . Blood rushed from a wound in the head,' Wilkinson wrote.

As he and his section advanced northwards to the east of the wood's eastern edge, Wilkinson came face to face with a German machine-gun position in a trench. He shot two of the gun team, leaving his mates to deal with the machine-gunner himself. 'I had done this with no more feeling than a boy firing with an airgun at a target in the garden,' he noted later, adding 'Now I had seen those dead Germans I sobered somewhat and began to take things more seriously.' But notwithstanding his best efforts, Wilkinson was equally fired up when he encountered the next trenchful of Germans:

They had already dropped their rifles and offered no resistance. I wanted to use the bayonet, but could not bring myself to do it. So I fired a couple of rounds at two yards range into the two nearest to me. This was nothing else but murder. I don't know what made me do it, as they could easily have been taken prisoner. I shall never forget the looks on their faces as I pointed my rifle at them. Such sickly grins which showed fear. They shrank backward before they were shot. We cleared that trench sending some of the Germans back as prisoners.

Perhaps the lines of Scottish corpses that Wilkinson had seen had something to do with it. His account refers to there being 'a lot of kilted troops lying about . . . Their bare legs were almost black, and the smell was terrible.' It was 'a sickly sweet smell that remained in one's nostrils for a week

afterwards'. Having taken his revenge, he and his unit soon found the tables were turned. Germans inside High Wood pinned them down by firing at them.[13] They only escaped thanks to steps taken by the trench mortar battery of 47th Division's 140th Brigade. Within the space of fifteen minutes it fired no fewer than 750 mortar rounds into the German stronghold inside the wood. After that the German garrison troops there had had enough and they began to surrender. By that night High Wood was at long last in British hands.[14]

We have already noted the ruthless tactics pursued by the New Zealanders in relation to their prisoners (see Chapter 35). In case readers are tempted to conclude from Vernon Wilkinson's account that British and New Zealander troops behaved more reprehensibly than others, it is interesting to mention at this point an account written by a soldier in the Canadian Army.

One of the impressionable young Canadians who went over the top on 15 September was Lance Cattermole, an eighteen-year-old private in the Canadian 21st Battalion. This was the left-hand battalion in the 2nd Canadian Division's 4th Brigade, whose job it was to take the Sugar Factory south of Courcelette. This was to be a preliminary operation carried out before the Canadian troops were ordered to take the village itself. If his platoon's officers or NCOs blew their whistles at zero hour to signify that the men should go over the top, Cattermole never heard them. At 6.20 a.m. precisely the noise made by the artillery became so loud that all extraneous sounds were blotted out. 'The air over our heads was suddenly filled with the coughing and sighing, whining and screaming of thousands of shells,' Cattermole recalled, and when he looked behind him, 'as far as the eye could see, there was a sheet of flame from the hundreds of guns lined up, almost wheel to wheel, belching fire and smoke. It was an awe-inspiring sight.'

Because his platoon was in the third wave, there was no question of his having to make the first move. Cattermole and the others in his twenty-man section merely had to follow the first waves over the parapet. However, he had barely started out when a German shell landed a short distance in front of him, throwing a column of earth up into the air and knocking him to the ground. Fortunately for Cattermole, the shell was a dud or he would not have survived to tell his tale. After picking himself up, and urging his comrades to move forwards, he caught sight of a man called John Robb: 'He was on his knees, sitting back on his heels with his arms hanging loosely at his sides. His helmet was off . . . his face turned to the sky . . . [Not] realizing he had been hit . . . I foolishly . . . shouted out: "Come on Robb!" But

as I moved in front of him . . . I saw the blood gushing from his neck . . .
He had obviously been hit in the jugular. [Then] I knew he was finished . . .
In any case, we were not allowed to stop to succour companions in an
advance. So there was nothing I could do.'

The rules of engagement were even harsher concerning the Germans.
Before the advance started, Cattermole was left in no doubt what action
had to be taken if any of the enemy attempted to surrender: 'We were given
strict instructions to take no prisoners, until our objective had been gained.
The reason for this was that so often in British advances when the Germans
had thrown down their arms in surrender and our men had moved through
them at the same time indicating to them to go to our rear, where they
would be collected as prisoners, the Germans had picked up their rifles
again and shot our men in the back, thereby bringing the advance to a halt.
No such risks could, or would, be taken in this important attack.'

According to Cattermole, it was this instruction that appeared to have
been instrumental in what he witnessed when he eventually reached the
German front-line trench.

In keeping with our no prisoners order, this trench was being 'mopped up', and
the occupants 'eliminated'. The trench was already half full of dead enemy, and
here and there little columns of steam rose [up] in the cool morning air either from
the hot blood [that had been spilt], or from the urine which I understand is released
on the death of any human body. Two Canadians stood over the trench, one on
the parapet, and the other on the parados, and they [had] exterminated the
Germans as they came out of their dugouts.

One young German, [who was] scruffy, bareheaded, [who had] cropped hair
and [who was] wearing steel-rimmed spectacles, ran [around] screaming with
fear, dodging in and out amongst us, [in a bid] to avoid being shot, crying out,
'Nein! Nein!' He pulled out from his breast pocket a handful of photographs, and
tried to show them to us – I suppose they were of his wife and children – in an
effort to gain our sympathy. It was all of no avail. As the bullets smacked into him,
he fell to the ground motionless, the pathetic little photographs fluttering down to
the earth around him.

In just about any other circumstances, what these Canadians had done
would have been viewed by witnesses as a disgusting, heartless, barbaric
act. Because it was seen in the context of all the other horrific sights on the
Somme, it did not seem to strike observers as being so terrible. It was not

just that all the corpses and the killing had made some of the participants callous. The torment on show wherever one looked ended up distorting the soldiers' moral compass. That being the case, it should be no surprise to find in the pages of any book about the Somme examples of similar acts of merciless bloodletting carried out by all the armies involved in the conflict. Cattermole may well have been affected by the same syndrome. His account appears to suggest that while he could see that the execution was very sad, he believed it really was necessary.

The Canadian 4th Brigade certainly was successful. By the time Cattermole had torn himself away from the scene of the mass execution and made it to the Sugar Factory, it had been captured, and the captain in charge of his company was hungrily eyeing Courcelette, which lay a short distance to the north. Gough prompted by Haig had the same idea.[15] Later that afternoon the 2nd Canadian Division was ordered to take that as well, and it was duly captured by troops within the Canadian 5th Brigade.

It was one of the crowning achievements of the 15 September attack. The previously mentioned capture of High Wood and the capture of Martinpuich were also highlights from the British viewpoint. And of course one should not forget the capture of Flers, which was famously described in one report in the following hyperbolic terms: 'Tank has been seen walking down High Street of Flers followed by large numbers of our troops cheering wildly.'[16]

The person who wrote this neglected to say that in fact the tank in question was on its last legs, to continue the metaphor. Its commander, Lieutenant Stuart Hastie, later admitted that because the tank's steering mechanism had been hit, the driver had to use its brakes when steering. This had put an enormous strain on the engine, so that by the time the tank was driven into Flers, the engine was 'beginning to knock very badly'. 'At this point, we'd to make our minds up what to do,' Hastie recalled, 'because the engine was in such a shocking state that it was liable to let us down at any moment . . . I had a look round, so far as it was possible to do that in the middle of a village being shelled at that time by both sides, and I could see no signs of the British Army coming up behind me. [So] . . . I slewed the tank round with great difficulty on the brakes and came back . . .'[17]

South of the British, the French had made good progress before 15 September, capturing Bois d'Anderlu and Bouchavesnes three days earlier, and Le Priez Farm on 14 September. Their attempts to advance alongside their ally next day were less successful. However, even the British efforts cannot be seen as anything but disappointing. Once again they had taken important landmarks without breaking through the German defences. And in the process the British had thrown away the surprise factor they could have retained if they had not used the tanks, and sustained many casualties.

The severe losses sustained by the Guards Division were particularly disappointing. This was one of the most prized assets in the British Army, yet it had failed to do more than dent the German defences west of Lesboeufs. At one point there had been concern that several of its battalions would be decimated. It was only rescued by the bravery of Lieutenant-Colonel Vaughan Campbell, commanding officer of the 3rd Coldstream Guards. Twice he rallied the guardsmen with blasts on his hunting horn, and transformed what at one time looked as if it might be a humiliating defeat into an honourable draw. Campbell deservedly won the Victoria Cross for his quick thinking and bravery.[18]

2nd Lieutenant Geoffrey Fildes of the 2nd Coldstream Guards, part of the Guards Division's 1st Guards Brigade, had been warned that his battalion's casualties had been particularly severe. He and some brother officers had been left out of the attack just in case this should happen. All battalions did this as a matter of course so that those left behind could fill in for those who did not come back. Perhaps it was just as well given the rumours that had come in. However, in spite of the warnings, Fildes had carried on hoping.

Fearing the worst, the battalion's sergeant-major and drummers had marched out to meet the survivors. They intended to raise their morale by playing them in. Then came the moment of truth. The battalion's casualties really were in excess of 400. Those within the Guards Division were approaching 5,000.[19] Fildes would never forget the homecoming scene outside the camp near Carnoy, which he recorded in his memoir in the following terms:

Over the skyline something flashed and whirled ... We knew it for the sergeant-drummer's stick. At last his head and shoulders appeared above the ridge and behind him surged . . . the drummers . . . He swaggered into full view and as he strode forward the full array of the Drums followed in his wake . . . Next over the crest loomed the figure of our Colonel marching at the head of the devoted band. Rank after rank . . . poured over the skyline. Eagerly we counted their strength, wondering every instant how many remained to follow. All too soon a gap appeared, but we, striving to disbelieve our fears, watched spellbound for the next body of men. But none came. The impossible was true. Before us marched all that remained of the old battalion.[20]

37: Hard Times

Flers, 16 September–1 October 1916

(See map 18)

The New Zealanders' successful advances on the Somme on 15 September, and afterwards, should not conceal the torment that they, like so many others, suffered in the process. Captain Lindsay Inglis for one, whose mistake on 15 September had created the need for an immediate advance the next morning in order to recapture Grove Alley, the trench he and his men had vacated, was suffering from a strong dose of guilt. As he admitted, this was made worse when Lieutenant-Colonel Robert Young of the 1st Battalion the Canterbury Regiment asked him rhetorically 'Why the hell didn't you stay there?' This question prompted Inglis to write: 'I was sore enough about that withdrawal without his rubbing it in, and at that moment could cheerfully have murdered him.'[1]

William Gibbard, a twenty-three-year-old private in the 1st Battalion the Wellington Regiment, which had been ordered to retake Grove Alley, might have wanted to do the same to Inglis if he had known that Inglis was responsible for what he had to endure over the next three days.[2] Gibbard later described it in a letter to his parents. His ordeal began at midnight on 15–16 September, when he and his fellow Wellingtonians were woken up and ordered to march to the front line. This was no easy task given that the manoeuvre required them to walk seven miles in the dark over a landscape pitted with shell holes. Needless to say, Gibbard fell into several of them, an experience made even more alarming because they were often found to be the last resting place of dead Germans and New Zealanders.

Even before the attack started at 9.35 a.m. on 16 September, Gibbard witnessed one of his comrades being wounded by a German shell. There were more casualties during the advance. However, the 1st Wellingtons' final approach to Grove Alley was something of an anticlimax, given that most of its garrison either bolted or surrendered.[3] But, as Gibbard related, it was the aftermath, when German artillery shelled the captured trench the next day, that he found so distressing. Reporting on it afterwards, he wrote:

We are just about in a panic. Some of [my] . . . fellows have run back to the next line. Major [Fleming] Ross is singing: 'Pack up your troubles in your old kit bag, and smile boys, smile. While he is singing, [a] . . . shell bursts right on top of him, and blows him to atoms. I am five yards from him round a corner. The next thing I remember is I am struggling for breath. I have been buried and am trying to release myself. [After getting out I realize] I have been shaken up a good deal. [But] I am better off than the fellow who was on the right of the Major. He has been buried [too], and [has] very bad shell shock. He . . . is . . . crying . . . When I see this, the tears come into my eyes [too].

Eventually the shelling targeted another area, leaving those who survived the grisly task of clearing away the mangled corpses from the partially filled-in trench. As if that was not enough, it then began to pour with rain. The bad weather persisted for the next twenty-four hours, by which time, as Gibbard put it, 'we were wet through . . . The mud is nearly up to our knees.'

Gibbard also mentioned his participation in another activity that was to become a regular feature for infantry on the Somme: shortly before they were relieved during the night of 18–19 September, they were ordered by the surviving lieutenant to bury their comrades' corpses. 'We carry four into a shell hole and cover them over with earth,' Gibbard recorded, describing how they marked the spot with a German gun, barrel downwards, stuck into the ground. 'It is a very rude burial but the best we can give in the circumstances.'[4]

At least it was less rudimentary than the burial accorded to two dead Germans whose waterlogged corpses were found floating in the well in Flers. Their discovery after breakfast on 18 September caused consternation at the battalion's advanced HQ located in a deep dugout nearby. According to the adjutant, it turned out that during the night, unaware of the presence of the bodies, the cooks had taken water from the well and had used it to make that morning's batch of hot cocoa. It was no wonder that everyone who drank it agreed it had 'a most unpleasant flavour'. The adjutant concluded: 'I am sorry to say the cocoa in most of those who had swallowed it did not rest in peace!'[5]

It is to be hoped that this expression in its normal sense did apply to the most severely wounded New Zealanders, who had been carried back to an advanced dressing station, probably that known as Bogle's Post, located near the junction of Fat and Flag Trenches south-west of Flers. The account by Sergeant John Russell of the 1st Wellingtons describes how he came across these 'no hopers' as they passed by the dressing station during one of the nights when his battalion still occupied the front line. The wounded men had been removed from the dressing station to make room for other casualties who needed immediate attention, and 'placed in rows on an exposed slope where they were being left to die. They had probably been given massive overdoses of morphia to help them out of this sorrowful world, but as there was no one in attendance on them, it seemed a very lonely way in which to be allowed to pass away.'[6]

What Russell referred to as 'this pathetic sight' was matched by his description of the packhorses, who at the beginning of the New Zealanders' tour carried the baskets containing shells up to the guns situated on the ridge between Longueval and Bazentin-le-Grand. 'Sometimes a shell would knock out some of the horses, but the remainder would continue to plod stoically forward at their normal walking pace as if nothing unusual had happened. In the bitterly cold and wet weather, they . . . looked the picture of misery.'

The quiet unappreciated persistence inherent in the slow fatalistic progress of the horses, and the heroism of their drivers, can be contrasted with the courage of a different kind exhibited by drivers of the speedy teams of six horses pulling ammunition wagons and limbers up the bumpy road leading from Delville Wood to Flers. This journey eventually became a regular event when the New Zealanders advanced again and the guns were moved forward on 29 September.[7] However, even before that, the teams supplying the artillery had to run the gauntlet up a portion of this road.

On 26 September, Archie Greves, a nineteen-year-old New Zealand Field Artillery 'driver', who on several occasions had to ride his horse, one of a team of six pulling an ammunition limber, part of the way up this road in order to supply his battery's guns positioned in Devil's Gully, became fixated on the corpse of a New Zealand Field Artillery corporal lying in their path. 'It is impossible to avoid running . . . it over,' he reported. '[The road] is under direct observation [of] Fritz . . . We do this particular stretch at a gallop . . . It would be suicide to attempt to stop and remove the body.' Two days later Greves referred to it again: 'Going down the Flers–Delville Wood road again. Some of remains of corporal are still there. The wheel of the ammunition limber passed down his backbone, the head being pushed into the mud.'[8]

Even when Greves returned exhausted to the horse lines that day, there was no escaping the corpses, which were everywhere, and turned up in the most unexpected places. 'After getting back from the guns, I went over to my selected shell hole for a wash. Previously I had noticed a boot but did not [take] . . . much heed of it. Today I required a boot lace so I got hold of the boot. [But] it did not come as easily as I had anticipated. There was a man attached to it. Now I have changed my "wash basin!"'

Eventually the crushed corporal's disappearance would become irrevocable, and he would become one of the missing, whose relations would never know what had become of him. The grinding-down of his body, along with those of so many others, prompted Greves to state: 'The road . . . has a foundation of horses, mules, wagons and human corpses.'

Greves' diary entry for 2 October mentions another killing field 'near the road [leading] from Delville Wood to the Flers turn off'. One of the dead Germans he spotted there 'had evidently been wounded in the "sit upon" and was bending over a log having it dressed when one of our shells exploded nearby, blowing his head off and killing his cobber (friend). On the other side [of the road], there is a dead Tommy laying on the broad of his back . . . his eyes wide open. He has got the wind up Charlie, the Maori driver, who will always turn his head away when passing him.' Horrific as such observations must have appeared to those members of Greves' family who subsequently pored over what he had described, as far as he was concerned, they were fascinating rather than upsetting. This might be explained by the fact that he passed the same sights on several occasions. As a result, they lost their shock factor.

Soldiers fighting on the front line appear to have found their one-off brush with traumatic events much harder to take. One such witness was Alexander Aitken. A twenty-one-year-old 2nd lieutenant serving in the 1st Battalion, the Otago Regiment, in September 1916, he would one day scale the heights of academia, becoming a mathematics professor at Edinburgh University.

That, along with his prowess as a musician, not to mention his bravery, made him ideally suited to lead his platoon during the New Zealand Division's next major advance. It formed part of the 4th Army's bid to seize a wide swathe of territory, including Morval, Lesboeufs and Gueudecourt, which took place at 12.35 p.m. on 25 September.[9] Aitken's ability to keep to a specified rhythm, a skill honed while practising playing classical music on his violin, and his facility for mental arithmetic, both came in useful when he was ensuring his troops timed their advance so that they hugged the creeping barrage as it moved forward to the German front-line position.

Aitken and his comrades in the 1st Otagos, on the left of the attack, had to advance around 700 yards northwards from the crest on which Grove Alley lay to the westward portion of the crest housing Goose Alley, the next communication trench, which connected the German third 'line' (Flers Trench and Flers Support Trench) with their fourth 'line' (Gird Trench and Gird Support Trench; see map 18). Given that the barrage was to creep forward 100 yards every two minutes with a brief intermission, as it targeted North Road in the valley between the two crests, the officer in charge of each assaulting unit had to work out a system to make sure he timed his assault so that the advance by infantry and artillery coincided.[10]

Aitken solved the problem of keeping time, and not counting the seconds too quickly or slowly, by making his counting comply with a basic rhythm while at the same time utilizing the kind of algebraic formula all mathematics students have to use when solving problems: rather than just counting the seconds and hoping that he was allowing the correct interval between each one, he whispered to himself the first three letters of the alphabet between each reference to a second (a, b, c, one: a, b, c, two: a, b, c, three, and so on), and had his men move forward one pace for each second he counted.

His system worked so well that his platoon reached the south-western end of Goose Alley just as the barrage lifted off it, and the cowed German defenders fled rather than waiting to take on the approaching mass of attackers. The other platoons from the 1st Otagos, and the 1st Battalions of the Auckland and Canterbury Regiments to their right, were equally successful. This meant that the 1st New Zealand Brigade ended up holding their objective, which ran from Factory Corner on North Road to the left portion of Goose Alley (south-west of Abbey Road), without suffering excessive casualties.[11] The New Zealanders' success secured the western flank of XV Corps' operation targeting Gueudecourt. The latter village was captured by British forces the next day.[12]

Aitken can be excused for wishing that the next attack by the 1st New Zealand Brigade, an advance to Gird Trench and Gird Support Trench, scheduled for 2.15 p.m. on 27 September, would run as smoothly. Unfortunately for him and his men, success appears to have blinded Major-General Andrew Russell, and Brigadier-General Francis Johnston of the 1st New Zealand Brigade, to the risks they would be running if they did not devise a sensible and clearly explained artillery plan. According to Aitken, the plan they came up with had two critical defects.

Firstly, it required Aitken, and his comrades in the 1st Otagos, once again on the left of the attack, to advance up Goose Alley and to its east with their left flank exposed, without sufficient protection from Germans in trenches on their left. Secondly, insufficient time was allowed for the attackers, who were supposed to be following a poorly defined creeping barrage, to reach the German front line at the same time as the artillery's shells: whereas two days earlier twenty-five minutes had been allowed for the attackers to cover the 700 yards separating Grove Alley from Goose Alley, a mere eight minutes had been specified for the 1,000-yard advance on 27 September.[13] It was not just Aitken who was concerned by the orders. He recalls that the 'drawbacks' of the plan were apparent to every man in the battalion, and he noticed that his company commander was 'grave and preoccupied all morning on the 27th, as though he already foresaw his death in the afternoon'.

Nevertheless at 2.15 p.m. Aitken, having led his platoon up the previously captured section of Goose Alley, climbed out of the trench at its junction with the sunken road connecting Flers and Eaucourt l'Abbaye (Abbey Road), accomplishing without loss the first stage of the attack. They then deployed parallel with Gird Trench, the German front line to the north that they were supposed to be attacking. They were following in the wake of the platoons from the 1st Otagos' other companies that had preceded them. The battalion's objectives encompassed the as yet uncaptured portion of Goose Alley, including its junctions with Gird Trench and Gird Support Trench, as well as the adjacent portions of the Gird Trenches to the southeast of those junctions (see map 18). That left the portions of the Gird Trenches further to the east, up to their junction with the Ligny Thilloy road, to the 1st Otagos' sister battalions within the 1st New Zealand Brigade, the 1st Battalions of the Auckland and Canterbury Regiments.[14] The British 55th Division was to be responsible for taking the German-held portion of Gird Trench on the New Zealand Division's right.

At first the men in Aitken's platoon were allowed to advance towards Gird Trench unmolested, protected by the gentle slope that before the advance had concealed their objective from the New Zealanders, and the advancing New Zealanders from the German garrison holding Gird Trench. But as they approached the road that ran along the crest from Factory Corner to Eaucourt L'Abbaye, cutting across the line of their advance, they were overwhelmed by the German shelling. One shell landed just ten yards away from Aitken, wiping out most of the men from another company who were walking in front of him. It was only then that he realized why ahead of him there was no sign of hundreds of the men from his battalion who had preceded his platoon out of Goose Alley. All that was left of them were a few scattered isolated figures.

Worse was to follow. Aitken's account reveals what was waiting for his platoon as they reached the Factory Corner to Eaucourt L'Abbaye road: 'From two directions, half right [and] half left, came the hissing of many bullets, the herring- bone weave of machine-gun cross fire . . . Many seemed to whiz past my ear, some to bury themselves under my feet . . . Suddenly at my left side my platoon sergeant dropped on one knee and looked up at me in a curious doubtful gaze. "Come on sergeant!" I said stepping forward.'

Depending on your point of view, some might praise such disregard for his own, and his men's, welfare as heroic, whereas others might brand it foolhardy. Aitken, analysing after the attack what went wrong, claimed it was neither. He says by this stage he was, as often happens during an attack, in a dream world, 'powerless to do anything but go mechanically on . . . On! On! . . . In an attack such as this, under deadly fire . . . the final shield from death removed . . . the will is fixed . . . At the same time all emotion is numbed . . .'

Aitken put the detached way he interpreted the traumatic events unfolding around him down to the hypnotic effect of his intense focus on reaching their target in such inhospitable surroundings. The following terse account of the moments after the blowing-up of the men in front of him and the lead-up to the annihilation of his platoon, certainly reflects the dream-like prism through which Aitken claims he witnessed his men's fate:

[The men ahead] vanished in [the] . . . smoke of the shell burst, some falling where they stood, the others walking on. [It was] dreamlike. I passed through the smoke . . . Close [to the] . . . road I heard a voice abusing the Germans. Crossing the road I realized it had been my own. As I took the bank [beside the road], I saw Private Nelson, one of my men, fall forward on his knees and elbows . . . I mentally registered . . . [his name, but then] the terrific . . . force [that was dominating me] pulled me on . . . I glanced right and left, and saw [most of the men in my] . . . platoon, thirty of them, crumple and fall, only two going on.

Seconds later Aitken was also hit. First came what felt like a sledgehammer blow to his right upper arm. It was followed by the shot that broke the bones in his right foot, and left him curled up in a shell hole, with blood soaking the sleeve of his tunic and seeping out of the holes in his boot. Luckily for him, his wounds, although painful, were not life-threatening. After lying out on the battlefield for the rest of the day, he eventually managed to crawl to safety. Others were less fortunate. There was to be no happy ending as far as the attack by the 1st Otagos was concerned. Let down by their commanders as badly as the 2nd Australian Division had been by Major-General Legge in the course of their first attempt to take the Pozières heights two months earlier, the 1st Otagos, which, according to Aitken, must have suffered around 350 casualties, had been decimated.[15]

Yet possibly because the generals' negligence on the Somme was so prevalent, the shortcomings of Major-General Russell, Brigadier-General Johnston and XV Corps' Lieutenant-General Horne appear to have passed unnoticed outside the confines of the New Zealand Division. Perhaps more might have been made of their failures had it not been for the division's previous success on 15 September. The fact that the right-hand side of the 27 September attack featuring the right flank of the 1st Battalion the Auckland Regiment, and the 1st Battalion the Canterbury Regiment, reached and held their objectives may also have helped to deflect criticism.[16] The successful capture of the section of Gird Trench on the New Zealand Division's right may have further sweetened the atmosphere at XV Corps, lessening the chance that Horne would seek a whipping boy concerning that day's events.[17] However, the high casualties incurred on the right, which appear to have reached the same level as the Otagos, leave one with the lingering suspicion that many more young lives than those mentioned by 2nd Lieutenant Aitken were needlessly lost or ruined as a result of the handling of the New Zealand Division and its supporting artillery.

Whether or not generals were responsible for at least some of the casualties during the attack itself, it is hard not to admire the fortitude with which survivors within the 1st Canterburys held on to their hard-won gains. The best source for what really happened on the right side of the German front line taken on 27 September is an account written by Howard Kippenberger. A nineteen-year-old private serving in the 1st Canterburys on 27 September, he was to rise through the ranks to become a major-general during World War II, quite an achievement for a man whose great-grandfather had been born in Germany, the country young Howard was fighting in World War I.

His Germanic roots do not appear to have left Kippenberger with a split allegiance. The following extract from his account suggests he had no sentimental misgivings concerning the fate of the Germans who had died during and in the aftermath of the 1st Canterburys' advance to, and beyond, Gird Trench and Gird Support Trench. 'In the space between our [new] trench [located about 50 yards north of Gird Support Trench], and Gird Trench, the German dead lay thick. I should say about ten of theirs to one of ours, and our losses are heavy enough . . . There were [also] many dead in front of our trench. We had killed most of their wounded, a matter of necessity . . . That probably accounts for the extraordinary number of [German] dead.'

Perhaps his callous attitude was a reaction to the horrors he witnessed. Kippenberger's heart seems to have hardened when a German bullet smashed into the head of his friend, Vic Hearn, while, in the immediate aftermath of the attack, they were trying to take a German strongpoint between Gird Trench and Gird Support Trench. The bullet killed Vic 'instantly'. Seeing his friend gunned down shocked this impressionable teenager. It was all the more traumatic, because when Kippenberger returned to the corpse next morning, after the fighting had subsided, Vic was 'quite unrecognizable'. Unable to countenance burying his remains, Kippenberger opted for a less extreme measure. After one last look, he covered his dead friend's face with a handkerchief before stumbling away, struggling to hold back his tears.

This was no time to be grieving. If he and his comrades were not to be blown out of the position they had just taken, they had to ensure their new trench was shell-proof. By daybreak on 28 September, they had dug a trench that was 4 feet deep and 18 inches wide. But while he was helping to deepen the extension, connecting it with the position held by another 1st Canterbury company, which had taken up a position about 50 yards away to their right, Kippenberger noticed they were being watched. There were Germans monitoring every movement from hot-air balloons that had ascended and were hovering in the distance. 'Didn't we curse them!' Kippenberger wrote in his account. His account also records what happened shortly afterwards: 'A shell pitched about ten yards past the trench, exploded in a muffled kind of fashion like a gas shell, and left behind a great ball of heavy white smoke, as big as a haystack, which took fully five minutes to disperse.' It was a ranging shot, and the battalion's Captain Still immediately warned the men to stop digging and to take what cover they could.

As Kippenberger reported, 'We did so, knowing that only chance could save us, as we had nothing worth calling "protection".' They were at the mercy of the German gunners. Minutes later their ordeal began. In his account Kippenberger concedes 'There was probably only one battery of 5.9s on to us, but they had the range exactly and fired at top speed.' He then listed the sights and sounds that terrorized them. First of all, there was the sound of 'an express train roaring . . . towards you'. Then there were the 'head-splitting bangs in the air' followed by 'stunning explosions close at hand' that sent up 'showers of earth' into the air. This was repeated again and again in quick succession for every shell. If you were lucky, the shell sailed harmlessly past, 'and the clods [of earth] shower onto you'. You could be considered less fortunate if 'the side of the trench falls in and you [have to] scramble frantically from under it' only 'to be knocked flat by [the blast accompanying] a vicious bang overhead'.

Kippenberger's account gives the following supplementary details about what he and his comrades had to endure:

The air is full of the smell of the explosive. You cannot see the sky through the drifting clouds of smoke which cast a shadow [over everything. There is] . . . no mercy, no respite. And then, [just when you are thinking all is lost] . . . stupefied and shaken, you realize that the shells are passing overhead . . . the sun is shining . . . onto you [once again and] . . . someone else is getting a turn.

Now you must pull yourself together, say unconcernedly to the next man – if he is alive – 'Some strafe that!' And get to work to help the situation. Round the corner, two men [are] already working, as if possessed, to clear the earth from the owner of two legs sticking stiffly out. Not much hope there. [The] next man [is] quite dead, half his head blown away. Step over him. Round another corner, [is] about 15 yards of straight trench. Every man down, and not a place to put your foot. The first man [is] dead, head between [his] knees. Put him out. The next is living, moaning softly, huddled on his knees . . . his face sweating with his agony . . . [His] right wrist and hand [are] smashed. [He has a] big gash in [his] right thigh, and [a] flesh wound in [the] neck. Put on the field dressings . . . Whatever his pain, he won't make your job harder by showing it. [He] thanks you in a pleasant voice, and settles down to wait, [for] hours probably, for the stretcher-bearers. You feel like choking to see their gameness.

About 100 yards of their trench was destroyed by this bombardment, which killed twelve men as well as wounding four others. It had resulted in a relatively short casualty list relative to countless similar incidents on the Somme. But given that Kippenberger's company was already down to just fifty-five men before the bombardment started, the effect was as damaging as if about 250 men had been lost out of a battalion of 800. If the Germans had only known how thinly the New Zealanders were now spread, they must have backed their chances of making a successful counter-attack.

When the immediate emergency was over, Kippenberger attempted to return to the position he had occupied previously, only to find it was almost impossible to progress up the trench without standing on the corpses. 'If they had been Germans, I would not have [been] troubled,' he confessed, 'but they were our own dear boys, and I hesitated. Corporal Macleod came [towards me] . . . from the opposite direction, looked a minute, climbed onto the parados, walked quickly along and suddenly toppled head first into the trench on top of the others. [Forgetting my worries about the corpses] I went straight . . . [to him], but the sniper had got him through the brain and he, [like those I had stepped on to get to him], was [already] dead.'[18]

Corporal Macleod's death was to be the last from his company recorded in Kippenberger's account during that spell in the trenches. That night, what remained of the 1st New Zealand Brigade was relieved, being replaced in the front line by the 2nd New Zealand Brigade. It was battalions from that unit which on 1 October made the New Zealand Division's final Somme attack.

That advance, which formed part of the Allied move towards Eaucourt L'Abbaye, was, like the New Zealand Division's other major advances on the Somme, successful in terms of territory seized, but relatively costly in terms of casualties. While the portions of Goose Alley, Gird Trench and Gird Support Trench targeted, but not captured, on 27 September were taken, along with Circus Trench – an extension to the west of the western-most section of Gird Trench before its lurch to the north-west (see map 18) – the 2nd Battalions of the Otago and Canterbury Regiments had each lost about 175 men.[19]

These losses, together with those sustained by the 2nd Battalion the Wellington Regiment – the former regiments' sister battalion in the 2nd New Zealand Brigade – during the attack, took the New Zealand Division's casualties close to 6,725.[20] This was a large figure for such a small country, but about par for the course on the Somme, considering the number of men committed to action, the number of actions fought, and the amount of time spent in the front line. The one consolation was that these latest casualties were suffered in the course of an advance that helped pave the way for the taking of Eaucourt L'Abbaye by British troops two days later.

Major-General Russell relinquished his command of the front line to the 41st Division on 4 October. The next day Haig sent Russell a message via the New Zealand government, congratulating his division 'on the splendid record it had achieved', pointing out that it had served in the front line for no fewer than twenty-three consecutive days, a period in which it had carried out 'with complete success every task set'.[21] It would be quibbling to interject that this airbrushed away the mistakes made on 27 September. The New Zealand Division had exhibited a remarkable capacity to get the job done, even if it had been helped along by ruthless tactics that could almost certainly be considered war crimes.

It would be misleading, however, not to at least mention one more stain on the New Zealand Division's reputation. At 5.44 a.m. on 2 October, just hours after the division's final Somme attack, John Sweeney, a thirty-seven-year-old private serving in the 1st Battalion the Otago Regiment, was executed near Russell's headquarters in Méaulte. The 'extreme penalty', carried out by a firing squad of twelve 1st Otago soldiers, was not punishment for any misdemeanour committed on a Somme battlefield. Private Sweeney had deserted on 25 July while the New Zealand Division was holding the line near Armentières and had only been apprehended on 3 September, after the regiment had travelled to the south to take part in the 'Big Push'.

Forty-one days was a long time to be away from your regiment during a war. However, the way Sweeney's case was presented leads one to question whether he received a fair trial. In the course of his court martial ten days after he was apprehended, Sweeney was sentenced without the court, consisting of three officers from the 1st New Zealand Brigade, being told about his work as a tunneller during the Gallipoli campaign. The relevant papers had gone missing, a factor that might have had a critical bearing on whether he was granted another chance, rather than being condemned to be shot.

No consideration appears to have been given to the fact that Sweeney had been born in Australia, a country that did not allow its soldiers to be executed. If anyone did speak to the court on Sweeney's behalf, no record of it appears in his file. If he had been represented, surely his commanding officer's suggestion that his 'conduct until . . . January 1915 was bad' would have been delved into.

Sweeney's chances of being treated leniently were further reduced after Brigadier-General Francis Johnston of the 1st New Zealand Brigade stated that discipline in the battalion in question was 'very fair' rather than very good, and that if the sentence was carried out, 'the seriousness of the offence will then be brought home to the [other] men of the Brigade'. Such reasoning, which amounted to punishing one man to encourage the others, might not have been accepted had the court been subject to today's standards of justice. Nevertheless on 28 September, General Rawlinson adopted this reasoning as well, recommending the sentence be carried out, as 'crimes of this nature have been prevalent in this Division and I can see no extenuating circumstances'.[22]

Sergeant Arthur Rhind, who saw Sweeney being marched out to his execution, reported in his diary on 2 October: 'A firing party [from 1st Battalion the Otago Regiment] arrived last night, and he was shot this morning in front of a dugout opposite our mess. A deserter twice over, he went out to be shot without showing any fear.'[23] After he had been despatched, New Zealand's Defence Minister, James Allen, was asked whether his parents should be told. Allen ruled that they should and a letter was duly sent to their last known address in Tasmania. Unfortunately the letter never reached them. They had moved from Tasmania to Bondi, a district of Sydney, before it was sent. That explains why John Sweeney's mother wrote to the Defence Minister on 28 November 1916 stating: 'I have got word that my son . . . has been killed at the front on October 2nd. Would you kindly let me know any particulars.' Only then did the military authorities realize that she still had not heard the worst, whereupon, on 18 December 1916, the missing letter was sent out again, this time to the right address.

Not surprisingly, its contents shocked the Sweeneys, despite the heartfelt sympathy expressed by Brigadier-General Robin, commander of the military forces in New Zealand, in its concluding paragraph: 'I can only in such a painful matter reiterate my sincerest regrets and offer you and the soldier's other relatives my deepest sympathy.' On 28 December, John's father Bernard wrote back to Robin, stating 'I must say it is a great blow to hear of my son's death in that way. He was the last I would have thought would do such a thing. Would you kindly let me know if there is any chance of ever hearing any more particulars of the case.' He also asked whether John had left anything for him, or his wife, adding 'The smallest article would be a comfort to us.'[24]

He was not the only parent who needed comforting in the wake of the New Zealand Division's trials and tribulations. Graphic evidence that this was the case was to be supplied to Private Claude Burley of the 2nd

Wellington Regiment during his last day on the Somme. In the course of
the lead-up to the New Zealand Division's first Somme action, he had
helped to carry the remains of Corporal Cliff Curran and Private Tommy
Mooney, the men who had been blown up by one of their own grenades
(see Chapter 35), to a nascent graveyard about half a mile away from where
they had died (probably the Quarry Cemetery, 500 yards north of Montauban, the location specified as Cliff Curran's last resting place in his
personal service file). Burley and his comrades then dug two graves and
buried the men side by side. As Burley wrote in his letter home:

They were the first New Zealanders to be buried there and among the first in this
[cemetery] . . .
    The Church of England minister . . . read a short service . . . and said he would
write home to their people. As the padre [spoke], trains, guns and all sorts of carts
and conveyances [passed by]. Even as we stood around the grave . . . shells were
bursting around us . . . One landed . . . on an ammunition train . . . causing a lot
of destruction, and as we left [the cemetery], two more poor fellows . . . [victims]
of this shell, were carried over.

Before leaving the cemetery following the service, Burley marked the
graves with two crosses fashioned out of wooden ammunition boxes, on
which he wrote 'their ages and particulars'. Presumably he hoped this
would help their relatives find them after the war. Perhaps he also intended
to return. His letter describes how his return happened sooner rather than
later: 'As we came away past the place (for the last time, the 2nd Wellingtons having been ordered to leave the Somme on 6 October) I . . . ran over
and had a last look . . . I could hardly find the grave[s]. There were so many
added since [I was] last there.'[25]

38: Ambushed

Thiepval and Feste Staufen, 26–28 September 1916

(See maps 2 and 19)

The big attack on 15 September had not resulted in a breakthrough, but it had given Haig the time and space to attack some of the old German front-line – and second-line – defences from a different direction. Within days of trying out the tanks, his new weapon, in a push principally focused on getting the 4th Army's front moving, Haig gave General Gough the green light to mount a major operation aimed at the Reserve Army's territory, whose principal landmark was the village of Thiepval.[1]

Thiepval in September 1916 was a very different type of place to what had existed there three to four months earlier. One German witness, reporting on its condition after the 1 July attack, stated:

The entire [Thiepval] sector is a scene of devastation and ruin. All the buildings have been razed to the ground apart from a few isolated walls. Nothing is left of the church and the château except for the château gates. They are the only remaining structure. The trenches and approach roads are only distinguishable as slight hollows in the ground, and are partly buried by tree trunks, rocks and rubble. They are blocked in places by mounds of earth and are intersected by deep craters. They are usually passed at a run.[2]

Trench repairs carried out afterwards made Thiepval just as hard a nut to crack as it had been before. That is why the following comments made by Major-General Ivor Maxse to the men in his 18th Division on the eve of their 26 September attack on the village were all the more uplifting. According to Private Reginald Emmett of the 54th Brigade's 11th Royal Fusiliers, Maxse's pre-battle morale booster was in essence: 'The 180th Württemburgers have withstood attacks on Thiepval for two years. But the 18th Division will take it tomorrow.'

Not that all those listening believed him. 'We thought: all very well for you . . . ,' Emmett recalled later, and that night, when he and his companions sang the well-known song 'I Want to Go Home', the knowledge that

they might not survive the coming battle probably added greater significance to the words than they had ever had before.[3]

The attack started at 12.35 p.m. on 26 September. British forces were
advancing from south to north rather than from west to east, which had
been the case on 1 July. The 18th Division's 54th Brigade was to operate on
the left (west) side of the attack, leaving the right (east) side to 54th Brigade's
sister brigade within the division, 53rd Brigade.

It is highly likely that the pessimists within the ranks of the 18th Division would have been correct about the push not being successful, had it
not been for one weapon that differentiated the two sides. The appearance
of a tank at a critical stage revived the British attack when it was faltering.
The report by Brigadier-General T. H. Shoubridge, commander of the
54th Brigade, admitted: 'It seems doubtful, if the château defence had not
been dealt with by the tank, whether the attack would have progressed
beyond that line. As it was, the assaulting companies of the 12th Middlesex
passed it right and left.'[4]

That tank, combined with a generous provision of guns and howitzers
(around one field gun or small-calibre howitzer per 10.5 yards of front, and
one heavier gun or howitzer per 26 yards of front, more or less the formula
that had been so successful on 15 September), was enough to help the 18th
Division take a substantial proportion of the Thiepval front-line system
with the initial thrust.[5] Progress thereafter was necessarily slower than the
troops might have hoped because it was not just the trench lines that had to
be quelled. There were also snipers lurking in many of the neighbouring
shell holes.[6]

When describing how he came to be in the German line, Private Emmett
does not say he was helped by a tank. But neither does his account refer to
his being held up by the German 'obstacle' which, it seems, the tank broke
through. If his following testimony is correct, it is likely that he made it
past the defences protecting the German front line after the tank had moved
on. 'We had been told to make for the ruin of a château,' Emmett recalled,
'and dazed and exhausted as I was, I dragged myself to a little hill where
there was a pile of stones. All that was left of the château I supposed.
Here . . . German machine-gun fire became fiercer than ever . . . sweeping . . . just above the ground. I threw myself into a shell hole.'

The following statement by signaller Sydney Fuller (the private mentioned in Chapter 15), serving with the 8th Suffolk regiment, part of the
18th Division's 53rd Brigade, suggests he may have witnessed the moment

when the tables were turned: 'I saw a long line of men running towards our rear, and for a moment I thought it was the beginning of another repulse. Then I saw they were holding their hands above their heads: [they were] Germans. They had surrendered, and left their trench like one man.'[7]

Special care was taken to winkle out the Germans who remained in their dugouts when the British swept past them. Emmett, who belonged to the assault battalion assigned this role by the 54th Brigade, wrote afterwards:

I started . . . telling any Germans left [in the dugouts] to come up. If there was no response, I fired a few shots, and then threw down a bomb. We got quite a few [Germans reacting to that]. Some came holding up their hands, and shouting, 'Kamerad!' Others held up photographs of their wives and children. We had to be very quick on them, for some still had a bit of kick in them.

[In] one dugout in particular . . . they could not be got out. The place was set on fire. Several were killed as they came out. The others died in the fire. [Other] prisoners were sent down the line in the charge of a corporal as escort. Many got shot on the way down. The escorts told us later that many of our boys were mad with what they had gone through, and the strain of it all, and just shot at anything in a German uniform.[8]

A similar tale was told by Private Fuller. As he moved around the battle-field he spotted two dead German soldiers, who were lying near one of the dugout entrances. They had been riddled with bullets. 'Another [German, who was still alive], was lying buried almost to the neck by a shell which had dropped near[by]. I shall never forget the expression on this man's face. [It was] ghastly white, [and] his eyes were staring with terror. He was unable to move, while our chaps threw bombs past him down the dugout stairs, and the enemy inside threw their bombs out.' According to Fuller, these explosions in the dugouts could be 'felt' rather than heard. The sound was muffled by the depth of the dugout. While he was watching, 'a little German popped out wearing his metal helmet, holding both hands above his head and crying, "Mercy! Mercy!" He was shot at once, and dropped like an empty sack.'[9]

The shooting was an evil act. But even if he had wanted to, Fuller could not have intervened effectively. The killing was going on all around him. What could one man do? While he was walking northwards, looking for Zollern Trench, the second objective, he saw two more Germans running towards him. They were sobbing. One was wearing a Red Cross armband.

Some British soldiers called out, ordering them to stop. But as Fuller said, 'they seemed to be mad with fear . . . too terrified to be reasonable'. They dodged past the British soldiers' bayonets, only to be shot by a passing party of 'bombers' – men who specialized in taking on the enemy with what the likes of Fuller called 'bombs', but which today we would refer to as grenades.

At the end of the day it was hard to be precise about exactly where each unit had reached due to the intermixing of personnel and units. That being said, the 54th Brigade's 12th Middlesex regiment reported that its right had pushed on past the northern edge of Thiepval, whereas the 53rd Brigade's 8th Suffolk regiment, after likewise advancing beyond the second objective, had been unable to find a secure spot and had opted to return to Zollern Trench, where they stayed that night.[10] However far north they had penetrated, they needed to be relieved eventually. One of the soldiers who was available was Private Thomas Jennings of the 6th Battalion, the Royal Berkshire Regiment, a 53rd Brigade unit. During the hours of darkness that followed the fighting he had to crouch down in a trench to avoid the massive bombardment by the German artillery. However, at dawn on 27 September the German gunners ceased firing, fearing that if they continued they would be pinpointed by the British planes and then fired at in their turn. That gave Jennings the chance to look around.

What he saw appalled him. Even the trench where he had been sitting was a scene of horror. As Jennings noted afterwards: 'Buried in its walls were dozens of bodies, both British and German, rotting in the wet earth. A khaki-clad leg or arm protruded from the sides, and a couple of [dead] Jerries wrapped in blankets, complete with jackboots, were acting as silent sentinels either side of a dugout.' As he wandered around outside the trench, Jennings stumbled across 'a huge crater . . . Its occupants were the dead of our soldiers who made the advance on 1st July . . . Laid, sat or reclined in all positions, [the] skeletons [were] covered with greenish skin and flesh [due to] . . . decomposition. One that I noticed in particular was lying on his back, his belly a moving mass of maggots.' Jennings was about to retreat back to the original trench where he had spent the night when his captain, noticing what he had been looking at, ordered him to search the bodies for anything that might enable them to be identified. 'It wasn't a pleasant task,' Jennings noted, which in the circumstances was a classic piece of British understatement.[11]

The offensive launched by Gough's Reserve Army did not just consist of the advance to Thiepval. Other Reserve Army units attempting to advance from south to north, alongside the 18th Division, included II Corps' 11th Division on the 18th Division's right, and then two Canadian Corps divisions on the 11th Division's right. Relatively little is known about the actions of most of these units, other than what is recorded in official war diaries and regimental histories. The one exception relates to the part played by the 9th West Yorkshire Regiment, part of the 11th Division's 32nd Brigade.

The regiment's 2nd Lieutenant Geoffrey Pratt, a journalist before he joined the Army, wrote a detailed account about his wartime experiences on the Somme. It makes for interesting reading. Not only does he write about the great events in which he participated, but unusually for a soldier Pratt also reveals his personal weaknesses and feelings as these events unfolded. For that reason it is an extraordinary and a rare piece of writing for an era when the officer class was expected to demonstrate the fortitude and lack of emotional expression characteristic of the 'stiff upper lip'.

Pratt's account starts with a shock. He had just been given one of those orders for which the Somme generals have become infamous: an instruction to stage an attack before the artillery barrage had started, even though it would have been impossible to reach the assembly point in time for the attack. Pratt was told at 2.45 p.m. on 27 September that he and his company needed to march the best part of a mile to the north from near Mouquet Farm where they were located, so that they could attempt to capture Feste Staufen (Stuff Redoubt) at 3 p.m. When Pratt remonstrated, pointing out that by the time they arrived at the assembly point, the Germans would have already put down their counter-barrage, his colonel lamely replied 'I am very sorry, but it is an order, and I am afraid you simply have to do your best.' Because there was no higher authority to whom he could appeal before zero hour, Pratt felt trapped. He could either refuse to obey orders or just go along with them knowing they could amount to a death sentence: 'It seemed next to certain we would give our lives for a failure,' he wrote afterwards.

By the time Pratt and his company arrived at the assembly point in Zollern Trench, ready to advance the 500 yards separating them from Feste Staufen, it was already 3.20 p.m. That was around twelve minutes after the first barrage was supposed to have lifted off their objective. In fact the bombardment had not yet materialized. The artillery programme had been changed, but Pratt and his colonel had not been informed. Nevertheless, once they had regained their breath Pratt and his men dutifully charged over the top. Predictably they were fired at by German guns, and were forced to take shelter in shell holes about 200 yards from their target. There they stopped, waiting for reinforcements.

At about 4 p.m. Pratt and his men noticed that the 6th Yorkshire Regiment, their sister unit within the 32nd Brigade, was attacking on their left. They took that as their cue to advance as well. They all ended up in Hessian Trench, with most of the 6th Yorkshires about 100 yards to the left of the 9th West Yorkshires, having to their surprise not met any serious opposition. The only Germans they saw in the captured trench were lined up on the stairs leading down to a dugout, and they were offering to surrender. Pratt saw that the rest of the German garrison were rushing away to the north, and ordered his men to fire at them. But that quickly petered out, after one of Pratt's men was shot in the head: Pratt saw a small spurt of brain come out behind his head, before the man fell in a crumpled heap onto the parapet.

As can be seen from map 19, Hessian Trench ran from east to west. The trench that Pratt and his men needed to occupy if they were to control Feste Staufen ran from Hessian Trench to the north for around 150 yards. It was along this trench, which represented the western edge of Feste Staufen, that Pratt and his men proceeded first. Their first task once there was to winkle the Germans out of their dugouts. To do this Pratt and his men employed tactics similar to those being used in Thiepval. 'We shouted to them to come out,' Pratt reported. 'If they came out, well and good. If not, we rolled a bomb down. Each dugout had two entrances into the same trench. A bomb went down one, and the Boche came up the other, all scrambling to get out first.' Some were very badly wounded. The one man who tried to run away was shot.

After extricating the Germans from the dugouts, Pratt and his sergeant walked to the northern end of this trench, stopping when they came to a fork in it. At this point they agreed they should retrace their steps so that they could help with the prisoners. They might have done better to have called for assistance and then proceeded up the left fork a little way further. If they had, they might have been able to catch the Germans up that fork in their dugout, and to nip any opposition in the bud. As it was, they not only failed to secure the approaches to their trench, but they also failed to set up a strongpoint at this northern spot while they had the opportunity. It was a mistake – albeit an understandable one given that there were so few of them in the Redoubt – which they would live to regret.

Having made their choice, they and their men proceeded to round up their prisoners and escort them down to the junction with Hessian Trench where they, the West Yorkshires, had entered the Redoubt. There they met Lieutenant H. A. Gough, another West Yorkshire officer, who reminded Pratt there was an order that all prisoners should be shot. However, when Pratt suggested that he, Gough, could shoot them if he wanted, Gough backed down. The prisoners were subsequently sent westwards along Hessian Trench to where the 6th Yorkshire Regiment were holding the line. Pratt was later told that the prisoners did not survive. Allegedly when this large group of Germans was seen approaching, a Lewis gun was turned onto them.

Shortly afterwards Archie White, a twenty-four-year-old captain in the 6th Yorkshire Regiment, appeared and took over as the Redoubt commander. There was not much that needed changing in the trench where they had congregated. Pratt had more or less secured the western edge. There were groups of soldiers every fifty yards, and a dugout in the centre that served as headquarters. But no move had yet been made to secure the south side, let alone the east and north sides. White ordered Pratt to tackle the south side the next morning (28 September) and supplied him with a thirteen-man Yorkshire Regiment team, including a grenade-thrower and enough backup in case there was a need to force their way through at the point of bayonets.

As it turned out they need not have worried. There was no opposition on the south side, and a post was duly set up complete with filled sandbags about twenty yards back from where the trench running along the southern edge forked. At that point everything looked rosy. But Pratt's subsequent report about what he witnessed when he returned to the headquarters dugout makes it clear just how tenuous their grip on the Redoubt really was:

I . . . found smoke and fire coming from the entrance . . . I . . . found that a shell had come straight down the stairs, blowing everyone there to pieces . . . I found two men, and we set to work clearing out the debris. Soon we came across mangled portions. I came across a man's shoulder and chest, mutilated and raw, and part of a severed head. There was an acrid smell of blood, [which I found] peculiarly repulsive . . . [There was also] a mass of loose earth in which the dead men were all mushed together.

We . . . then turned our attention to a lad who had been sitting on the bottom step when the shell entered, and was now half buried. As soon as we cleared up a bit, I could see his back was broken . . . He could not feel his legs . . . They lay twisted away from his body in an 'impossible' position.

Following on from this traumatic discovery, Pratt's equilibrium began to suffer. His state of mind became even more vulnerable as a result of having to respond to a string of unforeseen emergencies. One minute he was comforting a man who had been wounded trying to secure the northern edge of the Redoubt. The next minute it was a lad who had been shot in the head by a sniper. 'He fell down . . . in the trench,' Pratt recalled, 'and in an unearthly voice shouted out, "Mother! Mother!" Then he seemed to come to. The bullet had ploughed through the top of his head, taking part of the brain with it. I picked him up, but he said he could not move his left arm and leg.' Then there was the man who let off a Mills grenade by mistake. 'A piece had cut a big gash in his jugular vein, and blood was spurting out,' Pratt reported. 'With every breath, a stream of blood poured from his mouth. I knelt by his side. But there seemed nothing to do, and after perhaps a couple of minutes, he was dead in a pool of blood with a blue grey face.'

These and other incidents persuaded Pratt to move back the post he had organized on the western edge of the Redoubt. 'I was sick of blood and carnage,' he explained, justifying his movement of the post. But then he realized that was a mistake, since from the more southerly post he would not be able to see whether Germans were approaching from the northern end of the trench. So the post was moved back to where it had been originally. Once that was done Pratt appeared to recover. He cheered himself up by shooting at some Germans who were within range.

However, his sang-froid was disturbed again when Captain White informed Pratt that he had received an order requiring him to complete the capture of the Redoubt by taking its eastern and northern sides to add to what they already controlled. A British barrage was to be fired at the German positions on these sides. As soon as it finished, Pratt was to go round the northern end of the Redoubt, even though he would be enfiladed by the Germans in the post he had neglected to eliminate to the north-west, and troops from the 8th Duke of Wellington Regiment who had just arrived were to go round the southern end of the Redoubt. The two parties were to join forces on the eastern side. White's order finished with the most controversial part: 'All Boche prisoners must be bayoneted and thrown over the parapet.'

Pratt was upset at what White was telling him. He told White that the plan would not work, that they would never get past the German post to the north-west. But White would not be diverted from the path he had chosen. So it was that Pratt and the men who were to act under his command found themselves part of a plan that the man with the best knowledge of the conditions on the ground (Pratt) did not support.

The barrage had been requested for 6 p.m., but they had to wait another hour before it was delivered. When it came some shells appeared to target the German post to the north-west. 'Our spirits . . . rose,' Pratt commented later:

I had cleared away the barrier and entanglements, and immediately the barrage was over, we set off. . . As we were nearing the [German] post . . . I . . . whispered to Crochan: 'Have a bomb ready!' At that [very] moment some bombs exploded close to us . . . At first I thought someone had dropped some of our bombs. But immediately afterwards, it dawned on me it was the Boche. I chucked two bombs I was carrying as hard as I could in the direction of . . . [the German post to the north-west] and fired my pistol. Then a whole shower of bombs [exploded near us].[12]

As Pratt had warned, the Germans had been on the lookout for just such a move. Now the British were paying for their failure to take the German defenders seriously. They were being ambushed. And the wounded British soldiers squealed like stuck pigs, as they felt hard steel splinters piercing their feet, their legs, their hands and their sides, cut by whatever it was the Germans had shot or thrown at them. The attack was a total failure.

It was a disappointing development, all the more so because it had to be set against one of the most successful weeks for British forces on the Somme. On 26 September, Combles, Morval, Lesboeufs and Gueudecourt had all been captured in the Somme's eastern sector. Mouquet Farm was captured in the centre, and Thiepval was more or less in the bag in the western sector. The French, not to be outdone, had captured Frégicourt. However, their hopes of advancing to within attacking distance of the Moislains (about 2 miles east of Bouchavesnes) to Le Transloy defence system was thwarted.[13]

Pratt's account does not describe what happened next inside the Redoubt, other than to say that after he had been wounded in his foot, leg, hand and side, he somehow hobbled back to base and later was shipped back to Britain. While he had been in the Redoubt, it was Pratt who had taken all the risks. Yet after the Redoubt was finally captured by the British on

9 October, it was Captain Archie White who won the Victoria Cross.[14] White stayed on in the Redoubt after Pratt had been forced to leave because of his wounds. After the Germans had forced their way in, White helped to drive them out by leading the counter-attack. Perhaps Lieutenant-General Claud Jacob, commander of II Corps, wanted to reward White for his robust attitude. When Jacob had sent a messenger to White asking him how long he could hold out, White replied cheekily: 'Till the cows come home.'[15]

39: Weather Permitting

Serre, Beaucourt and Beaumont Hamel, 29 September 1916–17 March 1917

(See maps 20 and 21)

Just when Haig must have been hoping that all the weeks of striving to wear down the Germans were about to bear fruit, a new element was brought into the equation. It began to rain. It was no surprise that the Somme push would eventually be stopped by the weather. It was just that the rainy season arrived sooner than Haig had expected. The result was disappointing to put it mildly. The bad weather was to ruin all his best-laid plans, and leave him even more vulnerable to the criticism of his tactics and lack of progress that was brewing at home.

Haig's ideas for the next stage of the advance were sent out to Rawlinson and Gough while the fighting on the Thiepval ridge was still raging. On 29 September a letter from Haig's General Headquarters informed them what he had in mind for the 4th Army and the Reserve Army. The 4th Army was to capture the next German position running from Le Transloy to Loupart Wood (one mile east of Irles), via Beaulencourt, and the ridge beyond the Thilloy–Warlencourt valley. Gough's Reserve Army, advancing northwards from the Thiepval ridge, was to tackle Loupart Wood to Miraumont. At the same time another branch of his army was to advance eastwards from the original front line between Hébuterne and Beaumont Hamel with a view to joining forces with the southern thrust at Miraumont. This would have the effect of cutting off any German forces still remaining in the area north of the Ancre.[1]

If this additional blow had been landed, as Haig hoped, on or before 12 October, who knows how it would have affected the German Army. It was already reeling after the reverses it had suffered on 26 September. The following day Prince Rupprecht noted in his diary that his troops in the 1st and 2nd Armies, as well as the staff officers controlling them, were becoming more and more 'depressed' by the seemingly never-ending losses of terrain combined with the inability to strike back. Although he could see that such losses were not what really mattered, it was hard to convey that message to the average German soldier. This was all the more the case because the level of casualties had left the German Army short of well-trained officers and NCOs who could cajole and inspire the men in the front line to carry on fighting.[2]

It was then, when all seemed lost, that the weather intervened. At first the rain only came in one- or two-day spurts. It did not totally halt Haig's armies, or the French, in their tracks. After a long fight the French finally took most of Sailly during the night of 15–16 October.[3] During the first fifteen days of the month, the 4th Army nevertheless took Eaucourt l'Abbaye and Le Sars alongside the Albert to Bapaume road, and Gough's Reserve Army completed the capture of the Staufen and Schwaben Redoubts.[4] But the time taken for these preliminary actions convinced Haig that, once again, he had been too ambitious. On 17 and 18 October, after discussions with his army commanders and the French, he approved a variation of the 29 September plan 'weather permitting'. The new plan was to focus on separate attacks astride the River Ancre, and towards Le Transloy, with less emphasis on the area in between.[5]

But within twenty-four hours of the revised plan being finalized, even that was called into question by the weather. No sooner had the British Commander-in-Chief signed off on a series of four attacks to take place between 21 and 26 October, targeting Beaumont Hamel and Beaucourt (Gough's Reserve Army), and Le Transloy (Rawlinson's 4th Army), than the heavens opened again.

At first, it was hoped that the cloudburst on 19 October, the day after the revised plan was made, was just an isolated event. It was followed by three dry days. However, thereafter, it rained every day until after the beginning of November, resulting in the repeated postponements of the planned operations. It was not just the three generals whose mood was affected, as is demonstrated by the comments of Reverend Harold Davies, the chaplain who worked with the Royal Naval Division's 190th Brigade, a key unit for the coming offensive. Reverend Davies incorporated into the entries he made daily in his diary what amounted to a running commentary describing his charges' reaction to each new spate of bad weather. On 22 October he mused: 'It is curious how religion . . . tells on these occasions. Instead of giving way to petulance at the delay, which must be putting a terrible strain on them, [they] are quiet, and try to maintain the old spirit. It is rather like a dinner or lunch when certain individuals have had some grounds of quarrel, and are obliged to meet, and all are scrupulously determined to avoid the disagreeable topic.'

His diary entry the next day shows that there had been no change for the better: 'Once again . . . the day has been postponed. Instead of the 25th, it is now to be the 26th. I dropped into HQ mess. Here everything was hilarity and humour. They had decided to drop all shop talk. An imminent battle seemed the furthest thought from their minds.'⁶

The problem with all this rain was that it quickly transformed the innocuous-looking communication trenches, and surrounding country-side, into mantraps from which at times it seemed there was no escape. H. G. Hartnett, a twenty-five-year-old private serving in the 2nd Australian Battalion, described what he witnessed as he approached the front line north of Flers on 31 October in the following terms. 'The communication trench was . . . about two hundred yards long, and was half full of mud and water. Into this we sank . . . going down to our thighs in many cases. Per-spiration poured off the struggling men trying to force their way along . . . through the sticky black mud . . . [Some of them] were so exhausted that the tears ran down their cheeks, and they sobbed like children. In their despair, they would have welcomed death as a happy release from their torture.'

At least while proceeding down the communication trench the men were keeping warm, because they were moving. How much worse was their torment when, after reaching the front line, they had to more or less remain stationary in the mud all night. 'Rain fell all through the long night to add to our misery,' Hartnett recalled. He went on to describe what he witnessed when he woke up the next morning: 'Every man was standing bogged over his knees in the mud looking helpless. To sit down was impos-sible. The banks of the trench were so wet and soft that they broke and fell in everywhere. The only thing to do was to stand up and sink into the mud.'

They had to do this even though it was very cold. 'The blood seemed to stop circulating where our legs disappeared out of sight, our feet being like blocks of ice,' Hartnett recalled, adding 'As the day wore on, men became resigned to their fate . . . Here and there along the trench a man would be seen bogged in the mud leaning up against the bank sound asleep. It was the only way to have a rest.'⁷

Norman Collins, a nineteen-year-old 2nd Lieutenant in the 1st/6th Seaforth Highlanders, whose 152nd Brigade and 51st Highland Division were also going to be involved when the big offensive came off, had seen his men putting up with conditions that were even worse than those recounted by Hartnett. In the 23 October letter he sent to all of his folks back home he wrote: 'The mud is really awful. Even on main roads, it is up to our boot tops, and off the roads [it] will drag a man's boots off . . . In the trench, it varies from ankle to almost waist deep, and men have to be hauled out using ropes.'[8]

Notwithstanding these extreme conditions, which made it hard just to survive in a trench, let alone to do anything more proactive, General des Vallières, the French liaison officer with British GHQ, warned Haig on 23 October that because his French master Joffre was an 'underbred individual' he might make a scene about the British plans. Joffre had written to Haig complaining that the British Commander-in-Chief was not complying with their original strategy. At the beginning of the Battle of the Somme they had both agreed to attack on a wide front. Yet now Haig was restricting himself to narrow attacks, such as the one in the pipeline to be directed at Le Transloy.

Haig recorded in his diary how he had reacted to this slur: 'I at once replied that his letter seemed to have been written under a misapprehension on several points, viz. that I am losing time, that the scale of my attacks have been reduced, that my plans have been modified or changed. Not one of these suggestions is justified in fact. Meanwhile, to the utmost extent of the means at my disposal and so far as weather conditions render possible, I will continue to co-operate with you in exploiting to the full the successes already gained. But I must remind you that it lies with me to judge what I can undertake, and when I can undertake it.' It was apparently this last sentence that had upset Joffre. However, fortunately for Anglo-French relations, he had reconciled himself to what Haig was telling him. When Joffre arrived at GHQ, he could not have been more friendly or conciliatory.[9]

While British forces were struggling to adapt to the problems imposed by the weather, the Germans surprised the French by recapturing La Maisonnette on 29 October.[10] It was a sobering moment for Haig since it told him that whatever the extent of demoralization of the German troops, they were far from being down and out. The French capture of Pressoire and Ablaincourt on 7 November on the other hand suggested that it was still possible to attack notwithstanding the wintry conditions.[11]

On 5 November, Haig had told Gough that he should hold off making his attack until he had had four days of dry weather, which should have been sufficient to dry out the battlefield.[12] It was only on 11 November that it looked as if that precondition would be satisfied, and it was then that Gough finally felt he could fix the date for what was referred to as the 5th Army's offensive. The Reserve Army had been renamed the 5th Army with effect from 1 November.[13] The push forward was to begin at 5.45 a.m. on

13 November, and would feature two converging advances. The main thrust was to be made by the 5th Army's V Corps – commanded by the fifty-seven-year-old Lieutenant-General Edward Fanshawe – north of the Ancre. It would go from west to east and would employ four divisions (63rd [Royal Naval] Division, 51st [Highland] Division, and the 2nd and 3rd Divisions) against the area north of the Ancre running from the river to Serre. The villages of Beaumont Hamel and Beaucourt were also to be on the hit list.

The second thrust would be a northward attack towards the south side of the Ancre, and would feature the 19th and 39th Divisions, part of II Corps, whose commander was the fifty-two-year-old Lieutenant-General Claud Jacob (see map 20).

With hours to go before the attack commenced, General Kiggell visited Gough's headquarters on 12 November to check that he was not just attacking to please his Commander-in-Chief. Kiggell came away having been assured that the chances of the attack succeeding were 'quite good'. Haig received a similar message when he visited Gough's headquarters that afternoon. During that visit he mentioned to Gough that a victory would serve a multiple purpose. It would enable British forces to occupy a favourable position during the coming winter. But it would also help British foreign policy. Both Russia and Romania would be helped and heartened by a victory. (Romania had declared war on Austria-Hungary on 27 August, and the next day Germany declared war on Romania.) A victory would mean that the Germans would be unlikely to send units from the Somme to fight against Romania. It would also show the Russians – and the French – that the British really were intent on doing everything possible to defeat the Germans. Lastly, it would mean that Britain's suggestions would be taken more seriously at the military leaders' conference at Chantilly, which was to be held over the coming days.[14]

Even while Kiggell and Haig were talking to Gough about whether the push should go ahead, the preliminary bombardment was under way, designed to soften up the German defences before the attack. In an effort to minimize the chances of merely repeating the disastrous events that had taken place on V Corps' front on 1 July, lessons had been learned since then and action taken. It was hoped that the trench activity in the intervening nineteen weeks would have degraded the German powers of resistance somewhat, even though in this area it had not been as intense as on other parts of the front. Another factor which improved the chances of success was that the wide expanses of No Man's Land, which had been a major factor in the failures on 1 July, had been reduced to less than 250 yards in some areas.

However, the greatest changes related to the artillery. The catastrophe on 1 July had taught all commanders that it was necessary to make the forthcoming attack a surprise. With that in mind, on the days before the assault, the artillery was ordered to replicate the shelling programme it would adopt at, and just before, zero hour. It was hoped that as a result the Germans would not anticipate an attack when the same procedure was followed on 13 November.

Commanders had also learned that the number of guns per yard on 1 July was insufficient. With that in mind the ratio of guns per yard was to be substantially improved this time. On V Corps' front there was to be either a heavy gun or a heavy howitzer for every 31 yards, compared with for every 57 yards on 1 July. The number of field guns and light howitzers per yard of front was also increased: there was to be either a field gun or a light howitzer for every 13.5 yards on V Corps' front, compared with for every 21 yards of front on 1 July.[15] While these statistics were not quite as overwhelming as those laid on for the 15 September attack (a heavy gun or howitzer for each 21 yards of front, and a field gun or light howitzer for each 10 yards of front), or for the French attack on 1 July (a heavy gun or howitzer for each 21 yards of front), they were a marked improvement on what had been used last time this front was subjected to an all-encompassing attack.[16]

Perhaps even more important was the intention to use the newest artillery tactics, which had been honed since they were first used in a general attack on 15 September. While part of the barrage was to remain on the German front line at zero hour, a quarter of the 18-pounder guns were to fire 50 yards in front of it. Six minutes later, the shelling from these guns was to creep forward at the rate of twenty yards a minute, thereby enabling the infantry who advanced just behind the shelling to leap into the German trenches minutes, or even seconds, after it, and the remainder of the barrage was lifted from the German front line.[17]

The all-important right (south) side of V Corps' objectives was the responsibility of the 63rd (Royal Naval) Division. The south side was not just considered important because, if successful, this unit would end up taking one of the three villages north of the Ancre being targeted by the attack. What made the unit's success absolutely critical was that it represented the link which would join up the assault south of the Ancre with that being made to the north of the river. If all went according to plan the II Corps troops south of the Ancre would take the bridges across the river, thereby enabling those units to the south to communicate with, help and supply the British forces to the north, and vice versa.

It is surprising to find that the Royal Naval Division had been given this crucial role. Questions had been asked about its lack of battle experience, refusal to comply with army rules and protocol, and discipline, not least by Major-General Cameron Shute, who had taken over as its commander shortly before the battle. He feared that while the division had done well at Gallipoli, the men who manned it would be too undisciplined to make an impact when brought up against the more experienced German fighters.

Several examples of this indiscipline are mentioned in the regimental history of the division's Hawke Battalion. First of all there was the recurrent failure to post a guard. Time and again Shute would turn up to inspect the battalion, only to find that no one had seen him arrive. Then there was the repeated failure to keep the trenches tidy and clear of mud and rubbish. Lastly, the officers had not taken the trouble to clear the lining of ammunition boxes from the bottom of their trenches, even though Shute had requested that they should be removed.[18]

Although Shute's requests were perfectly reasonable, his criticism made him unpopular. He allegedly also made a complaint about the state of the Naval Division's latrines. Whether or not that particular story is apocryphal, it later became the subject of an uncomplimentary ditty written by the Hawke Battalion's Captain A. P. Herbert, later a well-known writer. The ditty started with the words:

> The general inspecting the trenches
> Exclaimed with a horrified shout:
> 'I refuse to command a division
> Which leaves its excreta about.'
>
> But nobody took any notice,
> No one was prepared to refute
> That the presence of shit was congenial
> Compared with the presence of Shute . . .

To combat these kinds of minor infractions, Shute would have preferred to replace at least some of the division's officers with regular army officers.[19] But before he could organize that, the division was ordered to take its place in the front line for the 13 November attack. Perhaps fearing that the men would not know how to react if they were given absolute discretion, he did not send them into the front line empty-handed. Shortly before they went into battle, he gave them one pointer they would never forget: 'I'm going to tell you this much. You know what you have got to do. The more prisoners you take, the less food you'll get, because we have to feed them with your rations.'[20]

It is hard for us to know how seriously the men who heard that terrible piece of advice took it. All that is certain is that, as in so many other units, there were extremes of behaviour at both ends of the heroic-cowardly spectrum. There is no doubt who was the best-known hero to come out of the fighting on 13 November 1916: it was Lieutenant-Colonel Bernard Freyberg, the twenty-seven-year-old commanding officer of the Royal Naval Division's Hood Battalion, whose actions during the battle that day won him the highest award for bravery, the Victoria Cross.

A fascinating insight into how Freyberg's leadership transformed a stalemate into victory has been provided by Captain the Honourable Lionel Montagu of the Hood Battalion, who was with him at the critical moment in the battle. This moment did not take place during the first hours of the fighting, or even during the first day. As Montagu has explained, it did not take any special act of heroism to break through the German front-line system alongside the Ancre on 13 November. That was down to the effective artillery bombardment, which combined with that morning's mist. If the account by the German soldier quoted below is accurate, the mist may have concealed the approach of the attackers.

Because of that, and because Freyberg had trained his men to follow the creeping barrage closely, the Hood Battalion, supported by the Drake Battalion, took the first three German trenches, and ended the day in or just short of Station Road, with just one more trench separating them from Beaucourt. Freyberg wanted to enter Beaucourt that day, only to be stood down by Major-General Shute on the grounds that the Royal Naval Division battalions to the north had not fared so well, and that Freyberg would receive no support if he went on alone.[21]

According to Montagu, Freyberg's heroic act, which ensured the village was captured, took place on 14 November:

Freyberg soon had things organized [for the attack on the 14th]. I was to lead the second wave in support of him from the second trench. The prospect seemed to me very doubtful. The snipers and machine guns were so active that it was dangerous to show your head even for an instant . . . We were to attack at 7.45 a.m . . . I had always heard it was impossible to advance against hostile machine guns unless our artillery had first knocked them out. These, and the snipers, were quite unaffected by our barrage, which seemed feeble. Such were my doubts, that I sent a message to Freyberg at 7.15 a.m. to ask him if he intended to attack . . . He told me that he had exactly the same doubts, and nearly called it off.

At 7.45 a.m., our barrage became a little more intense, but nothing like enough to stop the snipers and machine guns. I saw Freyberg leap out of the trench, and wave the men on. Three men followed from my trench, and I got out with my runner with bullets raining past us. The first wave stopped three times. Freyberg was knocked clean over by a bullet which hit his helmet, but he got up again. I and my runner dived into a shell hole, and waited about half a minute. I said I would go back, and get some more men out of the trench, and crawled about ten yards back to do so. Then about a dozen men came out, and I got up and waved the rest on. They all followed. We soon got into Beaucourt. And found that the Germans could not face our men, and were surrendering in hundreds. It was an amazing sight. They came out of their holes tearing off their equipment.

At that point they were hoping they were home and dry, but as Montagu put it, that was when 'It started'. 'It' was the artillery bombardment they had been dreading. 'They are ranging on this house!' Freyberg shouted, and he and Montagu scurried out of the building where they had been sheltering and took refuge in a shallow trench. They, and the troops with them, were far from safe. British forces in Beaucourt were all but overwhelmed by the enormous number of shells that rained down around them. As if that was not bad enough, both Freyberg and Montagu believed the Germans were about to counter-attack. 'I expected to see them on top of us at any minute,' Montagu recalled.

He first knew that something had gone badly wrong when he heard Freyberg speaking in a strange voice: 'Goodbye Montagu,' he said. Freyberg had been hit. There was a hole in his neck that was bleeding profusely. He was going a very bad colour, according to Montagu, who thought Freyberg was about to die. But after Montagu fed him a quarter grain of morphia, he recovered, and was even able to walk back to base once the barrage halted.[22] As for Montagu, he stayed on in Beaucourt until he was sure it was secured, which it was by 10.30 a.m. thanks to assistance from troops with the 37th Division's 111th Brigade, who seized the line running north-west from Beaucourt.[23] Montagu earned a DSO, but probably deserved the Victoria Cross as well.

Unfortunately, there appear to be no equivalent accounts describing the moment when Beaumont Hamel was taken. However, the beginning of the following report by a German soldier at least gives us a strong clue as to how British forces came to break through the German front line. The report was by Fähnrich Pukall, whose 3rd Company, part of the 1st Battalion of the 62nd Regiment, a 12th Division unit, was located in the front line just to the north of the Hawthorn Crater:

The mist was very thick [that morning]. It was unusually quiet . . . [However] Geisemeyer . . . called me over . . . to the left flank . . . and urged me to listen . . . Something was moving out there. [He was right.] When I listened, I heard muffled sounds. It was not the sound of digging, or the snipping of wire cutters. The British must be advancing! Stand to! I shouted . . .

I had to . . . warn the machine gunner. I ran toward the dip in the ground where the gunner was stationed, only to be stopped in my tracks by an extraordinary sight. A gigantic column of flames and smoke was ascending to the sky. (It was the Hawthorn Redoubt mine, which was exploded again at the British zero hour.) The mist distorted its shape and made it look bigger than it was . . . I was horrified . . . At the same time machine guns began firing all along the front and mortar bombs began to fall on our trench along with the shrapnel. I raced back to my platoon. The sentries dived for cover [shouting out their warning]: 'Attack!'[24]

Another German report suggests that the Scottish soldiers in the 51st (Highland) Division, the unit attacking Beaumont Hamel from the west, only reached the village that morning because of a penetration of the line by the Royal Naval Division to the south.[25] According to this theory, the soldiers who entered the German lines south of the village then turned northwards and captured the front-line positions protecting the village from the rear. It has to be said this is not how most of the 51st Division's penetrations of the German line are portrayed in the British official history. It suggests there was a straightforward entry into the German lines from the west. This makes one wonder whether the German report writer was too keen to exculpate his own unit in order to produce a reliable account.[26]

Whatever doubts exist concerning the direction of the 'breakthrough', no one could feel anything but sympathy for those who had to clear up the mess afterwards. Logic demanded that the medics and stretcher-bearers should be given the first crack of the whip so that they could rescue the living from the remaining trenches and dugouts. It was dangerous work. German gunners, who were still shelling the Beaumont Hamel sector, did not discriminate between combatants and medics. It was one such barrage that persuaded Captain David Rorie of the 1st/2nd Highland Field Ambulance to take refuge in one of the two-floored dugouts that required a descent down forty steps to get to the first chamber. The one he chose had a line of bunk beds down one side of the fifty-foot-long reception room, and it was full of wounded German soldiers: 'The place was . . . in utter darkness, and when we flashed our lights on and the wounded saw our escort with rifles at the ready, there was an outbreak of "Kamerad!", while a bevy of rats squeaked and scuttled away from their feast on the dead bodies on the floor. The stench was indescribably abominable, for many of the cases were gas-gangrenous.'[27]

It was only after the living cases had been picked up that the next stage of the clearing-up process began. Now it was the turn of the burial parties to do their work. 2nd Lieutenant Norman Collins of the 1st/6th Seaforth Highlanders had the misfortune to be appointed as the burial officer for his 152nd Brigade. He divided the dead into two categories. Those who had been killed during the 13 November attack, and those who had been lying out in No Man's Land since 1 July. He could not decide which job was worse. Removing the more recently killed ran the risk of upsetting his workers, who frequently came across friends and acquaintances, brothers or cousins. Alternatively there was the horrific task of moving the piles of bones covered with clothes, which was all that remained of those who had been sacrificed on the first day of the battle.

The latter were 'practically skeletons', Collins recalled later. However, what was particularly disturbing was not the smell (when bodies have lain out for a long time they have a sweet smell) but what was found inside each body. There was 'a rat's nest in the cage of each [man's] chest', and 'when you touched a body, the rats just poured out of the front,' he remembered.[28]

There was to be no similar clear-up at Serre. There the German garrison ruled supreme to the bitter end of the Battle of the Somme, having once again repulsed the British attempt to capture the village. The 3rd Division brigades who had tried and failed on 13 November had to recover and tend their wounds back in their own trenches. However, there was a victory of sorts south of the Ancre where II Corps' units had successfully advanced to the south bank of the river, in the process capturing St Pierre Divion.[29]

That was not quite the end of the Battle of the Somme. General Gough pleaded with Haig to be allowed one last roll of the dice just in case he could pull off another coup. The attack that targeted trenches north of Regina Trench (see map 20) as well as those south of Serre duly took place on 18 and 19 November. Like so many of the assaults that preceded it, the attackers' fortunes were mixed. Although some objectives were taken, there was to be no great breakthrough that might have changed the course of the battle. It is telling when describing this last – pointless – assault, which was made against a backdrop of driving snow, that the only achievement most people remember is the heroic but insignificant last stand made by 129 officers and men, mostly from the 16th Highland Light Infantry and the 11th Border Regiment, which held out for eight days behind the German front line.[30]

Although the capture by German troops of the survivors of that intrepid band of men represented the final act of the Battle of the Somme proper, its history would not be complete without a reference to its aftermath. First came the evacuation of the few remaining French civilians who had survived on the fringes of the area that British guns could reach. This took place on 13 December when Favreuil, less than a mile north of Bapaume, was shelled for the first time. The German district commandant did not even wait for the next morning to move the civilians out. He gave his order at 10 p.m., and within minutes they were being asked to leave.

Hugo Natt, a German doctor attached to the 118th Regiment's 2nd Battalion (a 56th Reserve Division unit), recorded in his diary the reaction of an eighty-year-old Frenchman and his forty-two-year-old daughter when ordered to vacate their house:

The way the old man wept as he went through the rooms [for the last time], and the daughter with a bedroll full of clothing, all she could take from a trunk, plucked at the heartstrings . . . They left in silence at about 10.30 p.m.

They were hardly out of the door before the Inspection Teams moved in, searching through all the cupboards for anything that might come in useful. The four small hens outside were killed within ten minutes. The order for their slaughter was given by Lieutenant Marchand, the 2nd Battalion's Provisions' officer . . . I found the looting so disgusting that I could hardly bring myself to speak to the gentlemen. I told them what I thought of what they were doing, but they could not understand how I could be so sentimental.[31]

But the evacuation of the French civilians was merely a preliminary step. Of far greater consequence was the move that Hindenburg and Ludendorff had been planning since September: the retreat from the Somme to the Siegfriedstellung (Hindenburg Line). This was designed to rescue the 1st and 2nd German Armies from the hellish conditions they had been enduring for months. It would give them a chance to recuperate in civilized conditions, and it would offer them the opportunity to take up secure positions in more normal surroundings.

The move was to be accompanied by a scorched-earth policy. Nothing that the British or French would find useful was to be left untouched. The French countryside and her towns and villages were to be put to the torch. Ernst Jünger, a twenty-one-year-old German officer, recorded what he witnessed during the retreat in the following terms:

The villages we passed . . . on our way had the look of vast lunatic asylums. Whole companies were set to knocking or pulling down walls, or sitting on rooftops, uprooting the tiles. Trees were cut down, windows smashed; wherever you looked, clouds of smoke and dust rose from vast piles of debris. We saw men dashing about wearing suits and dresses left behind by the inhabitants, with top hats on their heads. With destructive cunning, they found the roof-trees of the houses, fixed ropes to them, and, with concerted shouts, pulled till they all came tumbling down. Others were swinging pile-driving hammers, and went around smashing everything that got in their way, from the flowerpots on the windowsills to ornate conservatories.

As far back as the Siegfried Line, every village was reduced to rubble, every tree chopped down, every road undermined, every well poisoned, every basement blown up or booby trapped, every rail unscrewed, every telephone wire rolled up, everything burnable burned; in a word, we were turning the country that our advancing opponents would occupy into a wasteland.[32]

This was the legacy of all that fighting which historians and soldiers alike refer to as the Battle of the Somme.

★ ★ ★

There never will be a last word on the Battle of the Somme. Ever since the last shot was fired in November 1916, soldiers and historians have been commenting on what went wrong – and what went right. The most fundamental question posed by just about anyone who has ever written about the Somme's history is: was the 'Big Push' masterminded by Haig successful?

If confined to a single sentence, the short answer has to be: no, it was not. In spite of approximately 500,000 to 700,000 casualties sustained on the Somme by each side in the conflict, British forces were unable to break through the German lines other than superficially.[33] However, much had been achieved. For a start, by 11 July 1916 the German forces attacking at Verdun had been halted, so that troops could be sent to the Somme.[34] Stopping the attack at Verdun was one of the prime reasons for the Somme offensive. That being the case, Haig's 'Big Push' has to be rated a partial success.

German participants have also recorded the effect of the 'Big Push' on their own forces. General Ludendorff stated that 'the German Army had been fought to a standstill, and was utterly worn out'.[35] Field Marshal von Hindenburg, commenting at the 9 January 1917 conference where it was agreed that the Germans should wage a campaign of unrestricted U-boat warfare against its enemies, stated 'We must save the men from a second Somme battle.'[36] If the fighting on the Somme had pushed Germany to take that suicidal step – which was bound to prompt America to enter the war on the side of the Allies – it is another vindication of Haig's strategy.

The opinions of Hindenburg and Ludendorff were supported by Prince Rupprecht. In his diary he highlighted that the level of casualties on the Somme meant the average German soldier was not as capable, or as well trained, as those he replaced. 'The month of September brought the heaviest losses of the whole battle,' he commented, adding that the rein-forcements 'had not even covered one tenth of requirements'. By the end of November he was even more pessimistic, saying that 'what still remained of the old first-class peace-trained German infantry has been expended on the battlefield'.[37]

Rupprecht's Chief of the General Staff, General Hermann von Kuhl, explained the procedure that contributed to the degradation of the German troops: their divisions were too weak to remain in the field for more than fourteen days at a time. Consequently, a fresh division was needed every day, and there was insufficient time for rest and training between tours of service. As a result 'the quality and number of reinforcements were on the decline'.[38]

It has been said that the German Army never regained its former effi-ciency during World War 1. If that is true, the British generals at the Somme had arguably won a victory of sorts, also if one considers developments within the British Army as a result of the battle. There is no doubt that the commanders of the British forces learned valuable lessons during the fighting. To cite a well-known example, they developed the concept of the creeping barrage, making it possible for their soldiers to advance towards a German trench with much higher chances of success than had existed on 1 July 1916. Experiences with tanks also showed commanders how to and how not to deploy them most effectively, in other words not in a wood such as High Wood and not in small numbers. The successful use of tanks at the Battle of Cambrai in November 1917 can safely be said to have been partly due to lessons learned at the Battle of the Somme.

One could say that the British generals should have been better trained before being let loose on the battlefield, so that their soldiers were not needlessly sacrificed while their superiors learned their craft. There is a lot to be said for that, although certain lessons could not be learned except in battlefield conditions. Haig's ignorance concerning the use of artillery was astonishing. For example, prior to the Battle of Neuve Chapelle in March 1915, he even had to send out a note asking whether someone could tell him how many guns and shells were needed to cave in a German trench. At the time, incredibly, Haig was commander of the 1st Army.

Anyone judging the performance of the top generals during the Battle of the Somme will want to know whether they acted reasonably given the knowledge at the time. My final judgement on Haig and Rawlinson is as follows: Both of them failed to give sufficient weight to what they were told by their artillery experts, and neither applied common sense when planning the first attacks. You didn't need to be an inspired general to learn about the limitations of the artillery, which was the principal means of allowing a troop assault to succeed.

What is particularly frustrating about the way Haig exercised his command is that sometimes he was able to make the British Army perform efficiently. The clearest example of this relates to the second attack on the Pozières Heights. Readers of Chapter 28 will recall how, after the initial debacle, Haig visited the Australian headquarters and explained what steps had to be taken to make the next attack successful. Because his advice was taken to heart, the next advance was a triumph. One wonders whether Haig should not have learned from this, and realized that he could not be a successful commander if he was not at least checking on the attack plans of his generals.

In order to do so Haig might have had to pass a lot of his existing responsibilities as Commander-in-Chief over to someone else. However, the fact that he did not think that checking the attack plans of his commanders was necessary suggests he was lacking in two important respects. Not only did he show no signs of being a creative general who could devise new methods of defeating the enemy, but he also did not take measures that anyone with a bit of common sense could see were necessary. The fact that Rawlinson frequently had to be told by Haig to supervise his corps commanders suggests he was no more committed to overseeing the planning process than his Commander-in-Chief.

As well as highlighting some of the negative and positive aspects of the way British generals ran the battle, which became apparent in the course of my research, I would also like this book, published as it is during the centenary of the Battle of the Somme, to record how views on the conduct of the battle have altered over the years. Informed opinions were being given more or less immediately after the disastrous opening day, albeit in private. One man who was incensed by what had taken place was Major-General Oliver Nugent, commander of the 36th Ulster Division, which (as described in Chapters 11 and 12) lost so many young men north of Thiepval. On 11 July 1916 he wrote to his wife Kitty: 'I knew that unless everything went like clockwork on all sides of us, there was certain to be a failure. I pointed out in the strongest possible way that we were asked to do impossibilities, and I was told I was making difficulties . . . The man I loathe is Henry Rawlinson . . . whose senseless optimism is responsible for the practical wiping out of the Division.'[39]

No doubt Lord Cavan, commander of XIV Corps, had similar views about Rawlinson's, and Haig's, unreasonable demands, if not a hatred of the two generals in person. Haig had demanded that Cavan's troops should mount an attack against the Le Transloy line. When a preliminary assault failed on 3 November, Rawlinson believed that the corps commander's lack of conviction was the problem, rather than the enemy. Cavan objected when ordered to stage the follow-up assault, stating:

An attack from my present position with the troops at my disposal . . . has practically no chance of success.

I assert my readiness to sacrifice the British right rather than jeopardize the French . . . but . . . it does not appear that a failure would much assist the French, and there is a danger of this attack shaking the confidence of the men and officers in their commanders.

No-one who has not visited the front trenches can really know the state of exhaustion to which the men are reduced.

Before he would move, Lord Cavan insisted that Rawlinson come to the front to see for himself. After doing so, Rawlinson cancelled the planned attack, only for Haig to order that it go ahead. The result was another 2,000 casualties without any substantial progress.[40]

We have seen how hopeless attacks such as this had prompted Winston Churchill to complain as early as 1 August 1916 that Haig's strategy of grinding down the German Army without a realistic hope of a break-through meant the younger generation were being sacrificed for no purpose. David Lloyd George was equally negative, and famously asked the French general Ferdinand Foch for his opinion on Britain's generals. Haig was very upset, noting in his diary on 17 September: 'Unless I had been told of this conversation personally by General Foch, I would not have believed that a British minister could have been so ungentlemanly as to go to a foreigner and put such questions regarding his own subordinates.'[41]

But even more ungentlemanly conduct was to follow the end of the Battle of the Somme, after Lloyd George took over from Herbert Asquith as the British Prime Minister on 6 December. So disgusted was Lloyd George with Haig's and Rawlinson's tactics that he gave the French to understand in February 1917 that Haig and the BEF should be placed under the command of France's top general. The reputation of Robert Nivelle, the general in question, was riding high in the wake of a couple of victories he had masterminded at Verdun. He appeared even more attractive as a potential Allied commander after he boasted that he knew how to break through the German defences on a larger scale as well. That was one reason why towards the end of 1916 he was asked to replace Joffre as commander of the French Army. Lloyd George only backed down after learning that his demand would result in Haig's and Robertson's resignations.[42]

Lloyd George's verdict that Haig's tactics were immoral, if not wicked, was not endorsed by many of the first writers on the First World War after Germany's defeat. Some of them were authors of regimental histories. They did not hold back when it came to pointing out how mistaken tactics had led to unnecessary casualties in their regiments. But they rarely directed their criticism specifically against Rawlinson or Haig.[43]

Such neutral commentary was not to be found in the tide of anti-war literature that first hit the bookshops from the late 1920s. They included celebrated works like Robert Graves's *Goodbye to All That* (1929) and Siegfried Sassoon's *Memoirs of an Infantry Officer* (1930). Like so much of the war poetry, these books highlighted the appalling conditions endured in the trenches, and criticized the remote, out-of-touch commanders who were considered responsible for making the experience of war even more horrific than was necessary. The decisions taken on the Somme and at Passchendaele in 1917 were targeted in particular.

This critical attitude was reflected in the first of the participating countries' official histories. Volume III of the Australian official history written by Charles Bean, published in 1929, does not hold back in its castigation of Gough and Haig for the tactics employed on the Australians' fronts. The only counterbalance was Bean's judgement that, while Haig may have lacked imagination and the ability to surround himself with trustworthy subordinates, he did eventually learn from his mistakes. It is possible, Bean predicted, that history 'will assign him a greater share than is yet recognized in the responsibility for the victories with which the war ended'.[44] That was not a view shared by Churchill and Lloyd George when their accounts of what the generals achieved were published, although Lloyd George's autobiography, published during the 1930s, tended to switch the debate from the strategy at the Somme to the one pursued at Passchendaele.

Apart from the unexpectedly weak critical pronouncements voiced in the British official history, also published in the 1930s, the anti-war emphasis, including criticism of the generals, characterized many books on the First World War until the 1960s. That was when harsh criticism of Haig and his generals in works such as *The Donkeys* (1961) by Alan Clark caught the public's imagination. The theme in the book, which suggested that the brave lions (the British infantry) were sent to their deaths thanks to the dull donkeys (the generals), did not actually cover the Somme, but the impression left by it and the stage musical *Oh, What a Lovely War!*, produced for the first time in 1963, created an atmosphere which meant that any counter-argument had to be classified as revisionist.

It may be no coincidence, but the first of the more balanced biographies of Haig appeared two years after *The Donkeys* was published. In his *Douglas Haig: The Educated Soldier* (1963), John Terraine argued that even if Haig had made no errors, it would have been next to impossible to break through the German lines. That was because the poor battlefield communications and the dominance of artillery and machine guns favoured the defender over the attacker. It was this study that appears to have done more than any other work to have switched the debate about Haig's achievements from emotional polemic to rational debate. And it was the publication in 1971 of Martin Middlebrook's popular history *The First Day on the Somme: 1 July*

1916 that diverted this debate from Passchendaele to the Somme. Since then a flood of books have been published on the Somme, most of them including a revisionist pro-Haig and pro-Rawlinson slant even if they include strong condemnation of some of the decisions taken.

The most commonly held view of historians today is that serious mistakes were certainly made. However, the generals, who started the war as novices when it came to trench warfare, had to embark on a steep learning curve during which they struggled to grasp how to make the most of the weapons and technical developments available to them.[45]

The generals could not have made any headway on the Somme without the indomitable spirit of the British, Canadian and Australasian infantrymen. For this reason I feel it appropriate to end this study, on the centenary of this great battle, with the words of the men whose statements sum up the essence of the Somme. Out of the hundreds of accounts and letters I have chosen four.

The first describes the horror and the gallows humour that coexisted side by side on the Somme, as seen through the eyes of Major Philip Pilditch, the adjutant in the 7th London Brigade, Royal Field Artillery, while stumbling back from the front line to his brigade's headquarters on 30 August:

At one point I felt something soft brush my face, and a buzz of flies around my head. To my disgust I found I had kicked against the black outstretched hand and arm of a . . . dead German lying nearly over the trench and held there by a mass of congested telephone wires.

A different kind of disgust washed over Pilditch when around another corner he came across a line of ration-carriers:

The leading man, a great sandy-haired fellow, rested his load, and with a grin, slung off his steel hat and hung it on a 'peg' sticking out of the side of the trench. This seemed to amuse the others and provoked a roar of laughter. As I passed I saw the peg was a human leg, boot and all belonging to a body long since buried and partly uncovered by a shell burst.[46]

The second quotation comes from Reverend Harold Davies, the chaplain to the Royal Naval Division's 190th Brigade mentioned earlier in this chapter. He evidently admired the dutiful commitment of the men in the brigade who were willing to give their all during that penultimate battle on 13 November 1916, even though they knew in their hearts that nothing was to be gained by it apart from a meaningless bit of territory:

At Brigade HQ the prevalent idea is that the push is for political and not for military reasons. As one man expressed it, we are to jump off Westminster Bridge for the MPs to watch us. Most of them are impressed with the futility of the attack in the present state of the ground.[47]

The third quotation is from Lieutenant Vere Harmsworth, the twenty-one-year-old second son of Lord Rothermere, proprietor of the *Daily Mail*. By the light of a candle Harmsworth wrote the following words to his beloved uncle St John, when he believed he was about to go into action for the first time since moving from Gallipoli to France. As it turned out, he eventually went into action on 13 November 1916 with the Hawke Battalion of the Royal Naval Division. Harmsworth was shot and killed the same day as he tried to advance past a strongpoint that was holding up part of the battalion. I am quoting his words, not because they are the most poignant of the lines he wrote, but because they express a sentiment found in so many of the letters written by soldiers on the Somme before an attack:

Whether I am to emerge from this show I do not know . . . Surely it is a life fulfilled if one dies young and healthy fighting for one's country. I remember I read a French book just before the war . . . A man came before the monument of a young knight who had been killed. He remarked 'What could be finer than to die like that, full of youth and strength, never having known the troubles and infirmities of old age . . . The crowning consolation is that one will have done one's utmost to leave the world better than one found it.'[48]

The final word goes to Douglas Horton, the Australian lance corporal whose account, describing events at Pozières, was mentioned extensively in Chapters 24 and 25:

Pozières remains sacred to the memory of the Australian lads who gave their all for liberty. He has never lived who has not felt at some time that his life belonged to humanity. And surely those who not only fell but gave their lives for humanity . . . lived in the fullest sense. They lie there enshrouded by the soil they saved and [for]ever then live in our memory . . . as men whose praises shall go resounding down the ages while yet men love and revere liberty, and honour bravery.[49]

Notes

1: Great Expectations

1 30 April 1916 entry in 252 Tunnelling Company war diary, WO 95/406, brought to my attention by Simon Jones, *Underground Warfare 1914–1918*, pp. 115–20. The tunnel was 1,055 feet long.

2 An undated note in Lord Rawlinson's papers, RWLN 1/6, Churchill Archives Centre, states the number of infantry in the 4th Army on 26 June 1916 was 231,028.

3 Geoffrey H. Malins, *How I Filmed the War*, pp. 162–3.

4 Matthäus Gerster, *Das Württembergische Reserve-Infanterie-Regiment nr. 119 im Weltkrieg 1914–1918*, pp. 52–3.

5 Malins, *How I Filmed the War*, pp. 163–4.

6 Dudley Menaud-Lissenburg, a signaller in 97 Battery, 147 Brigade Royal Field Artillery, 29 Division, IWM Documents 7248.

7 Otto Lais, *Bilder aus der Sommeschlacht des Weltkrieges*, p. 16.

8 The 1 July 1916 entry in the 2nd Royal Fusiliers war diary states that there were around 500 casualties, including approaching 200 who were either killed or missing, in that battalion's file, NA WO 95/2301.

9 Gerster, *Das Württembergische Reserve-Infanterie-Regiment*, pp. 52–3.

10 Lais, *Bilder*, pp. 19–21 and 25.

11 Gerster, *Das Württembergische Reserve-Infanterie-Regiment*, p. 54.

12 'Summary of operations 1st July 1916' in the 1st July 1916 entry, 4th Army's war diary, the Fourth Army Papers of General Lord Rawlinson, Volume 1, in IWM Documents 20537.

13 Ibid.

14 Ibid.

15 Ibid. It is possible that some troops from the 4th or 31st Divisions reached Serre on 1 July 1916, but there was no evidence that a substantial proportion of any British unit held the village on that day (see Chapter 7, p. 84).

16 Ibid. Optimism was also particularly pronounced concerning III Corps' units.

17 Brigadier-General Sir James E. Edmonds, *History of the Great War: Military Operations: France and Belgium 1916, Volume 1 (1916 Official History, Vol. 1)*, pp. 342–3.

18 General Sir Henry Rawlinson, diary entry 1 July 1916, in Churchill College, Cambridge, RWLN 1/5.
19 General Sir Douglas Haig, diary entry 2 July 1916.
20 *1916 Official History*, Vol. 1, p. 483.
21 Ibid., pp. 312–476, refers to the following units being available for the Somme attack: sixteen infantry divisions under the 4th Army's corps, plus two in reserve, and the three under the 3rd Army. There was also a cavalry division in 4th Army's reserve.

2: Paradise Lost

 1 Brigadier-General Sir James E. Edmonds, *History of the Great War: Military Operations: France and Belgium 1916, Volume 1* (*1916 Official History*, Vol. 1), pp. 18–19. This figure includes two Canadian infantry and two Indian cavalry divisions.
 2 *1916 Official History*, Maps Volume: map 3.
 3 *1916 Official History*, Vol. 1, pp. 57 and 95.
 4 Ibid., pp. 150–1.
 5 Sergeant Harry Tawney, letter to his wife Jeannette 8 March 1915, LSE Tawney 27/8.
 6 Ibid., 22 September 1915, LSE Tawney/Vyvyan 1.
 7 Ibid., 8 March 1915, LSE Tawney 27/8.
 8 Captain Charlie May, diary entry 9 November 1915, in Gerry Harrison (ed.), *To Fight Among Friends: The First World War Diaries of Charlie May* (*The May Book*), pp. 4–5. Extracts are included in this book with the consent of Georgina Jay, daughter of Pauline May's brother-in-law (Pauline being Charlie May's daughter), who inherited the copyright, and Gerry Harrison.
 9 Sergeant Harry Tawney, letter to sister Mildred 22 November 1915, LSE Tawney/Vyvyan 45. The writings of Tawney, many of them contained in his biography, *The Life of R. H. Tawney* by Lawrence Goldman, were brought to my attention by Gerry Harrison (see note 8).
10 Location from 13–16 November 1915 entry in 22nd Manchesters war diary, NA WO 95/1669.
11 Captain Charlie May, diary entries 12–16 November 1915, *The May Book*, pp. 11–14.
12 *1916 Official History*, Vol. 1, p. 18.
13 Private R. W. Harpley, 55th Battalion, AIF, AWM 3DRL 3663.
14 Leslie Kenney, letter 8 July 1915, NZ NAM 1997.806.
15 Private Arthur Wrench, in IWM Documents 3834.

16 L. F. Ashurst, IWM Sound Archive 9875.

17 Captain Charlie May, diary entry 15 November 1915, *The May Book*, p. 40.

18 Eddie Bigwood, IWM Sound Archive 10116.

19 Frank Crozier, *A Brass Hat in No Man's Land*, p. 56.

20 Lieutenant Lawrence Gameson, IWM Documents 612.

21 Percy Jones, IWM Documents P246.

22 Captain Charlie May, diary entry 7 December 1915, *The May Book*, p. 35.

23 Ibid., 13 January 1916, *The May Book*, p. 69.

24 Ibid., 27 February 1916, *The May Book*, p. 110.

25 Ibid.

26 Captain Alfred Bland, letter to Violet 29 February 1916, in book containing copies of his letters (*Bland's Book*), IWM Documents 20673. Extracts from *Bland's Book* are included with the consent of Dan Mace, Alfred Bland's great-grandson.

27 Captain Charlie May, diary entry 18 January 1916, *The May Book*, p. 75.

28 Captain Alfred Bland, letter to Violet 20 March 1916, *Bland's Book*.

29 Ibid., 18 January 1916.

30 Ibid., 1 March 1916.

31 Ibid., 7 February 1916.

32 Ibid., 18 May 1916.

33 Sergeant Harry Tawney, letter to Jeannette 29 March 1915, LSE Tawney 27/8.

34 Ibid., 9 December 1915, LSE Tawney/Vyvyan 45.

35 Sergeant Harry Tawney, letter to William Beveridge 22 December 1915, LSE Beveridge 2A 106.

36 Sergeant Harry Tawney, letter to Jeannette 22 December 1915, LSE Tawney/Vyvyan 1.

37 Lieutenant Edgar Lord, IWM Documents 6559.

38 2nd Lieutenant P. G. Heath, 'Fifty Years After: Memoirs of a Combatant Officer of the 18th Division 1914/18 on the Western Front', in Liddle Archive, Leeds. A similar incident affecting the 9th Royal Irish Rifles is described in Chapter 11.

39 Sergeant Harry Tawney, letter to William Beveridge 22 December 1915, LSE Beveridge 2A 106.

3: A Gentleman's Agreement

1 Rawlinson does not mention Don Quixote in the surviving documents, but his critical views on Haig's excessively ambitious objectives, for example in relation to the 10–13 March 1915 objective at Neuve Chapelle (see the 25 March 1915 entry in his personal diary, Churchill College, Rawlinson papers RWLN 1/1), make it an appropriate analogy in this author's opinion.

2 General Sir Henry Rawlinson's letter 25 March 1915 to Major Clive Wigram, Army Museum Rawlinson Papers, Letter Book, Volume 1, October 1914– May 1915, p. 72, 1952-01-33-17.

3 General Sir Douglas Haig, diary entries 16–17 March 1915, a copy of which is in NA WO 256/3.

4 Major-General Sir Frederick Maurice, _The Life of General Lord Rawlinson of Trent_, pp. 110–12.

5 17 March 1916 entry in Rawlinson's personal diary, Rawlinson Papers, RWLN 1/1, Churchill College.

6 Ibid.

7 Ibid., and 12 April 1916 entry in the same diary.

8 Alfred Duff Cooper, _Haig, Volume 1_, p. 328.

9 Gary Mead, _The Good Soldier: The Biography of Douglas Haig_, p. 237.

10 Except for text covered by a note that specifically quotes another source, the information about Haig in this chapter comes from Gary Sheffield, _The Chief: Douglas Haig and the British Army_, and Mead, _The Good Soldier_.

11 Mead, _The Good Soldier_, pp. 36–44 and 67–8.

12 Brigadier-General Sir James E. Edmonds, _History of the Great War: Military Operations: France and Belgium 1917, Volume 1 (1916 Official History, Vol. 1)_, p. 297.

13 General Sir Douglas Haig, diary entry 1 May 1915.

14 Field Marshal Earl Kitchener, in Appendix 5 of Brigadier-General Sir James E. Edmonds, _History of the Great War: Military Operations: France and Belgium 1916: Sir Douglas Haig's Command to the 1st July: Battle of the Somme, Appendices_, p. 40, 'Instructions for General Sir D. Haig . . . Commanding the Expeditionary Force in France dated 28 December 1915'. General Joffre's age on 1 July 1916 has been specified.

15 David R. Woodward, _Field Marshal Sir William Robertson: Chief of the Imperial General Staff in the Great War (Robertson Biography)_, p. 40.

16 _1916 Official History, Vol. 1_, p. 44.

17 Ibid., p. 13.

18 The horse affair, which is dealt with in the 18 and 24 May 1916 War Committee Minutes, in NA CAB 42/14/2 and 42/14/10, was brought to my attention by Robin Prior and Trevor Wilson, _The Somme_, pp. 12–14.

19 General Sir Henry Rawlinson, diary entry 29 March 1916 (_Rawlinson's Diary_), Churchill College, 1/5.

20 War Committee minutes for 7 April 1916, NA CAB 42/12/5, brought to my attention by the _Robertson Biography_, p. 41.

21 War Committee minutes for 30 May 1916, NA CAB 42/14/12, brought to my attention by the _Robertson Biography_, pp. 41 and 43.

22 War Committee Minutes 7 June 1916, NA CAB 42/15/6.

23 *Rawlinson's Diary*, Churchill College 1/5; and Volume 5 of the Fourth Army papers of General Lord Rawlinson: GHQ Letters, (*4th Army Letters*), IWM Documents 20537.

24 As shown on Map 2, the portion of the German front line that was to be attacked ran in a south-easterly direction from Gommecourt until it turned sharply eastwards, so that it ran to the north and to the east of Maricourt rather than to the west and south of it, which it would have done but for this sharp turn. The aforementioned sharp turn eastwards meant that the British and French front lines jutted forward from the general line, creating a salient.

25 Brigadier-General Charles Budworth, Appendix A to 'Remarks based on recent IV Corps Artillery Operations', 6 October 1915, brought to my attention by Robin Prior and Trevor Wilson, *Command on the Western Front: The Military Career of Sir Henry Rawlinson 1914–1918*, p. 168.

26 The list of 'Resources available for 4th Army' sent to Rawlinson with Lieutenant-General L. S. Kiggell's letter of 26 March 1916, on the basis of which Rawlinson's 3 April attack plan was drawn up, stated that the 4th Army would have 223 howitzers with a calibre of at least 6 inches; they included 133 howitzers with a calibre of at least 8 inches, 4th Army letters, Volume 5, in IWM. A subsequent list of howitzers entitled 'Ammunition Expenditure' purporting to show the number of weapons actually used on 1 July states that the 4th Army had 265 howitzers with a calibre of at least 6 inches; they included 161 with a calibre of at least 8 inches, NA WO 158/327.

27 See Chapter 5's note 24 for the Somme front that was eventually attacked.

28 Budworth to IV Corps Headquarters, 5 October 1915.

29 Diary entries 3 and 4 April 1916 in *Rawlinson's Diary*.

30 Diary entry 30 March 1916 in *Rawlinson's Diary*.

31 Lieutenant-General Lancelot Kiggell, letters to Rawlinson 12 and 13 April 1916, *4th Army Letters*; diary entry 14 April 1916 in *Rawlinson's Diary*.

32 Diary entry 14 April 1916 in *Rawlinson's Diary*.

33 Kiggell, letters to Rawlinson 12 and 13 April 1916, *4th Army Letters*; diary entry 14 April 1916 in *Rawlinson's Diary*.

34 See Chapter 5's note 24 for the total front attacked on 1 July 1916.

35 General Sir Henry Rawlinson, letter to GHQ 10 May 1916, *4th Army Letters*.

36 Diary entry 18 April 1916 in *Rawlinson's Diary*.

37 Rawlinson letter to GHQ 19 April 1916, *4th Army Letters*.

38 Ibid.

39 Diary entry 13 May 1916 in *Rawlinson's Diary*; and letter from Kiggell to Rawlinson 16 May 1916, *4th Army Letters*.

4: The Build-Up

1 Captain Charlie May, diary entry 13 April 1916, in Gerry Harrison, *To Fight Among Friends: The First World War Diaries of Charlie May* (*The May Book*), p. 153.

2 Ibid., 2 June 1916, *The May Book*, p. 189.

3 Diary entry 2 June 1916 in 22nd Manchesters war diary, NA WO 95/1669; Captain Alfred Bland, letter to his wife Violet June 1916, in book containing copies of his letters (*Bland's Book*), IWM Documents 20673.

4 Bland, letter to his wife Violet, '*Bland's Book*'.

5 Captain Charlie May, diary entry 3 June 1916, *The May Book*, p. 190; 1 June 1916 entry in *Bland's Book*, presumably started on that date and finished after the raid.

6 5 June 1916 note written by Lieutenant-General Henry Horne to 7th Division in *The May Book*, p. 196.

7 Lieutenant William Gomersall's letters to his brother and sisters 6 and 25 December 1916, in internet site: www.gomersall.netau/unclewilliam (*Gomersall's Correspondence*). Gomersall's letters were brought to my attention by Gerry Harrison, who appears in note 1 above.

8 Captain Charlie May, diary entries 21 and 25 February 1916, *The May Book*, pp. 104 and 108.

9 Ibid., 6 April 1916, *The May Book*, pp. 147–8.

10 Letter 6 April 1916 in *Gomersall's Correspondence*.

11 Letter 15 April 1916 in ibid.

12 Captain Alfred Bland, letter 18 June 1916 in *Bland's Book*.

13 Ibid., 13 June 1916 in *Bland's Book*.

14 Captain Charlie May, diary entry 15 June 1916, *The May Book*, p. 202.

15 Ibid., 7 and 10 June 1916, *The May Book*, pp. 195 and 198.

16 Ibid., 16 June 1916, *The May Book*, pp. 202–3.

17 Brigadier-General Sir James E. Edmonds, *History of the Great War: Military Operations: France and Belgium 1916, Volume 1* (*1916 Official History, Vol. 1*), pp. 47–8.

18 Captain Charlie May, diary entry 17 June 1916, *The May Book*, p. 203.

19 Captain Alfred Bland, letter 18 June 1916 in *Bland's Book*.

20 Ibid.

21 Captain Alfred Bland, letter 22–25 June 1916 in *Bland's Book*.

22 General Sir Henry Rawlinson, letter to GHQ 21 June 1916, IWM 4th Army Records, Volume 5.

23 'Report of the Army Commander's remarks at the conference held at Fourth Army headquarters 22nd June 1916', IWM 4th Army Records, Volume 6.

24 Sergeant Karl Eisler, account (*Eisler's Account*), Freiburg BA/MA PH12 11/57, brought to my attention by Irina Renz, Gerd Krumeich and Gerhard Hirschfeld, *Scorched Earth: The Germans on the Somme 1914–1918* (*Scorched Earth*), p. 82.

25 Kronprinz von Rupprecht, *Mein Kriegstagebuch, Volume 1*, pp. 478–86, 9–26 June 1916 entries, and the 3 July entry on pp. 494–6.

26 2nd Lieutenant Roland Ingle, account (*Ingle's Account*), in IWM Documents 7087; and 23 June 2016 entry in Rawlinson's diary in Churchill College 1/5.

27 A. J. Peters, account, in IWM Documents 7450 (08/94/1).

28 *Ingle's Account.*

29 *Eisler's Account*, brought to my attention by *Scorched Earth*, p. 83.

30 Captain Charlie May, diary entry 24 June 1916, *The May Book*, p. 207.

31 Ibid., 25 June 1916, pp. 208–9.

32 Sergeant Harry Tawney, letter to his wife Jeannette 26 June 1916, LSE Tawney 27/8.

33 Ibid.

34 *Ingle's Account.*

35 Captain Charlie May, letter to Maude May 26 June 1916, *The May Book*, p. 214.

36 Maude May, letter to Captain Charlie May 30 June 1916, ibid., pp. 215–16.

37 Captain Charlie May, diary entry 27 June 1916, ibid., p. 210.

5: Fatal Flaw

1 Brigadier-General Hubert Rees, 94th Brigade file, NA WO 95/2363. The speech was ready for circulation on 28 June 1916, but it was probably circulated on 30 June. The circulation date is unclear in the 94th Brigade war diary.

2 29 June 1916 entry in 1st Lancashire Fusiliers war diary, NA WO 95/2300.

3 The Victoria Crosses were won during the Gallipoli landings on 25 April 1915.

4 The twenty-one divisions referred to appear to include the three divisions under the command of the 3rd Army, as well as the sixteen plus two reserves under the 4th Army.

5 De Lisle's comment about unlimited ammunition was either a white lie or wishful thinking (see text attached to note 22 in Chapter 4).

6 Approximately the same figure was quoted by Lieutenant-General Sir Aylmer Hunter-Weston in his papers, personal diary, volume 3, British Library ADD MS 48365. He said VIII Corps had 596 howitzers, guns and mortars.

7 Major-General Henry de Beauvoir de Lisle, 1st Lancashire Fusiliers file, NA WO 95/2300.

8 30 June 1916 letter, Lieutenant-General Sir Aylmer Hunter-Weston papers, British Library ADD MS 48365.

9 Private George Morgan, interview with Malcolm Brown (*Morgan Interview*), quoted in David Raw, *Bradford Pals*, pp. 171–2; Private Reginald Glenn, IWM Sound Archive 13082.

10 *Morgan Interview*.

11 Major J. Collis Browne, letter to the official historian 12 November 1929, NA CAB 45/132.

12 Ibid.

13 Major-General de Beauvoir de Lisle, letter to the official historian 12 November 1929, NA CAB 45/189. It should be noted that, in a letter to the official historian 12 December 1929, Lieutenant-General Hunter-Weston claimed that de Lisle and the commander of 86th Brigade objected to the mine being blown up at zero hour, NA CAB 45/138.

14 Percy Jones, IWM Documents P246.

15 Ibid.

16 Lieutenant-Colonel Kyme Cordeaux, letter to his wife 27 June 1916, IWM Documents 16975.

17 Lieutenant F. L. Cassel, IWM Documents 7405.

18 General Sir Henry Rawlinson, 9 October 1915 report addressed to Haig, NA WO 95/710.

19 23 June 1916 entry in 1st/5th North Staffordshire Regiment war diary, NA WO 95/2685.

20 'General Command XIV RK 1c secret 26.6.1916: Interrogation of Englishman of V North Staffordshire Regiment captured on 24.6.16', Hauptstaatsarchiv Stuttgart, M43 Bu4, brought to my attention by Phillip Robinson.

21 German records name two of the captured Englishmen as 'Coones' and 'Barrow' of the Newfoundland Regiment (88th Brigade, 29th Division), who were captured in the Beaumont Hamel sector during a failed raid. The very brief interrogation report of 5 July 1916 suggests one or both men confirmed an attack was expected four to five days after the commencement of the bombardment, i.e. on 28 or 29 June. Hauptstaatsarchiv Stuttgart, M43 B60, brought to my attention by Phillip Robinson. Curiously when specifying the casualties, the 27 June 1916 entry in the Newfoundland Regiment war diary (NA WO 95/2308) only refers to killed and wounded. There is no mention that anyone went missing. It is possible that the Germans incorrectly linked them with the Newfoundland Regiment.

22 In some reports his surname is written as Lipmann.

23 'Corps HQ Staff XIV RK 1c No.33, 28 June 1916: Interrogation of the deserter (11/R.Fus 29 Div 86 Brig) Josef Lipman, 23 yrs old, carpenter serving in the Army since 11/8/14', Hauptstaatsarchiv Stuttgart, M43 B60, brought to my attention by Phillip Robinson.

24 The figure of 21 miles has been arrived at by measuring the general direction of the Anglo-French line in Brigadier-General Sir James E. Edmonds, *History of the Great War: Military Operations: France and Belgium 1916 (1916 Official History)*, Maps Volume: maps 2 and 6. Of the 21 miles, the British attack accounted for nearly 15 miles (of this, the 3rd and 4th Army's fronts accounted for two miles and approaching 13 miles respectively), while the French attack accounted for nearly two miles north of the Somme, and in excess of four miles to the south of the Somme. Readers might like to compare the above statistics with front specifications mentioned in the *1916 Official History*, and in documents prepared by Rawlinson. The *1916 Official History*, Volume I, p. 250, states that the 4th Army's front on 1 July 1916 was about 25,000 yards (in excess of 14 miles). However, Rawlinson's documents refer to 20,000 yards, the width of the 4th Army front specified in the first version of his attack plan sent to Haig on 3 April 1916, plus 2,500 yards, the additional front, including Montauban, which Haig wanted the 4th Army to attack, totalling 22,500 yards (approaching 13 miles, as mentioned in my calculations at the top of this note). This suggests that Rawlinson might have been adopting a similar procedure to me when he was measuring the front.

25 27 June 1916 entry in 2nd Royal Fusiliers war diary, NA WO 95/2301.

26 28 June 1916 entry in 52nd Reserve Infantry Brigade combat report, translation in Newfoundland Centre, Beaumont Hamel, of German text in Hauptstaatsarchiv Stuttgart M410 Bu 239. Brought to my attention by Phillip Robinson.

27 General Sir Henry Rawlinson's diary, Churchill College 1/5.

28 Gerry Harrison (ed.), *To Fight Among Friends (The May Book)*, p. 211.

29 Sergeant Harry Tawney, letter to his wife 29 June 1916, LSE, Tawney 27/8.

30 *The May Book*, p. 213.

31 Apparatus for sending morse-code messages.

32 The Fourth Army papers of Lord Rawlinson: Vols 10 and 11, Daily Intelligence Summaries: 3 and 28 April 1916; 15 and 28 May 1916. IWM Documents 20537.

33 III Corps 22 June 1916 'Signal Traffic During Operations' notice, in III Corps file, NA WO 95/672.

34 Message 'To all units' sent at 3.10 a.m. on 1 July 1916, 4th Division's 12th Brigade file, NA WO 95/1502. The words quoted appear to have been sent to all 4th Army corps whose units were going over the top on 1 July, leaving it to the corps to circulate the message to their troops. The document cited is in the above-mentioned 12th Brigade file. A reference to that file has been given, rather than a reference to the file of the 34th Division or of one of its units, because I have not found it in any of those places. According to the *1916 Official History*, Volume 1, pp. 391–2, at 2.45 a.m. on 1 July 1916 the German 56th Reserve Brigade sent the 28th Reserve Division 'a fragment' of the British

34th Division message quoted, adding that the original 4th Army message was sent to the corps, Reserve Army and 4th Brigade R.F.C. at 10.17 p.m. on 30 June 1916. The *1916 Official History* has taken the aforementioned information about what the German 56th Reserve Brigade sent, and, from *Schlachten des Weltkrieges: Somme-Nord*, Volume 1, p. 54. (This publication is described in the *1916 Official History* as 'an official monograph . . . issued by the Reichsarchiv'.) The German text of this monograph states that the message was sent by the 56th Reserve Brigade at 3.45 a.m., that is, German time, which was one hour ahead of British time. Thus 3.45 a.m. German time is 2.45 a.m. British time, the time specified by the abovementioned note in the *1916 Official History*.

35 One reference to the circulation of the intelligence is in the 1 July 1916 entry in the German 28th Reserve Division's 'Kriegstagebuch mit Anlagen', May–December 1916, Karlsruhe Generallandesarchiv 456 F 16 Nr. 64.

6: The First Blows

1 Sergeant Karl Eisler, account, Freiburg BA/MA PH12 11/57. The '11' is a roman numeral 2 brought to my attention by Irina Renz, Gerd Krumeich and Gerhard Hirschfeld, *Scorched Earth: The Germans on the Somme 1914–1918*, pp. 81–9.

2 T. F. C. Downman, account, in 1/5 Sherwood Foresters file, NA WO 95/2695.

3 Lieutenant Beck, brochure *Treffen der 26 RD: am 5 July 1936*, brought to my attention by Jack Sheldon, who quoted from it in his book *The Germans at Beaumont Hamel*, pp. 85–8.

4 'Divisional Smoke Programme for Assault', 24 June 1916, 46th Division file, NA WO 95/2663; 'Report on the part played by the 169th Infantry Brigade in the action on the 1st of July 1916', 169th Brigade file, NA WO 95/2692; 168th Brigade's 'Report on operations 1st July 1916' (*168 Brigade's Report*), 168th Brigade file, NA WO 95/2951; 169th Brigade report to 56th Division 10 July 1916, NA WO 95/2957.

5 'Decisions at Conference', 13 June 1916, in VII Corps file, NA WO 95/804.

6 *168 Brigade's Report*.

7 Captain R. H. Lindsey-Renton in Major C. A. Cuthbert Keeson, *The History and Records of the Queen Victoria's Rifles 1792–1922*, p. 163.

8 Otto Lais, *Bilder aus der Sommeschlacht des Weltkrieges*, pp. 14–15.

9 Lieutenant F. L. Cassel, IWM Documents 76/208/1.

10 Jimmy Young, 'Notes on 179 Company RE', in Old Tunnellers Comrades Association Bulletin, No. 13, 1938, given to me by Phillip Robinson.

11 A compilation of Lieutenant Cecil Lewis, I W M Sound Archive 4162 and his book *Sagittarius Rising*, p. 104.

7: False Dawn

1 Lieutenant-General Sir Aylmer Hunter-Weston, papers, personal diary, Volume 3, British Library ADD MS 48365. I have assumed this 30 June 1916 letter is to his wife, although there is no addressee in the book into which the letter has been copied.

2 A note dated 20 June 1916 labelled 'Infantry of the IV Army' in Rawlinson's papers, Churchill College, RWLN 1/6, states that there were in excess of 52,000 infantry in the four divisions in VIII Corps. Hunter-Weston's thank-you message sent to his troops on 4 July 1916 stated that the troops in the corps, in addition to the infantry, took the total up to around 80,000: 94th Brigade file, NA WO 95/2363.

3 31st Division Order 31, 23 June 1916, that division's file, NA WO 95/2341; and Brigadier-General Sir James E. Edmonds, *History of the Great War: Military Operations: France and Belgium 1916, Volume 1 (1916 Official History, Vol. 1)*, pp. 426–7.

4 Marieux is about 14 miles north-east of Amiens, and about 10 miles north-west of Beaumont Hamel.

5 30 June 1916 letter in Hunter-Weston papers.

6 Elaine McFarland, *A Slashing Man of Action*, p. 126.

7 Lieutenant-General Sir Aylmer Hunter-Weston, papers, Private Diary, British Library ADD MS 48365.

8 'Note by Lieutenant-General Sir Aylmer Hunter-Weston commanding 8th Army Corps when acting as left flank of the general attack by the 4th Army within the limits of the present front near Fonquevillers to near the river Ancre', in Hunter-Weston papers, Official War Diaries with Appendices, British Library ADD MS 48357.

9 Brigadier-General W. P. Hore-Ruthven, note entitled: 'An appreciation of the probable line of defence which the enemy may reasonably be expected to adopt against an attack by the VIIIth Corps . . . ', in Hunter-Weston's papers, the Official War Diaries with Appendices, British Library ADD MS 48357.

10 General Sir Douglas Haig, diary, 8 April 1916, NA WO 256/9.

11 General Sir Henry Rawlinson, note 19 June 1916, Churchill College, RWLN 1/6.

12 Lieutenant-General Sir Aylmer Hunter-Weston, letter to his wife Grace 26 June 1916, papers, Private Diary, British Library ADD MS 48365. Once again, as

mentioned in note 1, I have assumed the letter is to Grace. In a letter written on 25 June 1916, possibly to his wife as well, he states that he has 359 guns including heavies, howitzers and field guns but excluding mortars.

13 Brigadier-General Hubert Rees, 'A Personal Record of the War 1915–1916–1917' (*Rees' Account*), IWM Documents 7166.

14 Elaine McFarland, *A Slashing Man of Action: The Life of Lieutenant-General Sir Aylmer Hunter-Weston MP*, p. 226.

15 (*Rees' Account*).

16 169 Regiment's Kriegstagebuch November 1915–July 1916 (*169 Regiment's KTB*), Generallandesarchiv, Karlsruhe 456 F42 Nr. 162, previously 456 EV 42 Band 114; the cutting of tape is mentioned in the 1 July 1916 entry of 12th York and Lancaster Regiment war diary, NA WO 95/2365; the laying of tape is mentioned in the 19 June 1916 'Instructions for the attack', and its not being in position on 1 July in B Company's report, both in 18th West Yorkshire file, NA WO 95/2362.

17 *169 Regiment's KTB*.

18 Lieutenant M. Gerster, History of the 52nd (Royal Württemberg) Reserve Infantry Brigade, Stuttgart M410 Bu 260.

19 There was also a fifth cricketer who played for Yorkshire's county side.

20 Private George Morgan, interview with Malcolm Brown, quoted in David Raw, *Bradford Pals* (*Bradford Pals Book*), p. 177; 30 June 1916 entry in 18th West Yorkshires war diary, NA WO 95/2362.

21 Private Jack Hindle, 22 July 1916 edition of *Accrington Observer & Times*, brought to my attention along with all Accrington Pals testimony in this chapter by Andrew Jackson, author of *Accrington Pals: The Full Story* (*Accrington Pals Book*), p. 103; 'Report on operations June 30th to 9.40 p.m. July 1st–Battle of the Somme' (*11 East Lancashire's Report*) with war diary in 11th East Lancashires file, NA WO 95/2366.

22 Private Walter Peart, 22 July 1916 edition of *Burnley Express & Advertiser*, brought to my attention by the *Accrington Pals Book*, p. 105.

23 Private James H. Roberts, 19 August 1916 edition of *Burnley Express & Advertiser*, brought to my attention by the *Accrington Pals Book*, p. 106.

24 *11th East Lancashire's Report*: 'Operations of 93rd Infantry Brigade: 1st July 1916' (*93rd Brigade's Report*), in 92nd Brigade file, NA WO 95/2356.

25 *Rees' Account*.

26 Private James H. Roberts, in the *Accrington Pals Book*, pp. 106–7.

27 Private Reginald Glenn, IWM Sound Archive 13082.

28 1 July 1916 entry in 12th York and Lancaster Regiment war diary, NA WO 95/2365.

29 1 July 1916 entry in 11 East Lancashires war diary stated only a few reached the German lines.

30 *93rd Brigade's Report*; 1 July 1916 entry in 15th West Yorkshires war diary, their file, NA WO 95/2361.

31 Anonymous account quoted in Laurie Milner, *Leeds Pals: A History of the 15th (Service) Battalion (1st Leeds), The Prince of Wales's Own West Yorkshire Regiment: 1914–1918 (Leeds Pals Book)*, pp. 140–1, referring to a memorial book: *Sec-Lieut T.A.R.R.E. Willey 15th West Yorks. Regt. (Leeds Pals) – 'Tribute' – Mort au champ d'honneur – July 1st 1916 (Willey Memorial Book)*, privately published by Tom Willey's father, Arthur, in the second half of 1916.

32 Private Arthur Hollings, letter to his father, *Yorkshire Evening Post*, 15 July 1916, quoted in the *Leeds Pals Book*, p. 141, and reprinted in the *Willey Memorial Book*.

33 *93rd Brigade's Report*; 1 July 1916 entry in 15 West Yorkshires war diary, their file, NA WO 95/2361.

34 *169 Regiment's KTB.*

35 Sergeant-Major George Cussins, 1 July 1916 entry in 16th West Yorkshires war diary, NA WO 95/2362.

36 Otto Lais, *Bilder aus der Sommeschlacht: Erlebnisbericht von Otto Lais*, pp. 16–19.

37 *Rees' Account.*

38 1 July 1916 entry in 93rd Brigade war diary, NA WO 95/2359.

39 'Operations of 94th Infantry Brigade on July 1st 1916', in 94th Brigade file, NA WO 95/2363.

40 Messages in 31st Division war diary, NA WO 95 2341.

41 *Rees' Account.*

42 Casualty list with 93rd Brigade war diary, NA WO 95/2359; 4 July entry in 94th Brigade war diary, NA WO 95/2363.

43 *Leeds Pals Book*, pp. 142–4.

44 *The Bickersteth Diaries*, ed. John Monier Bickersteth, p. 100.

45 Information about Robert Tolson supplied by Jonathan Tolson, Robert's great-nephew. The Tolson family has given me permission to use the letters about Robert Tolson quoted in this chapter. A copy of these letters is in the Liddle Collection.

46 C. R. Chappell to Zoe Tolson 2 July 1916.

47 Ibid., 10 July 1916.

48 HQ 93rd Brigade, 13 July 1916.

49 C. R. Chappell to Zoe Tolson 18 July 1916.

50 H. Sandland addressed to 'Miss' Tolson 22 July 1916.

51 H. Newcome Wright, letter to Whiteley Tolson 27 July 1916.

52 Whiteley Tolson to his son Gerald 28 July 1916.

53 Ibid., 2 August 1916.

54 Ibid., 6 August 1916.

55 British Red Cross and Order of St John: Enquiry department for wounded and missing dated 1 September 1916, enclosed in a letter from Whiteley Tolson to his son Gerald 5 September 1916.

56 Gerald Tolson to his uncle, Legh Tolson, 11 September 1916.

57 Whiteley Tolson to his son Gerald 12 September 1916.

58 Letter from Lance-Corporal (name illegible on letter) 24 October 1916.

59 C. R. Chappell, letter to 'Mr Tolson' 13 March 1917.

60 *Bradford Pals Book*, p. 232.

8: Hunter-Bunter's Folly

1 Geoffrey H. Malins, *How I Filmed the War*, pp. 156–8.

2 30 April 1916 entry in 252nd Tunnelling Company war diary, NA WO 95/406; this and all other sources in this chapter concerning the Hawthorn mine were brought to my attention by Simon Jones, *Underground Warfare: 1914–1918*, pp. 115–20.

3 20 May 1916 entry in 252nd Tunnelling Company war diary.

4 Alexander Barrie, IWM Documents 7307.

5 22 June 1916 entry in 252nd Tunnelling Company war diary.

6 H. N. Harvey, undated letter to Brigadier-General Sir James E. Edmonds, received 28 October 1929 (*Harvey's Letter*), NA CAB 45/189, said the original plan was the night before; Brigadier-General Sir James E. Edmonds, *History of the Great War: Military Operations: France and Belgium 1916, Volume 1 (1916 Official History, Vol. 1)*, p. 429, said it was four hours before zero hour.

7 Ibid.

8 Major-General de Beauvoir de Lisle, letter to the official historian 12 November 1929, NA CAB 45/189.

9 Captain Rex Trower, commander of 252nd Tunnelling Company, letter to Colonel R. N. Harvey, Inspector of Mines, 14 February 1930, stated that he could not be sure that the explosion would not kill some men if it occurred at zero hour, NA CAB 45/189.

10 'Narrative of Operations of 1st July 1916 showing the situation as it appeared to general staff VIII Corps from information received during the day', in VIII Corps file, NA WO 95/820; *Harvey's Letter*.

11 *1916 Official History, Vol. 1*. For the lifting of the heavy artillery, see 'Action of the Corps Heavy Artillery on July the 1st 1916', VIII Corps' Commander Heavy Artillery file, NA WO 95/825.

12 'Account of action 1st July 1916: Attack of 1st Lancashire Fusiliers on Beaumont Hamel' (*Lancashire Fusiliers' Report*), NA WO 95/2300.

13 *Lancashire Fusiliers' Report*, and 'Account of the 1st July Battle by the 86th Brigade' in the 86th Brigade file, NA WO 95/2298.

14 1 July 1916 entry in 2nd Royal Fusiliers war diary, NA WO 95/2301, says they retired at midday, although the *Lancashire Fusiliers' Report* refers to a retirement of troops on the battalion's right at 9.45 a.m.

15 Corporal George Ashurst, taken from his book *My Bit: A Lancashire Fusilier at War 1914–18*, pp. 99–102, and his account in IWM Sound Archive 9875.

16 Nigel McCrery, *Final Wicket: Test and First Class Cricketers Killed in the Great War*, p. 322.

17 *Lancashire Fusiliers' Report*. The latter report and Lieutenant-Colonel Magniac's messages contain different figures for the number of Lancashire Fusiliers who advanced at 12.30 p.m. and the number who arrived at the sunken road. I have relied on the numbers in the battalion's war diary. In the messages, forty men are said to have advanced and three other ranks are said to have reached the sunken road.

18 Matthäus Gerster, *Das Württembergische Reserve-Infanterie-Regiment nr. 119 im Weltkrieg 1914–1918*, p. 53.

19 Untitled report by 87th Brigade in its file, NA WO 95/2303, and 'Report on the operations of the 29th Division from the 30th June to the night of the 1st/2nd July' (*29th Division's Report*), in that division's file, NA WO 95/2280.

20 *29th Division's Report*.

21 Ibid.

22 *1916 Official History, Vol. 1*, p. 436.

23 Arthur Raley, interview, Oral Histories of the First World War: Veterans: 1914–1918, Library and Archives Canada.

24 Arthur Raley, *The Veteran Magazine*, 1.3, 21 September 1916, p. 40.

25 Arthur Raley, interview, Oral Histories of the First World War: Veterans: 1914–1918, Library and Archives Canada.

26 1 July 1916 entry in 1st Newfoundland Regiment war diary, NA WO 95/2308.

27 Joy B. Cave (ed.), *I Survived Didn't I? The Great War Reminiscences of Private 'Ginger' Byrne*, pp. 23, 26 and 43.

28 Private Bert Ellis, 22 July 1916 edition of *The Evening Telegram* newspaper.

29 *Newfoundland Quarterly*, vol. XVI, October 1916, p. 5, brought to my attention by Jenny Higgins, the writer and director of a documentary film about the Newfoundland Regiment, commissioned by the Labrador Heritage website of the Memorial University of Newfoundland.

30 Casualty figures in the 29th Division file, NA WO 95/2280, are specified as being 736, whereas in the *1916 Official History, Vol. 1*, p. 436, they are specified as being 710. Other facts are from the 1 July 1916 entry of the 1st Newfoundland Regiment war diary, NA WO 95/2308. The Governor of Newfoundland's

comments on the report sent to him by Lieutenant-Colonel Arthur Hadow, both of which are printed in the 29 July 1916 edition of the *St John's Daily Star*, state that 783 men were involved in the attack. This figure may be slightly out since it is possible a few men were not included in the count.

31 Private Bert Ellis, 22 July 1916 edition of *The Evening Telegram* newspaper.

32 Dudley Menaud-Lissenburg, IWM Documents 7248.

33 Casualty figures for the 1st Essex Regiment are specified as being 216 in the 29th Division file, NA WO 95/2280, whereas in the *1916 Official History, Vol. 1*, p. 436, they are specified as being 229.

34 *29th Division's Report.*

35 Ibid. The casualties of the 29th Division are stated as being 4,997 in the *1916 Official History, Vol. 1*, pp. 436–7, and 5,189 in the 29th Division file, NA WO 95/2280.

36 2nd Lieutenant Arthur Stanford, IWM Documents 16653.

37 Letter from Mrs Knight to her son William Knight 18 July 1916, Knight Papers, MF 344, Archives and Special Collections, Memorial University of Newfoundland (*Knight Papers*), brought to my attention by Jenny Higgins (see note 29).

38 Letter from Warren Knight to William Knight 18 July 1916, Knight Papers.

9: Rattling the Cage

1 Report under the heading 'Wirkung der Sprengung' (*Pioneers' Report*) in the 4 Feldpionier Kompanie Bataillon Nr. 13 file covering July 1916, Hauptstaatsarchiv Stuttgart M201 Bu200.

2 1 July 1916 entry in 1st/8th Battalion, the Royal Warwickshire Regiment war diary (*1/8 Royal Warwicks War Diary*), NA WO 95/2756.

3 Lieutenant Beck, account (*Beck's Account*), in the Brochure *Treffen der 26 RD: am 5 July 1936*, brought to my attention by Jack Sheldon, who quoted from it in his book *The Germans at Beaumont Hamel*, pp. 85–8.

4 Ibid.

5 *Pioneers' Report.*

6 Document entitled 'Letter by 2nd Lt G. W. Glover to Major G. W. Barclay' (*Glover's Letter*), in 1st Rifle Brigade file, NA WO 95/1496.

7 Martin Middlebrook, *The First Day on the Somme*, p. 134.

8 *Beck's Account.*

9 1 July entry, *1/8 Royal Warwicks War Diary*.

10 'Operations on 1st July 1916', in 4th Division file, NA WO 95/1445.

11 Captain W. J. Page, account (*Page's Account*), brought to my attention by Lieutenant-Colonel John Downham of the Queen's Lancashire Regiment; 'Narrative of 1st July 1916', in 11th Brigade file, NA WO 95/1490.

12 *Glover's Letter.*

13 1 July 1916 entry of *1/8 Royal Warwicks War Diary*; 1 July 1916 entry for 1st/8th Royal Warwicks, NA WO 95/2755.

14 *Beck's Account.*

15 *Glover's Letter.*

16 1 July 1916 entry in 2nd Seaforth Highlanders war diary (*2nd Seaforth Highlanders War Diary*), NA WO 95/1483.

17 *Glover's Letter*; and 6.20 p.m. 10th Brigade message to the 4th Division in '1st July 1916: Messages received on the Telephone', in 4th Division file, NA WO 95/1444.

18 *Beck's Account.*

19 *Page's Account.*

20 *2nd Seaforth Highlanders War Diary.*

21 'Report on action of 10th Infantry Brigade on 1st July 1916', NA WO 95/1479.

22 1 July 1916 entry in 1st Royal Irish Fusiliers war diary, NA WO 95/1482.

23 *Pioneers' Report.*

24 Captain M. G. Browne was brought to my attention by Lieutenant-Colonel John Downham of the Queen's Lancashire Regiment.

25 *Beck's Account.*

26 Ibid.

27 Hauptmann Freiherr Georg vom Holtz, *Das Württembergische-Reserve-Inf-Regiment Nr. 121 im Weltkrieg* (*121 Res. Inf. Reg. History*), p. 34.

28 4th Division file, NA WO 95/1445.

29 *Beck's Account.*

30 *121 Res. Inf. Reg. History*, p. 36.

31 2 July 1916 timed at 2.30 p.m. 1st/121st Reserve Regiment to the said Regiment, Hauptstaatsarchiv Stuttgart, M411 2550.

32 Ibid., 3 July 1916 in the afternoon.

33 *Page's Account.*

10: Neither Fish Nor Fowl

1 3rd Army order number 11 dated 21 June 1916, in VII Corps file, NA WO 95/804.

2 'Account of the operations of the VIIth Corps against Gommecourt on the 1st of July 1916', NA WO 95/804 (*VII Corps Account*).

3 Lieutenant Cyril Ashford, letter 2 August 1923, in 46th Division file, NA WO 95/2664; Brigadier-General C. T. Shipley, letter to Brigadier-General Sir James E. Edmonds 5 June 1929, NA CAB 45/137; and *VII Corps Account*.

4 23 and 24 June 1916 entries in the 46th Division war diary, NA WO 95/2663; and *VII Corps Account*.

5 10 July 1916 report by 169th Brigade's Brigadier-General E. S. Coke (*169th Brigade Report*), NA WO 95/2957; and *VII Corps Account*.

6 Brigadier-General Sir James E. Edmonds, *History of the Great War: Military Operations: France and Belgium 1916, Volume 1* (*1916 Official History, Vol. 1*), p. 460.

7 Major-General L. J. Bols, letter to Brigadier-General Sir James E. Edmonds (the official historian) 14 June 1929, NA CAB 45/132; *1916 Official History, Vol. 1*, p. 454.

8 *VII Corps Account*.

9 Lieutenant-Colonel Arthur Bates, 8 July 1916 report to 169th Brigade's Brigadier-General, *The History of the London Rifle Brigade 1850–1919* (*The London Rifle Brigade Report*), pp. 133–4; casualty figures are from *VII Corps Account*.

10 Private Arthur Schuman, account (*Schuman's Account*), in IWM Documents 4326.

11 *The London Rifle Brigade Report*; report of 1 July 1916 events attached to the war diary of 1st/16th Battalion, the London Regiment (Queen's Westminster Rifles), NA WO 95/2963; 168th Brigade's 'Report on Operations 1st July 1916', in 168th Brigade file, NA WO 95/2951; Lieutenant-Colonel W. H. W. Young (commander of 1st/13th Battalion, the London Regiment [Kensington]), letter to the official historian 10 October 1929, NA WO 95/2955.

12 Lance-Corporal Cecil Dixon, in Major C. A. Cuthbert Keeson, *History and Records of Queen Victoria's Rifles 1792–1922*, pp. 170–71.

13 'Report of Operations of 56th (London) Division culminating in the attack on the S. W. face of the Gommecourt Salient on July 1st 1916', NA WO 95/2931.

14 *The London Rifle Brigade Report*.

15 168th Brigade's 'Report on Operations 1st July 1916' (*168th Brigade Report*), NA WO 95/2951.

16 'Account of action on 1st July 1916 E. of Hebuterne', 5 July 1916, in 1st/14th Battalion file, the London Regiment (London Scottish), NA WO 95/2956; and *168th Brigade Report*.

17 2nd Lieutenant R. E. Petley, account (*Petley's Account*), in 1st/5th London Battalion (London Rifle Brigade) file, NA WO 95/2961.

18 Accounts by Sergeant W. M. Lilley, Sergeant H. Frost, Lance-Corporal J. H. Foaden and Corporal R. F. Ebbetts, and *Petley's Account*, all in *The History of the London Rifle Brigade 1850–1919*, pp. 139–47, and *Schuman's Account*.

19 *Petley's Account.*

20 4 July 1916 court of inquiry into actions by 46th Division's brigades on 1 July 1916 (*46th Division Inquiry*), NA WO 95/2663, a copy of which is lodged in the Liddle Collection.

21 46th Division's 'Divisional Smoke Programme for Assault', 24 June 1916, 46th Division file, NA WO 95/2663.

22 Lieutenant Cyril Ashford letter 2 August 1923; and 'Points of Interest, Action of 1st July' attached to 12 July 1916 'Narrative of Operations on July 1st 1916': both in the 46th Division file, NA WO 95/2663,

23 T. F. C. Downman, account, in 1st/5th Sherwood Foresters file, NA WO 95/2695.

24 Ibid.

25 Ibid. combined with explanatory extracts from Lieutenant Cyril Ashford, account (*The Ashford Account*), in 1st/6th Battalion file, the South Staffordshire Regiment, NA WO 95/2687.

26 Ibid.

27 Ibid.

28 Ibid.

29 Leutnant Adolf Kümmel, der Reserve, a. D., *Res. Inf. Regt. Nr. 91 im Weltkriege 1914–1918*, pp. 211–12.

30 'Report on the part played by the 139th Infantry Brigade in the action on the 1st July 1916', NA WO 95/2692; 'Narrative of Operations on July 1st 1916', 12 July 1916 (*46th Division Narrative*), NA WO 95/2663.

31 Corporal P. J. Murphy, account, in 139th Brigade file, NA WO 95/2692.

32 *The Ashford Account.*

33 *VII Corps Account.*

34 Testimony of Major R. Abadie, Captain F. E. Wenger and 2nd Lieutenant G. E. Cronk, cited in *46th Division Inquiry.*

35 *46th Division Narrative.*

36 Major-General Eddie Montagu-Stuart-Wortley, letter to the Military Secretary, War Office, 18 September 1919, NA WO 138/29, brought to my attention by the National Archives archivist William Spencer.

37 Lieutenant-General Thomas Snow, letter to General Allenby 2 July 1916, NA WO 138/29, brought to my attention by the BBC programme *My Family at War* featuring General Snow's great-grandson Dan Snow.

38 Lieutenant-General Thomas Snow, note to 3rd Army 10 July 1916 (*Snow's 10 July Note*), in 46th Division file, NA WO 2663.

39 Ibid., note to 3rd Army 8 August 1916, in VII Corps file, NA WO 95/804.

40 *Snow's 10 July Note.*

41 General Douglas Haig, letter to War Office 4 July 1916, NA WO 138/29.

42 *VII Corps Account.*

43 2nd Lieutenant C. E. Moy, serving with the 1st/16th London Regiment (Queen's Westminster Rifles), account, IWM Documents 17166; and Liddle Collection; F. H. Wallis, account, in 1st/5th London Regiment (London Rifle Brigade) file, NA CAB 45/131.

44 Based on a translation of the document entitled 'Remarks by the 55th Reserve Infantry Regiment', which along with the translation of the 55th Reserve Regiment's war diary is in the 56th Division's file, NA WO 95/2931.

11: Achilles Heel

1 F. P. Crozier, *A Brass Hat in No Man's Land* (*Crozier: Brass Hat*), pp. 53–4.

2 Ibid., pp. 60–2.

3 Crozier's age following his birthday in January 1916.

4 David Starrett, IWM Documents 6659; and Lieutenant John Leslie Stewart-Moore, 'Random Recollections' (*Stewart-Moore's Recollections*), the unpublished source cited in Philip Orr, *The Road to the Somme* (*Orr*), p. 115.

5 F. P. Crozier, *Impressions and Recollections*, p. 149.

6 *Orr*, pp. 53–4.

7 *Crozier: Brass Hat*, pp. 66–72.

8 *Stewart-Moore's Recollections.*

9 The execution took place on 27 February 1916, NA WO 71/450.

10 *Crozier: Brass Hat*, pp. 83–4.

11 Ibid., pp. 92–3.

12 36th Division's Order No. 34, 16 June 1916, NA WO 95/2491 (*36th Division's Attack Order*).

13 *Crozier: Brass Hat*, p. 61.

14 Ibid., p. 97; F. P. Crozier, *The Men I Killed*, pp. 81–2.

15 Shakespeare's play *Henry V* includes the reference to 'A little touch of Harry in the night', referring to the way the monarch reassured his troops before the battle of Agincourt in 1415.

16 *Crozier: Brass Hat*, pp. 98–9.

17 1 July 1916 entry in 14th Royal Irish Rifles war diary, NA WO 95/2511.

18 *36th Division's Attack Order.*

19 36th Division: as well as Billie McFadzean, Captain E. N. F. Bell, 9th Royal Inniskilling Fusiliers, Lieutenant G. S. Cather, 9th Royal Irish Fusiliers; Private R. Quigg, 12th Royal Irish Rifles; 49th Division: Captain G. Sanders, 1st/7th West Yorkshires; 32nd Division: Sergeant J. Y. Turnbull, 17th Highland Light Infantry.

20 Private Leslie Bell, account, Martin Middlebook Archive.

21 1 July 1916 entry in 9th and 10th Royal Inniskilling Fusiliers war diaries, NA WO 95/2510.

22 1 July 1916 entry in 10th Royal Inniskilling Fusiliers war diary, NA WO 95/2510.

23 Cyril Falls, *The History of the 36th Ulster Division*, p. 52.

24 1 July 1916 entry in 14th Royal Irish Rifles war diary, NA WO 95/2511.

25 J. K. Hope, volume of reminiscences, RURRM, brought to my attention by *Orr*, p. 201.

26 Major d.R. Paul Müller, Oberst a.D. Hans von Fabeck and Oberstleutnant a.D. Richard Riesel, *Geschichte des Reserve-Infanterie-Regiments Nr. 99*, p. 103.

27 Herbert Ritter von Wurmb, *Das K. B. Reserve-Infanterie-Regiment Nr. 8 (Wurmb History)*, p. 67.

28 'Report on Operations Culminating in the Allied Advance on 1.7.16', in 10th Royal Inniskilling Fusiliers file, and 1 July 1916 entry in 9th Royal Inniskilling Fusiliers file, both in NA WO 95/2510; 1 July 1916 entry in 11th Royal Irish Rifles war diary, NA WO 95/2506; 1:20,000 map in 36th Division file, NA WO 95/2491.

29 *Wurmb History*, p. 78.

30 Hugh Stewart, File on Formation and Training, held by Philip Orr, brought to my attention by *Orr*, p. 200.

31 Hugh Stewart, File on Somme, RURRM, brought to my attention by *Orr*, p. 210.

32 Ibid., pp. 200 and 204.

33 *Crozier: Brass Hat*, pp. 102–3.

34 1 July 1916 entry in 2nd King's Own Yorkshire Light Infantry war diary, WO 95/2402.

35 1 July 1916 entry in 11th Borders war diary, NA WO 95/2403; and 32nd Division's 'Report on Operations 21st June to 4th July and from 8th to 15th July' (*32nd Division Report*), NA WO 95/2368.

36 1 July 1916 entry in 1st Dorsets war diary, NA WO 95/2392.

37 *32nd Division Report*.

38 Ibid.

39 1 July 1916 entry in 19th Lancashire Fusiliers war diary, NA WO 95/2394.

40 1 July 1916 entry in 16th Northumberland Fusiliers war diary, NA WO 95/2398.

41 *Salford City Reporter* article quoted in Michael Stedman, *Salford Pals*, p. 119.

42 *32nd Division Report*.

43 11 August 1916 edition of *Eccles and Patricroft Journal*, in Stedman, *Salford Pals*, p. 126.

44 Lieutenant Charles S. Marriot, account, Lancashire Fusiliers Museum, brought to my attention by Stedman, *Salford Pals*, p. 122.

45 Brigadier-General Sir James E. Edmonds, *History of the Great War: Military Operations: France and Belgium 1916, Volume 1*, p. 402.

12: An Opportunity Missed

1 F. P. Crozier, *The Men I Killed*, p. 83; F. P. Crozier, *A Brass Hat in No Man's Land* (*Crozier: Brass Hat*), p. 106.

2 *Crozier: Brass Hat*, pp. 101–6.

3 David Starrett, IWM Documents 6659.

4 1 July 1916 entry in 9th Royal Irish Rifles war diary, NA WO 95/2503.

5 Tommy Ervine, in Philip Orr, *The Road to the Somme* (*Orr*), p. 208.

6 1 July 1916 entries in 8th and 9th Royal Irish Rifles war diaries, both in NA WO 95/2503.

7 Ralph J. Whitehead, *The Other Side of the Wire, Volume 2* (*Whitehead*), p. 202. Although the original account states the events occurred at 9 a.m. (8 a.m. British time), it is possible that the time given was mistaken. It is also possible that the account is unreliable, which is why I have been guarded concerning its authenticity in the main text.

8 Herbert Ritter von Wurmb, *Das K. B. Reserve-Infanterie-Regiment Nr. 8* (*Wurmb History*), p. 70; *Whitehead*, p. 234 .

9 *Wurmb History*, p. 69.

10 30 June and 1 July 1916 entries in 52nd Reserve Infantry Brigade war diary, translation in Newfoundland Centre, Beaumont Hamel, of original document in Hauptstaatsarchiv Stuttgart M410 Bu239.

11 1 July 1916 entry in 52nd Reserve Infantry Brigade war diary.

12 1 July 1916 entry in 52nd Reserve Infantry Brigade combat report, translation in Newfoundland Centre, Beaumont Hamel, of original document in Hauptstaatsarchiv Stuttgart M410 Bu239.

13 *Wurmb History*, pp. 69–70.

14 30 June and 1 July 1916 entries in Lieutenant-General Sir Thomas Morland, *War Diaries & Letters 1914–1918*, edited by Bill Thompson (*Morland's Diaries*), pp. 147–8.

15 1 July 1916 entry in 49th Division war diary, NA WO 95/2765; 8.38 a.m. message from X Corps to the 49th Division in X Corps file, NA WO 95/851.

16 1 July 1916 entry in 36th Division war diary, that division's file, NA WO 95/2491

17 Ibid.

18 36th Division message sent to X Corps at 10.10 a.m., in X Corps file, NA WO 95/851.

19 Situation report at 10.30 a.m. in 1 July 1916 entry in X Corps war diary, NA WO 95/851.

20 29 June and 1 July 1916 entries in *Morland's Diaries*, pp. 147–8.

21 Entries between 9.15 and 10 a.m. on 1 July 1916 in 36th Division war diary, in that division's file, NA WO 95/2491, referring inter alia to information given by the 36th Division to X Corps at 8.32 a.m.

22 1 July 1916 entry in the 32nd Division file, NA WO 95/2368.

23 9 a.m. and 2.37 p.m. on 1 July 1916 entries in the 32nd Division file.

24 1 July 1916 entry in the 32nd Division file.

25 *Morland's Diaries*, p. xxxi.

26 36th Division's message confirming its troops were consolidating on the 'C' line appears to have been sent to X Corps shortly before 10.30 a.m. on 1 July 1916. It is in X Corps file, NA WO 95/851.

27 Ibid.

28 Message at 2.45 p.m. on 1 July 1916 from X Corps to 49th Division, in X Corps file, NA WO 95/851, and confirmation that X Corps verbally passed on the message to Major-General Perceval at 2.46 p.m.; the entry for that time is in the 49th Division war diary, NA WO 95/2765.

29 Message at 12.20 p.m. on 1 July 1916 from X Corps to 36th and 49th Divisions, in X Corps file, NA WO 95/851.

30 Message at 5.10 p.m. from X Corps to 49th Division, in X Corps file, NA WO 95/851; 1 July 1916 entry in 146th Brigade war diary, in that brigade's file, NA WO 95/2792.

31 Order at 6.18 p.m. from X Corps to 32nd, 36th and 49th Divisions as well as the 4th Army, in X Corps file, NA WO 95/851.

32 1 July 1916 entry in 146th Brigade war diary, NA WO 95/2792; message from 107th Brigade to 146th Brigade, received at 7.48 p.m.; 3.58 p.m. message from X Corps to 49th and 36th Divisions, in X Corps file, NA WO 95/851; and account by Major H. D. Bousfield of the 1st/7th West Yorkshire Regiment, CAB 45/188.

33 'Report on action of 9th Battn. Royal Irish Fusiliers on July 1st 1916', in that battalion's file, NA WO 95/2505.

34 1 July 1916 entry in 8th and 9th Royal Irish Rifles war diaries, NA WO 95/2503.

35 Lieutenant Joseph Shannon, statement in WO 339/22396.

36 Captain John Berry, statement in WO 339/14325.

37 Major Adam Jenkins, statement in WO 339/14333.

38 1 July 1916 entry in 107th Brigade war diary, NA WO 95/2502.

39 1 July 1916 entry in 10th Royal Inniskilling Fusiliers war diary, NA WO 95/2510.

40 *Crozier: Brass Hat*, p. 108.

41 *Wurmb History*, p. 68.

42 Lieutenant-Colonel Francis Bowen, diary entry 1 July 1916, brought to my attention by his son Richard.

43 *Crozier: Brass Hat*, p. 110.

44 *Wurmb History*, p. 72.

45 1 July 1916 entry in 107th Brigade war diary, NA WO 95/2502.

46 *Wurmb History*, p. 72.

47 Casualty list, apparently covering 1 and 2 July, attached to '36th (Ulster) Division: Weekly Summary of Operations', 7 July 1916, in 36th Division file, NA WO 95/2491.

48 Ibid.

49 1 and 2 July 1916 entries in 107th Brigade war diary, NA WO 95/2502.

50 'Narrative of Events relating to 148th Infantry Brigade 1st–8th July 1916', in 148th Brigade file, NA WO 95/2803.

51 'Report on operations 21st June to 4th July and from 8th to 15th July', in 32nd Division file, NA WO 95/2368.

52 1 July 1916 entry in 2nd Manchester Battalion war diary, NA WO 95/2392.

53 *Wurmb History*, p. 78. These figures only cover 1 and 3 July 1916.

54 1 July 1916 entry in 52nd Reserve Infantry Brigade war diary.

55 Hugh Stewart, File on Somme, RURRM, brought to my attention by Orr, p. 238.

56 18 July 1916 edition of *Belfast Evening Telegraph*, brought to my attention by Orr, p. 239.

57 Ibid., 19 July 1916.

58 Hugh Stewart, File on Somme, RURRM, brought to my attention by Orr, p. 243.

13: Of Moles and Men

1 According to Charles Bean, *The Australian Imperial Force in France: Volume III: 1916*, p. 699, the Germans usually referred to the Pozières heights as Hill 160 or Hill 161.

2 Brigadier-General H. D. Tuson, quoted in 1 July 1916 entry in 2nd Scots Rifles war diary, 2nd Scots Rifles file, NA WO 95/1715.

3 Brigadier-General Sir James E. Edmonds, *History of the Great War: Military Operations: France and Belgium 1916, Volume 1 (1916 Official History, Vol. 1)*, p. 373, and its Map Volume, map 8.

4 Brigadier-General H. D. Tuson, quoted in 1 July 1916 entry in 2nd Scots Rifles war diary, 2nd Scots Rifles file, NA WO 95/1715.

5 Lieutenant-General Sir William Pulteney, letter to Edith Londonderry 22 June 1916, in *Putty: From Tel-el-Kebir to Cambrai: The Life and Letters of Lieutenant-General Sir William Pulteney 1861–1941 (Pulteney Biography)*, p. 399.

6 Ibid.

7 Lieutenant-General Sir William Pulteney, letter to Ettie Desborough 29 June 1916, in *Pulteney Biography*, p. 410.

8 Lieutenant-General Sir William Pulteney, letter to Edith Londonderry 22 June 1916, in *Pulteney Biography*, p. 399.

9 Lieutenant Alfred Bundy, account (*Bundy's Account*), IWM Documents 10828.

10 Reginald Leetham, account (*Leetham's Account*), IWM Documents 18567.

11 The first moves of the 25th Brigade's assault battalions were as follows: 1 July 1916 entry in 2nd Lincolnshire Regiment war diary states its troops advanced into No Man's Land before zero hour (NA WO 95/1730). The 1 July 1916 entry in the 2nd Royal Berkshires war diary (NA WO 95/1729) appears to suggest its troops only climbed out at zero hour, but this might not be the case, given that the 25th Brigade's Preliminary Operation Order No. 100 required the battalions to climb out into No Man's Land at 7.25 a.m. 'if circumstances permit', in 25th Brigade file, NA WO 95/1726. The first moves of the 23rd Brigade's assault battalions were as follows: 1 July 1916 entry in 2nd Devons war diary states the first wave made their preliminary advance 7–10 minutes before zero hour, NA WO 95/1712; 1 July 1916 entry in 2nd Middlesex war diary appears to suggest the first wave only advanced at 7.30 a.m., but the precise time of the advance is not clearly specified; 1 July 1916 entry in 23rd Brigade war diary states that the first waves of both battalions crawled forward before zero hour, NA WO 95/1709.

12 1 July entries in 2nd Royal Berkshires war diary and 2nd Devons war diary.

13 Captain Alan Hanbury-Sparrow, IWM Sound Archive 4770.

14 'Report on the part taken by the 2nd Battalion Devonshire Regiment during the attack on Pozières on the 1st July 1916', in 2nd Devonshires file, NA WO 95/1712.

15 1 July 1916 entry in 2nd Middlesex file, NA WO 95/1713.

16 *Bundy's Account*.

17 1 July 1916 entry in 2nd Lincolns war diary, in its file, NA WO 95/1730; Lieutenant-Colonel Reginald Bastard, letter to the official historian dated '19 March' with no year specified, in NA CAB 45/132.

18 2nd Lieutenant W. V. C. Lake, IWM Documents 22872.

19 *Leetham's Account*.

20 *1916 Official History, Vol. 1*, p. 385.

21 Ibid., p. 391.
22 Alfred Vischer, *Das 10. Württ. Infanterie-Regiment Nr. 180 in der Somme-Schlacht 1916*, p. 18.
23 'Report: 25th Infantry Brigade: Operation about Ovillers July 1st 1916', in 25th Brigade file, NA WO 95/1726.
24 Cyril José, letter to sister Ivy 16 November 1916, IWM Documents 19925.
25 Ibid., 13 July 1916.
26 Ibid., 16 July 1916.

14: Land of Hope and Glory

1 Major Henry Hance, letter to the official historian (*Hance Letter*) June 1930, NA CAB 45/189.
2 Captain James Young, 'Notes on 179 Company R. E.' (*Young Notes*), Tunnellers' Old Comrades Association Bulletin, No. 13, 1938, brought to my attention by Simon Jones and Phillip Robinson.
3 Ibid.
4 Captain Hugh Kerr, transcript of interview (*Kerr Interview*) given to Alexander Barrie, author of *War Underground*, Alexander Barrie papers, Royal Engineers Museum, Acc. 9007-01, brought to my attention by Simon Jones (see note 6).
5 It was started by the 185th Tunnelling Company.
6 Simon Jones, *Underground Warfare 1914–1918*, pp. 121–3; *Young Notes*; The 5 July 1916 Weekly Report written by 179 Tunnelling Company's Henry Hance, in the 34th Division file (*279 Tunnelling Company's Weekly Report*), NA WO 95/2432.
7 Henry Hance in the *Hance Letter* recalled that the tunnel was almost 350 yards long. The *279 Tunnelling Company's Weekly Report* stated that the tunnel was 1,008 feet (336 yards) long.
8 *Kerr Interview.*
9 *Hance Letter*; *Young Notes*; *279 Tunnelling Company's Weekly Report*. The latter states that 200 feet of the tamping consisted of alternating 6 feet of air space with 10 feet of tamping.
10 27 June 1916 order signed by 101st Brigade's Brigadier-General Gore, in 101st Brigade file, NA WO 95/2455.
11 Lieutenant-Colonel A. G. B. Urmison, letter to the official historian 11 June 1930, NA CAB 45/191.
12 Lieutenant-Colonel E. A. Osborne, letter to the official historian 14 April 1930, NA CAB 45/190.

13 Lieutenant-Colonel G. Steward, letter to the official historian 5 September 1930, NA CAB 45/191; 34th Division Operation Order 16 dated 15 June 1916, NA WO 95/2432.

14 Brigadier-General Sir James E. Edmonds, *History of the Great War: Military Operations: France and Belgium 1916, Volume 1*, p. 373, and its Map Volume, map 8.

15 34th Division's Operation Order No. 16 dated 15 June 1916, in 34th Division file, NA WO 95/2432.

16 Major Walter Vignoles, account, IWM Documents 77/3/1 or 6968.

17 29 June 1916 entry in 16th Royal Scots war diary, NA WO 95/2458.

18 Private Harry Baumber, account, brought to my attention by Peter Bryant, *Grimsby Chums: The Story of the 10th Lincolnshires in the Great War* (*Grimsby Chums*), p. 56.

19 *Kerr Interview.*

20 Major Kyme Cordeaux, letter 10 July 1916, IWM Documents 16975.

21 *Grimsby Chums*, p. 56.

22 Private Harry Baumber, brought to my attention in *Grimsby Chums*.

23 1 July 1916 smoke report by 2nd Lieutenant O. Behrendt, in 34th Division file, NA WO 95/2432.

24 Graham Stewart and John Sheen, *Tyneside Scottish: A History of the Tyneside Scottish Raised in the North-East in World War One* (*Tyneside Scottish*), p. 98.

25 Private J. Elliot, *Tyneside Scottish*, p. 99.

26 Ibid., p. 101.

27 1 July 1916 entry in 102nd Brigade war diary, in that unit's file, NA WO 95/2459.

28 Dr James Fiddian, letter to 2nd Lieutenant Andrew Wright, as he was in 1916, 20 January 1922, held by Andrew Wright's son Major Philip Wright. Andrew Wright later became Sir Andrew Wright.

29 Major Kyme Cordeaux, quoted in *Grimsby Chums*, p. 59.

30 Private Harry Baumber, quoted in ibid.

31 Anonymous, *Reserve-Infanterie-Regiment Nr. 110 im Weltkrieg 1914–1918* (*110th Reserve Regiment Book*), p. 125.

32 2nd Lieutenant J. H. Turnbull, account, quoted in *Grimsby Chums*, p. 62.

33 1 July 1916 entry in 102nd Brigade war diary, NA WO 95/2459.

34 Jack Alexander, *McCrae's Battalion: The Story of the 16th Royal Scots*, p. 159.

35 'Gefechtbericht . . . des Leutnant d. R. Heine', *110th Reserve Regiment Book*, p. 303.

36 1 July 1916 entry in 101st Brigade war diary, NA WO 95/2455.

37 1 July 1916 entry in 27th Northumberland Fusiliers war diary, NA WO 95/2467.

38 *Grimsby Chums*, pp. 63–4; 1 July 1916 entry 101st Brigade war diary, NA WO 95/2455. It should be noted that *Grimsby Chums* refers to Cordeaux ordering an attack on La Boisselle. Given what is written in the 101st Brigade war diary about the attack being directed at Bloater and Kipper Trenches, Heligoland and the German support line, it is thought that the reference in the book to La Boisselle is intended to mean the La Boisselle sector.

39 Account written by 2nd Lieutenant Andrew Wright as he then was (*Andrew Wright's Account*), brought to my attention by his son, Major Philip Wright.

40 'III Corps: Summary of Operations: 1st to 7th July 1916', III Corps file, NA WO 95/673.

41 *110th Reserve Regiment Book*, pp. 304–5.

42 Approximate casualty list under 6 July 1916 entry in 101st Brigade war diary, NA WO 95/2455.

43 Casualty list for 1–4 July 1916 in 103rd Brigade file, NA WO 95/2464.

44 Lieutenant-Colonel H. W. L. Waller, letter to the official historian 18 April 1930, NA CAB 45/191.

15: Bull's Eye

1 'Preliminary Examination of Oswald Lakemaker 109th R.I.R. who surrendered near Mansell Copse (F.11.c.4.6) on early morning 29th June 1916' (*Preliminary Lakemaker Report*), 4th Army papers, vol. 10.

2 The quote contains wording from the following two documents: 'Extracts from the examination of a deserter of the 1st Bn. 109th Res. Rgt. who came across to our lines south east of Mametz on the morning of June 29th' and 'Fourth Army Intelligence Summary 30th June 1916', 4th Army papers, vol. 10, IWM Documents; and *Preliminary Lakemaker Report*.

3 'Examination of Ernst Girndt and Arnold Fuchs 4th Co., 1st Bn., 62nd Regt., 12th Div., VI Corps, who surrendered at the Fleche on June 27th 1916', 'Fourth Army Intelligence Summary 29th June 1916', 4th Army papers, vol. 10, IWM Documents.

4 *Preliminary Lakemaker Report*.

5 'Fourth Army Intelligence Summary 30th June 1916', 4th Army papers, vol. 10, IWM Documents.

6 'Notes from examination of prisoners of the 111th Res. Inf. Regt. Captured night of 26th/27th June at Wicked Corner (F.3.c.67/37)', 'Fourth Army Intelligence Summary 29th June 1916', 4th Army papers, vol. 10, IWM Documents.

7 'Preliminary Examination' of prisoners from the Thiepval sector, attached to 'Fourth Army Intelligence Summary 29th June 1916', 4th Army papers, vol. 10, IWM Documents.

8 Private A. R. Brennan, account, IWM Documents 12116.

9 Private James Deary, Martin Middlebrook papers.

10 Lance Corporal Edward Fisher, Martin Middlebrook papers.

11 '53rd Infantry Brigade: Abbreviated report on operations 25th June 1916 to 22nd July 1916', in 53rd Brigade file, NA WO 95/2034.

12 Brigadier-General Sir James E. Edmonds, *History of the Great War: Military Operations: France and Belgium 1916, Volume 1 (1916 Official History, Vol. 1)*, pp. 301–2.

13 Lieutenant-Colonel Neil Fraser-Tytler, *Field Guns in France*, p. 81.

14 Private Sydney Fuller, diary (*Fuller Diary*), IWM Documents 2607.

15 Private Albert Andrews, account, IWM Documents 15946, reproduced with permission from Beryl Read, his daughter, and Susan Richardson, the widow of the publisher of the account that was published under the title *Orders are Orders: A Manchester Pal on the Somme*.

16 1 July 1916 entry in 18th Kings (Liverpool) war diary, NA WO 95/2330.

17 1 July 1916 entries in 17th and 20th Kings (Liverpool) war diaries, NA WO 95/2334 and 2335 respectively.

18 *1916 Official History, Vol.* 1, pp. 321–2, and its Map Volume, map 5. 'Plan of Operations', not dated, in XIII Corps file, NA WO 95/895.

19 2nd Lieutenant Kenneth Macardle, account, in the Manchester Regiment archives held by Tameside Local Archives and Study Centre, MR 1/3/2/6.

20 1 July 1916 entry in 90th Brigade war diary, NA WO 95/2337.

21 'The Account of the Operations of the 54th Infantry Brigade during the Battle of the Somme between the 23rd June and 20th July 1916', in 94th Brigade file, NA WO 95/2041.

22 Untitled report dated 26 July 1916, in 55th Brigade file, NA WO 95/2046.

23 *Fuller Diary*.

24 *1916 Official History, Vol.* 1, pp. 324–5.

25 Ibid., p. 343.

26 Ibid., p. 341.

27 Ibid., p. 345.

16: The Attack

1 2nd Lieutenant Siegfried Sassoon, *Memoirs of an Infantry Officer (Sassoon's Memoirs)*, p. 61.

2 *Sassoon's Memoirs*, p. 67.

3 Ibid., pp. 70–1.

4 Ibid., p. 73.

5 Brigadier-General Sir James E. Edmonds, *History of the Great War: Military Operations: France and Belgium 1916, Volume 1 (1916 Official History, Vol. 1)*, p. 348.

6 30 June 1916 entry in 22nd Middlesex war diary, NA WO 95/1669, states they left the Bois des Tailles at 9.30 p.m.; two hours were spent walking to the front line. I have assumed that 'some time to settle down' mentioned by Tawney means at least half an hour.

7 R. H. Tawney, *The Attack and Other Papers*, pp. 1–20.

8 1 July 1916 entry in 22nd Manchesters war diary, NA QO 95/1669.

9 The line is shown in Brigadier-General Sir James E. Edmonds, *History of the Great War: Military Operations: France and Belgium 1916,* Maps Volume: map 7, and the action is described in *1916 Official History, Vol. 1*, pp. 351–5 and 364–6.

10 *1916 Official History, Vol. 1*, pp. 356–7.

11 Ibid., pp. 356–61 and 366–8.

12 Lieutenant-Colonel Ronald Fife, diary, brought to my attention by Major Roger Chapman and Steve Erskine, IWM Documents 19219.

13 *1916 Official History, Vol. 1*, p. 368.

14 Sergeant Karl Eisler, account, Freiburg BA/MA PH12 II/57, brought to my attention in *Scorched Earth: The Germans on the Somme 1914–1918* by Irina Renz, Gerd Krumeich and Gerhard Hirschfeld, pp. 81–9.

15 *1916 Official History, Vol. 1*, p. 345.

16 O. Bezzel, *Das Koniglich Bayerische Reserve-Infanterie-Regiment, Nr. 6*, pp. 92–3, 111–13, 116–18.

17 Private Arthur Bunting, letter to his wife Effie, not dated, brought to my attention by his grandson Adrian Bunting.

17: Repercussions

1 I. L. ('Dick') Read, *Of Those We Loved*, p. 130.

2 Lieutenant Edgar Lord, account, IWM Documents 6559.

3 Reverend J. P. H. Halet, IWM Documents 19171.

4 Edith Appleton, *A Nurse at the Front: The Great War Diaries of Sister Edith Appleton*, ed. Ruth Cowen, quoted thanks to permission from her great-nephew Dick Robinson, and publishers Simon & Schuster and the Imperial War Museum. The full text of the diaries can be found via the website http://anurseatthefront.org.uk, or directly by using the following link 'formula' on the internet: http://anurseatthefront.org.uk-all-four-volumes/the-diaries-volume-3/. Please note that readers should change the number near the end of the aforementioned formula to define which volume of the diary they want to read. The formula phrased as it is would bring up volume 3.

5 Marjorie Beeton, diary, brought to my attention by Daniel Kirmatzis.

6 Nancy Peto, diary, brought to my attention by her grandson Jonathan Peto, and quoted with permission from the Peto family.

7 Brigadier-General L. A. E. Price Davies, letters, I WM Documents 7069.

8 Lieutenant-Colonel Kyme Cordeaux, letters, I WM Documents 16975.

9 General Sir Douglas Haig, 1 July 1916 entry in diary, Liddell Hart Centre.

10 Lieutenant-General Sir Aylmer Hunter-Weston, 1 July 1916 letter. I have assumed it is to his wife, although this is not specified. Private Diary, his papers, British Library, MS 48365.

11 Brigadier E. C. Anstey, *History of the Royal Artillery* (unpublished).

12 Lieutenant-General Sir Aylmer Hunter-Weston, 2 July 1916 letter to his wife Grace. Private Diary, his papers, British Library ADD MS 48365.

13 16 July 1916 diary entry in Brigadier Phillip Howell, Liddle Hart Centre for Military Archives, brought to my attention by Elaine McFarland, *A Slashing Man of Action: The Life of Lieutenant-General Sir Aylmer Hunter-Weston MP*, p. 246.

14 Kronprinz von Rupprecht, *Mein Kriegstagebuch*, vol. 1, pp. 494–5 and 503.

18: Can't See the Wood for the Trees

1 Lieutenant-Colonel Ronald Fife, diary, brought to my attention by Major Roger Chapman and Steve Erskine, I WM Documents 19219.

2 Brigadier-General Sir James E. Edmonds, *History of the Great War: Military Operations: France and Belgium 1916, Volume 2 (1916 Official History, Vol. 2)*, p. 20.

3 *1916 Official History, Vol. 2*, pp. 6–15.

4 3 July 1916 entry in Haig's diary (*Haig's Diary*), and 'Note of interview between Sir D. Haig and General Joffre on 3rd July 1916 at Val Vion . . .'. Both documents are in NA WO 256/11.

5 4 July 1916 entry in *Haig's Diary*.

6 *1916 Official History, Vol. 2*, pp. 15–17; 3 July 1916 entry in 1st Royal Welch Fusiliers war diary, NA WO 95/1665.

7 As with the extract from Sassoon's *Memoirs of an Infantry Officer* in Chapter 16, I have not found an account that corroborates the facts in this extract. All we know is that the account by the battalion's commanding officer, Lieutenant-Colonel Clifton Stockwell, confirms that Sassoon was commended for the part he played in the operation (see *Regimental Records of the Royal Welch Fusiliers*, p. 202). We also know that the battalion sent a patrol across the gap separating the eastern end of Quadrangle Trench and the western end of Wood Trench in a bid to help the 2nd Royal Irish Regiment (see 5 July 1916 entry in the battalion war diary, NA WO 95/1665). In addition, we know that men were killed during the 5 July operation. All these facts are consistent with Sassoon's account.

8 Siegfried Sassoon, *Memoirs of an Infantry Officer*, pp. 87–91.

9 Llewelyn Wyn Griffith, *Up to Mametz (Wyn Griffith Book)*, pp. 146–50.

10 *Wyn Griffith Book*, p. 200.

11 'Personal Notes on the operations about Mametz Wood as far as the 115th Brigade is concerned' by Brigadier-General Horatio Evans, Regimental Museum, The Royal Welch Fusiliers, brought to my attention by its curator Anne Pedley.

12 *Wyn Griffith Book*, p. 216.

13 The time is in the 7 July 1916 entry of the 115th Brigade war diary, NA WO 95/2560.

14 *Wyn Griffith Book*, p. 221

15 7 July 1916 entry in XV Corps war diary, NA WO 95/921.

16 7 July 1916 entries in 16th Welch Regiment and 11th South Wales Borderers war diaries, NA WO 95/2561 and 2562 respectively.

17 *Wyn Griffith Book*, pp. 219–28.

18 7 July 1916 entry in 12th Manchesters war diary, NA WO 95/2012.

19 'Narrative by Major-General T. D. Pilcher', NA WO 138/36, brought to my attention by William Spencer, the National Archives World War I expert.

20 *1916 Official History, Vol. 2*, pp. 57–8.

21 *Wyn Griffith Book*, p. 232.

22 Ibid., p. 243.

23 11 July 1916 entry in 115th Brigade war diary, NA WO 95/2560.

24 *Wyn Griffith Book*, p. 245.

25 *1916 Official History, Vol. 2*, p. 54.

26 Ibid.

27 '113th Infantry Brigade: Casualties for period July 6th–11th' in 113th Brigade file, NA WO 95/2552; '114th Infantry Brigade: Report on operations of 10th/11th July – attack on Mametz Wood' in 114th Brigade file, NA WO 95/2557; 12 July 1916 entry in 115th Brigade war diary, NA WO 95/2560.

28 *Wyn Griffith Book*, pp. 253–4.

19: Big Bang

1 General Sir Douglas Haig, letter to General Sir William Robertson 9 July 1916, 4th Army war diary, General Sir Henry Rawlinson, 4th Army papers, vol. 1, IWM Documents.

2 Lieutenant G. N. Kirkwood, note to 97th Brigade, 9 July 1916, file relating to 11th Borders' lack of discipline (*Borders' Enquiry File*), NA WO 32/17700.

3 Lieutenant-General Sir Hubert Gough, letter to Military Secretary, GHQ, 22 July 1916, in *Borders' Enquiry File*.

4 Adjutant General's letter to General Sir Douglas Haig 6 August 1916, *Borders' Enquiry File*.

5 10 July 1916 entry in Haig's diary, NA WO 256/11.

6 'Note of discussion as to attack on Longueval plateau and C-in-C's decision thereon' with 11 July 1916 entry in Haig's diary, NA WO 256/11.

7 General Sir Henry Rawlinson, letter to General Sir Douglas Haig 11 July 1916, with 11 July entries in Haig's diary, NA WO 256/11.

8 Note of 11 and 12 July 1916 telephone conversations between Rawlinson and Lieutenant-General Sir Launcelot Kiggell, Chief of the General Staff, with 11 July entries in Haig's diary NA WO 256/11.

9 Lieutenant-Colonel Frank Maxwell, 2 July 1916 letter in his papers, National Army Museum.

10 Lieutenant-Colonel Frank Maxwell, account, 12th Middlesex Regiment, NA WO 95/2044.

11 Brigadier-General Sir James E. Edmonds, *History of the Great War: Military Operations: France and Belgium 1916, Volume 2 (1916 Official History, Vol. 2)*, p. 67.

12 Ibid., pp. 69–74.

13 The artillery statistics in this chapter come from the note about comparative artillery used on 1 and 14 July 1916 in General Sir Henry Rawlinson's papers, Army Museum, 1952-01-33-71.

14 Major-General Sir H. H. Tudor, NA CAB 45/191.

15 Neil Fraser-Tytler, *Field Guns in France*, p. 89.

16 Major John Bates, letters, IWM Documents 2854.

17 *1916 Official History, Vol. 2*, pp. 86–7.

18 Pat Leonard, IWM Documents 16268.

19 J. M. Brereton, *A History of the 4th/7th Royal Dragoon Guards and their Predecessors 1685–1980*, pp. 326–7; *1916 Official History, Vol. 2*, p. 88.

20: Surrounded

1 17 July 1916 entry in Haig's diary.

2 14 and 15 July 1916 entries in 9th Division war diary, NA WO 95/1735.

3 1st South African Brigade report by Brigadier-General Tim Lukin to 9th Division's Major-General Bill Furse (*South African Brigade's Report*), that brigade's file, NA WO 95/1777.

4 Dudley Meredith, account (*Meredith's Memoir*), South African National Museum of Military History, acq. no. 4134, brought to my attention by Ian Uys.

5 Herbert Nock, account, NASA, Ian Uys collection, A2029, vol. 24.

6 Harry Cooper, in Ian Uys, *Delville Wood*, p. 80.

7 Ian Uys, *Roll Call*, p. 132.

8 *South African Brigade's Report*.

9 Uys, *Delville Wood*, p. 112.

10 *South African Brigade's Report*.

11 17 July 1916 entry in Henry Rawlinson's diary, Churchill College Archives Centre, RWLN 1/5.

12 Uys, *Roll Call*, p. 75.

13 Ibid.

14 Ibid., p. 78.

15 Alf Mandy, in Uys, *Roll Call*, p. 77.

16 17 and 18 July 1916 entries in 9th Division's 'Narrative of Events: From July 1st to July 19th 1916' (*9th Division Narrative*), NA WO 95/1777; and *South African Brigade's Report*.

17 18 July 1916 entry in *9th Division Narrative*.

18 Ernest Solomon, *Potchefstroom to Delville Wood* (*Solomon's Book*), pp. 63 and 65–9.

19 18 July 1916 entry in 9th Division war diary, NA WO 95/1777, and *South African Brigade's Report*.

20 18 July 1916 entry in 1st South African Battalion war diary, NA WO 95/1780.

21 Private Pauls, undated statement, *In Memoriam to the memory of two heroic brothers* (*Tatham Book*), p. 24, in NASA, Ian Uys collection, A2029, vol. 24.

22 Private William Poole, 30 July 1916 statement, *Tatham Book*, p. 27.

23 Private William Helfrich, 28 August 1916 statement, *Tatham Book*, pp. 31–4, with extra details supplied from statement recorded on 27 August 1916 by Cecile Tatham, Errol's sister, *Tatham Book*, p. 28.

24 *South African Brigade's Report*.

25 17 July 1916 entry in *9th Division Narrative*.

26 Private Frank Marillier, in Uys, *Roll Call*, pp. 93–4.

27 John A. Lawson, *Memories of Delville Wood: South Africa's Great Battle*, pp. 12–15.

28 Uys, *Roll Call*, p. 95, says the message was sent at 5.30 p.m. However, this statement should be treated with caution given that the content of the message and other testimony suggests it might have been sent earlier.

29 *Solomon's Book*, pp. 69–70.

30 *Meredith's Memoir*.

31 18 and 19 July 1916 entries in *9th Division Narrative* and 9th Division war diary; 'Attack on Longueval and Delville Wood', report by the commander of 53rd Brigade, in 53rd Brigade file, NA WO 95/2034.

32 Corporal Lilford, in Uys, *Roll Call*, pp. 89–90.

33 Ibid.

34 Captain Richard Medlicott, in NASA, Ian Uys collection, A2029, vol. 23.

35 Richard Unwin (the name he used while in the army; his real surname was Postlethwaite), interview transcript in NASA, Ian Uys collection, A2029, vol. 24; and Private Bernard Leffler, in Uys, *Roll Call*, p. 102.

36 *9th Division Narrative*; 20 July 1916 entry in 76th Brigade war diary, in its file, NA WO 95/1433.

37 Uys, *Roll Call*, pp. 106–7 and 113–14; and *South African Brigade's Report*.

38 Casualty list in South African Brigade file, NA WO 95/1777, referred to in the *South African Brigade's Report.*

39 Nigel Cave Delville Wood, *Pen and Sword,* p. 125. Everard Wyrall, *The 17th Battalion Royal Fusiliers,* and A. Hilliard Atteridge, *History of the 17th (Northern) Division,* p. 158.

40 Quoted in Uys, *Delville Wood,* p. 205.

21: Repulsed

1 Volume 5 of 4th Army records: GHQ Letters, IWM Documents.

2 Congratulations from Haig mentioned in 14 July 1916 entry in Haig's diary, NA WO 256/11.

3 In a successful bid to protect the left wing of the 14 July 1916 attack, III Corps' 1st Division had captured Contalmaison Villa at 3.45 p.m. that day, having taken Lower Wood (a short distance north of the north-west corner of Mametz Wood) at 10.45 p.m. on 13 July, as was noted in Brigadier-General Sir James E. Edmonds, *History of the Great War: Military Operations: France and Belgium 1916, Volume 2 (1916 Official History, Vol. 2),* p. 68.

4 34th Division order 14 July 1916 sent out at 11.55 p.m., NA WO 95/2432.

5 *1916 Official History, Vol.* 2, p. 101.

6 General Sir Henry Rawlinson, diary entry 16 June 1916, his documents, Churchill College, 1/5.

7 15 July 1916 entry in 10th Royal Fusiliers war diary, NA WO 95/2532.

8 16 July 1916 entry in 112th Brigade war diary, NA WO 95/2535, and 15–16 July 1916 entries in 10th Royal Fusiliers war diary, NA WO 95/2532.

22: A Terrible Mistake

1 'Note of Commander-in-Chief's instructions . . .' received by 4th Army, 21 June 1916, 4th Army Records: GHQ letters: Rawlinson's papers, vol. 5, IWM Documents.

2 Major-General C. H. Harington, in his capacity as Major-General 2nd Army, note to 1st and 2nd Army units and headquarters, 13 July 1916, 1st Army file, NA WO 95/165.

3 Ibid.

4 5th Australian Division Order No. 31, 16 July 1916, in AWM4 1/50/5 Part 2.

5 Waldo Zander, AWM 2DRL 171.

6 Brigadier-General Harold Elliott, letter to Captain C. E. W. Bean 17 August 1926, in Official History 1914–18 War: Records of C. E. W. Bean, Official

Historian: Diaries and Notebooks, AWM38 3DRL 606/243A/1 (*Bean's Fromelles Diaries and Notebooks A*), pp. 249–50.

7 Ross McMullin, *Pompey Elliott*, p. 208.

8 C. E. W. Bean, Historical Note, undated, and 12 July 1926 letter from McCay to Bean, in Official History 1914–18 War: Records of C. E. W. Bean, Official Historian: Diaries and Notebooks, AWM38 3DRL 606/243B/1, p. 19 and p. 65 respectively.

9 *The Australian Imperial Force in France: Volume III: 1916 (Australian Official History, Vol. III)*, p. 347.

10 Ibid.

11 Haking's letter to Monro, 17 July 1916, in XI Corps file, NA WO/95 881.

12 *Australian Official History, Vol. III*, pp. 349–50.

13 'Report on operations on front of XI Corps on 17th July and 19th/20th July 1916 against Enemy's trenches from Fauquissart to Trivelet Road to Ferme Delangre', in XI Corps file, AWM4 1/22/4 Part 2.

14 A note headed 'Attached Troops, Heavy Artillery', 16 July 1916, in 5th Australian war diary file, AWM4 1/50/5 Part 4, and in XI Corps war diary file, AWM4 1/22/4 Part 3, suggests that thirty-five howitzers with 6-inch or more than 6-inch calibres were available; *Australian Official History, Vol. III*, p. 337, states the number of such howitzers 'appears to have been' twenty-eight. As is often the case, it is hard to find documents that clearly give the precise number of howitzers used.

15 Haking's order to attacking divisions, 16 July 1916.

16 Brigadier-General Elliott's letter to his wife 19 July 1916, in Papers of Brigadier Harold Elliott, Series 5, Wallet 3, in AWM 2DRL/0513 (*Elliott's Fromelles Papers*).

17 Private Henry Williams, 17 July 1916 letter, in *Bean's Fromelles Diaries and Notebooks A*, p. 63.

18 Ibid.

19 Lieutenant-Colonel F. W. Toll, report dated 21 July 1916 in Appendix C (*Toll's C Report*) of 31st Battalion war diary, AWM4 23/48/12.

20 Kathleen Thyer's letter quoting a boyfriend who served in 8th Brigade's 32nd Battalion, in Eric Chinner's papers, SLV MSB 177: MS10191.

21 Sergeant Francis Law, *Recollections of the Battle of Fromelles, 19 July 1916*, undated, in *Bean's Fromelles Diaries and Notebooks A*, p. 134 (*Law's Report*).

22 Lieutenant-Colonel F. W. Toll, report on operation in Appendix D (*Toll's D Report*) of 31st Battalion file, AWM4 23/48/12.

23 *Law's Report*, *Toll's C Report* and *Toll's D Report*.

24 *Toll's D Report*.

25 The description of 2nd/7th Royal Warwickshire regiment's action comes from its commanding officer's *Report on Operations 19-7-1916*, dated 21 July

1916, and the *Report on Action of 19th July 1916* written by 182nd Brigade's commander on 21 July 1916 (*182nd Brigade Report*), both of which are with the 2nd/7th Royal Warwicks' war diary in NA WO/95 3056, and *Evidence from 2/7 Warwicks as to German Casualties* sent by 61st Division's commander to XI Corps, which is in the 61st Division file, NA WO/95 3033.

26 Untitled and undated list of messages sent to 61st Division's Artillery HQ, in 61st Division file (*61st Division Artillery Message List*), NA WO/95 3033.

27 2nd/6th Royal Warwickshire Regiment war diary, in NA WO/95 3056 and *182nd Brigade Report*, 61st Division's *Report on Proceedings 15th to 19th July 1916*, 184th Brigade's *Report on Operations 19th/20th July 1916* (*184th Brigade Report*).

28 2nd/1st Buckinghamshire Battalion war diary, in NA WO/95 3066, and *184th Brigade Report*.

29 *61st Division Artillery Message List*.

30 15th Australian Brigade *Report on Action 19th/20th July 1916*, in 15th Australian Brigade file, AWM4 23/15/5, p. 55.

31 *Operations 19th July 1916 (5th Australian Division Summary of Operations)*, a summary of operations in 5th Australian Division file, AWM4 1/50/5 July Part 6, p. 24.

32 Message in 15th Australian Brigade file, p. 76.

33 Ibid., p. 61.

34 Ibid., p. 78.

35 Ross McMullin, *Pompey Elliott*, p. 234.

36 Elliott papers, letter to his wife 20 July 1916, in *Elliott's Fromelles Papers*.

37 7.35 p.m. message in 15th Australian Brigade file, p. 73.

38 Permission to use 58th Battalion: at 7.35 p.m. according to 15th Australian Brigade file, p. 84. Reports of 60th Battalion in German lines: entries for 6.45 and 7.06 p.m. in *5th Australian Division Summary of Operations* in 5th Australian Division file, Part 6, pp. 25–6; 6.30 a.m. original message in 15th Australian Brigade file, p. 61, leading to the aforementioned 6.45 pm. entry; and 7.18 p.m. entry in *Narrative of events 17.7.1916 to 20/7/1916* in 14th Australian Brigade file, AWM4 23/14/4, p. 90.

39 184th Brigade to 15th Australian Brigade message, in 15th Australian Brigade file, p. 71.

40 *Report on Operations 15th to 19th July 1916*, in 61st Division file.

41 Message in 61st Division file.

42 Note of Elliott's comment in *Bean's Fromelles Diaries and Notebooks A*, p. 116.

43 5th Australian Division file, Part 6, p. 28, and the 9 p.m. order itself in XI Corps file, NA WO 95/881.

44 15th Australian Brigade file, p. 56.

45 *Australian Official History, Vol. III*, p. 395.

46 Ibid.

23: Sacrifice of the Australians

1 5th Australian Division file, Part 6, p. 28, under 10.10 p.m. entry, and 10.10 p.m. message from XI Corps to the 1st Army mentioning the sighting, in X Corps file.

2 'Notes on Interview with General McCay', in X Corps file.

3 Waldo Zander, AWM 2DRL 171 (*Zander's Report*).

4 Captain T. C. Barbour in Records of C. E. W. Bean, Official Historian: Diaries and Notebooks, AWM38 3DRL 606/243A/1 (*Bean's Fromelles Diaries and Notebooks A*), pp. 180–1.

5 'Instructions for Infantry Brigadiers' sent to them by 5th Australian Division's Major-General James McCay on 15 July 1916, in 14th Australian Brigade file, AWM4 23/14/4, pp. 39–41.

6 *The Australian Imperial Force in France: Volume III: 1916* (*Australian Official History, Vol. III*), p. 379, and Lieutenant-Colonel Cass's report 21 July 1916 (*Cass 14th Brigade Report*), in 14th Australian Brigade file, AWM4 23/14/4, p. 102.

7 22 July 1916 'Report on Condition of German Trenches' by Lieutenant-Colonel Cass, in 14th Australian Brigade file, p. 95.

8 *Bean's Fromelles Diaries and Notebooks A*, p. 38.

9 A. G. Butler, *The Official History of the Australian Army Medical Services in the War of 1914–1918, Volume 2: The Western Front*, p. 44.

10 Account by L. Colley-Priest, in SLNSW MLMSS 2439, Item 1.

11 Account by W. J. A. Allsop, 8th Field Ambulance, in SLNSW MLMSS 1606, Item 1.

12 *Bean's Fromelles Diaries and Notebooks A*, p. 47.

13 5th Australian Division, Summary of Operations, p. 25.

14 'Report on 19th/20th July 1916', in 15th Australian Brigade file, AWM4 23/15/5 (internet p. 56).

15 See note 43 and 10.16 p.m. 15th Brigade to 5th Australian Division in 5th Australian Division, Summary of Operations, 5th Australian Division file, Part 6, p. 28; 11.16 p.m. 15th Brigade to 5th Australian Division in 15th Australian Brigade file, p. 97.

16 15th Australian Brigade file, p. 102.

17 00.45 a.m. entry in 20 July 1916 entry in 'Operations 19 July 1916', 5th Australian Division file, Part 6, p. 45.

18 61st Division 'Report on operations 15th to 19th July 1916' in 61st Division file, NA WO/95 3033.

19 *Bean's Fromelles Diaries and Notebooks A*, p. 40.

20 Major R. O. Cowey's report in ibid., p. 217.

21 Captain Charles Mills, letter to Charles Bean 29 June 1926 in *Bean's Fromelles Diaries and Notebooks A*, p. 152.

22 Captain A. R. White, 'Report on operations 19/20 July 1916', in 32nd Battalion file, AWM4 23/49/12, p. 12, and his undated reply to Bean's 1 November 1926 letter in *Bean's Fromelles Diaries and Notebooks A*, p. 168.

23 Cass's messages from 3.20 a.m. until 4.20 a.m. in *Bean's Fromelles Diaries and Notebooks A*, p. 41, and 14th Australian Brigade file, pp. 152–3 and 155.

24 Note in 5th Australian Division file, Part 6, p. 51.

25 *Bean's Fromelles Diaries and Notebooks A*, p. 48, and 14th Australian Brigade narrative, in 14th Australian Brigade file, p. 92.

26 Report on Operation 'Assault on and attempt to consolidate enemy's trenches N10 c13 to N10 c14 on the 19th and 20th July 1916', dated 21 July 1916 in 31st Battalion file, AWM4 23/48/12.

27 *Zander's Report.*

28 Captain S. A. Pinkstone of 55th Battalion, letter to Bean 10 September 1926 in *Bean's Fromelles Diaries and Notebooks A*, pp. 228–9; *Australian Official History, Vol. III*, p. 429, suggests Pinkstone saw this counter-attack on the Australian right whereas it was on its left.

29 Sergeant Francis Law, *Recollections of the Battle of Fromelles, 19 July 1916*, undated, in *Bean's Fromelles Diaries and Notebooks A*, p. 134.

30 *Bean's Fromelles Diaries and Notebooks A*, p. 42.

31 Ibid., p. 43.

32 Ibid.

33 'Summary of Events at Adv. XI Corps HQ', in XI Corps file, AWM4 1/22/4 Part 3, p. 27.

34 *Bean's Fromelles Diaries and Notebooks A*, p. 48.

35 'Notes by Lt Colonel Cass, 54th Battalion, for Mr Bean's personal use' (*Cass Notes*), in *Bean's Fromelles Diaries and Notebooks A*, pp. 28–9; *Cass 14th Brigade Report* in 14th Australian Brigade file, pp. 103–4; 'Report by Lieut-Col DM McConaghy CMG Commanding 55th Battalion AIF on the operations of 55th Battalion during attack on German lines on the night of 19th–20th July', in 14th Australian Brigade file, p. 106.

36 3 April 1918 letter from 55th Battalion's Sergeant Bert White in *Bean's Fromelles Diaries and Notebooks A*, p. 60; *Cass Notes* in ibid., p. 29.

37 *Cass 14th Brigade Report* in 14th Australian Brigade file, p. 104; Lieutenant-Colonel F. W. Toll, report on operation in Appendix D of 31st Battalion file, p. 30.

38 Captain R. Hugh Knyvett, *'Over There' with the Australians* (*Knyvett*), p. 155.

39 'Report on Work done by Ambulance during action of 19th 20th 21st July', in 15th Field Ambulance file, AWM4 26/58/3, p. 24; 20 July 1916 entry in 5th Australian Division's Assistant Director of Medical Services war diary, AWM4 26/22/6 Part 1.

40 Sergeant Reginald Gray, account, Turnbull Library MS Papers 4134, Folder 2.

41 *Knyvett*, pp. 156–9.

42 Billy Miles, letter to Bean 30 July 1929, in *Bean's Fromelles Diaries and Notebooks A*, pp. 91–4; Major Murdoch, letters to Bean 19 and 24 May and 20 June 1926, *Bean's Fromelles Diaries and Notebooks B*, pp. 57 and 59.

43 General McCay, letter to Bean 6 June in *Bean's Fromelles Diaries and Notebooks B*, p. 61, and 5th Australian Division file, AWM4 1/50/5 Part 1, p. 6.

44 5th Australian Division file, AWM4 1/50/5 Part 1, p. 6.

45 Brigadier-General Elliott's letter to his wife 24 July 1916, in Papers of Brigadier-General Harold Elliott, Series 5, Wallet 3, AWM 2DRL/0513.

46 *Australian Official History, Vol. III*, p. 441.

47 Different casualty figures are given in: *Australian Official History, Vol. III*, p. 442; XI Corps Report, AWM4 1/22/4 Part 2, p. 18; 5th Australian Division file, Part 3, p. 33; 61st Division file in NA WO/95 3033.

48 Different casualty figures are given in: *Australian Official History, Vol. III*, p. 442; XI Corps Report, AWM4 1/22/4 Part 2, p. 18; 5th Australian Division file, Part 3, p. 33; 61st Division file in NA WO/95 3033; 60th Australian Battalion war diary, AWM4 23/77/7; 50th Australian Battalion war diary, AWM4 23/76/6.

49 Haking's report to 1st Army 24 July 1916 in XI Corps file; Haking's report to 1st Army 26 July 1916 in 5th Australian Division file, Part 3, p. 38.

50 Records of C. E. W. Bean, Official Historian: Diaries and Notebooks, AWM38 3DRL 606/52/1, pp. 26–7.

51 Ibid., AWM38 3DRL 606/237/1.

52 G. Christie-Miller, account, vol. 2 in IWM Documents 80/32/1.

53 XI Corps 18 July 1916 order, 'To the Troops of the 61st Division and the 5th Australian Division', in XI Corps file, AWM4 1/22/4 Part 2.

24: The Charge

1 C. E. W. Bean, *Official History of Australia in the War of 1914–1918, Volume 3* (*Australian Official History, Vol. 3*), p. 468.

2 Hubert Gough, *The Fifth Army*, pp. 102–23, 136–7; and his *Soldiering On, Being the Memoirs of General Sir Hubert Gough*, pp. 117, 122 and 126–8.

3 Brigadier-General Sir James E. Edmonds, *History of the Great War: Military Operations: France and Belgium 1916, Volume 2* (*1916 Official History, Vol. 2*), p. 102.

4 20 July 1916 entry in Haig's diary.

5 *Australian Official History, Vol. 3*, p. 483.

6 Ibid.

7 *1916 Official History, Vol. 2*, pp. 112–13.

8 Reserve Army Operation Order No. 13, 21 July 1916, in 5th Army file (the Reserve Army was later renamed 5th Army), NA WO 95/518.

9 Captain H. R. J. Harris, account, AWM 1DRL/0337 (*Harris's Report*).

10 3rd Australian Battalion war diary, AWM4 23/20/17.

11 Paul Maze, *A Frenchman in Khaki* (*Maze*), pp. 149–50.

12 Ibid., p. 142.

13 C. E. W. Bean, Official Historian, Diaries and Notebooks, AWM38 3DRL 606/244/1, p. 82.

14 A. H. Smith, NSW MLMSS 3046, letter to his mother 28 July 1916.

15 A. Dunlop, AWM PR00676.

16 Information concerning the 22 July 1916 attack taken from: 3rd Australian Brigade's Operation Memorandum no. 13 dated 21 July 1916, and 'Report on operations about Pozières 19th–26th July 1916', both in AWM4 23/3/9; 'Report on operations carried out by 9th (Australian) Infantry Battalion commencing 19th July and concluding 0400 25th July 1916', AWM4 23/26/19; and *Australian Official History, Vol. 3*, pp. 489–90.

17 Sergeant Philip Browne, AWM 1DRL/0428.

18 Fred Barbour, letter dated 24 November 1916 in Bean, Official Historian: Diaries and Notebooks, AWM38 3DRL 606/244/1, p. 105.

19 *Maze*, p. 158.

20 Douglas Horton, account, AWM 3DRL/0359.

21 'Short account of the operations of 1st Australian Infantry Brigade resulting in the capture of Pozières', in 1st Australian Brigade file, AWM4 23/1/12, p. 148.

22 *Harris's Report*.

23 Lieutenant Keith McConnel, AWM 2DRL/0029.

24 *Maze*, p. 161.

25 Lieutenant Keith McConnel, AWM 2DRL/0029.

26 *Australian Official History, Vol. 3*, pp. 499–500.

27 Quotes and information taken from: Lieutenant Arthur Blackburn, letter dated 4/9/1916, AWM 3DRL/6392; Blackburn report dated 28 July 1916 in Bean, Official Historian, Diaries and Notebooks, AWM38 3DRL 606/244/1, pp. 140–2; 10th Australian Battalion war diary, AWM4 23/27/9; and *Australian Official History, Vol. 3*, pp. 509–14.

28 Lieutenant E. W. D. Laing, 30 July 1916 letter, AWM 1DRL/0404; *Australian Official History, Vol. 3*, pp. 506–7.

25: An Eye for an Eye

1 Brigadier-General Sir James E. Edmonds, *History of the Great War: Military Operations: France and Belgium 1916, Volume 2* (*1916 Official History, Vol. 2*), pp. 136–41.

2 Douglas Horton (*Horton's Account*), AWM 3DRL/0359.

3 C. E. W. Bean, *Official History of Australia in the War of 1914–1918, Volume 3* (*Australian Official History, Vol. 3*), pp. 515–16.

4 Lieutenant Elmer Laing, AWM 1DRL/0404.

5 Ibid.

6 Corporal Archibald Barwick, NSW MLMSS 7229.

7 Lieutenant James Aitken, AWM 1DRL/0013.

8 Company Sergeant-Major Frederick Callaway, 2 August 1916 letter, AWM PR87/237.

9 Lieutenant Walter Host, Red Cross file: 21 November 1916 report by W. H. Shepard of 2nd Australian Battalion.

10 Ibid.: 9 February 1917 report by A. E. Ray of 2nd Australian Battalion.

11 Lieutenant Walter Waterhouse, NSW MLMSS 2792.

12 2nd Lieutenant J. E. G. Stevenson, AWM 3DRL/2995.

13 *Horton's Account.*

14 Colonel A. G. Butler, *The Official History of the Australian Army Medical Services in the War of 1914–1918. Volume 2: The Western Front*, p. 58.

15 Albert Coates, SLV MS 10345.

16 A. Dunlop, AWM PR00676.

17 Captain H. R. J. Harris, account, AWM 1DRL/0337.

18 'Report on situation at 1200 on 24/7/16 in line held by 4th Bn. in 1 Australian Brigade file', AWM4 23/1/12, pp. 170–1.

19 'Report on the operations of 1st Australian Division at Pozières in 1st Australian Division file', AWM4 1/42/18 July Part 2, p. 6.

20 7th Australian Battalion war diary, AWM4 23/24/17.

21 *Australian Official History, Vol. 3*, p. 560.

22 Ibid., pp. 564–7; and 5th Australian Battalion war diary, AWM4 23/22/17.

23 4th Australian Battalion war diary, AWM4 23/21/17; *Australian Official History, Vol. 3*, p. 571.

24 *Australian Official History, Vol. 3*, p. 573; and 8th Australian Battalion war diary, AWM4 23/25/19.

25 'Report on operations from 1200 24/7/16 to 2011 25th inst. in 1st Australian Brigade file' AWM4 23/1/12, pp. 176–7.

26 6th Australian Battalion war diary, AWM4 23/23/8.

27 Lieutenant-Colonel Iven Mackay, to 1st Infantry Brigade 25 July (no time given), in 1st Australian Brigade file, AWM4 23/1/12, p. 179.

28 *Australian Official History, Vol. 3*, pp. 575–8 and 582–5.

29 Ibid., pp. 587–8.

30 6th Australian Battalion war diary, AWM4 23/23/8, and *Australian Official History, Vol. 3*, p. 590.

31 7th Australian Battalion war diary, AWM4 23/24/17.

32 Ibid. and *Australian Official History, Vol. 3*, pp. 590–1.

33 7th Australian Battalion war diary, AWM4 23/24/17, and *Australian Official History, Vol. 3*, p. 591.

34 *Australian Official History, Vol. 3*, p. 592.
35 Ibid., p. 593.
36 Private V. A. Bowman, AWM IDRL/0141.
37 E. J. Rule, *Jacka's Mob*, p. 61.

26: The Check

1 C. E. W. Bean, *Official History of Australia in the War of 1914–1918, Volume 3 (Australian Official History, Vol. 3)*, p. 600.
2 Ibid., p. 604. His chief of staff on the Somme was Lieutenant-Colonel A. H. Bridges.
3 Legge's character sketch in Coulthard-Clark, *No Australians Need Apply (Legge Biography)*, pp. 63–5, 74–9, 106, 138, 155, and C. E. W. Bean, Official Historian, Diaries and Notebooks, AWM38 3DRL 606/40/1, pp. 46–54 (online pp. 45–9).
4 1st A. & N.Z.A.C. Order No. 16, 26 July 1916, in 2nd Australian Division file, AWM4 1/44/12; and Second Australian Divisional Orders Nos 35 and 36, 28 July 1916.
5 *Australian Official History, Vol. 3*, p. 621.
6 Second Australian Divisional Order No. 36, 28 July 1916, in AWM4 1/44/12 Part 2, p. 28, and First Australian Divisional Artillery: Narrative of Events in AWM4 13/10/22, p. 46.
7 *Legge Biography*, p. 206.
8 Bean, Official Historian, Diaries and Notebooks, AWM38 3DRL 606/40/1, pp. 46–54 (online pp. 45–9).
9 Captain Aubrey Wiltshire, account, in NSW MLMSS 3058.
10 Arthur Clifford, account (*Clifford's Account*), in Florence Breed, *From France with Love 1916–1918: The Deeds of Wimmera Diggers on the Somme*, pp. 62–4.
11 *Clifford's Account*.
12 Ibid.
13 Gellibrand told Bean that 22nd and 24th Battalion casualties were about 25 per cent of the men, AWM38 3DRL 606/54/1, p. 6 (online p. 5). 22nd Australian Battalion casualties in 27 July 1916 entry of its war diary, AWM4 23/39/11.
14 5th Australian Brigade war diary and file, AWM4 23/5/13 (online pp. 6 and 16).
15 Second Australian Divisional Order No. 35, 28 July 1916, AWM4 1/44/12 (online p. 24).
16 Peter S. Sadler, *The Paladin: A Life of Major-General Sir John Gellibrand*, p. 63.
17 Bean, Official Historian, Diaries and Notebooks, AWM38 3DRL 606/136/1, p. 5 (online p. 7).

18 Neville Browning, *The Blue & White Diamond (28th Australian Battalion's Regimental History)*, p. 148.

19 Ibid., p. 150.

20 Private Victor Graham, SLV MSB 4565/9.

21 Bean, Official Historian, Diaries and Notebooks, AWM38 3DRL 606/54/1, pp. 13–16 (online pp. 9–10).

22 Lieutenant-Colonel J. Walker, message sent at 2.28 a.m. on 29 July 1916, AWM4 23/7/11 (online pp. 43–4).

23 20th Australian Battalion and 5th Australian Brigade war diaries, AWM4 23/37/12 and 23/5/13 respectively.

24 Private Alec Macdonald, 28 November 1916 report under Lieutenant Patrick T. C. Bell (*Bell's Red Cross File*), in AWM 1DRL/0428; and Private Tom Young, in *28th Australian Battalion's Regimental History*, p. 154.

25 Private P. H. Parker, 31 July 1916, and John A. Glover, 4 December 1916, Frank Baker, 10 December 1916, Private Arnold Mills, 28 December (year unspecified but probably 1916), reports to Red Cross, in *Bell's Red Cross File*.

26 John A. C. Stuart, *28th Australian Battalion's Regimental History*, pp. 157–8.

27 Ibid., p. 158.

28 Private Fred Hocking, AWM PR88/161.

29 26th Australian Brigade war diary, AWM4 23/6/11.

30 'Brief Report on Operation carried out on 28th/29th July 1916', in 26th Australian Brigade file, AWM4 23/6/12 (internet p. 18).

31 25th and 28th Australian Battalions war diaries, 7th Australian Brigade file, and 'Second Australian Division Report on Operation 28/29 July 1916' in 2nd Australian Division file, AWM4 23/42/12, 23/45/16, 23/7/11 and 1/44/12 respectively.

32 Wisbey Sinclair, 26 November 1916 letter (*The Sinclair Letter*), in Private Noel George Sainsbury's personal file.

33 Arthur Bruce-Drayton, in report dated 7 January 1919, in Private Noel George Sainsbury's Red Cross file, AWM 1DRL/0428.

34 *The Sinclair Letter.*

35 Court of Inquiry conclusion dated 14 August 1916 in Lieutenant Robert Goldthorp Raws' personal file (*Goldthorp Raws' Personal File*) (internet p. 46).

36 Court of Inquiry dated 12 August 1916, in *Goldthorp Raws' Personal File* (internet p. 45).

37 Ibid.

38 Letter to brother Lennon Raws 3 August 1916, family file (*Raws' File*), in AWM 2DRL/0481.

39 Letter to sister 8 August 1916 in *Raws' File*.

40 Letter to brother-in-law 12 August 1916 in *Raws' File*.

41 Letter to sister 16 August 1916 in *Raws' File*.

42 Letter to father 19 August 1916 in *Raws' File*.

43 William Begley, 20 September 1916 report in Goldthorp Raws' Red Cross File, AWM 1DRL/0428, and Begley's personal file, in Series B2455.
44 Secretary, Wounded and Missing Persons Bureau, Australian Red Cross Society letter 12 January 1918, in Goldthorp Raws' Red Cross File.
45 Letter to Lennon Raws 19 August 1916 in *Raws' File*.

27: On Parole

1 Brigadier-General Sir James E. Edmonds, *History of the Great War: Military Operations: France and Belgium 1916, Volume 2 (1916 Official History, Vol. 2)*, pp. 163 and 167–9.
2 'Report on 30th Divn. operations July 24th–July 31st', in 30th Division file, NA WO 95/2310.
3 Ibid.
4 Sergeant A. E. Borland, 'Narrative of the part taken by D Coy., 2nd R.S.F. in the action at Guillemont on 30th July 1916', held by the Royal Highland Fusiliers Museum, brought to my attention by Major Ian Gordon, Greg Ward, Willie Gallacher and Sandy Leisham.
5 30 July 1916 entry in 18th Manchesters war diary, in its file, NA WO 95/2339.
6 30 July 1916 entries in 16th and 18th Manchesters war diaries, in their files, both in NA WO 95/2339.
7 *1916 Official History, Vol. 2*, p. 166.
8 Figures in war diary for 90th Brigade, in its file, NA WO 95/3327.
9 *1916 Official History, Vol. 2*, pp. 164, 166 and 171.
10 Ibid., pp. 167–9.
11 Winston Churchill, 1 August 1916 memorandum, NA CAB 37/153/3.
12 David R. Woodward, *Field Marshal Sir William Robertson: Chief of the Imperial General Staff in the Great War (Robertson Biography)*, p. 55.
13 Haig letter to Sir William Robertson 1 August 1916, in Robert Blake, ed., *The Private Papers of Douglas Haig 1914–1919*, pp. 157–8.
14 *Robertson Biography*, p. 57.
15 Edith Appleton, *A Nurse at the Front: The Great War Diaries of Sister Edith Appleton*, ed. Ruth Cowen (for full entry see Chapter 17, note 4), pp. 166–83.

28: Second Time Lucky

1 White's letter to Bean 1 May 1928, Bean's undated handwritten note of an interview with White in C. E. W. Bean, Official Historian, Diaries and Notebooks, AWM38 3DRL 606/244/1 (internet pp. 186 and 226), and the 29 July entry in Haig's diary.

2 2nd Australian Division war diary 29 July 1916, AWM4 1/44/12.

3 C. E. W. Bean, *Official History of Australia in the War of 1914–1918, Volume 3 (Australian Official History, Vol. 3)*, p. 650.

4 Ibid., p. 651.

5 Ibid., pp. 652–3.

6 Ibid., pp. 655–6, and 'Operations by 7th Field Company Australian Engineers: Battle of Somme' in 7th Field Company file, AWM4 14/26/7.

7 *Australian Official History, Vol. 3*, p. 664.

8 Bean's notes of interview with White on 6 August 1916 on pp. 118–19 of his notebook (internet pp. 98–9).

9 *Australian Official History, Vol. 3*, p. 652.

10 2nd Australian Division Order No. 37, 4 August 1916, AWM4 1/44/13 (internet August Part 2); 5th Australian Brigade Order No. 25, 4 August 1916, AWM4 23/5/14; 4 August 1916 entry in 6th Australian Brigade war diary, AWM4 23/6/12; 7th Australian Brigade Order No. 30, 4 August 1916, AWM4 23/7/12.

11 *Australian Official History, Vol. 3*, p. 664.

12 Alec Raws, letter to his sister 8 August 1916, in Lieutenant Robert Goldthorp Raws' family file (*Raws' File*). It does not specify what date he dug the assembly trench. I have assumed it was on the night of 31 July–1 August for the following reason: in his letter Alec Raws states that on the night in question a more senior officer was killed, and he (Alec) and another officer had to take over. The only officer in Alec's battalion who was killed during the time when the assembly trenches were being dug was Captain Frederick Ward. The sole report in Ward's Red Cross file that appears credible concerning the date states that Ward died of wounds incurred on the night of 31 July. However, that date may be incorrect. The 23rd Battalion war diary states Ward died on 3 August.

13 Ibid.

14 16 July 1916 letter to his brother-in-law in *Raws' File*.

15 12 August 1916 letter to his brother Lennon in ibid.

16 Ibid.

17 4 August 1916 letter to his friend Norman Bayles in *Raws' File*.

18 12 August 1916 letter to his brother Lennon in ibid.

19 Lieutenant-Colonel R. Smith, 22nd Australian Battalion, 8 August 1916 report to 6th Australian Brigade, in Bean, Official Historian, Diaries and Notebooks, AWM38 3DRL 606/244/1 (internet p. 174).

20 2nd Australian Division Order No. 37 dated 3 August 1916 in the 2nd Australian Division file, AWM4 1/44/13, contains bombardment times.

21 Sergeant Keith Anderson, AWM 2DRL/0151.

22 Lieutenant Blanchard in Lieutenant Leslie Pritchard's Red Cross file, AWM 1DRL/0428.

23 Casualties extracted from figures in the 22nd Australian Battalion war diary, July and August entries, in AWM4 23/39/11 and 23/39/12.

24 7th Australian Brigade to 2nd Australian Division, report dated 12 August 1916 (*7th Australian Brigade 4–5 August Report*), in 7th Australian Brigade file, AWM4 23/7/12.

25 Lieutenant Frank Corney, in AWM 2DRL 0948.

26 My version of what I have assumed to be the German, taking into account the translation reproduced in 'Extracts from diary of an officer of the 84th Regiment (sic) captured on night 4th/5th E. of Pozières', in Appendix to 1st Anzac Corps Summary (Intelligence) No. 14 (*1st Anzac Intelligence 14 Appendix*), from 6 p.m. on 6 August to 6 p.m. on 7 August 1916 (1 Anzac Intelligence 14 Appendix), AWM4 1/30/7.

27 My version of what I have assumed to be the German, taking into account the translation reproduced in 'Extract from a letter written by a prisoner of the 84th Regiment (sic) captured E. of Pozières on 4th/5th inst. Letter dated 2/8/16', in 1st Anzac Corps Summary (Intelligence) No. 13, from 6 p.m. on 5 August to 6 p.m. on 6 August 1916, AWM4 1/30/7.

28 *1st Anzac Intelligence 14 Appendix*.

29 *7th Australian Brigade 4–5 August Report*.

30 Ibid.

31 Report by 27th Battalion's adjutant Major Trevor Cunningham, Red Cross file, AWM 1DRL/0428.

32 Major Trevor Russell Cunningham, Personal File, NAA B2455.

33 *7th Australian Brigade 4–5 August Report*; 27th Australian Battalion's undated report to 7th Australian Brigade, AWM4 23/44/12; 28th Australian Battalion's 9 August 1916 report to 7th Australian Brigade, AWM4 23/45/17; and the story of the attack by 5th, 6th and 7th Brigade's battalions in *Australian Official History, Vol. 3*, pp. 674–7.

34 Department of Veterans' Affairs, *Simply Hell Let Loose: Stories of Australians at War*, pp. 51–2.

35 William Hatcher, personal file, NAA B2455.

29: Counter-Attack

1 2nd Australian Division message circulated to its brigades, in 7th Australian Brigade file, AWM4 23/7/12 (internet p. 126).

2 My version of what I have assumed to be the German, taking into account the translation that is reproduced in the report entitled 'Special Order of the Day' written by Lieutenant-Colonel Ray Leane, commanding officer of the 48th Australian Battalion, 10 August 1916.

3 C. E. W. Bean, *Official History of Australia in the War of 1914–1918, Volume 3* (*Australian Official History, Vol. 3*), pp. 707–8.

4 Major A. W. Leane of 28th Australian Brigade, 9 August 1916 report to 7th Australian Brigade in 28th Australian Battalion file, AWM4 23/45/17.

5 7th Australian Brigade file, AWM4 23/7/12 (internet p. 106).

6 Ibid.

7 Ibid., AWM4 23/7/12 (internet p. 110, 8 a.m. message, and p. 115, 8.44 a.m. message).

8 28th Australian Battalion report, 9 August 1916, in 28th Battalion file, AWM4 23/45/16.

9 12th Australian Brigade's 'Weekly report on operations between 4th and 11th August 1916', in 12th Australian Brigade file, AWM4 23/12/6.

10 Ray Leane, letter to Bean 6 June 1923 (*Ray Leane's Account*), in C. E. W. Bean, Official Historian, Diaries and Notebooks, AWM38 3DRL 606/244/1 (internet pp. 58–9).

11 Ben Leane, AWM 1DRL/0412.

12 Leane writing around seven years later specified 200 men lost; the war diary written contemporaneously specified about 100. Rightly or wrongly, I have assumed the latter figure is more likely to be correct.

13 *Ray Leane's Account*.

14 Ben Leane, AWM 1DRL/0412.

15 7th Australian Brigade message to 2nd Australian Division, 5 August 1916, 7th Australian Brigade file, AWM4 23/7/12 (internet p. 133).

16 Alec Raws, letter to his brother Lennon 12 August in Lieutenant Robert Goldthorp Raws' family file (*Raws' File*).

17 E. J. Rule, *Jacka's Mob*, pp. 62–70.

18 Lieutenant Lionel Carter, letter to Lieutenant-Colonel Ray Leane 8 August 1916; Lieutenant-Colonel Ray Leane, letter to Bean 7 June 1923; Professor H. Woollard, letter to Bean 21 July 1928: all in Bean, Official Historian, Diaries and Notebooks, AWM38 3DRL 606/244/1 (internet pp. 53–60 and 200); Ben Leane, AWM 1DRL/0412.

19 Brigadier-General Paton, report to 2nd Australian Division 7 August 1916, in 7th Australian Brigade file, AWM4 23/7/12 (internet p. 202).

20 *Australian Official History, Vol. 3*, pp. 718–20.

21 26th Battalion message to 7th Brigade in 7th Australian Brigade file, AWM4 23/7/12 (internet p. 199).

22 2nd Australian Division's Administrative Staff Headquarters file, AWM4 1/45/9 (internet pp. 16–25).

23 *Australian Official History, Vol. 3*, p. 723.

24 5 August 1916 entry in 25th Australian Battalion war diary, AWM4 23/42/13.

30: The Back Door

1 2nd Australian Division war diary, AWM4 1/44/13.

2 Roland Perry, *Monash: The Outsider Who Won a War*, p. 211.

3 C. E. W., Bean, Official Historian, Diaries and Notebooks, AWM38 3DRL 606/50/1 p.22 (internet p. 20).

4 Ibid., pp. 21–2 (internet pp. 19–20).

5 Eric Wren, *Randwick to Hargicourt: History of the 3rd Battalion, AIF*, p. 154.

6 Ibid., p. 19 (internet p. 17).

7 Perry, *Monash*, p. 247.

8 27 June 1916 letter to brother Lennon Raws, in Lieutenant Robert Goldthorp Raws' family file (*Raws' File*), AWM 2DRL/0481. Rightly or wrongly I have guessed what swear word was used by the British officer; in his letter Raws merely refers to the British officer using an 'Australian word'.

9 Ibid.

10 Ivan D. Chapman, *Iven G. Mackay: Citizen and Soldier*, p. 75.

11 4th Australian Division war diary, AWM4 1/48/4.

12 E. J. Rule, *Jacka's Mob*, p. 57.

13 4th Australian Division G.S. Circular No. 34, 14 July 1916, 4th Australian Division file, AWM4 1/48/4 (internet part 2 p. 17).

14 4th Australian Division war diary, AWM4 1/48/4.

15 Neville Browning, *Fix Bayonets: The History of the 51st Battalion A.I.F.*, pp. 26–7.

16 4th Australian Division war diary, AWM4 1/48/4.

17 1st Anzac Order No. 21, 7 August 1916, AWM4 1/29/7.

18 Haig to Rawlinson and Gough in 4th Army papers, GHQ letters, IWM Documents.

19 Brigadier-General Sir James E. Edmonds, *History of the Great War: Military Operations: France and Belgium 1916, Volume 2*, pp. 215–16.

20 16th Australian Battalion war diary, AWM4 23/33/9. Australian operations 8–11 August 1916 taken from C. E. W. Bean, *Official History of Australia in the War of 1914–1918, Volume 3 (Australian Official History, Vol. 3)*, pp. 734–51.

21 Armitage specified about 800 yards, but I have preferred his commanding officer's specification – 750 yards – in Major Jacob Ross's report in R. R. Freeman, *Hurcombe's Hungry Half Hundred: A Memorial History of the 50th Battalion A.I.F. 1916–1919 (Freeman's 50th Battalion History)*, p. 60; a three-minute bombardment of the German front line is confirmed by 'Artillery Order No. 5 by G.O.C.R.A. 1st A.N.Z.A.C.', 12 August 1916.

22 Captain H. E. S. Armitage, AWM 1DRL 0053.

23 *Australian Official History, Vol. 3*, pp. 755–6.

24 Captain Jim Churchill-Smith in *Freeman's 50th Battalion History* (*Churchill-Smith's Account in Freeman*), pp. 61–2.

25 Ibid., p. 63.

26 13th Australian Brigade war diary, AWM4 23/30/22.

27 *Australian Official History, Vol. 3*, pp. 753–5.

28 Ibid.

29 Ibid., p. 763.

30 Ibid.

31 Ibid.

32 *Churchill-Smith's Account in Freeman*, p. 63.

33 Corporal Duncan, undated statement in Lieutenant Victor Dridan, Red Cross file, AWM 1DRL/0428.

34 2nd Lieutenant A. Mills, 9 November 1916 statement in Lieutenant Victor Dridan, Red Cross file, AWM 1DRL/0428.

35 Ibid.

36 Commanding Officer (not named), letter 14 November 1916, 13th Australian Field Ambulance in Lieutenant Victor Dridan, Red Cross file, AWM 1DRL/0428.

37 Brigadier-General Brudenell White, letter 12 August 1916 to 4th Australian Division, in 4th Australian Division file, AWM4 1/48/5 (internet 4 August, Australian Division file Part 2, pp. 14–15).

38 *Australian Official History, Vol. 3*, p. 759.

39 Lieutenant-Colonel Arthur Ross to 13th Australian Brigade, in 51st Australian Battalion file, AWM4 23/68/6 (internet p. 16); and *Australian Official History, Vol. 3*, p. 764.

40 13th Australian Brigade, 20 August 1916, 'Summary of Operations: Period 12th to 16th August inclusive', in 13th Australian Brigade file, AWM4 23/13/7 (internet pp. 38–9).

41 'Artillery Order No. 6 by G.O.C.R.A. 1st Anzac', 14 August 1916, in 4th Australian Division file, AWM4 1/48/5 (internet Part 2 pp. 38–40).

42 Lieutenant-Colonel Arthur Ross to 13th Australian Brigade, in 51st Australian Battalion file, AWM4 23/68/6 (internet p. 16).

43 13th Australian Brigade message, which appears to have been sent at 4.20 p.m. on 15 August 1916, in 13th Australian Brigade file, AWM4 23/13/7 (internet p. 24); and 15 August entry in 4th Australian Division war diary, AWM4 1/48/5 (internet Part 1 p. 23).

44 12 and 14 August 1916 entries in 13th Australian Battalion war diary, AWM4 23/30/22.

45 'Amended Casualties', 21 August 1916, in 13th Australian Brigade file, AWM4 23/13/7.

46 Frank Dawson of 51st Australian Battalion's A Company, in 2nd Lieutenant Oscar M. Chilvers' Red Cross file, AWM 1DRL/0428.

47 Corporal F. B. Deane of 51st Australian Battalion, in 2nd Lieutenant Oscar M. Chilvers' Red Cross file, AWM 1DRL/0428.

48 2nd Lieutenant Oscar M. Chilvers, personal service record in NAA Series B2455.

49 'Summary of Operations: 13th Australian Infantry Brigade: Period 12th to 16th August inclusive', 20 August 1916, in 13th Australian Brigade file, AWM4 23/13/7 (internet p. 39); and 16 August 1916 entry of 1st Australian Division war diary, AWM4 1/42/19.

50 *Australian Official History, Vol. 3*, pp. 726–7; and 'Fourth Australian Division Casualties for 29-7-16 to 16-8-16' in 4th Australian Division file, AWM4 1/48/5 (internet Part 3 p. 15).

51 14 August 1916 entry in 4th Australian Division war diary, AWM4 1/48/5 (internet Part 1 p. 20).

31: Butchers

1 Lieutenant A. S. Lloyd, letter to his wife Margot 6 July 1916, in his file (*Lloyd File*), IWM Documents, Con Shelf.

2 Ibid., 13 July 1916, in *Lloyd File*.

3 Ibid., 19 July 1916, in *Lloyd File*.

4 Ibid., 22 July 1916, in *Lloyd File*.

5 Ibid., letter 21 July 1916: recipient not disclosed, quoted in Malcolm Brown, *The Imperial War Museum Book of the Somme* (*IWM Book*), p. 149.

6 Lieutenant A. S. Lloyd, letter 1 August 1916: recipient not disclosed, quoted in the *IWM Book*, p. 150.

7 Ibid., letter 1 August 1916: recipient not disclosed, quoted in the *IWM Book*, p. 149.

8 The IWM *Book*, p. 151.

9 Major F. W. Bewsher, *The History of the 51st (Highland) Division 1914–18*, p. 77, brought to my attention by Terry Norman, *The Hell of High Wood*, p. 161.

10 Captain J. C. Dunn, *The War the Infantry Knew 1914–1919* (*Dunn Book*), p. 251.

11 Private Frank Richards, *Old Soldiers Never Die*, p. 199.

12 'Narrative of attack on High Wood by 19th Infantry Bde', in 19th Brigade file, NA WO 95/2420.

13 *Dunn Book*, pp. 242–8.

14 'Report on Operations of 20th Infantry Brigade July 11th–20th 1916', in 20th Brigade file, NA WO 95/1653; and Brigadier-General Sir James E. Edmonds, *History of the Great War: Military Operations: France and Belgium 1916, Volume 2* (*1916 Official History, Vol. 2*), p. 110.

15 Arthur Russell, *The Machine Gunner*, p. 55.

16 98th Brigade report 21 August 1916, in its file, NA WO 95/2424.

17 *1916 Official History, Vol. 2*, pp. 190–3.

18 Lieutenant-General Launcelot Kiggell to Rawlinson 24 August 1916, in Rawlinson's 4th Army papers, IWM Documents.

19 Brigadier-General Frederick Carleton, papers, IWM Documents 20718.

32: The Human Factor

1 1st Australian Division war diary, in 1st Australian Division file, AWM4 1/42/19 (internet part 1, p. 4).

2 Ben Champion, AWM 2DRL/0512, brought to my attention by Scott Bennett, *Pozières: The Anzac Story*, p. 220.

3 Eric Moorhead, 5th Australian Battalion, in AWM 3DRL/7253.

4 Eric Moorhead, AWM 3DRL/7253, brought to my attention by Bennett, *Pozières*, p. 227.

5 C. E. W. Bean, Official Historian, Diaries and Notebooks (*Bean's Diaries and Notebooks*), AWM38 3DRL 606/55/1, pp. 32–3 (internet pp. 31–2).

6 Brigadier-General Sir James E. Edmonds, *History of the Great War: Military Operations: France and Belgium 1916, Volume 2* (*1916 Official History, Vol. 2*), p. 220.

7 19 August entry in 3rd Australian war diary, AWM4 23/20/18, and 18 August entry in 4th Australian war diary, AWM4 23/21/18.

8 Ivan D. Chapman, *Iven G. Mackay: Citizen and Soldier*, p. 79.

9 *1916 Official History, Vol. 2*, p. 221.

10 *Bean's Diaries and Notebooks*, AWM38 3DRL 606/55/1, p. 87 (internet p. 73).

11 Brigadier-General Brudenell White, letters to General Walker 19 August 1916, in 1st Australian Division file, AWM4 1/42/19 (internet part 4, pp. 4–7).

12 'Report of Operations 10th Batt AIF 19th to 23 August', in 10th Australian Battalion file, AWM4 23/27/10; '3rd Australian Infantry Brigade Report on Operations about Mouquet Farm and Pozières 19th to 23rd August 1916', in 3rd Australian Brigade file, AWM4 23/3/10; 'Report on operations of 1st Australian Division August 15th to August 23rd 1916', in 1st Australian Division file, AWM4 1/42/19 (internet part 6, p. 11).

13 *Bean's Diaries and Notebooks*, AWM38 3DRL 606/55/1, pp. 109–10 (internet pp. 88–9).

14 Ibid., pp. 113–14 (internet pp. 92–3).

15 3rd Australian Brigade file (internet p. 28).

16 C. E. W. Bean, *Official History of Australia in the War of 1914–1918, Volume 3*, p. 797; and Sergeant David Badger's service record file, NAA B2455.

17 Sergeant David Badger, Red Cross file, in AWM 1DRL/0428.
18 10th Australian Battalion file, AWM4 23/27/10 (internet p. 5).
19 2nd Lieutenant Herbert Crowle, AWM 1DRL/0227, brought to my attention by Bennett, *Pozières*, pp. 237–8; and war service records, NAA B2455.
20 Brigadier-General Brudenell White, letters to General Walker 19 August 1916, in 1st Australian Division file, AWM4 1/42/19 (internet Part 4, pp. 4–7).
21 2nd Lieutenant Alfred Hearps, war service records, NAA B2455.
22 3rd Australian Brigade file (internet p. 28).
23 *Bean's Diaries and Notebooks*, AWM38 3DRL 606/56/1, p. 29 (internet p. 29).
24 Ibid., AWM38 3DRL 606/55/1 (internet pp. 116–23).
25 Letter from Charles Bean's mother to him 2 September 1916, in *Bean's Diaries and Notebooks*, AWM38 3DRL 606/55/1 (internet pp. 129–30).
26 Letter from Charles Bean's mother 3 September 1916, *Bean's Diaries and Notebooks*, AWM38 3DRL 606/55/1 (internet pp. 131–3).
27 Ibid.
28 Letter from Amy Butler to Jack Bean 8 November 1916, *Bean's Diaries and Notebooks*, AWM38 3DRL 606/55/1 (internet pp. 133–6).
29 *Bean's Diaries and Notebooks*, AWM38 3DRL 606/56/1, pp. 8–33 (internet pp. 26–31).
30 Margaret Young and Bill Gammage, eds, *Hail and Farewell: Letters from Two Brothers Killed in France in 1916*, pp. 165, 172.
31 Goldthorp Raws, NAA war service records, B2455.

33: Shell-Shocked

1 4th Australian Division war diary, in 4th Australian file, AWM4 1/48/5 and AWM4 1/48/6 (internet August 1916, part 1, p. 30, and September 1916, part 1, p. 16).
2 Charles Bean, diary, in C. E. W. Bean, Official Historian, Diaries and Notebooks, AWM38 3DRL 606/57/1, pp. 8–11 (internet pp. 9–12).
3 'Daily Casualty Report' in 4th Australian Division file, AWM4 1/48/6 (internet September 1916, part 1, p. 38).
4 Brigadier-General Sir James E. Edmonds, *History of the Great War: Military Operations: France and Belgium 1916, Volume 2* (*1916 Official History, Vol. 2*), p. 228.
5 Lieutenant Pat Auld's account in R. R. Freeman, *Hurcombe's Hungry Half Hundred: A Memorial History of the 50th Battalion A.I.F. 1916–1919* (*Freeman's 50th Battalion History*), pp. 65–7; and 'Summary of operations of 50th Battalion from 7.30 p.m. 2nd September to 6.15 a.m. on 4th September 1916', 50th Battalion file, AWM4 23/67/3 (internet September 1916, pp. 11–13).

6   Quartermaster Sergeant L. A. Davies, report 21 April 1917, in Captain Howard Williams' Red Cross file, AWM 1DRL/0428.

7   Private T.E. Peake, 31 December 1918 report in Lieutenant Ernest Smythe's Red Cross file, AWM 1DRL/0428.

8   Ibid.; and Private Chas White undated report, both in Lieutenant Francis Bailey's Red Cross file, AWM 1 DRL/0428.

9   Private J. Morton, 27 December 1916 report in Lieutenant Albert Clifford's Red Cross file, AWM 1 DRL/0428.

10 51st Australian Battalion exploits from its file's 'Report on operation at Mouquet Farm 1st/4th September 1916', AWM4 23/68/7 (internet September 1916, pp. 5-6); and C. E. W. Bean, *Official History of Australia in the War of 1914–1918, Volume 3 (Australian Official History, Vol. 3)*, pp. 850–2.

11 Message from Lieutenant Duncan Maxwell to commanding officer 52nd Australian Battalion, in 52nd Australian Battalion file, AWM4 23/69/6 (internet September 1916, p. 10).

12 *Australian Official History, Vol. 3*, pp. 846–9 and 852–8; 50th Australian Battalion, 'Report on attack on Mouquet Farm', in 52nd Australian Battalion file, AWM4 23/69/6 (internet September 1916, pp. 5–8); and 51st Australian Battalion's 'Report on operation at Mouquet Farm 1st/4th September 1916', in 51st Australian Battalion file, AWM4 23/68/7 (internet September 1916, pp. 5–8).

13 *Australian Official History, Vol. 3*, p. 860; and 13th Australian Battalion 'Summary of operations near Mouquet Farm – period – 1st to 5th Sept 1916', in 13th Australian Battalion file, AWM4 23/13/8 (internet September 1916, p. 26).

14 *1916 Official History, Vol. 2*, pp. 255–6.

15 Ibid., p. 286.

16 *Australian Official History, Vol. 3*, p. 858.

17 Private G. H. Holdway, report, 19 October 1916, in Lieutenant Len Wadsley's Red Cross file, AWM 1DRL 0428.

18 John Wadsley, 'Dear Everybody At Home: A Tasmanian's Letters from the Great War', *Sabretache*, vol. XLVI, no. 4, December 2005, pp. 11–14.

19 Ralph Potter, report, 30 July 1917, in Private Edward Potter's Red Cross file, AWM 1DRL/0428.

20 War service records of Edward, Ralph and Thomas Potter, NAA B2455. The film is Steven Spielberg's *Saving Private Ryan*.

34: Last Throw of the Dice

1   The letter from Sir Launcelot Kiggell to Rawlinson and Gough 19 August 1916, Rawlinson's 4th Army documents, Volume 5, IWM Documents,

originally asked for suggestions by 25 August, but this appears to have been extended until 28 August.

2 Letter from Sir Launcelot Kiggell to Rawlinson and Gough 19 August 1916, Rawlinson's 4th Army documents, Volume 5, IWM Documents.

3 Letter from Rawlinson to Sir Launcelot Kiggell 28 August 1916, Rawlinson's 4th Army documents, Volume 5, IWM Documents.

4 29 August 1916 entry in Haig's diary, NA WO 256/12.

5 Letter from Sir Launcelot Kiggell to Rawlinson and Gough 31 August 1916, Rawlinson's 4th Army documents, Volume 5, IWM Documents.

6 30 August 1916 entry in Rawlinson diary, Rawlinson papers 1/5, Churchill College.

7 Letter from Rawlinson to Sir Launcelot Kiggell 31 August 1916, Rawlinson's 4th Army documents, Volume 5, IWM Documents.

8 Kronprinz von Rupprecht, *Mein Kriegstagebuch*, vol. 1, pp. 520–1.

9 2nd Lieutenant Arthur Conway Young, in Laurence Houseman, ed., *Of Fallen Englishwomen*, p. 309.

10 Letter from Haig to Robertson 22 August 1916, NA WO 158/21, mentioned in Gary Sheffield, *The Chief*, p. 189.

11 Sir Ernest D. Swinton, *Eyewitness*, p. 261.

12 Lord Hankey, *The Supreme Command, 1914–1918*, p. 513.

35: Bloodlust

1 Major-General Alexander Godley, letter to Colonel James Allen 10 December 1914, ANZ WA 252 1.

2 Ettie Rout, letter to Colonel Heaton Rhodes, the New Zealand Government Commissioner in Cairo, 12 March 1916, in the Personnel Venereal Disease General Correspondence file, in ANZ ADI 777, 24/46, R22431299.

3 New Zealand's Director General of Medical Services to his Minister of Defence written in the month of September 1917, in ANZ ADI 777 24/46/1.

4 J. M. Russell, ATL MS Papers 1696.

5 Cecil Malthus, *Armentières and the Somme*, p. 92.

6 Captain Lindsay Inglis, NZATL MS Papers 0421-48 (*Inglis Account*), pp. 19–20.

7 Major C. B. Brereton, *Tales of Three Campaigns*, pp. 185–6.

8 *Inglis Account*, pp. 19–20.

9 Letter from Mrs M. Hughes to Minister of Defence, James Allen, 26 September 1916 (*Frank Hughes' Execution file*), ANZ, AB00 W4344, Box 16, 325A, R8686440.

10 James Allen, letter to Mrs M. Hughes October 1916 (precise date not specified), *Frank Hughes' Execution file*.

11 New Zealand Division Order No. 41, 1 September 1916, in that division's file, NA WO 95/3658.

12 Stanley Brailsford, 2nd Battalion, 3rd New Zealand Rifle Brigade, NZNAM 1990.2491.

13 *Inglis Account*, pp. 21–2.

14 Captain Cuthbert Free, letter to his fiancée 10 September 1916, Free family's 'Letters from Cuthbert Free while on active service', ATL MS Papers 4387.

15 *Inglis Account*, p. 27.

16 Major Herbert Hart, in John Crawford, ed., *The Devil's Own War: The Diary of Herbert Hart*, p. 135.

17 *Inglis Account*, p. 21.

18 Sergeant Arthur Rhind, ATL MS Papers 3772.

19 2nd Lieutenant Alexander Aitken, *Gallipoli to the Somme: Recollections of a New Zealand Infantryman*, p. 130.

20 13 September 1916 entry in 2nd Wellington Battalion war diary, in that regiment's file, NA WO 95/3690, and Corporal Cliff Curran's personal service file.

21 Private Claude Burley, undated remains of letter to Ethel Sturm, ATL MS Papers 7514 (*Burley Letter*).

22 *Burley Letter*, and 13 and 14 September 1916 entries in 2nd Wellington Battalion war diary, NA WO 95/3690.

23 Sergeant Arthur Rhind, ATL MS Papers 3772.

24 George F. Hulme, in History of the War file, ANZ AD78 Box 25 F16/33, brought to my attention by Robert Cameron and his website: robertcameron.wordpress.com (*Robert Cameron*).

25 Leslie Kenney, diary, NZNAM 1997.806.

26 William Kingston Wilson, NZNAM 1994.2314 (*Wilson's Account*), brought to my attention by Ray Grover, *March to the Sound of the Guns*.

27 New Zealand Division Order No. 49, 13 September 1916, NA WO 95/3658; Brigadier-General W. G. Braithwaite's 'Report on operations 15th, 16th and 17th September 1916', 26 September 1916, 2nd New Zealand Brigade file, NA Wo 95/3693 (*2nd New Zealand Brigade Report*).

28 15 September 1916 entry, 2nd New Zealand Brigade war diary and the brigade's Order No. 20, 14 September 1916, in that brigade's file, NA WO 95/3693.

29 14 September 1916 entry, New Zealand Division war diary, that division's file, NA WO95/3658, *Inglis Account*, and Lieutenant-Colonel W. S. Austin, *The Official History of the New Zealand Rifle Brigade (the Earl of Liverpool's Own)*, pp. 119–20.

30 Austin, *The Official History of the New Zealand Rifle Brigade (the Earl of Liverpool's Own)*, p. 120.

31 3rd New Zealand Rifle Brigade Order No. 31, 14 September 1916, NA WO 95/3705.

32 *Inglis Account*, p. 27.

33 'Narrative of Events' dated 8 October 1916 by 3rd New Zealand Rifle Brigade's Brigadier-General Harry Fulton, in that brigade's file, NA WO 95/3705 (*3rd New Zealand Brigade Report*).

34 2nd Lieutenant George Tuck, ATL MS 2166 (*Tuck Account*).

35 'Report by Lt Col C. H. J. Brown commanding 2nd Battalion Auckland Regiment in the operation of 15th September 1916', NA WO 95/3688; and *2nd New Zealand Brigade Report*.

36 *Tuck Account*.

37 W. V. Graham, letter extract in the History of the War: France: Somme: Advance 1916, ANZ R23 247 105, AD 78 Box 25, F16/33, brought to my attention by Robert Cameron.

38 *2nd New Zealand Brigade Report* and *3rd New Zealand Brigade Report*.

39 *3rd New Zealand Brigade Report*.

40 *Wilson's Account*.

41 *3rd New Zealand Brigade Report*.

42 *Inglis Account*, p. 35.

43 Brigadier-General Sir James E. Edmonds, *History of the Great War: Military Operations: France and Belgium 1916, Volume 2*, pp. 318–28.

44 *Inglis Account*, p. 42.

45 Ibid., p. 39.

46 'Narrative of the Action' by 2nd Wellington Regiment, in 2nd New Zealand Brigade file, NA WO 95/3693 (*2nd Battalion the Wellington Regiment Report*).

47 *Burley Letter*.

48 Casualty figures gleaned from: 15 September war diary entries, 1st and 3rd Battalions the 3rd New Zealand Rifle Brigade; 'Summary of Casualties' attached to that brigade's 4th Battalion war diary; *2nd Battalion the Wellington Regiment Report*; and *2nd New Zealand Brigade Report*.

49 *Inglis Account*, p. 52.

36: The Caterpillars

1 Sergeant Harold Horne (*Horne's Account*), IWM Documents.

2 Sergeant-Major Douglas Pegler, IWM Documents 82/7/1.

3 Brigadier-General Sir James E. Edmonds, *History of the Great War: Military Operations: France and Belgium 1916, Volume 2* (*1916 Official History, Vol. 2*), p. 181.

4 Major C. A. Cuthbert Keeson, *The History and Records of Queen Victoria's Rifles 1792–1922*, pp. 191–2.

5 Lieutenant Basil Henriques, 'Lecture on the Attack on the Quadrilateral', delivered at Bovington Camp, 6 March 1917, brought to my attention by Colin Hardy, author of 'Dies Irae', a private study of the action of Lieutenant Henriques on 15 September 1916.

6 *1916 Official History, Vol. 2*, p. 294.

7 *Horne's Account*.

8 *1916 Official History, Vol. 2*, p. 310.

9 Ibid., pp. 309–10.

10 Quote in Trevor Pigeon, *The Tanks at Flers*, p. 83.

11 Letter from Brigadier-General W. L. Osborn to the British official historian 9 June 1935, NA CAB 45/136.

12 15 September 1916 entry in 47th Division 'Report on operations 15th/19th September 1916', in its file, NA WO 95/2701.

13 Private Vernon Wilkinson, information supplied by his daughter-in-law Hilary, and brought to my attention by Daniel Kirmatzis and Doug Goodman.

14 Ibid.

15 Private Lance Cattermole, account, IWM Documents 92/26/1.

16 GHQ war diary, N9657, 10.55 a.m., NA WO 95/7, as mentioned in Trevor Pigeon, *The Tanks at Flers*, pp. 168 and 178.

17 Lieutenant Stuart Hastie, IWM Sound Archive 4126.

18 *The Guards Division at the Somme*, pp. 491 and 494.

19 Ibid., p. 498. These statistics relate to the following dates: 10–17 September 1916. However, it is likely that most casualties were sustained on 15 September.

20 Captain C. P. Fildes, *Iron Times with the Guards*, p. 268.

37: Hard Times

1 Captain Lindsay Inglis, NZATL MS Papers 0421-48, p. 50.

2 16–19 September 1916 entries in 1st Battalion Wellington Regiment war diary, NA WO 95/3689 (*1st Wellington War Diary*).

3 16 September 1916 entry, *1st Wellington War Diary*.

4 Private William Gibbard, ATL MS Papers 4134-2.

5 Captain R. W. Wrightson, ANZ: History of the War (France – Somme Advance – 1916): AD 78, Box 25, F16/33, R23247105, brought to my attention by Robert Cameron and his website: robertcameron.wordpress.com.

6 Sergeant John Russell, ATL MS Papers 1696.

7 Lieutenant J. R. Byrne, *New Zealand Artillery in the Field 1914–1918*, p. 140.

8 Archie Greves, *A Sovereign in My Pocket: The Story of Bombardier Archibald K. Greves,* in NZ NAM 2006.122.

9 Brigadier-General Sir James E. Edmonds, *History of the Great War: Military Operations: France and Belgium 1916, Volume 2 (1916 Official History, Vol. 2),* pp. 379—80.

10 'Time table to accompany Operation Order No. 17', referred to in the said Order dated 23 September 1916, issued by 1st New Zealand Brigade, in that brigade's file, NA WO 95/3685.

11 Alexander Aitken, *Gallipoli to the Somme: Recollections of a New Zealand Infantry-man (Aitken's Memoirs),* pp. 148—57, and 25 September 1916 entry in 1st Battalion the Canterbury Regiment war diary, NA WO 95/3697.

12 *1916 Official History, Vol. 2,* p. 385.

13 'Appendix A: Time table to accompany Lack Operation Order No. 18', referred to in the said Order dated 27 September 1916, issued by the 1st New Zealand Brigade, in that brigade's file, NA WO 95/3685.

14 27 September 1916 entry of 1st Battalion the Wellington Regiment war diary, in its file, NA WO 95/3689.

15 *Aitken's Memoirs,* pp. 166—73.

16 27 September entries in 1st Battalions of the Auckland and Canterbury Regiments war diaries, in their files, NA WO 95/3688 and NA WO 95/3697 respectively; 28 September 1916 entry in 1st Battalion the Wellington Regiment, in that unit's file, NA WO 95/3689.

17 *1916 Official History, Vol. 2,* p. 387.

18 Private Howard Kippenberger, account, ATL MS Papers 8181-147, brought to my attention by Ray Grover, *March to the Sound of the Guns.*

19 Lieutenant A. E. Byrne, *Official History of the Otago Regiment, N. Z. E. F. in the Great War 1914—1918,* p. 136; 12 October 1916 entries in 2nd Battalions of the Canterbury and Otago Regiments war diaries, in those regiments' files, NA WO 95/3699 and NA WO 95/3703 respectively; Colonel H. Stewart, *The New Zealand Division 1916—1919: A Popular History Based on Official Records,* pp. 110—15.

20 'Summary of Casualties: New Zealand Division: Period 1st September to 7th October 1916', in that division's file, NA WO 95/3658.

21 5 October entry in New Zealand Division war diary, in that division's file, NA WO 95/3658.

22 J. J. Sweeney, Court Martial file (*Sweeney's File*), ANZ Record No. 22/30/72, Archives Reference No. AD1 Box 767, Container Code C912 242, R22430427.

23 Arthur Rhind, ATL MS Papers 3772.

24 *Sweeney's File.*

25 Private Claude Burley, undated remains of letter to Ethel Sturm, ATL MS Papers 7514, and 6 October 1916 entry in 2nd Battalion the Wellington Regiment war diary, in that regiment's file, NA WO 95/3690.

38: Ambushed

1 20 September entry in Haig diary, NA WO 256/13.

2 Hauptmann von Forster, undated comment in 'History of the 52nd (Royal Württemberg) Reserve Infantry Brigade: Part II: The Battle of the Somme 24 June 1916 to October 1916, based on the Brigade war diaries and compiled by M. Gerster, Leutnant of the Landwehr in Reserve Infantry Regiment 119', which is a translation of the original German document. The former is filed in the archive of the Newfoundland Memorial Park near Beaumont Hamel, and the latter is in the Hauptstaatsarchiv Stuttgart, M410 Bu 260.

3 Private Reginald Emmett, account (*Emmett Account*), IWM Sound Archive 16548.

4 'Report of operations of the 54th infantry brigade during the capture of Thiepval . . .', NA WO 95/2041.

5 Brigadier-General Sir James E. Edmonds, *History of the Great War: Military Operations: France and Belgium 1916, Volume 2 (1916 Official History, Vol. 2)*, p. 393.

6 Ibid.

7 Private Sydney Fuller, diary (*Fuller Diary*), IWM Documents.

8 *Emmett Account*.

9 *Fuller Diary*.

10 *1916 Official History, Vol. 2*, pp. 404 and 406.

11 Private Thomas Jennings, IWM Documents 6596, or 79/17/1.

12 2nd Lieutenant Geoffrey Pratt, IWM Documents 01/20/1.

13 *1916 Official History, Vol. 2*, pp. 376, 382, 383, 385, 401.

14 Ibid., pp. 418 and 453.

15 Colonel Archie White (he was a colonel when he wrote this article), 'The Somme Battle, 1916 and the Somme Commemoration, 1966', *The Green Howards Gazette*, vol. LXXIV, pp. 107–9, brought to my attention by Roger Chapman, *Beyond Their Duty: Heroes of the Green Howards*.

39: Weather Permitting

1 Brigadier-General Sir James E. Edmonds, *History of the Great War: Military Operations: France and Belgium 1916, Volume 2 (1916 Official History, Vol. 2)*, p. 427.

2 Kronprinz von Rupprecht, 27 September 1916 diary entry, *Mein Kriegstagebuch*, vol. 2, p. 34.

3 *1916 Official History, Vol. 2*, p. 444.

4 Ibid., pp. 430–2, 437, 453–4.

5 Ibid., p. 458.

6 Reverend Harold Davies, IWM Documents 03/30/1.

7 Private H. G. Hartnett, AWM 2DRL 0840.

8 2nd Lieutenant Norman Collins, 23 October 1916 letter in his papers, IWM Documents 16191.

9 23 October 1916 entry in Haig diary, NA WO 256/13.

10 *1916 Official History, Vol. 2*, p. 475.

11 Ibid., p. 474.

12 5 November 1916 entry in Haig diary, NA WO 256/14.

13 *1916 Official History, Vol. 2*, p. 460.

14 12 November 1916 entry in Haig diary, NA WO 256/14; *1916 Official History, Vol. 2*, p. 230.

15 *1916 Official History, Vol. 2*, p. 478.

16 Ibid. and ibid., p. 564.

17 Ibid., p. 479.

18 D. Jerrold, *The Hawke Battalion*, p. 130.

19 Ibid., pp. 129–30.

20 Ordinary Seaman Joe Murray, IWM Sound Archive 8201.

21 *1916 Official History, Vol. 2*, p. 489.

22 S. M. Holloway, *From Trench and Turret*, pp. 59–63.

23 *1916 Official History, Vol. 2*, p. 505.

24 Fähnrich Pukall, quoted in Oberstleutnant A. D. H. Reymann, *Das 3. Oberschlesichlesiche Infanterie-Regiment Nr. 62 im Kriege 1914–1918*, pp. 133–4, brought to my attention by Jack Sheldon, *The German Army on the Somme*, pp. 372–3, and *The Germans at Beaumont Hamel*, pp. 163–4.

25 Rittmeister von Dresky, account referred to in Jack Sheldon, *The Germans at Beaumont Hamel*, pp. 166–7.

26 *1916 Official History, Vol. 2*, pp. 491–4.

27 Captain David Rorie, *A Medico's Luck in the War*, p. 113.

28 2nd Lieutenant Norman Collins, IWM Sound Archive 12043, and Norman Collins, *Last Man Standing: The Memoirs of a Seaforth Highlander during the Great War*, ed. Richard van Emden, p. 110.

29 *1916 Official History, Vol. 2*, p. 483.

30 Michael Renshaw, *Redan Ridge*, pp. 81–100.

31 Hugo Natt, diary brought to my attention by Irena Renz, Gerd Krumeich and Gerhard Hirschfeld, *Scorched Earth: The Germans on the Somme*, pp. 138–9.

32 Ernst Jünger, *Storm of Steel*, pp. 127–8.

33 *1916 Official History, Vol. 2*, pp. xiii–vi.

34 Ibid., p. 60.

35 Ibid., p. 555.

36 Ibid.

37 Ibid., p. xii.

38 Ibid.

39 Major-General Oliver Nugent to Catherine (Kitty), his wife, on 11 July 1916, in Nicholas Perry, *Major-General Oliver Nugent and the Ulster Division 1915–1918*, p. 89.

40 J. P. Harris, *Douglas Haig and the First World War*, p. 268.

41 17 September 1916 entry in Haig diary, NA WO 256/13.

42 David R. Woodward, *Field Marshal Sir William Robertson: Chief of the Imperial General Staff in the Great War*, pp. 97–107.

43 Cuthbert Headlam, *History of the Guards Division in the Great War 1915–1918*.

44 C. E. W. Bean, *The Australian Imperial Force in France 1916*.

45 Peter Simkins, *From the Somme to Victory: The British Army's Experience on the Western Front 1916–1918*, pp. 12–58.

46 Major P. H. Pilditch, IWM Documents Conshelf 0332.

47 Reverend Harold Davies, IWM Documents 03/30/1.

48 Lieutenant Vere Harmsworth, letter to his uncle St John 24 October 1916, brought to my attention by Vyvyan Harmsworth.

49 Lance Corporal Douglas Horton, AWM 1 DRL/0359.

Select Bibliography

Aitken, 2nd Lieutenant Alexander, *Gallipoli to the Somme: Recollections of a New Zealand Infantryman*, London, 1963

Alexander, Jack, *McCrae's Battalion: The Story of the 16th Royal Scots*, Edinburgh, 2003

Anonymous, *Reserve-Infanterie-Regiment Nr. 110 im Weltkrieg 1914–1918*, Karlsruhe, 1934

Anonymous, *The History of the London Rifle Brigade, 1859–1919*, London, 1921

Ashurst, Corporal George, *My Bit: A Lancashire Fusilier at War 1914–18*, Ramsbury, 1987

Austin, Lieutenant-Colonel W. S., *The Official History of the New Zealand Rifle Brigade (the Earl of Liverpool's Own)*, Wellington, 1924

Barrie, Alexander, *War Underground*, London, 1962

Bean, C. E. W., *Official History of Australia in the War of 1914–1918, Volume 3, The Australian Imperial Force in France, 1916*, Melbourne, 1929

Bennett, Scott, *Pozières: The Anzac Story*, Melbourne, 2011

Bewsher, Major F. W., *The History of the 51st (Highland) Division, 1914–1918*, Edinburgh, 1921

Bezzel, Oberst a.D. Dr Oskar, *Das Königlich Bayerische Reserve-Infanterie-Regiment Nr. 6*, Munich, 1938

Bickersteth, John Monier (ed.), *The Bickersteth Diaries*, Barnsley, 1995

Blake, Robert (ed.), *The Private Papers of Douglas Haig 1914–1919*, London, 1952

Breed, Florence (ed.), *From France with Love 1916–1918: The Deeds of Wimmera Diggers on the Somme*, Donald, Australia, 1995

Brereton, J. M., *A History of the 4th/7th Royal Dragoon Guards and Their Predecessors 1685–1980*, Barnsley, 1982

Brereton, Major C. B., *Tales of Three Campaigns*, London, 1926

Brown, Malcolm, *The Imperial War Museum Book of the Somme*, London, 2006

Browning, Neville, *Fix Bayonets: The History of the 51st Battalion, A.I.F.*, Bayswater, Western Australia, 2000

Browning, Neville, *The Blue & White Diamond: The History of the 28th Battalion, 1915–1919*, Bassendean, Western Australia, 2003

Bryant, Peter, *Grimsby Chums: The Story of the 10th Lincolnshires in the Great War*, Hull, 1990

Butler, Colonel A. G., *The Official History of the Australian Army Medical Services in the War of 1914–1918, Volume 2: The Western Front*, Canberra, 1940

Byrne, Lieutenant A. E., *Official History of the Otago Regiment, N.Z.E.F., in the Great War, 1914–1918*, Auckland, 1921

Byrne, Lieutenant J. R., *New Zealand Artillery in the Field 1914–1918*, Auckland, 1922

Cave, Joy B. (ed.), *I Survived Didn't I? The Great War Reminiscences of Private 'Ginger' Byrne*, Barnsley, 1993

Chapman, Ivan D., *Iven G. MacKay: Citizen and Soldier*, Melbourne, 1975

Chapman, Roger, *Beyond Their Duty: Heroes of the Green Howards*, Green Howards Museum, Richmond, 2001

Coulthard-Clark, C. D., *No Australian Need Apply: The Troubled Career of Lieutenant-General Gordon Legge*, Sydney, 1988

Cowen, Ruth (ed.), *A Nurse at the Front: The Great War Diaries of Sister Edith Appleton*, London, 2012

Crawford, John (ed.), *The Devil's Own War: The Diary of Herbert Hart*, Auckland, 2008

Crozier, Brigadier-General Frank, *A Brass Hat in No Man's Land*, London, 1930

Crozier, Brigadier-General F. P., *Impressions and Recollections*, London, 1930

Crozier, Brigadier-General F. P., *The Men I Killed*, London, 1937

Department of Veterans' Affairs, *Simply Hell Let Loose: Stories of Australians at War*, Sydney, 2002

Duff Cooper, Alfred, *Haig, Volume 1*, London, 1935

Dunn, Captain J. C., *The War the Infantry Knew 1914–1919*, London, 1938

Edmonds, Brigadier-General Sir James E., *History of the Great War: Military Operations: France and Belgium 1916, Volume 1*, London, 1932 (for Volume 2, see under Miles)

Edmonds, Sir James E., *Military Operations: France and Belgium 1917*, London, 1940 and 1948

Falls, Cyril, *The History of the 36th Ulster Division*, London, 1922

Fildes, Captain G. P., *Iron Times with the Guards*, London, 1918 (author's name did not appear in the book when it was first published; it was said to be by 'an OE')

Fraser-Tytler, Lieutenant-Colonel Neil, *Field Guns in France*, London, 2006

Freeman, R. R., *Hurcombe's Hungry Half Hundred: A Memorial History of the 50th Battalion A.I.F. 1916–1919*, Norwood, South Australia, 1991

Gerster, Matthäus, *Das Württembergische Reserve-Infanterie-Regiment Nr. 119 im Weltkrieg 1914–1918*, Stuttgart, 1920

Goldman, Lawrence, *The Life of R. H. Tawney*, London, 2013

Gough, General Sir Hubert, *Soldiering On, Being the Memoirs of General Sir Hubert Gough,* London, 1954

Gough, General Sir Hubert, *The Fifth Army*, London, 1931

Griffith, Llewelyn Wyn, *Up to Mametz*, London, 1931

Grover, Ray, *March to the Sound of the Guns*, Dunedin, New Zealand, 2008

Hankey, Lord (Maurice), *The Supreme Command, 1914–1918*, London, 1961

Harris, J. P., *Douglas Haig and the First World War*, Cambridge, 2008

Harrison, Gerry (ed.), *To Fight Among Friends: The First World War Diaries of Charlie May*, London, 2014

Hart, Peter, *The Somme*, London, 2005

Holloway, S. M., *From Trench and Turret*: *Royal Marines Letters and Diaries 1914–1918,* Royal Marines Museum, Southsea, Hampshire, 2006

Holtz, Hauptmann Freiherr Georg vom, *Das Württembergische-Reserve-Infanterie Regiment Nr. 121 im Weltkrieg 1914–1918*, Stuttgart, 1922

Housman, Laurence (ed.), *War Letters of Fallen Englishmen*, London, 1930

Jackson, Andrew, *Accrington Pals: The Full Story*, Barnsley, 2013

Jerrold, D., *The Hawke Battalion*, London, 1925

Jones, Simon, *Underground Warfare 1914–1918*, Barnsley, 2010

Jünger, Ernst, *Storm of Steel*, Germany, 1920 (final altered edition 1961)

Keeson, Major C. A. Cuthbert, *The History & Records of the Queen Victoria's Rifles 1792–1922*, London, 1923

Knyvett, Captain R. Hugh, *'Over There' with the Australians*, London, 1918

Kümmel, Adolf, Leutnant d. Res. a.D., *Res. Inf.-Reg Nr. 91 im Weltkriege 1914–1918*, Oldenburg, 1926

Lais, Otto, *Bilder aus der Sommeschlacht des Weltkrieges*, Stuttgart, 1940

Lawson, Private John A., *Memories of Delville Wood: South Africa's Great Battle*, Cape Town, 1918

Leask, Anthony, *Putty: From Tel-el-Kebir to Cambrai: The Life and Letters of Lieutenant-General Sir William Pulteney 1861–1941*, Solihull, 2015

Lewis, Lieutenant Cecil, *Sagittarius Rising*, London, 1936

Macdonald, Andrew, *On My Way to the Somme: New Zealanders and the Bloody Offensive of 1916*, Auckland, 2005

Malins, Lieutenant Geoffrey H., *How I Filmed the War*, London, 1920

Malthus, Cecil, *Armentières and the Somme*, Auckland, 2002

Maurice, Major-General Sir Frederick, *The Life of General Lord Rawlinson of Trent*, London, 1928

Maze, Paul, *A Frenchman in Khaki*, London, 1936

McCrery, Nigel, *Final Wicket: Test and First-Class Cricketers Killed in the Great War*, Barnsley, 2015

McFarland, Elaine, *A Slashing Man of Action: The Life of Lieutenant-General Sir Aylmer Hunter-Weston MP*, Bern, 2014

McMullin, Ross, *Pompey Elliott*, Melbourne, 2002

Mead, Gary, *The Good Soldier: The Biography of Douglas Haig*, London, 2007

Middlebrook, Martin, *The First Day on the Somme: 1 July 1916*, London, 1971

Miles, Captain Wilfrid, *History of the Great War: Military Operations: France and Belgium 1916, Volume 2*, London, 1938 (for Volume 1, see under Edmonds)

Milner, Laurie, *Leeds Pals: A History of the 15th (Service) Battalion (1st Leeds) The Prince of Wales's Own West Yorkshire Regiment: 1914–1918*, Barnsley, 1991

Müller, Major d.R. Paul, Fabeck, Oberst a.D. Hans von, and Riesel, Oberstleutnant a.D. Richard, *Geschichte des Reserve-Infanterie-Regiments Nr. 99*, Munich, 1917

Norman, Terry, *The Hell They Called High Wood: The Somme 1916*, London, 1984

Orr, Philip, *The Road to the Somme*, Belfast, 1987

Perry, Nicholas, *Major-General Oliver Nugent and the Ulster Division 1915–1918*, Stroud, 2007

Perry, Roland, *Monash: The Outsider Who Won a War: A Biography of Australia's Greatest Military Commander*, Milson's Point, New South Wales, 2004

Pidgeon, Trevor, *The Tanks at Flers: An Account of the First Use of Tanks in War at the Battle of Flers–Courcelette: The Somme: 15th September 1916*, Cobham, 1995

Prior, Robin and Wilson, Trevor, *Command on the Western Front: The Military Career of Sir Henry Rawlinson 1914–1918*, London, 2004

Prior, Robin and Wilson, Trevor, *The Somme*, London, 2005

Raw, David, *Bradford Pals: A Comprehensive History of the 16th, 18th & 20th (Service) Battalions of the Prince of Wales Own West Yorkshire Regiment 1914–1918*, Barnsley, 2005

Read, I. L. ('Dick'), *Of Those We Loved*, Durham, 1994

Renz, Irina, Krumeich, Gerd and Hirschfeld, Gerhard, *Scorched Earth: The Germans on the Somme 1914–1918*, Barnsley, 2009

Reymann, Oberleutnant a.D. H., *Das 3 Oberschlesische Infanterie-Regiment im Kriege 1914–1918*, Germany, 1930

Richards, Private Frank, *Old Soldiers Never Die*, London, 1933

Rose-Bladensburg, Lieutenant-Colonel Sir John, *The Coldstream Guards 1914–1918*, London, 1928

Rule, E. J., *Jacka's Mob*, Sydney, 1933

Rupprecht von Bayern, Kronprinz von, *Mein Kriegstagebuch, Volumes 1 and 2*, Berlin, 1929

Russell, Arthur, *The Machine Gunner*, Kineton, 1977

Sadler, Peter S., *The Paladin: A Life of Major-General Sir John Gellibrand*, Melbourne, 2000

Sassoon, 2nd Lieutenant Siegfried, *Memoirs of an Infantry Officer*, London, 1930

Scott, Canon George Frederick, *The Great War as I Saw It*, Toronto, 1922

Sheffield, Gary, *The Chief: Douglas Haig and the British Army*, London, 2011

Sheldon, Jack, *The German Army on the Somme, 1914–1916*, Barnsley, 2005

Sheldon, Jack, *The Germans at Beaumont Hamel*, Barnsley, 2006

Simkins, Peter, *From the Somme to Victory: The British Army's Experience on the Western Front 1916–1918*, Barnsley, 2014

Solomon, Ernest, *Potchefstroom to Delville Wood*, Johannesburg, 1919

Stedman, Michael, *Salford Pals: 15th, 16th, 19th & 20th Battalion Lancashire Fusiliers: A History of the Salford Brigade*, Barnsley, 1993

Stewart, Graham, and Sheen, John, *Tyneside Scottish: A History of the Tyneside Scottish Raised in the North-East in World War One: 20th, 21st, 22nd & 23rd (Service) Battalions in the Northumberland Fusiliers*, Barnsley, 1999

Stewart, Colonel H., *The New Zealand Division 1916–1919: A Popular History based on Official Records*, Auckland, 1921

Swinton, Major-General Sir Ernest D., *Eyewitness: Being Personal Reminiscences of Certain Phases of the Great War including the Genesis of the Tank*, London, 1932

Tawney, R. H., *The Attack and Other Papers*, London, 1953

Thompson, Bill (ed.), *Great War Corps Commander: General Sir Thomas Morland KCB, KCMG, DSO: War Diaries & Letters 1914–1918*, Leicestershire, 2015

Uys, Ian, *Delville Wood*, Johannesburg, 1983

Uys, Ian, *Roll Call: The Delville Wood Story*, Johannesburg, 1991

Van Emden, Richard (ed.), *Last Man Standing: The Memoirs of a Seaforth Highlander during the Great War by Norman Collins*

Vischer, Oberstleutnant Alfred, *Das 10. Württembergische Infanterie-Regiment Nr. 180 in der Somme-Schlacht 1916*, Stuttgart, 1917

Ward, Dudley C. H., *Regimental Records of the Royal Welch Fusiliers (later the 23rd Foot), vol. 3, 1914–1918: France and Flanders*, London, 1928

Whitehead, Ralph J., *The Other Side of the Wire, Volume 2: The Battle of the Somme. With the German XIV Reserve Corps, 1 July 1916*, Solihull, 2011

Woodward, David R., *Field Marshal Sir William Robertson: Chief of the Imperial General Staff in the Great War*, Santa Barbara, California, 1998

Wren, Eric, *Randwick to Hargicourt: History of the 3rd Battalion, A.I.F.*, Sydney, 1935

Wurmb, Herbert Ritter von, *Das K.B. Reserve-Infanterie-Regiment Nr. 8*, Munich, 1929

Young, Margaret and Gammage, Bill (eds), *Hail and Farewell: Letters from Two Brothers Killed in France in 1916: Alec and Goldy Raws*, Sydney, 1995

Acknowledgements

One of my first steps after agreeing to write a book about the Battle of the Somme from the British point of view was to revisit Erich Maria Remarque's celebrated anti-war novel *All Quiet on the Western Front*. It showed me how it was possible to portray the torment suffered by a country's army in the trenches – and its soldiers' unbroken spirit – with a series of vignettes, without covering every action. My quest to find an original angle to this 100-year-old story was assisted by the contents of three other books.

The first was Robin Prior and Trevor Wilson's highly regarded, fascinating *Command on the Western Front: The Military Career of Sir Henry Rawlinson 1914–1918*. At first sight this academic tome might seem a strange choice for someone who has professed a desire to emulate the approach of Remarque's novel. However, there is method in my madness. Although Prior and Wilson's superficial aim appears to be an analysis of the tactics on the Somme in the light of the World War I battles that General Rawlinson, the Somme commander, and his chief, General Douglas Haig, had fought before 1 July 1916, under the surface there is a message which is almost hidden by the strength of what seems to be the authors' main point.

Unusually for a book about the Somme, it suggests that there was a straightforward answer to the question: how many guns and shells were necessary to enable the troops under Rawlinson's command to cross No Man's Land without suffering excessive losses? As far as Prior and Wilson were concerned, all Rawlinson had to do was to apply the lessons learned from the previous attacks that he and Haig had masterminded on the Western Front in order to come up with a workable plan for the Somme.

Although some of the information necessary to work out the number of guns and shells required was missing at the time the book was published, so that Prior and Wilson's calculations were often based on estimated figures, their clear-headed analysis set me thinking along the following lines. If there really was a method of calculating what was required, how come Rawlinson, an experienced, cautious general, had failed to use it in order to convince Haig that they should not be so ambitious? Only then did I latch on to the argument that perhaps the key to the whole battle really was the relationship between the two generals.

Perhaps the reason why Rawlinson was not able to stand up to Haig, so that there was a sensible plan in place for the first day of the 'Big Push', really was because Haig had once done him a favour and Rawlinson now felt constrained not to challenge his master's authority in return. In other words, perhaps Rawlinson was giving Haig what the Latin master who taught Rawlinson at Eton would have referred to as a quid pro quo. I have developed this suggestion in more detail in Chapter 3, and mention it in pride of place here since I suspect that it was the main reason for the British 'failure' to win the Battle of the Somme outright.

But it was two relatively unknown books, Scott Bennett's *Pozières: The Anzac Story* and Andrew Macdonald's *On My Way to the Somme: New Zealanders and the Bloody Offensive of 1916*, which showed me that there was another way of achieving what I have always believed should be the main objective of a book about the Somme battle: a description of what went on in and behind the German front-line trenches as the British Army and its allies attacked. Before I read these books, I had assumed that it would be impossible to focus on what was happening in the German front-line system. Such a focus had been sidelined if not excluded within most general Somme books for the simple reason that there were few vivid accounts on this subject available in the British archives. By way of contrast, the accounts I discovered in the Australian and New Zealand files, thanks to Scott Bennett and Andrew Macdonald, were a revelation. Armed with them, I was all of a sudden able to look at what actually happened as the strong, suntanned Aussies climbed into the German trenches protecting Pozières and Mouquet Farm, and as the ruthless tactics employed by the New Zealanders flushed the Germans out of their dugouts in and to the north of Flers. It was as if a veil had been torn aside revealing what had been hidden from British, and German, eyes for so many years. Authors Peter Stanley, Chris Pugsley and Ray Grover, and Robert Cameron, also helped me find the treasures in the Australasian files.

Once my research was underway, I was aided in particular by the work of six other historians. I could not help but be influenced by Martin Middlebrook's popular history, *The First Day on the Somme: 1 July 1916*, the book that many readers still regard as the best book they have read about World War I. I liked the impressionistic way he structured his book: he jumped from event to event as the minutes and hours ticked by, rather than dealing with the corps in a linear fashion, one after the other.

I am indebted to Malcolm Brown's *Imperial War Museum Book of the Somme*, and Peter Hart's magisterial book *The Somme*, which is also mostly based on the Imperial War Museum's archives. No one endeavouring to cover the complete battle can afford to ignore the magnificent array of accounts assembled by both these historians, and I was no exception. After much internal debate, I eventually decided to follow Hart's linear structure (dealing with one corps after the other) for most of my chapters about 1 July 1916.

So much for the first day of the 'Big Push'. I also needed assistance for what followed. I would not have been able to deal adequately with the events at Delville Wood had I not had the help of Ian Uys, the author of *Delville Wood* and a series of other books on the same subject.

I have, if anything, been even more reliant on Jack Sheldon, author of the ground-breaking book *The German Army on the Somme 1914–1916*, as well as a couple of books describing the Germans at Beaumont Hamel and at Thiepval. He has bent over backwards to ensure that I have been given every bit of assistance I have requested in connection with his area of expertise: the Germans. He also sent me any German texts I could not find in the main German libraries, and went through a long list of German units that I sent him so that he could tell me which had the most colourful regimental histories. It is not his fault that I have felt obliged to omit more German accounts than I would have wished in order to reduce this book to a reasonable size. I should also mention Ralph Whitehead, author of *The Other Side of the Wire, Volume 2*, who has been equally accommodating. As well as answering any questions on the Germans that I could not put to Jack Sheldon, Ralph Whitehead also sent me an index he had prepared of the entries about Germans in the British Official History, a useful aid given that the official historian left them out of his printed index.

I have to confess there is another reason why this book has turned out the way it has. It has been written in the shadow cast by a tragedy that devastated my family almost a hundred years ago. My great-grandfather Cecil Sebag-Montefiore, who served in the Royal Engineers on the Western Front, was severely wounded while in France. The legend passed down through my father spoke of Cecil's unbearable misery after returning to civilian life. His catchphrase was 'I haven't had a happy day since I came home.' Eventually he could not take it any more, and he shot himself. The waves created by that wild act have rippled through the generations. Some might say it has made me excessively sympathetic, not just to those we all class as the victims of this terrible war, but also to those whom today many would condemn. I am hoping readers will keep the reasons for my approach in mind as they read these pages, even if they do not agree with it.

Before mentioning my main helpers on this history of the Battle of the Somme, I want to acknowledge the special contribution provided by Richard Kemp, a retired solicitor, who has worked with me on the research from start to finish. At times his assistance has been so intense that he almost deserves to be known as the co-author. His greatest contribution has been to visit the Liddle Collection in Leeds repeatedly and sift through its material. He also helped to drastically reduce the time I needed to spend in the Imperial War Museum in London and the Australian War Memorial in Canberra by preparing lists of files that he thought I should see before my visits.

I should also mention the assistance I have been given by Lieutenant-Colonel Phillip Robinson, a British Army engineer who is currently writing a history of mining on the Western Front. He very generously gave me a series of translations of German war diaries, thereby saving me the time and expense of having to look for these files in Stuttgart and Munich. He also guided me about the mining under the Somme, and introduced me to the other expert on mining on the Western Front: Simon Jones, author of *Underground Warfare 1914–1918*, who ever since has been a tower of strength answering all my queries.

Another stalwart supporter has been Nigel Cave, the editor of Pen & Sword's very successful Battleground Europe series of books, which includes many titles on the Somme, some of them written by himself. His books include *Beaumont Hamel* and *Delville Wood*. He has taken me around the main sites of the Somme and has also recommended many of the books I have subsequently quoted in my chapter endnotes.

Jon Cooksey, editor of *Stand To*, the journal for the Western Front Association, has always made himself available to answer questions, and has frequently advised me on what books to read on the Somme.

It would be impossible to name all the people who have permitted me to use their relatives' or their family's papers. But the following documents were especially important: the published diary written by the 22nd Manchesters' Captain Charlie May (ed. Gerry Harrison) has to be one of the most moving documents written on the Somme during the lead-up to the battle; Sister Edith Appleton's diary, which records her work caring for Somme patients in the hospital at Étretat, is the best account by a World War I nurse that I have seen; Sergeant Richard Tawney's description of the part he played in the 22nd Manchesters' attack near Mametz is one of the most stirring accounts in this book; the account by Lieutenant Pat Auld of the 50th Australian Battalion's occupation of the front line near Mouquet Farm, and 2nd Lieutenant Geoffrey Pratt's description of the 9th West Yorkshires' stand in the front line at Feste Staufen, are noteworthy because as well as being vivid, they highlight the vulnerability of some of the junior officers who were required to lead the men into battle.

The following personnel were of great help in letting me use their collections:

Britain

British Library: Maps: Jim Carruth, Curator of Modern Mapping, Nicola Beech.

Camden, London Borough of: Library Loans: June Gronland.

Churchill College, Cambridge: Churchill Archives Centre: Allen Packwood, Director.

Imperial War Museum: Documents: Anthony Richards, Head of Department, Simon Robbins, Simon Offord; Printed Books: Jane Rosen; First World War Galleries Project: Senior Curator, Paul Cornish.

The National Archives: David Priest, Production Co-ordination Manager, Hazel Pocock, William Spencer.

The Tank Museum: David Fletcher.

Australia

Australian War Memorial, Canberra: Sue Ducker, Reading Room Manager, Research Centre; Craig Tibbitts, Senior Curator, Official and Private Records (at time of visit); Stuart Bennington: Acting Senior Curator, Official and Private Records.

State Library of New South Wales: Maggie Patton, Manager, Research and Discovery, Library & Information Services; Dr Tracy Bradford, Head of Manuscripts (has since left library); Robynne Hayward.

State Library Victoria: Dr Kevin Molloy, Manuscripts Collection Manager; Shona Dewar, Librarian Manuscripts Collection.

Germany

Freiburg: Bundesarchiv-Militärarchiv: Melanie Wehr, Achim Koch, Christiane Botzet.

Karlsruhe: Generallandesarchiv: Manfred Hennhöfer.

Munich: Bayerisches Hauptstaatsarchiv: Martina Haggenmüller.
Potsdam: Zentrum für Militärgeschichte und Sozialwissenschaften des Bundeswehr: Bibliothek: Gabriele Bosch. Militärgeschichtliches Forschungsamt: Markus Poehlmann.
Stuttgart: Hauptstaatsarchiv: Dr Wolfgang Mährle.

New Zealand

Alexander Turnbull Library: David Colquhoun, Curator, Manuscripts (now retired); Jocelyn Chalmers, Research Librarian, Manuscripts.
Archives New Zealand: Graham Langton, Senior Archivist, Research Services, David Knight.
National Army Museum, Waiouru: Dolores Ho, Archivist.

I have also been helped by the following advisers and researchers: Christopher Bailey, James Ball, Nikola Becker, Manuel Bollag, Sophie Bolton, Martin Böhm, Michael Börner, Julia Brandt, Emily Cohen, Nyla Davison, Eliot Dodd, Leighanna Driftmier, Dalila de Freitas, Felix Fuchs, Sandra George, Michael Griff, Will Hamilton, Leah Hancharuk, Katherine Har, Vanessa Hindinger, Jemima Kelly, Daniel Kirmatzis, Clarissa Kopanitsak, Jan Linke, Charlotte Long, Olaf Loschke, Will Manley, Lauren Markewicz, Elena Oyon, Colin du Plessis, Susan Resnik, Frederik Risse, Solvi Ryder, Katherine Saunders, Barbara Schatz, Anna Schrötter, Carl Seemann, Thuja Seidel, Elizabeth Smelloff, Edmond Smith, Mareike Spendl, Florian Spiegelhalter, Benjamin Spiel, Rachel Vaknin, Elliot Vick and Katie Watson.

My agent, David Godwin, helped me pitch to Penguin the idea of writing a book on World War I, and eventually a book on the Battle of the Somme.

It was Eleo Gordon, my editor at Penguin, who suggested that if I was to write a big book to link up with the World War I centenary, it had to be about the Battle of the Somme. Because of the need to get the book out in time for the centenary of the first day of the battle, she has taken on a lot of the work that would normally be done by the author. Thanks to her input the book has been completed in time. The text has been excellently copyedited by Richard Mason, and invaluable support was provided by Emma Brown. The very user-friendly maps were drawn by Jeff Edwards.

Finally, I am grateful to my mother, April Sebag-Montefiore, for correcting the first half of this book before passing it back to me, thus making my job thereafter that much easier.

Index